PACIFIC NORTHWEST CAMPING

PACIFIC NORTHWEST CAMPING

The Complete Guide
to Recreation Areas
in Washington and Oregon

Tom Stienstra
&
Julie Lancelle

Foghorn Press
San Francisco

Editor: JOSEPH HESSION
Senior Research Editor: JULIE LANCELLE
Maps: LASLO VESPREMI
Cover photo: JIM HUGHES/USDA Forest Service
Back cover photo: TERRY L. DUNCKEL
Technical Advisor: JON LANCELLE

Library of Congress Cataloging in Publication Data

Stienstra, Tom
Pacific Northwest Camping

1. Camping   2. Recreation   3. Washington   4. Oregon   I. Title

88-080733

ISBN 0-935701-21-4

Printed in the United States of America
Typography by BookPrep, Gilroy, California

CONTENTS

JOINING THE FIVE PERCENT CLUB

G oing on a camping trip can be like trying to put hiking boots on an octopus. You've tried it too, eh? Instead of the relaxing, exciting sojourn it was intended to be, a camping trip can turn into a scenario called "You Against The World." You want something easy? Try fighting an earthquake.

But it doesn't have to be that way, and that's what this book is all about. If you give it a chance, it can put the mystery, excitement and fun back into your camping vacations - and remove the fear of snarls, confusion and occasional temper explosions of volcanic proportions that keep people at home, locked away from the action.

Mystery? There are hundreds of hidden, rarely-used campgrounds listed and mapped in this book that you never dreamed of. Excitement? With many of these campsites comes the sizzle with the steak, the hike to a great lookout, the big fish at the end of the line. Fun? The how-to section of the book can take the futility out of your trips so you can put the fun back in. Add it up, put it in your cash register and you can turn camping into the satisfying adventure it is meant to be, whether for just an overnight quickie or for a month-long fortune hunt.

It has been documented that 95 percent of vacationers use only five percent of the available recreation areas. With this book you can leave the herd to wander and be free. You can join the inner circle, the five percenters who know the great hidden areas used by so few people. To join the Five Percent Club, you should take a hard look at the maps for the areas you wish to visit, and in turn, the numbered listings for the campgrounds that follow. As you study the camps, you will start to feel a sense of excitement building, a sense that you are about to unlock a door and catch a glimpse into a world that is rarely viewed. When you feel that excitement, act on it and parlay the energy into a great trip so you can spend your time making new memories rather than thinking of old ones.

We have tracked down and mapped more than 1,400 campgrounds in Washington and Oregon, organized them in distinct geographical areas and then detailed each of them in the corresponding listings.

This is how the campground guide works. Washington is divided into 12 geographical zones, with each of them given a locator number. For example, zone one is the Olympic Peninsula. Each zone map then identifies the individual campgrounds by number, and those numbers are then used for a corresponding listing.

Each campground is then given a logo that refers to the level of development—1. Boat-in; 2. Primitive; 3. Developed for tent camping; 4. Motorhome park.

1. Boat-in: A boat-in campground can be reached only by boat such as the many isolated campgrounds on islands in Puget Sound. Most are primitive, with few facilities and no piped water available.

2. Primitive: A primitive camp has few facilities, may not have piped water available, but is free or very low cost.

3. Developed for tents: A developed camp has piped water, facilities, and reservations are often necessary. A daily fee is often charged.

4. Motorhome park: A motorhome park has been expressly designed for recreational vehicles, providing hookups and full amenities. Some have space for tents available.

The campground maps and guide lists can serve two ways: 1. If you're on the road, it's late in the day and you're looking for a spot to spend the night, you can likely find one nearby. 2. Or, you can custom tailor a vacation to fit exactly into your plans, rather than heading off and hoping it turns out right.

For those interested in a tailor-made vacation, you may wish to obtain additional maps, particularly if you are venturing into areas governed by the U.S. Forest Service or Bureau of Land Management. Both are federal agencies and have low cost maps that detail all hiking trails, lakes, streams and back country camps that can be reached via logging roads. The back country camps are often in primitive and rugged settings, but provide the sense of isolation that many need on a trip. In addition, they can provide good jumpoff points for backpacking trips, if that is your calling. These camps are often free, and we have included hundreds of them in this book.

At the other end of the spectrum are the developed parks for motorhomes, parks that offer a home away from home with everything from full hookups to a grocery store to a laundromat. These spots are just as important as the remote camps with no facilities. Instead of isolation, RV parks provide a place to shower, get outfitted for food or find clean clothes. For the motorhome cruisers, they offer spots to stay in high style while touring the area. They tend to cost from $12 to $20 per night, with an advance deposit necessary in summer months.

Somewhere between the two - the remote, unimproved camps and the lavish motorhome parks - are hundreds and hundreds of campgrounds that provide a compromise; beautiful settings, some facilities, with a small overnight fee. Piped water, vault toilets and picnic tables tend to come with the territory, along with a fee of $4 to $10. Because they offer a bit of both worlds, this is where demand is highest, particularly during the summer season when you can expect company. But this does not mean they should be abandoned in search of a less confined environment. For one, most parks have set up quotas so you don't feel like you've been squeezed in with a shoehorn. And secondly, the same parks often provide off-season or weekday prospects when there can be virtually no use.

Prior to your trip, you will want to get organized, and that's where you will start putting boots on that giant octopus. The key to organization for any task is breaking it down to its key components, then solving each element independent of the others. Remember the octopus. Grab a moving leg, jam a boot on and make sure it's on tight before reaching for another leg. Do one thing at a time, in order, and all will get done.

We have isolated the different elements of camping and you should do the same when planning for your trip. There are separate sections on each of the primary ingredients for a successful trip: 1. Food and cooking gear; 2. Clothes and weather protection; 3. Foot wear, leg care and how to choose the right boots and socks; 4. Sleeping gear and how to get your rest; 5. Combatting bugs and some common sense first-aid; 6. Fishing and recreation gear; 7. How to obtain good maps and put them to use.

Each section has a list of needed gear at the end of its respective chapter. This can help you become completely organized for your trip in just one week by spending just a little time each evening, working a different section each night. In itself, getting organized is an unnatural act for many. By splitting it up, you take the pressure out and put the fun back in.

As a full time outdoors writer, the quetion I get asked more than any other is, "Where are you going this week?" All of the answers are in this book.

FOOD & COOKING GEAR

I was a warm, crystal clear day, the kind of day when if you had ever wanted to go sky diving, you would go sky diving. That was exactly the case for my old pal Foonsky, who had never before tried the sport. But a funny thing happened after he jumped out of the plane and pulled the ripcord for the first time: The parachute didn't open up.

In total free fall, Foonsky noticed the earth below started looking bigger and bigger. Not one to panic, he calmly pulled the ripcord on the emergency parachute. But nothing happened then either. No parachute, no nothing.

The ground was getting closer and closer, and as he tried to search out a soft place to land, Foonsky detected a small object shooting up toward him. It looked like a camper.

Foonsky figured this could be his last chance, so as they passed in mid-flight, he shouted, "Hey, do you know anything about parachutes!"

The other fellow just shouted back as he headed off into space, "Do you know anything about lighting camping stoves!"

Well, Foonsky got lucky and his parachute opened. But as for the other fellow, well, he's probably in orbit like a NASA weather satellite. If you've ever had a mishap lighting a camping stove, you know exactly what we're talking about.

When it comes to camping, all things are not created equal. Nothing is more important than having your stove light easily and reach full heat without feeling like you're playing with a short fuse to a miniature bomb. If your stove does not work right, your trip can turn into a disaster, regardless of how well you have planned the other elements. In addition, a bad stove will add an underlying feel of futility to your day, especially if you have carefully detailed out your cooking gear and food for the trip. You know that sure enough, that darn stove is going to foul up on you again.

CAMPING STOVES

If you are buying a camping stove, remember this one critical rule: Do not leave the store with a new stove unless you have been shown exactly how to use it.

Know what you are getting. Many stores that specialize in outdoor recreation equipment provide experienced campers/employees who will demonstrate the use of every stove they sell, and while they're at it, describe its respective strengths and weaknesses.

The second rule is to never buy a stove that uses kerosene for fuel. Kerosene is smelly, messy, provides low heat, needs priming, and in America is virtually obsolete as a camp fuel. As a test experience, I tried using a kerosene stove once. It could scarcely boil a pot of water, and when some kerosene leaked out, it ruined everything it touched. The smell of kerosene never did go away. Kerosene remains popular in Europe only because the campers haven't much heard of white gas yet. When they do, they will demand it.

That leaves white gas or butane as the best fuels, and either can be right for you, depending on your special preferences.

White gas is the most popular, because it can be purchased at most outdoor recreation stores, at many supermarkets, and is inexpensive and effective. It burns hot, has virtually no smell, and evaporates quickly if it should spill. If you get caught in wet, miserable weather and can't get a fire going, you can use it as an emergency fire starter—though its use as such should be sparing and never on an open flame.

White gas is a popular fuel both for car campers who use the large, two-burner stoves equipped with a fuel tank and pump, or for hikers who use the lightweight backpacking stoves. On the latter, lighting can require priming with a gel called priming paste, which some people dislike. Another problem with white gas is that it can be extremely explosive.

As an example, I once burned my beard completely off in a mini-explosion while lighting one of the larger stoves styled for car camping. I was in the middle of cooking dinner when the flame suddenly shut down. Sure enough, the fuel tank was empty, and after re-filling it, I pumped the tank 50 or 60 times to regain pressure. When I lit a match, the sucker ignited from three feet away. The concussion from the explosion was like a stick of dynamite going off, and immediately, the smell of burning beard was in the air. In the quick flash of an erred moment, my once thick, dark beard had been reduced to a mass of little, burned curly cues.

My error? After filling the tank, I forgot to shut the fuel cock off while pumping up the pressure in the tank. As a result, as I pumped the tank, the stove burners were slowly producing the gas/air mixture, filling the air space above the stove. The strike of a match—even from a few feet away—and ka-boom!

That problem can be solved by using stoves that consume bottled butane fuel. On the plus side, butane requires no pouring, pumping or priming, and stoves that use butane are the easiest to light of all camping stoves. Just turn a knob and light, that's it. On the minus side, because it comes in bottles, you never know precisely how much fuel you have left, and when a bottle is emptied, you have a potential piece of litter. The person who tosses an empty butane cartridge on the ground and leaves it behind is perpetrating a gross insult to his camping brethren.

The other problem with butane as a fuel is that it just plain does not work well in cold weather, or when there is little fuel left in the cartridge. Since you cannot predict mountain weather in spring or fall, and will eventually use most of the fuel in the cartridge, butane can thus make a frustrating choice. If there is any chance of the temperature falling below freezing, you must sleep with your butane cartridge to keep it warm, or otherwise forget its use come morning. Believe it or not, that is exactly the case.

Personally, I prefer using a small, lightweight stove that consumes white gas so I can closely gauge fuel consumption. My pal Foonsky uses one with a butane bottle because it lights so easily. We have contests to see who can boil a pot of water faster and the difference is usually negligible. Thus, other factors are important when choosing a stove.

Of the other elements, ease of cleaning the burner is the most important. If you camp much, especially with the smaller stoves, the burner holes will eventually become clogged. Some stoves have a built-in cleaning needle; a quick twist of a knob and you're in business. On the other hand, others require disassembling and a protracted session using special cleaning tools. If a stove is difficult to clean, you will tend to put off doing it, and your stove will sputter and pant while you watch the cold pot of water sitting atop it.

Thus, before making a purchase, require the salesman to show you how to clean the burner head. Except in the case of the large, multi-burner camping stoves, which rarely require cleaning, this test can do more to determine the long-term value of a stove than any other factor.

BUILDING FIRES

One summer expedition took me to the Canadian wilderness in British Columbia for a 75-mile canoe trip on the Bowron Lake Circuit, a chain of 13 lakes, six rivers and seven portages. It is one of the true great canoe trips in the world, a loop trip where you never repeat your route and end just a few hundred feet distant from where you started. But at the first camp at little Kibbee Lake, my camp stove developed a fuel leak at the base of the burner and the nuclear-like blast that followed just about turned Canada into a giant crater.

As a result, the final 70 miles of the trip had to be completed without a stove, cooking on open fires each night. The problem was compounded by the weather, raining eight of the 10 days. Rain? In Canada, raindrops the size of silver dollars fall so hard that they actually bounce on the lake surface. We actually had to stop paddling a few times in order to empty the rain water out of the canoe. At the end of the day, we'd make camp, and then came the test. Either make a fire, or go to bed cold and hungry.

With an axe, at least we had a chance for success. As soaked as all the downed wood was, I was able to make my own fire-starting tinder from the chips of splitting logs. No matter how hard it rains, the inside of a log is always dry.

In miserable weather, matches don't stay lit long enough to get the tinder started. Instead, we used either a candle or the little, wax-like fire-starter cubes that stay lit for several minutes. From that, we could get the tinder going. Then we added small, slender strips of wood that had been axed from the interior of the logs. When the flame reached a foot high, we added the logs, with the dry interior of them facing in. By the time the inside of the logs had caught fire, the outside would be drying from the heat. It wasn't long and a royal blaze was brightening the rainy night.

That's a worst-possible case scenario and perhaps you will never face anything like it. Nevertheless, being able to build a good fire and cook on it can be one of the more satisfying elements of a camping trip. At times, just looking into the flames can provide a special satisfaction at the end of a good day.

However, never expect to build a fire for every meal, or in some cases, even build one at all. Many state and federal campgrounds have been picked clean of downed wood, or forest fire danger prohibits them altogether during the fire season. In either case, you either use your camp stove or go hungry.

But when you can build a fire, and the resources are available to do so, it will add depth and a personal touch to your camping trip. Of the campgrounds listed in the directory of this book, the sites that allow for fires will likely already have fire rings available. In primitive areas where you can make your own, you should dig a ring eight inches deep, line the edges with rock, and clear all the needles and twigs in a five-foot radius. The next day, when the fire is dead out, you can discard the rocks, spread dirt over the black charcoal, then scatter pine needles and twigs over it. Nobody will ever know you camped there. That's the best way I know to keep a secret spot a real secret.

When you start to build a campfire, the first thing you will notice is that no matter how good your intentions, your fellow campers will not be able to resist moving the wood around. Just watch. You'll be getting ready to add a key piece of wood at just the right spot, and your companion will stick his mitts in, quietly believing he has a better idea, shift the fire around and undermine your best thought-out plans.

So I make a rule on camping trips. One person makes the fire and everybody else stands clear, or is involved with other camp tasks, like gathering wood, getting water, putting up tents or planning dinner. Once the fire is going strong, then it's fair game; anyone adds logs at their discretion. But in the early, delicate stages of the campfire, it's best to leave it to one person at a time.

Before a match is first struck, a complete pile of firewood should be gathered alongside. Then start small, with the tiniest twigs you can find, and slowly add in larger twigs as you go, criss-crossing them like a miniature teepee. Eventually, you will get to the big chunks that will produce high heat. The key is to get one piece of wood burning into another, which then burns to another, setting off what I call the chain of flame. Conversely, single pieces of wood, set apart from each other, will not burn.

On a dry, summer evening at a campsite where plenty of wood is available, about the only way you can blow the deal is to get impatient and try to add the big pieces too quickly. Do that and you'll just get smoke, not flames, and it won't be long before every one of your fellow campers will be poking at your fire. It will drive you crazy, but they just can't help it.

COOKING GEAR

I like traveling light, and I've found all one needs is a cooking pot, small frying pan, metal pot grabber, fork, knife, cup, and matches for a cook kit. In fact, I keep it all in one small bag, which fits into my pack. If I'm camping out of my 4-wheel drive rig, the little bag of cooking gear is easy to keep track of. Simple, not complicated, is the key to keeping a camping trip on the right track.

You can get more elaborate by purchasing complete cook kits with plates, a coffee pot, large pots and other cookware, but what really counts is having one single pot you're happy with. It needs to be just the right size, not too big or small, and be stable enough so it won't tip over, even if it is at a slight angle on a fire, full of water at a full boil. Mine is just 6 inches wide and 4½ inches deep, holds better than a quart of water, and has served well for several hundred camp dinners.

The rest of your cook kit is easy to complete. The frying pan should be small, light-gauge aluminum, teflon-coated, with a fold-in handle so it's no hassle to store. A pot grabber is a great addition, that is, a little aluminum gadget that will clamp to the edge of pots and allow you to lift them and pour water with total control and without burning your fingers. A fork, knife and cup are at your discretion. For cleanup, take a small bottle filled with dish cleanser and a plastic scrubber, and you're in business.

A Sierra Cup, which is a wide aluminum cup with a wire handle, is ideal because you can eat out of them as well as use them for drinking (although not at the same time). This means no plates to clean after dinner, so cleanup is quick and easy. In addition, if you go for a hike, you can clip it to your belt with the wire handle.

If you want a more formal setup, complete with plates, glasses, silverware, and the like, you can end up spending more time preparing and cleaning up from meals than you do enjoying the country you are exploring. In addition, the more equipment you bring, the more loose ends you will have to deal with—and loose ends can cause plenty of frustration. If you have a choice, choose simple.

And remember what Thoreau said: "A man is rich in proportion to what he can do without."

FOOD AND COOKING TRICKS

On a trip to the Bob Marshall Wilderness in western Montana, I woke up one morning, yawned, and said, "What've we got for breakfast?"

The silence was ominous. "Well," finally came the response, "we don't have any food left."

"What!?"

"Well, I figured we'd catch trout for meals every other night."

En route to civilization, we ended up eating wild berries, buds, and yes, even tried a root (not too tasty). When we finally landed the next day at a Kalispell pizza parlor, we nearly ate the wooden tables.

Running out of food on a camping trip can do more to turn reasonable people into violent grumps than any other event. There's no excuse for it, not when a system for figuring meals can be outlined with precision and little effort. You should not go out and buy a bunch of food, throw it in your rig, and head off for yonder. That leaves too much to chance. And if you've ever been in the woods and real hungry, you'll know to take a little effort to make sure a day or two of starvation will not re-occur.

A three-step process offers a solution:

- 1. Make a general meal-by-meal plan and be sure your companions like what is on it. Never expect to catch fish for any meals.

● 2. Tell your companions to buy any speciality items on their own, and not to expect you to take care of everything, like some special brand of coffee.

● 3. Put all the food on your living room floor and literally figure every day of your trip meal-by-meal, bagging the food in plastic bags as you go. You will know exact food quotas and the only way you will go hungry is if you knowingly exceed them.

Fish for meals? There's a guaranteed rule for that. If you expect to catch fish for meals, you will most certainly get skunked. If you don't expect to catch fish for meals, you will probably catch so many they'll be coming out of your ears. I've seen it a hundred times.

One of the best camp dinner meals you can make is a self-designed soup/ stew mix. After bringing a pot of water to a full boil, add in ramen or pasta, then cut up a potato, carrot, onion and garlic clove and let it simmer—then add in a soup mix or two. Because vegetables can take 10 minutes to cook, it is often a good idea to add in the soup mix well after the vegetables. Read the directions on the soup mix to determine cooking time. Make sure you stir it up, otherwise your concoction may fall victim to "The Clumps." That done, pull a surprise bottle of wine out of your pack and we're talking about a gourmet dinner in the outback.

If you are car camping and have a big ice chest, you can bring virtually anything to eat and drink. If you want to go on the trail, well, then the rules of the game change.

There will be no steaks, beer, or french fries waiting in your pack when you reach the top of the mountain. But that doesn't mean you don't have to eat well. Some of the biggest advances in the outdoor industry have come in freeze-dried dinners now available for campers. Some of them are almost good enough to serve in restaurants. Sweet-and-sour pork over rice, tostadas, burgundy chicken . . . it sure beats the poopy goop we used to eat, like the old, soupy chili mac dinners that tasted bad and looked so unlike "food" that its consumption was near impossible, even for my dog.

To provide an idea of how to plan a menu, consider what my companions and I ate while hiking 250 miles on California's John Muir Trail.

● Breakfast: Instant soup, oatmeal (never get plain), one beef jerky stick, coffee or hot chocolate.

● Lunch: One beef stick, two jerky sticks, one Granola bar, dried fruit, half cup of pistachio nuts, Tang, small bag of M&M's.

● Dinner: Instant soup, freeze-dried dinner, milk bar, rainbow trout.

What was that last item? Rainbow trout? Right! Unless you plan on it, you can catch them every night.

COOKING GEAR LIST

Matches bagged in different zip-lock bags
Fire-starter cubes or candle
Camp stove
Camp fuel

Pot, pan, cup
Pot grabber
Knife, fork
Dish soap and scrubber
Salt, pepper, spices
Itemized food
Plastic spade

OPTIONAL

Axe or hatchet
Wood or charcoal for barbeque
Ice chest
Spatula
Grill

CLOTHING & WEATHER PROTECTION

What started as the innocent pursuit of the perfect campground had evolved into one heck of a predicament for Foonsky and me.

We had parked at the end of a logging road and then bushwhacked our way down a canyon to a pristine trout stream. On my first cast, a little flip into the plunge pool of a waterfall, I caught a 16-inch rainbow trout, a real beauty that jumped three times. Magic stuff.

Then, just across the stream, we saw it - The Perfect Camping Spot. On a sandbar on the edge of the forest, there lay a flat area high and dry above the river. Nearby was plenty of downed wood collected by past winter storms that could be used for firewood. And of course, this beautiful trout stream was bubbling along just 40 yards from the site.

But nothing is perfect, right? To reach it, we had to wade across the river, though it didn't appear too difficult a task. The cold water tingled a bit, and the river came up surprisingly high, just above belt level. But it would be worth it to camp at The Perfect Spot.

Once across the river, we put on some dry clothes, set up camp, explored the woods, and fished the stream, catching several nice trout for dinner. But late that afternoon, it started raining. What, rain in the summertime? Nature makes its own rules. The next morning it was still raining, pouring like a Yosemite waterfall from a solid gray sky. We both looked skyward and with our mouths open, almost drowned.

That's when we noticed The Perfect Camping Spot wasn't so perfect. The rain had raised the river level too high for us to wade back across. We were marooned, wet and hungry.

"Now we're in a heck of a predicament," said Foonsky, the water streaming off him.

Getting cold and wet on a camping trip—with no way to get warm—is not only unnecessary and uncomfortable, but it can be a fast ticket to hypothermia, the number one killer of outdoorsmen. By definition, hypothermia is a condition in which body temperature is lowered to the point that it causes illness. It is particularly dangerous because the afflicted are usually unaware it is setting in. The first sign is a sense of apathy, then a state of confusion over decisions, which can lead eventually to collapse (or what appears sleep), then death.

You must always have a way to get warm and dry in short order, regardless of any condition you may face. If you have no way of getting dry, then to prevent hypothermia, you must take emergency steps, which are detailed in the chapter on first-aid.

But you should never reach that point. For starters, always have different sets of clothes tucked away so no matter how cold and wet you might get, you are not far from putting on something dry. On hiking trips, I always carry a second set of clothes, sealed in a plastic garbage bag to stay dry, and keep another set waiting back at the truck.

If you are car camping, the vehicle can cause an illusionary sense of security. But with an extra set of dry clothes stashed safely away, there is no illusion. The security is real. For finishers, make sure those clothes can make you warm and keep you that way. And no matter how hot the weather is when you start on your trip, always be prepared for the worst. Foonsky and me were taught the hard way.

Both of us were soaking wet on that sandbar, so we tried holing up in the tent for the night. A sleeping bag with Quallofil, or another polyester fiber fill, can retain warmth, even when wet, because the fill is hollow and retains its loft. So as miserable as it was, we made it through the night.

The rain finally stopped the next day, and the river dropped a bit, but it was still rolling big and angry. Using a stick as a wading staff, Foonsky made it 80 percent across the stream before he was dumped, but he made a jump for it and managed to scramble to the river bank. He waved for me to follow. "No problem," I thought.

It took me some 20 minutes to reach nearly the same spot where Foonsky was dumped. The heavy river current was above my belt and pushing hard—then, in the flash of an instant—my wading staff slipped on a rock. I teetered in the river current, and then was knocked over like a bowling pin, completely submerged. I went tumbling down the river, heading right toward the waterfall. While underwater, I looked up at the river surface and can remember how close it appeared, yet how out of control I was. Right then, this giant hand appeared, and I grabbed it. It was Foonsky. If it wasn't for that hand, I would have sailed right over the waterfall.

My momentum drew Foonsky right into the river, and we scrambled in the current, but I suddenly sensed the river bottom under my knees. On all fours, the two of us clambered ashore. We were safe.

"Thanks 'ol buddy," I said.

"Man, we're wet," he responded. "Let's get to the rig and get some dry clothes on."

DRESSING IN LAYERS

After falling in the river, Foonsky and me looked like a couple of cold swamp rats. When we eventually reached the truck, and changed into warm clothes, a strange phenomenon hit both of us. Once we started warming up, we began to shiver and shake like an old engine trying to start. It's the body's built-in heater. Shivering is how the body tries to warm itself, producing as much heat as if you were jogging.

To retain that heat, you should dress in "layers." The interior layer, what you wear closest to your skin, and the exterior layer, what you wear to repel the weather, are the most important.

In the good 'ol days, campers wore long underwear made out of wool, which was scratchy, heavy, and sometimes sweaty. Well, times have changed. You can now wear long underwear made of Polypropylene, a synthetic material that is warm, light, and wicks dampness away from your skin. It's ideal to wear in a sleeping bag on cold nights, during cool evenings after the sun goes down, or for winter snow sports. Poly shirts come in three weights, light, medium, and heavy, and medium can be a perfect garment for campers. The light weight seems to cling to your body. We call it Indian Underwear, because it keeps creeping up on you. The heavy weight is very warm and can be bulky. For most folks, the medium is just right.

The next layer of clothes should be a light cotton shirt or a long-sleeve cotton/wool shirt, or both, depending on coolness of the day. For pants, many just wear blue jeans when camping, but blue jeans can be hot and tight. And once wet, jeans tend to stay that way. Putting on wet blue jeans on a cold morning is an agonizing way to start the day. I have suffered that fate a number of times. A better choice are pants made from a cotton/canvas mix, which are available at outdoor shops. They are light, have a lot of give, and dry quickly. If the weather is quite warm, shorts that have some room to them can be the best choice.

VESTS, PARKAS

In cold weather, you should take the layer system one step further with a warm vest and a parka jacket. Vests are especially useful because they provide warmth without the bulkiness of a parka.

The warmest vests and parkas are either filled with down, Quallofil, or are made with a cotton/wool mix. Each has its respective merits and problems. Downfill provides the most warmth for the amount of weight, but becomes useless when wet, taking a close resemblance to a wet dish rag. Quallofil keeps much of its heat-retaining qualities even when wet, but is expensive. Vests made of cotton/wool mixes are the most attractive and also are quite warm, but can be as heavy as a ship's anchor when wet.

Sometimes the answer is combining the two. My favorite camping companion, Little Foot, wears a good-looking, cotton-wool vest, and a parka filled with Quallofil. The vest never gets wet, so weight is less of a factor.

RAIN GEAR

One of the most miserable nights I ever spent in my life was on a camping trip where I didn't bring my rain gear or a tent. Hey, it was early August, the temperature had been in the 90's for weeks, and if anybody told me it was going to rain, I would have told them to consult a brain doctor. But rain it did. And as I got wetter and wetter, I kept saying to myself, "Hey, it's summer, it's not supposed to rain." Then I remembered one of the Ten Commandments of camping: Forget your rain gear and you can guarantee it will rain.

To stay dry, you need some form of water repellent shell. It can be as simple as a $5 poncho made out of plastic or as elaborate as Gore-Tex rain jacket and pants that cost $300 a set. What counts is not how much you spend, but how dry you stay.

Some can do just fine with a cheap poncho, and note that ponchos can serve other uses in addition to that as a rain coat. Ponchos can be used as a ground tarp, a rain cover for supplies or a backpack, or in a pinch, can be roped up to trees to provide a quick storm ceiling if you don't have a tent. The problem with ponchos is that in a hard rain, you just don't stay dry. First your legs get wet, then they get soaked. Then your arms follow the same pattern. If you're wearing cotton, you'll find that once part of the garment gets wet, the water will spread until, alas, you are completely wet anyway, poncho and all. Before long you start to feel like a walking refrigerator.

One high-cost option is buying a Gore-Tex rain jacket and pants. Gore-Tex is actually not a fabric, as is commonly believed, but a laminated film that coats a breathable fabric. The result is a lightweight, water repellent, breathable jacket and pants. They are perfect for campers—but they cost a fortune.

Some hiking buddies of mine have complained that their older Gore-Tex rain gear has lost some of its water repellent qualities. However, manufacturers insist that this is the result of water seeping through seams, not leaks in the jacket. At each seam, tiny needles will have pierced through the fabric, and as tiny as the holes are, water will find a way through. An application of Seam Lock, especially at the major seams at the shoulders of a jacket, can usually end the problem.

If you don't want to spend the big bucks for Gore-Tex rain gear, but want to stay drier than from wearing a poncho, a coated nylon jacket is the middle road that many choose. They are inexpensive, have the highest water repellent qualities of any rain gear, and are warm, providing a good outer shell for your layers of clothing. But they are not without fault. These jackets don't breathe at all, and if you zip it up tight, you can sweat like an Eskimo.

My brother, Rambob, gave me a $20 nylon jacket prior to an expedition where we climbed Northern California's Mt. Shasta, one of America's most impressive peaks at 14,162 feet. I wore that $20 special all the way to the top with no complaints; it's warm and 100 percent waterproof. At $20, it seems like a treasure, especially compared to the $180 Gore-Tex jackets. That feeling intensifies every time it rains.

OTHER GEAR, AND A FEW TIPS

What are the three items most commonly forgotten on a camping trip? "A cook, a dish washer, and a fish cleaner," said my pal, the Z-Man.

C'mon now, bucko, the real answers? A hat, sunglasses, and chapstick. A hot day is unforgiving without them.

A hat is crucial, especially when you are visiting high elevations. Without one you are constantly exposed to everything nature can give you. The sun will dehydrate you, sap your energy, sunburn your head, and in worst cases, cause sunstroke. Start with a comfortable hat. Then finish with sunglasses, chapstick and sunscreen for additional protection. That will help protect you from extreme heat.

To help against extreme cold, it's a good idea to keep a pair of thin ski gloves stashed away with your emergency clothes, along with a wool ski cap. The gloves should be thick enough to keep your fingers from stiffening up, but pliable enough to allow full movement, so you don't have to take them off to complete simple tasks, like lighting a stove. An option to gloves are glovelets, which look like gloves with no fingers. In any case, just because the weather turns cold doesn't mean that your hands have to.

And if you fall into a river like Foonsky and me did, well, I hope you have a set of dry clothes waiting back at your rig. And a helping hand reaching out for you.

CAMPING CLOTHES LIST

Polypropylene underwear
Cotton shirt
Long sleeve cotton/wool shirt
Cotton/canvas pants
Vest
Parka
Rain jacket, pants, or poncho
Hat
Sunglasses
Chapstick
Sunscreen

OPTIONAL

Seam Lock
Shorts
Swimming suit
Gloves

HIKING AND FOOT CARE

We had set up a nice, little camp in the woods, and my buddy, Foonsky, sitting against a big Douglas fir, was strapping on his hiking boots.

"New boots," he said with a grin. "But they seem pretty stiff."

We decided to hoof it on down the trail for a few hours, exploring the mountain wildlands that are said to hide Bigfoot and other strange creatures. These woods are quiet and secret, and after even a short while on the trail, a sense of peace and calm seems to settle in. The forest provides the chance to be cleansed with clean air and the smell of trees, freeing you from all troubles.

But it wasn't long before the look of trouble was on Foonsky's face. And no, it wasn't from seeing Bigfoot.

"Got a hot spot on a toe," he said.

Immediately we stopped. He pulled off his right boot, then socks, and inspected the left side of his big toe. Sure enough, a blister had bubbled up, filled with fluid, but not popped. From his medical kit, Foonsky cut a small piece of moleskin to fit over the blister, then taped it to hold it in place. A few minutes later, we were back on the trail.

A half hour later, there was still no sign of Bigfoot. But Foonsky stopped again and pulled off his other boot. Another hot spot. A small blister had started on the little toe of his left foot, over which he taped a band-aid to keep it from further chafing against the inside of his new boot.

In just a few days, 'ol Foonsky—a big, strong guy who goes 6-foot-5, 200-plus pounds—was walking around like a sore-hoofed hoss that had been loaded with a month of supplies and then ridden over sharp rocks. Well, it wasn't the distance that had done Foonsky in, it was those blisters. He had them on eight of his ten toes and was going through band-aids, moleskin and tape like he was a walking emergency ward. If he used any more tape, he was going to look like a mummy from an Egyptian tomb.

If you've ever been in a similar predicament, then you know the frustration of wanting to have a good time, wanting to hike and explore the area at which you have set up a secluded camp, only to be turned gimpy legged by several blisters. No one is immune, not big, strong guys nor small, innocent-looking women. All are created equal before the blister god. You can be forced to bow to it unless you get your act together.

That means wearing the right style boots for what you have in mind—and then protecting your feet with a careful selection of socks. If you are still so unfortunate as to get a blister or two, it means knowing how to treat them fast so they don't turn your walk into a sore-footed endurance test.

What causes blisters? In almost all cases, it is the simple rubbing of your foot against the rugged interior of your boot. That act can be worsened by several factors:

- 1. A very stiff boot, that is, one in which your foot moves inside the boot as you walk, instead of the boot flexing as if it was another layer of skin.
- 2. Thin, holey, or dirty socks. This is the fastest route to blister death. Thin socks will allow your feet to move inside of your boots, holey socks will allow your skin to chafe directly against the boot's interior, and dirty socks will wrinkle and fold, also rubbing against your feet instead of cushioning them.
- 3. Soft feet. By itself, soft feet will not cause blisters, but in combination with a stiff boot or thin socks, can cause terrible problems. This often afflicts men more than women because females in general go barefoot more than men, and the bottoms of their feet thus become tougher. In fact, some of the biggest, toughest-looking guys you'll ever see—from Hells Angels to pro football players—have feet that are as soft as a baby's butt. Why? Because they never go barefoot and don't hike much.

SELECTING THE RIGHT BOOTS

One summer I hiked 400 miles, including 250 miles in three weeks along the crest of California's Sierra Nevada, and another 150 miles over several months in an earlier general training program. In that span, I got just one blister, suffered on the fourth day of the 250-miler. I treated it immediately, and suffered no more. One key is wearing the right boot, and for me, that means a boot that acts as a thick layer of skin that is flexible and pliable to my foot. I want my feet to fit snugly in them with no interior movement.

There are three kinds of boots: Hiking shoes, backpacking boots and mountaineering boots. Either select the right one or pay the consequences.

The stiffest of the lot is the mountaineering boot. These boots are often identified by mid-range tops, laces that extend almost as far as the toe area, and ankle areas that are as stiff as a board. The lack of "give" in them is what enamors them to mountaineers. The stiffness is preferred when rock climbing, walking off-trail on craggy surfaces, or hiking down the edge of stream beds where small rocks can cause you to turn your ankle. Because these boots don't give on rugged, craggy terrain, it reduces ankle injuries and provides better traction.

The backlash of stiff boots is that if careful selection of socks is not made, and your foot starts slipping around in them, you will get a set a blisters that would raise even Foonsky's eyebrows. But if you just want to go for a nice walk, or even a good romp with a backpack, then hiking shoes or backpacking boots are better designed for those respective uses.

Hiking shoes are the lightest of all boots, designed for day walks or short backpacking trips. Some of the newer models are like rugged tennis shoes, designed with a canvas top for lightness and a lug sole for traction. These are perfect for people who like to walk, but rarely carry a backpack. Because they are flexible, they are easy to break in, and with fresh socks, rarely cause blister problems. And because they are light, general hiking fatigue is greatly reduced.

On the negative side, because they have shallow lug soles, traction can be far from good on slippery surfaces. In addition, canvas hiking shoes provide less than ideal ankle support, which can be a problem in rocky areas, such as along a stream where you might want to go trout fishing. Turn your ankle and your trip can be ruined.

My preference is for a premium backpacking boot, the perfect medium between the stiff mountaineering boots and the soft canvas hiking shoes. The deep lug bottom provides traction, high ankle coverage provides support, yet the soft, waterproof leather body gives each foot a snug fit—add it up and that means no blisters. On the negative side, they can be quite hot, weigh a ton, and if they get wet, take days to dry.

There are a zillion styles, brands and price range of boots to choose from. If you wander about, looking at them equally, you will get as confused as a kid in a toy store. Instead go into the store with your mind clear about what you want, then find it and buy it. If you want the best, expect to spend $60 to $80 for hiking shoes, from $100 to $140 and sometimes more for backpacking or mountaineering boots. This is one area you don't want to scrimp on, so try not to yelp about the high cost. Instead, walk out of the store believing you just bought the best.

If you plan on using the advice of a shoe salesman for your purchase, first look at what kind of boots he is wearing. If he isn't even wearing boots, then any advice he might attempt to tender may not be worth a plug nickel. Most people I know who own quality boots, including salesmen, will wear them almost daily if their job allows, since boots are the best footware available. However, even these well-meaning folks can offer skeptical advice. Every hiker I've ever met will tell you he wears the world's greatest boot.

Instead, enter the store with a precise use and style in mind. Rather than fishing for suggestions, tell the salesman exactly what you want, and try two or three different brands of the same style. Always try on the matching pair of boots simultaneously so you know exactly how they'll feel. If possible, walk up and down stairs with them. Are they too stiff? Are your feet snug yet comfortable, or do they slip? Do they have that "right" kind of feel when you walk?

If you get the right answers to those questions, then you're on your way to blister-free, pleasure-filled days of walking.

SOCKS

The poor gent was scratching his feet like ants were crawling over them. I looked closer. Huge yellow calluses had covered the bottoms of his feet. At the ball and heel, the calluses were about a quarter of an inch thick, cracking and sore.

"I don't understand it," he said. "I'm on my feet a lot, so I bought a real good pair of hiking boots. But look what they've done to my feet. My feet itch so much I'm going crazy."

People can spend so much energy selecting the right kind of boot, that they can virtually overlook wearing the right kind of socks. One goes with the other.

Your socks should be thick enough to provide a cushion for your foot, as well as a good, snug fit. Without good socks, you might try to get the boot laces real tight—and that's like putting a tourniquet on your feet. You should have plenty of clean socks on hand, or plan on washing what you have on your trip. As socks are worn, they become compressed, dirty, and damp. Any one of those factors can cause problems.

My camping companions believe I go overboard when it comes to socks, that I bring too many and wear too many. But it works, and that's where the complaints stop. So how many do I wear? Well, would you believe three socks on each foot? It may sound like overkill, but each has its purpose, and like I said, it works.

The interior sock is thin, lightweight and made out of Polypropylene or Thermax, synthetic materials that actually transport moisture away from your skin. With a poly interior sock, your foot stays dry when it sweats. Without a poly sock, your foot can get damp, mix with dirt, which in turn can cause a "hot spot" to start on your foot. Eventually you get blisters, lots of them.

The second sock is for comfort and can be cotton, but a thin wool-based composite is ideal. Some made of the latter can wick moisture away from the skin, much like the qualities of Polypropylene. If wool itches your feet, a thick cotton sock can be suitable, though cotton collects moisture and compacts more quickly than other socks. If you're on a short hike rather than a long one, cotton will do just fine.

The exterior sock should be made of high quality, thick wool—at least 80 percent wool. It will cushion your feet, provide that "just right" snug fit in your boot, and in cold weather, give you some additional warmth and insulation. It is critical to keep the wool sock clean. If you wear a dirty wool sock over and over again, it will compact and lose its cushion, start wrinkling while you hike, and with that chain of events, your feet will catch on fire from the blisters that starting popping up.

A FEW TIPS

If you are like most folks, the bottoms of your feet are rarely exposed and quite soft. Therefore, you should take additional steps for their care. The best tip is keeping a fresh foot pad in your boot made of sponge rubber. Another cure for soft feet is to get out and walk or jog on a regular basis prior to your camping trip.

If you plan to use a foot pad and wear three socks, you will need to use these items when sizing boots. It is an unforgiving error to wear thin cotton socks when buying boots, then later trying to squeeze all this stuff, plus your feet, into your boots. There just won't be enough room.

The key to treating blisters is fast work at the first sign of a hot spot. But before you remove your socks, first check to see if the sock has a wrinkle in it, a likely cause to the problem. If so, either change socks or get them pulled tight, removing the tiny folds, after taking care of the blister. Cut a piece of moleskin to cover the offending toe, securing the moleskin with white medical tape. If moleskin is not available, small band-aids can do the job, but they have to be replaced daily, and sometimes even more frequently. At night, clean your feet and sleep without socks.

Two other items that can help your walking is an Ace bandage and a pair of Gaters.

For sprained ankles and twisted knees, an Ace bandage can be like an insurance policy to get you back on the trail and out of trouble. Over the years, I have had serious ankle problems and have relied on a good wrap with a four-inch bandage to get me home. The newer bandages come with the clips permanently attached, so you don't have to worry about losing them.

Gaters are leggings made of plastic, nylon or Gore-Tex which fit from just below your knees, over your calves, and attach under your boots. They are of particular help when walking in damp areas, or places where rain is common. As your legs brush against ferns or low-lying plants, gaters will deflect the moisture. Without them your pants will be soaking wet in short order.

Should your boots become wet, a good tip is to never try to force dry them. Some well-meaning folks will try to speed dry them at the edge of a campfire or actually put the boots in an oven. While this may dry the boots, it can also loosen the glue that holds them together, ultimately weakening your shoe until one day they fall apart in a tattered heap.

A better bet is to treat the leather so the boots become water repellent. Silicone-based liquids are the easiest to use and least greasy of the treatments available.

A final tip is to have another pair of lightweight shoes or mocassins that you can wear around camp, and in the process, give your feet the rest they deserved.

HIKING AND FOOT CARE LIST

Quality hiking boots
Backup lightweight shoes
Polypropylene socks
Thick cotton socks
80 percent wool socks
Strong boot laces
Innersole or foot cushion
Ace bandage
Moleskin and medical tape
Band-Aids
Gaters

CHAPTER FOUR

SLEEPING GEAR

One mountain night in the pines on an eve long ago, my dad, brother and I rolled out our sleeping bags and were bedded down for the night. After the pre-trip excitement, a long drive, an evening of trout fishing and a barbeque, we were like three tired doggies.

But as I looked up at the stars, I was suddenly wide awake. The kid was still wired. A half hour later? No change—wide awake.

And as little kids can do, I had to wake up ol' dad to tell him about it. "Hey, dad, I can't sleep."

"This is what you do," he said. "Watch the sky for a shooting star and tell yourself that you cannot go to sleep until you see at least one. As you wait and watch, you will start getting tired and it will be difficult to keep your eyes open. But tell yourself you must keep watching. Then you'll start to really feel tired. When you finally see a shooting star, you'll go to sleep so fast you won't know what hit you.

Well, I tried it that night and I don't even remember seeing a shooting star, I went to sleep so fast.

It's a good trick, and along with having a good sleeping bag, ground insulation, maybe a tent—or a few tricks for bedding down in a pickup truck or motorhome—you can get a good night's sleep on every camping trip.

Some 20 years after that camping episode with my dad and brother, we made a trip to the Planetarium at the Academy of Sciences in San Francisco to see a show on Halley's Comet. The lights dimmed, and the ceiling turned into a night sky, filled with stars and a setting moon. Meanwhile, a scientist began explaining phenomenons of the heavens.

After a few minutes, I began to feel drowsy. Just then, a shooting star zipped across the Planetarium ceiling. I went into a deep sleep so fast it was like I was in a coma. I didn't wake up until the show was over, the lights were turned back on and people were leaving the auditorium.

Drowsy, I turned to see if ol' Dad had liked the show. He had not only gone to sleep too, but apparently had no intention of waking up. Just like a camping trip.

SLEEPING BAGS

What could be worse than trying to sleep in a cold, wet sleeping bag on a rainy night without a tent in the mountains?

The answer is trying to sleep in a cold, wet sleeping bag on a rainy night without a tent in the moutains—when your sleeping bag is filled with down.

Water will turn a down-filled sleeping bag into a mushy heap. Many campers do not like a high-tech approach, but state-of-the-art polyester sleeping bags can keep you warm even when wet. That factor, along with temperature rating and weight are key factors when selecting a sleeping bag.

A sleeping bag is basically a shell filled with heat-retaining insulation. By themselves, they are not warm. Your body provides the heat, and the sleeping bag's ability to retain that heat is what makes them warm or cold.

The old-styled canvas bags are heavy, bulky, cold, and when wet, useless. With other options available, their use is limited. Anybody who sleeps outdoors or backpacks should choose otherwise.

Instead, buy and use a sleeping bag filled with down or one of the quality polyfills. Down is light, warm, and aesthetically pleasing to those who don't think camping and technology mix. If you like down bags, be sure to keep them double wrapped in plastic garbage bags on your trip in order to keep dry. Once wet, you'll spend your nights howling at the moon.

The polyfiber-filled bags are not necessarily better than those filled with down, but can be. The one key advantage is that even when wet, some poly-fills can retain 80 to 85 percent of your body heat. This allows you to sleep and get valuable rest even in miserable conditions. And my camping experience shows that no matter how lucky you may be, there comes a time when you will get caught in an unexpected, violent storm and everything you've got will get wet, including your sleeping bag. That's when the value of a poly-fill bag becomes priceless. You either have one and can sleep—or you don't have one and suffer. It is that simple. Of the synthetic fills, Quallofil made by Dupont is the leader of the industry.

But as mentioned, just because a sleeping bag uses a high-tech poly-fill doesn't necessarily make it a better bag. Other factors come into play.

The most important factors are a bag's temperature rating and weight. The temperature rating of a sleeping bag refers to how cold it can get before you start actually feeling cold. Many campers make the mistake of thinking "I only camp in the summer, so a bag rated at 30 or 40 degrees should be fine." Later, they find out it isn't so fine, and all it takes is one cold night to convince them of that. When selecting the right temperature rating, visualize the coldest weather you might ever confront, and then get a bag rated for even colder weather.

For instance, if you are a summer camper, you may rarely experience a night in the low 30's or high 20's. A sleeping bag rated at 20 degrees would thus be appropriate, keeping you snug, warm, and asleep. For most campers, I advise a bag rated at zero or 10 degrees.

If you buy a poly-filled sleeping bag, never leave it squished in your stuff sack between camping trips. Instead keep it on a hanger in a closet or use it as a blanket. One thing that can reduce a poly-filled bag's heat-retaining qualities is if you lose the loft out of the tiny hollow fibers that make up the fill. You can avoid this with proper storage.

The weight of a sleeping bag can also be a key factor, especially for backpackers. When you have to carry your gear on your back, every ounce becomes important. To keep your weight to a minimum, sleeping bags that weigh just three pounds are available, though expensive. But if you hike much, it's worth the price. For an overnighter, you can get away with a 4 or 4 1/2 pound bag without much stress. However, bags weighing five pounds and up should be left back at the car.

I have two sleeping bags: a 7-pounder that feels like I'm sleeping in a giant sponge, and a little 3-pounder. The heavy duty model is for pickup truck camping in cold weather and doubles as a blanket at home. The lightweight bag is for hikes. Between the two, I'm set.

INSULATION PADS

Even with the warmest sleeping bag in the world, if you just lay it down on the ground and try to sleep, you will likely get as cold as a winter cucumber. That is because the cold ground will suck the warmth right out of your body. The solution is to have a layer of insulation between you and the ground. For this, you can use a thin Insulite pad, a lightweight Therm-a-Rest inflatable pad, or an air mattress. Here is a capsule summary of them:

● Insulite pads: They are light, inexpensive, roll up quick for transport, and can double as a seat pad at your camp. The negative side is that at night, they will compress, making it feel like you are sleeping on granite.

● Therm-a-Rest pads: They are a real luxury, because they do everything an Insulite pad does, but also provide a cushion. The negative side to them is that they are expensive by comparison, and if they get a hole in them, become worthless unless you have a patch kit.

● Air mattress: Adequate for car campers, but their bulk, weight and the amount of effort necessary to blow them up makes them a nuisance for any other purpose.

A FEW TRICKS

When surveying a camp area, the most important consideration should be to select a good spot to sleep. Everything else is secondary. Ideally, you want a flat spot that is wind sheltered on ground soft enough to drive stakes into. Yeah, and I want to win the lottery.

Sometimes the ground will have a slight slope to it. In that case, always sleep with your head on the uphill side. If you sleep parallel to the slope, every time you roll over in your sleep, you can find yourself rolling right down the hill. If you sleep with your head on the downhill side, you can get a headache that feels like an axe is embedded in your brain.

When you have found a good spot, clear it of all branches, twigs, and rocks, of course. A good tip is to then dig a slight indentation in the ground where your hip will fit. Since your body is not flat, but has curves and edges, it will not feel comfortable on flat ground. Some people even get severely bruised on the sides of their hips when sleeping on flat, hard ground. For that reason alone, they learn to hate camping. Instead, bring a spade, dig a little depression in the ground for your hip, and sleep well.

After the ground is prepared, throw a ground cloth over the spot, which will keep most of the morning dew off you. In some areas, particularly where fog is a problem, morning dew can be heavy and get the outside of your sleeping bag quite wet. In that case, you either need a tent or some kind of roof, like that of a poncho or tarp, with its ends tied to trees.

TENTS AND WEATHER PROTECTION

All it takes is to get caught in the rain once without a tent and you will never go anywhere without one again. A tent provides protection from rain, wind and mosquito attacks. In exchange, you can lose a starry night's view, though some tents now even provide moon roofs.

A tent can be as complex as a four-season, tubular-jointed dome with rain fly, or nothing more complicated than two ponchos snapped together and roped up to a tree. They can be as cheap as a $10.00 tube tent, which is nothing more than a hollow piece of plastic, or as expensive as a $500.00 five-person deluxe expedition dome model. They vary greatly in size, price, and put-up time. If you plan on getting a good one, then plan on doing plenty of shopping and asking lots of questions. The key ones are: Will it keep me dry? How hard is it to put up? Is it roomy enough? How much does it weigh?

With a little bit of homework, you can get the right answers to these questions.

● Will it keep me dry? On many one and two-person tents, the rain fly does not extend far enough to keep water off the bottom sidewalls of the tent. In a driving rain, water can also drip from the rain fly and to the bottom sidewalls of the tent. Eventually, the water can leak through to the inside, particularly through the seams where the tent has been sewed together. Water can sneak through the tiny needle holes.

You must be able to stake out your rain fly so it completely covers all of the tent. If you are tent shopping and this does not appear possible, then don't buy the tent. To prevent potential leaks, use seamlock, a glue-like substance, to close potential leak areas on tent seams. On the large umbrella tents, keep a patch kit handy and dig a small canal around your tent to channel rain water.

Another way to keep water out of your tent is to store all wet garments outside the tent, under a poncho. Moisture from wet clothes stashed in the tent will condense on the interior tent walls. If you bring enough wet clothes in the tent, by the next morning you will feel like you're camping in a duck blind.

● How hard is it to put up? If a tent is difficult to erect in full sunlight, you can just about forget it at night. Some tents can go up in just a few minutes without requiring help from another camper. This might be the kind of tent you want.

The way to compare put-up time of tents when shopping is to count the number of connecting points from the tent poles to the tent, and also the number of stakes required. The fewer, the better. Think simple. My tent has seven connecting points and, minus the rain fly, requires no stakes. It goes up in a few minutes. If you need a lot of stakes, it is a sure tipoff to a long put-up time. Try it at night or in the rain, and you'll be ready to cash your chips and go for broke.

Another factor are the tent poles themselves. Some small tents have poles that are broken into small sections and are connected by Bungy cords. It only takes an instant to convert it to a complete pole.

Some outdoor shops have tents on display on their showroom floor. Before buying the tent, have the salesman take the tent down and put it back up. If it takes him more than five minutes, or he says he "doesn't have time," then keep looking.

● Is it roomy enough? Don't judge the size of a tent on floor space alone. Some tents small on floor space can give the illusion of roominess with a high ceiling. You can be quite comfortable in them, snug yet not squeezed in.

But remember that a one- person or two-person tent is just that. A two-person tent has room for two people plus gear. That's it. Don't buy a tent expecting it to hold more than it is intended to.

● How much does it weigh? If you're a hiker, this becomes the preeminent question. If it's much more than six or seven pounds, forget it. A 12-pound tent is bad enough, but get it wet and it's like carrying a piano on your back. On the other hand, weight is scarcely a factor if you camp only where you can take your car. My dad, for instance, used to have this giant canvass umbrella tent that folded down to this neat little pack that weighed about 500 pounds.

AN OPTION

If you like going solo and choose not to own a tent at all, a biffy bag can provide the weather protection you require. A biffy bag is a water repellent shell in which your sleeping bag fits. They are light and tough, and for some, are a perfect option to a heavy tent. On the down side, however, there is a strange sensation when you try to ride out a rainy night in one. You can hear the rain hitting you, sometimes even feel the pounding of the drops through the biffy bag. It can be difficult to sleep under such circumstance.

PICKUP TRUCK CAMPERS

If you own a pick-up truck with a camper shell, you can turn it into a self-contained campground with a little bit of work. This can be an ideal way to go because it is fast, portable and you are guaranteed a dry environment.

But that does not necessarily mean it is a warm environment. In fact, without insulation from the metal truck bed, it can feel like sleeping on an iceberg. That is because the metal truck bed will get as cold as the air temperature. Without insulation, it can be much colder in your camper shell than it would be on the open ground.

When I camp in my rig, I use a large piece of foam for a mattress and insulation. The foam measures four inches thick, is 48 inches wide and 76 inches long. It makes for a bed as comfortable as anything one might ask for. In fact, during the winter, if I don't go camping for a few weeks because of writing obligations, I sometimes will throw the foam on the living room floor, lay down the old sleeping bag, light a fire and camp right in my living room. It's in my blood, I tell you.

If you camp in cold areas in your pick-up truck camper shell, a Coleman catalytic heater can keep you toasty. When urging a catlytic heater, it is a good idea to keep ventilation windows partially open to keep the air fresh. Don't worry about how cold it is - the heater will take the snap out of it.

MOTORHOMES

The problems motorhome owners encounter come from two primary sources: Lack of privacy and light intrusion.

The lack of privacy stems from the natural restrictions of where a "land yacht" can go. Without careful use of the guide portion of this book, motorhome owners can find themselves in parking lot settings, jammed in with plenty of neighbors. Because motorhomes often have large picture windows, you lose your privacy, causing some late nights, and come daybreak, light intrusion forces an early wakeup. The result is you get short on sleep.

The answer is to always carry inserts to fit over the inside of your windows. This closes off the outside and retains your privacy. And if you don't want to wake up with the sun at daybreak, you don't have to. It will still be dark.

GOOD NIGHT'S SLEEP LIST

Sleeping bag
Insulite pad or Therm-a-rest
Tent
Ground tarp

OPTIONAL

Air pillows
Mosquito netting
Foam pad for truck bed
Windshield light screen for motorhome
Catalytic heater

FIRST AID & PROTECTION AGAINST INSECTS

A mountain night could not have been more perfect, I thought as I lay in my sleeping bag.

The sky looked like a mass of jewels and the air tasted sweet and smelled of pines. A shooting star fireballed across the sky, and I remember thinking, "It just doesn't get any better."

Just then, as I was drifting into sleep, this mysterious buzz appeared from nowhere and deposited itself inside my left ear. Suddenly awake, I whacked my ear with the palm of a hand about hard enough to cause a minor concussion. The buzz disappeared. I pulled out my flashlight and shined it on my palm, and there, lit in the blackness of night, lay the squished intruder. A mosquito, dead amid a stain of blood, both his and mine.

Satisfied, I turned off the light, closed my eyes, and thought of the fishing trip planned for the next day. Then I heard them. It was a squadron of mosquitos, flying landing patterns around my head. I tried to grab them with an open hand, but they dodged the assault and flew off. Just 30 seconds later another landed in my left ear, though I promptly dispatched the invader with a rip of the palm.

Now I was completely awake, so I got out of my sleeping bag to retrieve some mosquito repellent. While en route, several of the buggers swarmed and nailed me in the back and arms. Later, after application of the repellent and again snug in my sleeping bag, the mosquitos would buzz a few inches from my ear. After getting a whiff of the poison, they would fly off. It was like sleeping in a sawmill.

The next day, drowsy from little sleep, I set out to fish. I'd walked but 15 minutes when I brushed against a bush and felt this stinging sensation on the inside of my arm, just above the wrist. I looked down. A tick had got his clamps into me. I ripped it out before he could embed his head into my skin.

After catching a few fish, I sat down against a tree to eat lunch, and just watch the water go by. My dog, Rebel, sat down next to me and stared at the beef jerky I was munching as if it was a T-bone steak. I finished eating, giving him a small piece, and patted him on the head. Right then, I noticed an itch on my arm where a mosquito had drilled me. I unconsciously scratched it. Two days later, in that exact spot, some nasty red splotches started popping up. Poison oak. By petting my dog and then scratching my arm, I had transfered the oil residue of the poison oak leaves from Rebel's fur to my arm.

On returning home, Foonsky asked me about the trip.

"Great," I said. "Mosquitos, ticks, poison oak. Can hardly wait to go back."

"I'd like to go too," he said.

"On the next trip," I answered, "We'll declare war on those buggers."

MOSQUITOS, NO-SEE-UMS, HORSEFLIES

On a trip to Canada, Foonsky and me were fishing a small lake from the shore when suddenly a black horde of mosquitos could be seen moving across the lake toward us. It was like when the Frency Army looked across the Rhine and saw the Wehrmacht coming. There was a literal buzz in the air. We fought them off for a few minutes, then made a fast retreat to the truck and jumped in, content the buggers had been fooled. But somehow, still unknown to us, the mosquitos started gaining entry to the truck. In 10 minutes, we squished 15 of them while they attempted to plant their oil derricks in our skin. Just outside the truck, the black horde waited for us to make a tactical error, like rolling down a window. It took a sudden hailstorm to wipe out the attack.

When it comes to mosquitos, no-see-ums, gnats and horseflies, there are times when there is nothing you can do. Said episode was one of those times. However, in most situations you can muster a defense to repel the attack.

The first key with mosquitos is to wear clothing too heavy for them to drill through. Expose a minimum of skin, wear a hat, and around your neck, tie a bandana, one that has preferably been sprayed with repellent. If you try to get by with just a cotton T-shirt, you will become a federal mosquito sanctuary.

So first your skin must be well covered, exposing only your hands and face. Second, you should have your companion spray your clothes with repellent from an aerosol can. Third, you should dab liquid repellent directly on your skin.

Taking Vitamin B1 and eating garlic are reputed to act as natural insect repellents, but I've met a lot of mosquitos that are not convinced. A better bet is to take the mystery out of the task and examine the contents of the repellent in question. The key is the percentage of the ingredient called "Non-diethyl-metatoluamide." That is the poison, and the percentage of it in the container must be listed and will indicate that brand's effectiveness. "Inert ingredients" are just excess fluids used to fill the bottles.

At night, the easiest way to get a good night's rest without mosquitos buzzing in your ear is to sleep in a bug-proof tent. If the night's are warm and you want to see the stars, new tent models are available that have a skylight covered with mosquito netting. If you don't like tents on summer evenings, mosquito netting rigged with an air space at your head can solve the problem. Otherwise prepare to get bit, even with the use of mosquito repellent.

If you're problems are with no-see-ums or biting horseflies, then you need a slightly different approach.

No-see-ums are a tiny, black insect that can look like nothing more than a sliver of dirt on your skin. Then you notice something stinging—and when you rub the area, you scratch up a little no-see-um. The results are similar to mosquito bites, making your skin itch, splotch, and when you get them bad, puffy. In addition to using the techniques described to repel mosquitos, you should go one step further.

The problem is no-see-ums are tricky little devils. Somehow they can actually get under your socks around the ankles, where they will bite to their heart's content all night long while you sleep, itch, sleep, and itch some more. The best solution is to apply a liquid repellent to your ankles, then wear clean socks.

Horseflies are another story. They are rarely a problem, but when they get their dander up, they can cause problems you'll never forget.

One such episode occurred when Foonsky and I were paddling a canoe along the shoreline of a large lake. This giant horsefly, about the size of a fingertip, started divebombing the canoe. After 20 minutes, it landed on his thigh, and not one accustomed to such trespasses, Foonsky immediately slammed it with an open hand—then let out a blood-curdling "yeeeee-ow" that practically sent ripples across the lake. When Foonsky whacked it, the horsefly had somehow turned around and bit him in the hand, leaving a huge, red welt.

In the next 10 minutes, that big fly strafed the canoe on more divebomb runs, until I finally got ready with my canoe paddle, swung like a baseball player and nailed that horsefly like I'd hit a home run. It landed about 15 feet from the boat, still buzzing, and shortly thereafter was eaten by a large rainbow trout, which was comforting to Foonsky.

If you have horsefly or yellowjacket problems, you'd best just leave the area. One, two or a few can be dealt with. More than that and your camping trip will be about as fun as being roped to a tree and stung by an electric cattle prod.

On most trips, you will spend time doing everything possible to keep from getting bit by mosquitos or no-see-ums. When that fails, you must know what to do next—and fast if you're among those ill-fated campers who get big, red lumps from a bite inflicted from even a microscopic-sized mosquito.

A fluid called "After Bite," or a dab of ammonia, should be applied immediately to the bite. To start the healing process, apply a first-aid gel, not liquid, such as Campho-Phenique.

TICKS

Ticks are a nasty, little vermin that will wait in ambush, jump on unsuspecting prey, and eventually crawl to a prime location before trying to fill his body with his victim's blood.

I call them the Dracula Bug, but by any name they can be a terrible camp pest. Ticks rest on grasses and low plants and attach themselves to those who brush against the vegetation. Dogs are particularly vulnerable. Typically, they are no more than 18 inches above ground. If you stay on the trails, you can usually avoid them.

There are two common species of ticks. The common coastal tick is larger, colored brownish, and prefers to crawl around prior to putting the clamps on you. The latter habit can give you the creeps, but when you feel it crawling, you can just pick it off and dispatch it. Their preferred destination is usually the back of your neck, just where the hairline starts. The other species, a wood tick, is small, black, and when he puts the clamps in, immediately painful. When a wood tick gets into a dog for a few days, it can cause a large, red welt.

In either case, ticks should be removed as soon as possible. If you have hiked in an area infested with them, it is advisable to shower as soon as possible, discarding and washing your clothes immediately. If you just leave your clothes in a heap, a tick can crawl from your clothes and thus invade your home. They like warmth, and one way or another, they can end up in your bed. Waking up in the middle of the night with a tick crawling across your chest can really give you the creeps.

Once a tick has the clampers on you, you must decide how long it has been there. If it has been a short time, the most painless and effective method is to just take a pair of sharp tweezers and grasp the little devil, making certain to isolate the mouth area, then pull him out.

If the tick has been in longer, you may wish a doctor to extract it. Some people will burn it with a cigarette, or poison it with lighter fluid. In any case, you must take care to remove all of it, especially its claw-like mouth.

The wound, however small, should then be cleansed and dressed. This is done by applying liquid peroxide, which cleans and sterilizes the wound, and then coating on a dressing such as First-Aid Cream, Campho-Pehnique gel, or Neosporin ointment.

POISON OAK

After a nice afternoon hike, about a five miler, I was concerned about possible exposure to poison oak, so I immediately showered and put on clean clothes. Then I settled into a chair with my favorite foamy body-building elixer to watch the end of a baseball game. The game went 18 innings, and meanwhile, my dog, tired from the hike, had gone to sleep on my bare ankles.

A few days later I had a case of poison oak. My feet looked like they had been on fire and put out with an ice pick. The lesson? Don't always trust your dog, give him a bath, and beware of extra-inning ballgames.

You can get poison oak only from direct contact with the oil residue from the leaves. It can be passed in a variety of fashions, as direct as skin/leaf contact or as indirect as leaf to dog, dog to sofa, sofa to skin. Once you have it, there is little you can do but want to itch yourself to death. Applying Caladryl lotion or its equivalent can help because it contains antihistamines, which attack and dry the itch.

A tip that may sound crazy but seems to work is advised by my pal Furni. You should expose the afflicted area to the hottest water you can stand, then suddenly emerse it in cold water. The hot water opens the skin pores and gets the "itch" out. The cold water then quickly seals the pores.

In any case, you're a lot better off if you don't get poison oak to begin with. Remember the old Boy Scout saying: "Leaves of three, let them be." Also remember that poison oak can disguise itself. In the spring it is green, then gradually turns reddish in the summer. By fall, it becomes a bloody, ugly-looking red. In the winter, it loses its leaves altogether and appear to be nothing more than barren, brown sticks of small plant. However, at any time and in any form, skin contact can cause quick infection.

Some people are more easily afflicted than others, but if you are one of the lucky few, don't cheer too loud. While some people can be exposed to the oil residue of poison oak with little or no effect, the body's resistance can be gradually worn down by repeated exposures. At one time, I could practically play in the stuff and the only problems would be a few little bumps on the inside of my wrist. Now, some 15 years later, times have changed. My resistance has broken down. If I merely rub against poison oak now, in a few days the exposed area can look like it has been used for a track meet.

So regardless if you consider yourself vulnerable or not, you should take heed to reduce exposure. That can be done by staying on trails when you hike and making sure your dog does the same. Remember, the worst stands of poison oak are usually brush-infested areas just off the trail. It can also be done by dressing so your skin is completely protected, wearing long-sleeve shirts, long pants, and boots. If you suspect you've been exposed, immediately wash your clothes, then wash yourself with aloe vera, rinsing with a cool shower.

And don't forget to give your dog a bath.

SUNBURN

The most common injury suffered on camping trips is sunburn, yet some people wear it as a badge of honor, believing that it somehow enhances their virility. Well it doesn't. Neither do suntans. And too much sunburn can lead to serious burns or sunstroke, or at the least, result in leathery skin at an early age.

It is easy enough to avoid. Use a high-level sunscreen on your skin, chapstick on your lips, and wear sunglasses and a hat. If any area gets burned, apply First-Aid Cream, which will soothe and provide moisture for the parched, burned skin.

The best advice from Doctor Bogney is not to worry about getting a suntan. Those that do are involved in a practice that is not only one of the ultimate wastes of time, but eventually ruinous to their skins as well.

A WORD ABOUT GIARDIA

Some mountain streams may be clear, cold and taste as clean as the granite rocks they polish, but BEWARE, they may contain an invisible stomach killer. Giardia, a relatively new danger to mountain campers, is a microscopic organism that can cause severe diarrhea and abdominal cramps. It's a painful souvenir of your camping trip and it can last for weeks.

The simplest ways to protect yourself is to drink piped water, carry water to your camping spot, or use one of the lightweight water filtration systems available at backpacking stores. They are fast and effective. A slower yet inexpensive route when unsure about drinking water is to boil it for at least two minutes. At higher altitudes, boil water for at least five minutes. However, this can be frustrating since few thirsty campers like to drink hot water. In addition, boiled water can taste like ashes from the campfire.

Water purification tablets, such as iodine or chlorine, do a good job in killing bacteria, but are unreliable against Giardia. The tablets work slowly, requiring as much as 30 minutes, and even then may not be 100 percent effective.

If you are without a filtration device and are in an area where no piped water is available, such as a wilderness area, then special care must be used to determine what streams have drinkable water. Michael Furniss, a hiking buddy and hydrologist, has shown me how to identify "safe" streams, but all were the headwaters of small feeder creeks in high, mountain pass areas. In many cases, we would climb high above the trail to obtain water from a source in order to be certain that no one had camped above the waterway.

"Major rivers, and any creek that meanders through a meadow, should be avoided at all costs," Furniss advised.

The reason is that Giardia is transferred from affected individuals into a watershed through waste products. When it rains, the organism can be washed from the waste and into the river. Eventually, somewhere downstream, it can be consumed by an unsuspecting camper, and the cycle continues.

To prevent the spread of Giardia, National Park Service law mandates that waste be buried no closer than 100 yards from natural waters and at least eight inches deep.

This is dead serious business. If you have any doubts about the water you plan to drink, the purchase of a water purification unit will not only solve those doubts, but allow you to enjoy your trip free of worry.

HYPOTHERMIA

No matter how well planned your trip might be, a sudden change in weather can turn it into a puzzle for which there are few answers. Bad weather, or an accident, can result in a dangerous chain of events.

Such a chain of episodes occurred for my brother, Rambob, and myself on a fishing trip one fall day just below the snow line. The weather had suddenly turned very cold and ice was forming along the shore of the lake. Suddenly, the canoe was placed in terrible unbalance and just that quick, it flipped. The little life vest seat cushions were useless, and using the canoe as a paddle board, we tried to kick our way back to shore where my dad was going crazy at the thought of his two sons drowning before his eyes.

It took 17 minutes in that 38-degree water, but we finally made it to the shore. When they pulled me out of the water, my legs were dead, not strong enough to even hold up my weight. In fact, I didn't feel so much cold as tired, and I just wanted to lay down and go to sleep.

I closed my eyes, and my brother-in-law, Lloyd Angal, slapped me in the face several times, then got me on my feet and pushed and pulled me about.

In the celebration over making it to shore, only Lloyd had realized that hypothermia was setting in—where the temperature of the body is lowered to the point that it causes poor reasoning, apathy and collapse. It can look like the endangered is just tired and needs to sleep, but that sleep can become a coma.

Ultimately, my brother and I shared what little dry clothing remained. We then began hiking to get muscles functioning, creating internal warmth. We shivered, another way the body creates warmth for itself. We ate whatever munchies were available because the body produces heat by digestion. And most important, we got our heads as dry as possible. More body heat is lost through wet hair than any other single factor.

A few hours later, we were in a pizza parlor replaying the incident, talking about how only a life vest can do the job of a life vest. We decided never again to rely on those little floatation seat cushions that disappear when the boat flips.

Almost by instinct we had done everything right to prevent hypothermia: Don't go to sleep, get dry clothes on, dry your head, induce shivering, start a physical activity, and eat something. That's how you fight hypothermia. In a dangerous setting, whether you fall in a lake, a stream, or get caught unprepared in a storm, that's how you can stay alive.

After being in that ice-bordered lake for almost 20 minutes, and then finally pulling ourselves to the shoreline, a strange, eerie phenomenon occured. My canoe was flipped over and gone was almost all of its contents; tackle box, flotation cushions and cooler. But remaining was one paddle and one fishing rod, the trout rod my grandfather had given me for my 12th birthday.

Lloyd gave me a smile. "This means that you are meant to paddle and fish again," he said with a laugh.

FIRST-AID KIT LIST

Band-aids
Sterile gauze pads
Roller gauze
Athletic tape
Moleskin
Thermometer
Aspirin
Ace bandage

SECONDARY KIT LIST

Mosquito repellent
After Bite or ammonia
Campho-Phenique gel
First Aid cream
Sunscreen
Neosporin ointment
Caladryl
Biodegradable soap
Towelettes

OPTIONAL

Water purification system
Coins for emergency phone call
Extra set of matches
Tweezers

Fishing & Recreational Equipment

F eet tired and hot, stomachs hungry, we stopped our hike for a lunch break aside a beautiful little river pool that was catching the flows from a long but gentle waterfall. My brother, Rambob, passed me a piece of jerky. I took my boots off, then slowly dunked my feet into the cool, foaming water.

I was gazing at a towering peak across a canyon, when suddenly—Wham!— there was a jolt at the heel of my right foot. I pulled my foot out of the water. Incredibly, a trout had bitten it.

My brother looked at me like I had antlers growing out of my head. "Wow!" he exclaimed, "that trout almost caught himself an outdoors writer!"

It's true that in remote areas trout sometimes bite on almost anything, even feet. In California's High Sierra, I have caught limits of trout using nothing but a bare hook. The only problem is the fish will often hit the splitshot sinker instead of the hook. Of course, fishing isn't usually that easy. But it gives you an idea of what is possible.

America's wildlands are home for a remarkable abundance of fish and wildlife. Deer browse with little fear of man, bear keep an eye out for your food, and little critters like squirrels and chipmunks are daily companions. Add in the fishing and you can get some real zing to your camping trip.

Your trips will evolve into premium outdoor experiences if you can parlay in a few good fishing trips, avoid bear problems, and occasionally add a little offbeat fun with some camp games.

TROUT AND BASS

He creeps up on the stream as quiet as an old Indian, keeping his shadow off the water. With his little spinning rod, he'll zip his lure within an inch or two of its desired mark, probing along rocks, the edges of riffles and pocket water; wherever he can find a change in river habitat. It's my brother, Rambob, trout fishing, and he's a master at it.

In most cases, he'll catch a trout on his first or second cast. After that it's time to move upriver, giving no spot much more than five minutes due. Stick and move, stick and move, stalking the stream like a bobcat zeroing in on an unsuspecting rabbit. He might keep a few for dinner, but mostly he releases what he catches. Rambob doesn't necessarily fish for food. It's the feeling that comes with it.

You can feel a sense of exhilaration, like you've taken a good shower after being coated with dust. On your walk back to camp, the steps come easy. You suddenly understand what John Muir meant when he talked of developing a oneness with nature, because you have it. That's what fishing can help provide.

You don't need a million dollars worth of fancy gear to catch fish. What you need is the right outlook, and that can be learned. That goes regardless if you are fishing for trout or bass, the two most popular fisheries in America. Your fishing tackle selection should be as simple and as clutter-free as possible.

At home I've got every piece of fishing tackle you might imagine, more than 30 rods and many tackle boxes, racks and cabinets filled with all kinds of stuff. I've got one lure that looks like a chipmunk and another that resembles a miniature can of beer with hooks. If I hear of something new, I want to try it, and usually do. It's the result of a lifelong fascination with the sport. But if you just want to catch fish, there's an easier way to go. And when I go fishing, I take that path. I don't try to bring everything. It would be impossible anyway.

Instead I bring a relatively small amount of gear. At home I will scan my tackle boxes for equipment and lures, make my selections, and bring just the essentials. Rod, reel and tackle, everything will fit into a side of my backpack or a small carrying bag.

So, what kind of rod should be used on an outdoors trip? For most camper/anglers, I suggest the use of a light, multi-piece spinning rod that will break down to a small size. One of the best deals on the fishing market is the six-piece Daiwa 6½-foot pack rod, No. 6752. It retails for as low as $30, yet is made of a graphite/glass composite that gives it qualities of much more expensive models. And it comes in a hard plastic carrying tube for protection. Other major rod manufacturers, such as Fenwick, Sabre, and Contender, offer similar premium rods, and it's tough to miss with any of them.

The use of graphite/glass composites in fishing rods has made them lighter, more sensitive, yet stronger. The only downside to graphite as a rod material is that it can be brittle. If you rap your rod against something, it can crack or cause a weak spot. That weak spot can eventually snap, even under light pressure, like setting a hook or casting. A small bit of care will prevent that from ever occurring.

If you haven't bought a fishing reel in some time, you will be surprised at the quality and price of micro spinning reels on the market. The reels come tiny, and strong, with rear-control drag systems. Sigma, Shimano, Cardinal, Abu and others all make premium reels. They also come expensive, usually $50 to $75. They're worth it. With your purchase, you've got a reel that will last for years.

The one downside to spinning reels is that after longterm use, the bail spring will weaken. The result is that after casting and beginning to reel, the bail will sometimes not flip over and allow the reel to retrieve the line. You then have to do it by hand. This can be incredibly frustrating, particularly when stream fishing where instant line pickup is essential. The solution is to have a new bail spring installed every few years, a cheap, quick operation for a tackle expert.

You might own a giant tackle box filled with lures, but on your fishing trip you are better off to fit just the essentials into a small container. One of the best ways to do that is to use the Plano Micro-Magnum 3414, a tiny two-sided tackle box for trout fishermen that fits into a shirt pocket. In mine, I can fit 20 lures in one side of the box and 20 flies, splitshot, and snap swivels in the other. For bass lures, which are larger, you need a slightly larger box, but the same principle can apply.

There are more fishing lures on the market than you can imagine, but a few special ones can do the job, and I make sure they are in my box on every trip. For trout, a few of my favorites are a small, black Panther Martin spinner with yellow spots, small gold Kastmaster, yellow Roostertail, gold Z-Ray with red spots, Super Duper and a Mepps Lightning spinner.

You can take it a step further using an insider's wisdom. My old pal, Ed the Dunk, showed me his trick of taking a tiny Dardevle spoon, then spraypainting it flat black and dabbing five tiny red dots on it. It's a real killer, particularly in tiny streams where the trout are spooky.

The best trout catcher I've ever used on rivers is a small metal lure called a Met-L Fly. On days when nothing else works, it can be like going to a shooting gallery. The problem is that the lure is near impossible to find. Rambob and I consider the few we have left so valuable that if the lure is snagged on a rock, a cold swim is deemed mandatory for their retrieval. These lures are as elusive to find in tackle shops as trout can be to catch without one.

For bass, you can also fit all you need into a small plastic tackle box. I have fished with many bass pros and all of them actually use just a few lures: A white spinner bait, a small jig called a Git's It, a surface plug called a Zara Spook, and plastic worms. At times, like when the bass move into shoreline areas during the spring, shad minnow imitations such as made by Rebel or Rapala can be dynamite. For instance, my favorite is the one-inch, blue/silver Rapala. Every spring, as the lakes begin to warm and the fish snap out of their winter doldrums, I like to float and paddle around small lakes in my small raft. I'll cast that little Rapala along the shoreline and catch and release hundreds of bass, bluegill and sunfish. The fish are usually sitting right along the shoreline, waiting for my offerings.

A FEW TRICKS

There's an old angler's joke about how you need to "think like a fish." But if you're the one getting zilched, you may not think it's so funny.

The irony is that it really is your mental approach, what you see and what you miss, that often determines your fishing luck. Some people will spend a lot of money on tackle, lures and fishing clothes, and that done, just saunter up to a stream or lake, cast out and wonder why they are not catching fish. The answer is their mental outlook. They are not attuning themselves to their surroundings.

You must try living on nature's level, not your own. Do the former and you will start to feel things you never believed even exisited. Soon you will see things that will allow you to catch fish. You can get a headstart by reading about fishing, but to get your degree in fishing, you must attend the University of Nature.

On every fishing trip, regardless what you fish for, try to follow three hard-and-fast rules:

    ● 1. Always approach the fishing spot so you will be undetected by the fish.

    ● 2. Present your lure, fly or bait in a manner that appears completely natural, as if no line was attached.

● 3. Stick and move, hitting one spot, working it the best you can, then move to the next.

Here's a more detailed explanation:

1. APPROACH: No one can just walk up to a stream or lake, cast out, and start catching fish as if someone had waved a magic wand. Instead, give the fish credit for being smart. After all, they live there.

Your approach must be completely undetected by the fish. Fish can sense your presence through sight and sound, though this is misinterpreted by most people. By sight, this only rarely means the fish actually see you. More likely, they will see your shadow on the water, or the movement of your arm or rod while casting. By sound, it doesn't mean they hear you talking. It means they will detect the vibrations of your footsteps along the shore, kicking a rock, or the unnatural plunking sound of a heavy cast hitting the water. Any of these elements can spook them off the bite. In order to fish undetected, you must walk softly, keep your shadow off the water, and keep your casting motion low. All of these keys become easier at sunrise or sunset, when shadows are on the water. At mid-day, a high sun causes a high level of light penetration in the water, which can make the fish skittish to any foreign presence.

Like hunting, you must stalk the spots. When my brother Rambob sneaks up on a fishing spot, he looks like a burglar sneaking through an unlocked window.

2. PRESENTATION: Your lure, fly, or bait must appear in the water as if no line was attached, so it appears as natural as possible.

My pal Mo Furniss has skindived in rivers to watch what the fish see when somebody is fishing.

"You wouldn't believe it," he said. "When the lure hits the water, every trout within 40 feet, like 15, 20 trout, will do a little zig-zag. They all see the lure, they're all aware something is going on. Meanwhile, onshore the guy casting doesn't get a bite and thinks there aren't any fish in the river."

If you're trying to fool a fish into striking, your offering must appear as part of its natural habitat, as if it is an insect just hatched or a small fish looking for a spot to hide. That's where you come in.

After you have sneaked up to a fishing spot, you should zip your cast upstream, then start your retrieve as soon as it hits the water. If you let the lure sink to the bottom, then start the retrieve, you have no chance. A minnow, for instance, does not sink to the bottom then start swimming. On rivers, the retrieve should be more of a drift, as if the "minnow" was in trouble and the current was sweeping it downstream.

When fishing on trout streams, always hike and cast upriver, then retrieve as the offering drifts downstream in the current. This is effective because trout will sit almost motionless, pointed upstream, finning against the current. This way they can see anything coming in their direction, and if a potential food morsel arrives, all they need to do is move over a few inches, open their mouths, and they've got an easy lunch. Therefore, you must cast upstream.

Conversely, if you cast downstream, your retrieve will bring the lure from behind the fish, where he cannot see it approaching. And I've never seen a trout that had eyes in its tail. In addition, when retrieving a downstream lure, the river current will tend to sweep your lure inshore to the rocks.

3. FINDING SPOTS: A lot of fishermen don't catch fish and a lot of hikers never see any wildlife. The key lies in where they are looking.

The rule of the wild is that fish and wildlife will congregate wherever there is a distinct change in the habitat. This is where you should begin your search. To find deer, for instance, forget probing a thick forest, but look for where a forest breaks into a meadow, or a clear-cut has splayed a stand of trees. That's where the deer will be. Look for the change.

In a river, it can be where a riffle pours into a small pool, a rapid that plunges into a deep hole and flattens, a big boulder in the middle of a long riffle, a shoreline point, a rock pile, a submerged tree. Look for the changes. On the other hand, long straight stretches of shoreline will not hold fish—the habitat is lousy.

On rivers, the most productive areas are often where short riffles tumble into small oxygenated pools. After sneaking up from the downstream side and staying low, you should zip your cast so the lure plops gently in the white water just above the pool. Starting your retrieve instantly, the lure will drift downstream and plunk into the pool. Bang! That's where the trout will hit. Take a few more casts, then head upstream to the next spot.

With a careful approach and lure presentation, and by fishing in the right spots, you have the ticket to many exciting days on the water.

OF BEARS AND FOOD

The first time you come nose-to-nose with a bear, it will make your skin quiver.

Even mild-mannered black bears, the most common bear in America, can send shockwaves through your body. They range from 250 to 400 pounds and have big claws and teeth that are custom made for scaring campers. When they bound, muscles on their shoulders seem to roll like ocean breakers.

Bears in camping areas are accustomed to sharing the mountains with hikers and campers. They have become specialists in the food raiding business. As a result, you must be able to make a bear-proof food hang, or be able to scare the beast off. Many campgrounds provide bear and raccoon-proof food lockers, which also solves the problem. You can also stash your food in your vehicle, but that puts a limit on your trip.

If you are in a particularly remote area, there will be no food lockers available. Your car will not be there, either. The answer is making a bear-proof food hang—suspending all of your food wrapped in a plastic garbage bag from a rope in mid-air, often 10 feet from the trunk of a tree, 20 feet off the ground.

This is accomplished by tying a rock to a rope, then throwing it over a high but sturdy tree limb. Next, tie your food bag to the rope, and hoist it up in the air. When you are satisfied with the position of the food bag, you then tie off the end of the rope on another tree. Nothing else will do, especially for hikers in bear-troubled areas, such as Yosemite, Sequoia or Kings Canyon National Parks. One day in Yosemite near Tuolumne Meadows, I met five consecutive teams of hikers heading the other direction. Every one of them had lost food to bears.

I've been there. On one trip, Foonsky and Rambob had left to fish while I was stoking up an evening campfire. Suddenly, I felt the eyes of an intruder on my back. I turned around and this big bear was heading straight for our camp. In the next half hour, I scared the bear off twice, but then he got a whiff of something sweet in my brother's pack.

In most situations you can spook a black bear by banging on a pot and shouting like a lunatic. But some bears are on to the old banging-the-pot trick. If so, and he gets a whiff of your Tang, banging on a pot and shouting can be like trying to stop a steamroller with a roadblock.

In this case, the bear rolled into camp like a semi-truck, grabbed my brother's pack, ripped it open and plucked out the Tang and the Swiss Miss. The bear, a 350-pounder, then sat astride a nearby log and lapped at the goodies like a thirsty dog finding water.

I took two steps toward the pack and that bear jumped off the log and galloped across the camp right at me. Scientists say a man can't outrun a bear, but they've never seen how fast I can go up a granite block with a bear on my tail. Once a bear gets his mitts on your gear, he considers it his.

Shortly thereafter, Foonsky returned while I was still perched on top of the rock, and demanded to know how I could let a bear get our Tang. But it took all three of us, Foonsky, Rambob and myself, all charging at once and shouting like madmen to clear the bear out of the camp and send him off over the ridge. It was a lesson to never let food sit unattended.

FUN AND GAMES

You can bring an added dimension to your camping trip with a few recreational tools.

One such tool is an inexpensive star chart. They allow you to identify stars, constellations and planets on clear mountain nights. Another good addition is a pocket-size handbook on tree identification. Both of these can provide a unique perspective to your trip and make you feel more a participant of the wild, rather than an observer.

If you want more excitement, and maybe a little competition with your companions, a good game using twigs or rocks is called "3-5-7." You set up the game by laying out three rows of twigs, with three twigs in one row, five in another, seven in the other. Alternating turns with one competitor, you are allowed to remove all or as few as one twig from a row, but from only one row per turn. You alternate turns removing twigs and whoever is left picking up the last twig is the loser.

Some folks bring a deck of cards and a tiny cribbage board, or will set up a poker game. Of the latter, I've been in a few doozies on backpacking trips. Money is meaningless in the woods, but something like penny candy has a high value. Betting a pack of M&Ms and a beef stick in an outback poker game is like laying down a million dollars in Las Vegas.

In a game of seven-card stud, I caught a straight on the last card of the deal, but Foonsky was showing three sevens and bluffing full house. When I bet five

M&M's with nuts and two Skittles, Rambob folded. "Too much for me." But Foonsky matched my bet, and then with painful slowness, raised me a grape stick.

All was quiet. It was the highest bet ever made. I felt nervous, my heart started pounding, and again I looked hard at my cards. The decision came tough. I folded. The potential of losing a grape stick, even with a great hand like I had, was just too much to gamble.

But I still had my grape stick.

FISHING/RECREATION GEAR LIST

Fishing rod
Fishing reel with fresh line
Small tackle box with lures, splitshot, and snap swivels
Pliers
Knife
Firecrackers for bear protection

OPTIONAL

Rope for bearproof food hang
Stargazing chart
Tree identification handbook
Deck of cards

CHAPTER SEVEN

MAPS & HOW TO USE THEM

Now you're ready to join the Five Percent Club, that is, the five percent of people in Washington and Oregon who know the secret spots where you can camp, fish and hike, and have the time of your life doing it.

To aid in that pursuit, there are a number of contacts, map sources and reservation systems available for your use. These include contacts for national forests, state parks, national parks and motorhome parks. The state and federal agencies listed can provide detailed maps at low costs and any additional information you might require.

NATIONAL FORESTS

The Forest Service provides many secluded camps and also permits camping anywhere except where it is specifically prohibited. If you ever want to clear the cobwebs and get away from it all, this is the way to go.

Many Forest Service campgrounds are quite remote, have no water and require no reservations or check-in. In addition, there is no charge for their use. At those Forest Service campgrounds that provide piped water, the camp fee is often only a few dollars, with payment done on the honor system. Because most of these camps are in mountain areas, they are subject to closure from snow or mud during the winter.

Dogs are permitted on National Forests with no extra charge, and no hassle. Conversely, in state and national parks, dogs are not allowed on trails.

Maps for National Forests are among the best you can get, detailing all back country streams, lakes, hiking trails and logging roads for access. They cost $1 and are available by writing USDA-Forest Service, Outdoor Recreation Information Office, 1018 First Ave., Seattle, WA 98104.

I've found the Forest Service personnel to be the most helpful of any government agency when obtaining camping or hiking trail information. Unless you are buying a map, it is advisable to phone, not write, to get the best service. For specific information on a National Forest, write or phone at the following addresses and phone numbers.

Washington
 ● **Gilford Pinchot National Forest**, 500 West 12th St., Vancouver, WA 98660, 206-696-7500

● **Olympic National Forest**, P.O. Box 2288., Olympia, WA 98507, 206-753-9534

● **Mt. Baker-Snoqualmie National Forest**, Holyoke Building, 1022 First Ave., Seattle, WA 98104 206-442-5400

● **Colville National Forest**, 695 South Main St., Colvilee, WA 99114, 509-684-3711

● **Wenatchee National Forest**, P.O. Box 811, Wenatchee, WA 98801, 509-662-4335

● **Okanogan National Forest**, P.O. Box 950, Okanogan, WA 98840 509-422-2704

Oregon

● **Deschutes National Forest**, 1645 Highway 20 East, Bend, OR 97701, 503-388-2715

● **Fremont National Forest**, 34 North D St., Lakeview, OR 97630, 503-947-2151

● **Malheur National Forest**, 139 NE Dayton St., John Day, OR 97845, 503-474-1731

● **Mount Hood National Forest**, 2955 NW Division St., Gresham, OR 97030, 503-447-6247

● **Ochoco National Forest**, Federal Building, Prineville, OR 97754, 503-447-6247

● **Rogue River National Forest**, 333 West 8th St., Medford, OR 97501, 503-776-3600

● **Siskiyou National Forest**, 200 NE Greenfield, Grants Pass, OR 97526, 503-479-5301

● **Siuslaw National Forest**, 545 SW Second, Corvallis, OR 97330, 503-757-4480

● **Umatilla National Forest**, 2517 SW Hailey Ave., Pendleton, OR 97801, 503-276-3811

● **Umpqua National Forest**, 2900 NW Stewert Parkway, Roseburg, OR 97470, 503-672-6601

● **Wallowa-Witman National Forest**, P.O. Box 907, Baker, OR 97814, 503-883-7761

● **Willamette National Forest**, 211 East Seventh Ave., Eugene, OR 97401, 503-883-7761

● **Winema National Forest**, P.O. Box 1390, Klamath Falls, OR 97601, 503-883-7761

STATE PARKS

The Washington and Oregon State Park systems provide many popular camping spots. Reservations are often a necessity during the summer months. However, reservations are not needed at many others, as indicated in the zone-by-zone camping guide. The camps include drive-in sites, tent space and picnic tables, with showers and a bathroom provided nearby. Although some parks are well known, there are still some little-known gems in the State Park system where campers can get seclusion even in summer months.

In Washington, there are nine parks that offer a reservation service. Reservations are accepted from the second Monday in January until 14 days before Labor Day. You can request camping dates within the current calendar year only. There is a $3 non-refundable fee for each reservation made at each park. The $3 payment and the "standard campsite fee" for the first night must accompany your request for a reservation.

For more information, Washington State Parks provide a toll-free campsite information number at 1-800-562-0990.

Washington
- **Belfair State Park**, N.E. 410 Beck Road, Belfair WA 98528 206-478-4625
- **Birch Bay State Park**, 5105 Helwig Rd., Blaine, WA 98230 200-371-2800
- **Fort Canby State Park**, P.O. Box 488, Ilwaco, WA 98630 206-642-3078
- **Fort Flagler State Park**, Norland WA 98358 206-385-1259
- **Lake Chelan State Park**, Route 1, Box 90, Chelan WA 98816 509-687-3710
- **Moran State Park**, Star Route, Box 22, Eastsound, WA 98245 206-376-2326
- **Pearrygin Lake State Park**, Route 1, Box 300, Winthrop, WA 98862 509-996-2370
- **Steamboat Rock State Park**, P.O. Box 352, Electric City, WA 99123 509-633-1304
- **Twin Harbors/Grayland Beach**, c/o Twin Harbors State Park, Westport, WA 98595 206-753-4055

Oregon
- **State Parks and Recreation Division**, 525 Trade St., SE, Salem, OR 97310, 503-378-6305
- **State Parks Portland Office**, 3554 So. 82nd Ave., Portland, OR 97266, 503-238-7488
- **State Parks Tillamook Office**, 3600 E. Third St., Tillamook, OR 97141, 503-842-5501
- **State Parks Coos Bay Office**, 1155 So. 5th St., Coos Bay, OR 97420, 503-269-9410
- **State Parks Bend Office**, 63055 No. Highway 97, Bend, OR 97701, 503-388-6211
- **State Parks La Grande Office**, 211 Adams Ave., La Grande, OR 97850, 503-963-6444

NATIONAL PARKS

The National Parks in Washington and Orgeon are natural wonders, ranging from the spectacular Mount Rainer National Park to the lava-strewn Mount St. Helens National Monument and the often fog-bound Olympic National Forest.

For information on each of the five national parks in Washington, you should contact the parks directly at the following numbers or addresses.

Washington
- **Olympic National Park**, 600 East Park Ave., Port Angeles, WA 98362 206-452-9235
- **Mount St. Helens National Volcanic Monument**, Amboy, WA 98601 206-247-5473
- **Mount Rainer National Park**, Tahoma Woods, Star Route, Ashford, WA 98304 206-855-1331
- **North Cascades National Park**, Ross Lake and Lake Chelan National Recreation Areas, 800 State St., Sedro Wooley, WA 98284 206-855-1331
- **Coulee Dam National Recreation Area**, P.O. Box 37, Coulee Dam, WA 99116 509-633-1360

Oregon
- **Crater Lake National Park**, P.O. Box 7, Crater Lake, OR 97604, 503-594-2211
- **Fort Clatsop National Memorial**, Route 3, Box 604-FC, Astoria, OR 97103, 503-861-2471
- **John Day Fossil Beds National Monument**, 420 W. Main St., John Day, OR 97845, 503-575-0721
- **Oregon Caves National Monument**, 19000 Caves Highway, Cave Junction, OR 97523, 503-592-2100

DEPARTMENT OF NATURAL RESOURCES

The Department of Natural Resources manages about five million acres of public land in Washington.

All of it is managed under the concept of "multiple use," designed for the greatest recreational opportunities while still protecting the natural resources of the area.

The campgrounds on these areas are among the most primitive, remote and least known of the camps listed in this book. The cost is usually free and you are asked to remove all litter and trash from the area, leaving only your footprints behind.

In addition to maps of the area it manages, the Department of Natural Resources also has U.S. Geological Survey maps and U.S. Army maps. For information, write or phone:

- **Department of Natural Resources**, Photo and Map Sales, AW-11, 1065 South Capitol Way, Olympia, WA 98504 206-753-5338

BUREAU OF LAND MANAGEMENT

- **Oregon State Office**, 825 NE Multnomah St., Portland, OR 97208, 503-231-6274
- **Burns District**, 74 So. Alvord St., Burns, OR 97720, 503-573-2071
- **Coos Bay District**, 333 So. 4th St., Coos Bay, OR 97420, 503-269-5880
- **Eugene District**, 1255 Pearl St., Eugene, OR 97401, 503-687-6651

● **Lakeview District**, 1000 So. Ninth St., Lakeview, OR 97630, 503-947-2177

● **Medford District**, 3040 Biddle St., Medford, OR 97630, 503-776-4174

CAMP GEAR
CHECK LIST

1. Cooking gear list:

> Matches bagged in different zip-lock bags
> Fire-starter cubes or candle
> Camp stove
> Camp fuel
> Pot, pan, cup
> Pot grabber
> Knife, fork
> Dish soap and scrubber
> Salt, pepper, spices
> Itemized food
> Plastic spade
>
> —Optional:
> Axe or hatchet
> Wood or charcoal for barbeque
> Ice chest
> Spatula
> Grill
> Tin foil

2. Hiking and foot care list:

> Quality hiking boots
> Backup lightweight shoes
> Polypropylene socks
> Thick cotton socks
> 80 percent wool socks
> Strong boot laces
> Innersole or foot cushion
> Ace bandage
> Moleskin and medical tape

Band-Aids
Gaters
Water repellent boot treatment

3. **Camping clothes list:**

Polypropylene underwear
Cotton shirt
Long sleeve cotton/wool shirt
Cotton/canvas pants
Vest
Parka
Rain jacket, pants, or poncho
Hat
Sunglasses
Chapstick
Sunscreen

—Optional:
Seam Lock
Shorts
Swimming suit
Gloves
Ski cap

4. **Good night's sleep list:**

Sleeping bag
Insulite pad or Therm-a-rest
Tent
Ground tarp

—Optional:
Air pillow
Mosquito netting
Foam pad for truck bed
Windshield light screen for motorhome
Catalytic heater

5. **First-aid kit list:**

Bandaids
Sterile gauze pads
Roller gauze
Athletic tape
Moleskin
Thermometer

Aspirin
Ace bandage
Mosquito repellent
After Bite or ammonia
Campho-Phenique gel
First Aid cream
Sunscreen
Neosporin ointment
Caladryl
Biodegradable soap
Towelette

—Optional:
Water purification system
Coins for emergency phone call
Extra set of matches
Tweezers
Mirror for signaling

6. **Fishing/recreation gear list**

Fishing rod
Fishing reel with fresh line
Small tackle box with lures, splitshot, and snap swivels
Pliers
Knife

—Optional:
Stargazing chart
Tree identification handbook
Deck of cards
Backpacking cribbage board

7. **Miscellaneous essentials**

Maps
Flashlight
Nylon rope for food hang
Handkerchief
Camera and film
Plastic garbage bags
Toilet paper
Compass
Watch

—Optional:
Binoculars
Notebook and pen
Towel

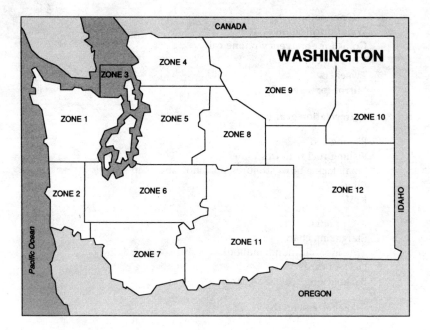

GUIDE TO WASHINGTON CAMPING AREAS

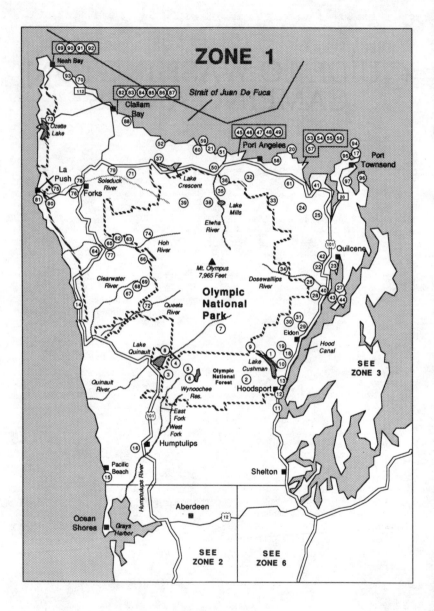

OLYMPIC PENINSULA

BIG CREEK
Site **1**

Campsites, facilities: There are 23 tent sites and 23 sites for trailers or motorhomes up to 21 feet long. Picnic tables are provided. Piped water, sanitary services, showers, firewood, wheelchair facilities, store and cafe are available. Pets are permitted. Boat dock and ramp are located at nearby Lake Cushman.

Reservations, fee: No reservations necessary; $4 fee per night. Open from May through mid-November.

Who to contact: Phone Olympic National Forest at 206-877-5254, or write at P.O. Box 68, Hoodsport, WA 94548.

Location: From town of Hoodsport, drive eight miles northwest on Highway 44 to the "T" intersection and you're there.

Trip note: This camp is a good alternative to campsites 9 and 10, which are set right along Lake Cushman and get heavier use. The park is set at about 1,000-feet elevation and covers 30 acres.

BROWN CREEK
Site **2**

Campsites, facilities: There are 22 tent sites and 12 sites for trailers or motorhomes up to 21 feet long. Picnic tables are provided. Well water, vault toilets and firewood are available. Pets are permitted.

Reservations, fee: No reservations necessary; $3 fee per night. Open late-May to early-September.

Who to contact: Phone Olympic National Forest at 206-426-8265, or write at Shelton, WA 98584.

Location: Drive north out of Shelton on US 101, then turn left at the Skokomish Valley on County Route 23 and drive for about 14 miles on Route 23 and Forest Service Roads. A Forest Service Map is essential.

Trip note: This camp is virtually unknown to outsiders. It is accessible to two-wheel drive vehicles, but the road connects to a network of primitive, back country Forest Service roads. Camp is small, just six acres, but is within the vast Olympic National Forest. Obtain Forest Service map to expand trip.

WILLABY
Site **3**

Campsites, facilities: There are 19 tent sites and 12 sites for trailers or motorhomes up to 21

feet long. Picnic tables are provided. Piped water, flush toilets, electricity in the bathrooms and firewood are available. Pets are permitted. Boat docks, launching facilities and rentals are available at nearby Quinault Lake.

Reservations, fee: No reservations necessary; $6 fee per night. Open early-May to mid-September.

Who to contact: Phone Olympic National Forest at 206-288-2525, or write to Quinault Ranger Station, Quinault, WA 98575.

Location: Drive on US 101 to Quinault turn-off (County Route 5), then drive 1½ miles to where the camp is located along the shore of Quinault Lake.

Trip note: This seven-acre camp is set on the shore of Quinault Lake at 200-feet elevation. The Quinault Rain Forest Nature Trail and the Quinault Recreation Loop Trail are nearby. Quinault Lake covers about six square miles.

FALLS CREEK

Site **4**

Campsites, facilities: There are 22 tent sites and 17 sites for trailers or motorhomes up to 15 feet long. Picnic tables are provided. Piped water, flush toilets, electricity in the bathrooms and firewood are available. Pets are permitted. Boat docks, launching facilities and rentals are available at nearby Quinault Lake. Wheelchair facilities are available.

Reservations, fee: No reservations necessary; $6 fee per night. Open mid-May to early-October.

Who to contact: Phone Olympic National Forest at 206-288-2525, or write to Quinault Ranger Station, Quinault, WA 98575.

Location: Drive on US 101 to Quinault turn-off (County Route 5), and drive three miles to where camp is located on the shore of Quinault Lake.

Trip note: This three-acre camp is set at 200-foot elevation, on the shore of Quinault Lake where Falls Creek empties into it. The Quinault Rain Forest Nature Trail and Quinault Recreation Loop Trail are nearby. A rustic setting on the edge of Olympic National Park.

CAMPBELL TREE GROVE

Site **5**

Campsites, facilities: There are six tent sites and three sites for trailers or motorhomes up to 21 feet long. Picnic tables are provided. Vault toilets, drinking water and firewood are available. Pets are permitted.

Reservations, fee: No reservations necessary; $3 fee per night. Open from Memorial Day to Labor Day.

Who to contact: Phone Olympic National Forest at 206-288-2525, or write at Quinault Ranger Station, Quinault, WA 98575.

Location: This is located on the edge of the Colonel Bob Wilderness. To reach it you drive 26 miles northeast of Humptulips on Forest Service roads. A Forest Service map is essential.

Trip note: This 14-acre camp is set at about 1,100-feet elevation. Trails leading into the Colonel Bob Wilderness are nearby, see Forest Service map for locations. The West Fork of the Humptulips River runs near the camp. A prime base camp for wilderness expedition.

COHO

Site **6**

Campsites, facilities: There are 46 tent sites and 46 sites for trailers or motorhomes up to 36 feet long. Picnic tables are provided. Flush toilets, piped water and wheelchair facilities are available. Pets are permitted. Boat docks and launching facilities are available at Wynoochee Lake.

Reservations, fee: No reservations necessary; $6 fee per night. Open late-May to early-September.

Who to contact: Phone Olympic National Forest at 206-426-8265, or write at P.O. Box 520, Shelton, WA 98584.

Location: From the town of Montesano drive 12 miles north on County Route 58, then continue north for another 22 miles on Forest Service roads to where camp is located on the west shore of Wynoochee Lake. A Forest Service map would be helpful.

Trip note: This eight-acre camp is set on the shore of Wynoochee Lake at 900-feet elevation. Points of interest include a natural trail, Wynoochee Dam Viewpoint, and a 10-mile National Recreation Trail that goes around the lake. This is one of the most idyllic drive-to settings you could hope to find.

GRAVES CREEK

Site **7**

Campsites, facilities: There are 45 tent sites and 45 sites for trailers or motorhomes up to 21 feet long. Picnic tables, drinking water and restrooms are available. Pets are permitted.

Reservations, fee: No reservations necessary; no fee. Open all year with limited winter facilities.

Who to contact: Phone Olympic National Park at 206-452-4501, or write at 600 East Park, Port Angeles, WA 98362.

Location: Drive 15 miles northeast of Quinault on an all-weather Forest Service road. Campground and Graves Creek Ranger Station are located at road's end.

Trip note: This camp is set at 540-feet elevation and set a short distance from trailhead leading into many areas in the backcountry of Olympic National Park. See Olympic Forest Service-National Park map for details. The upper Quinalt River is nearby, but there are lakes in the area.

JULY CREEK

Site **8**

Campsites, facilities: There are 31 primitive tent sites. Picnic tables are provided. Toilets and drinking water are available.

Reservations, fee: No reservations necessary; no fee. Open all year.

Who to contact: Phone Olympic National Park at 206-452-4501, or write at 600 East Park, Port Angeles, WA 98362.

Location: Drive two miles north of the town of Amanda Park on US 101, then turn right and drive for two miles along north shore of Quinault Lake to camp where July Creek empties into Quinault Lake.

Trip note: A primitive alternative, located on the north shore of Quinault Lake. Full supplies are available on the southern shoreline of the lake, which has a marina.

STAIRCASE

Site **9**

Campsites, facilities: There are 63 tent sites and 63 sites for trailers or motorhomes up to 16 feet long. Picnic tables are provided. Restrooms, drinking water and wheelchair facilities are available.

Reservations, fee: No reservations necessary; $5 fee per night. Open all year.

Who to contact: Phone Olympic National Park at 206-452-4501, or write at 600 East Park, Port Angeles, WA 98362.

Location: From town of Hoodsport, drive 19 miles northwest via Staircase and Skokomish River Roads to where camp is located on the Staircase Rapids of the North Fork of the Skokomish River, about one mile from where it empties into Lake Cushman.

Trip note: A take-your-pick spot. Lake Cushman is located just south, the Skokomish River runs adjacent and the Wonder Mountain Wilderness is set to the northeast. A major trailhead at the camp leads to many areas in the backcountry of Olympic National Park. See Olympic National Park and Forest Map for details. In the summer there are ranger programs and a nature trail is nearby.

LAKE CUSHMAN STATE PARK

Site **10**

Campsites, facilities: There are 50 tent sites and 30 sites with full hook-ups for trailers or motorhomes up to 60 feet long. Picnic tables are provided. Sanitary services, drinking water, restrooms, showers and wheelchair facilities are available. Store, cafe and ice are available within one mile. Firewood is available for an extra fee. Pets are permitted. Boat docks and launching facilities are available at nearby Lake Cushman.

Reservations, fee: No reservations necessary; $6 fee per night. Open all year.

Who to contact: Phone the Lake Cushman State Park at 206-877-5491, or write at P.O. Box 128, Hoodsport, WA 98548.

Location: Drive seven miles west of Hoodsport on Staircase Road.

Trip note: This 603-acre camp is set at on the shore of Lake Cushman and has beach access. Good trout fishing. Lake Cushman is a 10-mile long lake that is surrounded by the Olympic Mountains. Nearby recreation options include an 18-hole golf course and marked hiking trails.

POTLATCH STATE PARK

Site **11**

Campsites, facilities: There are 17 tent sites and 18 drive-through sites with full hook-ups for trailers or motorhomes up to 60 feet long. Picnic tables and drinking water are provided. Sanitary services and restrooms with showers are available. Firewood is available for an extra fee. Pets are permitted. Boat docks are available at nearby Hood Canal.

Reservations, fee: No reservations necessary; $6 fee per night. Open all year.

Who to contact: Phone Potlatch State Park at 206-877-5361, or write at P.O. Box D, Hoodsport, WA 98548.

Location: Drive 12 miles north of Shelton on US 101 to where park is located along the shoreline of Hood Canal.

Trip note: A good camp for vacationers towing boats with drive-through sites providing plenty of space. This 57-acre park is set along Hood Canal which offers opportunities for fishing, clamming, crabbing and scuba diving. Nearby recreation options include marked hiking trails.

Site **12** | **GLEN AYR**
RV PARK

Campsites, facilities: There are 57 drive-through sites for trailers or motorhomes of any length. Electricity, piped water, sewer hookups and picnic tables are provided. Bottled gas, toilets, showers, recreation hall and laundry are available. Store, cafe and ice are within one mile. Pets are permitted.

Reservations, fee: Reservations accepted; $12 fee per night. Mastercard and Visa/Bank-Americard accepted. Open all year.

Who to contact: Phone the park at 206-877-9522, or write P.O. Box 217, Hoodsport, WA 98548.

Location: Drive one mile north of Hoodsport on US 101.

Trip note: A fully-developed park located at sea level. This nine-acre park is on Hood Canal, where there are opportunities to fish and scuba dive. Nearby recreation options include an 18-hole golf course.

Site **13** | **REST A WHILE**

Campsites, facilities: There are 15 tent sites and 92 drive-through sites for trailers or motorhomes of any length. Electricity, piped water, sewer hookups and picnic tables are provided. Bottled gas, toilets, firewood, recreation hall, store, laundry, ice are available, and a cafe is less than a mile from the park. Showers are available for an extra fee. Pets and motorbikes are permitted. Boat docks and launching facilities are available at nearby Hood Canal.

Reservations, fee: Reservations accepted; $13 fee per night. Open all year.

Who to contact: Phone the park at 206-877-9474, or write at N 27001 Highway 101, Hoodsport, WA 98548.

Location: Drive three miles north of Hoodsport on US 101.

Trip note: This seven-acre park, located at sea level, is on Hood Canal. There are numerous opportunities to fish and scuba dive. An alternative to parks 11 and 12.

Site **14** | **KALALOCH** ▲

Campsites, facilities: There are 179 sites for tents or motorhomes up to 21 feet long. Picnic tables are provided. Restrooms, drinking water, wheelchair facilities and trailer sanitary station are available. A store and cafe are within one mile. Pets are permitted.

Reservations, fee: No reservations necessary; $5 fee per night. Open all year.

Who to contact: Phone Olympic National Park at 206-452-4501, or write at 600 East Park, Port Angeles, WA 98362.

Location: Drive 25 miles south of Forks on US 101.

Trip note: This camp is located on the beach, and like other camps set on the coast of the Olympic Peninsula, gets heavy rain in winter and spring. It's often foggy in summer. Set along the coastal National Wildlife Refuge.

Site 15
PACIFIC BEACH STATE PARK

Campsites, facilities: There are 118 tent sites and 20 sites for trailers or motorhomes up to 45 feet long. Picnic tables are provided, and sanitary disposal station and toilets are available. Electricity, piped water and showers are available for an extra fee. Pets are permitted.

Reservations, fee: No reservations necessary; $6 fee per night. Open all year.

Who to contact: Phone the state park at 206-289-3553, or write at Route 4, Box 2900, Hoquiam, WA 98550.

Location: Camp is in the town of Pacific Beach on Highway 109.

Trip note: This nine-acre in-town campground is on the beach where motor vehicles are allowed. It tends to get crowded since there are no other coastal camps in the immediate vicinity.

Site 16
RIVERVIEW RV PARK AND CAMPGROUND

Campsites, facilities: There are 12 tent sites and 24 drive-through sites for trailers or motorhomes of any length. Picnic tables are provided. Sanitary services, toilets and firewood are available. A store, cafe and ice are within one mile. Electricity, piped water, sewer hookups and showers are available for an extra fee. Pets and motorbikes are permitted. Boat launching facilities are available at nearby Humptulip River.

Reservations, fee: No reservations necessary; $5.50 fee per night. Open all year.

Who to contact: Phone the park at 206-987-2216, or write at P.O. Box 57, Humptulips, WA 98552.

Location: In Humptulips drive ¼ mile west on Beach Cutoff Road.

Trip note: This five-acre camp is set at about 1000-feet elevation along the Humptulips River. Good layover if you're cruising Highway 101.

Site 17
FORT WORDEN

Campsites, facilities: There are 50 sites for trailers or motorhomes up to 50 feet long. Picnic tables are provided. Toilets, cafe, laundry, store, playground and conference facilities are available. Electricity, piped water, sewer hookups, showers and firewood are available for an extra fee. Pets are permitted. Boat docks, buoys, floats and launching facilities are nearby. Wheelchair facilities are available.

Reservations, fee: Reservations required; $6 fee per night. Open all year.

Who to contact: Phone the State Park at 206-385-4730, or write at Box 574, Townsend, WA 98368.

Location: This park is set on the northeastern tip of the Olympic Peninsula, at the northern end of the town of Port Townsend. From Highway 101, turn north on Highway 20 and drive about 10 miles to Port Townsend.

Trip note: The highlight here is the great lookout over the Strait of Juan De Fuca as it feeds into Puget Sound. This 339-acre park is at historic Fort Worden and includes buildings from the turn of the century. Nearby recreation options include marked hiking trails, marked bike trails and tennis courts.

MELBOURNE
Site **18**

Campsites, facilities: There are five primitive campsites for tents or small trailers. Picnic tables, fire grills and tent pads are provided. Pit toilets are available. There is no water, so bring your own. Firearms are prohibited.

Reservations, fee: No reservations necessary; no fee. Open all year.

Who to contact: Phone Department of Natural Resources at 800-527-3305, or write at AW-11, 1065 South Capitol Way, Olympia, WA 98504.

Location: Drive 11 miles north from Hoodsport on US 101, then turn left on Jorsted Creek Road (Forest Service Road 24) and drive 5½ miles. Turn left and travel on a gravel road for 1¾ miles, then bear left and drive ¾ mile to the camp which is on Melbourne Lake.

Trip note: This primitive camp is on Melbourne Lake at about 1000-feet elevation. A little-known, rustic setting. If you want quiet, and don't mind a lack of facilities, this is a good drive-to option.

LILLIWAUP CREEK
Site **19**

Campsites, facilities: There are 13 campsites for tents or small trailers. Picnic tables, fire grills and tent pads are provided. Pit toilets and piped water are available.

Reservations, fee: No reservations necessary; no fee. Open all year.

Who to contact: Phone the Department of Natural Resources at 800-527-3305, or write the Department at AW-11, 1065 South Capitol, Olympia, WA 98504.

Location: Drive 11 miles north of Hoodsport on US 101, then turn left on Jorsted Creek Road (Forest Service Road 24) and drive 6½ miles to camp, which is on the right of Lilliwaup Creek.

Trip note: An alternative to campsite 18. A primitive, quiet setting with no facilities provided. Lilliwaup Creek makes for a nice setting.

DUNGENESS
Site **20**   RECREATION AREA

Campsites, facilities: There are 65 tent sites and 65 drive-through sites for trailers or motorhomes of any length. Picnic tables are provided. Sanitary services, toilets and playground are available. Showers and firewood are available for an extra fee. Pets are permitted.

Reservations, fee: No reservations necessary; $6 fee per night. Open February to October with limited winter facilities.

Who to contact: Phone the park at 206-683-5847, or write at 223 East 4th, Port Angeles, WA 98362.

Location: From Sequim drive five miles west on US 101, then turn right on Kitchen Road and drive four miles to park.

Trip note: This park overlooks the Strait of Juan De Fuca, and is set along the Dungeness National Wildlife Refuge. Nearby recreation options include marked hiking trails. Toll ferry at Port Angeles can take you to Victoria.

Site **21**   SALT CREEK RECREATION AREA   ▲

Campsites, facilities: There are 65 tent sites and 65 sites for trailers or motorhomes of any length. Picnic tables are provided. Sanitary services, toilets, showers, playground are available. Firewood is available for an extra fee. Pets are permitted.

Reservations, fee: No reservations necessary; $6 fee per night. Open all year.

Who to contact: Phone the park at 206-928-3441, or write at 223 East 4th, Port Angeles, WA 98362.

Location: From Port Angeles, drive 10 miles west on Highway 112, then turn right on Camp Hayden Road and drive three miles to the park.

Trip note: This 192-acre camp overlooks the Strait of Juan De Fuca. Nearby recreation options include marked hiking trails. A good layover spot if you're planning to take the ferry out of Port Angeles to Victoria.

Site **22**   FALLS VIEW   ▲

Campsites, facilities: There are 16 tent sites and 30 sites for trailers or motorhomes up to 31 feet long. Picnic tables are provided. Piped water, flush toilets and electricity in the restrooms are available. Pets are permitted. Boat docks and launching facilities are on nearby Big Quilcene River. Wheelchair facilities are available.

Reservations, fee: No reservations necessary; $5 fee per night. Open May to mid-September.

Who to contact: Phone Olympic National Forest at 206-765-3368, or write to the Quilcene Ranger Station in Quilcene, WA 98376.

Location: From Quilcene drive four miles southwest on US 101. Camp is located on the Big Quilcene River.

Trip note: A rustic spot on the edge of Olympic National Forest, yet with most facilities available.

Site **23**   RAINBOW

Campsites, facilities: There are nine tent sites. Picnic tables are provided. Restrooms, drinking water and firewood are available. A store, cafe, laundry and ice are within five miles. Pets are permitted.

Reservations, fee: This campground is subject to closure, a phone call is mandatory. No reservations necessary; $3 fee per night. Open late-May to early-September.

Who to contact: Phone Olympic National Forest at 206-765-3368, or write to the Quilcene Ranger Station at Quilcene, WA 98376.

Location: Drive five miles southwest of Quilcene on US 101. Camp is located on the right.

Trip note: If closed, campsite 22 provides nearby option. A rugged, primitive setting on edge of Olympic National Forest, with back country access provided on Forest Service roads. Advisable to obtain Forest Service map.

Site **24**
DUNGENESS FORKS

Campsites, facilities: There are nine tent sites. Picnic tables are provided. Well water, vault toilets and firewood are available. Pets are permitted.

Reservations, fee: No reservations necessary; $4 fee per night. Open late-May to early-September.

Who to contact: Phone Olympic National Forest at 206-765-3368, or write to the Quilcene Ranger Station in Quilcene, WA 98376.

Location: From Sequim drive four miles southeast on US 101, then turn right and drive eight miles on county and Forest Service roads to get to camp. A Forest Service map is essential.

Trip note: A little-known, little-used, primitive camp. No significant lakes or streams nearby. If you want quiet, you'll find it here.

Site **25**
EAST CROSSING

Campsites, facilities: There are nine tent sites and nine sites for trailers or motorhomes up to 16 feet long. Picnic tables are provided. Well water and vault toilets are available. Pets are permitted.

Reservations, fee: No reservations necessary; $4 fee per night. Open late-May to early-September.

Who to contact: Phone Olympic National Forest at 206-765-3368, or write to Quilcene Ranger Station in Quilcene, WA 98376.

Location: From Sequim drive four miles southeast on US 101, then turn right and drive 11 miles on county and Forest Service roads to get to camp. A Forest Service map is essential.

Trip note: A nearby option to camp 25. This seven-acre camp is set at about 1200-feet elevation. Some improvements, but still for individuals seeking out-of-the-way spot.

Site **26**
ELKHORN

Campsites, facilities: There are 16 tent sites and 20 sites for trailers or motorhomes up to 21 feet long. Picnic tables are provided. Well water, vault toilets and firewood are available. Pets are permitted.

Reservations, fee: No reservations necessary; $3 fee per night. Open mid-May to September.

Who to contact: Phone Olympic National Forest at 206-877-5254, or write to Hoodsport Ranger Station, Hoodsport, WA 98548.

Location: From Brinnon, drive one mile north on US 101 then turn left and drive 10 miles west on County Route 10 and Forest Service Road 2610 (same road). Camp is on left.

Trip note: This eight-acre camp is set on the Dosewallips River at 600-feet elevation. It is in the Brothers Wilderness about five miles from a major trailhead into the Olympic National Park backcountry. Camp 34 is more primitive option.

SEAL ROCK
Site **27**

Campsites, facilities: There are 35 tent sites and 35 sites for trailers or motorhomes up to 31 feet long. Picnic tables are provided. Well water, vault toilets and wheelchair facilities are available. Pets are permitted. Boat docks and launching facilities are nearby on the Hood Canal and in Dabob Bay.

Reservations, fee: No reservations necessary; $6 fee per night. Open mid-April to November.

Who to contact: Phone Olympic National Forest at 206-877-5254, or write to Hoodsport Ranger Station at P.O. Box 68, Hoodsport, WA 98548.

Location: From Brinnon, drive two miles north on US 101. Camp is on the shore at Seal Rock.

Trip note: This 30-acre camp is set along the shore near the mouth of Dabob Bay. Modern, developed setting, that is a good spot for boat owners.

COLLINS
Site **28**

Campsites, facilities: There are 14 tent sites and five sites for trailers or motorhomes up to 21 feet long. Picnic tables are provided. Well water, vault toilets and firewood are available. Pets are permitted.

Reservations, fee: No reservations necessary; $4 fee per night. Open late-May to early-September.

Who to contact: Phone Olympic National Forest at 206-877-5254, or write to the Hoodsport Ranger Station at P.O. Box 68, Hoodsport, WA 98548.

Location: From Brinnon drive two miles south on US 101, then turn right and drive five miles west on Forest Service Road 2515. Camp is on the left.

Trip note: Tourists cruising Highway 101 don't have a clue about this spot, yet it's not far from the highway. This four-acre camp is set on the Duckabush River at 200-feet elevation. Rustic, some improvements.

HAMMA HAMMA
Site **29**

Campsites, facilities: There are 15 tent sites and 15 sites for trailers or motorhomes up to 21 feet long. Picnic tables are provided. Well water, vault toilets and firewood are available. Pets are permitted. Some facilities are wheelchair accessible.

Reservations, fee: No reservations necessary; $3 fee per night. Open mid-May to September.

Who to contact: Phone Olympic National Forest at 206-877-5254, or write to the Hoodsport Ranger Station at P.O. Box 68, Hoodsport, WA 98548.

Location: From Eldon drive two miles north on US 101, then turn left and drive 6½ miles west to camp on Forest Service Route 25.

Trip note: Good holdover for vacationers cruising Highway 101. This camp is set on the Hamma Hamma River at about 600-feet elevation.

LENA CREEK
Site **30**

Campsites, facilities: There are 14 tent sites and seven sites for trailers or motorhomes up to 16 feet long. Picnic tables are provided. Well water, vault toilets and firewood are available. Pets are permitted. Wheelchair facilities are available.

Reservations, fee: No reservations necessary; $3 fee per night. Open mid-May to September.

Who to contact: Phone Olympic National Forest at 206-877-5254, or write to the Hoodsport Ranger Station at P.O. Box 68, Hoodsport, WA 98548.

Location: From Eldon drive two miles north on US 101, then turn left and drive nine miles on Forest Service Route 25 to camp.

Trip note: This seven-acre camp is set where Lena Creek empties into the Hamma Hamma River. A trail from camp leads two miles to Lena Lake and four miles to Upper Lena Lake. Map of Olympic National Forest details trail and road system. Rustic, some improvements.

LENA LAKE
Site **31**

Campsites, facilities: There are 29 rustic tent sites at this hike-in campground. Pit toilets are available, but there is no piped water. Pets are permitted.

Reservations, fee: No reservations necessary; no fee. Open late-May to early-September.

Who to contact: Phone Olympic National Forest at 206-877-5254, or write at Eldon, WA 98320.

Location: From Eldon drive two miles north on US 101, then head west for nine miles on Forest Service Route 25 to Lena Creek Camp. Hike two miles to Lena Lake, and campsites are scattered around the lake.

Trip note: Can't beat the price— free. This 135-acre camp is set on Lena Lake. Popular in the summer. Two-mile hike from Lena Creek to campground is suitable for entire family.

HEART O'
THE HILLS
Site **32**

Campsites, facilities: There are 105 tent sites and 21 sites for trailers or motorhomes. Picnic tables are provided. Restrooms and drinking water are available. Pets are permitted. Wheelchair facilities are available.

Reservations, fee: No reservations necessary; $5 fee per night. Open all year.

Who to contact: Phone Olympic National Park at 206-452-4501, or write to 600 East Park, Port Angeles, CA 98362.

Location: From Port Angeles, drive five miles south on Hurricane Ridge Road. Camp is on the left.

Trip note: Set on the northern edge of Olympic National Park. You can drive deeper into the interior of the park on Hurricane Ridge Road and take one of numerous hiking trails. This camp is set at 1800-feet elevation. Evening Ranger programs are available in the summer.

DEER PARK
Site **33**

Campsites, facilities: There are 18 tent sites. Picnic tables are provided. Restrooms and drinking water are available. Pets are permitted.

Reservations, fee: No reservations necessary; no fee. Open mid-June to late- September with limited winter facilities.

Who to contact: Phone Olympic National Park at 206-452-4501, or write to 600 East Park,

Port Angeles, CA 98362.

Location: From Port Angeles drive six miles east on US 101, then turn right and drive 18 miles south on Deer Park Road.

Trip note: This camp is set in the Olympic Peninsula's high country at 5400-feet elevation, just below 6000-foot Blue Mountain. Numerous trails in area, including major trailhead into backcountry of Olympic National Park and the Buckhorn Wilderness.

DOSEWALLIPS
Site 34

Campsites, facilities: There are 33 tent sites. Picnic tables are provided. Restrooms, drinking water and wheelchair facilities are available. Pets are permitted.

Reservations, fee: No reservations necessary; no fee. Open June to late-September.

Who to contact: Phone Olympic National Park at 206-452-4501, or write to 600 East Park, Port Angeles, WA 98362.

Location: From Quicene drive 13 miles south on US 101, then turn right and drive 15 miles west along Dosewallips River.

Trip note: More remote option to camps 26 and 28. This camp is set on the Dosewallips River at 1600-feet elevation. Major trailhead into backcountry of Olympic National Park. Trail follows Dosewallips River over Anderson Pass then along Quinault River and ultimately reaches Quinault Lake.

ALTAIRE
Site 35

Campsites, facilities: There are 29 tent sites and 29 sites for trailers or motorhomes up to 18 feet long. Picnic tables are provided. Restrooms and drinking water are available. Pets are permitted.

Reservations, fee: No reservations necessary; $5 fee per night. Open June to late-September.

Who to contact: Phone Olympic National Park at 206-452-4501, or write to 600 East Park, Port Angeles, WA 98362.

Location: From Port Angeles drive nine miles west on US 101, then turn left and drive four miles south along Elwha River.

Trip note: This camp is set on the Elwha River about a mile from Lake Mills. Nice layover spot for a one-nighter before taking ferry boat at Port Angeles to Victoria.

ELWHA
Site 36

Campsites, facilities: There are 41 tent sites and 41 sites for trailers or motorhomes up to 21 feet long. Picnic tables are provided. Restrooms and drinking water are available. Pets are permitted.

Reservations, fee: No reservations necessary; $5 fee per night. Open all year.

Who to contact: Phone Olympic National Park at 206-452-4501, or write to 600 East Park, Port Angeles, WA 98362.

Location: From Port Angeles drive nine miles west on US 101, then turn right and drive three miles south along Elwha River.

Trip note: This camp is set along the Elwha River and gets regular use. Some trails available, with evening ranger programs popular in the summer.

FAIRHOLM
Site 37

Campsites, facilities: There are 87 tent sites and 87 sites for trailers or motorhomes up to 21 feet long. Picnic tables are provided. Sanitary services, restrooms, drinking water and wheelchair facilities are available. Store and cafe are within one mile. Pets are permitted. Boat launching facilities are nearby on Lake Crescent.

Reservations, fee: No reservations necessary; $5 fee per night. Open all year.

Who to contact: Phone Olympic National Park at 206-452-4501, or write to 600 East Park, Port Angeles, WA 98362.

Location: From Port Angeles drive 26 miles west on US 101, then turn right and drive one mile to camp on North Shore Road.

Trip note: This camp is set on the shore of Lake Crescent, a pretty lake within boundaries of Olympic National Forest. Since it is only a mile from Highway 101, it gets heavy use during tourist months.

BOULDER CREEK
Site 38

Campsites, facilities: There are 50 primitive tent sites at this hike-in campground. Picnic tables are provided. Restrooms and drinking water are available. Pets are permitted.

Reservations, fee: No reservations necessary; no fee. Open mid-June to late-September with limited winter facilities.

Who to contact: Phone Olympic National Park at 206-452-4501, or write to 600 East Park, Port Angeles, WA 98362.

Location: From Port Angeles drive nine miles west on US 101, then 12 miles southwest along Elwaha River. Backpack a short distance to campground.

Trip note: A primitive option in national park setting, 2000-feet elevation, with some walking necessary. This camp is along Boulder Creek, near the Olympic Hot Springs. The trail here leads into the backcountry and eventually to Boulder Lake.

SOLEDUCK
Site 39

Campsites, facilities: There are 84 sites for tents or motorhomes up to 21 feet long. Picnic tables are provided. Sanitary services, restrooms, drinking water and wheelchair facilities are available. A store and cafe are within one mile. Pets are permitted.

Reservations, fee: No reservations necessary; $5 fee per night. Open May to late-October with limited winter facilities.

Who to contact: Phone Olympic National Park at 206-452-4501, or write to 600 East Park, Port Angeles, WA 98362.

Location: From Port Angeles drive 27 miles west on US 101, then fork left at Soleduck turn-off and drive 12 miles to camp.

Trip note: A nice hideaway with Sol Duc Hot Springs a highlight. Camp set at 2000-feet elevation along Soleduck River.

Site 40 — DOSEWALLIPS STATE PARK

Campsites, facilities: There are 113 tent sites and 40 sites for trailers or motorhomes up to 60 feet long. Picnic tables are provided. Restrooms and drinking water are available. Recreation hall, store, cafe and laundry are within one mile. Electricity, piped water, sewer hookups, and showers are available for an extra fee. Pets and motorbikes are permitted. Wheelchair facilities are available.

Reservations, fee: No reservations necessary; $6 fee per night. Open all year.

Who to contact: Phone Dosewallips State Park at 206-796-4415, or write to Drawer K, Brinnon, WA 98320.

Location: From Brinnon drive one mile south on US 101. Park is located on shore of the Hood Canal.

Trip note: This 425-acre park is set at the mouth of Dosewallips Creek, which gets a fair run of steelhead in winter months. In Hood Canal, salmon and rockfishing is popular. Beachcombers might consider clamming.

Site 41 — SEQUIM BAY

Campsites, facilities: There are 60 tent sites and 26 sites for trailers or motorhomes up to 30 feet long. Picnic tables are provided. Sanitary services, toilets, drinking water and a playground are available. Electricity, piped water, sewer hookups, showers and firewood are available for an extra fee. Pets are permitted. Boat docks, launching facilities and moorage camping are nearby on Sequim Bay. Wheelchair facilities are available.

Reservations, fee: No reservations necessary; $6 fee per night. Open all year.

Who to contact: Phone the Sequim Bay State Park at 206-683-4235, or write to 1872 Highway 101 East, Sequim, WA 98382.

Location: From Sequim drive four miles southeast on US 101.

Trip note: This 90-acre camp is on Sequim Bay. Nearby recreation options include marked hiking trails and tennis courts. Because of its unique location, it gets far less rain than other areas on the Olympic Peninsula.

Site 42 — TRANQUILCENE TRAILER PARK

Campsites, facilities: There are 12 sites for tents or motorhomes of any length. Electricity, piped water, sewer hookups and picnic tables are provided. Firewood is available. Bottled gas, sanitary services, store, cafe, laundry and ice are within one mile. Pets and motorbikes are permitted. Boat launching facilities are nearby on Quilcene Bay.

Reservations, fee: Reservations accepted; $7.50 fee per night. Open all year.

Who to contact: Phone the park at 206-765-3409, or write to P.O. Box 188, Quilcene, WA 98376.

Location: From Quilcene drive ½ mile south on US 101.

Trip note: Set at about 1000-feet elevation, this five-acre camp is near the shore of Quilcene Bay in a wooded setting. Nearby recreation options include marked hiking trails and a full service marina. A developed, private camp.

Site 43   FLOCK IN RV PARK

Campsites, facilities: There are 23 drive-through sites for trailers or motorhomes of any
length. Electricity, piped water, sewer hookups and picnic tables are provided.
Toilets, showers, recreation hall and cafe are available. Bottled gas, sanitary services,
store, laundry and ice are within one mile. Pets and motorbikes are permitted.
Reservations, fee: Reservations accepted; $8.50 fee per night. Open all year.
Who to contact: Phone the park at 206-796-4707, or write to P.O. Box 172, Brinnon, WA
98320.
Location: This park is on US 101 in the town of Brinnon.
Trip note: A private, developed RV park set near the Hood Canal and the Dosewallips
River.

Site 44   COVE PARK CAMPGROUND

Campsites, facilities: There are 35 sites for trailers or motorhomes up to 30 feet long.
Electricity, piped water, sewer hookups and picnic tables are provided. Bottled gas,
sanitary services, toilets, store, laundry and ice are available. Showers are available for
an extra fee. Pets are permitted. Boat docks and launching facilities are nearby on the
Hood Canal.
Reservations, fee: Reservations accepted; $9.50 fee per night. Open all year.
Who to contact: Phone the park at 206-796-4723, or write to 28453 Highway 101, Brinnon,
WA 98320.
Location: From Brinnon, drive three miles north on Highway 101.
Trip note: This five-acre camp is in a rural setting near the shore of Dabob Bay at sea level.
Private camp, fully developed.

Site 45   ELMER'S TRAVEL TRAILER PARK

Campsites, facilities: There are five tent sites and 12 sites for trailers or motorhomes up to
31 feet long in this adult only campground. Electricity, piped water and sewer
hookups are provided. Sanitary services, toilets and laundry are available. Bottled
gas, store, cafe and ice are within one mile. Showers are available for an extra fee. Pets
are permitted.
Reservations, fee: No reservations necessary; $10 fee per night. Open all year.
Who to contact: Write Elmer's Travel Trailer Park at 2430 Highway 101, Port Angeles, WA
98362.
Location: From Port Angeles drive two miles east on US 101.
Trip note: Located at about 1000-feet elevation, this 10-acre camp is near the ocean yet in
urban setting. Nearby recreation options include an 18-hole golf course, marked
hiking trails and a full service marina.

Site 46   AL'S RV TRAILER PARK

Campsites, facilities: There are 31 sites for trailers or motorhomes up to 33 feet long in this
adult only campground. Electricity, piped water and sewer hookups are provided.

Bottled gas, toilets, showers and laundry are available. Store, cafe and ice are within one mile. Boat docks and launching facilities are nearby.

Reservations, fee: No reservations necessary; $8 fee per night. Open all year.

Who to contact: Phone the park at 206-457-6563, or write at 522 N Lee Creek, Port Angeles, WA 98362.

Location: From Port Angeles drive two miles east on US 101, then turn left on Lee Creek Road and drive ½ mile to park.

Trip note: A good choice for motorhome owners. It is set in the country at about 1000-feet elevation, yet not far from the Straight of Juan De Fuca. Nearby recreation options include an 18-hole golf course and a full service marina.

Site 47   CITY CENTER TRAILER PARK

Campsites, facilities: There are 30 sites for trailers or motorhomes of any length. Electricity, piped water and sewer hookups are provided. Bottled gas, sanitary services, toilets and laundry are available. Store, cafe and ice are within one mile. Showers are available for an extra fee. Pets are permitted. Boat docks, launching facilities and rentals are nearby.

Reservations, fee: Reservations accepted; $10 fee per night. Open all year.

Who to contact: Phone the park at 206-457-7092, or write to 127 South Lincoln, Port Angeles, WA 98362.

Location: In Port Angeles drive on US 101 to the corner of Lincoln and 2nd.

Trip note: Private camp. This three-acre RV park is next to a river and in the woods. Nearby recreation options include an 18-hole golf course, marked biking trails, a full service marina and tennis courts.

Site 48   THUNDERBIRD BOATHOUSE

Campsites, facilities: There are 18 sites for trailers or motorhomes of any length. Sanitary services, toilets, a cafe and ice are available. Pets and motorbikes are permitted. Boat docks, launching facilities and rentals are nearby.

Reservations, fee: Reservations accepted; $6.50 fee per night with MasterCard and Visa accepted. Open April to late-October.

Who to contact: Phone the park at 206-457-3595, or write to P.O. Box 787, Port Angeles, WA 98362.

Location: In Port Angeles from the junction of US 101 and Front Street, drive west on Front Marina Drive.

Trip note: Good vehicle camp for boat owners with park set along Strait of Juan De Fuca. Nearby recreation options include an 18-hole golf course, a full service marina and tennis courts.

Site 49   WELCOME INN TRAILER AND RV PARK

Campsites, facilities: There are 15 tent sites and 130 drive-through sites for trailers or motorhomes of any length. Electricity, piped water, sewer hookups and picnic tables are provided. Bottled gas, sanitary services, toilets and laundry are available. Store, cafe and ice are within one mile. Showers are available for an extra fee. Pets and motorbikes are permitted. Boat docks and launching facilities are nearby.

Reservations, fee: Reservations accepted; $11 fee per night. Open all year.

Who to contact: Phone the park at 206-457-1553, or write to 112 Highway 101 West, Port Angeles, WA 98362.

Location: From Port Angeles drive 1 ½ miles west on US 101 to the park.

Trip note: A privately developed campground for motorhomes and tent campers. An eight-acre camp set in the woods. Nearby recreation options include an 18-hole golf course, marked hiking trails, a full service marina and tennis courts.

ELWHA RESORT
Site **50** AND CAMPGROUND

Campsites, facilities: There are nine tent sites and seven sites for trailers or motorhomes up to 32 feet long. Electricity, piped water, sewer hookups and picnic tables are provided. Bottled gas, toilets, store, cafe, ice, playground are available. Sanitary services and laundry are located within one mile. Showers and firewood are available for an extra fee. Pets and motorbikes are permitted. Boat docks, launching facilities and rentals are nearby at the Elwha River.

Reservations, fee: Reservations accepted; $7.50 fee per night with MasterCard and Visa accepted. Open all year.

Who to contact: Phone the park at 206-457-7011, or write at 464 Highway 101 West, Port Angeles, WA 98362.

Location: From Port Angeles drive nine miles west on US 101.

Trip note: A small, private campground set at sea level next to the Elwha River. More seclusion than nearby camps 45-49. Nearby recreation options include marked hiking trails, Lake Adwell.

LYRE RIVER
Site **51** PARK

Campsites, facilities: There are 15 tent sites and 60 drive-through sites for trailers or motorhomes of any length. Electricity, piped water, sewer hookups and picnic tables are provided. Bottled gas, sanitary services, toilets, store, laundry and ice are available. Showers and firewood are available for an extra fee. Pets and motorbikes are permitted.

Reservations, fee: Reservations accepted; $10.50 fee per night. Open all year.

Who to contact: Phone the park at 206-928-3436, or write at 5960 Lyre River, Port Angeles, WA 98362.

Location: From Port Angeles drive five miles west on US 101, then get on Highway 112 and drive 15 miles west. Turn right on Lyre River Road and drive ½ mile to the park.

Trip note: This 80-acre camp is in a wooded area tucked between the Strait of Juan De Fuca and the Lyre River. Marked hiking trails are accessible in the immediate area.

SILVER KING
Site **52** RESORT

Campsites, facilities: There are 10 tent sites and 165 sites for trailers or motorhomes of any length. Electricity, piped water and picnic tables are provided. Bottled gas, sanitary services, toilets, firewood, store, laundry and ice are available. Showers are available for an extra fee. Pets and motorbikes are permitted. Boat docks and launching facilities are at nearby Pillar Point Recreation Area.

Reservations, fee: Reservations required; $9.50 fee per night. Open all year.

Who to contact: Phone the park at 206-928-3858, or write at Star Route 2, Box 10A, Clallam Bay, WA 98326.

Location: From Port Angeles drive five miles west on US 101 then get on Highway 120 and drive west for 30 miles. At Jim Creek, turn right and drive ½ mile to the park.

Trip note: A good summer camp for salmon fishermen, with mooching the most popular technique for big salmon in Strait of Juan De Fuca. Camp is privately run, developed.

Site 53   SUNSHINE MOBILE AND RV PARK

Campsites, facilities: There are 12 tent sites and 35 drive-through sites for trailers or motorhomes of any length. Electricity, piped water, sewer hookups and picnic tables are provided. Toilets, showers, recreation hall, laundry and ice are available. Sanitary services, store and cafe are located within one mile. Pets and motorbikes are permitted.

Reservations, fee: Reservations accepted; $10.50 fee per night. Open all year.

Who to contact: Phone the park at 206-683-4769, or write at 1875 Highway 101 West, Sequim, WA 98382.

Location: From Sequim, drive four miles west on US 101 to park.

Trip note: Private camp. Set at about 1000-feet elevation, this six-acre camp is in a wooded area outside of Sequim. Nearby recreation options include an 18-hole golf course and a full service marina at Sequim Bay.

Site 54   SEQUIM WEST RV PARK

Campsites, facilities: There are 28 drive-through sites for trailers or motorhomes of any length. Electricity, piped water, sewer hookups and picnic tables are provided. Toilets, showers, laundry and ice are available. Bottled gas, sanitary services, store, cafe are located within one mile. Pets are permitted.

Reservations, fee: Reservations accepted; $14.50 fee per night with American Express, MasterCard and Visa accepted. Open all year.

Who to contact: Phone the park at 206-683-4144, or write at 740 West Washington, Sequim, WA 98382.

Location: The park is in the town of Sequim, on the west end of Highway 101.

Trip note: This two-acre camp is near the Dungeness River within 10 miles of Dungeness Spit State Park. Nearby recreation options include an 18-hole golf course and a full service marina at Sequim Bay.

Site 55   SOUTH SEQUIM BAY RV PARK

Campsites, facilities: There are 10 tent sites and 30 drive-through sites for trailers or motorhomes of any length. Picnic tables are provided. Bottled gas, sanitary services, toilets, showers and playground are available. Electricity, piped water, sewer hookups and firewood are available for an extra fee. Pets and motorbikes are permitted. Boat rentals are at nearby Sequim Bay.

Reservations, fee: Reservations accepted; $9 fee per night. Open early-April to mid-November.

Who to contact: Phone the park at 206-683-7194, or write at Box 152, Old Bly Highway, Sequim, WA 98382.

Location: From Sequim, drive five miles southeast on US 101 to park.

Trip note: This six-acre park set along Sequim Bay is especially good when salmon are running. Nearby recreation options include an 18-hole golf course, marked bike trails and tennis courts.

Site **56**   **SEQUIM BAY MARINA**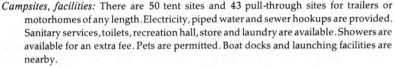

Campsites, facilities: There are 50 tent sites and 43 pull-through sites for trailers or motorhomes of any length. Electricity, piped water and sewer hookups are provided. Sanitary services, toilets, recreation hall, store and laundry are available. Showers are available for an extra fee. Pets are permitted. Boat docks and launching facilities are nearby.

Reservations, fee: No reservations necessary; $9 fee per night. Open all year.

Who to contact: Phone the park at 206-683-4050, or write at 630 West Sequim Bay, Sequim, WA 98382.

Location: From Sequim, drive one mile east on US 101 then turn left on West Sequim Bay Rd and drive three miles to marina.

Trip note: Headquarters on Sequim Bay for salmon fishermen. Nearby recreation options include an 18-hole golf course.

Site **57**   **RAINBOW'S END**

Campsites, facilities: There are 15 tent sites and 37 sites for trailers or motorhomes of any length. Electricity, piped water, sewer hookups and picnic tables are provided. Sanitary services, toilets, showers and laundry are available. Bottled gas, store, cafe and ice are located within one mile. Firewood is available for an extra fee. Pets and motorbikes are permitted.

Reservations, fee: Reservations accepted; $14.75 fee per night. Open all year.

Who to contact: Phone the park at 206-683-3863, or write at 1464 Highway 101 West, Sequim, WA 98382.

Location: From Sequim, drive two miles west on US 101 to the park.

Trip note: Of the group of five camps on Sequim Bay (camps 53-57) this is one of the nicest. Nearby recreation options include an 18-hole golf course, marked bike trails, a full service marina and tennis courts.

Site **58**   **DIAMOND POINT RV PARK AND CAMPGROUND**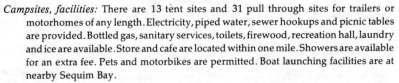

Campsites, facilities: There are 13 tent sites and 31 pull through sites for trailers or motorhomes of any length. Electricity, piped water, sewer hookups and picnic tables are provided. Bottled gas, sanitary services, toilets, firewood, recreation hall, laundry and ice are available. Store and cafe are located within one mile. Showers are available for an extra fee. Pets and motorbikes are permitted. Boat launching facilities are at nearby Sequim Bay.

Reservations, fee: Reservations accepted; $13 fee per night. Open all year.

Who to contact: Phone the park at 206-683-2284, or write at 137 Industrial Parkway, Sequim, WA 98382.

Location: From Sequim, drive 10 miles east on US 101 then turn left on Diamond Point Road and drive 3 ½ miles to camp.

Trip note: Privately developed and operated. Good layover before heading to Victoria by ferry.

Site 59   WHISKEY CREEK BEACH

Campsites, facilities: There are 40 tent sites and 11 sites for trailers or motorhomes of any length. Piped water, sewer hookups and picnic tables are provided. Sanitary services and laundry are available. Pets are permitted. Boat launching facilities are nearby.

Reservations, fee: Reservations accepted; $5 fee per night. Open May to late-September.

Who to contact: Phone the park at 206-928-3489, or write at Joyce, WA 98343.

Location: From Port Angeles, travel five miles west on US 101, 13 miles west on Highway 112, then turn north on Schmitt Rd.

Trip note: Set at beach along Strait of Juan De Fuca. Agate Beach is nearby. Campground covers 400 acres.

Site 60   LOG CABIN RESORT

Campsites, facilities: There are 10 tent sites and 40 sites for trailers or motorhomes of any length. Electricity, piped water, sewer hookups and picnic tables are provided. Sanitary services, toilets, store, cafe, laundry, ice, playground are available. Showers and firewood are available for an extra fee. Pets are permitted. Boat docks, launching facilities and rentals are located at Lake Crescent.

Reservations, fee: Reservations accepted; $10 fee per night with MasterCard and Visa accepted. Open April to November.

Who to contact: Phone the park at 206-928-3325, or write at 6540 East Beach, Port Angeles, WA 98362.

Location: From Port Angeles, drive 16 miles west on US 101, then turn right on East Beach Road and drive three miles to camp.

Trip note: A pretty spot along the shore of Lake Crescent. Good spot for boaters. Marked hiking trail traces lake's shoreline.

Site 61   KOA PORT ANGELES-SEQUIM

Campsites, facilities: There are 50 tent sites and 90 drive-through sites for trailers or motorhomes of any length. Picnic tables are provided. Bottled gas, sanitary services, toilets, showers, store, laundry, ice, playground and swimming pool are available. A cafe is located within one mile. Electricity, piped water, sewer hookups and firewood are available for an extra fee. Pets and motorbikes are permitted.

Reservations, fee: Reservations accepted; $12 fee per night with MasterCard and Visa accepted. Open May to late-October.

Who to contact: Phone the park at 206-457-5916, or write at 2065 Highway 101 East, Port Angeles, WA 98362.

Location: From Port Angeles, drive six miles east on US 101 then turn left on O'Brien Road and go one block to campground.

Trip note: A private, developed camp that covers 41 acres but located in country setting. Nearby recreation options include an 18-hole golf course, marked hiking trails and tennis courts.

Site **62**
WILLOUGHBY
CREEK

Campsites, facilities: There are three campsites for tents or small trailers. Picnic tables, fire grills and tent pads are provided. Pit toilets are available. There is no water, so bring your own.

Reservations, fee: No reservations necessary; no fee. Open all year.

Who to contact: Phone the Department of Natural Resources at 1-800-527-3305, or write Department of Natural Resources AW-11, 1065 South Capitol Way, Olympia, WA 98504.

Location: Drive 14 miles south of Forks on US 101 and turn east on Hoh Rain Forest Road. Drive 3 ½ miles to camp. Camp is on the right.

Trip note: This is a little-known, tiny and rustic camp set along Willoughby Creek and the Hoh River. Area gets heavy rainfall.

Site **63**
MINNIE PETERSON

Campsites, facilities: There are six campsites for tents or small trailers. Picnic tables, fire grills and tent pads are provided. Pit toilets and piped water are available. Firearms prohibited.

Reservations, fee: No reservations necessary; no fee. Open all year.

Who to contact: Phone the Department of Natural Resources at 1-800-527-3305, or write Department of Natural Resources AW-11, 1065 South Capitol Way, Olympia, WA 98504.

Location: Drive 14 miles south of Forks on US 101 and turn east on Hoh Rain Forest Road. Drive 4 ½ miles to camp on left.

Trip note: This is a primitive camp, set on the Hoh River on the edge of the Hoh Rain Forest. Bring your rain gear. Not many folks know about this spot.

Site **64**
COTTONWOOD

Campsites, facilities: There are six campsites for tents or small trailers. Picnic tables, fire grills and tent pads are provided. Pit toilets, piped water and a boat launch are available.

Reservations, fee: No reservations necessary; no fee. Open all year.

Who to contact: Phone the Department of Natural Resources at 1-800-527-3305, or write Department of Natural Resources AW-11, 1065 South Capitol Way, Olympia, WA 98504.

Location: Drive 15 miles south of Forks on US 101, and then go west on Oil City road for 2 ⅓ miles. Turn left on a gravel road (H-4060) and drive one mile to camp.

Trip note: An option to camps 62-65, primitive and little-used, and also set along Hoh River.

Site **65**
HOH OXBOW

Campsites, facilities: There are five campsites for tents or small trailers. Picnic tables, fire grills and tent pads are provided. Pit toilets, piped water and a hand boat launch are available. Firearms are prohibited.

Reservations, fee: No reservations necessary; no fee. Open all year.

Who to contact: Phone the Department of Natural Resources at 1-800-527-3305, or write Department of Natural Resources AW-11, 1065 South Capitol Way, Olympia, WA 98504.

Location: Drive 14 miles south of Forks on US 101 and camp east of highway next to the river.

Trip note: The most populated of the five camps on the Hoh River. Primitive, close to highway, and the price is right.

Site **66**   SOUTH FORK HOH

Campsites, facilities: There are three campsites for tents or small trailers. Picnic tables, fire grills and tent pads are provided. Pit toilets are available. There is no water so bring your own.

Reservations, fee: No reservations necessary; no fee. Open all year.

Who to contact: Phone the Department of Natural Resources at 1-800-527-3305, or write Department of Natural Resources AW-11, 1065 South Capitol Way, Olympia, WA 98504.

Location: Drive 15 miles south of Forks, then go east on Hoh Mainline Road for 6 ½ miles. Turn left on H-1000 Road and drive 7 ½ miles to camp on right. A Forest Service map is essential.

Trip note: This one is way out there. Rarely used camp, and not many folks know about it. Set along South Fork of Hoh River.

Site **67**   COPPER MINE BOTTOM

Campsites, facilities: There are nine campsites for tents or small trailers. Picnic tables, fire grills and tent pads are provided. Pit toilets and a hand boat launch are available. There is no piped water available.

Reservations, fee: No reservations necessary; no fee. Open all year.

Who to contact: Phone the Department of Natural Resources at 1-800-527-3305, or write Department of Natural Resources AW-11, 1065 South Capitol Way, Olympia, WA 98504.

Location: On US 101 begin at milepost 147, go north on Hoh Clearwater Mainline Rd for 12 ½ miles, then right on C1010 (gravel one-lane road) for 1 ½ miles. Camp is on the left.

Trip note: A primitive and hidden campground that few tourists ever visit. Set on Clearwater River, a tributary to the Queets River, which runs to the ocean. River dory launching.

Site **68**   UPPER CLEARWATER

Campsites, facilities: There are six campsites for tents or small trailers. Picnic tables, fire grills and tent pads are provided. Pit toilets, piped water and a hand boat launch are available.

Reservations, fee: No reservations necessary; no fee. Open all year.

Who to contact: Phone the Department of Natural Resources at 1-800-527-3305, or write

Department of Natural Resources AW-11, 1065 South Capitol Way, Olympia, WA 98504.

Location: From US 101 milepost 147, go north on Hoh Clearwater Mainline Rd. for 13 miles, then turn right on C3000 (gravel one-lane road) and drive 3 ⅓ miles. Camp entrance is on right.

Trip note: One of three primitive camps set along Clearwater River. River dory launching.

YAHOO LAKE
Site **69**

Campsites, facilities: There are six tent sites and a group shelter at this primitive hike-in camp. Pit toilets, a group shelter and a boat dock are available. There is no piped water so bring your own.

Reservations, fee: No reservations necessary; no fee. Open all year.

Who to contact: Phone the Department of Natural Resources at 1-800-527-3305, or write Department of Natural Resources AW-11, 1065 South Capitol Way, Olympia, WA 98504.

Location: Follow directions to Upper Clearwater camp and continue on C3000 (gravel road) for ¾ mile. Turn right on C3100 (gravel two-lane road) keep left and continue on C3100 another ¾ mile to trailhead. Hike in.

Trip note: This camp is set at about 2000-feet elevation on the edge of tiny Yahoo Lake. An idyllic setting that few people take advantage of.

PILLAR POINT
Site **70**   RECREATION AREA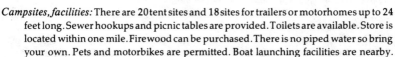

Campsites, facilities: There are 20 tent sites and 18 sites for trailers or motorhomes up to 24 feet long. Sewer hookups and picnic tables are provided. Toilets are available. Store is located within one mile. Firewood can be purchased. There is no piped water so bring your own. Pets and motorbikes are permitted. Boat launching facilities are nearby.

Reservations, fee: No reservations necessary; $6 fee per night. Open mid-May to mid-September.

Who to contact: Phone the park at 206-928-3201, or write at Star Route 2, Box 8, Clallam Bay, WA 98326.

Location: From Clallam Bay, drive 14 miles east on Highway 112, then ½ mile north on Pillar Point Road to campground.

Trip note: This camp is set in the northwestern end of the Olympic Peninsula, near the mouth of the Strait of Juan De Fuca. Fishermen will launch here and try to intercept migrating salmon.

KLAHOWYA
Site **71**

Campsites, facilities: There are 73 tent sites and 36 sites for trailers or motorhomes up to 31 feet long. Picnic tables are provided. Piped water, vault toilets and firewood are available. Pets are permitted. Wheelchair facilities are available. Boat ramp is nearby.

Reservations, fee: No reservations necessary; $5 fee per night. Open May to mid-October.

Who to contact: Phone Olympic National Forest at 206-374-6522, or write at Soleduck

Ranger Station, Star Route 1, Box 185, Forks, WA 98331.

Location: From Forks, drive 20 miles northeast on US 101. Camp is on the north side of the road.

Trip note: A good choice if you don't want to venture far from Highway 101, yet want to retain the feel of Olympic National Forest. Camp is 32 acres and set along the headwaters of the Soleduck River.

QUEETS
Site 72

Campsites, facilities: There are 26 primitive tent sites. Picnic tables are provided. Toilets are available, but there is no piped water. Pets are permitted.

Reservations, fee: No reservations necessary; no fee. Open June to late-September.

Who to contact: Phone Olympic National Park at 206-452-4501, or write at 600 East Park, Port Angeles, WA 98362.

Location: From Queets, drive five miles east on US 101, then 14 miles northeast on unpaved road along Queets River. Campground is located at the end of the road.

Trip note: This is a gem of a find if you don't mind bringing your own water, or purifying river water. Camp is little-known, primitive, and set on the shore of the Queets River. A trailhead is available for hikes into interior of Olympic National Park.

ERICKSON'S BAY
Site 73

Campsites, facilities: There are 15 primitive tent sites at this boat-in camp. Picnic tables and pit toilets are provided. No piped water is available. Pets are permitted.

Reservations, fee: No reservations necessary; no fee. Open all year.

Who to contact: Phone Olympic National Park at 206-452-4501, or write at 600 East Park, Port Angeles, WA 98362.

Location: From Ozette, drive ½ mile south to Lake Ozette (Boat/backpack access only).

Trip note: Very few people visit this site, set on the shore of Ozette Lake and just a few miles from the Pacific Ocean. This is a boaters' delight. Access is limited to boaters and backpackers.

HOH RAIN FOREST
Site 74

Campsites, facilities: There are 95 sites for tents or motorhomes up to 21 feet long. Picnic tables are provided. Sanitary services, restrooms and drinking water are available. Pets are permitted.

Reservations, fee: No reservations necessary; $5 fee per night. Open all year.

Who to contact: Phone Olympic National Park at 206-452-4501, or write at 600 East Park, Port Angeles, WA 98362.

Location: From Forks, drive 14 miles south on US 101, then 19 miles east along the Hoh River until you arrive at the campground.

Trip note: This camp is at the trailhead leading into the interior of Olympic National Park. An option to campsites 62-65, which are set downriver on the Hoh. In the summer there are evening ranger programs.

MORA

Site 75

Campsites, facilities: There are 91 sites for tents or motorhomes up to 21 feet long. Picnic tables are provided. Drinking water, sanitary services and restrooms are available. Pets are permitted. Wheelchair facilities are available.

Reservations, fee: No reservations necessary; $5 fee per night. Open all year.

Who to contact: Phone Olympic National Park at 206-452-4501, or write at 600 East Park, Port Angeles, WA 98362.

Location: From Forks, drive two miles north on US 101 then west 12 miles on La Push Highway to campground.

Trip note: A good out-of-the-way choice set near Pacific Ocean and coastal National Wildlife Refuge. Soleduck River feeds into the ocean near here.

BOGACHIEL STATE PARK

Site 76

Campsites, facilities: There are 41 sites for tents or small motorhomes up to 35 feet long. Picnic tables are provided. Sanitary services, restrooms and drinking water are available. Store and ice are located within one mile. Showers and firewood are available for an extra fee. Pets are permitted.

Reservations, fee: No reservations necessary; $6 fee per night. Open all year.

Who to contact: Phone the state park at 206-374-6356, or write at HC 80 Box 500, Forks, WA 98331.

Location: From Forks, drive six miles south on US 101 to the park.

Trip note: Good base camp for salmon or steelhead fishing trip. This 119-acre park is set on the Bogachiel River. Marked hiking trails in the area.

HOH RIVER RESORT

Site 77

Campsites, facilities: There are eight tent sites and 27 drive-through sites for trailers or motorhomes of any length. Electricity, piped water, sewer hookups and picnic tables are provided. Toilets, store, laundry and ice are available. Showers and firewood are available for an extra fee. Pets and motorbikes are permitted.

Reservations, fee: No reservations necessary; $11.50 fee per night. Open all year.

Who to contact: Phone the park at 206-374-5566, or write at Star HC 80-750, Forks, WA 98331.

Location: From Forks, drive 15 miles south on US 101.

Trip note: A nice camp set right along Highway 101. Marked hiking trails are in the area.

FORKS 101 RV PARK

Site 78

Campsites, facilities: There are 10 tent sites and 50 sites for trailers or motorhomes of any length. Electricity, piped water and sewer hookups are provided. Bottled gas, sanitary services, toilets and laundry are available. Store, cafe and ice are located within one mile. Showers are available for an extra fee. Pets and motorbikes are permitted.

Reservations, fee: Reservations accepted; $10 fee per night. Open May to December.

Who to contact: Phone the park at 206-374-6970, or write at Box 1533, Forks, WA 98331.

Location: This park is in Forks, on US 101 near the south edge of town.

Trip note: A four-acre urban camp primarily for motorhomes. A tennis court is available nearby.

Site 79   BEAR CREEK MOTEL AND RV PARK

Campsites, facilities: There are eight tent sites and 15 drive-through sites for trailers or motorhomes of any length. Electricity, piped water, sewer hookups and picnic tables are provided. Bottled gas, sanitary services, toilets, showers and firewood are available. Cafe is located within one mile. Pets are permitted. Boat launching facilities are nearby.

Reservations, fee: No reservations necessary; $10 fee per night with American Express, MasterCard and Visa accepted. Open all year.

Who to contact: Phone the park at 206-327-3660, or write at Box 213, Beaver, WA 98305.

Location: From Forks, drive 15 miles north on US 101, watch for milepost 206. Camp is nearby.

Trip note: A quiet, little spot set where Bear Creek empties into the Soleduck River. Private and developed.

Site 80   THREE RIVERS RESORT

Campsites, facilities: There are 15 tent sites and 10 sites for trailers or motorhomes of any length. Picnic tables are provided. Bottled gas, toilets, store, cafe, laundry and ice are available. Electricity, piped water, sewer hookups, showers and firewood can be purchased for an extra fee. Pets are permitted.

Reservations, fee: Reservations accepted; $5 fee per night with MasterCard and Visa accepted. Open all year.

Who to contact: Phone the park at 206-374-5300, or write at Star Route 2, Bx 280, Forks, WA 98331.

Location: From Forks, drive nine miles west on Forks-La Push Highway.

Trip note: A small, private camp set on the Soleduck River. The coastal National Wildlife Refuge and Pacific Ocean are a short drive to the west.

Site 81   SHORELINE RESORT AND TRAILER PARK

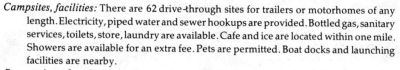

Campsites, facilities: There are 62 drive-through sites for trailers or motorhomes of any length. Electricity, piped water and sewer hookups are provided. Bottled gas, sanitary services, toilets, store, laundry are available. Cafe and ice are located within one mile. Showers are available for an extra fee. Pets are permitted. Boat docks and launching facilities are nearby.

Reservations, fee: No reservations necessary; $9 fee per night with MasterCard and Visa accepted. Open all year.

Who to contact: Phone the park at 206-374-6488, or write at Box 26, La Push, WA 98350.

Location: From Forks, drive 14 miles west on Forks-La Push Highway to the ocean.

Trip note: Set along the Pacific Ocean and the coastal National Wildlife Refuge. Private park, developed.

Site 82   COHO RESORT AND TRAILER PARK

Campsites, facilities: There are 25 tent sites and 100 sites for trailers or motorhomes of any 0length. Electricity, piped water, sewer hookups and picnic tables are provided. Sanitary services, toilets, cafe, laundry and ice are available. Bottled gas and store are located within one mile. Showers are available for an extra fee. Pets and motorbikes are permitted. Boat docks, launching facilities and rentals are nearby.

Reservations, fee: No reservations necessary; $8 fee per night. Open February to October.

Who to contact: Phone the park at 206-963-2333, or write at Sekiu, WA 98381.

Location: From Sekiu, drive one mile east on Highway 112 to park.

Trip note: One of seven camps in immediate area besides campsites 83-88. A full service marina nearby provides boating access.

Site 83   SURFSIDE RESORT

Campsites, facilities: There are 20 tent sites and 24 drive-through sites for trailers or motorhomes of any length. Electricity, piped water, sewer hookups and picnic tables are provided. Sanitary services, toilets and showers are available. Bottled gas, store, cafe, laundry and ice are located within one mile. Firewood is available for an extra fee. Pets and motorbikes are permitted. Boat docks, launching facilities and rentals are nearby.

Reservations, fee: Reservations accepted; $9 fee per night. Open May to September.

Who to contact: Phone the park at 206-963-2723, or write at P.O. Box 151, Sekiu, WA 98381.

Location: In Sekiu, on the east edge of town.

Trip note: Nearby recreation options include marked hiking trails, marked bike trails and a full service marina.

Site 84   CURLEY'S RESORT

Campsites, facilities: There are 12 sites for trailers or motorhomes up to 22 feet long. Electricity, piped water and sewer hookups are provided. Toilets, showers and ice are available. Bottled gas, sanitary services, store, cafe and laundry are located within one mile. Pets and motorbikes are permitted. Boat docks, launching facilities and rentals are nearby.

Reservations, fee: Reservations accepted; $8 fee per night with MasterCard and Visa accepted. Open April to late-October.

Who to contact: Phone the park at 206-963-2281, or write at Box 265, Sekiu, WA 98381.

Location: In the town of Sekiu.

Trip note: A small RV Park set on the edge of Clallam Bay.

Site **85**
OLSON'S RESORT

Campsites, facilities: There are 30 tent sites and 100 sites for trailers or motorhomes of any length. Electricity, piped water, sewer hookups and picnic tables are provided. Toilets, showers, store, cafe and ice are available. Sanitary services and laundry are located within one mile. Pets and motorbikes are permitted. Boat docks, launching facilities and rentals are nearby.

Reservations, fee: No reservations necessary; $8 fee per night with MasterCard and Visa accepted. Open February to mid-October.

Who to contact: Phone the park at 206-963-2311, or write at Box 216, Sekiu, WA 98381.

Location: In Sekiu, off Highway 112 at the north end of Front Street.

Trip note: A large, private camp developed with full services. A marina nearby is salmon fishing headquarters.

Site **86**
VAN RIPERS'S RESORT
HOTEL AND CAMPGROUND

Campsites, facilities: There are 60 drive-through sites for trailers or motorhomes of any length. Electricity, piped water and picnic tables are provided. Sanitary services, toilets, showers and ice are available. Bottled gas, store, cafe and laundry are located within one mile. Sewer hookups and firewood are available for an extra fee. Pets and motorbikes are permitted. Boat docks, launching facilities and rentals are nearby.

Reservations, fee: No reservations necessary; $8.50 fee per night with MasterCard and Visa accepted. Open April to late-September.

Who to contact: Phone the park at 206-963-2334, or write at Box 246, Sekiu, WA 98381.

Location: In Sekiu, off Highway 112, north on Front Street.

Trip note: For motorhomes and trailers only, urban camping along Clallam Bay.

Site **87**
RICE'S RESORT

Campsites, facilities: There are 41 tent sites and 16 sites for trailers or motorhomes up to 30 feet long. Electricity, piped water, sewer hookups and picnic tables are provided. Sanitary services, toilets, showers, firewood, ice and playground are available. Bottled gas, store, cafe and laundry are located within one mile. Pets and motorbikes are permitted. Boat docks, launching facilities and rentals are nearby.

Reservations, fee: Reservations accepted; $8 fee per night. Open all year with limited winter facilities.

Who to contact: Phone the park at 206-963-2300, or write at Box 218, Sekiu, WA 98381.

Location: In Sekiu off Highway 112, ½ mile north and ⅛ mile west on Rice Street.

Trip note: Of the seven campgrounds in immediate area around Clallam Bay, this one is set up more for tent campers than the others.

Site **88**
SAM'S TRAILER
AND RV PARK

Campsites, facilities: There are 10 tent sites and 20 drive-through sites for trailers or motorhomes of any length. Electricity, piped water, sewer hookups and picnic tables are provided. Sanitary services, toilets, showers and laundry are available. Bottled gas, store, cafe and ice are located within one mile. Pets and motorbikes are permitted. Boat docks, launching facilities and rentals are nearby.

Reservations, fee: Reservations accepted; $7 fee per night. Open all year.

Who to contact: Phone the park at 206-963-2402, or write at Box 45, Clallam Bay, WA 98326.

Location: In Clallam Bay on Highway 112.

Trip note: An option to campsites 82-86 on Clallam Bay.

Site 89   THE VILLAGE CABINS/RV PARK

Campsites, facilities: There are 32 sites for trailers or motorhomes of any length. Electricity, piped water and sewer hookups are provided. Sanitary services, toilets and showers are available. Bottled gas, store, cafe, laundry, ice are located within one mile. Pets are permitted. Boat docks, launching facilities and rentals are nearby.

Reservations, fee: Reservations accepted; $9 fee per night with MasterCard and Visa accepted. Open April to October.

Who to contact: Phone the park at 206-645-2659, or write at Box 654, Neah Bay, WA 98357.

Location: In Neah Bay on Highway 112.

Trip note: This is one of six camps/RV parks set on northwestern tip of the Olympic Peninsula. It's for motorhome and trailers only. Looks over the Strait of Juan De Fuca where it enters Pacific Ocean.

Site 90   THUNDERBIRD RV PARK

Campsites facilities: There are five tent sites and 45 pull through sites for trailers or motorhomes of any length. Electricity, piped water and sewer hookups are provided. Bottled gas, toilets, laundry and ice are available. Sanitary services, store, cafe are located within one mile. Showers are available for an extra fee. Pets and motorbikes are permitted. Boat docks, launching facilities and rentals are nearby.

Reservations, fee: Reservations accepted; $9.50 fee per night with MasterCard and Visa accepted. Open April to late-September.

Who to contact: Phone the park at 206-645-2450, or write at Box 218, Neah Bay, WA 98357.

Location: In Neah Bay on Highway 112.

Trip note: Three-acre RV park with safety valve option of five tent sites. OK base of operations for anglers when salmon migrating through area. Full service marina nearby.

Site 91   TYEE MOTEL AND RV PARK

Campsites facilities: There are 40 pull through sites for trailers or motorhomes of any length. Electricity, piped water and sewer hookups are provided. Bottled gas, sanitary services, toilets, laundry and ice are available. Store and cafe are located within one mile. Showers are available for an extra fee. Pets and motorbikes are permitted. Boat docks, launching facilities and rentals are nearby.

Reservations, fee: Reservations accepted; $9.50 fee per night with MasterCard and Visa accepted. Open all year.

Who to contact: Phone the park at 206-645-2223, or write at Box 193, Neah Bay, WA 98357.

Location: In Neah Bay on Highway 112.

Trip note: For motorhomes and trailers only. Private and developed campground near northwestern tip of Olympic Peninsula.

Site 92   WESTWING RESORT

Campsites facilities: There are 10 tent sites and 26 sites for trailers or motorhomes up to 30 feet long. Electricity, piped water, sewer hookups and picnic tables are provided. Toilets, showers, laundry and ice are available. Bottled gas, store, cafe are located within one mile. Pets are permitted. Boat docks, launching facilities and rentals are nearby.

Reservations, fee: Reservations accepted; $8.50 fee per night with MasterCard and Visa accepted. Open May to October.

Who to contact: Phone the park at 206-645-2751, or write at Box 918, Neah Bay, WA 98357.

Location: In Neah Bay on Highway 112.

Trip note: This is one of the better choices in immediate area for tent campers.

Site 93   NEAH BAY RESORT

Campsites facilities: There are 10 tent sites and 38 sites for trailers or motorhomes of any length. Electricity, piped water, sewer hookups and picnic tables are provided. Bottled gas, sanitary services, toilets, showers, store, cafe and ice are available. Pets are permitted. Boat docks, launching facilities and rentals are nearby.

Reservations, fee: Reservations accepted; $12 fee per night. Open May to mid-September.

Who to contact: Phone the park at 206-645-2288, or write at Box 97, Neah Bay, WA 98357.

Location: From Neah Bay, drive five miles east on Highway 112 to resort.

Trip note: A private camp. Good alternative to campsites 89-92, all on tip of Olympic Peninsula. Set near Makah Indian Reservation and Cape Flattery.

Site 94   POINT HUDSON CAMPGROUND

Campsites facilities: There are 18 drive-through sites for trailers or motorhomes of any length. Picnic tables and full hookups are provided. Flush toilets, a store, cafe, laundromat, and ice are available. Showers are available for an extra fee. A boat dock and launching ramp is nearby.

Reservations, fee: Reservations accepted; $10 fee per night. Open all year.

Who to contact: Phone 206-385-2828, or write to the campground in Port Townsend, WA 98368.

Location: In Port Townsend, from the junction of Highway 20 and Water Street, drive to the Port Hudson Boat Basin.

Trip note: Nearby recreation options include an 18-hole golf course, a full-service marina, Old Fort Townsend State Park, Fort Flagler State Park and Fort Worden State Park.

SEA BREEZE CENTER
Site **95**   MOTORHOME AND RV PARK

Campsites: There are 32 sites for self-contained motorhomes or trailers of any size. Full hookups are provided. A store, laundromat, boat dock, launch ramp and ice are available. A sanitary dump station, bottled gas, and a cafe are nearby.

Reservations, fee: Reservations accepted; $8.50 fee per night. Visa and Mastercard accepted. Open all year.

Location: Drive to the west edge of the town of Port Townsend on Highway 20 and you'll see the park.

Trip note: Nearby recreation options include an 18-hole golf course, horseback riding rentals, tennis courts, Old Fort Townsend State Park, Fort Flagler State Park and Fort Worden State Park.

FORT FLAGLER
Site **96**   STATE PARK

Campsites facilities: There are 116 sites for tents or motorhomes up to 50 feet long. Picnic tables are provided. Flush toilets, a sanitary dump station, a store, cafe, boat buoys and floats, and a boat launch are available. Facilities are wheelchair accessible. Showers are available for an extra fee.

Reservations, fee: Reservations accepted; $6 fee per night.

Who to contact: Phone 206-385-1259, or write at Nordland, WA 98358.

Location: Drive to Marrowstone Island just south of Port Townsend. State Park is eight miles northeast of the town of Hadlock.

Trip note: The campgrounds are right on the beach. A good place for fisherman with year around rockfishing and salmon fishing. Crabbing and clamming are good in season. Tours are available for Fort Flagler, which was built in 1898.

OLD FORT TOWNSEND
Site **97**   STATE PARK

Campsites facilities: There are 40 sites for tents or motorhomes up to 40 feet long. Picnic tables are provided, and flush toilets, a playground and boat buoys are available. Firewood and showers are available for an extra fee.

Reservations, fee: No reservations; $6 fee per night. Open all year, but with limited winter facilities.

Who to contact: Phone 206-385-3595, or write at Route 1, Port Townsend, WA 98368.

Location: From Quilcene, drive 12 miles north on Highway 101, then go north on Highway 20 for seven miles to the park.

Trip note: This fort was built in 1859, one of the oldest remaining in the state. The campground has access to a good clamming beach, and there are stables nearby.

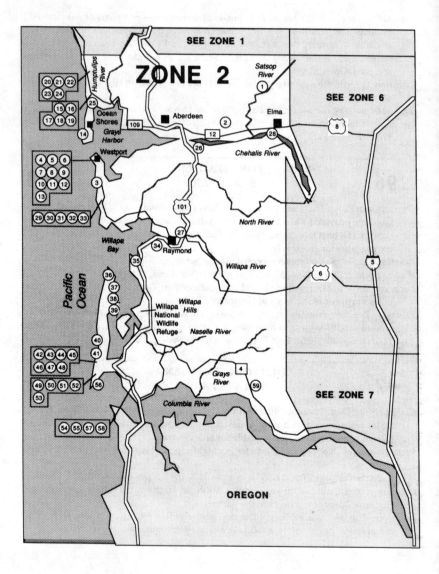

SOUTHWEST COAST

Site 1
SCHAFER
STATE PARK

Campsites, facilities: There are 47 tent sites and six sites with water and electric hookups for trailers or motorhomes up to 40 feet long. Picnic tables are provided. Sanitary services, toilets and a playground are available. Water, showers and firewood are an additional charge. Some facilities are wheelchair accessible. Pets are permitted.

Reservations, fee: No reservations necessary; $6 fee per night. Open all year with limited winter facilities.

Who to contact: Phone at 206-482-3852, or write at Route 1, Box 87, Elma, WA 98541.

Location: Drive four miles east of Montesano on Highway 12, then head north for eight miles on East Satsop Road to the Park.

Trip note: This heavily-wooded, rural camp covers 119 acres and is on the East Fork of the Satsop River. There are good canoe and kayaking spots, some with Class II and Class III rapids, along the Middle and West Forks of the Satsop River. At one time this park was the Schafer Company Park and was used by the employees and their families.

Site 2
LAKE SYLVIA

Campsites, facilities: There are 35 tent sites which also can accommodate vehicles or motorhomes up to 30 feet long. Picnic tables are provided. There is no piped water. Sanitary dump services, toilets, store, fishing supplies, a car-top boat launch, boat rentals and playground are available. Showers and firewood are available for an extra fee. Laundry and ice are located within one mile. Some facilities are wheelchair accessible. Pets are permitted.

Reservations, fee: No reservations necessary; $6 fee per night. Open all year.

Who to contact: Phone at 206-249-3621, or write at Box 701, Montesano, WA 98563.

Location: From Montesano, drive north one mile to the park.

Trip note: This camp is on the shore of Lake Sylvia and covers 234 acres. There are numerous marked hiking trails. Additional facilities found within five miles of the campground include an 18-hole golf course. If this camp is full, nearby options are Campsites 1, 26 and 28.

Site 3
TWIN HARBORS
STATE PARK

Campsites, facilities: There are 283 tent sites and 49 sites for trailers or motorhomes up to

35 feet long. Picnic tables are provided. Sanitary services, toilets and playground are available. Store, cafe and ice are available within one mile. Electricity, piped water, sewer hookups, showers and firewood are available for an extra fee. Some facilities are wheelchair accessible. Pets are permitted.

Reservations, fee: Reservations accepted; $6 fee per night. Open all year.

Who to contact: Phone at 206-753-4055, or write to Twin Harbors State Park, Westport, WA 98595.

Location: The park is three miles south of Westport on Highway 105.

Trip note: This park covers 1881 acres, and has beach access and marked hiking trails. Nearby in Westport there are fishing boats to charter. One of the largest campgrounds on the coast.

Site **4**
WESTPORT WATERFRONT RV PARK

Campsites, facilities: There are 30 sites with full hookups for trailers or motorhomes of any length. Sanitary services, toilets and ice and showers are available. Boat docks, launching facilities and rentals are located at the park. Bottled gas, store and laundry are within one mile.

Reservations, fee: Reservations accepted; $11 fee per night. Open May to late-October.

Who to contact: Phone the park at 206-268-0137, or write at 609 Revetment, Westport, WA 98595.

Location: In Westport, take Revetment Drive to boat basin to the park at 609 Revetment.

Trip note: This motorhome park and marina covers two acres. Westport Light and Westhaven State Parks are both nearby and offer day use facilities on the beach. Good salmon fishing in summer months along local coast.

Site **5**
LIGHTHOUSE RV RESORT

Campsites, facilities: There are 15 tent sites and 43 drive-through sites for trailers or motorhomes of any length. Electricity, piped water, sewer hookups and picnic tables are provided. Toilets, showers and laundry are available. Bottled gas, sanitary services, store, cafe and ice are within one mile. Pets and motorbikes are permitted. Boat docks and launching facilities are available nearby.

Reservations, fee: Reservations accepted; $8 fee per night. Open all year.

Who to contact: Phone at 206-268-0001, or write at P.O. Box 1237, Westport, WA 98595.

Location: In Westport, drive three blocks east on Tacoma Avenue from Highway 109 and you're there.

Trip note: This private park covers three acres and is near Gray's Harbor and Westport Light State Park, a day-use park popular for surfing, scuba diving and rock collecting. There is a full service marina within five miles of the campground at Gray's Harbor.

Site **6**
ISLANDER RV PARK

Campsites, facilities: There are 60 drive-through sites with full hookups for trailers or motorhomes of any length. Toilets, showers, cafe, laundry, ice, swimming pool, boat docks, launching facilities and rentals are available. Bottled gas, sanitary services and store are located within one mile. Pets and motorbikes are permitted.

Reservations, fee: Reservations accepted; $8 fee per night. American Express, MasterCard and Visa accepted. Open all year.

Who to contact: Phone at 206-268-9166, or write at P.O. Box 488, Westport, WA 98595.

Location: In Westport, drive to boat basin on Revetment Drive.

Trip note: This park covers three acres and is on Grays Harbor, not far from Westport Light and Westhaven State Parks, which offer ocean-front day-use facilities. Additional facilities found within five miles of the campground include a full service marina.

G & M CHARTER
Site **7** ### TRAILER PARK

Campsites, facilities: There are 10 tent sites and 30 drive-through sites with full hookups for trailers or motorhomes of any length. Picnic tables are provided. Sanitary services, toilets, boat docks, launching facilities, rentals and ice are available, and showers are available for an extra fee. Bottled gas, store, cafe and laundry are available within one mile. Pets and motorbikes are permitted.

Reservations, fee: Reservations accepted; $8 fee per night. Open April to October.

Who to contact: Phone the park at 206-268-0265, or write at P.O. Box 342, Westport, WA 98595.

Location: In Westport, drive to Point Chehalis on Revetment Drive. Park is at the Westport Docks.

Trip note: This park covers one acre and is near Westport Harbor. There are several state parks nearby that offer day-use facilities along the ocean.

COHO
Site **8** ### TRAILER PARK

Campsites, facilities: There are 80 drive-through sites with full hookups for trailers or motorhomes of any length. Picnic tables are provided. Sanitary services, toilets, showers, laundry and ice are available. Bottled gas, a store and a cafe are within one mile. Pets are permitted. Boat docks, launching facilities and rentals also are located at this park.

Reservations, fee: Reservations accepted; $10 fee per night. Open all year.

Who to contact: Phone at 206-268-0111, or write at 2501 Nyhus, Westport, WA 98595.

Location: In Westport, from Highway 105 drive north on Nyhus Street to the Westport Docks.

Trip note: This park covers two acres, one of 10 camp options in the immediate area. Both Westhaven and Westport Light State Parks are nearby. They are popular places for rock hounds, scuba divers and surf fishermen. Additional facilities found within five miles of the campground include a full service marina.

HAMMOND
Site **9** ### TRAILER PARK

Campsites, facilities: There are eight tent sites and 25 sites with full hookups for trailers or motorhomes of any length. Picnic tables are provided. Sanitary services, toilets, showers, firewood and laundry are available. Bottled gas, store, cafe and ice are within one mile. Pets are permitted. Boat docks, launching facilities and boat rentals are nearby.

Reservations, fee: Reservations accepted; $7 fee per night. Open all year.

Who to contact: Phone at 206-268-9645, or write at P.O. Box 1648, Westport, WA 98595.

Location: In Westport, drive ¼ mile south on Montesano Street to 1845 Roberts Road.

Trip note: This park covers five acres. Additional facilities found within five miles of the campground include a full service marina.

HOLAND CENTER

Site **10**

Campsites, facilities: There are 80 drive-through sites with full hookups for trailers or motorhomes of any length. Picnic tables are provided. Toilets and showers are available. Bottled gas, store, cafe, laundry and ice are located within one mile. Pets are permitted. Boat docks and launching facilities are nearby.

Reservations, fee: Reservations accepted; $9 fee per night. Open all year.

Who to contact: Phone at 206-268-9582, or write at P.O. Box 468, Westport, WA 98595.

Location: In Westport, this park is at the corner of Highway 105 and Wilson Street.

Trip note: This camp covers 18 acres. Additional facilities found within five miles of the campground include a full service marina.

ERIN MOTEL
AND TRAILER PARK

Site **11**

Campsites, facilities: There are seven sites for trailers or motorhomes of any length. Electricity, piped water, sewer hookups and picnic tables are provided. Sanitary services, toilets and showers are available. Bottled gas, store, cafe, laundry and ice are located within one mile. Pets and motorbikes are permitted. Boat docks and launching facilities are nearby.

Reservations, fee: Reservations accepted; $8 fee per night. MasterCard and Visa accepted. Open April to late-October.

Who to contact: Phone at 206-268-9614, or write at P.O. Box 346, Westport, WA 98595.

Location: This motel and RV park is located in the town of Westport on Ocean Avenue.

Trip note: The park covers one acre and is close to the services of Gray's Harbor, and Westport Light and Westhaven State Parks. Additional facilities found within five miles of the campground include a full service marina.

TOTEM RV
AND TRAILER PARK

Site **12**

Campsites, facilities: There are 10 tent sites and 77 drive-through sites for trailers or motorhomes of any length. Electricity, piped water, sewer hookups and picnic tables are provided. Sanitary services, toilets, showers, store, laundry and ice are available. Bottled gas and cafe are located within one mile. Pets and motorbikes are permitted. Boat docks, launching facilities and rentals are nearby.

Reservations, fee: Reservations accepted; $9 fee per night. Open March to October.

Who to contact: Phone at 206-268-0025, or write at P.O. Box 1166, Westport, WA 98595.

Location: In Westport, from the junction of Highway 105 and Montesano Street, drive 1 ½ miles north on Highway 105, then two blocks northeast to Nyhus (1st Avenue).

Trip note: This park covers two acres and is near Westhaven State Park which offers day-use facilities. Additional facilities found within five miles of the campground include marked bike trails, a full service marina and tennis courts.

Site **13**
PACIFIC MOTEL
AND TRAILER PARK

Campsites, facilities: There are 40 tent sites and 80 drive-through sites for trailers or motorhomes of any length. Electricity, piped water and sewer hookups are provided. Sanitary services, toilets, recreation hall and swimming pool are available, and showers are available for an extra fee. Bottled gas, store, cafe, laundry and ice are located within one mile. Pets and motorbikes are permitted. Boat docks and launching facilities are nearby.

Reservations, fee: Reservations accepted; $10 fee per night. MasterCard and Visa accepted. Open all year.

Who to contact: Phone at 206-268-9325, or write at 330 W. Forrest, Westport, WA 98595.

Location: The motel and trailer park are in Westport. To get there, drive two miles north of Twin Harbor State Park on Highway 105.

Trip note: This park covers five acres and is near Twin Harbors and Westport Light state parks, both of which have beach access. Additional facilities found within five miles of the campground include a full service marina.

Site **14**
MARINA VIEW
RV PARK

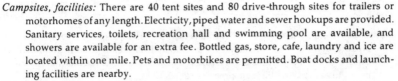

Campsites, facilities: There are 50 tent sites and 93 drive-through sites for trailers or motorhomes of any length. Electricity, piped water, sewer hookups and picnic tables are provided. Sanitary services, toilets, showers, store, cafe and ice are available. Pets and motorbikes are permitted. Boat docks, launching facilities and rentals are nearby.

Reservations, fee: Reservations accepted; $9 fee per night. American Express, MasterCard and Visa accepted. Open all year.

Who to contact: Phone at 206-289-3391, or write at P.O. Box 1291, Ocean Shores, WA 98569.

Location: From Ocean Shores, drive five miles south on Point Brown Avenue and you're there.

Trip note: This camp covers 13 acres and is on Point Brown. Additional facilities found within five miles of the campground include an 18-hole golf course, marked hiking trails, marked bike trails and a riding stable.

Site **15**
STURGEON
TRAILER HARBOR

Campsites, facilities: There are 66 drive-through sites for trailers or motorhomes of any length. Electricity, piped water, sewer hookups and picnic tables are provided. Toilets, showers and recreation hall are available. Bottled gas, store, cafe and ice are located within one mile. Pets and motorbikes are permitted.

Reservations, fee: Reservations accepted; $12 fee per night. Open all year.

Who to contact: Phone at 206-289-2101, or write at P.O. Box 536, Ocean City, WA 98569.

Location: This trailer park is on Highway 109 in Ocean City at the southern end of town.

Trip note: This park covers five acres and offers beach access. Additional facilities found within five miles of the campground include an 18-hole golf course, marked hiking trails, a full service marina and a riding stable.

Site 16
OCEAN CITY STOVE AND RV PARK

Campsites, facilities: There are 20 sites for trailers or motorhomes of any length. Electricity, piped water and sewer hookups are provided. Toilets and showers are available. Bottled gas, sanitary services, store, cafe and ice are located within one mile. Pets and motorbikes are permitted. Boat rentals are nearby.

Reservations, fee: Reservations accepted; $8 fee per night. MasterCard and Visa accepted. Open all year.

Who to contact: Phone the park at 206-289-3589, or write at Route 4, Box 230, Ocean City, WA 98569.

Location: This park is in the town of Ocean City on Highway 109.

Trip note: This park covers two acres and offers beach access. Additional facilities found within five miles of the campground include an 18-hole golf course, marked hiking trails and a riding stable.

Site 17
LOOKOUT RV PARK

Campsites, facilities: There are 23 sites for trailers or motorhomes of any length. Electricity, piped water, sewer hookups and picnic tables are provided. Sanitary services, toilets, showers and recreation hall are available. Bottled gas, store, cafe and ice are located within one mile. Pets are permitted.

Reservations, fee: Reservations accepted; $10 fee per night. Open all year.

Who to contact: Phone at 206-289-2220, or write at Route 4, Box 570, Ocean City, WA 98569.

Location: Follow the signs in Ocean City to the Lookout RV Park.

Trip note: This park covers one acre and has beach access. One of 11 campgrounds on six miles of coastline.

Site 18
BLUE PACIFIC MOTEL AND TRAILER PARK

Campsites, facilities: There are 19 sites for trailers or motorhomes up to 30 feet long. Electricity, piped water, sewer hookups and picnic tables are provided. Toilets, showers and a playground are available. Bottled gas, store, cafe and ice are located within one mile. Pets are permitted.

Reservations, fee: Reservations accepted; $10 fee per night. MasterCard and Visa accepted. Open all year, but with limited winter facilities.

Who to contact: Phone at 206-289-2262, or write at Route 4, Box 615, Ocean City, WA 98569.

Location: Drive north from Ocean City on Highway 109 for ½ mile to this park.

Trip note: This park covers two acres and has beach access. An 18-hole golf course is available nearby.

Site **19**
ROD'S BEACH RESORT

Campsites, facilities: There are 85 drive-through sites for trailers or motorhomes of any length. Electricity, piped water, sewer hookups and picnic tables are provided. Sanitary services, toilets, showers, recreation hall, store, cafe, ice and playground are available. Bottled gas located within one mile. A swimming pool is available for an extra fee. Pets are permitted.

Reservations, fee: Reservations accepted; $12 fee per night. MasterCard and Visa accepted. Open February to late-November.

Who to contact: Phone the park at 206-289-2222, or write to Rod's Beach Resort, Copalis Beach, WA 98535.

Location: Drive south from Copalis Beach on Highway 109 for 1 ½ miles to this park.

Trip note: This park covers 10 acres and has beach access. Nice sunsets.

Site **20**
TIDELANDS ON THE BEACH

Campsites, facilities: There are 100 tent sites and 60 drive-through sites for trailers or motorhomes of any length. Electricity, piped water, sewer hookups and picnic tables are provided. Sanitary services, toilets, firewood and playground are available. Bottled gas, store, cafe and ice are located within one mile. Showers are available for an extra fee. Pets are permitted.

Reservations, fee: Reservations accepted; $12 fee per night. Open all year.

Who to contact: Phone at 206 289 8963, or write at P.O. Box 36, Copalis Beach, WA 98535.

Location: Drive south from Copalis Beach on Highway 109 for one mile.

Trip note: This wooded park covers 47 acres and has beach access. A more remote option to campsites 15-19.

Site **21**
SURF AND SAND RV PARK

Campsites, facilities: There are 45 drive-through sites for trailers or motorhomes of any length. Electricity, piped water, sewer hookups and picnic tables are provided. Sanitary services, toilets, showers, cafe and ice are available. Bottled gas and store are located within one mile. Pets are permitted.

Reservations, fee: Reservations accepted; $14 fee per night. MasterCard and Visa accepted. Open all year.

Who to contact: Phone at 206-289-2707, or write at P.O. Box 87, Copalis Beach, WA 98535.

Location: In Copalis Beach, take the the Copalis Beach Access Road off Highway 109 and drive ¼ mile to park.

Trip note: This park covers five acres and has beach access. Decent layover for motorhome vacation.

Site **22**
DRIFTWOOD ACRES OCEAN CAMPGROUND

Campsites, facilities: There are 30 tent sites and 70 sites for trailers or motorhomes of any

length. Piped water, sewer hookups and picnic tables are provided. Electricity, showers, sanitary services, toilets and firewood are available. Bottled gas, store, cafe and ice are located within one mile. Pets are permitted.

Reservations, fee: Reservations accepted; $14 fee per night. Open April to late-October.

Who to contact: Phone at 206-289-3484, or write at P.O. Box 216, Copalis Beach, WA 98535.

Location: Drive ¼ mile south of Copalis Beach on Highway 109 to park.

Trip note: This wooded campground covers 150 acres and has beach access and marked hiking trails. Additional facilities found within five miles of the campground include an 18-hole golf course and a riding stable.

Site 23 HIDEAWAY RV PARK

Campsites, facilities: There are eight tent sites and 35 sites for trailers or motorhomes of any length. Electricity, piped water, sewer hookups and picnic tables are provided. Sanitary services, toilets and firewood are available, and showers are available for an extra fee. Bottled gas, store, cafe and ice are located within one mile. Pets and motorbikes are permitted.

Reservations, fee: Reservations accepted; $14 fee per night. MasterCard and Visa accepted. Open all year.

Who to contact: Phone at 206-289-2182, or write at P.O. Box 67, Copalis Beach, WA 98535.

Location: This park is in Copalis Beach, at the north end of town on Highway 109.

Trip note: The park covers 20 acres and offers beach and river access. An 18-hole golf course is a short drive distant.

Site 24 RIVERSIDE TRAILER COURT

Campsites, facilities: There are 15 tent sites and 53 drive-through sites for trailers or motorhomes of any length. Electricity, piped water, sewer hookups and picnic tables are provided. Bottled gas, sanitary services, toilets, showers, firewood and recreation hall are available. Store, cafe and ice are located within one mile. Pets and motorbikes are permitted.

Reservations, fee: Reservations accepted; $12 fee per night. MasterCard and Visa accepted. Open all year.

Who to contact: Phone at 206-289-2111, or write at P.O. Box 132, Copalis Beach, WA 98535.

Location: From Copalis Beach, drive across the river to the park.

Trip note: This park covers three acres and has beach and river access.

Site 24 OCEAN CITY STATE PARK

Campsites, facilities: There are 149 tent sites and 29 sites with full hookups for trailers or motorhomes up to 55 feet long. Picnic tables are provided, and sanitary services and toilets are available. Showers and firewood (in the summer) are available for an extra fee. Some facilities are wheelchair accessible. Pets are permitted.

Reservations, fee: No reservations necessary; $6 fee per night. Open all year.

Who to contact: Phone the state park at 206-289-3553, or write at Route 4, Box 2900,

Hoquiam, WA 98550.

Location: Drive 20 miles west from Aberdeen on Highway 109, then turn left on Highway 105 and drive three miles to park.

Trip note: One of the choice spots in the area for tent campers. This camp is on the ocean and covers 131 acres. It is near many interesting shops and restaurants in town, and a short drive from an 18-hole golf course.

Site 26   ARTIC RV PARK

Campsites, facilities: There are 12 tent sites and 10 sites for trailers or motorhomes of any length. Electricity, piped water and sewer hookups are provided. Sanitary services and cafe are available. Firewood can be purchased for an extra fee. Pets and motorbikes are permitted.

Reservations, fee: Reservations accepted; $7 fee per night. Open all year.

Who to contact: Phone at 206-532-9811, or write at HCR 77, Box 64, Cosmopolis, WA 98537.

Location: Drive seven miles south of Aberdeen on Highway 101.

Trip note: This wooded park covers four acres and provides access to the North River. It offers a more remote setting compared to campsites 3-25 on Grays Harbor. An 18-hole golf course is a short drive distant.

Site 27   TIMBERLAND RV PARK

Campsites, facilities: There are six tent sites and 24 drive-through sites for trailers or motorhomes of any length. Electricity, piped water, sewer hookups and picnic tables are provided. Toilets and showers are available. Bottled gas, sanitary services, store, cafe, laundry and ice are located within one mile. Pets and motorbikes are permitted. Boat docks are nearby where the Willapa River empties into Willapa Bay.

Reservations, fee: Reservations accepted; $8 fee per night. Open mid-March to November.

Who to contact: Phone at 206-942-3325, or write at 1402 Vail, Raymond, WA 98577.

Location: To get to this park, drive on Highway 101 to Raymond, then turn west on Highway 105 and drive six blocks. Turn left on Crescent for two blocks and you're there.

Trip note: This park covers three acres and has access to the Willapa River, a popular river during salmon or steelhead runs. Additional facilities found within five miles of the campground include an 18-hole golf course and tennis courts.

Site 28   RL'S RV PARK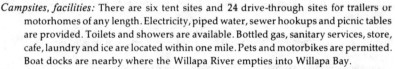

Campsites, facilities: There are 20 tent sites and 100 drive-through sites for trailers or motorhomes of any length. Electricity, piped water and sewer hookups are provided. Bottled gas, sanitary services, toilets, showers and laundry are available. Store and cafe are located within one mile. Pets and motorbikes are permitted. Boat docks, launching facilities and rentals are nearby on the Chehalis River.

Reservations, fee: Reservations accepted; $8 fee per night. Open all year.

Who to contact: Phone at 206-482-5623, or write at P.O. Box K2, Elma, WA 98541.

Location: From Elma, drive ½ mile south of Highway 12 to the park.

Trip note: This rural park covers eight acres and sits along the Chehalis River. Additional facilities found within five miles of the campground include an 18-hole golf course, a riding stable and tennis courts.

Site 29   OCEAN GATE RESORT

Campsites, facilities: There are 20 tent sites and 24 drive-through sites for trailers or motorhomes of any length. Electricity, piped water, sewer hookups and picnic tables are provided. Toilets, showers, laundry and playground are available, and firewood is available for an extra fee. Bottled gas, store, cafe and ice are found within one mile. Pets and motorbikes are permitted.

Reservations, fee: Reservations accepted; $9 fee per night. Open all year.

Who to contact: Phone at 206-267-1956, or write at P.O. Box 67, Grayland, WA 98547.

Location: Drive to Grayland on Highway 105. The park is located in town.

Trip note: This is a privately-run park that provides an option to campsite 33, the public-run Grayland Beach State Park. This park covers seven acres and has beach access.

Site 30   SOUTH BEACH RV PARK

Campsites, facilities: There are five tent sites and 10 sites for trailers or motorhomes of any length in this adult-only campground. Electricity, piped water and sewer hookups are provided. Sanitary services and toilets are available, and showers are available for an extra fee. Bottled gas, store, cafe, laundry and ice are found within one mile. Pets are permitted.

Reservations, fee: Reservations accepted; $6 fee per night. Open all year.

Who to contact: Phone at 206-267-5121, or write at Route 1, Box 50A, Grayland, WA 98547.

Location: Drive to Grayland on Highway 105. The park is located in town.

Trip note: No kids are permitted here. This is a small park, just three acres, and provides beach access.

Site 31   WESTERN SHORES TRAILER PARK

Campsites, facilities: There are 10 tent sites and 25 drive-through sites for trailers or motorhomes of any length. Electricity, piped water, sewer hookups and picnic tables are provided. Bottled gas, toilets, recreation hall, ice and playground are available, and showers are available for an extra fee. Sanitary services, firewood, store and cafe are located within one mile. Pets and motorbikes are permitted.

Reservations, fee: Reservations accepted; $7 fee per night. MasterCard and Visa accepted. Open all year.

Who to contact: Phone at 800-562-0189, or write at Star Route 1, Box 79, Grayland, WA 98547.

Location: Drive to Grayland on Highway 105. The camp is located in town.

Trip note: A small, private park designed for families. This is a good option to campsite 31, since kids are welcome.

Site **32**
TWIN SPRUCE
RV PARK

Campsites, facilities: There are 12 tent sites and 49 drive-through sites for trailers or
motorhomes of any length. Electricity, piped water, sewer hookups and picnic tables
are provided. Toilets, recreation hall and laundry are available, showers are available
for an extra fee. Bottled gas, store, cafe and ice can be found within one mile. Pets and
motorbikes are permitted.

Reservations, fee: Reservations accepted; $9 fee per night. Open March to November.

Who to contact: Phone at 206-267-1275, or write at P.O. Box 120, Grayland, WA 98547.

Location: Drive to Grayland on Highway 105, then go east on Schmid Road. Follow the
signs to Twin Spruce RV Park.

Trip note: This wooded park covers five acres and has beach access.

Site **33**
GRAYLAND BEACH
STATE PARK

Campsites, facilities: There are 60 campsites with full hookups for trailers or motorhomes
up to 40 feet long. Picnic tables are provided, toilets are available and showers are
available for an extra fee. Some facilities are wheelchair accessible.

Reservations, fee: Reservations accepted; $6 fee per night. Open all year.

Who to contact: Write Grayland State Park, Westport, WA 98595.

Location: Drive to Grayland on Highway 105. The park is just south of town.

Trip note: This ocean-front park covers 317 acres and has a self-guided interpretive trail.
One of the best parks in the immediate area, and quite popular to out-of-towners,
especially in the summer season.

Site **34**
GYPSY
RV PARK

Campsites, facilities: There are two tent sites and 12 drive-through sites for trailers or
motorhomes of any length. Electricity, piped water and sewer hookups are provided.
Toilets, showers, recreation hall and laundry are available. Bottled gas, store, cafe and
ice can be found within one mile. Pets and motorbikes are permitted. Boat docks and
launching facilities are nearby where the Willapa River empties into Willapa Bay.

Reservations, fee: Reservations accepted; $8 fee per night. Open all year.

Who to contact: Phone at 206-875-5165, or write at P.O. Box 191, South Bend, WA
98586.

Location: Drive to South Bend on US 101, then go south on Central. The camp is located in
town.

Trip note: This wooded park covers two acres and is on the Willapa River. Additional
facilities found within five miles of the campground include an 18-hole golf course.

Site **35**
KOA
HAPPY TRAILS

Campsites, facilities: There are 10 tent sites and 32 drive-through sites for trailers or
motorhomes of any length. Piped water and picnic tables are provided. Bottled gas,
sanitary services, toilets, showers, recreation hall, store, laundry and ice are available.
Electricity, sewer hookups and firewood can be purchased for an extra fee. There is a

cafe nearby. Pets and motorbikes are permitted. Boat docks and launching facilities are about three miles from camp on Willapa Bay.

Reservations, fee: Reservations accepted; $10 fee per night. MasterCard and Visa accepted. Open March to December.

Who to contact: Phone at 206-875-6344, or write at P.O. Box 315, Bay Center, WA 98527.

Location: Take the Bay Center exit off Highway 101 and drive one mile south to campground.

Trip note: This camp covers 11 acres and is on the shore of Willapa Bay. A trail from the campground leads to the beach.

Site 36   EVERGREEN COURT

Campsites, facilities: There are 16 tent sites and 18 sites for trailers or motorhomes of any length. Electricity, piped water, sewer hookups and picnic tables are provided. Sanitary services, toilets, showers, firewood and a playground are available. A store, cafe and laundry can be found within one mile. Pets and motorbikes are permitted.

Reservations, fee: Reservations accepted; $6 fee per night. MasterCard and Visa accepted. Open all year.

Who to contact: Phone the park at 206-665-5100, or write at P.O. Box 488, Ocean Park, WA 98640.

Location: Drive seven miles north of Ocean Park on Highway 103 to get to park.

Trip note: This wooded campground covers five acres and has beach access. Nearby is Leadbetter Point State Park, a day-use park and natural area that adjoins a wildlife refuge. The trails at Leadbetter Point State Park lead through the dunes and woods and provide opportunities for seeing both marine birds and waterfowl, especially in the spring and fall. There is also a boat launch there. Additional facilities found within five miles of the campground include an 18-hole golf course and marked bike trails.

Site 37   OCEAN AIRE

Campsites, facilities: There are 40 drive-through sites for trailers or motorhomes of any length. Electricity, piped water, sewer hookups and picnic tables are provided. Bottled gas, sanitary services, toilets, showers, laundry and ice are available. Store and cafe can be found within one mile. Pets are permitted. Boat rentals are nearby on Willapa Bay.

Reservations, fee: Reservations accepted; $8 fee per night. Open all year.

Who to contact: Phone at 206-665-4027, or write at P.O. Box 155, Ocean Park, WA 98640.

Location: Drive 12 miles north of Logan Beach on Highway 103, then turn east on 259th Street, drive two blocks and you're there.

Trip note: This camp covers two acres and has access to the shoreline of Willapa Bay. Additional facilities found within five miles of the campground include tennis courts. About eight miles north of this campground is Leadbetter Point State Park which is open for day use and provides footpaths for walking through the state-designated natural area and wildlife refuge.

OCEAN PARK
Site **38**   RESORT

Campsites, facilities: There are six tent sites and 120 drive-through sites for trailers or motorhomes of any length. Electricity, piped water, sewer hookups and picnic tables are provided. Bottled gas, toilets, recreation hall, laundry, ice, playground and swimming pool are available, and showers are available for an extra fee. Firewood, store and cafe can be found within one mile. Pets and motorbikes are permitted. Boat docks and launching facilities are nearby on Willapa Bay.

Reservations, fee: Reservations accepted; $9 fee per night. MasterCard and Visa accepted. Open all year.

Who to contact: Phone the park at 206-665-4585, or write at P.O. Box 339, Ocean Park, WA 98640.

Location: Drive nine miles north of Long Beach on Highway 103. This resort is in Ocean Park.

Trip note: This wooded campground covers 10 acres and has access to the shoreline of Willapa Bay. Primarily for motorhomes.

WESTGATE MOTOR
Site **39**   AND TRAILER COURT

Campsites, facilities: There are 34 drive-through sites for trailers or motorhomes of any length. Electricity, piped water and sewer hookups are provided. Bottled gas, toilets, showers, recreation hall and ice are available. Store, cafe and laundry can be found within one mile. Pets are permitted. Boat docks and launching facilities are nearby on Willapa Bay.

Reservations, fee: Reservations accepted; $9 fee per night. MasterCard and Visa accepted. Open all year.

Who to contact: Phone the park at 206-665-4211, or write at Route 1, Box 394, Ocean Park, WA 98640.

Location: Drive seven miles north of Long Beach on Highway 103. The park sits along highway—you'll see it.

Trip note: This camp covers four acres and has beach access. Additional facilities found within five miles of the campground include an 18-hole golf course.

PEGG'S OCEANSIDE
Site **40**   TRAILER PARK

Campsites, facilities: There are six tent sites and 30 sites for trailers or motorhomes of any length. Electricity, piped water, sewer hookups and picnic tables are provided. Sanitary services, toilets, recreation hall and ice are available, and showers are available for an extra fee. Bottled gas, store, cafe and laundry can be found within one mile. Pets and motorbikes are permitted.

Reservations, fee: Reservations accepted; $7 fee per night. Open mid-April to mid-September.

Who to contact: Phone at 206-642-2451, or write at Route 1, Box 460, Long Beach, WA 98631.

Location: Drive four miles north of Long Beach on Highway 103 and you're there.

Trip note: This wooded campground covers three acres and has beach access. Additional facilities found within five miles of the campground include an 18-hole golf course.

ANDERSEN'S TRAILER
Site **41**   COURT AND MOTEL

Campsites, facilities: There are 10 tent sites and 56 sites for trailers or motorhomes of any length. Electricity, piped water, sewer hookups and picnic tables are provided. Sanitary services, toilets, showers, recreation hall, laundry, ice and playground are available. Bottled gas, store and cafe can be found within one mile. Pets are permitted.

Reservations, fee: Reservations accepted; $9 fee per night. Open mid-February to late-November.

Who to contact: Phone at 206-642-2231, or write at Route 1, Box 480, Long Beach, WA 98631.

Location: Drive 3 ½ miles north of Long Beach on Highway 103 and you're there.

Trip note: This camp covers five acres and has beach access. Additional facilities found within five miles of the campground include an 18-hole golf course, a riding stable and tennis courts.

CRANBERRY
Site **42**   ADULT PARK

Campsites, facilities: There are 24 drive-through sites for trailers or motorhomes of any length in this adult-only campground. Electricity, piped water, sewer hookups and picnic tables are provided. Sanitary services, toilets, showers and ice are available. Bottled gas, store, cafe and laundry can be found within one mile. Pets are permitted.

Reservations, fee: Reservations accepted; $7 fee per night. Open all year.

Who to contact: Phone at 206-642-2027, or write at Route 1, Box 522B, Long Beach, WA 98631.

Location: Drive three miles north of Long Beach on Highway 103 and you're there.

Trip note: This wooded park covers two acres and has beach access. Additional facilities found within five miles of the campground include an 18-hole golf course, a riding stable and tennis courts.

PACIFIC PARK
Site **43**   TRAILER PARK

Campsites, facilities: There are 53 sites for trailers or motorhomes of any length. Electricity, piped water, sewer hookups and picnic tables are provided. Toilets, laundry and ice are available, and showers are available for an extra fee. Bottled gas, store and cafe can be found within one mile. Pets are permitted.

Reservations, fee: Reservations accepted; $7 fee per night. Open all year.

Who to contact: Phone at 206-642-3253, or write at Route 1, Box 543, Long Beach, WA 98631.

Location: Drive two miles north of Long Beach on Highway 103 and you're there.

Trip note: This park covers two acres, and has beach access. Additional facilities found within five miles of the campground include an 18-hole golf course, marked bike trails and a riding stable.

Site 44
SAND-LO MOTEL AND RV PARK

Campsites, facilities: There are five tent sites and 14 sites for trailers or motorhomes of any length. Electricity, piped water and sewer hookups are provided. Sanitary services, toilets, showers and laundry are available. Bottled gas, store, cafe and ice are available within one mile. Pets and motorbikes are permitted.

Reservations, fee: Reservations accepted; $7 fee per night. MasterCard and Visa accepted. Open all year.

Who to contact: Phone at 206-642-2600, or write at P.O. Box 736, Long Beach, WA 98631.

Location: Drive one mile north of Long Beach on Highway 103 and you're there.

Trip note: This park covers three acres and has beach access. Additional facilities found within five miles of the campground include an 18-hole golf course, a full service marina and a riding stable.

Site 45
DRIFTWOOD RV TRAV-L PARK

Campsites, facilities: There are 50 drive-through sites for trailers or motorhomes of any length. Electricity, piped water, sewer hookups and picnic tables are provided. Toilets, showers, recreation hall and ice are available. Bottled gas, store, cafe and laundry can be found within one mile. Pets are permitted.

Reservations, fee: Reservations accepted; $9 fee per night. Open March to November.

Who to contact: Phone at 206-642-2711, or write at P.O. Box 296, Long Beach, WA 98631.

Location: Drive ¾ mile north of Long Beach on Highway 103 and you're there.

Trip note: This park covers two acres and has beach access. Additional facilities found within five miles of the campground include an 18-hole golf course and a full service marina.

Site 46
ANTHONY'S HOME COURT MOTEL PARK

Campsites, facilities: There are 20 sites for trailers or motorhomes. Electricity, piped water, sewer hookups and picnic tables are provided. Toilets, laundry, ice and playground are available, and showers are available for an extra fee. Bottled gas, sanitary services, store and cafe are located within one mile. Pets are permitted.

Reservations, fee: Reservations accepted; $8 fee per night. MasterCard and Visa accepted. Open all year.

Who to contact: Phone at 206-642-2802, or write at Route 1, Box 610, Long Beach, WA 98631.

Location: Drive ½ mile north of Long Beach on Highway 103 and you're there.

Trip note: This park covers two acres and has beach access. Additional facilities found within five miles of the campground include an 18-hole golf course, marked bike trails and a riding stable.

Site 47   OCEANIC RV PARK

Campsites, facilities: There are 18 drive-through sites for trailers or motorhomes of any length. Electricity, piped water and sewer hookups are provided. Toilets and showers are available. Bottled gas, sanitary services, store, cafe, laundry and ice are located within one mile. Pets are permitted. Boat docks, launching facilities and rentals are nearby.

Reservations, fee: Reservations accepted; $7 fee per night. MasterCard and Visa accepted. Open all year.

Who to contact: Phone at 206-642-3836, or write at P.O. Box 441, Long Beach, WA 98631.

Location: This park is in Long Beach at the junction of Pacific Highway and 5th Avenue.

Trip note: This camp covers two acres and has beach access. Additional facilities found within five miles of the campground include an 18-hole golf course, marked bike trails and a full service marina.

Site 48   WHITMAN'S RV PARK

Campsites, facilities: There are 10 tent sites and 29 drive-through sites for trailers or motorhomes of any length. Electricity, piped water, sewer hookups and picnic tables are provided. Sanitary services, toilets, laundry and ice are available, and showers are obtained for an extra fee. Bottled gas, store and cafe can be found within one mile. Pets and motorbikes are permitted. Boat docks, launching facilities and rentals are nearby.

Reservations, fee: Reservations accepted; $8 fee per night. Open all year.

Who to contact: Phone at 206-642-2174, or write at Route 1, Box 614, Long Beach, WA 98631.

Location: This park is in Long Beach on Highway 103 at the north end of town.

Trip note: This park covers two acres and has beach access. Additional facilities found within five miles of the campground include an 18-hole golf course, marked bike trails, a full service marina and a riding stable.

Site 49   SOUWESTER LODGE AND TRAILER PARK

Campsites, facilities: There are 10 tent sites and 60 drive-through sites for trailers or motorhomes of any length. Electricity, piped water and sewer hookups are provided. Toilets, showers and laundry are available. Bottled gas, sanitary services, store, cafe and ice are located within one mile. Pets and motorbikes are permitted. Boat launching facilities are nearby.

Reservations, fee: Reservations accepted; $9 fee per night. Open all year.

Who to contact: Phone the park at 206-642-2542, or write at P.O. Box 102, Seaview, WA 98644.

Location: From the junction of US 101 and Highway 103 in Seaview, drive one block south on US 101, then one block west on 38th Place and you're there.

Trip note: One of the few spots in immediate area that provides spots for tent camping. This covers three acres and has beach access. Additional facilities found within five miles of the campground include an 18-hole golf course, a full service marina and a riding stable.

Site 50
WILDWOOD RV PARK
AND CAMPGROUND

Campsites, facilities: There are 20 tent sites and 30 sites for trailers or motorhomes of any length. Electricity, piped water, sewer hookups and picnic tables are provided. Sanitary services and toilets are available, and showers can be obtained for an extra fee. Bottled gas, firewood, store, cafe, laundry and ice are located within one mile. Pets and motorbikes are permitted.

Reservations, fee: Reservations accepted; $8 fee per night. Open mid-May to mid-September.

Who to contact: Phone the park at 206-642-2131, or write at Route 1, Box 76, Long Beach, WA 98631.

Location: From the junction of US 101 and Highway 103 in Seaview, drive ½ mile east on US 101, and ¾ mile north on Sand Ridge Road and you're there.

Trip note: This wooded park covers five acres and has beach access. Additional facilities found within five miles of the campground include an 18-hole golf course, a full service marina and tennis courts. See campsite 53 for attractions at nearby Ft. Canby State Park.

Site 51
THE BEACON-CHARTERS
RV PARK

Campsites, facilities: There are 39 drive-through sites for trailers or motorhomes of any length. Electricity, piped water and sewer hookups are provided. Toilets and ice are available, and showers can be obtained for an extra fee. Bottled gas, store, cafe and laundry are located within one mile. Pets are permitted. Boat docks and launching facilities are nearby.

Reservations, fee: Reservations accepted; $9 fee per night. Open late-May to mid-September.

Who to contact: Phone at 206-642-2138, or write at P.O. Box 74, Ilwaco, WA 98624.

Location: Drive to Ilwaco. The park is on the corner of Howerton and Elizabeth.

Trip note: This park covers two acres and has beach and river side access. Ft. Canby State Park is nearby which offers an interpretive center on maritime and military history, and numerous hiking trails. Additional facilities found within five miles of the campground include an 18-hole golf course.

Site 52
COVE RV AND
TRAILER PARK

Campsites, facilities: There are three tent sites and 25 sites for trailers or motorhomes of any length. Electricity, piped water, sewer hookups and picnic tables are provided. Sanitary services, toilets and laundry are available. Showers can be obtained for an extra fee. Bottled gas, store, cafe and ice are located within one mile. Pets are permitted. Boat docks, launching facilities and rentals are nearby.

Reservations, fee: Reservations accepted; $9 fee per night. Open all year.

Who to contact: Phone at 206-642-3689, or write at P.O. Box 38, Ilwaco, WA 98624.

Location: Drive to Ilwaco. Turn south on 2nd Street and drive four blocks to the park.

Trip note: This park covers five acres and has beach access. Additional facilities found within five miles of the campground include a maritime museum and hiking trails at nearby Ft. Canby State Park, a full service marina and a riding stable.

KOA ILWACO

Site **53**

Campsites, facilities: There are 50 tent sites and 120 drive-through sites for trailers or motorhomes of any length. Picnic tables are provided. Bottled gas, sanitary services, toilets, showers, firewood, recreation hall, store, laundry, ice and playground are available. Electricity, piped water and sewer hookups can be obtained for an extra fee. Pets are permitted.

Reservations, fee: Reservations accepted; $11 fee per night. MasterCard and Visa accepted. Open April to November.

Who to contact: Phone the park at 206-642-3292, or write at P.O. Box 549, Ilwaco, WA 98624.

Location: This campground is in Ilwaco at the junction of US 101 South and US 101 Alternate.

Trip note: This campground covers 17 acres and has ocean and river access. Additional facilities found within five miles of the campground include a maritime museum and hiking trails at nearby Ft. Canby State Park, and an 18-hole golf course.

MAUCH'S SUNDOWN
Site **54**   ## RV PARK

Campsites, facilities: There are 10 tent sites and 50 drive-through sites for trailers or motorhomes of any length. Electricity, piped water, sewer hookups and picnic tables are provided. Sanitary services, toilets, firewood, laundry and ice are available, and showers can be obtained for an extra fee. Bottled gas, store and cafe are located within one mile. Pets and motorbikes are permitted. Boat docks and launching facilities are nearby on the Columbia River.

Reservations, fee: Reservations accepted; $8 fee per night. Open all year.

Who to contact: Phone at 206-777-8713, or write at P.O. Box 129, Chinook, WA 98614.

Location: This park is in Chinook near the Astoria Bridge, ½ mile west of town on US 101.

Trip note: Mauch's covers four acres and has riverside access. It is near Ft. Columbia State Park which has a newly renovated interpretive center featuring the history of coastal artillery.

RIVER'S END
Site **55**   ## CAMPGROUND

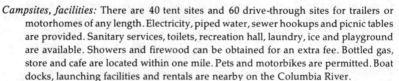

Campsites, facilities: There are 40 tent sites and 60 drive-through sites for trailers or motorhomes of any length. Electricity, piped water, sewer hookups and picnic tables are provided. Sanitary services, toilets, recreation hall, laundry, ice and playground are available. Showers and firewood can be obtained for an extra fee. Bottled gas, store and cafe are located within one mile. Pets and motorbikes are permitted. Boat docks, launching facilities and rentals are nearby on the Columbia River.

Reservations, fee: Reservations accepted; $8 fee per night. Open April to late-October.

Who to contact: Phone at 206-777-8317, or write at P.O. Box 66, Chinook, WA 98614.

Location: The campgound is in Chinook at the north end of town on US 101.

Trip note: This wooded campground covers five acres and has riverside access. Additional facilities found within five miles of the campground include marked bike trails and a full service marina. Also nearby is Ft. Columbia State Park which has an interpretive center featuring the history of coastal artillery.

FORT CANBY
Site **56**

Campsites, facilities: There are 190 tent sites and 60 sites for trailers or motorhomes up to 45 feet long. Electricity, piped water, sewer hookups and picnic tables are provided. Sanitary services and toilets are available. Showers can be obtained for an extra fee. A store and cafe are located within one mile. Pets are permitted. Boat launching facilities are nearby.

Reservations, fee: Reservations accepted; $6 fee per night. Open all year.

Who to contact: Phone the state park at 206-642-3078, or write at P.O. Box 488, Ilwaco, WA 98624.

Location: From Ilwaco drive two miles southwest on US 101 to the park.

Trip note: The choice spot of the area for tent campers. This park covers 1881 acres and provides hiking trails and opportunities for surf, jetty and ocean fishing by boat. There is an interpretive center that highlights Lewis and Clark, maritime and military history.

OLSENS
Site **57**

Campsites, facilities: There are 40 tent sites and 60 drive-through sites for trailers or motorhomes. Electricity and piped water are provided. Sanitary services, toilets, store and ice are available. Showers can be obtained for an extra fee. Bottled gas, cafe and laundry are located within one mile. Pets are permitted. Boat docks, launching facilities and rentals are nearby on the Columbia River.

Reservations, fee: No reservations necessary; $8 fee per night. Open May to late-October.

Who to contact: Phone at 206-777-8475, or write at P.O. Box 44, Chinook, WA 98614.

Location: This park is in Chinook on US 101.

Trip note: This camp covers seven acres and has river access. Additional facilities found within five miles of the campground include a full service marina.

CHINOOK
COUNTY PARK
Site **58**

Campsites, facilities: There are 100 tent sites and 100 drive-through sites for trailers or motorhomes of any length. Picnic tables are provided. Toilets, showers, firewood and playground are available, but there is no water. Bottled gas, store, cafe and ice are located within one mile. Pets are permitted. Boat docks and launching facilities are nearby on the Columbia River.

Reservations, fee: No reservations necessary; $5 fee per night. Open May to mid-October.

Who to contact: Phone at 206-777-8442, or write at P.O. Box 42, Chinook, WA 98614.

Location: This park is just east of Chinook on US 101.

Trip note: This campsite covers 15 acres and is near Ft. Columbia State Park.

SKAMOKAWA
VISTA PARK
Site **59**

Campsites, facilities: There are four tent sites and 15 sites for trailers or motorhomes of any length. Electricity and picnic tables are provided, but no water is available. Sanitary services, toilets, showers, firewood and playground are available. Bottled gas, store, cafe and ice are located within one mile. Pets and motorbikes are permitted. Boat docks and launching facilities are nearby.

Reservations, fee: Reservations accepted; $7 fee per night. Open all year.

Who to contact: Phone the park at 206-795-8605, or write at 13 School Road, Skamokawa, WA 98647.

Location: In Skamokawa on Highway 4, turn ¼ mile west on County School Road.

Trip note: This camp covers 30 acres and has access to the Columbia River. Additional facilities found within five miles of the campground include a full service marina and tennis courts.

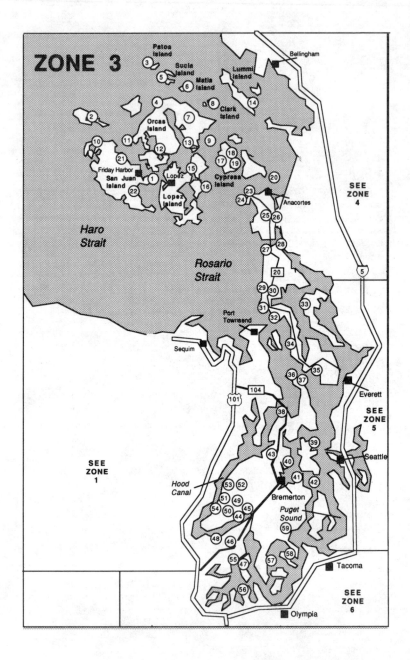

PUGET SOUND

Site 1
TURN ISLAND
STATE PARK

Campsites, facilities: There are 12 primitive campsites which are accessible only by boat. Picnic tables are provided and pit toilets are available. There is no piped water. Boat buoys can be obtained for overnight moorage.

Reservations, fee: No reservations necessary; $6 fee per night. Open all year.

Who to contact: Phone at 206-376-2326, or write at 6158 Lighthouse Road, Friday Harbor, WA 98250.

Location: This little island is just east of Friday Harbor and San Juan Island, and is accessible only by boat.

Trip note: This is one of about 30 campgrounds we detail in Zone three that can be reached only by boat. Quiet, primitive and beautiful, this spot offers good hiking trails and year around rockfishing. No cars allowed, unless they float.

Site 2
STUART ISLAND
MARINE STATE PARK

Campsites, facilities: There are 19 primitive campsites. Picnic tables are provided and pit toilets are available. There is no piped water. Boat buoys and floats can be obtained for overnight moorage.

Reservations, fee: No reservations necessary; $6 fee per night. Open all year.

Who to contact: Phone at 206-378-2044, or write at 6158 Lighthouse Road, Friday Harbor, WA 98250.

Location: Stuart Island is located northwest of San Juan Island and is accessible only by boat.

Trip note: This is really stalking the unknown. A remote little island on the edge of Canadian waters that covers 153 acres and has good harbors for mooring. There is good fishing at nearby Reed and Provost Harbors.

Site 3
PATOS ISLAND
STATE PARK

Campsites, facilities: There are four primitive campsites. Pit toilets are available, but there is no piped water. Boat buoys are available for overnight moorage.

Reservations, fee: No reservations necessary; $3 fee per night. Open all year.

Who to contact: Phone at 206-378-2044, or write at 6158 Lighthouse Road, Friday Harbor, WA 98250.

Location: Patos Island is four miles northwest of Sucia Island and is accessible only by boat.

Trip note: If you are going to get stranded on an island, this is not a bad choice, providing you like your companion. There are good hiking trails and excellent salmon and bottom fishing opportunities here.

Site 4
POINT DOUGHTY
MULTIPLE USE AREA

Campsites, facilities: There are two primitive campsites. Picnic tables are provided and pit toilets are available. There is no piped water.

Reservations, fee: No reservations necessary; no fee. Open all year.

Who to contact: Phone at 1-800-527-3305, or write at Department of Natural Resources, 919 North Township, Sedro Woolley, WA 98284.

Location: This campground was closed in 1987. It will be open when the management funds become available. Call 1-800-527-3305. These sites are located on the north shore of Orcas Island and are accessible only by boat (see trip note for details).

Trip note: Reaching this spot is quite an adventure. Strong currents and submerged rocks can make landing a boat dangerous. You are better off anchoring, then land using a raft or kayak. In return, you get guaranteed solitude.

Site 5
SUCIA ISLAND
MARINE STATE PARK

Campsites, facilities: There are 51 primitive campsites. Picnic tables are provided and vault toilets are available. There is no piped water. Boat buoys and floats can be obtained for overnight moorage.

Reservations, fee: No reservations necessary; $6 fee per night. Open all year.

Who to contact: Phone at 206-376-2044, or write at Star Route Box 28, Eastsound, WA 98245.

Location: Sucia Island is 2 ½ miles north of Orcas Island and is accessible only by boat.

Trip note: A classic spot, with rocky outcrops for lookout points and good beach and fishing areas. This island covers 562 acres, and provides opportunites for hiking, clamming, crabbing, canoeing and scuba diving.

Site 6
MATIA ISLAND
STATE PARK

Campsites, facilities: There are six primitive campsites. Pit toilets are available. There is no piped water. There is a boat dock, and buoys and floats can be obtained for overnight moorage.

Reservations, fee: No reservations necessary; $3 fee per night. Open all year.

Who to contact: Phone at 206-378-2044, or write at 6158 Lighthouse Road, Friday Harbor, WA 98250.

Location: Matia Island is 2 ½ miles northeast of Orcas Island and is accessible only by boat.

Trip note: The campsites are located just a short walk from the docking facilities. Many of the other island campgrounds don't have docks. Good fishing and beachcombing are among the highlights.

Site 7
MORAN
STATE PARK

Campsites, facilities: There are 135 campsites for tents or motorhomes up to 45 feet long, but there are no hookups. Picnic tables are provided, and flush toilets, showers and firewood are available. Some facilities are wheelchair accessible. Pets are permitted. Boat docks, fishing supplies, launching facilities and boat rentals are located at the concession stand in the park.

Reservations, fee: Reservations accepted; $6 fee per night. Open all year.

Who to contact: Phone at 206-378-2044, or write at 6158 Lighthouse Road, Friday Harbor, WA 98250.

Location: This park is on Orcas Island and is accessible by ferry from the town of Anacortes, which is five miles west of Burlington.

Trip note: This is a big park, 4604 acres, that offers hiking trails and lake fishing. If you drive to the top of Mt. Constitution, you will have a view of Vancouver, Mt. Baker and the San Juan Islands. No motorhomes are allowed on this winding road. Nearby recreation options include an 18-hole golf course.

Site 8
CLARK ISLAND
STATE PARK

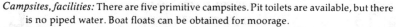

Campsites, facilities: There are eight primitive campsites. Pit toilets are available, but there is no piped water. Boat buoys can be obtained for overnight moorage.

Reservations, fee: No reservations necessary; $3 fee per night. Open all year.

Who to contact: Phone at 206-378-2044, or write at 6158 Lighthouse Road, Friday Harbor, WA 98250.

Location: These campsites are on Clark Island northeast of Orcas Island, and are accessible only by boat.

Trip note: This island state park offers beautiful beaches with opportunities for scuba diving. There are excellent views of the other islands.

Site 9
DOE ISLAND
STATE PARK

Campsites, facilities: There are five primitive campsites. Pit toilets are available, but there is no piped water. Boat floats can be obtained for moorage.

Reservations, fee: No reservations necessary; $3 fee per night. Open all year.

Who to contact: Phone at 206-378-2044, or write at 6158 Lighthouse Road, Friday Harbor, WA 98250.

Location: This small, secluded island is southeast of Orcas Island and accessible only by boat.

Trip note: This island has a rocky shoreline, which makes for an ideal fish habitat. Scuba diving and fishing are exceptional.

Site 10
POSEY ISLAND
STATE PARK

Campsites, facilities: There is one primitive campsite. No piped water is available.

Reservations, fee: No reservations necessary; $3 fee per night. Open all year.

Who to contact: Phone at 206-378-2044, or write at 6158 Lighthouse Road, Friday Harbor,

WA 98250.

Location: This little island is at the north end of Roche Harbor and is reached only by small boat.

Trip note: If you want a beautiful little spot all to yourself, this is it, the smallest campground in Washington. It is difficult to get there, however. The best way to approach is by kayak or canoe, a short paddle from San Juan Island.

Site 11   JONES ISLAND MARINE STATE PARK

Campsites, facilities: There are 20 primitive campsites. Picnic tables are provided and pit toilets are available. There is no piped water. Boat buoys and floats can be obtained for overnight moorage.

Reservations, fee: No reservations necessary; $6 fee per night. Open all year.

Who to contact: Phone at 206-378-2044, or write at 6158 Lighthouse Road, Friday Harbor, WA 98250.

Location: This island is one mile off the southwest tip of Orcas Island and is accessible only by boat.

Trip note: This little island is another hidden spot that gets little use. The campground is near the beach, so you don't have to carry your gear very far. The area provides good fishing and scuba diving.

Site 12   BLIND ISLAND STATE PARK

Campsites, facilities: There are four primitive campsites. Pit toilets are available, but there is no piped water. Boat buoys can be obtained for overnight moorage.

Reservations, fee: No reservations necessary; $3 fee per night. Open all year.

Who to contact: Phone at 206-378-2044, or write at 6158 Lighthouse Road, Friday Harbor, WA 98250.

Location: This island is north of Shaw Island and is accessible only by boat.

Trip note: This island has few trees and is known for its rocky shoreline. It is dangerous and ill advised to try beaching cruiser-style boats. Bring a life raft to paddle ashore.

Site 13   OBSTRUCTION PASS MULTIPLE USE AREA

Campsites, facilities: There are nine primitive campsites. Picnic tables are provided and vault toilets are available. There is no piped water. Boat buoys can be obtained for overnight moorage.

Reservations, fee: No reservations necessary; no fee. Open all year.

Who to contact: Phone at 800-527-3305, or write the Department of Natural Resources at 1065 South Capitol Way, Olympia, WA 98504.

Location: On Orcas Island, start at the town of Olga and go east on Doe Bay Road for 1/2 mile, then turn right on Obstruction Pass Road and go 2/3 mile. Keep right for 1/3 mile, then go straight for one mile to the parking area. Hike ½ mile to campground.

Trip note: It takes a ferry boat ride and a tricky drive and then a short walk to reach this campground, but that helps set it apart from others—a unique, primitive spot set in a forested area near the shore of Orcas Island. Good hiking.

LUMMI ISLAND
Site **14**

Campsites, facilities: There are five primitive campsites. Picnic tables are provided, and vault toilets are available. There is no piped water. Boat buoys can be obtained for overnight moorage.

Reservations, fee: No reservations necessary; no fee. Open all year.

Who to contact: Phone at 800-527-3305, or write at 1065 South Capitol Way, Olympia, WA 98504.

Location: This campground was closed in 1987. It will be open when the management funds become available. Call 1-800-527-3305. This camp is on the southeast shore of Lummi Island and is accessible only by boat.

Trip note: This little-known camp is set on the eastern edge of Lummi Island, facing Bellingham Bay. A nice, little spot with good lookouts at night of coastal lights to the east.

SPENCER SPIT
STATE PARK
Site **15**

Campsites, facilities: There are 20 campsites here for tents or self-contained motorhomes up to 60 feet long. Picnic tables are provided, and sanitary services and toilets are available. Boat docks are nearby.

Reservations, fee: No reservations necessary; $6 fee per night. Open all year.

Who to contact: Phone at 206-468-2251, or write at Route 2, Box 3600, Lopez, WA 98261.

Location: From Anacortes take the ferry to the east shore of Lopez Island.

Trip note: One of the few island campgrounds accessible to cars, via a ferry boat ride. A long sliver of sand extends far into the water and provides good access to prime clamming areas.

JAMES ISLAND
STATE PARK
Site **16**

Campsites, facilities: There are 13 primitive campsites that are accessible only by boat. Pit toilets are available, but there is no piped water. Boat floats and buoys can be obtained for overnight moorage off the east side of the island. A moorage dock on the west side of the island is open from early April through Labor Day.

Reservations, fee: No reservations necessary; $3 fee per night. Open all year.

Who to contact: Phone at 206-468-2251, or write at Route 2, Box 3600, Lopez, WA 98261.

Location: This island is east of Decatur Island on Rosario Strait and is only accessible by boat.

Trip note: A small, hidden island that provides good opportunities for hiking, fishing and scuba diving. Quiet and primitive.

STRAWBERRY ISLAND
MULTIPLE USE AREA
Site **17**

Campsites, facilities: There are three primitive campsites. Picnic tables are provided, and vault toilets are available. There is no piped water.

Reservations, fee: No reservations necessary; no fee. Open all year.

Who to contact: Phone at 800-527-3305, or write the Department of Natural Resources at 1065 South Capitol Way, Olympia, WA 98504.

Location: This island is off the west coast of Blakeley Island and is accessible only by small boat.

Trip note: Because of strong currents and submerged rocks, boat landing is difficult and this camp is rarely used. Boaters should anchor, then make shore using a raft or kayak.

Site 18   PELICAN BEACH
MULTIPLE USE AREA

Campsites, facilities: There are four primitive campsites. Picnic tables are provided and vault toilets are available. There is no piped water available. Buoys can be obtained for overnight moorage.

Reservations, fee: No reservations necessary; no fee. Open all year.

Who to contact: Phone at 800-527-3305, or write the Department of Natural Resources at 1065 South Capitol Way, Olympia, WA 98504.

Location: This camp is set on the east shore of Cypress Island and is accessible only by boat.

Trip note: This forested island campground offers a group shelter, beach access and hiking trails. The one mile trail to Eagle Cliff is a must.

Site 19   CYPRESS HEAD
MULTIPLE USE AREA

Campsites, facilities: There are five primitive campsites. Picnic tables are provided, and vault toilets are available. There is no piped water. Boat buoys are available for overnight moorage. The float is for off-loading only.

Reservations, fee: No reservations necessary; no fee. Open all year.

Who to contact: Phone at 800-527-3305, or write the Department of Natural Resources at 1065 South Captol Way, Olympia, WA 98504.

Location: This camp is set on the east shore of Cypress Island and is accessible only by boat.

Trip note: An option to campsite 18. Dock makes off-loading equipment a lot easier than most island campgrounds.

Site 20   SADDLEBAG ISLAND
STATE PARK

Campsites, facilities: There are five primitive campsites. Pit toilets are available, but there is no piped water.

Reservations, fee: No reservations necessary; $3 fee per night. Open all year.

Who to contact: Phone at 206-378-2044, or write at 6158 Lighthouse Road, Friday Harbor, WA 98250.

Location: This little island is north of Anacortes and east of Guemes Island. It is accessible only by boat.

Trip note: A good cruise from Anacortes. This island is quiet and primitive. There's a nice beach nearby for beachcombing, good crabbing in the bay for boaters.

Site **21**   LAKEDALE
CAMPGROUND

Campsites, facilities: There are 84 tent sites and 12 drive-through sites for trailers or motorhomes up to 34 feet long. Electricity, piped water and picnic tables are provided. Toilets, a store and ice are available. Showers and firewood are available for an extra fee. Pets and motorbikes are permitted. Boat docks and boat rentals are nearby.

Reservations, fee: Reservations accepted; $11 fee per night. MasterCard and Visa accepted. Open April to late-September.

Who to contact: Phone at 206-378-2350, or write at 2627 Roche Harbor, Friday Harbor, WA 98250.

Location: Take the ferry from Anacortes to Friday Harbor on San Juan Island, then drive 4 1/2 miles north on Roche Harbor Road to campground.

Trip note: A real nice spot for visitors who want the solitude of an island camp, yet all the amenities of a privately-run campground.

Site **22**   GRIFFIN BAY
MULTIPLE USE AREA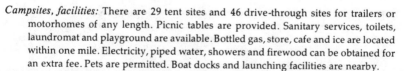

Campsites, facilities: There is one primitive campsite and three picnic sites. Piped water and picnic tables are provided, and pit toilets are available. Boat buoys can be obtained for overnight moorage.

Reservations, fee: No reservations necessary; no fee. Open all year.

Who to contact: Phone at 800-527-3305, or write the Department of Natural Resources at 1065 South Capitol Way, Olympia, WA 98504.

Location: Griffin Bay is on San Juan Island south of Friday Harbor and is accessible only by boat.

Trip note: This campground was closed in 1987. It will be open when the management funds become available. Call 1-800-527-3305. Hardly anybody knows about this spot, yet San Juan Island is one of the prettiest in the area. The camp is within a few miles of the San Juan National Historic Park, a day-use area. Two buoys provide mooring.

Site **23**   WASHINGTON PARK

Campsites, facilities: There are 29 tent sites and 46 drive-through sites for trailers or motorhomes of any length. Picnic tables are provided. Sanitary services, toilets, laundromat and playground are available. Bottled gas, store, cafe and ice are located within one mile. Electricity, piped water, showers and firewood can be obtained for an extra fee. Pets are permitted. Boat docks and launching facilities are nearby.

Reservations, fee: No reservations necessary; $10 fee per night. Open April to October and some off-season weekends. Limited winter facilities.

Who to contact: Phone at 206-293-4541, or write at P.O. Box 547, Anacortes, WA 98221.

Location: This campground is located just outside of Anacortes. To get to it drive four miles west on Highway 20 (12th Street), then go 3/4 miles past the Ferry Terminal.

Trip note: This wooded city park covers 220 acres and is set along the shore, allowing good beach lookouts. Nearby recreation options include an 18-hole golf course, a full service marina and tennis courts.

Site 24

SKYLINE
RV PARK

Campsites, facilities: There are 35 sites for trailers or motorhomes of any length in this adult only campground. Electricity, piped water and sewer hookups are provided. Sanitary services, toilets, showers and laundromat are available. Bottled gas, store, cafe and ice are located within one mile. Pets are permitted. Boat docks, launching facilities and boat rentals are nearby.

Reservations, fee: No reservations necessary; $13 fee per night. Open all year.

Who to contact: Phone at 206-293-4277, or write at 5809 Sands Way, Anacortes, WA 98221.

Location: This park is located just outside of Anacortes. To get there drive 4 1/4 miles west on Highway 20 (12th Street), then go 1/2 mile west on Sunset, and 1/4 mile south on Skyline Way.

Trip note: One of several options to campsites 23-28, which are located in the vicinity. Nearby recreation options include a full service marina and tennis courts.

Site 25

FERN HILL
CAMPGROUND

Campsites, facilities: There are 35 tent sites and 77 drive-through sites for trailers or motorhomes of any length. Electricity, piped water, sewer hookups and picnic tables are provided. Bottled gas, sanitary services, toilets, recreation hall, laundromat, ice and playground are available. Store and cafe are located within one mile. Showers and firewood can be obtained for an extra fee. Pets and motorbikes are permitted.

Reservations, fee: Reservations accepted; $14 fee per night. MasterCard and Visa accepted. Open all year.

Who to contact: Phone at 206-293-5355, or write at 527 Miller, Anacortes, WA 98221.

Location: From Anacortes, drive west on Highway 20 to Deception Pass junction, then go 3/4 miles south to Miller Road, and west to 527 Miller Road.

Trip note: Nearby recreation options include an 18-hole golf course, a full service marina and tennis courts.

Site 26

ANACORTES
RV PARK

Campsites, facilities: There are six tent sites and 40 sites for trailers or motorhomes of any length. Electricity, piped water, sewer hookups and picnic tables are provided. Bottled gas, sanitary services, toilets, showers, recreation hall, laundromat and playground are available. Store and cafe are located within one mile. Firewood can be purchased. Pets and motorbikes are permitted.

Reservations, fee: Reservations accepted; $15 fee per night. Open all year.

Who to contact: Phone at 206-293-3700, or write at 1255 Highway 20, Anacortes, WA 98221.

Location: From Mount Vernon or the junction of I-5 and Highway 20, drive 18 miles west to Whidbey Island junction. Campground is one block south at 1255 Highway 20.

Trip note: This wooded park covers six acres and is set along the shoreline. Nearby recreation options include an 18-hole golf course, a full service marina and tennis courts.

Site **27**
DECEPTION PASS
STATE PARK

Campsites, facilities: There are 251 tent sites. Picnic tables are provided. Sanitary services, toilets, store and playground are available. Cafe and ice are located within one mile. Showers and firewood can be obtained for an extra fee. Some facilities are wheelchair accessible. There is no piped water. Pets are permitted. Boat docks, launching facilities and boat rentals are found at the concession stand in the park.

Reservations, fee: No reservations necessary; $6 fee per night. Open all year.

Who to contact: Phone at 206-676-2417, or write at 5175 NSH 20, Oak Harbor, WA 98277.

Location: From Oak Harbor on Whidbey Island, drive 10 miles north of Highway 525 to get to this state park.

Trip note: This is a popular and large park that offers a little bit of everything. That includes trout fishing at Pass Lake, swimming, or watching nice sunsets across the Strait of Juan De Fuca.

Site **28**
HOPE ISLAND
STATE PARK

Campsites, facilities: There are five primitive campsites. No piped water is available.

Reservations, fee: No reservations necessary; $3 fee per night.

Who to contact: Phone at 206-676-2417, or write at 5175 NSH 20, Oak Harbor, WA 98277.

Location: This little island is in Skagit Bay, two miles north of the entrance to Swinomish Bay. It is accessible only by boat.

Trip note: A primitive alternative to the nearby and more developed campgrounds 23-27. The only catch is you must have a boat to reach it.

Site **29**
WESTERN VILLAGE
MOBILE ESTATES

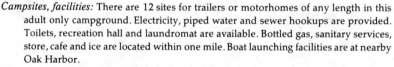

Campsites, facilities: There are 12 sites for trailers or motorhomes of any length in this adult only campground. Electricity, piped water and sewer hookups are provided. Toilets, recreation hall and laundromat are available. Bottled gas, sanitary services, store, cafe and ice are located within one mile. Boat launching facilities are at nearby Oak Harbor.

Reservations, fee: No reservations necessary; $9 fee per night. Open all year.

Who to contact: Phone at 206-675-1210, or write at 6451 60th NW, Oak Harbor, WA 98277.

Location: Take Highway 20 to the town of Oak Harbor. Turn northwest at 60th Street and drive one block to the park.

Trip note: This is a privately developed RV park located in town. It provides beach access. Nearby recreation options include an 18-hole golf course, marked bike trails, a full service marina and tennis courts.

Site **30**
OAK HARBOR
CITY BEACH PARK

Campsites, facilities: There are 55 sites for trailers or motorhomes of any length. Elec-

tricity, piped water and picnic tables are provided. Sanitary services, toilets and playground are available. Bottled gas, store, cafe, laundromat and ice are located within one mile. Showers can be obtained for an extra fee. Pets are permitted. Boat launching facilities are at nearby Oak Harbor.

Reservations, fee: No reservations necessary; $7 fee per night. Open mid-April to late-October.

Who to contact: Phone at 206-679-5551, or write at 3075-300 Avenue West, Oak Harbor, WA 98277.

Location: Take Highway 20 to the town of Oak Harbor. Turn south on Pioneer Way and drive one block to the park.

Trip note: A developed park that offers no tent camping, but has beach access. Nearby recreation options include an 18-hole golf course, a full service marina and tennis courts.

Site 31   FORT EBEY STATE PARK

Campsites, facilities: There are 50 campsites for tents or self-contained motorhomes up to 50 feet long. Picnic tables are provided. Sanitary services, toilets and showers are available. Pets and motorbikes are permitted.

Reservations, fee: No reservations necessary; $6 fee per night. Open mid-April to late-September.

Who to contact: Phone at 206-678-4636, or write at 395 North Fort Ebey Road, Coupeville, WA 98239.

Location: To get to the park, drive eight miles south of Oak Harbor on Highway 20.

Trip note: This park covers 228 acres and has access to a beach that is rocky and good for hiking. It is the site of an historic World War II bunker. There is also a freshwater lake.

Site 32   FORT CASEY STATE PARK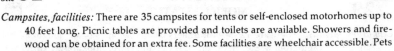

Campsites, facilities: There are 35 campsites for tents or self-enclosed motorhomes up to 40 feet long. Picnic tables are provided and toilets are available. Showers and firewood can be obtained for an extra fee. Some facilities are wheelchair accessible. Pets are permitted. Boat launching facilities are located in the park.

Reservations, fee: No reservations necessary; $6 fee per night. Open all year.

Who to contact: Phone at 206-678-4519, or write at 1280 Ft. Casey, Coupeville, WA 98239.

Location: To get to the park drive three miles south of Coupeville on Highway 20.

Trip note: A good spot to set up a base camp for a fishing trip. There is good rockfishing year around, and good salmon and steelhead fishing in season. This park covers 137 acres and is the site of an historic U.S Defense Post.

Site 33   CAMANO ISLAND STATE PARK

Campsites, facilities: There are 87 campsites for tents or self-enclosed motorhomes up to 30 feet long, and two primitive campsites. Picnic tables are provided. Sanitary services, toilets and playground are available. Showers and firewood can be obtained for an extra fee. Some facilities are wheelchair accessible. Pets are permitted. Boat launching facilities are located in the park.

Reservations, fee: No reservations necessary; $6 fee per night. Open all year.

Who to contact: Phone at 206-387-3031, or write at 2269 South Park Road, Stanwood, WA 98292.

Location: Take Highway 532 off I-5 at Stanwood and drive eight miles southwest to the park.

Trip note: The campsites are quiet and private in this wooded park. Good inshore rock-fishing is available year around and salmon fishing is also good in season. Clamming is excellent during low tides in winter and spring. There is a five mile self-guided nature trail.

Site 34   SOUTH WHIDBEY STATE PARK

Campsites, facilities: There are 54 campsites for tents or self-contained motorhomes up to 45 feet long, and six primitive campsites. Picnic tables are provided, and sanitary services and toilets are available. Showers and firewood can be obtained for an extra fee. Some facilities are wheelchair accessible. Pets are permitted.

Reservations, fee: No reservations necessary; $6 fee per night. Open all year.

Who to contact: Phone at 206-321-4559, or write at 4128 Smugglers Cove Road, Freeland, WA 98429.

Location: This park is located on the west side of Whidbey Island. To get there drive 4 1/2 miles southwest of Highway 525.

Trip note: This wooded park covers 85 acres and provides opportunities for hiking, scuba diving, picnicking, beachcombing and clam digging along a sandy beach. There are spectacular views of Puget Sound and the Olympic Mountains.

Site 35   MUTINY BAY RESORT

Campsites, facilities: There are 20 sites for trailers or motorhomes up to 28 feet long. No tent sites. Electricity, piped water, sewer hookups and picnic tables are provided. Toilets, showers and ice are available. Bottled gas, store, cafe and laundromat are located within one mile. Boat docks and launching facilities are nearby.

Reservations, fee: Reservations accepted; $10 fee per night. MasterCard and Visa accepted. Open all year.

Who to contact: Phone at 206-321-4500, or write at P.O. Box 249, Freeland, WA 98429.

Location: This park is located on the southwest side of Whidbey Island. To get there drive 10 miles northwest of Clinton on Highway 525, then go one mile west on Fish Road to the resort.

Trip note: A privately-operated park that provides an option to the nearby South Whidbey State Park.

Site 36   POINT NO POINT BEACH RESORT

Campsites, facilities: There are four tent sites and 38 drive-through sites for trailers or motorhomes up to 32 feet long. Electricity, piped water, sewer hookups and picnic tables are provided. Bottled gas, toilets, showers, cafe, laundromat and ice are available. A store is located within one mile. Boat docks and boat rentals are nearby.

Reservations, fee: Reservations accepted; $10 fee per night. Open mid-May to mid-October.

Who to contact: Phone at 206-638-2233, or write at 8708 NE Point No Point Road, Hansville, WA 98340.

Location: This park is at the northern tip of Bremerton Island. You can get to Hansville via Highway 16 or Highway 104, then go 1/2 mile east of Hansville on Point No Point Road.

Trip note: A summer resort with beach access.

FORBES LANDING
Site **37**

Campsites, facilities: There are 40 tent sites and 22 drive-through sites for trailers or motorhomes of any length. Electricity, piped water, sewer hookups and picnic tables are provided. Bottled gas, sanitary services, toilets, showers, store and ice are available. Pets are permitted. Boat docks, launching facilities and boat rentals are nearby.

Reservations, fee: Reservations accepted; $10 fee per night. Open all year.

Who to contact: Phone at 206-638-2257, or write at P.O. Box 113, Hansville, WA 98340.

Location: This park is at the northern tip of Bremerton Island. You can get to Hansville via Highway 16 or Highway 104. The park is located in town.

Trip note: An option to campsite 36 for tent campers. Nearby recreation options include an 18-hole golf course and a full service marina.

KITSAP MEMORIAL
Site **38** STATE PARK

Campsites, facilities: There are 43 tent sites. Picnic tables are provided, and sanitary services, toilets and playground are available. Showers and firewood can be obtained for an extra fee. Pets are permitted. Boat docks are nearby.

Reservations, fee: No reservations necessary; $6 fee per night. Open all year.

Who to contact: Phone at 206-779-3205, or write at 202 NE Park Street, Poulsbo, WA 98370.

Location: To get to this park, drive on Highway 3 to Poulsbo, and then go north past the Hood Canal Ferry Terminal to the park.

Trip note: A nice spot for tent campers along the Hood Canal. Nearby recreation options include an 18-hole golf course.

FAY-BAINBRIDGE
Site **39** STATE PARK

Campsites, facilities: There are 36 sites for trailers or motorhomes. Picnic tables are provided, and sanitary services, toilets and playground are available. A store and cafe are located within one mile. Piped water, showers and firewood can be obtained for an extra fee. Some facilities are wheelchair accessible. Pets are permitted. Boat docks and launching facilities are nearby.

Reservations, fee: No reservations necessary; $6 fee per night. Open all year.

Who to contact: Phone at 206-842-3931, or write at 15546 Sunrise, Bainbridge Island, WA 98110.

Location: Drive to Bainbridge Island via Highway 305. The park is located at the southern tip of the island.

Trip note: Set on the edge of Puget Sound, this site provides beautiful night vistas of Seattle.

Site 40 ILLAHEE STATE PARK

Campsites, facilities: There are 25 tent sites. Picnic tables are provided, and sanitary services, toilets and a playground are available. Showers and firewood can be obtained for an extra fee. A laundromat and ice are located within one mile. Some facilities are wheelchair accessible. Pets and motorbikes are permitted. Boat docks and launching facilities are nearby.

Reservations, fee: No reservations necessary; $6 fee per night. Open all year.

Who to contact: Phone at 206-478-6460, or write at 3540 Bahia Vista, Bremerton, WA 98310.

Location: Drive three miles northeast of Bremerton on Highway 303, then take the east turn off to the park.

Trip note: A nice spot just three miles from civilization in Bremerton, yet unknown to out-of-towners touring the area.

Site 41 MANCHESTER STATE PARK

Campsites, facilities: There are 50 tent sites. Picnic tables are provided. Sanitary services and toilets are available. Showers and firewood can be obtained for an extra fee. Some facilities are wheelchair accessible. Pets are permitted.

Reservations, fee: No reservations necessary; $6 fee per night. Open all year with limited winter facilities.

Who to contact: Phone at 206-871-4065, or write at P.O. Box 36, Manchester, WA 98353.

Location: Coming from Olympic Peninsula in the northwest, take Highway 3 to Highway 16, then take the Highway 160-Port Orchard exit. Stay on Highway 160 and signs will direct you to the park. Coming from the Seattle area and Highway 5, take the Highway 16 exit to Bremerton, then take the Sedgwick exit off Highway 16. Follow the signs that direct you to the park.

Trip note: Set on the edge of Point Orchard, with good lookouts across Puget Sound of boats, ferries, and at night, the lights of Seattle. Good hiking in the park.

Site 42 BLAKE ISLAND STATE PARK

Campsites, facilities: There are 44 tent sites. Picnic tables are provided. Sanitary services, toilets, showers, firewood and a unique restaurant (see trip note) are available. Some facilities are wheelchair accessible. Pets are permitted. Boat docks are located at the park.

Reservations, fee: No reservations necessary; $6 fee per night. Open all year.

Who to contact: Phone at 206-947-0905, or write at P.O. Box 287, Manchester, WA 98353.

Location: This little island is three miles west of Seattle and is accessible only by boat.

Trip note: Set right in the middle of the massive Seattle metropolitan area on a small island, yet offers a combination of primitive settings and developed facilities. Tillicum Village offers unique northwest Indian dining.

Site 43
GREEN MOUNTAIN
CAMP

Campsites, facilities: There are nine primitive campsites for tents or small trailers. Picnic tables, fire grills and tent pads are provided. Pit toilets, piped water and facilities for horses are available.

Reservations, fee: No reservations necessary; no fee. Open all year.

Who to contact: Phone at 800-527-3305, or write the Department of Natural Resources at 1065 South Capitol Way, Olympia, WA 98504.

Location: Start on State Route 3 south of Silverdale and go west on Newberry Hill Road for three miles, then turn left on Seabeck Highway and drive for two miles. Turn right on Holly Road and go four miles, then turn left on Tahuya Lake Road and drive one mile. Turn left again on Green Mountain Road (gravel) and drive 2 1/2 miles to the junction, then turn left and drive one mile to the campground.

Trip note: A prime spot, primitive yet with piped water provided. This campground is operated by the Department of Natural Resources and is located in Tahuya State Forest. There are facilities for horses here and trails for hiking and horseback riding.

Site 44
SNOOZE JUNCTION
TRAILER PARK

Campsites, facilities: There are 38 drive-through sites for trailers or motorhomes of any length. Electricity, piped water, sewer hookups and picnic tables are provided. Bottled gas, sanitary services, toilets, showers and recreation hall are available. A store, cafe, laundromat and ice are located within one mile. Pets and motorbikes are permitted. Boat docks and launching facilities are nearby.

Reservations, fee: Reservations accepted; $7 fee per night. Open all year.

Who to contact: Phone at 206-275-2381, or write at P.O. Box 468, Belfair, WA 98528.

Location: Drive to Belfair (eight miles southwest of Bremerton on Highway 3) on Bremerton Island. From the junction of Highways 3 and 300, go one block northwest, then turn southwest and drive 2 3/4 miles and turn south on Gladwin Beach Road.

Trip note: Good holdover spot for motorhome campers preparing to head north. Nearby recreation options include an 18-hole golf course and marked bike trails.

Site 45
BELFAIR
STATE PARK

Campsites, facilities: There are 147 tent sites and 47 sites for trailers or motorhomes up to 20 feet long. Picnic tables are provided. Sanitary services, toilets and playground are available. Store and cafe are located within one mile. Electricity, piped water, sewer hookups, showers and firewood can be obtained for an extra fee. Pets are permitted.

Reservations, fee: Reservations accepted; $6 fee per night. Open all year.

Who to contact: Phone at 206-478-4625, or write at NE 410 Beck Road, Belfair, WA 98528.

Location: Drive to Belfair (eight mile southwest of Bremerton on Highway 3) on Bremerton Island, and go west th e miles on Highway 300. Then turn north on access road to the park.

Trip note: Tent campers will consider this a good alternative to campsite 44. Set along edge of the Hood Canal.

Site 46
TWANOH
STATE PARK

Campsites, facilities: There are 38 tent sites and nine sites for trailers or motorhomes up to 20 feet long. Picnic tables are provided. Toilets, store and playground are available. Electricity, piped water, sewer hookups, showers and firewood can be obtained for an extra fee. Some facilities are wheelchair accessible. Pets are permitted. Boat docks and launching facilities are nearby.

Reservations, fee: No reservations necessary; $6 fee per night. Open all year, but with limited winter facilities.

Who to contact: Phone at 206-275-2222, or write at P.O. Box 2520, Belfair, WA 98528.

Location: Drive five miles east of the town of Union on Highway 106 to get to the park.

Trip note: If you are cruising Highway 101, this camp is only a short drive east off Highway 106. It is often bypassed by visitors touring Washington. A nice spot with option of visiting Mason Lake to the south, or Hood Canal to the north.

Site 47
JARELLS'S COVE
MARINA

Campsites, facilities: There are 4 tent sites and 16 drive-through sites for trailers or motorhomes up to 27 feet long. Piped water and picnic tables are provided, and bottled gas, toilets, store, laundromat and ice are available. Electricity, showers and firewood are obtained for an extra fee. Pets are permitted. Boat docks and boat rentals are available.

Reservations, fee: Reservations accepted; $8 fee per night. MasterCard and Visa accepted. Open all year.

Who to contact: Phone at 206-426-8823, or write at E. 220 Wilson Rd, Shelton, WA 98584.

Location: From the town of Shelton, drive eight miles north on Highway 3, then drive four miles east on Spencer Lake Road. Cross Hartstone Bridge and continue north on Island Drive, then turn west on Haskell Hill Road and drive one mile to the marina.

Trip note: Marina and boat rentals are the big bonus. The drive-through sites are ideal for pickup campers towing trailered boats.

Site 48
ROBIN HOOD
TRAILER VILLAGE

Campsites, facilities: There are 10 tent sites and 16 sites for trailers or motorhomes of any length. Electricity, piped water, sewer hookups and picnic tables are provided. Toilets, showers, cafe and laundromat are available. Bottled gas, sanitary services, store and ice are located within one mile. Pets and motorbikes are permitted. Boat docks and launching facilities are nearby.

Reservations, fee: Reservations accepted; $10 fee per night. MasterCard and Visa accepted. Open all year.

Who to contact: Phone at 206-898-2163, or write at East 6780 Highway 106, Union, WA 98592.

Location: To get to the park, drive eight miles southwest of Bremerton to Belfair, then continue southwest on Highway 106 for 13 miles to E. 6780 Highway 106.

Trip note: This wooded park has access to the Hood Canal. Nearby recreation options include an 18-hole golf course and a full service marina. An option to campsites 44, 45 and 55.

Site **49** TOONERVILLE MULTIPLE USE AREA

Campsites, facilities: There are four primitive campsites for tents or small trailers. Picnic tables, fire grills and tent pads are provided. Pit toilets are available, but there is no piped water. Motorbikes are permitted.

Reservations, fee: No reservations necessary; no fee. Open all year.

Who to contact: Phone at 800-527-3305, or write the Department of Natural Resources at 1065 South Capitol Way, Olympia, WA 98504.

Location: Drive eight miles southwest of Bremerton on Highway 3 to the town of Belfair. From Belfair take State Route 300 for 1/3 mile, then bear left and continue for another 3 1/3 miles. Turn right on Belfair-Tahuya Road and go 1/2 mile, then turn right on Elfendahl Pass Road for 2 1/2 miles (past the Tahuya 4x4 trailhead). Go straight through the intersection with Goat Ranch Road and drive 3 1/3 miles to the camp, which is on the left.

Trip note: Primitive and rustic, this wooded campground is managed by the Department of Natural Resources and has trails for use by hikers, horses and motorbikes.

Site **50** HOWELL LAKE

Campsites, facilities: There are six primitive campsites for tents or small trailers. Picnic tables, fire grills and tent pads are provided. Pit toilets and piped water are available. A boat launch for small craft is located at Howell Lake.

Reservations, fee: No reservations necessary; no fee. Open all year.

Who to contact: Phone at 800-527-3305, or write the Department of Natural Resources at 1065 South Capitol Way, Olympia, WA 98504.

Location: Drive eight miles southwest of Bremerton on Highway 3 to the town of Belfair. From Belfair, take State Route 300 for 1/3 mile and then follow it left for another 3 1/3 mile. Turn right on Belfair-Tahuya Road and go 4 1/2 miles. Camp is on the left.

Trip note: A little-known jewel. This campground is managed by the Department of Natural Resources and set along Lake Howell. There are trails for use by hikers, horses, or motorbikes.

Site **51** TAHUYA RIVER HORSE CAMP

Campsites, facilities: There are nine primitive campsites for tents or small trailers. Picnic tables, fire grills and tent pads are provided. Pit toilets, piped water and equestrian facilities are available. Motorbikes are permitted.

Reservations, fee: No reservations necessary; no fee. Open all year.

Who to contact: Phone at 800-527-3305, or write the Department of Natural Resources at 1065 South Captiol Way, Olympia, WA 98504.

Location: Drive eight miles southwest of Bremerton on Highway 3 to the town of Belfair. From Belfair, take State Route 300 for 1/3 mile and follow it left for 3 1/3 miles, then turn right on Belfair-Tahuya Road and go 1 3/4 miles. Turn right on Spillman Road for two miles, then turn left and drive 3/4 mile to campground.

Trip note: This camp is set along the Tahuya River and is a good base camp for trips into the Tehuya State Forest. The trails can be used by hikers, horses or motorbikes.

CAMP SPILLMAN
Site **52**   **MULTIPLE USE AREA**

Campsites, facilities: There are six primitive campsites for tents or small trailers. Picnic tables, fire grills and tent pads are provided. Pit toilets and piped water are available. Motorbikes are permitted.

Reservations, fee: No reservations necessary; no fee. Open all year.

Who to contact: Phone at 800-527-3305, or write the Department of Natural Resources at 1065 South Capitol Way, Olympia, WA 98504.

Location: Drive eight miles southwest of Bremerton on Highway 3 to the town of Belfair. From Belfair, drive ⅓ mile on State Route 300, continue to follow it left for 3 ⅓ miles, turn right on Belfair-Tahuya Road and go ½ mile, then turn right on Elfendahl Pass Road and drive 2½ miles. At Twin Lakes Road turn left and drive ⅔ mile to camp.

Trip note: One of four (50-53) campsites set in the immediate vicinity of the Tahuya Forest. This one sits along the Tahuya River.

TWIN LAKES
Site **53**   **MULTIPLE USE AREA**

Campsites, facilities: There are six primitive campsites for tents or small trailers. Picnic tables, fire grills and tent pads are provided. Pit toilets are available, but there is no piped water. A hand launch for small boats is available at the lake.

Reservations, fee: No reservations necessary; no fee. Open all year.

Who to contact: Phone at 800-527-3305, or write the Department of Natural Resources at 1065 South Capitol Way, Olympia, WA 98504.

Location: From Camp Spillman (see campground 52), continue west on Twin Lakes Road for one mile, then turn right and drive 1/2 mile to camp.

Trip note: Little known, free and quiet. This wooded campground is in Tehuya State Forest and is managed by the Department of Natural Resources.

ALDRICH LAKE
Site **54**   **MULTIPLE USE AREA**

Campsites, facilities: There are four primitive campsites for tents or small trailers. Picnic tables, fire grills and tent pads are provided. Pit toilets and piped water are available. A hand launch for small boats is located at the lake.

Reservations, fee: No reservations necessary; no fee. Open all year.

Who to contact: Phone at 800-527-3305, or write the Department of Natural Resources at 1065 South Capitol Way, Olympia, WA 98504.

Location: From the town of Tahuya, drive north on Belfair-Tahuya Road for four miles, turn left on Dewatto Road and drive two miles, turn left again on Robbins Lake Road and drive 1/2 mile. Then turn right and drive 2/3 mile, turn right again and drive 200 yards to campsites.

Trip note: This campground is on Aldrich Lake and is managed by Department of Natural Resources. Robbins Lake is nearby and has day-use facilities and a hand launch for small boats. To reach Robbins Lake, follow the directions above—except that after turning left on Robbins Lake Road and driving 1/2 mile, you make another left and drive one mile to Robbins Lake.

Site 55
JARRELL COVE
STATE PARK

Campsites, facilities: There are 20 tent sites. Picnic tables are provided and flush toilets are available. Showers can be obtained for an extra fee. Some facilities are wheelchair accessible. Pets and motorbikes are permitted. Boat docks are available for overnight moorage.

Reservations, fee: No reservations necessary; $6 fee per night. Open all year.

Who to contact: Phone at 206-426-9226, or write at East 391 Wingert Road, Shelton, WA 98584.

Location: From the town of Shelton, drive east on Highway 3 to Hartstene Island. The park is at the northwest end of the island.

Trip note: This wooded park is rarely crowded and offers a protected cove for boating and docking facilities. A private marina is nearby.

Site 56
SQUAXIN ISLAND
STATE PARK

Campsites, facilities: There are 31 primitive campsites. Picnic tables are provided and pit toilets are available. There is no piped water. Pets are permitted. Boat docks can be obtained for overnight moorage.

Reservations, fee: No reservations necessary; $6 fee per night. Open all year.

Who to contact: Phone at 206-426-9226, or write at East 391 Wingert Road, Shelton, WA 98584.

Location: This camp is on Squaxin Island, which is north of the city of Olympia and accessible only by boat.

Trip note: Very few people know about this spot. It's a secluded island, yet not far from Olympia. This island covers 31 acres and has trails for hiking.

Site 57
PENROSE POINT
STATE PARK

Campsites, facilities: There are 83 campsites for tents or self-contained motorhomes. Picnic tables are provided, and sanitary services and toilets are available. Showers and firewood can be obtained for an extra fee. Some facilities are wheelchair accessible. Pets are permitted. Boat docks are nearby.

Reservations, fee: No reservations necessary; $6 fee per night. Open all year.

Who to contact: Phone at 206-884-2514, or write at 321-158th KPS, Lakebay, WA 98439.

Location: From Tacoma, drive 10 miles north on Highway 16, then take Highway 302 and drive 17 miles to the park.

Trip note: This park overlooks Lake Bay in the Puget Sound near Tacoma. Because of the circle-like driving route it takes to get here, a lot of people bypass it.

Site 58
KOPACHUEK
STATE PARK

Campsites, facilities: There are 41 campsites for tents or self-contained motorhomes. Picnic tables are provided, and sanitary services and toilets are available. Showers and firewood can be obtained for an extra fee. Some facilities are wheelchair accessible. Pets are permitted. Boat docks are nearby.

Reservations, fee: No reservations necessary; $6 fee per night. Open all year.

Who to contact: Phone at 206-265-3606, or write at 11101-56th Street NW, Gig Harbor, WA 98335.

Location: From Tacoma, drive seven miles north on Highway 16, then take turn-off west and drive five miles to park.

Trip note: This park overlooks Lake Bay in the Puget Sound, near Tacoma. A nice, developed park with full facilities for tent campers.

Site 59   KOA TACOMA-GIG HARBOR

Campsites, facilities: There are 40 tent sites and 100 drive-through sites for trailers or motorhomes of any length. Electricity, piped water, sewer hookups and picnic tables are provided. Bottled gas, sanitary services, toilets, showers, recreation hall, store, cafe, laundromat, ice, playground and swimming pool are available. Firewood can be obtained for an extra fee. Pets and motorbikes are permitted.

Reservations, fee: Reservations accepted; $16 fee per night. MasterCard and Visa accepted. Open all year.

Who to contact: Phone at 206-858-8138, or write at 9515 Burnham, Gig Harbor, WA 98335.

Location: Take the Highway 16 exit off I-5 in Tacoma and drive 12 miles northwest on Highway 16. There will be signs showing the way to the KOA.

Trip note: Nearby recreation options include an 18-hole golf course, a full service marina and tennis courts.

Site 60   R.F. KENNEDY MULTIPLE USE AREA

Campsites, facilities: There are eight primitive campsites for tents or small trailers. Picnic tables, fire grills and tent pads are provided. Pit toilets, piped water, boat launching facilities and a floating dock are available.

Reservations, fee: No reservations necessary; no fee. Open all year.

Who to contact: Phone at 800-527-3305, or write the Department of Natural Resources at 1065 South Capitol Way, Olympia, WA 98504.

Location: Drive 10 miles northwest of Tacoma via Highway 16, then go west for about 15 miles on Highway 302 to the town of Home. Start at the bridge in Home and follow Longbranch Road south for 1 1/3 miles, turn right on Whiteman Road and drive 2 1/3 miles, then turn right on Bay Road and drive one mile to campsite.

Trip note: A beautiful yet free camp set along the shore of the peninsula. Piped water makes it a sure winner.

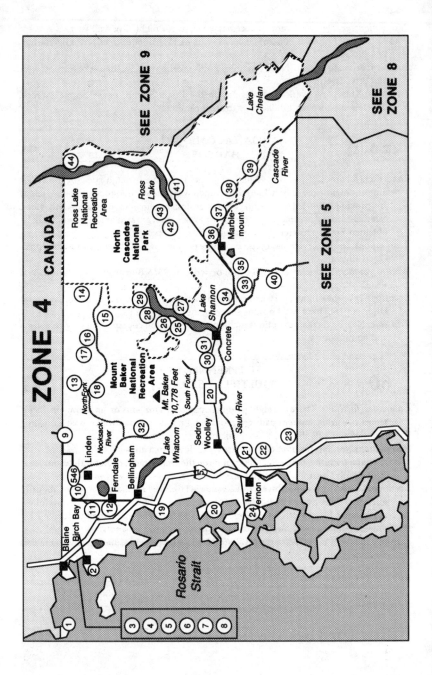

NORTH CASCADES

Site 1
WHALEN'S
RV PARK

Campsites, facilities: There are 100 tent sites and 65 sites for trailers or motorhomes of any length. Electricity, piped water and picnic tables are provided. Flush toilets, bottled gas, sanitary services, firewood and showers are available. A store, cafe, laundromat and ice are located. Pets are permitted. Boat docks, launching facilities and rentals are nearby.

Reservations, fee: Reservations accepted; $13 fee per night. Open May to late-October.

Who to contact: Phone at 206-945-2874, or write at Box 985, Point Roberts, WA 98281.

Location: This campground is located on Point Roberts. To get there, go north on Highway 99N to the Lander exit, west on Highway 10 to Highway 17, south on Highway 17 to 56th Street, south on 56th Street to Roosevelt Way, then turn east and drive to the campground.

Trip note: This is a one in a million, little-known spot that is very special to the few people who know about it. A mix of mountains and water. Nearby recreational options include an 18-hole golf course, a full service marina and tennis courts.

Site 2
BIRCH BAY
STATE PARK

Campsites, facilities: There are 147 tent sites and 20 sites for trailers or motorhomes up to 70 feet long, some have electricity and water hookups. Picnic tables are provided. Flush toilets, showers, firewood and sanitary services are available. A store, cafe, laundromat and ice are located within one mile. Some facilities are wheelchair accessible. Pets are permitted.

Reservations, fee: Reservations accepted; $6 fee per night. Open all year.

Who to contact: Phone at 206-371-2800, or write at 5105 Helwig Rd., Blaine, WA 98230.

Location: The easiest route is from Blaine by driving eight miles south on a paved road to the park. Other routes on county roads from the towns of Custer and Pleasant Valley are available.

Trip note: This park covers 193 acres and includes a mile-long beach. More than 300 different species of bird, many which are migrating on the Pacific Flyway, can be seen here. An 18-hole golf course is available nearby.

Site 3
BAYWOOD PARK

Campsites, facilities: There are 50 tent sites and 164 drive-through sites for trailers or

motorhomes of any length. Electricity, piped water and sewer hookups are provided. Flush toilets, sanitary services, showers, a recreation hall, laundromat and playground are available. Bottled gas, a store, cafe and ice are located within one mile. Pets are permitted. Boat launching facilities are nearby.

Reservations, fee: Reservations accepted; $12 fee per night. Open all year.

Who to contact: Phone at 206-371-7211, or write at 4672 Birch Bay-Lynden Road, Blaine, WA 98230.

Location: Take the 270 exit off I-5 south of Blaine, then drive three miles west on Birch Bay-Lynden Road to park.

Trip note: This camp provides opportunities for clamming and saltwater fishing. Nearby recreational options include an 18-hole golf course, a full service marina and a riding stable.

Site 4 — BIRCH BAY TRAILER PARK

Campsites, facilities: There are 25 tent sites and 320 drive-through sites for trailers or motorhomes of any length. Electricity, piped water, sewer hookups and picnic tables are provided. Flush toilets, bottled gas, sanitary services, showers, a recreation hall and laundromat are available. A store, cafe and ice are located within one mile. Pets and motorbikes are permitted. Boat launching facilities are nearby.

Reservations, fee: Reservations accepted; $14 fee per night. MasterCard and Visa accepted. Open all year.

Who to contact: Phone at 206-371-7922, or write at 8080 Harbor Vie, Blaine, WA 98230.

Location: Take the 270 exit off I-5 south of Blaine and drive four miles west on Birch Bay-Lynden Road, then 1/2 mile south on Harbor View to the park.

Trip note: This private campground provides good ocean access on Birch Bay. Nearby recreational options include a full service marina and tennis courts.

Site 5 — BORDER LINE RV PARK

Campsites, facilities: There are 10 tent sites and 48 drive-through sites for trailers or motorhomes of any length. Electricity, piped water, sewer hookups and picnic tables are provided. Flush toilets, bottled gas, sanitary services, showers, a cafe and ice are available. A store and laundromat are located within one mile. Pets and motorbikes are permitted. Boat docks and launching facilities are nearby.

Reservations, fee: Reservations accepted; $17 fee per night. MasterCard and Visa accepted. Open April to October.

Who to contact: Phone at 206-332-6909, or write at 1690 Peace Portal, Blaine, WA 98230.

Location: Take the 274 exit off I-5 south of Blaine, then drive 200 yards west on Peace Portal Way.

Trip note: This small private camp is one of six in the immediate area. Nearby recreational options include an 18-hole golf course, marked bike trails and a full service marina.

Site 6 — MAPLE LEAF TRAILER PARK

Campsites, facilities: There are eight tent sites and eight drive-through sites for trailers or motorhomes of any length. Electricity, piped water, sewer hookups and picnic tables are provided. Bottled gas, sanitary services, a store, playground, cafe, laundromat and ice are available within one mile. Pets and motorbikes are permitted. A boat ramp and boat rentals are located on California Creek.

Reservations, fee: Reservations accepted; $8 fee per night. Open all year.

Who to contact: Phone at 206-371-7006, or write at 8586 Harbor Drive, Blaine, WA 98230.

Location: Take the 274 exit off I-5 south of Blaine and drive west on Peace Portal Way to Blaine Road, turn south and follow the signs to the park.

Trip note: This campground is on California Creek, which is a nice little river that provides some boating access. One of six campgrounds in immediate area.

PLAZA PARK

Site **7**

Campsites, facilities: There are 100 tent sites and 49 drive-through sites for trailers or motorhomes of any length. Electricity, piped water, sewer hookups and picnic tables are provided. Flush toilets, bottled gas, sanitary services, showers, firewood and a laundromat are available. A store, cafe and ice are located within one mile. Pets and motorbikes are permitted.

Reservations, fee: Reservations accepted; $11 fee per night. Open all year.

Who to contact: Phone at 206-371-7822, or write at 4414 Birch Bay, Blaine, WA 98230.

Location: Take the 270 exit off I-5 and drive two miles west on Lynden-Birch Bay Road to 4414 Birch Bay.

Trip note: An option to campsites 3-8, which are also located in vicinity.

RICHMOND RESORT

Site **8**

Campsites, facilities: There are 50 sites for trailers or motorhomes up to 33 feet long. Electricity, piped water, sewer hookups and picnic tables are provided. Flush toilets, showers and a laundromat are available. Bottled gas, sanitary services, a store, cafe and ice are located within one mile. Boat launching facilities are nearby.

Reservations, fee: Reservations accepted; $14 fee per night. Open April to early-October.

Who to contact: Phone at 206-371-2262, or write at 8086 Birch Bay, Blaine, WA 98230.

Location: Take the 270 exit off I-5 and drive two miles west on Lynden-Birch Bay Road, go south one block on Harbor View, then northwest on Birch Bay Road to 4414 Birch Bay Road.

Trip note: An option to campsites 3-7.

SUMAS
RV PARK

Site **9**

Campsites, facilities: There are 25 tent sites and 30 drive-through sites for trailers or motorhomes of any length. Electricity, piped water and picnic tables are provided. Flush toilets, sanitary services, showers, firewood and a playground are available. Bottled gas, a store, cafe, laundromat and ice are located within one mile. Pets and motorbikes are permitted.

Reservations, fee: Reservations accepted; $10 fee per night. Open all year.

Who to contact: Phone at 206-988-8875, or write at 9600 Easterbrook, Sumas, WA 98295.

Location: The park is located in Sumas which is 25 miles northeast of Bellingham. To get there, drive to the junction of Highways 9 and 547, then go 1/4 mile south on Cherry Street. Campground is in the center of town.

Trip note: Set on edge of U.S.-Canada border. A holdover spot to spend American dollars before heading into British Columbia. Nearby recreational options include an 18-hole golf course and tennis courts.

KOA LYNDEN

Site **10**

Campsites, facilities: There are 80 tent sites and 100 drive-through sites for trailers or motorhomes of any length. Electricity, piped water, sewer hookups and picnic tables are provided. Flush toilets, bottled gas, sanitary services, showers, firewood, recreation hall, store, cafe, laundromat, ice, playground and swimming pool are available. Pets are permitted. Boat rentals nearby.

Reservations, fee: Reservations accepted; $16 fee per night. MasterCard and Visa accepted. Open March to November.

Who to contact: Phone at 206-354-4772, or write at 8717 Line Road, Lynden, WA 98264.

Location: From Bellingham, drive 14 miles north on Highway 539, then go east for three miles on Highway 546.

Trip note: A holdover spot for vacationers heading north to Canada via highways 539/546. Nearby recreational options include 18-hole golf course and tennis courts. Set in a rural area with many small farms.

WINDMILL INN

Site **11**

Campsites, facilities: There are 11 sites for trailers or motorhomes of any length. Electricity, piped water, sewer hookups and picnic tables are provided. Flush toilets, showers, bottled gas, a store, cafe, laundromat and ice are available within one mile. Pets and motorbikes are permitted. Boat launching facilities are nearby.

Reservations, fee: Reservations accepted; $10 fee per night. MasterCard and Visa accepted. Open all year.

Who to contact: Phone at 206-354-3424, or write at 8022 Guide Meridian, Lynden, WA 98264.

Location: From Bellingham, drive 10 miles north on Highway 539.

Trip note: A nice little spot set near the Nooksack River and Wiser Lake.

FERNDALE EVERGREEN MOBILE PARK

Site **12**

Campsites, facilities: There are 16 sites for trailers or motorhomes of any length in this adults-only campground. Electricity, piped water and sewer hookups are provided. Flush toilets, showers, bottled gas, a laundromat and playground are available. A store and ice are located within one mile. Pets are permitted.

Reservations, fee: Reservations accepted; $10 fee per night. Open all year.

Who to contact: Phone at 206-384-1241, or write at 6800 Enterprise, Ferndale, WA 98248.

Location: This park is located in Ferndale. To get there, take the 266 exit off I-5 and drive 1/2 mile east on Grandview, then one block south to the campground.

Trip note: An option to campsites 10 and 11, with this one providing more direct access from Interstate 5. A golf course and riding stable provide nearby options.

CANYON CREEK

Site **13**

Campsites, facilities: There are several primitive sites for tents or trailers up to 16 feet long. Picnic tables, and firegrills are provided. Firewood is available. No piped water or toilets are available. Pets are permitted.

Reservations, fee: No reservations necessary; $3 fee per night. Open mid-May to mid-September.

Who to contact: Phone Mt. Baker-Snoqualmie National Forest at 206-856-5700 or 206-599-2714, or write the Forest Service in Glacier, WA 98244.

Location: From the town of Glacier, drive two miles northeast on Highway 542, then go north on Forest Service Road 31 for seven miles to campground. A Forest Service map is essential.

Trip note: This campground is set on Canyon Creek about three miles from the Canadian Border. Secluded, little known, with Forest Service roads in area providing access.

HANNEGAN

Site **14**

Campsites, facilities: There are six primitive sites for tents or trailers up to 15 feet long. Picnic tables are provided, but no piped water is available. Firewood and a horse loading ramp are available. Pets are permitted.

Reservations, fee: No reservations necessary; $3 fee per night. Open mid-May to mid-September.

Who to contact: Phone Mt. Baker-Snoqualmie National Forest at 206-856-5700 or 206-599-2714, or write at the U.S. Forest Service in Glacier, WA 98244.

Location: From the town of Glacier, drive 12 1/2 miles east on Highway 542, then turn east on Forest Service Road 32 and drive four miles to campground. A Forest Service map is essential.

Trip note: This rustic spot has everything but piped water. The campground is set on Ruth Creek on the border of the Mt. Baker Wilderness, and is at the trailhead that leads into the Mt. Baker Wilderness across Hannegan Pass.

SILVER FIR

Site **15**

Campsites, facilities: There are 21 sites for tents, trailers or motorhomes up to 31 feet long. Picnic tables are provided. Piped water, firewood, a community kitchen and group picnic area are available. Pets are permitted.

Reservations, fee: No reservations necessary; $6 fee for the first night and $3 for each following night. Open May to October.

Who to contact: Phone Mt. Baker-Snoqualmie National Forest at 206-856-5700 or 206-599-2714, or write the U.S. Forest Service in Glacier, WA 98244.

Location: From the town of Glacier, drive 12 1/2 miles east on Highway 542 to the campground.

Trip note: This campground is set on the North Fork of the Nooksack River, just a short distance from the North Fork Nooksack Research Natural Area. Strongly advised to obtain a Forest Service map in order take maximum advantage of recreational opportunity.

Site 16
EXCELSIOR
GROUP CAMP

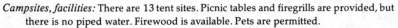

Campsites, facilities: There are 13 tent sites. Picnic tables and firegrills are provided, but there is no piped water. Firewood is available. Pets are permitted.

Reservations, fee: No reservations necessary; $3 fee per night. Open mid-May to mid-September.

Who to contact: Phone Mt. Baker-Snoqualmie National Forest at 206-856-5700 or 206-599-2714, or write the U.S. Forest Service in Glacier, WA 98244.

Location: From the town of Glacier, drive 6 1/2 miles east on Highway 542 to the campground.

Trip note: This campground is set near the Nooksack River less than a mile from Nooksack Falls and 1 1/2 miles from the site of the Excelsior Mine. Remember to bring your own water.

Site 17
NOOKSACK

Campsites, facilities: There are 20 sites for tents, trailers or motorhomes up to 31 feet long. Picnic tables and firegrills are provided. Piped water, vault toilets and firewood are available. A store, cafe, laundromat and ice are available within five miles. Pets are permitted.

Reservations, fee: No reservations necessary; $3 fee per night. Open mid-May to mid-September.

Who to contact: Phone Mt. Baker-Snoqualmie National Forest at 206-856-5700 or 206-599-2714, or write the U.S. Forest Service in Glacier, WA 98244.

Location: From the town of Glacier, drive 4 1/2 miles east on Highway 542 to the campground.

Trip note: This campground is set along the Nooksack River about three miles west of Nooksack Falls. An option to campsite 17, but with piped water available.

Site 18
DOUGLAS FIR

Campsites, facilities: There are 30 sites for tents, trailers or motorhomes up to 31 feet long. Picnic tables and firegrills are provided. Piped waters and firewood are available. A store, cafe, laundromat and ice are located within five miles. Pets are permitted.

Reservations, fee: No reservations necessary; $5 fee per night. Open May to October.

Who to contact: Phone Mt. Baker-Snoqualmie National Forest at 206-856-5700 or 206-599-2714, or write the U.S. Forest Service at Glacier, WA 98244.

Location: From the town of Glacier, drive two miles northeast on Highway 542 to the campground.

Trip note: This campground is set along the Nooksack River. An option to campsites 15-18.

Site 19
LARRABEE
STATE PARK

Campsites, facilities: There are 74 tent sites and 26 sites for trailers or motorhomes up to 60

feet long. Picnic tables are provided. Flush toilets, sanitary dump services, electricity, piped water, sewer hookups, showers and firewood are available. Pets are permitted. Boat launching facilities are available nearby.

Reservations, fee: No reservations necessary; $6 fee per night. Open all year.

Who to contact: Phone at 206-676-2093, or write at 245 Chuckanut, Bellingham, WA 98225.

Location: From Bellingham, drive seven miles south on Chuckanut Drive (Highway 11) to the park.

Trip note: This 1885-acre state park is on Samish Bay in Puget Sound. It offers tidepools and eight miles of hiking trails, including two that go to small lakes.

Site **20**   BAY VIEW STATE PARK

Campsites, facilities: There are 100 tent sites and nine sites for trailers or motorhomes up to 32 feet long. Picnic tables are provided. Flush toilets, a playground, swimming pool, electricity, piped water, sewer hookups and showers are available. Store and laundromat are located within one mile. Pets are permitted.

Reservations, fee: No reservations necessary; $6 fee per night. Open all year.

Who to contact: Phone at 206-757-0227, or write at 1093 Bay View-Edison Road, Brighton, WA 98233.

Location: From Burlington, drive five miles west on Highway 20, then turn north and drive two miles to the park.

Trip note: This is a good family campground with a large play area for kids. Set on Padilla Bay.

Site **21**   RIVERBEND PARK

Campsites, facilities: There are 25 tent sites and 95 drive-through sites for trailers or motorhomes of any length. Electricity, piped water, sewer hookups and picnic tables are provided. Flush toilets, sanitary services, showers, a laundromat and playground are available. Bottled gas, a store, cafe, ice and swimming pool are located within one mile. Pets are permitted.

Reservations, fee: Reservations accepted; $13 fee per night. MasterCard and Visa accepted. Open all year.

Who to contact: Phone at 206-428-4044, or write at 305 Stewart, Mount Vernon, WA 98273.

Location: In Mount Vernon, take the College Way exit off I-5 and drive one block west to Freeway Drive, then turn north and go 1/2 mile to the park.

Trip note: Access to the Skagit River here is a highpoint. Nearby recreational options include an 18-hole golf course, marked bike trails and tennis courts.

Site **22**   MOUNTAIN VIEW MOBILE HOME PARK

Campsites, facilities: There are 14 sites for trailers or motorhomes of any length in this adults-only campground. Electricity, piped water and sewer hookups are provided. Flush toilets, sanitary services and laundromat are available. Bottled gas, store, cafe, showers and ice are located within one mile. Pets are permitted. Boat launching facilities are nearby.

Reservations, fee: No reservations necessary; $10 fee per night. Open all year.

Who to contact: Phone at 206-424-3775, or write at 1685 Highway 99, Mount Vernon, WA 98273.

Location: In Mount Vernon, take the 225 exit off I-5 and drive 1/4 mile west, then turn north and drive 1/4 mile to 1685 Highway 99.

Trip note: This camp is an alternative to campsite 22, both on Skagit River, not far off I-5.

Site 23 LAKE MCMURRAY RESORT

Campsites, facilities: There are 10 tent sites and 35 drive-through sites for trailers or motorhomes of any length. Electricity, piped water and picnic tables are provided. Flush toilets, firewood, showers and sanitary dump services are available. A store, cafe and ice are located within one mile. Pets and motorbikes are permitted. Boat docks, launching facilities and rentals are nearby. There are also four rustic, one-room cabins available with wood stoves and electricity.

Reservations, fee: Reservations accepted; $9 fee per night. Open mid-April to November.

Who to contact: Phone at 206-445-4555, or write at 2294 McMurray, Mount Vernon, WA 98273.

Location: South of Mount Vernon, take the Highway 534 exit east and drive five miles, then go 1 1/4 miles southeast on Highway 9, then 1/2 mile north on Lakeview Road.

Trip note: This pleasant resort is on the shore of Lake McMurray, a small fishing lake stocked with rainbow and cutthroat trout. Perch and crappie are native to the lake. Sailboats are allowed.

Site 24 POTLATCH RV RESORT

Campsites, facilities: There are eight tent sites and 73 sites for trailers or motorhomes of any length. Electricity, piped water, sewer hookups and picnic tables are provided. Flush toilets, showers, bottled gas, a club house, cafe, laundromat, ice, large indoor swimming pool, spas, and cable TV are available. A store is located within one mile. Pets and motorbikes are permitted. Boat docks, launching facilities and rentals are nearby on Skagit Bay.

Reservations, fee: Reservations accepted; $13 fee per night. MasterCard and Visa accepted. Open all year.

Who to contact: Phone at 206-466-4468, or write at P.O. Box 344, La Conner, WA 98257.

Location: This resort is near LaConner. From the junction of I-5 and Highway 20, take the 230 exit and drive west on Highway 20, then go south on LaConner-Whitney Road, then north on 3rd Street.

Trip note: This park has access to the shore of Skagit Bay. Nearby recreation options include an 18-hole golf course, marked bike trails and a full service marina.

Site 25 HORSESHOE COVE

Campsites, facilities: There are eight tent sites and eight sites for trailers or motorhomes up to 21 feet long. Picnic tables are provided. Piped water, flush toilets, sanitary services and firewood are available. Pets are permitted. Boat launching facilities are located nearby on Baker Lake.

Reservations, fee: No reservations necessary; $5 fee per night. Open May to October.

Who to contact: Phone Mt. Baker-Snoqualmie National Forest at 206-856-5700, or write the Mt. Baker Ranger District in Sedro Woolley, WA 98284.

Location: From the town of Concrete, drive 9 1/2 miles north on County Road 25, then 2 1/2 miles north on Forest Service Road 11. Take Forest Service Road 1118 east for two miles to the campground. A Forest Service map is essential.

Trip note: This campground is set on the shore of 5000-acre Baker Lake, a good fishing lake for rainbow trout, kokanee salmon, cutthroat trout, dolly varden trout and whitefish.

BOULDER CREEK
Site 26
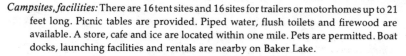

Campsites, facilities: There are 10 sites for tents or trailers up to 15 feet long. Picnic tables and firegrills are provided. Firewood and pit toilets are available, but there is no piped water. A store, cafe and ice are located within five miles. Pets are permitted. Boat docks and launching facilities are nearby on Baker Lake.

Reservations, fee: No reservations necessary; $3 fee per night. Open mid-May to mid-September.

Who to contact: Phone Mt. Baker-Snoqualmie National Forest at 206-856-5700, or write the Mt. Baker Ranger District in Sedro Woolley, WA 98284.

Location: From the town of Concrete, drive 9 1/2 miles north on County Road 25, then head north for 5 1/2 miles on Forest Service Road 11. Campground is on the left, set on Boulder Creek.

Trip note: This campground is an alterantive to camp 26, set on Boulder Creek about one mile from the shore of Baker Lake. A boat launch is located at Panorama Point.

MAPLE GROVE
Site 27

Campsites, facilities: There are 6 primitive tent sites which are only accessible by boat or on foot. Picnic tables are provided. Firewood is available, but there is no piped water. Pets are permitted. Boat launching facilities are located nearby on Baker Lake.

Reservations, fee: No reservations necessary; $3 fee per night. Open mid-May to mid-September.

Who to contact: Phone Mt. Baker-Snoqualmie National Forest at 206-856-5700, or write the Mt. Baker Ranger District in Sedro Woolley, WA 98284.

Location: From the town of Concrete, drive 9 1/2 miles north on County Road 25, then turn north on Forest Service Road 11 and drive 2 1/2 miles. Turn east on Forest Service Road 1118 and go two miles, then park your car, launch your boat and go one mile northeast across Lake Baker to the campground. A Forest Service map is essential.

Trip note: You want a quiet spot on the edge of a lake? OK, here it is. This rustic campground is on the shore of Lake Baker and is hike-in or boat-in only.

PANORAMA POINT
Site 28

Campsites, facilities: There are 16 tent sites and 16 sites for trailers or motorhomes up to 21 feet long. Picnic tables are provided. Piped water, flush toilets and firewood are available. A store, cafe and ice are located within one mile. Pets are permitted. Boat docks, launching facilities and rentals are nearby on Baker Lake.

Reservations, fee: No reservations necessary; $5 fee per night. Open May to October.

Who to contact: Phone Mt. Baker-Snoqualmie National Forest at 206-856-5700, or write the Mt. Baker Ranger District in Sedro Woolley, WA 98284.

Location: From the town of Concrete, drive 9 1/2 miles north on County Road 25, then drive 6 1/2 miles north on Forest Service Road 11 to campground.

Trip note: This well-maintained campground is on the shore of Baker Lake. The reservoir is one of the better fishing lakes in the area.

PARK CREEK
Site 29

Campsites, facilities: There are 12 sites for tents or trailers up to 15 feet long. Picnic tables are provided. Firewood and pit toilets are available, but there is no water. A store and cafe are located within one mile. Pets are permitted. Boat docks, launching facilities and rentals are nearby on Lake Baker.

Reservations, fee: No reservations necessary; $3 fee per night. Open mid-May to mid-September.

Who to contact: Phone Mt. Baker-Snoqualmie National Forest at 206-856-5700, or write Mt. Baker Ranger District in Sedro Woolley, WA 98284.

Location: From the town of Concrete, drive 9 1/2 miles north on County Road 25, then 7 1/2 miles north on Forest Service Road 11. Take Forest Service Road 1144 about 200 yards northwest and you're there. A Forest Service map is essential.

Trip note: This campground is set on Park Creek a short distance from the north shore of Baker Lake.

KOA GRADY CREEK
Site 30

Campsites, facilities: There are 30 tent sites and 40 drive-through sites for trailers or motorhomes of any length. Picnic tables are provided. Flush toilets, sanitary services, showers, recreation hall, store, laundromat, ice, playground, electricity, piped water, sewer hookups, firewood and swimming pool are available. Bottled gas and cafe are located within one mile. Pets and motorbikes are permitted.

Reservations, fee: Reservations accepted; $10 fee per night. MasterCard and Visa accepted. Open mid-April to late-October.

Who to contact: Phone at 206-826-3554, or write at 736 Russell, Concrete, WA 98237.

Location: From the town of Concrete, drive six miles west on Highway 20, then turn north on Russell Road and go 1/4 mile to the campground.

Trip note: This wooded campground is a good base for trips to Skagit River and Baker Lake. There are numerous hiking trails nearby.

CREEKSIDE RV PARK
Site 31

Campsites, facilities: There are two tent sites and 25 drive-through sites for trailers or motorhomes of any length. Electricity, piped water, sewer hookups and picnic tables are provided. Flush toilets, sanitary services, store, laundromat, ice, playground and showers are available. A store and a cafe are located within one mile. Pets and motorbikes are permitted.

Reservations, fee: Reservations accepted; $8 fee per night. Open all year.

Who to contact: Phone at 206-826-3566, or write at 761 Baker Lake Road, Concrete, WA

98237.

Location: From the town of Concrete, drive seven miles west on Highway 20, then turn north on Baker Lake Road and go 1/2 mile to the campground.

Trip note: This wooded campground is centrally located to the nearby recreational opportunities at Baker Lake and the Skagit River.

HUTCHISON CREEK
Site **32**

Campsites, facilities: There are 11 sites for tents or small trailers. Picnic tables, firegrills and tent pads are provided. Vault toilets and firewood are available, but there is no piped water. A store is located within one mile.

Reservations, fee: No reservations necessary; no fee. Open all year.

Who to contact: Phone the Department of Natural Resources at 1-800-527-3305, or write Department of Natural Resources AW-11, 1065 South Capitol Way, Olympia, WA 98504.

Location: Start on State Route 9 at Acme, just north of the Nooksack River Bridge, go east for 2 1/2 miles on Mosquito Lake Road, then turn right on a gravel road for 1/2 mile to campground.

Trip note: This campground is set in the forest along Hutchinson Creek near the South Fork of the Nooksack River. Managed by the Department of Natural Resources. Rustic, beautiful, primitive and unknown to out-of-towners.

HOWARD MILLER
Site **33**   STEELHEAD

Campsites, facilities: There are 40 tent sites and 20 sites for trailers or motorhomes of any length. Electricity, piped water and picnic tables are provided. Flush toilets, sanitary services, showers and a playground are available. Bottled gas, store, cafe and ice are located within one mile. Pets and motorbikes are permitted. Boat launching facilities are nearby on Skagit River.

Reservations, fee: No reservations necessary; $8 fee per night. Open all year.

Who to contact: Phone at 206-853-8808, or write at P.O. Box 97, Rockport, WA 98283.

Location: This city park is located in the town of Rockport. To get there, drive to the junction of Highway 20 and Rockport Darrington Road, then turn south and drive to campground.

Trip note: This city park has access to the Skagit River, which has been designated a wild and scenic river. Good steelhead fishing in season.

ROCKPORT
Site **34**   STATE PARK

Campsites, facilities: There are 12 tent sites and 50 sites for trailers or motorhomes up to 20 feet long. Picnic tables are provided. Flush toilets, sanitary services, electricity, piped water, sewer hookups, showers and firewood are available. Facilities are wheelchair accessible. A store, cafe and ice are located within one mile. Pets are permitted.

Reservations, fee: No reservations necessary; $6 fee per night. Open April to late-October.

Who to contact: Phone at 206-853-8461, or write at Route 1, Box 296, Concrete, WA 98237.

Location: Rockport is 40 miles east of Mt. Vernon. This state park is located one mile west of Rockport on Highway 20.

Trip note: This state park covers 457 acres and offers five miles of hiking trails, some of which are wheelchair accessible. The campground is set among old-growth Douglas Firs, and is near the Skagit River, a good steelhead stream.

Site 35   WILDERNESS VILLAGE AND RV PARK

Campsites, facilities: There are 20 tent sites and 40 drive-through sites for trailers or motorhomes of any length. Electricity, piped water, sewer hookups and picnic tables are provided. Flush toilets, sanitary services, showers, recreation hall and laundromat are available. Cafe and ice are located within one mile. Pets are permitted.

Reservations, fee: Reservations accepted; $8 fee per night. Open all year.

Who to contact: Phone at 206-873-2571, or write at 5570 Highway 20, Rockport, WA 98283.

Location: From the town of Rockport, drive five miles east on Highway 20. The park is near mile post 102.

Trip note: This park is near the Skagit River. Rockport State Park and hiking trails are nearby.

Site 36   ALPINE RV PARK AND CAMPGROUND

Campsites, facilities: There are 15 tent sites and 30 drive-through sites for trailers or motorhomes of any length. Electricity, piped water, sewer hookups and picnic tables are provided. Flush toilets, firewood, laundromat, showers and playground are available. Bottled gas, store, cafe and ice are located within one mile. Pets and motorbikes are permitted.

Reservations, fee: Reservations accepted; $8 fee per night. MasterCard and Visa accepted. Open all year.

Who to contact: Phone at 206-873-4142, or write at P.O. Box 148, Marblemount, WA 98267.

Location: Drive east of Rockport on Highway 20 to the town of Marblemount, then go past town 1 1/2 miles and you'll see the campground.

Trip note: This campground has access to the Skagit River. A trail from the nearby National Park Service Ranger Station ascends to Helen Buttes.

Site 37   CASCADE ISLANDS

Campsites, facilities: There are 15 tent sites. Picnic tables, firegrills and tent pads are provided. Vault toilets, piped water and firewood are available. Store, cafe and ice are located within one mile.

Reservations, fee: No reservations necessary; no fee. Open all year.

Who to contact: Phone the Department of Natural Resources at 1-800-527-3305, or write Department of Natural Resources AW-11, 1065 South Capitol Way, Olympia, WA 98504.

Location: Start on Highway 20 in Marblemount. Go east for 2/3 mile on Old Cascade Road, then turn right on Rockport Cascade Road, go 200 yards and turn left on South Cascade Road. Drive 1 1/4 miles to campground, which is on the left.

Trip note: This Department of Natural Resources campground is set on the shore of the

Cascade River about two miles upstream from its confluence with the Skagit River. The price is right, and so is the streamside setting.

MARBLE CREEK
Site **38**

Campsites, facilities: There are 13 tent sites and 15 sites for trailers or motorhomes up to 31 feet long. Picnic tables and firegrills are provided. Pit toilets and firewood are available, but there is no piped water. Pets are permitted.

Reservations, fee: No reservations necessary; no fee. Open mid-May to mid-September.

Who to contact: Phone Mt. Baker-Snoqualmie National Forest at 206-856-5700, or write Mt. Baker Ranger District in Sedro Woolley, WA 98284.

Location: From the town of Marblemount, drive east for eight miles on County Road 3528, then turn south on Forest Service Road 1530 and drive one mile to campground. A Forest Service map is essential.

Trip note: This rustic campground is set on Marble Creek. Continuing on Forest Service Road 1530 will take you up to Bush Lake. A trailhead to Hidden Lake just inside the boundary of North Cascades National Park can be found about five miles from camp at the end of Forest Service Road 1540. See Forest Service map for details.

MINERAL PARK
Site **39**

Campsites, facilities: There are four primitive sites for trailers up to 15 feet long. Picnic tables are provided. Firewood is available, but there is no piped water. Pets are permitted.

Reservations, fee: No reservations necessary; $3 fee per night. Open mid-May to mid-September.

Who to contact: Phone Mt. Baker-Snoqualmie National Forest at 206-856-5700, or write Mt. Baker Ranger District in Sedro Woolley, WA 98284.

Location: From the town of Marblemount, drive east on County Road 3528 for 15 miles and you'll find the campground.

Trip note: Here's another classic unknown camp spot that can provide a jumpoff for many adventures. This rustic site is set on the Cascade River and is near numerous trails leading into Glacier Peak Wilderness.

WILLIAM C. DEARINGER
Site **40**

Campsites, facilities: There are 12 primitive sites for tents or small trailers. Picnic tables, firegrills and tent pads are provided. Vault toilets and firewood are available, but there is no piped water.

Reservations, fee: No reservations necessary; no fee. Open all year.

Who to contact: Phone the Department of Natural Resources at 1-800-527-3305, or write Department of Natural Resources AW-11, 1065 South Capitol Way, Olympia, WA 98504.

Location: Start on State Route 530 and drive 1/3 mile north of Darrington, then go east on Mountain Loop Road for 1/2 mile. Continue straight for five miles, then turn left and drive 2/3 mile on East Sauk Prairie Road. Stay right on SW-D-5000 Road and go 2 2/3 miles, then bear right for one mile. Turn left on SW-D-5400 Road and drive about 400 yards to the campground.

Trip note: This wooded campground is on the Sauk River and is managed by the Department of Natural Resources. It may be a little difficult to get there, but that's why you'll probably be the only one there. Turn what is a negative for others into a positive for yourself.

Site 41   COLONIAL CREEK CAMPGROUND

Campsites, facilities: There are 162 campsites for tents or motorhomes up to 22 feet long. Picnic tables and fireplaces are provided. Flush toilets, piped water, a sanitary dump station and a boat ramp are available.

Reservations, fee: No reservations; $5 fee per night. Open from mid-April to early November.

Who to contact: Phone the Skagit District of the North Cascades National Park at 206-873-4590, or write them in Marblemount, WA 98267.

Location: Drive 25 miles east of Marblemount on Highway 20 and you'll see the campground.

Trip note: This campground is located at 1200 feet elevation along Colonial Creek in the Ross Lake National Recreation Area. Numerous hiking and fishing possibilities.

Site 42   NEWHALEM CREEK CAMPGROUND

Campsites, facilities: There are 129 campsites for tents or motorhomes. Picnic tables and fireplaces are provided. Flush toilets, piped water and a sanitary dump station are available.

Reservations, fee: No reservations; $5 fee per night. Open from mid-June to Labor Day.

Who to contact: Phone the Skagit District of the North Cascades National Park at 206-873-4590, or write them in Marblemount, WA 98267.

Location: Drive 15 miles northeast of Marblemount on Highway 20 and you'll see the entrance to the campground.

Trip note: A popular spot in North Cascades National Park, set along the Skagit River below Diablo Dam. Ross Lake is a short drive away. There are good hiking possibilities in the immediate area.

Site 43   GOODELL CREEK CAMPGROUND

Campsites, facilities: There are 22 campsites for tents or motorhomes up to 22 feet long. Picnic tables and fireplaces are provided. Pit toilets, piped water, a sanitary dump station and group sites are available.

Reservations, fee: No reservations; $3 fee per night.

Who to contact: Phone the Skagit District of the North Cascades National Park at 206-873-4590, or write them in Marblemount, WA 98267.

Location: Drive 15 miles east of Marblemount on Highway 20 to Newhalem and then go 1/2 mile further and you'll see the campground.

Trip note: This campground is an alternative to the nearby and larger camp 43. This one is set on Goodell Creek near the Skagit River in the Ross Lake National Recreation Area.

HOZOMEEN
Site **44**

Campsites, facilities: There are 122 campsites for tents or motorhomes up to 22 feet long.
  Picnic tables and fireplaces are provided. Pit toilets, piped water, a sanitary dump
  station and a boat launch on Ross Lake are available.

Reservations, fee: No reservations; $5 fee per night. Open from mid-May to late November.

Who to contact: Phone the Skagit District of the North Cascades National Park at 206-873-
  4590, or write them in Marblemount, WA 98267.

Location: Drive 40 miles south of the town of Hope (British Columbia) on Silver Skagit
  Road and you'll find the campground on the north end of Ross Lake.

Trip note: This camp is set just inside the border at the U.S./Canada line on the north shore
  of Ross Lake. Note that access is best from the north, leaving from the town of Hope.
  Takes an effort to get here. To some, it is worth that effort.

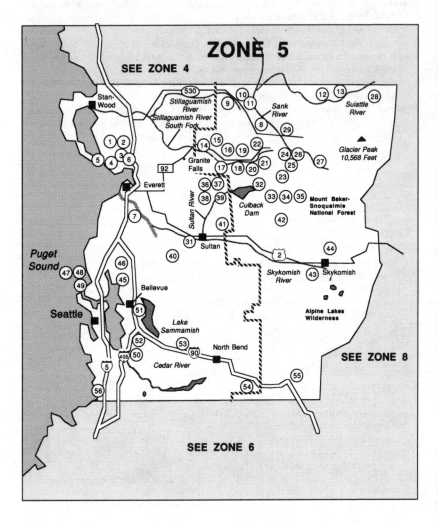

MOUNT BAKER

WENBERG
STATE PARK

Campsites, facilities: There are 65 tent sites and 10 sites for trailers or motorhomes up to 50 feet long. Picnic tables are provided and sanitary services, flush toilets, piped water, a store, cafe and playground are available. Electricity, piped water, hookups and showers are obtained for an extra fee. Some facilities are wheelchair accessible. Pets and motorbikes are permitted. Boat launching facilities and rentals are located on Lake Goodwin.

Reservations, fee: No reservations necessary; $6 fee per night. Open all year.

Who to contact: Phone at 206-652-7417, or write at 15430 East Lake Goodwin Road, Stanwood, WA 98292.

Location: Drive 13 miles north of Everett on I-5 to the 206/Smokey Point exit, then head west for five miles to the park.

Trip note: This state park is set along the shore of Lake Goodwin, where the trout fishing can be great. Power boats are allowed and there is a concession stand that provides food and fishing supplies. Lifeguards are on duty in the summer. There is a large day-use area and hiking trails nearby.

Site **2**

LAKE GOODWIN
RESORT

Campsites, facilities: There are 20 tent sites and 85 drive-through sites for trailers or motorhomes of any length. Electricity, piped water, sewer hookups and picnic tables are provided. Flush toilets, bottled gas, sanitary services, a recreation hall, store, cafe, laundromat, ice, playground, showers and firewood are available. Boat docks, launching facilities and rentals are nearby on Lake Goodwin.

Reservations, fee: Reservations accepted; $13 fee per night. American Express, Master-Card and Visa accepted. Open all year.

Who to contact: Phone at 206-652-8169, or write at 4726 176th NW, Stanwood, WA 98292.

Location: From Everett, drive 13 miles north on I-5 to the 206 exit, then drive west for five miles and you'll see the park.

Trip note: This private campground is set on Lake Goodwin, a lake known for good trout fishing. Motorboats are permitted on the lake and there is an 18-hole golf course nearby.

Site 3
CEDAR GROVE RESORT

Campsites, facilities: There are 10 tent sites and 47 sites for trailers or motorhomes. Electricity, piped water, sewer hookups and picnic tables are provided. Flush toilets, showers, playground and firewood are available. Bottled gas, sanitary services, a store, cafe, laundromat and ice are located within one mile. Boat docks, launching facilities and rentals are nearby on Lake Goodwin.

Reservations, fee: Reservations accepted; $12 fee per night. Open all year.

Who to contact: Phone at 206-652-7083, or write at 16529 52nd NW, Stanwood, WA 98292.

Location: From Everett, drive 13 miles north on I-5, then take the 206/Smokey Point exit and drive five miles west to 52nd Avenue NW, then turn south and go 1/2 mile to park.

Trip note: This wooded resort is set on the shore of Lake Goodwin near Wenberg State Park. Trout fishing and swimming are the highlights. Nearby recreation options include an 18-hole golf course.

Site 4
JIM MARION'S LAKE MARTHA RESORT

Campsites, facilities: There are seven tent sites and 24 drive-through sites for trailers or motorhomes of any length. Electricity, piped water, sewer hookups and picnic tables are provided. Flush toilets, sanitary services, showers and a laundromat are available. A store and ice are located within one mile. Boat docks and launching facilities are nearby on Lake Martha.

Reservations, fee: Reservations accepted; $12 fee per night. Open all year.

Who to contact: Phone at 206-652-8412, or write at 8105 Lakewood Road, Stanwood, WA 98292.

Location: From Everett, drive 13 miles north on I-5 to the 206/Smokey Point exit, then go seven miles west and bear left at fork in the road. Lake Martha is 1/2 mile away.

Trip note: Camping here is an option to the nearby and slightly larger Lake Goodwin. Good summer spot for fishing and swimming. Nearby recreation options include an 18-hole golf course.

Site 5
KAYAK POINT COUNTY PARK

Campsites, facilities: There are nine tent sites and 23 drive-through sites for trailers or motorhomes up to 25 feet long. Piped water and picnic tables are provided. Flush toilets, firewood and a playground are available. Pets are permitted. Boat docks and launching facilities are nearby on Puget Sound.

Reservations, fee: No reservations necessary; $7 fee per night. Open May to late-September.

Who to contact: Phone at 206-339-1208, or write at P.O. Box 310, Monroe, WA 98272.

Location: From Everett, drive north on I-5, then take the 199/Tulalip exit at Marysville. The road winds for 14 miles through the Tulalip Indian Reservation, then you'll see the park entrance on your left.

Trip note: This large, wooded county park is set on the shore of Puget Sound. Nearby recreation options include an 18-hole golf course.

Site 6
SMOKEY POINT
RV PARK

Campsites, facilities: There are 127 drive-through sites for trailers or motorhomes of any
length. Piped water and picnic tables are provided. Flush toilets, sanitary services,
showers, a recreation hall, laundromat, playground, electricity and sewer hookups
are available. Bottled gas, firewood, a store, cafe and ice are located within one mile.
Pets are permitted.

Reservations, fee: Reservations accepted; $12 fee per night. MasterCard and Visa accepted.
Open all year.

Who to contact: Phone at 206-652-7300, or write at 22910 15th Avenue SE, Bothell, WA
98021.

Location: From Everett, drive 13 miles north on I-5 to the 206/Smokey Point exit. Go west
for 1/10 mile on 172nd Street and you'll see the park on the south side.

Trip note: This is an ideal stopover for motorhome cruisers heading up I-5 and looking for a
place to spend the night. It is located just off the freeway and is only five miles from the state
park and resorts on Lake Goodwin. Nearby recreation options include marked bike trails.

Site 7
SILVER SHORES
RV PARK

Campsites, facilities: There are 10 tent sites and 83 sites for trailers or motorhomes.
Electricity, piped water and picnic tables are provided. Flush toilets, sanitary services,
showers and laundromat are available. Firewood, a store, cafe and ice are located
within one mile.

Reservations, fee: Reservations accepted; $15 fee per night. Open all year.

Who to contact: Phone at 206-337-8741, or write at 11621 West Silver Lake Road, Everett,
WA 98204.

Location: From Everett, take the 186 exit off I-5, and head east. You will see signs showing
you the way to the park.

Trip note: This is a good option to campsite 6 for travelers heading up I-5. This wooded
park is set along the shores of Silver Lake, a quiet lake with an eight-mph speed limit,
good trout fishing and swimming opportunities. Centrally located, close to shopping
and Seattle. There are tennis courts nearby.

Site 8
CLEAR CREEK

Campsites, facilities: There are seven tent sites and seven sites for trailers or motorhomes
up to 21 feet long. Picnic tables are provided. Pit or vault toilets, and firewood are
available. There is no piped water. Store, cafe, laundromat and ice are located within
two miles. Pets are permitted.

Reservations, fee: No reservations necessary; no fee. Open late-May to early-September.

Who to contact: Phone Mt. Baker-Snoqualmie National Forest at 206-436-1155, or write at
Darrington Ranger District, Darrington, WA 98241.

Location: From Darrington, drive 2 1/2 miles south on Highway 20, and you'll see the
campground entrance.

Trip note: A nice, secluded spot that does not get heavy use. This campground is set at the
confluence of Clear Creek and the Sauk River, which has been designated as a wild
and scenic river. A trail from camp leads about one mile up to Frog Lake.

FRENCH CREEK
Site **9**

Campsites, facilities: There are 24 tent sites and 24 sites for trailers or motorhomes up to 21 feet long. Picnic tables are provided. Pit or vault toilets, and firewood are available. There is piped water. A store is located within one mile. Some facilities are wheelchair accessible. Pets are permitted.

Reservations, fee: No reservations necessary; no fee. Open late-May to late-September.

Who to contact: Phone Mt. Baker-Snoqualmie National Forest at 206-436-1155, or write at Darrington Ranger Station, Darrington, WA 98241.

Location: From Darrington, drive eight miles west on Highway 530, then go south for 2/3 mile on Forest Service Road 2010 and you'll see the campground.

Trip note: This campground is set along French Creek about four miles from the boundaries of the Boulder River Wilderness. Visitors are strongly advised to obtain a Forest Service map, which details back roads and hiking trails.

SQUIRE CREEK
Site **10**   COUNTY PARK

Campsites, facilities: There are 30 drive-through sites for trailers or motorhomes up to 25 feet long. Piped water, sewer hookups and picnic tables are provided. Flush toilets, sanitary services and firewood are available. Pets are permitted. A store is located nearby in Darrington.

Reservations, fee: No reservations necessary; $5 fee per night. Open mid-May to mid-September.

Who to contact: Phone at 206-339-1208, or write at P.O. Box 310, Monroe, WA 98272.

Location: From Darrington, drive three miles west on Highway 530 and you'll see the park.

Trip note: This wooded park is set along Squire Creek about three miles from the boundaries of the Boulder River Wilderness. A low-cost motorhome park set near the outback.

CASCADE KAMLOOP
Site **11**   TROUT PARK

Campsites, facilities: There are eight tent sites and 24 sites for trailers or motorhomes of any length. Electricity, piped water, sewer hookups and picnic tables are provided. Flush toilets, sanitary services, showers, firewood and recreation hall are available. Bottled gas, a store, cafe, laundromat and ice are located within one mile. Motorbikes are permitted.

Reservations, fee: Reservations accepted; $8 fee per night. American Express, MasterCard and Visa accepted. Open all year.

Who to contact: Phone at 206-436-1003, or write at P.O. Box 353, Darrington, WA 98241.

Location: This campground is in Darrington. To get there take the 208 exit off I-5, then drive 31 miles east on Highway 530 and follow the "camping and fishing" signs to the campground.

Trip note: A little bit of both worlds, rustic yet all facilities available. A bonus is a nearby trout pond, which is stocked in season. No boats allowed. Nearby recreation options include marked hiking trails and tennis courts.

BUCK CREEK
Site **12**

Campsites, facilities: There are 19 tent sites and one site for a trailer or motorhome up to 21 feet long. Picnic tables are provided. Pit and vault toilets, and firewood are available. There is no piped water. Pets are permitted.

Reservations, fee: No reservations necessary; $3 per night. Open late-May to early-September.

Who to contact: Phone Mt. Baker-Snoqualmie National Forest at 206-436-1155, or write at Darrington Ranger District, Darrington, WA 98241.

Location: From Darrington, drive 7 1/2 miles north on Highway 530, then turn southeast on Forest Service Road 26 and drive 15 1/4 miles to the campground. A Forest Service map is essential.

Trip note: This primitive campground is set along Buck Creek near its confluence with the Suiattle River in the Glacier Peak Wilderness. Quiet and remote.

DOWNEY CREEK
Site **13**

Campsites, facilities: There are six tent sites and six sites for trailers up to 15 feet long. Picnic tables are provided. Pit or vault toilets and firewood are available. There is no piped water. Pets are permitted.

Reservations, fee: No reservations necessary; $3 fee per night. Open late-May to early-September.

Who to contact: Phone Mt. Baker-Snoqualmie National Forest at 206-436-1155, or write at Darrington Ranger District, Darrington, WA 98241.

Location: From Darrington, drive 7 1/2 miles north on Highway 530, then turn southeast on Forest Service Road 26 and drive 21 miles to the campground. A Forest Service map is essential.

Trip note: This is an option to camps 12 or 28. It is set deep in Glacier Peak Wilderness along Downey Creek near the Suiattle River. Two miles from the campground at Sulphur Creek camp is the trailhead that leads into the backcountry. A good spot to get away from it all.

TURLO
Site **14**

Campsites, facilities: There are 19 sites for tents or motorhomes up to 31 feet long. Picnic tables are provided. Pit or vault toilets, piped water and firewood are available. A store, cafe and ice are located within one mile in the town of Robe. Pets are permitted.

Reservations, fee: No reservations necessary; $6 fee per night. Open mid-May to late-September.

Who to contact: Phone Mt. Baker-Snoqualmie National Forest at 206-436-1155, or write at Mount Baker-Snoqualmie National Forest, Granite, WA 98252.

Location: From Granite Falls, go 10 2/3 miles east on Highway 92 and you'll see the campground entrance.

Trip note: This campground is set along the South Fork of the Stillaguamish River, the most westerly of six campgrounds located on this stretch of Highway 92. A Forest Service Public Information Center is nearby.

VERLOT

Site **15**

Campsites, facilities: There are 18 tent sites and 18 sites for trailers or motorhomes up to 31 feet long. Picnic tables are provided. Flush toilets, firewood and piped water are available. A store, cafe and ice are located within one mile. Pets are permitted.

Reservations, fee: No reservations necessary; $6 fee per night. Open mid-May to late-September.

Who to contact: Phone Mt. Baker-Snoqualmie National Forest at 206-436-1155, or write at Mount Baker-Snoqualmie National Forest, Granite, WA 98252.

Location: From Granite Falls, go 11 miles east on Highway 92 and you'll see the campground entrance.

Trip note: This campground is set along the South Fork of the Stillaguamish River, a short distance from the Lake Twenty-Two Research Natural Area and the Maid of the Woods Trail. A Forest Service map details back roads and hiking trails.

GOLD BASIN

Site **16**

Campsites, facilities: There are 93 tent sites and 83 sites for trailers or motorhomes up to 31 feet long. Picnic tables are provided. Vault toilets, piped water and firewood are available. A store, cafe and ice are located nearby. Some facilities are wheelchair accessible. Pets are permitted.

Reservations, fee: No reservations necessary; $6 fee per night. Open mid-May to early-September.

Who to contact: Phone Mt. Baker-Snoqualmie National Forest at 206-436-1155, or write at Mount Baker-Snoqualmie National Forest, Granite, WA 98252.

Location: From Granite Falls, go 13 1/2 miles east on Highway 92 and you'll see the campground entrance.

Trip note: One of the larger parks in the vicinity. With all facilities available this site is preferable for most motorhome campers. Set along the South Fork of the Stillaguamish River.

ESSWINE

Site **17**

Campsites, facilities: There are six tent sites and one site for trailers or motorhomes of any length. Picnic tables are provided. Pit or vault toilets and firewood are available, but there is no water. A store, cafe and ice are located within one mile. Pets are permitted.

Reservations, fee: No reservations necessary; $3 fee per night. Open mid-May to early-September.

Who to contact: Phone Mt. Baker-Snoqualmie National Forest at 206-436-1155, or write at Mount Baker-Snoqualmie National Forest, Granite, WA 98252.

Location: From Granite Falls, go 16 miles east on Highway 92 and you'll see the campground entrance.

Trip note: Only three miles from camp 16, but a very small, quiet and secluded camp. The lack of piped water is the only drawback.

BOARDMAN CREEK

Site **18**

Campsites, facilities: There are eight tent sites and three sites for trailers or motorhomes. Picnic tables are provided. Pit or vault toilets and firewood are available, but there is no piped water. Pets are permitted.

Reservations, fee: No reservations necessary; no fee. Open mid-May to early-September.

Who to contact: Phone Mt. Baker-Snoqualmie National Forest at 206-436-1155, or write at Mount Baker-Snoqualmie National Forest, Granite, WA 98252.

Location: From Granite Falls, go 16 1/2 miles east on Highway 92 and you'll see the campground entrance.

Trip note: Nearby Forest Service Roads will take you to several backcountry lakes, including Boardman Lake, Lake Evan, Clear Lake and Ashland Lakes. Get a Forest Service map, set up your camp, and go for it.

RIVER BAR

Site **19**

Campsites, facilities: There are 15 tent sites and 15 sites for trailers or motorhomes up to 31 feet long. Picnic tables are provided. Pit or vault toilets are available, but there is no piped water. Pets are permitted.

Reservations, fee: No reservations necessary; $3 fee per night. Open mid-May to late-September.

Who to contact: Phone Mt. Baker-Snoqualmie National Forest at 206-436-1155, or write at Mount Baker-Snoqualmie National Forest, Granite, WA 98252.

Location: From Granite Falls, go 18 miles east on Highway 92 and you'll see the campground entrance. A Forest Service map is essential.

Trip note: This campground is set along the South Fork of the Stillaguamish River, a shore distance from the boundary of Boulder River Wilderness.

RED BRIDGE

Site **20**

Campsites, facilities: There are 16 tent sites and 16 sites for trailers or motorhomes up to 31 feet long. Picnic tables are provided. Pit or vault toilets are available, but there is no piped water. Pets are permitted.

Reservations, fee: No reservations necessary; no fee. Open late-May to early-September.

Who to contact: Phone Mt. Baker-Snoqualmie National Forest at 206-436-1155, or write at Mount Baker-Snoqualmie National Forest, Granite, WA 98252.

Location: From Granite Falls, go 18 miles east on Highway 92 and you'll see the campground entrance.

Trip note: Another classic spot, one of several in vicinity. This campground is set on the South Fork of the Stillaguamish River near Mahardy Creek. A trailhead two miles east of camp leads to Granite Pass in the Boulder River Wilderness. Good base camp for backpacking expedition.

TULALIP MILLSITEE GROUP CAMP

Site **21**

Campsites, facilities: There are 12 tent sites and 12 sites for trailers or motorhomes up to 31

feet long. Picnic tables are provided. Pit or vault toilets are available, but no piped water is available. Pets are permitted.

Reservations, fee: Reservations required; no fee. Open mid-May to late-September.

Who to contact: Phone Mt. Baker-Snoqualmie National Forest at 206-436-1155, or write at Mount Baker-Snoqualmie National Forest, Granite, WA 98252.

Location: From Granite Falls, go 18 1/2 miles east on Highway 92 and you'll see the campground entrance.

Trip note: Like camps 14-22, this campground is set along the South Fork of the Stillaguamish River. A trailhead about one mile east of camp leads north into the Boulder River Wilderness. There are numerous creeks and streams that criss-cross this area.

Site 22   COAL CREEK BAR

Campsites, facilities: There are five tent sites and five sites for trailers up to 15 feet long. Picnic tables are provided. Pit or vault toilets and firewood are available. There is no piped water. Pets are permitted.

Reservations, fee: No reservations necessary; no fee. Open mid-May to late-September.

Who to contact: Phone Mt. Baker-Snoqualmie National Forest at 206-436-1155, or write at Mount Baker-Snoqualmie National Forest, Granite, WA 98252.

Location: From Granite Falls, go 23 1/2 miles east on Highway 92 and you'll see the campground entrance.

Trip note: This campground is set along the South Fork of the Stillaguamish River near Coal Creek. Nearby Forest Service roads lead to Coal Lake and a trailhead which then leads to other backcountry lakes. A Forest Service map will unlock this beautiful country for you.

Site 23   TWIN BRIDGES

Campsites, facilities: There are 10 tent sites and 10 sites for trailers or motorhomes up to 31 feet long. Picnic tables are provided. Pit or vault toilets are available, but there is no piped water.

Reservations, fee: No reservations necessary; no fee. Open June to early-September.

Who to contact: Phone Mt. Baker-Snoqualmie National Forest at 206-436-1155, or write at Mount Baker-Snoqualmie National Forest, Granite, WA 98252.

Location: From Granite Falls, go 30 miles east on Highway 92, then turn south on an all weather Forest Service road and go one mile to the campground. A Forest Service map is essential.

Trip note: This campground is out there in what we call "booger country." A beautiful spot set along the South Fork of the Sauk River. A trail one mile south of camp leads to Foggy and Weden Lakes.

Site 24   SOUTH FORK

Campsites, facilities: There are eight tent sites and three sites for trailers or motorhomes up to 15 feet long. Picnic tables are provided. Pit or vault toilets are available, but there is no piped water.

Reservations, fee: No reservations necessary; $3 fee per night. Open June to early-September.

Who to contact: Phone Mt. Baker-Snoqualmie National Forest at 206-436-1155, or write at Mount Baker-Snoqualmie National Forest, Granite, WA 98252.

Location: From Granite Falls, go 30 miles east on Highway 92, then head northeast for 4 1/2 miles on Forest Service Road 20. A Forest Service map is essential.

Trip note: An option to campsites 24-27. This campground is set along the South Fork of the Sauk River near the boundary of the Henry M. Jackson Wilderness. Nearby trails lead up Elliot Creek to Goat Lake, and up Bedal Creek to Sloan Peak at 7,835 feet elevation.

CHOKWICH
Site **25**   ▲

Campsites, facilities: There are six tent sites and five sites for trailers or motorhomes up to 21 feet long. Picnic tables are provided. Pit or vault toilets are available, but there is no piped water.

Reservations, fee: No reservations necessary; $3 fee per night. Open June to early-September.

Who to contact: Phone Mt. Baker-Snoqualmie National Forest at 206-436-1155, or write at Mount Baker-Snoqualmie National Forest, Granite, WA 98252.

Location: From Granite Falls, go 30 miles east on Highway 92, then head northeast for 4 1/2 miles on Forest Service Road. A Forest Service map is essential.

Trip note: This campground is adjacent to campsite 24 and offers the same possibilities.

BEDAL
Site **26**   ▲

Campsites, facilities: There are 16 tent sites and 16 sites for trailers or motorhomes up to 21 feet long. Picnic tables are provided. Pit or vault toilets are available, but there is no piped water. A Forest Service district office is nearby.

Reservations, fee: No reservations necessary; $3 fee per night. Open June to early-September.

Who to contact: Phone Mt. Baker-Snoqualmie National Forest at 206-436-1155, or write at Mount Baker-Snoqualmie National Forest, Granite, WA 98252.

Location: From Granite Falls, go 30 miles east on Highway 92, then head northeast for 6 1/2 miles on Forest Service Road 20. A Forest Service map is essential.

Trip note: This campground is set at the confluence of the North and South Forks of the Sauk River. North Fork Falls is about a mile up the North Fork of the Sauk from camp and worth the trip.

SLOAN CREEK
Site **27**   🌲

Campsites, facilities: There are seven tent sites. Picnic tables are provided. Pit or vault toilets are available, but there is no piped water. Firewood and a horse loading ramp are available.

Reservations, fee: No reservations necessary; $3 fee per night. Open June to early-September.

Who to contact: Phone Mt. Baker-Snoqualmie National Forest at 206-436-1155, or write at Mount Baker-Snoqualmie National Forest, Granite, WA 98252.

Location: From Granite Falls, go 30 miles east on Highway 92, then head northeast for seven miles on Forest Service Road 20, then 6 1/2 miles southeast on Forest Service Road 49. A Forest Service map is essential.

Trip note: This is the most remote of the drive-to campgrounds in the area. This one is a primitive spot, set at the confluence of Sloan Creek and the North Fork of the Sauk River. The camp acts as a trailhead for a hike that leads deep into Glacier Peak Wilderness, eventually connecting with the Pacific Crest Trail.

SULPHER CREEK
Site **28**

Campsites, facilities: There are nine tent sites and one site for a trailer to 15 feet long. Picnic tables are provided. Pit or vault toilets and firewood are available. There is no piped water.

Reservations, fee: No reservations necessary; $3 fee per night. Open June to early-September.

Who to contact: Phone Mt. Baker-Snoqualmie National Forest at 206-436-1155, or write at Mount Baker-Snoqualmie National Forest, Darrington, WA 98252.

Location: From Darrington, drive 7 1/2 miles north on Highway 530, then go 22 1/2 miles southeast on Forest Service Road 26. Forest Service map is advisable.

Trip note: This campground is set along the Suiattle River near the border of Glacier Peak Wilderness. A horse ramp and a trailhead leading deep into the backcountry can be found about a mile south of the campground. The trail hooks up with the Pacific Crest Trail. A good base camp for wilderness expedition.

WHITECHUCK
Site **29**

Campsites, facilities: There are 12 tent sites and six sites for trailers or motorhomes up to 15 feet long. Picnic tables are provided. Pit or vault toilets and firewood are available. There is no piped water.

Reservations, fee: No reservations necessary; $3 fee per night. Open June to early-September.

Who to contact: Phone Mt. Baker-Snoqualmie National Forest at 206-436-1155, or write at Mount Baker-Snoqualmie National Forest, Darrington, WA 98252.

Location: From Darrington, drive 1 1/3 miles north on Highway 530, then go 10 miles southeast on Forest Service Road 22.

Trip note: Very few people know of this spot, but it is one of the best if you like to hike and camp in primitive, rugged settings. This campground is set at the confluence of the White Chuck and the Sauk Rivers. Nearby trails lead to Peek-A-Boo Lake and Beaver Lake. A Forest Service map is essential.

FLOWING LAKE
COUNTY PARK
Site **30**

Campsites, facilities: There are eight tent sites and 29 drive-through sites for trailers or motorhomes up to 25 feet long. Electricity, piped water, sewer hookups and picnic tables are provided. Flush toilets, sanitary services, firewood and playground are available. Pets are permitted. Boat docks and launching facilities are nearby.

Reservations, fee: No reservations necessary; $7 fee per night. Open mid-May to mid-September.

Who to contact: Phone at 206-339-1208, or write at P.O. Box 310, Monroe, WA 98272.

Location: Drive eight miles northeast of Snohomish.

Trip note: A little something for everyone. The recreational possibilities include swimming, power boating and water skiing. Good fishing at the lake.

THUNDERBIRD PARK
Site **31**

Campsites, facilities: There are 40 tent sites and 68 sites for trailers or motorhomes of any length. Electricity, piped water, sewer hookups and picnic tables are provided. Flush toilets, sanitary services, recreation hall, store, laundromat, ice, playground and swimming pool are available. Showers and firewood are available for an extra fee. Pets are permitted. Boat launching facilities are nearby.

Reservations, fee: Reservations accepted; $12 fee per night. Open all year.

Who to contact: Phone at 206-794-8987, or write at 26426 Ben Howard Road, Monroe, WA 98272.

Location: Drive to the town of Monroe at the junction of Highways 2 and 203, then go south on Highway 203 for 1 1/4 miles, turn left on Ben Howard Road and drive five miles to the park.

Trip note: A good layover for Interstate 5 travelers who don't mind going a little out of their way. This park is set along the Skykomish River, is privately operated with all amenities available, and is just far enough away from the Seattle metropolis to give you a feeling of isolation.

CUTTHROAT LAKES
Site **32**

Campsites, facilities: There are 10 tent sites at this primitive, hike-in campground. Picnic tables, fire grills and tent pads are provided. Pit toilets are available, but there is no piped water.

Reservations, fee: No reservations necessary; no fee. Open all year.

Who to contact: Phone the Department of Natural Resources at 1-800-527-3305, or write Department of Natural Resources AW-11, 1065 South Capitol Way, Olympia, WA 98504.

Location: Start on Highway 2, 1/2 mile east of Sultan, go north on Sultan Basin Road for 14 miles, then keep left on SLS-4200 Road for two miles. Continue straight on P-5800 Road for one mile, then turn right on P-5000 Road and go 7 1/2 miles. Continue on SLS-6000 for 1 2/3 miles, then turn left on SLS-6100 Road and go 1 1/2 miles to the East Bald Mountain Trailhead. From East Bald Mountain Trailhead, hike three miles to the campsite.

Trip note: To reach this spot requires following difficult directions, but it is worth the effort because of the beautiful lakeside camps. Good trout fishing and hiking.

LITTLE GREIDER LAKE
Site **33**

Campsites, facilities: There are nine tent sites at this primitive hike-in campground. Picnic tables, fire grills and tent pads are provided. Pit toilets and firewood are available. There is no piped water.

Reservations, fee: No reservations necessary; no fee. Open all year.

Who to contact: Phone the Department of Natural Resources at 1-800-527-3305, or write

Department of Natural Resources AW-11, 1065 South Capitol Way, Olympia, WA 98504.

Location: Start on Highway 2, 1/2 mile east of the town of Sultan and go north on Sultan Basin Road for 13 1/2 miles, then go straight on the middle road (SLS-4000 Road) for about 8 1/2 miles to the Greider Lake Trailhead. From Greider Lake Trailhead, hike 2 1/2 miles to campsite.

Trip note: Prime country for hiking, backpacking, and trout fishing. This primitive, wooded campground is on Little Grieder Lake. Detailed map of area from Department of Natural Resources is essential before taking off for back country.

Site 34   BIG GREIDER LAKE

Campsites, facilities: There are five tent sites at this primitive hike-in campground. Picnic tables, fire grills and tent pads are provided. Pit toilets and firewood are available, but there is no piped water.

Reservations, fee: No reservations necessary; no fee. Open all year.

Who to contact: Phone the Department of Natural Resources at 1-800-527-3305, or write Department of Natural Resources AW-11, 1065 South Capitol Way, Olympia, WA 98504.

Location: Start on Highway 2, 1/2 mile east of the town of Sultan and go north on Sultan Basin Road for 13 2/3 miles. Take the middle road (SLS-4000 Road) for about 8 1/2 miles to the Greider Lake Trailhead. From Greider Lake Trailhead, hike three miles to campsite.

Trip note: This primitive campground is on Big Greider Lake. A good alternative to campsite 33, which is on Little Grieder Lake.

Site 35   BOULDER LAKE

Campsites, facilities: There are nine campsites for tents at this primitive hike-in campground. Picnic tables, fire grills and tent pads are provided. Pit toilets and firewood are available. There is no piped water.

Reservations, fee: No reservations necessary; no fee. Open all year.

Who to contact: Phone the Department of Natural Resources at 1-800-527-3305, or write Department of Natural Resources AW-11, 1065 South Capitol Way, Olympia, WA 98504.

Location: Start on Highway 2, 1/2 miles east of the town of Sultan and go north on Sultan Basin Road for 13 1/2 miles. Then go straight on the middle road (SLS-4000 Road) for about 8 1/2 miles to the Greider Lake Trailhead. Stay right on SLS-7000 Road and drive one mile to the Boulder Lake Trailhead. From Boulder Lake Trailhead hike 3 1/2 miles to campsite.

Trip note: This primitive hike-in campground is on Boulder Lake. One of three hike-in camps, 33-35, spotlighted in immediate area.

Site 36   BEAVER PLANT LAKE

Campsites, facilities: There are six tent sites at this primitive, hike-in campground. Picnic tables, firegrills and tentpads are provided. Pit toilets and firewood are available. There is no piped water.

Reservations, fee: No reservations necessary; no fee. Open all year.

Who to contact: Phone the Department of Natural Resources at 1-800-527-3305, or write Department of Natural Resources AW-11, 1065 South Capitol Way, Olympia, WA 98504.

Location: Start at the east end of the town of Granite Falls on Highway 92 and go north on Mountain Loop Highway for 15 miles, then turn north on Forest Service Road 4020 and drive 2 1/2 miles. Turn right on Forest Service Road 4021 and drive two miles to the Ashland Lakes Trailhead. From Ashland Lakes Trailhead hike one mile to campsite.

Trip note: This campground is on Beaver Plant Lake, one of four campgrounds, besides 36-39, highlighted in area. Map from Department of Natural Resources details trails and backcountry.

Site 37   UPPER ASHLAND LAKE

Campsites, facilities: There are six tent sites at this primitive, hike-in campground. Picnic tables, firegrills and tentpads are provided. Pit toilets and firewood are available, but there is no piped water.

Reservations, fee: No reservations necessary; no fee. Open all year.

Who to contact: Phone the Department of Natural Resources at 1-800-527-3305, or write Department of Natural Resources AW-11, 1065 South Capitol Way, Olympia, WA 98504.

Location: Start at the east end of the town of Granite Falls on Highway 92, go north on Mountain Loop Highway for 15 miles, then turn north on Forest Service Road 4020 and drive 2 1/2 miles. Turn right on Forest Service Road 4021 and drive two miles to the Ashland Lakes Trailhead. From Ashland Lakes Trailhead hike 1 1/2 miles to campsite.

Trip note: The lake is just a short hike away and well worth the effort. Detailed map of area essential.

Site 38   LOWER ASHLAND LAKE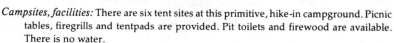

Campsites, facilities: There are six tent sites at this primitive, hike-in campground. Picnic tables, firegrills and tentpads are provided. Pit toilets and firewood are available. There is no water.

Reservations, fee: No reservations necessary; no fee. Open all year.

Who to contact: Phone the Department of Natural Resources at 1-800-527-3305, or write Department of Natural Resources AW-11, 1065 South Capitol Way, Olympia, WA 98504.

Location: Start at the east end of the town of Granite Falls on Highway 92. Go north on Mountain Loop Highway for 15 miles, then turn north on Forest Service Road 4020 and drive 2 1/2 miles. Turn right on Forest Service Road 4021 and drive two miles to the Ashland Lakes Trailhead, then hike two miles to campsite.

Trip note: This campground is on Lower Ashland Lake, set adjacent to campsite 37.

Site 39   TWIN FALLS LAKE

Campsites, facilities: There are five tent sites. Picnic tables are provided. Pit or vault toilets and firewood are available.

Reservations, fee: No reservations necessary; no fee. Open all year.

Who to contact: Phone the Department of Natural Resources at 1-800-527-3305, or write Department of Natural Resources AW-11, 1065 South Capitol Way, Olympia, WA 98504.

Location: Start at the east end of the town of Granite Falls on Highway 92. Go north on Mountain Loop Highway for 15 miles, then turn north on Forest Service Road 4020 and drive 2 1/2 miles. Turn right on Forest Service Road 4021 and drive two miles to the Ashland Lakes Trailhead. From Ashland Lakes Trailhead hike 3 1/2 miles to campsite.

Trip note: Good hiking, backpacking and trout fishing for people willing to grunt a little. A beautiful and secluded area, yet not a long drive from Seattle.

ELWELL
Site **40**

Campsites, facilities: There are 18 campsites for tents or small trailers. Picnic tables, firegrills and tentpads are provided. Pit toilets, piped water and firewood are available.

Reservations, fee: No reservations necessary; no fee. Open all year.

Who to contact: Phone the Department of Natural Resources at 1-800-527-3305, or write Department of Natural Resources AW-11, 1065 South Capitol Way, Olympia, WA 98504.

Location: From the junction of I-90 and Highway 202 in North Bend, drive north on 202 for eight miles to Fall City, then head north on 203 for about 10 miles to the town of Stillwater. Go north on Kelley Road for three miles, then turn right on Stossel Creek Road and go 4 1/2 miles. Stay left and continue 1 1/2 miles, then stay left again and go 1 1/2 miles. The campground is on the right.

Trip note: This camp was closed in 1987, but will be open to the public when management funds become available. Phone 1-800-527-3305. An obscure and primitive camp that is rarely visited, yet not all that far from Seattle. That combination makes it a winner, and it's free to boot.

WALLACE FALLS
Site **41**   STATE PARK

Campsites, facilities: There are six tent sites. Picnic tables are provided. Flush toilets and piped water are available. Pets and motorbikes are permitted. Some facilities are wheelchair accessible.

Reservations, fee: No reservations necessary; $6 fee per night. Open all year.

Who to contact: Phone at 206-793-0420, or write at P.O. Box 106, Goldbar, WA 98251.

Location: Drive 38 miles north and east of Bellevue via I-405, Highway 522 and Highway 2. The park is two miles northeast of the town of Goldbar.

Trip note: A beautiful and tiny spot nestled in the forest near the scenic Wallace Falls. Seattle is loaded with people, but very few of them know of this jewel.

TROUBLESOME
Site **42**   CREEK A & B

Campsites, facilities: There are 27 tent sites and 27 sites for trailers or motorhomes up to 21 feet long. Picnic tables are provided. Pit or vault toilets and firewood are available.

Pets are permitted.

Reservations, fee: Reservations required; no fee. Open mid-May to mid-September.

Who to contact: Phone Mt. Baker-Snoqualmie National Forest at 206-677-2414, or write at Skykomish Ranger District, Skykomish, WA 98288.

Location: From the junction of Highways 2 and 522, head east for 20 miles until you get to the town of Index. From there, drive 12 miles northeast on County Road 63 to the campground.

Trip note: Here's another one we bet you never heard of. This campground is set along the North Fork of the Skykomish River. There is a nature trail adjacent to camp, and a mineral springs about three miles to the east along the county road.

MILLER RIVER
Site **43**

Campsites, facilities: There are 24 tent sites and 24 sites for trailers or motorhomes up to 21 feet long. Picnic tables are provided. Pit or vault toilets are available, but there is no piped water. A store, cafe, laundromat and ice are available within one mile. Pets are permitted.

Reservations, fee: Reservations required; no fee. Open mid-May to October.

Who to contact: Phone Mt. Baker-Snoqualmie National Forest at 206-677-2414, or write at Skykomish Ranger District, Skykomish, WA 98288.

Location: From the town of Skykomish, drive 2 1/2 miles west on Highway 2, then go south on County Road 6400 for one mile. Turn on Forest Service Road 6410 and go two miles south.

Trip note: This campground is set along the Miller River a short distance from the boundary of the Alpine Lakes Wilderness. It is prime mountain territory. If you continue another four miles on Forest Service Road 6412 you will get to a trailhead leading to Lake Dorothy and many other backcountry lakes. A Forest Service map is essential.

BECKLER RIVER
Site **44**

Campsites, facilities: There are 10 tent sites and 10 sites for trailers or motorhomes up to 21 feet long. Picnic tables are provided. Vault toilets, piped water and firewood are available. Store, cafe, laundromat and ice are located within one mile. Pets are permitted.

Reservations, fee: No reservations necessary; $8 fee per night. Open mid-May to mid-September.

Who to contact: Phone Mt. Baker-Snoqualmie National Forest at 206-677-2414, or write at Skykomish Ranger District, Skykomish, WA 98288.

Location: From the town of Skykomish, go one mile east on Highway 2, then two miles north on Forest Service Road 65.

Trip note: This spot is on the Beckler River and is a good option to campsite 43. Located just 60 miles from Seattle, yet little known.

Site **45**
BOTHELL CANYON
MOTORHOME AND RV PARK

Campsites, facilities: There are 26 sites for trailers or motorhomes of any length. Elec-

tricity, piped water and sewer hookups are provided. Flush toilets, piped water and a laundromat are available. Showers are obtained for an extra fee. Bottled gas, sanitary services, store, cafe and ice are located within one mile. Pets are permitted.

Reservations, fee: Reservations accepted; $12 fee per night. Open all year.

Who to contact: Phone at 206-481-3005, or write at 22625 31st Avenue SE, Bothell, WA 98021.

Location: Drive eight miles north of Bellevue on I-405 to Bothell. In Bothell, take the 26 exit off I-405 and drive south to 228th Street, then turn east and drive 1 1/4 miles to 22625 31st Avenue SE.

Trip note: This wooded park is near Seattle and is for motorhomes and trailers only. Nearby recreation options include an 18-hole golf course, hiking trails, marked bike trails and a riding stable.

Site 46   SEATTLE NORTH RV PARK

Campsites, facilities: There are an unspecified number of tent sites and 180 drive-through sites for trailers or motorhomes of any length. Piped water and picnic tables are provided. Flush toilets, bottled gas, sanitary services, showers, firewood, recreation hall, store, laundromat, ice and playground are available. Electricity, sewer hookups and a swimming pool are obtained for an extra fee. Pets are permitted.

Reservations, fee: Reservations accepted; $18 fee per night. MasterCard and Visa accepted. Open all year.

Who to contact: Phone at 206-481-1972, or write at 22121 17th Avenue SE, Bothell, WA 98021.

Location: Take the Highway 405 exit off I-5 north of Seattle and drive three miles southeast to Highway 527. From there, go one block south, then one block east on 228th Avenue. On 15th go two blocks and you'll see the park.

Trip note: One of the Seattle options for motorhome campers. Nearby recreation options include an 18-hole golf course and tennis courts.

Site 47   TRAILER HAVEN

Campsites, facilities: There are 15 sites for trailers or motorhomes of any length in this adult only campground. Electricity, piped water and sewer hookups are provided. Flush toilets, bottled gas, showers and laundromat are available. Store, cafe and ice are located within one mile.

Reservations, fee: No reservations necessary; $15 fee per night. Open all year.

Who to contact: Phone at 206-362-4211, or write at 11724 Aurora Avenue North, Seattle, WA 98133.

Location: From I-5 in Seattle, take the 173 exit and go west to North Gateway and then to Highway 99. When you get to Aurora, turn north and go to 11724 Aurora Avenue North.

Trip note: Nearby recreation options include an 18-hole golf course, hiking trails, a full service marina and tennis courts.

Site 48   HOLIDAY PARK RESORT

Campsites, facilities: There are 22 sites for trailers or motorhomes up to 32 feet long.

Electricity, piped water, sewer hookups and picnic tables are provided. Flush toilets, showers, a cafe and laundromat are available. Bottled gas, sanitary services, store and ice are located within one mile.

Reservations, fee: Reservations accepted; $12 fee per night. Open all year.

Who to contact: Phone at 206-542-2760, or write at 19250 Aurora Avenue North, Seattle, WA 98133.

Location: From I-5 in Seattle, take the 175th Avenue exit off I-5 and go west to Aurora Avenue. Turn north and head to 19250 Aurora Avenue North.

Trip note: An alternative to campsite 47 situated nearby. Recreation options include an 18-hole golf course, marked bike trails and tennis courts.

Site 49 ORCHARD TRAILER PARK

Campsites, facilities: There are 10 sites for trailers or motorhomes of any length. Electricity, piped water and sewer hookups are provided. Flush toilets, showers and a laundromat are available. Bottled gas, store, cafe and ice are located within one mile. Pets are permitted.

Reservations, fee: No reservations necessary; $12 fee per night. Open all year.

Who to contact: Phone at 206-243-1210, or write at 4011 South 146th Street, Seattle, WA 98168.

Location: From I-5 in Seattle, take the 154 or Burien exit and go one mile west to Highway 99. Drive north for 3/4 mile to South 146th Avenue, turn east and drive to trailer park.

Trip note: The smallest and most intimate of the motorhome parks in the Seattle area. Nearby recreation options include an 18-hole golf course.

Site 50 LAKE SHORE MANOR

Campsites, facilities: There are 25 sites for trailers or motorhomes of any length. Electricity, piped water and sewer hookups are provided. Flush toilets, Showers, recreation hall and laundromat are available. Store, cafe and ice are located within one mile. Pets are permitted.

Reservations, fee: No reservations necessary; $11 fee per night. Open all year.

Who to contact: Phone at 206-772-0299, or write at 11448 Rainier South, Seattle, WA 98178.

Location: From the junction of I-5 and Highway 405 in Seattle, take the Renton exit and drive three miles north to Rainier Avenue and 11448 Rainier South.

Trip note: Nearby recreation options include an 18-hole golf course, hiking trails, marked bike trails and a full service marina.

Site 51 VASA PARK RESORT

Campsites, facilities: There are 16 tent sites and five sites for trailers or motorhomes of any length. Piped water, sewer hookups and picnic tables are provided. Flush toilets, sanitary services, a playground, electricity and showers are available. Bottled gas, firewood, store, cafe and laundromat are located within one mile. Pets and motorbikes are permitted. Boat launching facilities are nearby on Lake Sammamish.

Reservations, fee: Reservations accepted; $10 per night. Open mid-May to October.

Who to contact: Phone at 206-746-3260, or write at 3560 West Lake Sammamish, Bellevue, WA 98008.

Location: From I-90 in Bellevue, take the 13 exit and drive one mile north. The campground is on the west side of Lake Sammamish.

Trip note: The most rustic of the parks in the immediate Seattle area. This resort is on Lake Sammamish. The State Park is at the south end of the lake. Nearby recreation options include an 18-hole golf course, hiking trails, marked bike trails and a riding stable.

Site 52   TRAILER INNS RV PARK AND RECREATION CENTER

Campsites, facilities: There are 115 drive-through sites for trailers or motorhomes of any length. Electricity, piped water, sewer hookups and picnic tables are provided. Flush toilets, bottled gas, showers, recreation hall, swimming pool, laundromat, ice and playground are available. Sanitary services, store and cafe are available within one mile. Pets and motorbikes are permitted.

Reservations, fee: Reservations accepted; $14 fee per night. MasterCard and Visa accepted. Open all year.

Who to contact: Phone at 206-747-9181, or write at 15531 I-90, Bellevue, WA 98006.

Location: From the junction of Highway 405 and I-90 in Bellevue, go east on Highway 90 for two miles to exit 11A, then go south on the frontage road to the park.

Trip note: A nice spot for motorhome travelers, with nearby Lake Sammamish State Park a highlight. Nearby recreation options include an 18-hole golf course, hiking trails, marked bike trails and tennis courts.

Site 53   SNOQUALMIE RIVER CAMPGROUND

Campsites, facilities: There are 100 tent sites and 80 drive-through sites for trailers or motorhomes of any length. Piped water and picnic tables are provided. Flush toilets, sanitary services, showers and playground are available. Electricity and firewood can be obtained for an extra fee. Bottled gas, store, cafe, laundromat and ice are located within one mile. Pets and motorbikes are permitted. Boat launching facilities are nearby.

Reservations, fee: Reservations accepted; $7 fee per night. Open April to late-October and some off-season weekends.

Who to contact: Phone at 206-222-5545, or write at P.O. Box 16, Fall City, WA 98024.

Location: Go 14 miles east of Bellevue on I-90 until you get to the Preston-Fall City exit 22. Go five miles north on Highway 203 and follow the signs to the campground.

Trip note: If you're in the Seattle area and stuck for a place for the night, this is a prime choice. This wooded campground is set along the Snoqualmie River. Nearby recreation options include an 18-hole golf course, hiking trails and marked bike trails.

Site 54   TINKHAM

Campsites, facilities: There are 13 tent sites and 27 sites for trailers or motorhomes up to 21 feet long. Picnic tables are provided. Pit or vault toilets, firewood and piped water are available. Some facilities are wheelchair accessible. Pets are permitted.

Reservations, fee: No reservations necessary; $5 fee per night. Open mid-May to mid-September.

Who to contact: Phone Mt. Baker-Snoqualmie National Forest at 206-888-1421, or write at North Bend Ranger District, North Bend, WA 98045.

Location: Drive 31 miles southeast of Bellevue on I-90 (10 miles southeast of North Bend), then go 1 1/2 miles southeast on Forest Service Road 55 to campground. A Forest Service map is advisable.

Trip note: This campground is set along the Snoqualmie River, and is a good layover for the night for travelers heading west to Seattle. Nearby back-country roads are detailed on Forest Service map.

COMMONWEALTH
Site **55**

Campsites, facilities: There are six tent sites and six sites for trailers or motorhomes. Picnic tables are provided. Pit or vault toilets and firewood are available. There is no piped water. A cafe is located within one mile. Pets are permitted.

Reservations, fee: No reservations necessary; $3 fee per night. Open June to mid-September.

Who to contact: Phone Mt. Baker-Snoqualmie National Forest at 206-888-1421, or write at North Bend Ranger District, North Bend, WA 98045.

Location: Drive 43 miles southeast of Bellevue on I-90 (22 miles southeast of North Bend), then go 200 yards north on Forest Service Road 58 and you'll see the campground. A Forest Service map is essential.

Trip note: This campground is set along the Snoqualmie River near the Snoqualmie Summit Ski Area. There are several trails nearby that lead into the Alpine Lakes Wilderness backcountry. Massive Keechulus Lake is about three miles south from camp, across Highway 90.

SALTWATER
STATE PARK
Site **56**

Campsites, facilities: There are 53 sites for self-contained motorhomes up to 50 feet long. Picnic tables are provided. Flush toilets, sanitary services, showers, playground and firewood are available. A store, cafe and ice are located within one mile. Some facilities are wheelchair accessible. Pets are permitted. Boat buoys are nearby on Puget Sound.

Reservations, fee: No reservations necessary; $6 fee per night. Open all year.

Who to contact: Phone at 206-764-4128, or write at 25205 8th Place South, Kent, WA 98031.

Location: Drive eight miles south of Seattle on I-5 to Des Moines, then go two miles south on Highway 509 to the park.

Trip note: A nice state park for motorhome campers set on the edge of Seattle and beautiful Puget Sound. Beaches offer clamming and picnic facilities. There are also foot trails that lead through Kent Smith Canyon.

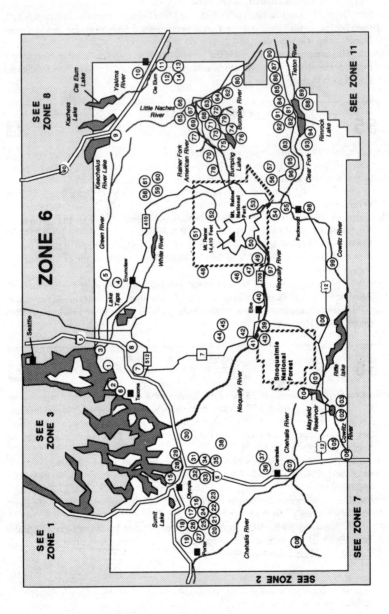

MOUNT RAINIER

Site 1
DASH POINT
STATE PARK

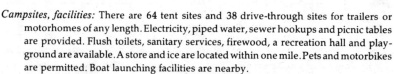

Campsites, facilities: There are 110 tent sites and 28 sites for trailers or motorhomes up to 35 feet long. Picnic tables are provided. Flush toilets, sanitary services, playground, electricity, piped water, showers and firewood are available. Pets are permitted.

Reservations, fee: No reservations necessary; $6 fee per night. Open all year.

Who to contact: Phone at 206-593-2206, or write at 5700 West Dash Point Road, Federal Way, WA 98003.

Location: From Tacoma, drive five miles northeast on Highway 509 and you'll see the park.

Trip note: This urban state park has beach access. Nearby recreation options include an 18-hole golf course and marked hiking trails. The city of Tacoma offers a variety of activities and attractions, including the Tacoma Art Museum with a childrens' gallery, the Washington State Historical Society Museum, the Seymour Botanical Conservatory at Wrights Park, Point Defiance Park, Zoo and Aquarium, the Western Washington Forest Industries Museum and the Fort Lewis Military Museum. The Old Town area along the waterfront has been renovated and there are two public fishing piers there.

Site 2
RIVERBEND
RV PARK

Campsites, facilities: There are 64 tent sites and 38 drive-through sites for trailers or motorhomes of any length. Electricity, piped water, sewer hookups and picnic tables are provided. Flush toilets, sanitary services, firewood, a recreation hall and playground are available. A store and ice are located within one mile. Pets and motorbikes are permitted. Boat launching facilities are nearby.

Reservations, fee: Reservations accepted; $9 fee per night. Open all year.

Who to contact: Phone at 206-456-1741, or write at 3802 Sixth Avenue, Tacoma, WA 98406.

Location: In Tacoma, take the 116 exit off I-5 and go 3 1/4 miles south on Old Pacific Highway. Turn east on Durgin Road and drive to the park.

Trip note: This wooded campground is on the river. Nearby recreation options include an 18-hole golf course, marked hiking trails and marked bike trails. For information on the attractions in Tacoma, see the trip note for campsite 1.

Site 3
CEDARS TRAILER
AND RV PARK

Campsites, facilities: There are 19 sites for trailers or motorhomes of any length. Electricity, piped water and sewer hookups are provided. Flush toilets and showers are available for an extra fee. Bottled gas, a store, cafe, laundromat and ice are located within one mile. Pets are permitted.

Reservations, fee: Reservations accepted; $10 fee per night. Open all year.

Who to contact: Phone at 206-922-3119, or write at 8425 Pacific Highway East, Tacoma, WA 98422.

Location: Take the 136 exit near Fife off I-5 and drive north to the Pacific Highway. Head northeast to 8425 Pacific Highway East.

Trip note: This wooded park is in a more rural area of Tacoma. For information on the activities and attractions in Tacoma, see the trip note for campsite 1.

Site 4
KANASKAT-PALMER
RECREATION AREA

Campsites, facilities: There are 31 tent sites and 19 drive-through sites for trailers or motorhomes up to 35 feet long. Electricity and picnic tables are provided. Flush toilets, showers and sanitary services are available. Some facilities are wheelchair accessible. Pets and motorbikes are permitted. Boat rentals are available on the Green River.

Reservations, fee: No reservations necessary; $6 fee per night. Open all year, with limited facilities in the winter.

Who to contact: Phone at 206-886-0148, or write at 23700 Flamingo Geyser, Auburn, WA 98002.

Location: Drive 28 miles east of Tacoma on Highway 164/410 to the town of Enumclaw, then go northeast on Farman Road for 11 miles, and you'll see the park.

Trip note: This wooded campground offers private campsites set along the Green River. In summer, the river is ideal for rafting and kayaking. In winter, it attracts a nice run of steelhead. Year around you can explore the area's hiking trils.

Site 5
GREEN RIVER
GORGE RESORT

Campsites, facilities: There are 60 tent sites and 20 drive-through sites for trailers or motorhomes up to 30 feet long. Piped water, sewer hookups and picnic tables are provided. Flush toilets, sanitary services, laundromat, ice and playground are available. Electricity, showers and firewood can be obtained for an extra fee. Pets and motorbikes are permitted.

Reservations, fee: Reservations accepted; $8 fee per night. MasterCard and Visa accepted. Open all year.

Who to contact: Phone at 206-886-2302, or write at 29500 Green River Gorge Road, Enumclaw, WA 98022.

Location: Drive 28 miles east of Tacoma on Highway 164/410 to the town of Enumclaw, then go eight miles north on Highway 169 to Black Diamond Road and four miles east on Green River Gorge Road to the resort.

Trip note: A nice spot, yet not far from the Tacoma/Seattle metroplex. This resort is set along the Green River, where you can raft or fish. Nearby recreation options include marked hiking trails and tennis courts.

Site **6**
FIR ACRES MOTORHOME AND RV PARK

Campsites, facilities: There are 20 sites for trailers or motorhomes of any length. Electricity, piped water, sewer hookups and picnic tables are provided. Flush toilets, showers and a laundromat are available. Bottled gas, sanitary services, store, cafe and ice are located within one mile. Pets are permitted.

Reservations, fee: Reservations accepted; $12 fee per night. Open all year.

Who to contact: Phone at 206-588-7894, or write at 12623 Bridgeport Way SW, Tacoma, WA 98499.

Location: Take the 125 exit off I-5 near Tacoma and drive 1/4 mile east to the park.

Trip note: Nearby recreation options include an 18-hole golf course and a full service marina. See the trip note for campsite 1 for list of attractions in Tacoma.

Site **7**
KARWAN VILLAGE MOTORHOME AND RV PARK

Campsites, facilities: There are 10 sites for trailers or motorhomes up to 32 feet long in this adults only campground. Electricity, piped water and sewer hookups are provided. Flush toilets, showers, laundromat, bottled gas, sanitary services, store, cafe and ice are available. Pets are permitted.

Reservations, fee: Reservations accepted; $8 fee per night. Open all year.

Who to contact: Phone at 206-588-2501, or write at 2621 South 84th Street, Tacoma, WA 98409.

Location: Take the 128 exit off I-5 near Tacoma and drive 200 yards west on 84th Street to the park.

Trip note: Nearby recreation options include an 18-hole golf course and Wapato Park. See the trip note for campsite 1 for a list of attractions in Tacoma.

Site **8**
MAJESTIC MOBILE MANORE

Campsites, facilities: There are five tent sites and 123 drive-through sites for trailers or motorhomes of any length. Electricity, piped water and sewer hookups are provided. Flush toilets, bottled gas, sanitary services, showers, recreation hall, store, laundromat, ice and swimming pool are available. A cafe is located within one mile. Pets and motorbikes are permitted.

Reservations, fee: Reservations accepted; $12 fee per night. Open all year.

Who to contact: Phone at 206-845-3144, or write at 6906 52nd Street East, Puyallup, WA 98371.

Location: Take the 135 exit off I-5 near Tacoma and drive four miles east on Highway 167 (River Road) to the park.

Trip note: This park is set along the Puyallup River. Nearby recreation options include an 18-hole golf course, a full service marina and tennis courts. For information on the attractions in Tacoma, see the trip note for campsite 1.

Site 9 LAKE EASTON STATE PARK

Campsites, facilities: There are 100 tent sites and 45 sites for trailers or motorhomes up to 20 feet long. Picnic tables are provided. Flush toilets, sanitary services, playground, electricity, piped water, sewer hookups, showers and firewood are available. A cafe and ice are located within one mile. Some facilities are wheelchair accessible. Pets are permitted. Boat launching facilities and floats are located on Lake Easton.

Reservations, fee: No reservations necessary; $6 fee per night. Open all year.

Who to contact: Phone at 206-656-2230, or write at P.O. Box 26, Easton, WA 98925.

Location: This state park is about 80 miles east of Tacoma. To get there, take Highway 18 to I-90 and head east for 45 miles to the town of Easton. The park is one mile west of town on I-90.

Trip note: This campground offers a multitude of recreational opportunity. For starters, it is set along the shore of Lake Easton, with Kachess Lake and Keechelus Lake just a short drive. The park provides opportunites for both summer and winter recreation, including swimming, fishing, boating, cross-country skiing and snowmobiling. Nearby recreation options include an 18- hole golf course and hiking trails.

Site 10 SUN COUNTRY GOLF

Campsites, facilities: There are five tent sites and 23 sites for trailers or motorhomes up to 32 feet long. Electricity, piped water, sewer hookups and picnic tables are provided. Flush toilets, showers, recreation hall and cafe are available. Pets and motorbikes are permitted.

Reservations, fee: Reservations accepted; $8 fee per night. Open mid-April to mid-October.

Who to contact: Phone at 509-674-2226, or write at P.O. Box 364, Cle Elum, WA 98922.

Location: Drive six miles west of Cle Elum on I-90, then take the 78 exit and follow the signs to the park.

Trip note: This park provides an option to campsite 9, also set near the Yakima River. Nearby recreation options include an 18-hole golf course, marked hiking trails and marked bike trails.

Site 11 MCKEAN'S TRAILER PARK

Campsites, facilities: There are 15 sites for trailers or motorhomes. Electricity, piped water, sewer hookups and picnic tables are provided. A cafe is available. Bottled gas, sanitary services, a store, laundromat and ice are located within one mile. Pets are permitted.

Reservations, fee: Reservations accepted; $9 fee per night. Open March to late-December.

Who to contact: Phone at 309-674-2254, or write at 1011 East 1st Street, Cle Elum, WA 98922.

Location: This park is in the town of Cle Elum at 1011 East 1st Street.

Trip note: You can rent rafts and canoes in Cle Elum and take a 16-mile raft trip down the Yakima River to Thorp, where they offer to pick you up and bring you back to Cle Elum. Cle Elum is the Indian word for "swift water". The Cle Elum Historical Telephone Museum is also in town. Campsites 9, 10 and 12 are also set near the Yakima River.

TRAILER CORRAL
Site **12**

Campsites, facilities: There are 10 tent sites and 20 sites for trailers or motorhomes of any length. Electricity, piped water, sewer hookups and picnic tables are provided. Flush toilets, sanitary services, showers, firewood, laundromat and ice are available. A store is located within one mile. Pets are permitted. Boat launching facilities are nearby.

Reservations, fee: Reservations accepted; $8 fee per night. Open all year.

Who to contact: Phone at 509-674-2433, or write at Route 2, Box 128, Cle Elum, WA 98922.

Location: From the town of Cle Elum, drive one mile east on I-90 to the 85 exit, then head east on Highway 970 for one mile to the park.

Trip note: This wooded campground is set along the Yakima River. See trip note about campsite 11 for river rafting information. Nearby recreation options include an 18-hole golf course, marked hiking trails and tennis courts.

TANEUM
Site **13**

Campsites, facilities: There are 11 tent sites and 13 sites for trailers or motorhomes up to 21 feet long. Picnic tables are provided. Piped water and firewood are available. Some facilities are wheelchair accessible. Pets are permitted.

Reservations, fee: No reservations necessary; $4 fee per night. Open May to late-November.

Who to contact: Phone Wenatchee National Forest at 509-674-4411, or write at Cle Elum Ranger District, West 2nd Street, Cle Elum, WA 98922.

Location: From the town of Cle Elum, drive 12 miles southeast on I-90, then go south on County Road 9123 for three miles. Turn west on County Road 51 and go two miles, then drive four miles northwest on Forest Service Road 33.

Trip note: A rustic spot set along Taneum Creek. It is just far enough out of the way to keep it from getting much use.

BUCK MEADOWS
Site **14**

Campsites, facilities: There are five sites for tents, trailers or motorhomes up to 14 feet long. Picnic tables are provided. Pit toilets are available, but there is no piped water. Pets are permitted.

Reservations, fee: No reservations necessary; $2 fee per night. Open June to mid-November.

Who to contact: Phone Wenatchee National Forest at 509-674-4411, or write at Cle Elum Ranger District, West 2nd Street, Cle Elum, WA 98922.

Location: From the town of Cle Elum, drive 12 miles southeast on I-90, then go south on County Road 9123 for three miles. Drive west on County Road 51 for two miles and continue six miles northwest on Forest Service Road 33 until you see the campground.

Trip note: This park is set along Taneum Creek and is an option to nearby campsite 13. It doesn't get heavy use because few out-of-towners know of it.

Site 15   COACH POST TRAILER PARK

Campsites, facilities: There are 20 drive-through sites for trailers or motorhomes of any length. Electricity, piped water, sewer hookups and picnic tables are provided. Flush toilets, showers and a laundromat are available. Bottled gas, a store, cafe and ice are located within one mile. Pets are permitted.

Reservations, fee: Reservations accepted; $8 fee per night. Open all year.

Who to contact: Phone at 206-754-7580, or write at 3633 7th Avenue SW, Olympia, WA 98502.

Location: Take the 104 exit off I-5 in Olympia and drive north on US 101 for three miles to the park.

Trip note: This wooded park is in a rural area just west of Olympia. Nearby recreation options include an 18-hole golf course, a full service marina, a riding stable and tennis courts.

Site 16   BLACK LAKE RV PARK

Campsites, facilities: There are 10 tent sites and 46 drive-through sites for trailers or motorhomes of any length. Electricity, piped water, sewer hookups and picnic tables are provided. Flush toilets, bottled gas, sanitary services, a recreation hall, store, ice, showers and firewood are available. A cafe is located within one mile. Pets are permitted. Boat docks, launching facilities and rentals are nearby.

Reservations, fee: Reservations accepted; $9 fee per night. Open all year.

Who to contact: Phone at 206-357-6775, or write at 4325 Black Lake-Belmore Road, Olympia, WA 98502.

Location: Take the 102 (Tumwater/Black Lake) exit off I-5 in Tumwater and take Trosper Road to Black Lake. Follow signs to park.

Trip note: Here's a good spot for campers traveling I-5 who don't want to get stuck in a hotel for the night. This campground is set along the shore of Black Lake. Nearby recreation options include an 18-hole golf course and a full service marina.

Site 17   COLUMBUS PARK

Campsites, facilities: There are 76 drive-through sites for trailers or motorhomes of any length. Electricity, piped water, sewer hookups and picnic tables are provided. Flush toilets, sanitary services, a recreation hall, store, laundromat, ice, showers, firewood and playground are available. Bottled gas and a cafe are located within one mile. Pets are permitted. Boat docks and launching facilities are nearby.

Reservations, fee: Reservations required; $9 fee per night. Open all year.

Who to contact: Phone at 206-786-9460, or write at 5700 Black Lake Boulevard, Olympia, WA 98502.

Location: Take the US 101 exit in Olympia and go northwest on US 101 for 1 3/4 miles, then go south on Black Lake Boulevard for 3 1/2 miles to park.

Trip note: This spot is an option to campsites 16 and 18. It is a wooded area set along the shore of Black Lake. Nearby recreation options include an 18-hole golf course and a full service marina.

Site 18
SALMON SHORES
RESORT

Campsites, facilities: There are 20 tent sites and 45 drive-through sites for trailers or motorhomes of any length. Electricity, piped water, sewer hookups and picnic tables are provided. Flush toilets, bottled gas, sanitary services, showers, a store, laundromat, ice, firewood and playground are available. A cafe is located within one mile. Boat docks, launching facilities and rentals are nearby on Black Lake.

Reservations, fee: Reservations accepted; $9 fee per night. MasterCard and Visa accepted. Open all year.

Who to contact: Phone at 206-357-8618, or write at 5446 Black Lake Boulevard, Olympia, WA 98502.

Location: Take the US 101 exit in Olympia and go northwest on US 101 for 1 3/4 miles, then go south on Black Lake Boulevard for 3 1/2 miles to the resort.

Trip note: This resort is set along the shore of Black Lake. Nearby recreation options include an 18-hole golf course, a full service marina and a riding stable. One of three camps in immediate vicinity.

Site 19
PORTER CREEK

Campsites, facilities: There are 14 primitive campsites for tents or small trailers. Picnic tables, fire grills and tent pads are provided. Pit toilets, piped water and horse loading ramps are available. Motorbikes are permitted.

Reservations, fee: No reservations necessary; no fee. Open all year.

Who to contact: Phone the Department of Natural Resources at 1-800-527-3305, or write Department of Natural Resources AW-11, 1065 South Capitol Way, Olympia, WA 98504.

Location: Sixteen miles south of Olympia on I-5, take Highway 12 west and drive 21 miles to the town of Porter. Go northeast on Porter Creek Road for three miles and then continue straight for another 1/2 mile and you'll see the campground on your left.

Trip note: Primitive and rustic, yet less than 20 miles from Olympia. This campground is in Capitol Forest and is managed by the Department of Natural Resources. It is set along the shore of Porter Creek and offers trails for hiking, horseback riding, or motorbiking.

Site 20
NORTH CREEK

Campsites, facilities: There are five primitive campsites for tents or small trailers. Picnic tables, fire grills and tent pads are provided. Pit toilets and piped water are available.

Reservations, fee: No reservations necessary; no fee. Open all year.

Who to contact: Phone the Department of Natural Resources at 1-800-527-3305, or write Department of Natural Resources AW-11, 1065 South Capitol Way, Olympia, WA 98504.

Location: Sixteen miles south of Olympia off I-5, take Highway 12 west for 12 miles to Oakville. Continue 2 1/2 miles west of Oakville on Highway 12 to D-Line Road then head east for two miles. Take the fork that goes to the right and drive three miles. You'll see the camp on your right.

Trip note: This little-known, wooded campground is set along Porter Creek and is managed by the Department of Natural Resources. There are trails for hikers only. An option is visiting Chehalis Reservoir, a short drive to the east.

SHERMAN VALLEY
Site **21**

Campsites, facilities: There are seven primitive campsites for tents or small trailers. Picnic tables, fire grills and tent pads are provided. Pit toilets and piped water are available.

Reservations, fee: No reservations necessary; no fee. Open all year.

Who to contact: Phone the Department of Natural Resources at 1-800-527-3305, or write Department of Natural Resources AW-11, 1065 South Capitol Way, Olympia, WA 98504.

Location: Sixteen miles south of Olympia off I-5 take Highway 12 west for 12 miles to the town of Oakville. Continue west on Highway 12 for 2 1/2 miles to D-Line Road and turn east. Go 1 2/3 miles and take the fork on the right, then go 4 1/2 miles to the campground which will be on the right.

Trip note: One of nine secluded camp spots set in the Capitol Forest, which is managed by the Department of Natural Resources. It is set along the shore of Porter Creek and there are hiking trails nearby.

MIMA FALLS
Site **22**   TRAILHEAD

Campsites, facilities: There are five primitive campsites for tents or small trailers. Picnic tables, fire grills and tent pads are provided. Pit toilets, piped water and a horse loading ramp are available.

Reservations, fee: No reservations necessary; no fee. Open all year.

Who to contact: Phone the Department of Natural Resources at 1-800-527-3305, or write Department of Natural Resources AW-11, 1065 South Capitol Way, Olympia, WA 98504.

Location: Take the Highway 121 exit off I-5 south of Olympia and drive four miles to Littlerock. Go west for one mile, turn left on Mima Road and drive 1 1/2 miles, then turn right on Bordeaux Road and go 1/2 miles. At Marksman Road, turn right and continue 2/3 mile and turn left and the campground is about 200 yards away.

Trip note: A highlight here is the trail that leads to Mima Falls. Excellent for hikers or horseback riders. Very quiet.

MARGARET MCKENNY
Site **23**

Campsites, facilities: There are 12 primitive campsites for tents or small trailers. Picnic tables, fire grills and tent pads are provided. Pit toilets, piped water and a horse loading ramp are available.

Reservations, fee: No reservations necessary; no fee. Open all year.

Who to contact: Phone the Department of Natural Resources at 1-800-527-3305, or write Department of Natural Resources AW-11, 1065 South Capitol Way, Olympia, WA 98504.

Location: Take the Highway 121 exit off I-5 south of Olympia and drive four miles to Littlerock. Go west for one mile and turn right on Waddell Creek Road. Drive 2 1/2 miles, then turn left and drive about 200 yards to the campground.

Trip note: This streamside campground is in the Capitol Forest and managed by the Department of Natural Resources. There are trails nearby that can be used by hikers or horseback riders.

MIDDLE WADDELL
Site **24**

Campsites, facilities: There are three primitive campsites for tents or small trailers. Picnic tables, fire grills and tent pads are provided. Pit toilets are available, but there is no piped water. Motorbikes are permitted.

Reservations, fee: No reservations necessary; no fee. Open all year.

Who to contact: Phone the Department of Natural Resources at 1-800-527-3305, or write Department of Natural Resources AW-11, 1065 South Capitol Way, Olympia, WA 98504.

Location: Take the Highway 121 exit off I-5 south of Olympia and drive four miles to the town of Littlerock. Continue west for one mile and turn right on Waddell Creek Road. Drive three miles, turn left and go 100 yards. You'll see the campsite on your left.

Trip note: This wooded campground is set along Waddell Creek in the Capitol Forest. The trails are used primarily for motorbikes. Remember that no piped water is available here.

YEW TREE
Site **25**

Campsites, facilities: There are three primitive campsites for tents or small trailers. Picnic tables, fire grills and tent pads are provided. Pit toilets are available, but there is no piped water. Motorbikes are permitted.

Reservations, fee: No reservations necessary; no fee. Open all year.

Who to contact: Phone the Department of Natural Resources at 1-800-527-3305, or write Department of Natural Resources AW-11, 1065 South Capitol Way, Olympia, WA 98504.

Location: Take the Highway 121 exit off I-5 south of Olympia and drive four miles to the town of Littlerock. Go west for one mile and then turn right on Waddell Creek Road. From there go 3 1/2 miles, turn left and drive 100 yards to the campsites, which are on the left.

Trip note: This wooded camp is set along Waddell Creek in Capitol Forest. The trails are used primarily by motorbikers.

MT. MOLLY
Site **26**

Campsites, facilities: There are 10 primitive campsites for tents or small trailers. Picnic tables, fire grills and tent pads are provided. Pit toilets are available, but there is no piped water. Motorbikes are permitted.

Reservations, fee: No reservations necessary; no fee. Open all year.

Who to contact: Phone the Department of Natural Resources at 1-800-527-3305, or write Department of Natural Resources AW-11, 1065 South Capitol Way, Olympia, WA 98504.

Location: Start four miles west of Olympia at the Mud Bay exit off US 101 and go south on Delphi Road for six miles. Drive straight on Waddell Creek Road for three miles, turn right and go 1 1/2 miles. Take the left fork and drive one mile to the campsites on the left.

Trip note: This campground is set in the forest. The nearby trails are used primarily for motorbiking. Week days are often quiet. The campground is managed by Department of Natural Resources.

FALL CREEK
Site **27**

Campsites, facilities: There are eight primitive campsites for tents or small trailers. Picnic tables, fire grills and tent pads are provided. Pit toilets, piped water and a horse loading ramp are available.

Reservations, fee: No reservations necessary; no fee. Open all year.

Who to contact: Phone the Department of Natural Resources at 1-800-527-3305, or write Department of Natural Resources AW-11, 1065 South Capitol Way, Olympia, WA 98504.

Location: Start four miles west of Olympia at the Mud Bay exit off US 101 and go south on Delphi Road for six miles. Continue straight on Waddell Creek Road for three miles, turn right and go 1 1/2 miles. Take the left fork and drive two miles on C-Line Road and then turn left onto C-4000 Road and drive 2 1/2 miles. Turn right and go 200 yards to campground.

Trip note: A good option to campsites 24-26, since the trails here are for hikers and horseback riders only. This wooded campground is set along Fall Creek in Capitol Forest.

MARTIN WAY MOTORHOME AND RV PARK
Site **28**

Campsites, facilities: There are 11 drive-through sites for trailers or motorhomes of any length in this adult only campground. Electricity, piped water and sewer hookups are provided. Flush toilets, showers and a laundromat are available. Bottled gas, sanitary services, a store, cafe and ice are located within one mile.

Reservations, fee: No reservations necessary; $10 fee per night. Open all year.

Who to contact: Phone at 206-491-6840, or write at 8103 Martin Way SE, Olympia, WA 98506.

Location: From I-5 in Olympia take the 111 exit and drive 3/4 mile south to Martin Way, turn west and go 1/4 mile to the park.

Trip note: This park is in urban Olympia. Nearby recreation options include an 18-hole golf course, a full service marina, tennis courts and the Nisqually National Wildlife Refuge. The refuge offers seven miles of foot trails along which you may view a great variety of plant and animal life.

NASQUALLY PLAZA RV PARK
Site **29**

Campsites, facilities: There are 60 drive-through sites for trailers or motorhomes of any length. Electricity, piped water, sewer hookups and picnic tables are provided. Flush toilets, bottled gas, sanitary services, a store, cafe, laundromat, ice, playground and swimming pool are available. Showers and firewood can be obtained for an extra fee. Pets are permitted. Boat launching facilities are nearby.

Reservations, fee: Reservations accepted; $11 fee per night. Open all year.

Who to contact: Phone at 206-491-3831, or write at 10220 Martin Way East, Olympia, WA 98503.

Location: From I-5 in Olympia take the 114 exit and go 200 yards south on Old Nasqually Road, then 1/8 mile west on Martin Way to the park.

Trip note: Nearby recreation options include an 18-hole golf course and Nisqually National Wildlife Refuge, which offers seven miles of foot trails along which you may view a great variety of flora and fauna.

Site 30   PLEASANT ACRES RESORT

Campsites, facilities: There are 20 tent sites and 60 drive-through sites for trailers or motorhomes of any length. Electricity, piped water, sewer hookups and picnic tables are provided. Flush toilets, sanitary services, showers, recreation hall, a store, cafe and laundromat are available. Firewood is available for an extra fee. Bottled gas and ice are available within one mile. Pets and motorbikes are permitted. Boat docks, launching facilities and rentals are available nearby.

Reservations, fee: Reservations accepted; $7 fee per night. Open all year.

Who to contact: Phone at 206-491-3660, or write at 7225 14th Avenue SE, Olympia, WA 98503.

Location: From I-5 in Olympia, take the 109 exit and drive one mile east on Martin Way, then turn south and go 1 1/2 miles on Carpenter Road. Turn east on 14th Avenue and drive to the resort.

Trip note: A nice layover spot for I-5 travelers. This wooded park is set along the shore of Long Lake, a narrow, 4 1/2-mile long lake. The best fishing is at either end of the lake. Nearby recreation options include an 18-hole golf course, hiking trails, marked bike trails and a full service marina.

Site 31   STAN'S RV PARK

Campsites, facilities: There are 20 tent sites and 41 drive-through sites for trailers or motorhomes of any length. Electricity, piped water and picnic tables are provided. Flush toilets, showers and sanitary services are available. Bottled gas, store and cafe are located within one mile. Pets are permitted.

Reservations, fee: Reservations accepted; $9 fee per night. Open all year.

Who to contact: Phone at 206-943-3614, or write at 2430 93rd Avenue SW, Olympia, WA 98502.

Location: From Olympia, drive five miles south on I-5 to the 99 exit. The park is on the northeast corner of the junction.

Trip note: This convenient spot is set just off the highway. Nearby recreation options include an 18-hole golf course and tennis courts.

Site 32   KOA OLYMPIA

Campsites, facilities: There are 35 tent sites and 75 drive-through sites for trailers or motorhomes of any length. Piped water and picnic tables are provided. Flush toilets, bottled gas, sanitary services, showers, recreation hall, a store, laundromat, ice, playground, a heated swimming pool, electricity, sewer hookups and firewood are available. A cafe is available within one mile. Pets and motorbikes are permitted.

Reservations, fee: Reservations accepted; $11 fee per night. MasterCard and Visa accepted. Open all year.

Who to contact: Phone at 206-352-2551, or write at 1441 83rd Avenue SW, Olympia, WA 98502.

Location: From Olympia, drive five miles south on I-5 to the 99 exit and go east for 1/2 mile on 93rd Ave. Drive one mile north on Kimmie Street, then go 1/2 mile east on 83rd Ave. SW to the campground.

Trip note: This wooded campground has all the comforts. Nearby recreation options include an 18-hole golf course, hiking trails, marked bike trails and tennis courts. One of three campsites (31,32,33) in immediate area.

Site 33   AMERICAN HERITAGE KOA

Campsites, facilities: There are 33 tent sites and 72 sites for trailers or motorhomes of any length. Piped water and picnic tables are provided. Flush toilets, bottled gas, sanitary services, showers, recreation hall, recreation program, a store, cafe, laundromat, ice, playground, heated swimming pool, electricity, sewer hookups and firewood are available. Pets and motorbikes are permitted.

Reservations, fee: Reservations accepted; $13 fee per night. MasterCard and Visa accepted. Open mid-May to mid-September.

Who to contact: Phone at 206-943-8778, or write at 9610 Kimmie Street SW, Olympia, WA 98502.

Location: From Olympia, drive five miles south on I-5 to the Highway 99 exit and go 1/2 mile east to Kimmie Street. At Kimmie Street, turn south and go 1/4 mile to the campground.

Trip note: This spacious, wooded campground is near an 18-hole golf course, hiking trails, marked bike trails and tennis courts. In addition, it's not far from the highway to boot.

Site 34   DEEP LAKE RESORT

Campsites, facilities: There are five tent sites and 43 sites for trailers or motorhomes up to 35 feet long. Electricity, piped water, sewer hookups and picnic tables are provided. Flush toilets, sanitary services, a recreation hall, store, cafe, laundromat, ice, bicycle rentals, playground, showers and firewood are available. Pets and motorbikes are permitted. Boat docks, launching facilities and rentals are nearby at the resort.

Reservations, fee: Reservations accepted; $10 fee per night. MasterCard and Visa accepted. Open mid-April to late-September.

Who to contact: Phone at 206-352-7388, or write at 12405 Tilley South, Olympia, WA 98502.

Location: Take the 95 exit off I-5 in south Olympia and drive east on Maytown Road for 2 1/2 miles, then turn north on Tilley Road and go 1/2 mile to the park.

Trip note: This wooded and well-maintained campground is set along the shore of Deep Lake near Millersylvania State Park, and offers swimming, fishing and boating opportunities. Other nearby recreation options include an 18-hole golf course and marked bike trails.

Site 35   MILLERSYLVANIA STATE PARK

Campsites, facilities: There are 139 tent sites and 52 sites for trailers or motorhomes up to 35 feet long. Picnic tables are provided. Flush toilets, Sanitary services, playground, electricity, piped water, showers and firewood are available. Store, cafe and ice are located within one mile. Some facilities are wheelchair accessible. Pets are permitted. Boat docks and launching facilities are nearby on Deep Lake.

Reservations, fee: No reservations necessary; $6 fee per night. Open all year.

Who to contact: Phone at 206-753-1519, or write at 1224 Tilley Road South, Olympia, WA 98502.

Location: Drive 10 miles south of Olympia on I-5 and take the 95 exit. Go east on Maytown Road and then 1/2 mile north on Tilly Road to the park.

Trip note: A popular park, not too far from Olympia, yet offers a lot of choices. It is set along the shore of Deep Lake where you can swim or go trout fishing. There are hiking trails and a fitness trail in among the old growth trees.

Site 36   PEPPERTREE WEST RV PARK

Campsites, facilities: There are 20 tent sites and 40 drive-through sites for trailers or motorhomes of any length. Electricity, piped water and sewer hookups are provided. Flush toilets, sanitary services, showers, recreation hall, laundromat, ice, swimming pool, bottled gas, a store and cafe are available. Pets and motorbikes are permitted. Boat launching facilities are available nearby.

Reservations, fee: Reservations accepted; $11 fee per night. MasterCard and Visa accepted. Open all year.

Who to contact: Phone at 206-736-9362, or write at 1208 Alder Street, Centralia, WA 98531.

Location: Take the 81 exit off I-5 in Centralia (about 23 miles south of Olympia), and drive to the southeast corner of town. You'll see the park.

Trip note: If you're driving I-5 and looking for a stopover, this spot, along with campsite 37, offers a good layover for tent campers or motorhomes. Surrounded by Chehalis Valley farmland, this campground is near an 18-hole golf course, hiking trails and tennis courts.

Site 37   TRAILER VILLAGE

Campsites, facilities: There are 16 drive-through sites for trailers or motorhomes of any length. Electricity, piped water, sewer hookups and picnic tables are provided. Flush toilets and showers are available. Bottled gas, sanitary services, a store, cafe, laundromat and ice are located within one mile. Pets are permitted.

Reservations, fee: Reservations accepted; $10 fee per night. Open all year.

Who to contact: Phone at 206-736-9260, or write at 1313 Harrison, Centralia, WA 98531.

Location: Take the Harrison/82 exit off I-5 in Centralia (about 23 miles south of Olympia) and go four blocks northwest on Harrison to the park.

Trip note: This is an option to campsite 36, but for motorhomes only. This park is in urban Centralia. Nearby recreation options include an 18-hole golf course.

Site 38   OFFUT LAKE RESORT

Campsites, facilities: There are 26 tent sites and 33 drive-through sites for trailers or motorhomes of any length. Electricity, piped water, sewer hookups and picnic tables are provided. Flush toilets, bottled gas, sanitary services, firewood, recreation hall, store, cafe, laundromat, ice and playground are available. Showers can be obtained for an extra fee. Pets and motorbikes are permitted. Boat docks and rentals are nearby.

Reservations, fee: Reservations accepted; $12 fee per night. MasterCard and Visa accepted. Open April to November.

Who to contact: Phone at 206-264-2438, or write at 4005 120th SE, Tenino, WA 98589.

Location: Take Highway 507 east off I-5 about 16 miles south of Olympia and drive eight miles to the town of Tenino. Go north on Old Highway 99 for four miles and then turn east on Offut Lake Resort Road.

Trip note: This wooded campground is on Offut Lake. Just enough off the beaten track to provide a bit of seclusion, yet not a long drive from Highway 5.

Site 39   ALDER LAKE

Campsites, facilities: There are 25 primitive campsites for tents or small trailers. Picnic tables, fire grills and tent pads are provided. Pit toilets, piped water, a group shelter and a boat launch are available.

Reservations, fee: No reservations necessary; no fee. Open all year.

Who to contact: Phone the Department of Natural Resources at 1-800-527-3305, or write Department of Natural Resources AW-11, 1065 South Capitol Way, Olympia, WA 98504.

Location: Take Highway 7 and drive south of Elbe for two miles, then turn right on Pleasant Valley Road and go 3 1/2 miles. Bear left on a paved, one-lane road for 100 yards and you'll see the campground on your right.

Trip note: This campground is set along the shore of Alder Lake in an area managed by the Department of Natural Resources. One option is the Mt. Rainier Scenic Railroad excursion that travels from Elbe through the forests to Mineral Lake. One of a kind.

Site 40   ELBE HILLS

Campsites, facilities: There are three primitive campsites for tents or small trailers. Picnic tables, fire grills and tent pads are provided. Pit toilets and a group shelter are available, but there is no piped water.

Reservations, fee: No reservations necessary; no fee. Open all year.

Who to contact: Phone the Department of Natural Resources at 1-800-527-3305 or 206-825-1631, or write Department of Natural Resources AW-11, 1065 South Capitol Way, Olympia, WA 98504.

Location: From the town of Elbe go east on Highway 706 for six miles, then turn left on a dead end road and go three miles. Keep right and continue 1/2 mile, then turn left and drive about 100 yards to the 4-wheel drive trailhead.

Trip note: Here's a spot for 4-wheel drive cowboys. The Department of Natural Resources manages this wooded campground and provides eight miles of trails for short wheelbase four-wheel drive vehicles. Beware. Trucks often get stuck here or can't make it up the hills when it is wet and slippery. Can yours?

Site 41   EAGLE'S NEST
ALDER LAKE

Campsites, facilities: There are eight sites for trailers or motorhomes up to 25 feet long. Electricity, piped water and sewer hookups are provided. Sanitary services and firewood are available. Pets are permitted. Boat launching facilities are located on Alder Lake.

Reservations, fee: Reservations accepted; $8 fee per night. MasterCard and Visa accepted. Open all year.

Who to contact: Phone at 206-569-2533, or write at 52120 Mountain Highway East, Eatonville, WA 98328.

Location: From Tacoma, drive 29 miles south on Highway 7 and you'll see the turn-off for the park.

Trip note: A wooded RV park set on the shore of Alder Lake. A cozy, little spot with all amenities.

Site 42   ELBE
TRAILER PARK

Campsites, facilities: There are 10 tent sites and 14 sites for trailers or motorhomes of any length. Electricity, piped water and sewer hookups are provided. Bottled gas, a store, cafe and ice are available within one mile. Pets are permitted. Boat launching facilities are located nearby.

Reservations, fee: No reservations necessary; $7 fee per night. Open all year.

Who to contact: Write at Star Route, Elbe, WA 98330.

Location: From Tacoma, drive 37 miles south on Highway 7 to the town of Elbe. The park is in town.

Trip note: This campground is near Alder Lake. The Mount Rainier Scenic Railroad leaves from Elbe regularly and makes its way through the forests to Mineral Lake. It features open deck cars, live music and restored passenger cars.

Site 43   ALDER LAKE
PARK

Campsites, facilities: There are 20 tents sites and 15 sites for trailers or motorhomes of any length. Electricity and piped water are provided. Vault toilets are available. Boat docks and launching facilities are located on Alder Lake.

Reservations, fee: No reservations; $4 to $6 fee per night. Open all year, with limited facilities in the winter.

Who to contact: Phone at 206-569-2778, or write 50324 School Road, Alder WA 98330.

Location: From Tacoma, drive 35 miles south on Highway 7 to Alder Lake. Go left to the park.

Trip note: This municipal park is set along the shore of Alder Lake. Decent spot to spend a weekend.

Site 44
TANWAX LAKE RESORT

Campsites, facilities: There are five tent sites and 25 sites for trailers or motorhomes of any length. Electricity, piped water, sewer hookups and picnic tables are provided. Flush toilets, showers, a cafe, laundromat and playground are available. Bottled gas, a store and ice are located within one mile. Boat docks, launching facilities and rentals are nearby.

Reservations, fee: Reservations accepted; $8 fee per night. Open mid-April to late-October.

Who to contact: Phone at 206-879-5533, or write at 34023 Tanwax Court East, Eatonville, WA 98328.

Location: From Tacoma, drive 27 miles south on Highway 7, then turn east to Eatonville on Highway 161. From there, drive seven miles north to Tanwax Drive. Go east on Tanwax Drive for 1/2 mile and you'll see the resort.

Trip note: This wooded resort is set along the shore of Tanwax Lake. About one mile south of the turn-off to Tanwax Lake on Highway 161 is "Northwest Trek," which is open from Memorial Day through Labor Day. It is a guided tram trip through a 600-acre wildlife preserve where you can see bison, caribou and many other animals in their natural habitat.

Site 45
RAINBOW RESORT

Campsites, facilities: There are 10 tent sites and 50 drive-through sites for trailers or motorhomes up to 30 feet long. Electricity, piped water, sewer hookups and picnic tables are provided. Flush toilets, bottled gas, firewood, recreation hall, showers, store, laundromat, ice and playground are available. A cafe is located within one mile. Boat docks, launching facilities and rentals are nearby.

Reservations, fee: Reservations accepted; $10 fee per night. Open all year.

Who to contact: Phone at 206-879-5115, or write at Route 1, Box 223, Eatonville, WA 98328.

Location: From Tacoma, drive 27 miles south on Highway 7, then turn east to Eatonville on Highway 161 and drive seven miles north to Tanwax Drive. Turn and drive east to the resort on Lake Tanwax.

Trip note: This wooded park is set along the shore of Lake Tanwax. Good fishing. Nearby recreation options include a riding stable. See trip notes to campsite 44 for information about Northwest Trek.

Site 46
GATEWAY INN AND RV PARK

Campsites, facilities: There are 18 sites for trailers or motorhomes of any length. Electricity, piped water and picnic tables are provided. Bottled gas, laundromat, firewood, sanitary services, cafe and ice are available. Pets are permitted.

Reservations, fee: Reservations accepted; $10 fee per night. MasterCard, Visa and American Express accepted. Open April to November.

Who to contact: Phone at 206-569-2506, or write to Gateway Inn and RV Park, Ashford, WA 98304.

Location: This park is located near the southwestern entrance to Mount Rainier National

Park, about 12 miles east of the town of Elbe on Highway 706.

Trip note: This wooded park is very close to Mount Rainier National Park, one of the most spectacular mountains in the hemisphere. After entering at the southwestern or Nisqually entrance to the park and driving on Nisqually Paradise Road, you will find the Longmire Visitor Center about five miles into the park. It offers exhibits on the plants, and geology of the area, and general park information. Continuing into the park for 10 more miles you will arrive at the Paradise Visitor Center, which has more exhibits and an observation deck. This is the only road into the park that is open all year.

Site 47   MOUNTHAVEN AT CEDAR PARK

Campsites, facilities: There are 20 sites for trailers or motorhomes of any length. Electricity, piped water, sewer hookups and picnic tables are provided. Flush toilets, showers, laundromat, firewood, cafe, ice and playground are available. Pets are permitted.

Reservations, fee: Reservations accepted; $12 fee per night. MasterCard and Visa accepted. Open all year.

Who to contact: Phone at 206-569-2594, or write at 38210 State Route 706 East, Ashford, WA 98304.

Location: This park is located near the southwestern entrance to Mount Rainier National Park, about 11 miles east of the town of Elbe on Highway 706.

Trip note: This wooded campground is near the Nisqually entrance to Mount Rainier National Park. See the trip note for campsite 46 for information about nearby sights at the National Park.

Site 48   EVANS CREEK

Campsites, facilities: There are 26 tent sites and 26 sites for trailers or motorhomes up to 31 feet long. Picnic tables are provided. Pit toilets and firewood are available, but there is no piped water. Pets are permitted.

Reservations, fee: No reservations necessary; no fee. Open mid-June to late-September.

Who to contact: Phone Mount Baker-Snoqualmie National Forest at 206-825-6585, or write at the White River Ranger District, Wilkeson, WA 98396.

Location: Drive eight miles east of Tacoma on Highway 167, then continue east on Highway 410 to Buckley. Go 11 miles south on Highway 165 and turn left on Forest Service Road 7930. Drive 1 1/2 miles to the campground.

Trip note: This primitive campground is set near Evans Creek in an ORV area near the northwestern corner of Mount Rainier National Park. The two nearby roads that lead into the park are secondary or gravel roads and provide access to several other primitive campgrounds and backcountry trails in the park. A National Forest map details the back roads and hiking trails.

Site 49   SUNSHINE POINT

Campsites, facilities: There are 18 sites for tents or motorhomes up to 25 feet long. Picnic tables are provided. Some facilities are wheelchair accessible. Pets are permitted.

Reservations, fee: No reservations necessary; $4 fee per night. Open all year.

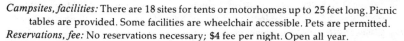

Who to contact: Phone Mt. Rainier National Park at 206-569-2211, or write at Mount Rainier National Park, Tahoma Woods, Ashford, WA 98304.

Location: Drive 12 miles east of the town of Elbe on Highway 706 and you'll see the entrance to the park. The campground is just inside the park entrance.

Trip note: This is one of just five campgrounds in Mount Rainier National Park, set near the Nisqually entrance. Campsites 50-53 are also located in the park. See the trip note for campsite 46 for information about the nearby sights and visitor serving facilities.

COUGAR ROCK
Site 50

Campsites, facilities: There are 200 sites for tents or motorhomes up to 30 feet long. Picnic tables are provided. Flush toilets, piped water and sanitary services are available. Some facilities are wheelchair accessible. Pets are permitted.

Reservations, fee: No reservations necessary; $5 fee per night. Open mid-June to mid-October.

Who to contact: Phone Mt. Rainier National Park at 206-569-2211, or write at Mount Rainier National Park, Tahoma Woods, Ashford, WA 98304.

Location: Drive about 12 miles east of the town of Elbe on Highway 706 and enter the park. You'll see the campground entrance on the left about two miles past the Longmire Visitor Center.

Trip note: This camp is at 3,180 feet elevation. The park provides a recreation program, and trout fishing is allowed without a permit. See the trip note for campgound 46 for information on the nearby park sights and visitor serving centers.

IPSUT
Site 51

Campsites, facilities: There are 31 sites for tents or motorhomes up to 20 feet long. Picnic tables are provided. Pit toilets and piped water are available. Pets are permitted.

Reservations, fee: No reservations necessary; $4 fee per night. Open Memorial Day to Labor Day.

Who to contact: Phone Mt. Rainier National Park at 206-569-2211, or write Mount Rainier National Park, Tahoma Woods, Ashford, WA 98304.

Location: Drive eight miles east of Tacoma on Highway 167, then continue east on Highway 410 for 13 miles to Buckley. From there, head southeast on Highway 165 for about 13 miles to the Carbon River Park entrance. The campground is five miles into the park.

Trip note: This camp is at the end of Carbon River Road and at the beginning of several trails that lead into the backcountry of Mount Rainier National Park, past lakes and glaciers, waterfalls and many other wonders. Obtain a map from the National Park Service for details, and get a permit if you plan to do some overnight backpacking.

WHITE RIVER
Site 52

Campsites, facilities: There are 117 sites for tents or motorhomes up to 20 feet long. Picnic tables are provided. Flush toilets and piped water are available. Some facilities are wheelchair accessible. Pets are permitted.

Reservations, fee: No reservations necessary; $5 fee per night. Open mid-June to mid-September.

Who to contact: Phone Mt. Rainier National Park at 206-569-2211, or write Mount Rainier National Park, Tahoma Woods, Ashford, WA 98304.

Location: From Enumclaw, drive 27 miles southeast on Highway 410 to the White River entrance into the park. Take White River Road to the right and drive about seven miles to the campground.

Trip note: This campground is set on the White River at 4,400 feet elevation. A trail near camp leads a short distance to the Sunrise Visitor Center. From there you can take several trails that lead to backcountry lakes and glaciers. You name it, it's got it.

OHANAPECOSH

Site **53**

Campsites, facilities: There are 232 sites for tents or motorhomes up to 30 feet long. Picnic tables are provided. Flush toilets, piped water and sanitary services are available. Some facilities are wheelchair accessible. Pets are permitted.

Reservations, fee: No reservations necessary; $5 fee per night. Open mid-May to November.

Who to contact: Phone Mount Rainier National Park at 206-569-2211, or write the Mount Rainier National Park, Tahoma Woods, Ashford, WA 98304.

Location: Drive 11 miles northeast of the town of Packwood on Highways 12 and 123 to the Ohanapecosh entrance to the park. The camp is next to the visitor center as you enter the park.

Trip note: This campground is set along the Ohanapecosh River. The nearby visitor center provides exhibits on the history of the forest and visitor information. Highway 706 heading east is closed by snowfall in winter.

Site **54**

HATCHERY
RV CAMP

Campsites, facilities: There are 30 sites for tents, trailers or motorhomes up to 21 feet long. Picnic tables are provided. Pit toilets and firewood are available, but there is no piped water. Some facilities are wheelchair accessible. Pets are permitted.

Reservations, fee: No reservations necessary; $2 fee per night. Open late-May to late-September.

Who to contact: Phone Gifford Pinchot National Forest at 206-494-5515, or write at Packwood Ranger District, Packwood, WA 98361.

Location: From the town of Packwood, drive seven miles northeast on Highway 12, then go one mile west on Forest Service Road 1272.

Trip note: This campground is set along the Ohanapecosh River about six miles south of the Ohanapechosh Hot Springs and the southeastern entrance to Mount Rainier National Park. There is a Forest Service information center about a mile from camp. A National Forest map details the back country roads and trails.

LA WIS WIS

Site **55**

Campsites, facilities: There are 10 sites for tents, trailers or motorhomes up to 15 feet long. Picnic tables are provided. Flush and pit toilets, piped water and firewood are available. Pets are permitted.

Reservations, fee: No reservations necessary; $8 fee per night. Open late-May to late-September.

Who to contact: Phone Gifford Pinchot National Forest at 206-494-5515, or write at Packwood Ranger District, Packwood, WA 98361.

Location: From the town of Packwood, drive seven miles northeast on Highway 12, then go 1/2 mile west on Forest Service Road 1272.

Trip note: This campground is set along the Ohanapecosh River and offers nature trails. It is about seven miles south of the entrance to Mount Rainier National Park and the Ohanapecosh Hot Springs.

SODA SPRINGS

Site 56

Campsites, facilities: There are eight primitive tent sites. Picnic tables are provided. Pit toilets and firewood are available, but there is no piped water. Pets are permitted.

Reservations, fee: No reservations necessary; $2 fee per night. Open mid-June to early-September.

Who to contact: Phone Gifford Pinchot National Forest at 206-494-5515, or write at Packwood Ranger District, Packwood, WA 98361.

Location: From the town of Packwood, drive nine miles northeast on Highway 12, then go one mile east on Highway 12. Turn north on Forest Service Road 4510 and drive about seven miles to the end of the road.

Trip note: This campground is set along Summit Creek, a good base camp for a backpacking expedition or daily hiking trips in the Cascade Range. There are many trails and lakes to choose from as destinations. Obtain a Forest Service map for details.

SUMMIT CREEK

Site 57

Campsites, facilities: There are seven primitive tent sites. Picnic tables are provided. Pit toilets and firewood are available, but there is no piped water. Pets are permitted.

Reservations, fee: No reservations necessary; $2 fee per night. Open mid-June to early-September.

Who to contact: Phone Gifford Pinchot National Forest at 206-494-5515, or write at Packwood Ranger District, Packwood, WA 98361.

Location: From the town of Packwood, drive nine miles northeast on Highway 12. Turn north on Forest Service Road 4510 and drive about three miles to the campground.

Trip note: Set along Summit Creek, this campground is another good base camp for trips into the Cascade Range backcountry. See trip note for campsite 56.

THE DALLES

Site 58

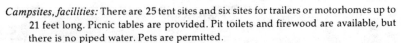

Campsites, facilities: There are 25 tent sites and six sites for trailers or motorhomes up to 21 feet long. Picnic tables are provided. Pit toilets and firewood are available, but there is no piped water. Pets are permitted.

Reservations, fee: No reservations necessary; $3 fee per night. Open mid-May to late-September.

Who to contact: Phone Mt. Baker-Snoqualmie National Forest at 206-825-6585, or write at White River Ranger District, Enumclaw, WA 98022.

Location: Drive to the town of Enumclaw 21 miles east of Tacoma. From there, go 25 1/2 miles southeast on Highway 410 and you'll see the campground on your left.

Trip note: This campground is set along the White River. There is a nature trail nearby, and the White River entrance to Mount Rainier National Park is about 14 miles south on Highway 410.

SILVER SPRINGS
Site **59**

Campsites, facilities: There are 52 tent sites and 36 sites for trailers or motorhomes up to 21 feet long. Electricity and picnic tables are provided. Pit toilets, piped water and firewood are available. A store, cafe and ice are located within one mile. Pets are permitted.

Reservations, fee: No reservations necessary; $4 fee per night. Open mid-May to late-September.

Who to contact: Phone Mt. Baker-Snoqualmie National Forest at 206-825-6585, or write at White River Ranger District, Enumclaw, WA 98022.

Location: Drive to the town of Enumclaw 21 miles east of Tacoma. From there, go 31 miles southeast on Highway 410 and you will see the campground entrance on your left.

Trip note: This campground is set along the White River about eight miles from the White River entrance to Mount Rainier National Park. A Forest Service information center is nearby.

CORRAL PASS
Site **60**

Campsites, facilities: There are 12 tent sites. Picnic tables are provided. Pit toilets, a horse loading ramp and firewood are available, but there is no piped water. Pets are permitted.

Reservations, fee: No reservations necessary; $3 fee per night. Open July to late-September.

Who to contact: Phone Mt. Baker-Snoqualmie National Forest at 206-825-6585, or write at White River Ranger District, Enumclaw, WA 98022.

Location: Drive to the town of Enumclaw 21 miles east of Tacoma. From there, go 31 miles southeast on Highway 410, then six miles east on Forest Service Road 7174. It is a windy, dirt road.

Trip note: This is the most remote of the campgrounds in the area. Primitive, quiet and an ideal base camp for a hiking trip. This campground is at 5,700 feet elevation. There are several trails near camp that lead to backcountry fishing lakes and streams. See a Forest Service map for details.

ECHO LAKE
Site **61**

Campsites, facilities: There are six primitive tent sites at this hike-in campground. Picnic tables are provided. Pit toilets are available, but there is no piped water.

Reservations, fee: No reservations necessary; $3 fee per night. Open July to mid-September.

Who to contact: Phone Mt. Baker-Snoqualmie National Forest at 206-825-6585, or write at White River Ranger District, Enumclaw, WA 98022.

Location: Drive to the town of Enumclaw 21 miles east of Tacoma. From there, go 31 miles southeast on Highway 410, then six miles east on Forest Service Road 7174. Park at the Corral Pass campground and hike five miles on Trail 1176 to Echo Lake.

Trip note: This hike-in campground is set on the shore of Echo Lake, and a visit is worth the five-mile tramp. The trail to the campground follows the Greenwater River. You can continue on the trail past the lake. It forks one mile north of the lake. The east fork goes into Norse Peak Wilderness. See a Forest Service map for details.

COTTON WOOD
Site 62

Campsites, facilities: There are 16 sites for tents, trailers or motorhomes up to 21 feet long. Piped water and picnic tables are provided. Pit toilets, firewood, sanitary services, a store, cafe and ice are available. Pets are permitted.

Reservations, fee: No reservations necessary; $4 fee per night. Open April to December.

Who to contact: Phone Wenatchee National Forest at 509-653-2205, or write at Naches Ranger District, 510 Highway 12, Naches, WA 98937.

Location: Thirteen miles northwest of Yakima on Highway 12 is the town of Naches. From there, go 4 1/2 miles west on Highway 12, then 17 1/2 miles northwest on Highway 410 to the campground.

Trip note: This campground is set along the Naches River. Camps 63, 64 and 80 provide nearby options if this one doesn't grab your fancy.

HALFWAY FLAT
Site 63

Campsites, facilities: There are 12 sites for tents, trailers or motorhomes up to 15 feet long. Picnic tables are provided. Pit toilets and firewood are available, but there is no piped water. Pets are permitted.

Reservations, fee: No reservations necessary; $4 fee per night. Open April to late-November.

Who to contact: Phone Wenatchee National Forest at 509-653-2205, or write at Naches Ranger District, 510 Highway 12, Naches, WA 98937.

Location: Thirteen miles northwest of Yakima on Highway 12 is the town of Naches. From there, go 4 1/2 miles west on Highway 12, 21 miles northwest on Highway 410, then three miles northwest on Forest Service Road 175 to the campground.

Trip note: This campground is set along the Naches River. A trail leads from camp into the backcountry of the William O. Douglas Wilderness, which can also be reached by car. Try hoofing it.

SAWMILL FLAT
Site 64

Campsites, facilities: There are 27 sites for tents, trailers or motorhomes up to 21 feet long. Piped water and picnic tables are provided. Pit toilets and firewood are available. Some facilities are wheelchair accessible. Pets are permitted.

Reservations, fee: No reservations necessary; $4 fee per night. Open April to December.

Who to contact: Phone Wenatchee National Forest at 509-653-2205, or write at Naches Ranger District, 510 Highway 12, Naches, WA 98937.

Location: Thirteen miles northwest of Yakima on Highway 12 is the town of Naches. From there, drive 4 1/2 miles west on Highway 12, then 23 1/2 miles northwest on Highway 410 to the campground.

Trip note: This campground is set on the Naches River near the Halfway Flat Campground. It's not quite all the way flat, just sorta flat.

CROW CREEK
Site **65**

Campsites, facilities: There are 15 sites for tents, trailers or motorhomes up to 15 feet long. Picnic tables are provided. Pit toilets and firewood are available, but there is no piped water. Pets are permitted.

Reservations, fee: No reservations necessary; $4 fee per night. Open mid-April to late-November.

Who to contact: Phone Wenatchee National Forest at 509-653-2205, or write at Naches Ranger District, 510 Highway 12, Naches, WA 98937.

Location: Thirteen miles northwest of Yakima on Highway 12 is the town of Naches. From there, go 4 1/2 miles west on Highway 12, 24 1/2 miles northwest on Highway 410, 2 1/2 miles northwest on Forest Service Road 197, then turn west on Forest Service Road 182 and go 1/2 mile to the campground.

Trip note: This campground is set along the Naches River. A trail from camp leads into the backcountry and then forks in several directions. One way leads to the American River, another follows West Quartz Creek, and another goes along Fife's Ridge into the Norse Peak Wilderness. See a Forest Service map for details.

KANER FLAT
Site **66**

Campsites, facilities: There are 41 sites for tents, trailers or motorhomes up to 21 feet long. Piped water and picnic tables are provided. Pit toilets and firewood are available. Pets are permitted.

Reservations, fee: No reservations necessary; $4 fee per night. Open mid-April to late-November.

Who to contact: Phone Wenatchee National Forest at 509-653-2205, or write at Naches Ranger District, 510 Highway 12, Naches, WA 98937.

Location: Thirteen miles northwest of Yakima on Highway 12 is the town of Naches. From there, go 4 1/2 miles west on Highway 12, then 25 miles northwest on Highway 410, and 2 1/2 miles northwest on Forest Service Road 197 and you'll see the campground.

Trip note: This campground is on the site of an old wagon trail campsite on the Old Naches Trail. It is set near the Naches River. A nice spot, even has piped water.

INDIAN FLAT
Site **67**

Campsites, facilities: There are 11 sites for tents, trailers or motorhomes up to 15 feet long. Piped water and picnic tables are provided. Pit toilets and firewood are available. Pets are permitted.

Reservations, fee: No reservations necessary; $4 fee per night. Open late-May to mid-September.

Who to contact: Phone Wenatchee National Forest at 509-653-2205, or write at Naches Ranger District, 510 Highway 12, Naches, WA 98937.

Location: Thirteen miles northwest of Yakima on Highway 12 is the town of Naches. From there, go 4 1/2 miles west on Highway 12, then drive 27 miles northwest on Highway 410 and you'll see the campground.

Trip note: This campground is set along the American River. A trail from camp leads into the backcountry west along Fife's Ridge, or further north to the West Quartz Creek drainage. A Forest Service map details the adventures.

AMERICAN FORKS
Site 68

Campsites, facilities: There are 15 sites for tents, trailers or motorhomes up to 21 feet long.
Piped water is provided. Pit toilets are available. Pets are permitted.

Reservations, fee: No reservations necessary; $4 fee per night. Open late-May to mid-September.

Who to contact: Phone Wenatchee National Forest at 509-653-2205, or write at Naches Ranger District, 510 Highway 12, Naches, WA 98937.

Location: Thirteen miles northwest of Yakima on Highway 12 is the town of Naches. From there go 4 1/2 miles west on Highway 12, 28 miles northwest on Highway 410, then turn southwest and go 200 yards on Forest Service Road 174 to campground.

Trip note: This campground is set at the confluence of the Bumping and American Rivers. A trail from nearby Cedar Springs campground is one of several in the area that lead into the backcountry. See a Forest Service map for details.

PINE NEEDLE
Site 69

Campsites, facilities: There are six sites for tents, trailers or motorhomes. Picnic tables are provided. Pit toilets and firewood are available, but there is no piped water. Pets are permitted.

Reservations, fee: No reservations necessary; $4 fee per night. Open late-April to mid-September.

Who to contact: Phone Wenatchee National Forest at 509-653-2205, or write at Naches Ranger District, 510 Highway 12, Naches, WA 98937.

Location: Thirteen miles northwest of Yakima on Highway 12 is the town of Naches. From there, go 4 1/2 miles west on Highway 12, 30 1/2 miles northwest on Highway 410 to the campground.

Trip note: This campground is set along the American River. Easy to reach, but rustic and beautiful.

PLEASANT VALLEY
Site 70

Campsites, facilities: There are 14 sites for tents, trailers or motorhomes up to 21 feet long. Picnic tables are provided. Pit toilets and firewood are available, but there is no piped water. Pets are permitted.

Reservations, fee: No reservations necessary; no fee. Open mid-June to late-November.

Who to contact: Phone Wenatchee National Forest at 509-653-2205, or write at Naches Ranger District, 510 Highway 12, Naches, WA 98937.

Location: Thirteen miles northwest of Yakima on Highway 12 is the town of Naches. From there go 4 1/2 miles west on Highway 12, then drive 37 miles northwest on Highway 410 and you'll see the campground on your left.

Trip note: This campground is set along the American River and is a good base camp for a hiking trip. A trail from camp follows Kettle Creek up to the American Ridge and Kettle Lake in the William O. Douglas Wilderness. It joins another trail there that follows the ridge and then drops down to Bumping Lake. A Forest Service map is essential.

LITTLE NACHES
Site **71**

Campsites, facilities: There are five sites for tents, trailers or motorhomes up to 15 feet long. Picnic tables are provided. Pit toilets and firewood are available, but there is no piped water. Pets are permitted.

Reservations, fee: No reservations necessary; $4 fee per night. Open late-May to late-November.

Who to contact: Phone Wenatchee National Forest at 509-653-2205, or write at Naches Ranger District, 510 Highway 12, Naches, WA 98937.

Location: Thirteen miles northwest of Yakima on Highway 12 is the town of Naches. From there go 4 1/2 miles west on Highway 12, 25 miles northwest on Highway 410, and then 100 yards northwest on Forest Service Road 197 to the campground.

Trip note: This campground is set on the Little Naches River near the American River. It is set just one-tenth of a mile off the highway, yet is known by relatively few and gets little use.

CEDAR SPRINGS
Site **72**

Campsites, facilities: There are 15 sites for tents, trailers or motorhomes up to 21 feet long. Piped water and picnic tables are provided. Pit toilets and firewood are available. Pets are permitted.

Reservations, fee: No reservations necessary; $4 fee per night. Open late-May to late-November.

Who to contact: Phone Wenatchee National Forest at 509-653-2205, or write at Naches Ranger District, 510 Highway 12, Naches, WA 98937.

Location: Thirteen miles northwest of Yakima on Highway 12 is the town of Naches. From there, go 4 1/2 miles west on Highway 12, 28 1/2 miles northwest on Highway 410, then turn and go 1/2 mile southwest on Forest Service Road 174 to the campground.

Trip note: This campground is set along the Bumping River a short distance from American Forks. If you continue driving southwest for 11 miles on Forest Service Road 174, you will get to Bumping Lake.

COUGAR FLAT
Site **73**

Campsites, facilities: There are 12 sites for tents, trailers or motorhomes up to 15 feet long. Piped water and picnic tables are provided. Pit toilets and firewood are available. Pets are permitted.

Reservations, fee: No reservations necessary; $4 fee per night. Open late-May to mid-September.

Who to contact: Phone Wenatchee National Forest at 509-653-2205, or write at Naches Ranger District, 510 Highway 12, Naches, WA 98937.

Location: Thirteen miles northwest of Yakima on Highway 12 is the town of Naches. From there, go 4 1/2 miles west on Highway 12, 28 1/2 miles northwest on Highway 410, then six miles southwest on Forest Service Road 174 to the campground.

Trip note: This campground is set along the Bumping River. A trail from camp follows the river and then heads up the tributaries. One of several camps in immediate vicinity on Forest Service Road 174. See map for Zone 6.

BUMPING CROSSING
Site **74**

Campsites, facilities: There are 12 sites for tents, trailers or motorhomes up to 15 feet long. Picnic tables are provided. Pit toilets and firewood are available, but there is no piped water. Store, cafe and ice are located within one mile. Pets are permitted. Boat docks, launching facilities and rentals are nearby on Bumping Lake.

Reservations, fee: No reservations necessary; $4 fee per night. Open late-May to late-November.

Who to contact: Phone Wenatchee National Forest at 509-653-2205, or write at Naches Ranger District, 510 Highway 12, Naches, WA 98937.

Location: Thirteen miles northwest of Yakima on Highway 12 is the town of Naches. From there, go 4 1/2 miles west on Highway 12, 28 1/2 miles northwest on Highway 410, and then drive 10 miles southwest on Forest Service Road 174 to the campground.

Trip note: This campground is set along the Bumping River about a mile from the boat landing at Bumping Lake. Good spot for a weekender.

BUMPING DAM
Site **75**

Campsites, facilities: There are 28 tent sites and 28 sites for trailers or motorhomes up to 15 feet long. Picnic tables are provided. Pit toilets and firewood are available, but there is no piped water. Store is located within one mile. Pets are permitted. Boat docks, launching facilities and rentals are nearby.

Reservations, fee: No reservations necessary; $4 fee per night. Open mid-May to late-November.

Who to contact: Phone Wenatchee National Forest at 509-653-2205, or write at Naches Ranger District, 510 Highway 12, Naches, WA 98937.

Location: Thirteen miles northwest of Yakima on Highway 12 is the town of Naches. From there go 4 1/2 miles west on Highway 12, 28 miles northwest on Highway 410, then drive 11 miles southwest on Forest Service Road 174 and 1/2 mile north on Forest Service Road 1602.

Trip note: This campground is next to the dam on Bumping Lake, a popular lake for fishing, swimming and water skiing.

BUMPING LAKE
AND BOAT LANDING
Site **76**

Campsites, facilities: There are 12 sites for tents, trailers or motorhomes up to 21 feet long. Piped water and picnic tables are provided. Pit toilets and firewood are available. Pets are permitted. Boat docks, launching facilities and rentals are nearby.

Reservations, fee: No reservations necessary; $4 fee per night. Open mid-May to late-November.

Who to contact: Phone Wenatchee National Forest at 509-653-2205, or write at Naches Ranger District, 510 Highway 12, Naches, WA 98937.

Location: Thirteen miles northwest of Yakima on Highway 12 is the town of Naches. From there, go 4 1/2 miles west on Highway 12, 28 1/2 miles northwest on Highway 410, then drive 11 miles southwest on Forest Service Road 174, and 300 yards west on Forest Service Road 174D.

Trip note: Woods and water, this spot has them both. A variety of water activities are allowed at Bumping Lake, including water skiing, fishing and swimming. There are also several hiking trails that go into the wilderness area surrounding the lake.

HELLS CROSSING
Site **77**

Campsites, facilities: There are 17 sites for tents, trailers or motorhomes up to 15 feet long. Piped water and picnic tables are provided. Pit toilets and firewood are available. Pets are permitted.

Reservations, fee: No reservations necessary; $4 fee per night. Open late-May to late-November.

Who to contact: Phone Wenatchee National Forest at 509-653-2205, or write at Naches Ranger District, 510 Highway 12, Naches, WA 98937.

Location: Thirteen miles northwest of Yakima on Highway 12 is the town of Naches. From there, go 4 1/2 miles west on Highway 12, then drive 33 1/2 miles northwest on Highway 410 and you'll see the campground entrance.

Trip note: This campground is set along the American River. A steep trail from camp leads up to Goat Peak and follows the American Ridge in the William O. Douglas Wilderness. Other trails join the ridgetop trail and connect with lakes and streams. A Forest Service map details the backcountry.

LODGE POLE
Site **78**

Campsites, facilities: There are 34 sites for tents, trailers or motorhomes up to 21 feet long. Piped water and picnic tables are provided. Pit toilets and firewood are available. Pets are permitted.

Reservations, fee: No reservations necessary; $4 fee per night. Open mid-June to mid-September.

Who to contact: Phone Wenatchee National Forest at 509-653-2205, or write at Naches Ranger District, 510 Highway 12, Naches, WA 98937.

Location: Thirteen miles northwest of Yakima on Highway 12 is the town of Naches. From there, go 4 1/2 miles west on Highway 12, then drive 40 1/2 miles northwest on Highway 410 to the campground.

Trip note: This campground is set along the American River about seven miles west of the western boundary of Mount Rainier National Park. See trip note for campsite 46 for information on Mount Rainier.

SODA SPRINGS
Site **79**

Campsites, facilities: There are 19 sites for tents, trailers or motorhomes up to 15 feet long. Piped water and picnic tables are provided. Pit toilets and firewood are available. Pets are permitted.

Reservations, fee: No reservations necessary; no fee. Open May to clate-November.

Who to contact: Phone Wenatchee National Forest at 509-653-2205, or write at Naches Ranger District, 510 Highway 12, Naches, WA 98937.

Location: Naches is 13 miles northwest of Yakima on Highway 12. From Naches, continue 4 1/2 miles west on Highway 12, then go 28 1/2 miles northwest on Highway 410. Turn and go five miles southwest on Forest Service Road 174 and you'll see the campground.

Trip note: This campground is set along Bumping Creek and offers natural mineral springs and a nature trail.

Site 80   SQUAW ROCK RESORT

Campsites, facilities: There are 25 tent sites and 60 drive-through sites for trailers or motorhomes of any length. Electricity, piped water and picnic tables are provided. Flush toilets, bottled gas, sanitary services, showers, a recreation hall, store, cafe, laundromat, ice, playground and swimming pool are available. Sewer hookups can be obtained for an extra fee. Pets and motorbikes are permitted.

Reservations, fee: Reservations accepted; $11 fee per night. MasterCard and Visa accepted. Open all year.

Who to contact: Phone at 509-658-2926, or write at 15690 Highway 410, Naches, WA 98937.

Location: Thirteen miles northwest of Yakima on Highway 12 is the town of Naches. From there go five miles west on Highway 12, 15 miles northwest on Highway 410.

Trip note: This park is near the Naches River. Nearby recreation options include hiking trails, marked bike trails and a riding stable. The nearby town of Nile, located southeast of the campground on Highway 410, offers all services.

Site 81   SILVER COVE RESORT

Campsites, facilities: There are 10 tent sites and 35 sites for trailers or motorhomes. Electricity, piped water, sewer hookups and picnic tables are provided. Bottled gas, cafe, ice, boat docks, launching facilities and rentals are available. Store is located within one mile. Pets and motorbikes are permitted.

Reservations, fee: Reservations accepted; $8 fee per night. Open all year with limited winter facilities.

Who to contact: Write at P.O. Box 985, Yakima, WA 98907.

Location: From Yakima go 40 miles west on Highway 12 and you'll see the resort on Rimrock Lake.

Trip note: This resort is set along the shore of Rimrock Lake, one of several camps in the immediate area. See Zone 6 map. Nearby recreation options include hiking trails, marked bike trails, a full service marina and a riding stable.

Site 82   TWELVE WEST RESORT

Campsites, facilities: There are 34 sites for trailers or motorhomes up to 32 feet long. Picnic tables are provided. Flush toilets, bottled gas, electricity, piped water, showers, firewood, cafe and ice are available. Pets are permitted. Boat docks, launching facilities and rentals are nearby.

Reservations, fee: Reservations accepted; $10 fee per night. Open all year with limited winter facilities.

Who to contact: Write at Star Route, Box 206, Naches, WA 98937.

Location: From Yakima, go 42 miles west on Highway 12 and you'll see the resort on Rimrock Lake.

Trip note: This resort is set along the shore of Rimrock Lake. Nearby recreation options include hiking trails, marked bike trails, a full service marina and a riding stable.

Site 83
RIMROCK LAKE
RESORT AND MARINA

Campsites, facilities: There are 30 tent sites and 80 drive-through sites for trailers or motorhomes of any length. Electricity, piped water and picnic tables are provided. Flush toilets, sewer hookups, bottled gas, showers, sanitary services, recreation hall, store, cafe and ice are available. Pets and motorbikes are permitted. Boat docks, launching facilities and rentals are nearby.

Reservations, fee: Reservations accepted; $11 fee per night. American Express, Master-Card and Visa accepted. Open all year.

Who to contact: Phone at 509-452-1010, or write at Star Route, Box 212, Naches, WA 98937.

Location: From Yakima, go 45 miles west on Highway 12 and you'll see the resort.

Trip note: This resort is set along the shore of Rimrock Lake. Nearby recreation options include hiking trails, marked bike trails, a full service marina and a riding stable.

Site 84
HAUSE CREEK

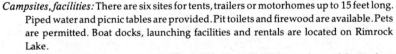

Campsites, facilities: There are 42 sites for tents, trailers or motorhomes up to 21 feet long. Piped water and picnic tables are provided. Flush toilets and firewood are available. Some facilities are wheelchair accessible. Pets are permitted. Boat docks, launching facilities and rentals are located on Rimrock Lake.

Reservations, fee: No reservations necessary; $5 fee per night. Open late-May to late-November.

Who to contact: Phone Wenatchee National Forest at 509-653-2205, or write at Naches Ranger District, 510 Highway 12, Naches, WA 98937.

Location: Drive 22 miles west of Naches on Highway 12 and you'll see the campground entrance.

Trip note: This campground is set along the Tieton River, where several creeks converge. The Teiton Dam, which creates Rimrock Lake, is just upstream.

Site 85
RIVER BEND

Campsites, facilities: There are six sites for tents, trailers or motorhomes up to 15 feet long. Piped water and picnic tables are provided. Pit toilets and firewood are available. Pets are permitted. Boat docks, launching facilities and rentals are located on Rimrock Lake.

Reservations, fee: No reservations necessary; $4 fee per night. Open April to mid-September.

Who to contact: Phone Wenatchee National Forest at 509-653-2205, or write at Naches Ranger District, 510 Highway 12, Naches, WA 98937.

Location: Drive 22 miles west of Naches on Highway 12 and you'll see the campground entrance.

Trip note: This campground is located near campsite 84. It is set on the Tieton River about five miles from Rimrock Lake.

WILD ROSE
Site **86**

Campsites, facilities: There are eight sites for tents, trailers or motorhomes up to 31 feet long. Picnic tables are provided. Pit toilets and firewood are available, but there is no piped water. Pets are permitted.

Reservations, fee: No reservations necessary; no fee. Open April to late-November.

Who to contact: Phone Wenatchee National Forest at 509-653-2205, or write at Naches Ranger District, 510 Highway 12, Naches, WA 98937.

Location: Drive 20 1/2 miles west of Naches on Highway 12 and you'll see the campground entrance.

Trip note: This campground is set along the Tieton River. An option to campsites 84, 85, 87 and 90.

WILLOWS
Site **87**

Campsites, facilities: There are 16 sites for tents, trailers or motorhomes up to 15 feet long. Picnic tables are provided. Pit toilets and firewood are available, but there is no piped water. Pets are permitted.

Reservations, fee: No reservations necessary; $4 fee per night. Open April to late-November.

Who to contact: Phone Wenatchee National Forest at 509-653-2205, or write at Naches Ranger District, 510 Highway 12, Naches, WA 98937.

Location: Drive 20 miles west of Naches on Highway 12 and you'll see the campground entrance.

Trip note: This campground is set along the Tieton River. Primitive, beautiful and easy access provided.

SOUTH FORK
Site **88**

Campsites, facilities: There are nine sites for tents, trailers or motorhomes up to 15 feet long. Picnic tables are provided. Pit toilets and firewood are available, but there is no piped water. Pets are permitted. Boat docks are nearby.

Reservations, fee: No reservations necessary; no fee. Open late-May to mid-September.

Who to contact: Phone Wenatchee National Forest at 509-653-2205, or write at Naches Ranger District, 510 Highway 12, Naches, WA 98937.

Location: Naches is 13 miles northwest of Yakima on Highway 12. From Naches continue 22 1/2 miles west on Highway 12, then go four miles south on Forest Service Road 143. Turn south on Forest Service Road 1000 and drive 1/2 mile to campground.

Trip note: This campground is set along the South Fork of the Tieton River, less than a mile from where it empties into Rimrock Lake. Often a good spot for trout fishing.

PENINSULA AND BOAT LANDING
Site **89**

Campsites, facilities: There are 19 sites for tents, trailers or motorhomes up to 15 feet long. Picnic tables are provided. Pit toilets and firewood are available, but there is no piped water. Pets are permitted. Boat docks and launching facilities are nearby.

Reservations, fee: No reservations necessary; no fee. Open mid-April to late-November.

Who to contact: Phone Wenatchee National Forest at 509-653-2205, or write at Naches Ranger District, 510 Highway 12, Naches, WA 98937.

Location: Naches is 13 miles northwest of Yakima on Highway 12. From Naches, continue 22 1/2 miles west on Highway 12, then go three miles south on Forest Service Road 143. At Forest Service Road 1382, turn west for one mile and you'll see the campground.

Trip note: This campground is set along the shore of Rimrock Lake. Swimming, fishing and water skiing are all allowed. One of several lakeside camps.

WINDY LAKE POINT

Site **90**

Campsites, facilities: There are 15 sites for tents, trailers or motorhomes up to 21 feet long. Piped water and picnic tables are provided. Pit toilets and firewood are available. Pets are permitted.

Reservations, fee: No reservations necessary; $4 fee per night. Open April to late-November.

Who to contact: Phone Wenatchee National Forest at 509-653-2205, or write at Naches Ranger District, 510 Highway 12, Naches, WA 98937.

Location: Drive 13 miles west of Naches on Highway 12 and you'll see the campground entrance.

Trip note: This campground is set along the Tieton River. More isolated than the camps set westward toward Rimrock Lake. Piped water is a bonus.

RIMROCK PUBLIC BOAT LANDING

Site **91**

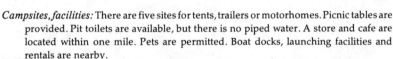

Campsites, facilities: There are five sites for tents, trailers or motorhomes. Picnic tables are provided. Pit toilets are available, but there is no piped water. A store and cafe are located within one mile. Pets are permitted. Boat docks, launching facilities and rentals are nearby.

Reservations, fee: No reservations necessary; no fee. Open mid-April to late-November.

Who to contact: Phone Wenatchee National Forest at 509-653-2205, or write at Naches Ranger District, 510 Highway 12, Naches, WA 98937.

Trip note: A small but good spot for campers trailering boats. This campground is set along the shore of Rimrock Lake where fishing, swimming and water skiing are allowed.

INDIAN CREEK

Site **92**

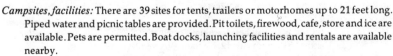

Campsites, facilities: There are 39 sites for tents, trailers or motorhomes up to 21 feet long. Piped water and picnic tables are provided. Pit toilets, firewood, cafe, store and ice are available. Pets are permitted. Boat docks, launching facilities and rentals are available nearby.

Reservations, fee: No reservations necessary; $5 fee per night. Open late-May to mid-September.

Who to contact: Phone Wenatchee National Forest at 509-653-2205, or write at Naches Ranger District, 510 Highway 12, Naches, WA 98937.

Location: Drive 31 1/2 miles west of Naches on Highway 12 and you'll see the campground entrance.

Trip note: This campground is set along the shore of Rimrock Lake. Fishing, swimming and waterskiing are allowed.

Site 93   CLEAR LAKE NORTH

Campsites, facilities: There are 35 sites for tents, trailers or motorhomes up to 21 feet long. Picnic tables are provided. Pit toilets and firewood are available, but there is no piped water. Pets are permitted. Boat docks, launching facilities and rentals are nearby.

Reservations, fee: No reservations necessary; no fee. Open mid-April to late-November.

Who to contact: Phone Wenatchee National Forest at 509-653-2205, or write at Naches Ranger District, 510 Highway 12, Naches, WA 98937.

Location: Naches is 13 miles northwest of Yakima on Highway 12. From Naches continue 35 1/2 miles west on Highway 12, then go one mile south on Forest Service Road 143. Continue 1/2 mile south on Forest Service Road 1312.

Trip note: This campground is set along the shore of Clear Lake, which is the forebay for Rimrock Lake. No swimming. Fishing only.

Site 94   CLEAR LAKE SOUTH AND BOAT LANDING

Campsites, facilities: There are 26 sites for tents, trailers or motorhomes up to 21 feet long. Piped water and picnic tables are provided. Pit toilets and firewood are available, but there is no piped water. Pets are permitted. Boat docks, launching facilities and rentals are nearby.

Reservations, fee: No reservations necessary; no fee. Open mid-April to late-November.

Who to contact: Phone Wenatchee National Forest at 509-653-2205, or write at Naches Ranger District, 510 Highway 12, Naches, WA 98937.

Location: Naches is 13 miles northwest of Yakima on Highway 12. From Naches continue 35 1/2 miles west on Highway 12, then go one mile south on Forest Service Road 143 to Forest Service Road 1312.

Trip note: This campground is located on Clear Lake, which is the forebay for Rimrock Lake. Fishing only.

Site 95   DOG LAKE AND BOAT LANDING

Campsites, facilities: There are 11 sites for tents, trailers or motorhomes up to 15 feet long. Picnic tables are provided. Pit toilets and firewood are available, but there is no piped water. Pets are permitted. Boat docks and launching facilities are nearby.

Reservations, fee: No reservations necessary; $2 fee per night. Open late-May to late-November.

Who to contact: Phone Wenatchee National Forest at 509-653-2205, or write at Naches Ranger District, 510 Highway 12, Naches, WA 98937.

Location: From the town of Packwood, drive 22 miles northeast on Highway 12.

Trip note: This campground is on the shore of Dog Lake. Nearby trails lead into the William O. Douglas Wilderness. See a Forest Service map for details.

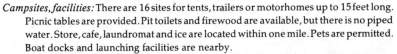

Site 96   WHITE PASS LAKE AND BOAT LANDING

Campsites, facilities: There are 16 sites for tents, trailers or motorhomes up to 15 feet long. Picnic tables are provided. Pit toilets and firewood are available, but there is no piped water. Store, cafe, laundromat and ice are located within one mile. Pets are permitted. Boat docks and launching facilities are nearby.

Reservations, fee: No reservations necessary; $2 fee per night. Open June to late-November.

Who to contact: Phone Wenatchee National Forest at 509-653-2205, or write at Naches Ranger District, 510 Highway 12, Naches, WA 98937.

Location: From the town of Packwood, drive 21 miles northeast on Highway 12, then turn north on Forest Service Road and drive 200 yards to Leech Lake.

Trip note: This campground is on the shore of Leech Lake. Nearby trails lead into the Goat Rock Wilderness to the south and the William O. Douglas wilderness to the north.

Site 97   BIG CREEK

Campsites, facilities: There are 30 sites for tents, trailers or motorhomes up to 21 feet long. Piped water and picnic tables are provided. Pit toilets and firewood are available. Some facilities are wheelchair accessible. Pets are permitted.

Reservations, fee: No reservations necessary; $5 fee per night. Open late-May to early-September.

Who to contact: Phone Gifford Pinchot National Forest at 206-494-5515, or write at Packwood Ranger District, Packwood, WA 98361.

Location: From the junction of Highways 7 and 706 at the town of Elbe, drive east about six miles to the town of Ashford. Continue 2 1/2 miles east on Highway 706, 1 1/2 miles south on a County Road, then continue 1/2 miles east on Forest Service Road 152.

Trip note: This campground is on the shore of Big Creek, just a short drive east to Mount Rainier National Park. See trip note for campsite 46 for details about Mount Rainier.

Site 98   PACKWOOD TRAILER AND RV PARK

Campsites, facilities: There are 15 tent sites and 57 drive-through sites for trailers or motorhomes of any length. Electricity, piped water, sewer hookups and picnic tables are provided. Flush toilets, sanitary services, showers, bottled gas, store, cafe, laundromat and ice are available. Pets and motorbikes are permitted.

Reservations, fee: Reservations accepted; $10 fee per night. MasterCard and Visa accepted. Open all year.

Who to contact: Phone at 206-494-5145, or write at P.O. Box 309, Packwood, WA 98361.

Location: This park is in the town of Packwood 25 miles south of Mount Rainier National Park.

Trip note: Nearby recreation options include a riding stable and tennis courts.

Site 99   MAPLE GROVE CAMPGROUND AND RV PARK

Campsites, facilities: There are six tent sites and 64 drive-through sites for trailers or motorhomes of any length. Electricity, piped water and picnic tables are provided. Flush toilets, sanitary services, firewood, recreation hall, store, cafe, laundromat, showers, bottled gas, ice and playground are available. Pets are permitted.

Reservations, fee: Reservations accepted; $10 fee per night. Open mid-April to December.

Who to contact: Phone at 206-497-2741, or write at P.O. Box 205, Randle, WA 98377.

Location: This park is located in the town of Randle, 16 miles east of Packwood on Highway 12.

Trip note: This RV park is set along the shore of the Cowlitz River. Nearby recreation options include hiking trails. One good drive is along winding Highway 26, which starts at Randle and heads up to Strawberry Mountain (5,464 feet). It's a good lookout point to Mt. St. Helens to the west.

Site **100** REDMON'S RV PARK

Campsites, facilities: There are 10 tent sites and six drive-through sites for trailers or motorhomes of any length. Electricity, piped water and sewer hookups are provided. Flush toilets, bottled gas, sanitary services, cafe, store and ice are available. Pets are permitted.

Reservations, fee: Reservations accepted; $12 fee per night. MasterCard and Visa accepted. Open all year.

Who to contact: Phone at 206-498-5425, or write at 8136 Highway 12, Glenoma, WA 98336.

Location: Drive 14 miles south of the town of Centralia on I-5 to the junction with Highway 12, then go east for 50 miles to the park.

Trip note: Recreation options include visiting huge Riffe Lake to the southeast, or driving up Strawberry Mountain or to the edge of Mt. St. Helens National Park—from Randle, drive south on Highway 26.

Site **101** HARMONY LAKESIDE RV PARK

Campsites, facilities: There are 14 tent sites and 52 drive-through sites for trailers or motorhomes of any length. Electricity, piped water, sewer hookups and picnic tables are provided. Flush toilets, sanitary services, showers, firewood, recreation hall and ice are available. Pets and motorbikes are permitted. Boat docks and launching facilities are nearby.

Reservations, fee: Reservations accepted; $9 fee per night. Open mid-April to mid-October.

Who to contact: Phone at 206-983-3804, or write at 563 Harmony Road, Silver Creek, WA 98585.

Location: Drive 14 miles south of the town of Centralia on I-5 to the junction with Highway 12, then go east for 18 miles. From there, drive 2 1/2 miles north on Harmony Road to the park.

Trip note: This park is set between three lakes. Campsites 102, 103, 104 provide nearby options.

Site **102** LAKE MAYFIELD MARINA RESORT

Campsites, facilities: There are 50 tent sites and 100 drive-through sites for trailers or

motorhomes of any length. Electricity, piped water, sewer hookups and picnic tables are provided. Flush toilets, sanitary services, showers, recreation hall, firewood, store, cafe and ice are available. A laundromat is located within one mile. Pets are permitted. Boat docks and launching facilities are nearby.

Reservations, fee: Reservations accepted; $10 fee per night. Open all year.

Who to contact: Phone at 206-985-2357, or write at 350 Lake Mayfield Resort, Mossy Rock, WA 98564.

Location: Drive 14 miles south of the town of Centralia on I-5 to the junction with Highway 12, then go east for 15 miles. From there, go one mile south on Winston Creek Road to the resort.

Trip note: This wooded resort is on the shore of Mayfield Reservoir. Nearby recreation options include hiking trails, marked bike trails and a riding stable.

Site **103**   WINSTON CREEK

Campsites, facilities: There are 11 primitive campsites for tents or small trailers. Picnic tables, fire grills and tent pads are provided. Pit toilets and piped water are available.

Reservations, fee: No reservations necessary; no fee. Open all year.

Who to contact: Phone the Department of Natural Resources at 1-800-527-3305, or write Department of Natural Resources AW-11, 1065 South Capitol Way, Olympia, WA 98504.

Location: Drive 14 miles south of the town of Centralia on I-5 to the junction with Highway 12, then go east for 15 miles. From there, go 3 1/2 miles south on Winston Creek Road. Turn left on Longbell Road and drive one mile. Camp is on the right.

Trip note: This campground is on the shore of Winston Creek, a primitive, quiet spot with lakeside beauty.

Site **104**   IKE KINSAWA STATE PARK

Campsites, facilities: There are 60 tent sites and 41 sites for trailers or motorhomes up to 20 feet long. Picnic tables are provided. Flush toilets, Sanitary services, store, cafe, playground, electricity, piped water, sewer hookups, showers and firewood are available. Some facilities are wheelchair accessible. Pets are permitted. Boat docks and launching facilities are nearby.

Reservations, fee: Reservations accepted; $6 fee per night. Open all year.

Who to contact: Phone at 206-983-3402, or write at 873 Harmony Road, Silver Lake, WA 98585.

Location: This state park is on Mayfield Lake, just north of the town of Mossy Lake, which is 18 miles east of I-5 on Highway 12.

Trip note: This campground is on the shore of Mayfield Reservoir, an option to campsite 103. This site provides more amenities. Nearby recreation options include hiking trails.

Site **105**   LEWIS & CLARK STATE PARK
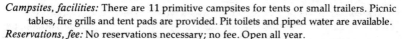

Campsites, facilities: There are 33 tent sites. Picnic tables are provided. Flush toilets, piped water, firewood and a playground are available. Pets are permitted.

Reservations, fee: No reservations necessary; $6 fee per night. Open all year.

Who to contact: Phone at 206-864-2643, or write at 4583 Jackson Highway, Winlock, WA 98596.

Location: From the town of Chehalis, drive 12 miles southeast on Jackson Highway 99 and you'll see the park.

Trip note: This state park has an interpretive center for Mt. St. Helens. There is also a kids' fishing pond stocked with trout, and a 1 1/2 mile nature trail.

Site 106   FROST ROAD TRAILER PARK

Campsites, facilities: There are 15 tent sites and 20 drive-through sites for trailers or motorhomes of any length. Electricity, piped water, sewer hookups and picnic tables are provided. Flush toilets, bottled gas, sanitary services, showers, recreation hall and ice are available. Pets are permitted.

Reservations, fee: Reservations accepted; $8 fee per night. MasterCard and Visa accepted. Open all year.

Who to contact: Phone at 206-785-3616, or write at 762 Frost Road, Winlock, WA 98596.

Location: Take the 63 exit off I-5 near Winlock, drive 3/4 mile east, 1 1/2 mile north and 1/2 mile west and you'll see the park.

Trip note: The Lewis and Clark State Park (campsite 105) is nearby. See trip note.

Site 107   STAN HEDWALL PARK

Campsites, facilities: There are 30 sites for trailers or motorhomes of any length. Electricity, piped water and picnic tables are provided. Flush toilets, showers, sanitary services and playground are available. Bottled gas, store, cafe and laundromat are available within one mile. Pets are permitted.

Reservations, fee: Reservations accepted; $7 fee per night. Open March to November.

Who to contact: Phone at 206-748-0271, or write at P.O. Box 871, Chehalis, WA 98532.

Location: Take the 76 exit off I-5 near Chehalis, then drive 1/8 mile south on Rice Road.

Trip note: This park is set along the Chehalis River. Nearby recreation options include an 18-hole golf course and hiking trails. Possible layover for I-5 travelers.

Site 108   RAINBOW FALLS STATE PARK

▲

Campsites, facilities: There are 50 tent sites. Picnic tables are provided. Flush toilets, piped water, sanitary services, showers, firewood and playground are available. Pets are permitted.

Reservations, fee: No reservations necessary; $6 fee per night. Open all year.

Who to contact: Phone at 206-291-3767, or write at 4008 Highway 6, Chehalis, WA 98532.

Location: Take Highway 6 west off I-5 in Chehalis, travel four miles south, then go west on Highway 6 for 18 miles and you'll see the park entrance.

Trip note: About a 25-minute drive from I-5, but out-of-towners pass it every time. A nice spot, with a swinging bridge over the Chehalis River, a pool at the base of Rainbow Falls for swimming, trout fishing opportunities and a self-guided nature trail through the old growth forest.

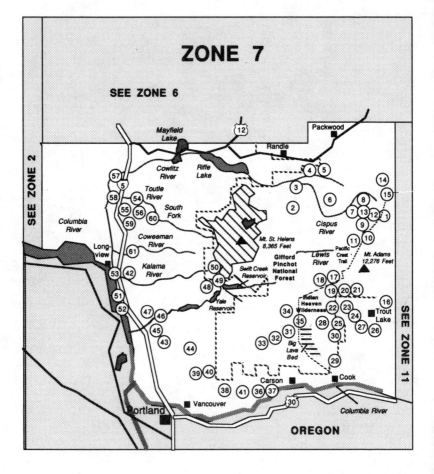

MOUNT ST. HELENS

KEENE'S
Site **1** HORSE CAMP

Campsites, facilities: There are 14 sites for tents, trailers or motorhomes up to 21 feet long.
 Picnic tables are provided. Pit toilets and firewood are available, but there is no piped
 water. Boat docks and launching facilities are nearby.

Reservations, fee: No reservations necessary; no fee. Open July to mid-September.

Who to contact: Phone Gifford Pinchot National Forest at 206-497-7565, or write at Randle
 Ranger District, Randle, WA 98377.

Location: Take County Road 3 off Highway 12 in Randle and drive two miles south, then
 go 29 miles southeast on Forest Service Road 23. Turn northeast on Forest Service
 Road 2329 and go seven miles, then turn west on Forest Service Road 82 and drive
 100 yards to the campground. A Forest Service map is essential.

Trip note: This campground is set at 4200 feet elevation along the South Fork of Spring
 Creek on the northwest flank of Mount Adams (elevation 12,276 feet) The Pacific
 Crest Trail passes within a couple of miles of camp. There are a number of trails from
 camp leading into the backcountry and to several alpine meadows. The meadows are
 fragile, so it is best to walk along their outer edges, where they meet the forest.

POLE PATCH
Site **2**

Campsites, facilities: There are 12 tent sites and four sites for trailers or motorhomes up to
 21 feet long. Picnic tables are provided. Pit toilets and firewood are available, but
 there is no piped water.

Reservations, fee: No reservations necessary; no fee. Open July to mid-September.

Who to contact: Phone Gifford Pinchot National Forest at 206-497-7565, or write at Randle
 Ranger District, Randle, WA 98377.

Location: Take County Route 3 south off Highway 12 in the town of Randle and go two
 miles. Continue south for 20 miles on Forest Service Road 25, then go east on Forest
 Service Road 28 for three miles. Turn north on Forest Service Road 77 for six miles to
 the campground. A Forest Service map is essential.

Trip note: This primitive camp is at 4400 feet elevation and is in an isolated alpine area near
 French Butte. Before taking your first step, you should obtain a map of the Gifford
 Pinchot National Forest, which details all back country roads, trails, lakes and
 streams.

IRON CREEK
Site **3**

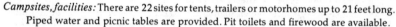

Campsites, facilities: There are 54 sites for tents, trailers or motorhomes up to 31 feet long. Piped water and picnic tables are provided. Pit toilets and firewood are available.

Reservations, fee: No reservations necessary; $5 fee per night. Open mid-May to late-October.

Who to contact: Phone Gifford Pinchot National Forest at 206-497-7565, or write at Randle Ranger District, Randle, WA 98377.

Location: Take County Route 3 south off Highway 12 in the town of Randle and go two miles. Continue south for 7 1/2 miles on Forest Service Road 25 and you'll see the campground entrance.

Trip note: One of the more popular Forest Service campgrounds. This spot is set along the Cispus River near its confluence with Iron Creek. A Forest Service Visitors Center is nearby which provides information about the Mount St. Helens-Mount Adams area.

TOWER ROCK
Site **4**

Campsites, facilities: There are 22 sites for tents, trailers or motorhomes up to 21 feet long. Piped water and picnic tables are provided. Pit toilets and firewood are available.

Reservations, fee: No reservations necessary; $5 fee per night. Open mid-May to late-September.

Who to contact: Phone Gifford Pinchot National Forest at 206-497-7565, or write at Randle Ranger District, Randle, WA 98377.

Location: Take County Road 3 off Highway 12 in Randle and drive south for two miles, then head southeast on Forest Service Road 23 for 5 1/2 miles. Turn south on Forest Service Road 28 and drive 1 1/2 miles and then go two miles west on Forest Service Road 76 to the campground. A Forest Service map is essential.

Trip note: This campground is set along the Cispus River.

NORTH FORK
Site **5**

Campsites, facilities: There are 33 sites for tents, trailers or motorhomes up to 31 feet long. Piped water and picnic tables are provided. Pit toilets and firewood are available.

Reservations, fee: No reservations necessary; $5 fee per night. Open mid-May to late-September.

Who to contact: Phone Gifford Pinchot National Forest at 206-497-7565, or write at Randle Ranger District, Randle, WA 98377.

Location: Take County Road 3 off Highway 12 in Randle and drive south for two miles, then turn southeast on Forest Service Road 23 and drive nine miles to the campground.

Trip note: This campground is set along the North Cispus River. In addition to fishing, there are nature trails and bike paths. A National Forest map details the back country.

BLUE LAKE
Site **6**   CREEK

Campsites, facilities: There are 11 sites for tents, trailers or motorhomes up to 31 feet long. Picnic tables are provided. Pit toilets, piped water and firewood are available.

Reservations, fee: No reservations necessary; no fee. Open mid-May to late-September.

Who to contact: Phone Gifford Pinchot National Forest at 206-497-7565, or write at Randle Ranger District, Randle, WA 98377.

Location: Take County Road 3 off Highway 12 in Randle and drive south for two miles, then turn southeast on Forest Service Road 23 and drive 13 miles to the campground.

Trip note: This is a classic Washington hideaway. The campground is set along Blue Lake Creek, a good base camp for the two-mile hike to Blue Lake. The trailhead is about a half-mile walk from camp.

ADAMS FORK
Site **7**

Campsites, facilities: There are 27 sites for tents, trailers or motorhomes up to 21 feet long. Piped water and picnic tables are provided. Pit toilets and firewood are available. Boat docks and launching facilities are nearby on the Upper Cispus River.

Reservations, fee: No reservations necessary; no fee. Open mid-May to late-September.

Who to contact: Phone Gifford Pinchot National Forest at 206-497-7565, or write at Randle Ranger District, Randle, WA 98377

Location: Take County Route 3 off Highway 12 in Randle and drive south for two miles, then turn southeast on Forest Service Road 23 and go 16 miles. Turn southeast on Forest Service Road 20 and drive 4 1/2 miles, then turn east and go 200 yards on Forest Service Road 56 to the campground.

Trip note: This campground is set along the Upper Cispus River near Adams Creek at an elevation of 2600 feet. A nearby trail leads north to Blue Lake, about a half-mile walk from camp.

CAT CREEK
Site **8**

Campsites, facilities: There are six sites for tents, trailers or motorhomes up to 15 feet long. Picnic tables are provided. Pit toilets and firewood are available, but there is no piped water.

Reservations, fee: No reservations necessary; no fee. Open mid-May to late-September.

Who to contact: Phone Gifford Pinchot National Forest at 206-497-7565, or write at Randle Ranger District, Randle, WA 98377.

Location: Take County Route 3 off Highway 12 in Randle and drive south for two miles, then turn southeast on Forest Service Road 23 and go 16 miles. Turn east on Forest Service Road 21 and drive six miles to the campground.

Trip note: This pretty spot is set along Cat Creek at its confluence with the Cispus River about 10 miles from the summit of Mount Adams. A trail that starts less than a mile from camp leads up along Blue Lake Ridge to Blue Lake. See a Forest Service map for details.

OLALLIE LAKE

Site **9**

Campsites, facilities: There are six sites for tents, trailers or motorhomes up to 21 feet long. Picnic tables are provided. Pit toilets and firewood are available, but there is no piped water. Boat docks and launching facilities are nearby.

Reservations, fee: No reservations necessary; no fee. Open July to mid-September.

Who to contact: Phone Gifford Pinchot National Forest at 206-497-7565, or write at Randle Ranger District, Randle, WA 98377.

Location: Take County Route 3 off Highway 12 in Randle and drive south for two miles, then turn southeast on Forest Service Road 23 and go 29 miles. Turn north on Forest Service Road 2329 and drive 1/2 mile, then continue north on Forest Service Road 5601 for 1/2 mile to the campground. A Forest Service map is essential.

Trip note: This campground is set along the shore of Olallie Lake at 4000 feet elevation. This small alpine lake is one of several in the area fed by streams coming off the glaciers on nearby Mount Adams (elevation 12,326 feet). A word to the wise: Mosquitos can be a problem in the spring and early summer; see Chapter 5 on protection against insects.

TAKHLAKH

Site **10**

Campsites, facilities: There are seven sites for tents, trailers or motorhomes up to 21 feet long. Piped water and picnic tables are provided. Pit toilets and firewood are available. Boat docks and launching facilities are available nearby on the lake.

Reservations, fee: No reservations necessary, with a fee of $2 per night. Open mid-June to late-September.

Who to contact: Phone Gifford Pinchot National Forest at 206-497-7565, or write at Randle Ranger District, Randle, 98377.

Location: Take County Route 3 off Highway 12 in Randle and drive south for 2 miles, then turn southeast on Forest Service Road 23 and go 29 miles. Go north on Forest Service Road 2329 for 1 ½ miles to the campground.

Trip note: This campground is set along the shore of Takhlakh Lake. This is one of five lakes in the area, all accessible by car.

COUNCIL LAKE

Site **11**

Campsites, facilities: There are 11 sites for tents, trailers or motorhomes up to 15 feet long. Picnic tables are provided. Pit toilets and firewood are available, but there is no piped water. Boat docks are nearby.

Reservations, fee: No reservations necessary; $2 fee per night. Open July to mid-September.

Who to contact: Phone Gifford Pinchot National Forest at 206-497-7565, or write at Randle Ranger District, Randle, WA 98377.

Location: Take County Route 3 off Highway 12 in Randle and drive south for two miles, then turn southeast on Forest Service Road 23 and go 30 miles. Turn west on Forest Service Road 2334 and drive one mile to the campground.

Trip note: This campground is set along the shore of Council Lake at about 4000 feet elevation along the northwest flank of Mount Adams. One of three lakeside campgrounds in immediate area.

KILLEN CREEK
Site **12**

Campsites, facilities: There are six tent sites and eight sites for trailers or motorhomes up to 21 feet long. Picnic tables are provided. Pit toilets and firewood are available, but there is no piped water.

Reservations, fee: No reservations necessary; no fee. Open July to mid-September.

Who to contact: Phone Gifford Pinchot National Forest at 206-497-7565, or write at Randle Ranger District, Randle, WA 98377.

Location: Take County Route 3 off Highway 12 in Randle and drive south for two miles, then turn southeast on Forest Service Road 23 and go 29 miles. Turn southeast on Forest Service Road 2329 and go six miles, then go 200 yards west on Forest Service Road 72.

Trip note: This campground is set along Killen Creek at the foot of Mount Adams (elevation 12,326 feet). A trail from camp leads up the mountain and connects with the Pacific Crest Trail, about a three-mile hike. It's worth the grunt.

HORSESHOE
Site **13** LAKE

Campsites, facilities: There are 10 sites for tents, trailers or motorhomes up to 15 feet long. Picnic tables are provided. Pit toilets and firewood are available, but there is no piped water. Boat docks and launching facilities are available on the lake.

Reservations, fee: No reservations necessary; no fee. Open mid-June to late-September.

Who to contact: Phone Gifford Pinchot National Forest at 206-497-7565, or write at Randle Ranger District, Randle, 98377.

Location: Take County Route 3 off Highway 12 in Randle and drive south for three miles, then turn southeast on Forest Service Road 23 and go 29 miles. Turn northeast on Forest Service Road 2329 and drive six miles, then turn west and go 1 1/2 miles on Forest Service Road 78.

Trip note: This campground is set along the shore of Horseshoe Lake. A trail from camp goes up nearby Green Mountain (elevation 5000 feet). Another trail heads up the north flank of Mount Adams. See a Forest Service map for details.

WALUPT LAKE
Site **14**

Campsites, facilities: There are 35 tent sites and 35 sites for trailers or motorhomes up to 21 feet long. Picnic tables are provided. Pit and vault toilets, and firewood is available. Some facilities are wheelchair accessible. There is no piped water. Boat docks are located nearby on Walupt Lake.

Reservations, fee: No reservations necessary; no fee. Open mid-June to early-September.

Who to contact: Phone Gifford Pinchot National Forest at 206-494-5515, or write at Packwood Ranger District, Packwood, WA 98361.

Location: Drive 2 1/2 miles southwest of Packwood on Highway 12, then go southeast on Forest Service Road 1302 for 16 1/2 miles. Head east on Forest Service Road 1114 for 4 1/2 miles and you'll arrive at the campground.

Trip note: A good base-camp for a multi-day vacation. For starters, this camp is set along the shore of Walupt Lake. For finishers, several nearby trails lead into the backcountry and other smaller alpine lakes. See a Forest Service map for details.

Site **15**
WALUPT LAKE
HORSE CAMP

Campsites, facilities: There are six sites for tents, trailers or motorhomes up to 15 feet long. Picnic tables are provided. Pit toilets and firewood are available, but there is no piped water.

Reservations, fee: No reservations necessary; no fee. Open mid-June to early-September.

Who to contact: Phone Gifford Pinchot National Forest at 206-494-5515, or write at Packwood Ranger District, Packwood, WA 98361.

Location: Drive 2 1/2 miles southwest of Packwood on Highway 12, then go southeast on Forest Service Road 2100 for 16 1/2 miles. Head east on Forest Service Road 2160 for 3 1/2 miles to the campground.

Trip note: Walupt Lake is just a mile away from the camp, where you can fish or use the boat dock. Several trails lead out from Walupt Lake into the backcountry of southern Goat Rocks Wilderness, which has 85 miles of trails that can be used by horses. If you have planned a multi-day horsepack trip, you need to bring in your own feed for the horses.

Site **16**
MORRISON
CREEK

Campsites, facilities: There are 12 tent sites. Picnic tables are provided. Pit toilets and firewood are available, but there is no piped water.

Reservations, fee: No reservations necessary; no fee. Open July to late-September.

Who to contact: Phone Gifford Pinchot National Forest at 509-395-2501, or write at Mount Adams Ranger District, Trout Lake, WA 98650.

Location: From Trout Lake, drive 200 yards southeast on Highway 141, then go north on County Route 17 for two miles. Continue north on Forest Service Road 8000 for 3 1/2 miles and head six miles north on Forest Service Road 8040.

Trip note: Here is a premium yet little-known spot. This campground is set along Morrison Creek at an elevation of 4600 feet near the southern slopes of Mount Adams, the second highest mountain in Washington (highest is Rainier). Nearby trails will take you to the ice fields and alpine meadows of the Mount Adams Wilderness.

Site **17**
SADDLE

Campsites, facilities: There are eight tent sites and two sites for trailers or motorhomes up to 15 feet long. Picnic tables are provided. Pit toilets and firewood are available, but no piped water is available.

Reservations, fee: No reservations necessary, with a fee of $2 per night. Open mid-June to late-September.

Who to contact: Phone Gifford Pinchot National Forest at 509-395-2501, or write at Mount Adams Ranger District, Trout Lake, 98650.

Location: From Trout Lake, drive 5 ½ miles southwest on Highway 141, then turn northwest on Forest Service Road 2400 and go 19 miles. Take Forest Service Road 2480 north for 1 ½ miles to the campground.

Trip note: One of eight campgrounds in immediate vicinity, we've numbered them Camps 17-24. There are two lakes nearby called Big and Little Mosquito Lakes which are fed by Mosquito Creek. So, while we're on the subject...mosquito attacks in late spring and early summer can be like squandrons of Russian bombers moving in. A sidelight is that the Pacific Crest Trail passes right by camp.

TILLICUM
Site 18   🚗

Campsites, facilities: There are 12 tent sites and 37 sites for tents, trailers or motorhomes up to 15 feet long. Piped water and picnic tables are provided. Pit toilets and firewood are available.

Reservations, fee: No reservations necessary; $4 fee per night. Open mid-June to late-September.

Who to contact: Phone Gifford Pinchot National Forest at 509-395-2501, or write at Mount Adams Ranger District, Trout Lake, WA 98650.

Location: From Trout Lake, drive 5 1/2 miles southwest on Highway 141, then turn northwest on Forest Service Road 2400 and drive 19 miles to the campground.

Trip note: A trail from camp leads southwest past little Meadow Lake to Squaw Butte, then over to Big Creek. Give it a try, a nice jaunt.

SURPRISE LAKES
INDIAN
Site 19   ▲

Campsites, facilities: There are nine tent sites and six sites for trailers or motorhomes up to 15 feet long. Picnic tables are provided. Pit toilets and firewood are available, but there is no piped water.

Reservations, fee: No reservations necessary; $2 fee per night. Open mid-June to late-September.

Who to contact: Phone Gifford Pinchot National Forest at 509-395-2501, or write at Mount Adams Ranger District, Trout Lake, WA 98650.

Location: From Trout Lake, drive 5 1/2 miles southwest on Highway 141, then turn northwest on Forest Service Road 2400 and drive 16 miles to the campground.

Trip note: This campground is set near a cluster of small lakes called the Surprise Lakes. The Pacific Crest Trail passes by camp and continues south into the Indian Heaven Wilderness area which is accessible only by foot path. Mosquito repellent is advised in early summer. This area is of Indian historical significance. Mosquito repellent advised in early summer.

COLD SPRINGS
INDIAN
Site 20   ▲

Campsites, facilities: There are nine sites for tents, trailers or motorhomes up to 15 feet long. Picnic tables are provided. Pit toilets and firewood are available, but there is no piped water.

Reservations, fee: No reservations necessary; $2 fee per night. Open mid-June to late-September.

Who to contact: Phone Gifford Pinchot National Forest at 509-395-2501, or write at Mount Adams Ranger District, Trout Lake, WA 98650.

Location: From Trout Lake, drive 5 1/2 miles southwest on Highway 141, then turn northwest on Forest Service Road 2400 and go 15 miles. Turn northeast on Forest Service Road 220 and go one mile to camp.

Trip note: If you like to hike to remote mountain lakes, this is a great jumpoff point. The camp is about a mile from the Pacific Crest Trail, which travels south through the

Indian Heaven Wilderness where you will find over 100 small lakes and ponds.

Site 21
MEADOW CREEK
INDIAN

Campsites, facilities: There are eight tent sites. Picnic tables are provided. Pit and vault toilets, and firewood are available. There is no piped water.

Reservations, fee: No reservations necessary; $2 fee per night. Open mid-June to late-September.

Who to contact: Phone Gifford Pinchot National Forest at 509-395-2501, or write at Mount Adams Ranger District, Trout Lake, WA 98650.

Location: From Trout Lake, drive 5 1/2 miles southwest on Highway 141, then turn northwest on Forest Service Road 2400 and drive 14 miles to the campground.

Trip note: This campground is a mile south of campsite 19. A map of Gifford Pinchot National Forest details back roads, trails, lakes and streams.

Site 22
CULTUS
CREEK

Campsites, facilities: There are 57 tent sites and seven sites for trailers or motorhomes up to 15 feet long. Piped water and picnic tables are provided. Pit toilets and firewood are available. Some facilities are wheelchair accessible.

Reservations, fee: No reservations necessary; $4 fee per night. Open mid-June to late-September.

Who to contact: Phone Gifford Pinchot National Forest at 509-395-2501, or write at Mount Adams Ranger District, Trout Lake, WA 98650.

Location: From Trout Lake, drive 5 1/2 miles southwest on Highway 141, then turn northwest on Forest Service Road 2400 and drive 12 1/2 miles to the campground.

Trip note: This campground is set at an elevation of 4000 feet, along Cultus Creek and on the edge of Indian Heaven Wilderness. Nearby trails will take you into this backcountry area, which has numerous small meadows and lakes among the stands of firs and pines.

Site 23
LITTLE GOOSE

Campsites, facilities: There are 28 tent sites and 10 sites for trailers or motorhomes up to 15 feet long. Piped water and picnic tables are provided. Pit toilets and firewood are available.

Reservations, fee: No reservations necessary; $2 fee per night. Open June to late-October.

Who to contact: Phone Gifford Pinchot National Forest at 509-395-2501, or write at Mount Adams Ranger District, Trout Lake, WA 98650.

Location: From Trout Lake, drive 5 1/2 miles southwest on Highway 141, then turn northwest on Forest Service Road 2400 and drive 10 miles to the campground.

Trip note: This campground is near Little Goose Creek and the backcountry of the Indian Heaven Wilderness. Since this camp has piped water available, it gets heavier use that most of the others in the immediate vicinity.

Site **24** SMOKEY CREEK CAMPGROUND

Campsites, facilities: There are five sites for tents, trailers or motorhomes up to 21 feet long. Picnic tables are provided. Pit toilets and firewood are available, but there is no piped water.

Reservations, fee: No reservations necessary; no fee. Open June to late-October.

Who to contact: Phone Gifford Pinchot National Forest at 509-395-2501, or write at Mount Adams Ranger District, Trout Lake, WA 98650.

Location: From Trout Lake, drive 5 1/2 miles southwest on Highway 141, then turn northwest on Forest Service Road 2400 and drive 7 1/2 miles to the campground.

Trip note: A primitive, little-used campground that is set along Smokey Creek. A trail leading into the Indian Lake Wilderness passes through camp. See trip notes to campsites 15-21 for details of the recreation options of the immediate area.

Site **25** FORLORN LAKES

Campsites, facilities: There are eight sites for tents, trailers or motorhomes up to 15 feet long. Picnic tables are provided. Pit toilets and firewood are available, but there is no piped water. Boat docks are available.

Reservations, fee: No reservations necessary; $3 fee per night. Open June to late-October.

Who to contact: Phone Gifford Pinchot National Forest at 509-395-2501, or write at Mount Adams Ranger District, Trout Lake, WA 98650.

Location: From Trout Lake, drive 5 1/2 miles southwest on Highway 141, then turn west on Forest Service Road 2400 and go one mile. Continue west on Forest Service Road 6000 for five miles, then turn north on Forest Service Road 6040 and go 2 1/2 miles to the campground.

Trip note: This campground is set among a group of small lakes about two miles from the edge of the Big Lava Bed and about four miles from the 500-foot deep crater from which it came. How big is this Big Lava Bed? About 12,000 acres, with lava tubes and other strange formations. The Forest Service cautions: "No trails or roads traverse the lava field, generally limiting exploration to the perimeter. If you choose to explore the interior, choose your route carefully. Compasses are not always reliable due to local magnetic influences in the vast expanse of rock."

Site **26** ICE CAVE

Campsites, facilities: There are 12 sites for tents, trailers or motorhomes up to 15 feet long. Picnic tables are provided. Pit toilets and firewood are available, but there is no piped water.

Reservations, fee: No reservations necessary; $2 fee per night. Open June to late-October.

Who to contact: Phone Gifford Pinchot National Forest at 509-395-2501, or write at Mount Adams Ranger District, Trout Lake, WA 98650.

Location: From Trout Lake, drive 5 1/2 miles southwest on Highway 141, then turn west on Forest Service Road 2400 and go one mile. Turn south on Forest Service Road 31 and go 200 yards to the campground.

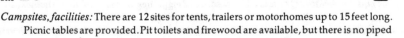

Trip note: This campground is located near 400-foot deep Ice Cave, one of the many lava tubes in the area. It looks like a different planet out here. This is the closest campground to the town of Trout Camp.

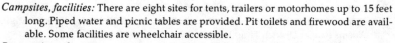

Site 27   PETERSON PRAIRIE

Campsites, facilities: There are eight sites for tents, trailers or motorhomes up to 15 feet long. Piped water and picnic tables are provided. Pit toilets and firewood are available. Some facilities are wheelchair accessible.

Reservations, fee: No reservations necessary; $6 fee per night. Open mid-May to late-September.

Who to contact: Phone Gifford Pinchot National Forest at 509-395-2501, or write at Mount Adams Ranger District, Trout Lake, WA 98650.

Location: From Trout Lake, drive 5 1/2 miles southwest on Highway 141, then turn west on Forest Service Road 2400 and drive 2 1/2 miles to the campground.

Trip note: This spot provides a good base camp if you want to have a short ride to town as well as access to the nearby wilderness areas. The Sno-park area provides winter recreation, including snowmobiling and cross-country skiing tracks.

Site 28   GOOSE LAKE

Campsites, facilities: There are 25 tent sites and one site for trailers or motorhomes up to 15 feet long. Picnic tables are provided. Pit toilets and firewood are available, but there is no piped water. A boat ramp is nearby.

Reservations, fee: No reservations necessary; $2 fee per night. Open mid-June to late-September.

Who to contact: Phone Gifford Pinchot National Forest at 509-395-2501, or write at Mount Adams Ranger District, Trout Lake, WA 98650.

Location: From Trout Lake, drive 5 1/2 miles southwest on Highway 141, then turn west on Forest Service Road 2400 and drive 2 1/2 miles, then go southwest on Forest Service Road 6000 for five miles and you'll arrive at the campground.

Trip note: This campground is set at an elevation of 3200 feet along the shore of Goose Lake. The northern edge of the Big Lava Bed and nearby crater are adjacent to camp.

Site 29   MOSS CREEK

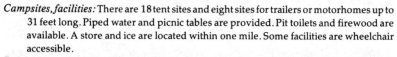

Campsites, facilities: There are 18 tent sites and eight sites for trailers or motorhomes up to 31 feet long. Piped water and picnic tables are provided. Pit toilets and firewood are available. A store and ice are located within one mile. Some facilities are wheelchair accessible.

Reservations, fee: No reservations necessary; $4 fee per night. Open mid-May to mid-September.

Who to contact: Phone Gifford Pinchot National Forest at 509-395-2501, or write at Mount Adams Ranger District, Trout Lake, WA 98650.

Location: From the town of Cook on Highway 14, go north on County Route 1800 for eight miles and you'll see the campground.

Trip note: This campground is set along the Little White Salmon River, a short distance from the town of Willard and Big Cedars County Park.

OKLAHOMA
Site **30**

Campsites, facilities: There are 21 tent sites and nine sites for trailers or motorhomes up to
    21 feet long. Piped water and picnic tables are provided. Pit toilets and firewood are
    available. Some facilities are wheelchair accessible.
Reservations, fee: No reservations necessary; $4 fee per night. Open mid-May to mid-
    October.
Who to contact: Phone Gifford Pinchot National Forest at 509-395-2501, or write at Mount
    Adams Ranger District, Trout Lake, WA 98650.
Location: From the town of Cook on Highway 14, go north on County Route 1800 for 14 1/2
    miles and you'll see the campground entrance.
Trip note: This campground is set along the Little White Salmon River. The Big Lava Bed is
    set just west and detailed in the trip note for campsite 25. As to why they named this
    camp "Oklahoma," who knows? Guess they had to name it something.

PANTHER CREEK
Site **31**

Campsites, facilities: There are seven sites for tents, trailers or motorhomes up to 21 feet
    long. Piped water and picnic tables are provided. Pit toilets and firewood are available.
Reservations, fee: No reservations necessary; $6 fee per night. Open mid-May to mid-
    September.
Who to contact: Phone Gifford Pinchot National Forest at 509-427-5645, or write at Wind
    River Ranger District, Carson, WA 98610.
Location: From the town of Carson on Highway 14, go nine miles northwest on County
    Route 92135. Turn east on Forest Service Road 6517 and go 1 1/2 miles, then turn
    south on Forest Service Road 65 for 100 yards to the campground.
Trip note: This campground is set along Panther Creek, several miles from the Wind River
    Ranger Station. Just west of the ranger station is the Wind River Nursery, a tree
    nursery that has the capacity to produce 27 million seedlings per year. Tours are
    available.

BEAVER
Site **32**

Campsites, facilities: There are five sites for tents, trailers or motorhomes up to 21 feet
    long. Piped water and picnic tables are provided. Pit toilets and firewood are avail-
    able. Some facilities are wheelchair accessible.
Reservations, fee: No reservations necessary; $8 fee per night. Open mid-May to late-
    October.
Who to contact: Phone Gifford Pinchot National Forest at 509-427-5645, or write at Wind
    River Ranger District, Carson, WA 98610.
Location: From the town of Carson on Highway 14, go 12 miles northwest on County
    Route 92135 and you'll see the campground entrance.
Trip note: This campground is set along Wind River about four miles from Trapper Creek
    Wilderness. A nice spot, small and remote, yet with piped water.

Site 33
LITTLE SODA SPRINGS

Campsites, facilities: There are seven sites for tents, trailers or motorhomes. Piped water and picnic tables are provided. Pit toilets and firewood are available.

Reservations, fee: No reservations necessary; $2 fee per night. Open mid-May to October.

Who to contact: Phone Gifford Pinchot National Forest at 509-427-5645, or write at Wind River Ranger District, Carson, WA 98610.

Location: From the town of Carson on Highway 14, go 13 miles northwest on County Route 92135 then turn and go one mile south on Forest Service Road 5401 to the campground.

Trip note: If campsite 32 is full, this provides a close option in virtually the same setting. It is situated along the Wind River about two miles from Trapper Creek Wilderness. There appear to be several mineral springs in the area. Ask at the ranger station in Wind River.

Site 34
PARADISE CREEK

Campsites, facilities: There are eight sites for tents, trailers or motorhomes up to 31 feet long. Piped water and picnic tables are provided. Pit toilets and firewood are available. Some facilities are wheelchair accessible.

Reservations, fee: No reservations necessary; $6 fee per night. Open mid-May to mid-September.

Who to contact: Phone Gifford Pinchot National Forest at 509-427-5645, or write at Wind River Ranger District, Carson, WA 98610.

Location: From the town of Carson on Highway 14, go 13 miles northwest on County Route 92135 then turn and go 6 1/2 miles north on Forest Service Road 30.

Trip note: Set fairly deep in the Gifford Pinchot National Forest, this campground is located at the confluence of Paradise Creek and the Wind River. Lava Butte is a short distance from camp and accessible by trail.

Site 35
FALLS CREEK/ CREST HORSE CAMP

Campsites, facilities: There are five sites for tents, trailers or motorhomes up to 15 feet long. Picnic tables are provided. Pit toilets and firewood are available, but there is no piped water.

Reservations, fee: No reservations necessary; no fee. Open mid-June to late-September.

Who to contact: Phone Gifford Pinchot National Forest at 509-427-5645, or write at Wind River Ranger District, Carson, WA 98610.

Location: From the town of Carson on Highway 14, go 13 miles northwest on County Route 92135, 1 1/2 miles east on Forest Service Road 6517, and then 12 1/2 miles north on Forest Service Road 65 to the campground.

Trip note: This camp is set along the Pacific Crest Trail and adjacent to the Big Lava Beds near the crater. See trip note to campsite 25 for details. The southern boundary of Indian Heaven Wilderness is two miles north of camp and is accessible by the Pacific Crest Trail.

Site **36**

BEACON ROCK
TRAILER PARK

Campsites, facilities: There are six tent sites and 15 drive-through sites for trailers or motorhomes of any length. Electricity, piped water, sewer hookups and picnic tables are provided. Flush toilets, bottled gas, sanitary services, showers, firewood, a recreation hall, laundromat and ice are available. A store and cafe are located within one mile. Pets are permitted. Boat launching facilities are nearby on the Columbia River.

Reservations, fee: Reservations accepted; $8 fee per night. Open all year.

Who to contact: Phone at 509-427-8473, or write at Beacon Rock Trailer Park, Skamania, WA 98648.

Location: Drive 15 miles west of the town of Carson on Highway 14 and you will see the park in the town of Skamania.

Trip note: This trailer park is set along the Columbia River, a short distance from Beacon Rock State Park. Nearby recreation options include an 18-hole golf course.

Site **37**

BEACON ROCK
STATE PARK

Campsites, facilities: There are 35 sites for tents or motorhomes up to 50 feet long. Picnic tables are provided. Flush toilets, showers, firewood, sanitary services and a playground are available. Some facilities are wheelchair accessible. Boat docks, launching facilities and rentals are nearby.

Reservations, fee: No reservations necessary; $6 fee per night. Open all year with limited winter facilities.

Who to contact: Phone at 509-427-8265, or write at MP34 83L, State Route 14, Skamania, WA 98648.

Location: Drive 35 miles east of the the town of Vancouver (Washington) on Highway 14 and you'll see the park entrance.

Trip note: This state park is set along the Columbia River with hiking trails heading inland. One of the trails leads to Beacon Rock, the second largest monolith in the world, which overlooks the Columbia River Gorge. If you like to fish, sturgeon are popular in the Columbia. Remember, there is a 6-foot maximum size limit for Mr. Sturgeon. A riding stable is in the area.

Site **38**

JONES CREEK

Campsites, facilities: There are nine campsites for tents or small trailers. Picnic tables, fire grills and tent pads are provided. Pit toilets and piped water are available. Motorbikes are permitted.

Reservations, fee: No reservations necessary; no fee. Open all year.

Who to contact: Phone the Department of Natural Resources at 1-800-527-3305, or write Department of Natural Resources AW-11, 1065 South Capitol Way, Olympia, WA 98504.

Location: Drive six miles east of Vancouver, WA on Highway 14 to the town of Camas. From the junction of Highways 14 and 500, go north on State Route 500 for 3 1/2 miles to Fern Prairie. Turn right on 19th Street and go one mile. Turn left on 292 Avenue and go two miles, then turn right on Ireland Drive and go about 200 yards.

Turn left on Lessard Road and go two miles, then continue straight on Winters Road for 1 1/2 miles and you'll arrive at the campground.

Trip note: A lot of folks cruising the Columbia River Highway miss this spot by a mile, but it's worth a look. It is set along Jones Creek. A motorbike trail adjacent to camp makes a seven-mile loop through the nearby area.

COLD CREEK
Site 39

Campsites, facilities: There are six campsites for tents or small trailers. Picnic tables, fire grills and tent pads are provided. Pit toilets and piped water are available.

Reservations, fee: No reservations necessary; no fee. Open all year.

Who to contact: Phone the Department of Natural Resources at 1-800-527-3305, or write Department of Natural Resources AW-11, 1065 South Capitol Way, Olympia, WA 98504.

Location: Start five miles north of Vancouver, WA at Exit 9 off I-5. Go east on NE 179th Street for 5 1/2 miles. Turn right on State Route 503 and go 1 1/2 miles. Turn left on NE 159th Street and go three miles, and then turn right on 182nd Avenue and drive one mile. Turn left on NE 139th (L-1400 Road) and go eight miles, and then turn left on L-1000 Road and drive three miles. Make another left and go 800 yards and you'll see the campground.

Trip note: OK, the directions are a little complicated, but few things worth remembering come easy, right? This campground is set along Cold Creek. There are trails nearby for hiking and horseback riding. It gets minimal use yet has piped water available.

ROCK CREEK
Site 40

Campsites, facilities: There are 19 campsites for tents or small trailers. Picnic tables, fire grills and tent pads are provided. Pit toilets and piped water are available. A horse loading ramp is nearby.

Reservations, fee: No reservations necessary; no fee. Open all year.

Who to contact: Phone the Department of Natural Resources at 1-800-527-3305, or write Department of Natural Resources AW-11, 1065 South Capitol Way, Olympia, WA 98504.

Location: Start five miles north of Vancouver, WA at Exit 9 off I-5. Go east on NE 179th Street for 5 1/2 miles. Turn right on State Route 503 and go 1 1/2 miles. Turn left on NE 159th Street and go three miles, and then turn right on 182nd Avenue and drive one mile. Turn left on NE 139th (L-1400 Road) and go eight miles, and then turn left on L-1000 Road and drive 3 1/2 miles (you'll pass the Cold Creek Campground after three miles). Turn left on L-1200 Road and go about 200 yards to the campground, which will be on your right.

Trip note: A nearby option to campsite 39, also managed by the Department of Natural Resources. This camp is set in a wooded area along Rock Creek. Nearby trails are for use by hikers and horseback riders.

DOUGAN CREEK
Site 41

Campsites, facilities: There are seven campsites for tents or small trailers. Picnic tables, fire grills and tent pads are provided. Pit toilets and piped water are available.

Reservations, fee: No reservations necessary; no fee. Open all year.

Who to contact: Phone the Department of Natural Resources at 1-800-527-3305, or write Department of Natural Resources AW-11, 1065 South Capitol Way, Olympia, WA 98504.

Location: Drive 19 1/2 miles east of Vancouver, WA on Highway 14 and turn north on Highway 140 and go five miles to Washogal River Road. Turn right on Washougal River Road and go about seven miles until you see the campground on your right.

Trip note: This campground is set along Dougan Creek near where it empties into the Washougal River. Small, remote and with piped water, it may have just what you are looking for.

Site 42   RAINBOW PARK CAMPGROUND

Campsites, facilities: There are 50 tent sites and 48 sites for trailers or motorhomes of any length. Electricity, piped water, sewer hookups and picnic tables are provided. Flush toilets, showers, sanitary services, a recreation hall, store and ice are available. Bottled gas and a cafe are available within one mile. Pets are permitted. Boat launching facilities are nearby.

Reservations, fee: Reservations accepted; $12 fee per night. Open all year.

Who to contact: Phone at 206-673-4574, or write at 299 Modrow Road, Kalama, WA 98625.

Location: Take Exit 32 off I-5 near Kalama and drive 1 1/2 miles east on Kalama River Road. Cross the bridge at Modrow Road and go 300 yards to the campground.

Trip note: This campground is set on the Kalama River where you can enjoy fishing and swimming. Nearby recreation options include hiking trails, a full service marina and tennis courts. If you visit Marine Park in Kalama you can see a single-tree totem pole that is 140 feet tall, believed to be the tallest in the world.

Site 43   BIG FIR CAMPGROUND

Campsites, facilities: There are 100 tent sites and 28 sites for trailers or motorhomes of any length. Electricity, piped water, sewer hookups and picnic tables are provided. Flush toilets, sanitary services, recreation hall, store, showers and ice are available. Pets and motorbikes are permitted. Boat launching facilities are nearby.

Reservations, fee: Reservations accepted; $13 fee per night. Open all year.

Who to contact: Phone at 206-887-8970, or write at 5515 NE 259th Street, Ridgefield, WA 98642.

Location: Take the Ridgefield Exit 14 off I-5 and drive four miles east. Follow the signs to the campground.

Trip note: This wooded campground is in a rural area not far from Paradise Point State Park. See trip note to campsite 45 for details.

Site 44   BATTLE GROUND LAKE STATE PARK

Campsites, facilities: There are 35 sites for tents or self-contained motorhomes up to 50 feet long. Piped water and picnic tables are provided. Flush toilets, sanitary services, WA 98604.

showers, firewood, a store, cafe and playground are available. Some facilities are wheelchair accessible. Pets are permitted. Boat launching facilities and rentals are available.

Reservations, fee: No reservations necessary; $6 fee per night. Open all year.

Who to contact: Phone at 206-687-4621, or write at 17612 NE Palmer Road, Battleground,

Location: Drive 21 miles northeast of Vancouver, WA. To get there take Highway 503 out of Vancouver and drive until you get to the Battleground crossroads, then head east for three miles, turn north and go 1 1/2 miles to the lake.

Trip note: This state park has horseback riding trails and some primitive campsites that will accommodate campers with horses. It is a good lake for swimming as well as fishing and it has a nice beach area. Travelers on I-5 looking for a quiet layover will find this to be an ideal spot and only about a 15-minute drive from the highway.

Site 45   PARADISE POINT STATE PARK

Campsites, facilities: There are 70 sites for tents or self-contained motorhomes up to 45 feet long. Piped water and picnic tables are provided. Flush toilets, sanitary services, firewood and showers are available. Pets are permitted. Boat launching facilities are nearby on the East Fork of the Lewis River.

Reservations, fee: No reservations necessary; $6 fee per night. Open all year.

Who to contact: Phone at 206-263-2350, or write at Route 1, Box 33914, Ridgefield, WA 98642.

Location: Drive 15 miles north of Vancouver, WA on I-5. The park is to the east of the freeway.

Trip note: This park is set along the East Fork of the Lewis River and has a two-mile hiking trail. Nearby recreation options include an 18-hole golf course. A good motorhome layover spot for cruisers on I-5.

Site 46   WOODLAND

Campsites, facilities: There are 10 campsites for tents or small trailers. Picnic tables, fire grills and tent pads are provided. Pit toilets, piped water, firewood and a childrens' playground are available. Some facilities are wheelchair accessible.

Reservations, fee: No reservations necessary; no fee. Open all year.

Who to contact: Phone the Department of Natural Resources at 1-800-527-3305, or write Department of Natural Resources AW-11, 1065 South Capitol Way, Olympia, WA 98504.

Location: Take Exit 21 off I-5 in Woodland and go 100 yards east on Highway 503. Turn right to East CC Street and go just south of the bridge. Turn right on County Road #1 and drive 300 yards. Then turn left on County Road #38 and drive 2 1/2 miles and you'll see the campground to your left.

Trip note: This is an optimum spot for people who are touring Washington up Interstate 5 but want a quiet setting along the way. This campground is set in a forested area that is managed by the Department of Natural Resources. It's quiet, near the main highways, and with playground equipment for the kids.

Site 47   LEWIS RIVER RV PARK

Campsites, facilities: There are 75 sites for tents, trailers or motorhomes of any length. Electricity, piped water, sewer hookups and picnic tables are provided. Flush toilets, bottled gas, sanitary services, showers, a store, cafe, laundromat, firewood, ice and swimming pool are available. Pets are permitted. Boat docks, launching facilities and rentals are nearby on the Lewis River.

Reservations, fee: Reservations accepted, with a fee of $12 per night; MasterCard and Visa accepted. Open all year.

Who to contact: Phone at 206-225-9556, or write at 3125 Lewis River, Woodland, WA 98674.

Location: Take Exit 21 off I-5 in Woodland and drive four miles east on Highway 503 to 3125 Lewis River Road.

Trip note: This park is set along the Lewis River, where the salmon and the steelhead can run thick in season. Nearby recreation options include an 18-hole golf course.

Site 48   VOLCANO VIEW CAMPGROUND

Campsites, facilities: There are 30 tent sites and 47 drive-through sites for trailers or motorhomes of any length. Electricity, piped water, sewer hookups and picnic tables are provided. Flush toilets, sanitary services, showers, firewood, recreation hall, store and ice are available. Cafe is located within one mile. Pets and motorbikes are permitted.

Reservations, fee: Reservations accepted; $10 fee per night. Open all year.

Who to contact: Phone at 206-231-4329, or write at 230 Highway 503, Ariel, WA 98603.

Location: Take Exit 21 off I-5 in Woodland and drive 25 miles east to "Jack's," then turn south and go 1 1/2 miles to campground.

Trip note: This campground is close to Mount St. Helens and along the edge of Yale Reservoir. Merrill Lake and Swift Creek Reservoir are nearby.

Site 49   LONE FIR RESORT

Campsites, facilities: There are five tent sites and 32 sites for trailers or motorhomes of any length. Electricity, piped water, sewer hookups and picnic tables are provided. Flush toilets, a laundromat, ice, showers and swimming pool are available. Bottled gas, sanitary services, a store and cafe are located within one mile. Pets and motorbikes are permitted. Boat docks and launching facilities are nearby.

Reservations, fee: Reservations accepted; $10 fee per night. MasterCard and Visa accepted. Open all year.

Who to contact: Phone at 206-238-5210, or write at Lone Fir Resort, Cougar, WA 98616.

Location: Take Exit 21 off I-5 in Woodland and drive 29 miles east on Highway 503 (Lewis River Road) and you'll see the resort.

Trip note: This campground is near Yale Lake, the smallest of four lakes in the area. A private camp, designed primarily for motorhome use.

LAKE MERRILL
Site **50**

Campsites, facilities: There are 11 campsites for tents or small trailers. Picnic tables, fire grills and tent pads are provided. Pit toilets, firewood and piped water are available. Boat launching facilities are available on Lake Merrill.

Reservations, fee: No reservations necessary; no fee. Open all year.

Who to contact: Phone the Department of Natural Resources at 1-800-527-3305, or write Department of Natural Resources AW-11, 1065 South Capitol Way, Olympia, WA 98504.

Location: Take Exit 21 off I-5 in Woodland and drive 29 miles east on Highway 503 to the town of Cougar. Go north on Cougar Road for 5 1/2 miles, then turn left on Forest Service Road 81 and drive 4 1/2 miles. Turn left on the access road to the campground.

Trip note: This is the choice of the area for campers seeking a primitive, quiet setting. This wooded campground is nestled on the shore of Lake Merrill, very near Mount St. Helens.

LOUIS RASMUSSEN
Site **51**   RV PARK

Campsites, facilities: There are 50 tent sites and 22 drive-through sites for trailers or motorhomes of any length. Electricity, piped water and sewer hookups are provided. Flush toilets, showers and sanitary services are available. Bottled gas, a store, cafe, laundromat and ice are located within one mile. Pets and motorbikes are permitted. Boat docks and launching facilities are nearby.

Reservations, fee: Reservations accepted; $8 fee per night. Open all year.

Who to contact: Phone at 206-673-2626, or write at P.O. Box 7, Kalama, WA 98625.

Location: Take Exit 30 off I-5 near Kalama and drive 100 feet west then go south for 1/2 mile to the RV park.

Trip note: This park is in an urban area along the shore of the Columbia River. Nearby recreation options include a full service marina and tennis courts. Good motorhome stopover for travelers on I-5.

CAMP KALAMA
Site **52**   CAMPGROUND

Campsites, facilities: There are 30 tent sites and 75 drive-through sites for trailers or motorhomes of any length. Electricity, piped water, sewer hookups and picnic tables are provided. Flush toilets, bottled gas, sanitary services, showers, firewood, a store, cafe, laundromat, ice and playground are available. Pets and motorbikes are permitted. Boat launching facilities are nearby.

Reservations, fee: Reservations accepted; $11 fee per night. MasterCard and Visa accepted. Open all year.

Who to contact: Phone at 206-673-2456, or write at 5055 North Meeker Drive, Kalama, WA 98625.

Location: Take Exit 32 off I-5 near Kalama and drive one block south of the frontage road and you'll see the campground.

Trip note: An option to campsite 51 with a more rustic setting and some accommodations for tent campers. It is set along the Columbia River. Nearby recreation options include a full service marina.

Site 53   OAKS TRAILER AND RV PARK

Campsites, facilu. · There are 62 drive-through sites for trailers or motorhomes of any length. Electricity, piped water, sewer hookups and picnic tables are provided. Flush toilets, sanitary services, showers, a laundromat, ice and playground are available. Bottled gas, a store and cafe are located within one mile. Pets are permitted.

Reservations, fee: Reservations accepted; $11 fee per night. MasterCard and Visa accepted. Open all year.

Who to contact: Phone at 206-425-2708, or write at 636 California Way, Longview, WA 98632.

Location: Take Exit 36 off I-5 near Longview and drive west on Highway 432 for 3 1/2 miles to Commerce. Go one block south and then turn southeast.

Trip note: This park is in an urban area near Longview. Nearby recreation options include an 18-hole golf course, marked bike trails and a full service marina.

Site 54   SILVER LAKE MOTEL AND RESORT

Campsites, facilities: There are 13 tent sites and 22 sites for trailers or motorhomes of any length. Electricity, piped water, sewer hookups and picnic tables are provided. Flush toilets, a store, showers, ice and playground are available. Sanitary services and a cafe are located within one mile. Pets and motorbikes are permitted. Boat docks, launching facilities and rentals are nearby.

Reservations, fee: Reservations accepted; $12 fee per night. MasterCard and Visa accepted. Open all year.

Who to contact: Phone at 206-274-6141, or write at 3201 Sport Lake Highway, Silver Lake, WA 98645.

Location: Take Exit 49 off I-5 and go 6 1/2 miles east on Highway 504 to the park.

Trip note: This park is set along the shore of Silver Lake, one of Washington's better bass fishing lakes.

Site 55   MERMAC STORE AND RV PARK

Campsites, facilities: There are 10 tent sites and 13 drive-through sites for trailers or motorhomes of any length. Electricity, piped water, sewer hookups and picnic tables are provided. Flush toilets, showers, firewood, a store and ice are available. Pets and motorbikes are permitted. Boat launching facilities are nearby.

Reservations, fee: Reservations accepted; $8 fee per night. MasterCard and Visa accepted. Open all year.

Who to contact: Phone at 206-274-6785, or write at 112 Burma Road, Castle Rock, WA 98611.

Location: Take Exit 52 off I-5 at Castle Rock and drive 100 yards east to the park.

Trip note: This wooded park is one-quarter of a mile from the Toutle River and one-half of a mile from the Cowlitz River. Take your pick.

Site 56 — TOUTLE VILLAGE

Campsites, facilities: There are six tent sites and 10 drive-through sites for trailers or motorhomes of any length. Electricity, piped water, sewer hookups and picnic tables are provided. Flush toilets, sanitary services, showers, recreation hall, a cafe, laundromat and ice are available. A store is located within one mile. Pets and motorbikes are permitted. Boat docks, launching facilities and rentals are nearby.

Reservations, fee: Reservations accepted; $10 fee per night. Open all year.

Who to contact: Phone at 206-274-7343, or write at 5037 Spirit Lake Highway, Toutle, WA 98649.

Location: Take Exit 49 off I-5 and drive 10 miles east on Highway 504 and you'll see the park.

Trip note: This campground is set on the shore of Silver Lake. Nearby recreation options include a full service marina. Bass fishing can be quite good in early summer when they pop out of their winter doldrums.

Site 57 — ESTES RV PARK

Campsites, facilities: There are 20 tent sites and 20 drive-through sites for trailers or motorhomes of any length. Electricity, piped water, sewer hookups and picnic tables are provided. Flush toilets, bottled gas, sanitary services, a store, showers, cafe, laundromat and ice are available. Pets and motorbikes are permitted. Boat docks are nearby.

Reservations, fee: Reservations accepted; $11 fee per night. American Express, Master-Card and Visa accepted. Open all year.

Who to contact: Phone at 206-864-2386, or write at 193 Foster Creek Drive, Toledo, WA 98591.

Location: Take Exit 57 off I-5 and drive on Foster Creek Drive for 100 yards west to the park.

Trip note: When the steelhead are running on the nearby Cowlitz River, this spot can make a good base camp for a multi-day fishing trip. Just a 7-iron shot from I-5.

Site 58 — COWLITZ BEND CAMPGROUND

Campsites, facilities: There are 20 tent sites and 24 drive-through sites for trailers or motorhomes of any length. Piped water and picnic tables are provided. Flush toilets, electricity, showers, sanitary services and ice are available. Bottled gas, a store, cafe and laundromat are located within one mile. Pets and motorbikes are permitted. Boat launching facilities are nearby.

Reservations, fee: Reservations accepted; $9 fee per night. Open all year.

Who to contact: Phone at 206-864-2895, or write at 491 Highway 506, Castle Rock, WA 98611.

Location: Take Exit 59 off I-5 near Castle Rock and drive west on Highway 506 for 400 yards to the campground.

Trip note: A good option to campsite 57, this one is set right on the Cowlitz River. A large smelt run arrives every spring. When they come, they come thick. Use a dip net and you can fill a 5-gallon bucket with just a couple of dips. Whoo-ya.

Site **59**

SEQUEST STATE PARK

Campsites, facilities: There are 54 tent sites and 16 sites for trailers or motorhomes up to 50 feet long. Picnic tables are provided. Flush toilets, playground, electricity, piped water, sewer hookups, showers and firewood are available. A store is located within one mile. Some facilities are wheelchair accessible.

Reservations, fee: No reservations necessary; $6 fee per night. Open all year.

Who to contact: Phone at 206-274-8633, or write at Box 3030, Spirit Lake Highway, Castle Rock, WA 98611.

Location: Take Exit 49 off I-5 and drive seven miles east on Highway 504 to the park.

Trip note: This state park is located across from Silver Lake and is considered to be one of western Washington's finest bass fishing lakes.

Site **60**

VOLCANO VIEW RESORT

Campsites, facilities: There are 15 tent sites and 26 drive-through sites for trailers or motorhomes of any length. Electricity, piped water, sewer hookups and picnic tables are provided. Sanitary services, a cafe and ice are available. Bottled gas, a store and laundromat are located within one mile. Pets and motorbikes are permitted. Boat docks, launching facilities and rentals are nearby on Silver Lake.

Reservations, fee: Reservations accepted; $12 fee per night. MasterCard and Visa accepted. Open all year.

Who to contact: Phone at 206-274-7087, or write at 4220 Spirit Lake Highway, Silver Lake, WA 98645.

Location: Take Exit 49 off I-5 and drive nine miles east on Highway 504 to the resort.

Trip note: This resort is set along the shore of Silver Lake, one of three campgrounds on the lake.

Site **61**

THE CEDARS RV PARK

Campsites, facilities: There are seven tent sites and 20 drive-through sites for trailers or motorhomes of any length. Electricity, piped water and picnic tables are provided. Flush toilets, Bottled gas, sanitary services, showers, laundromat and ice are available. Pets and motorbikes are permitted.

Reservations, fee: Reservations accepted; $8 fee per night. Open April to November.

Who to contact: Phone at 206-274-7019, or write at 115 Beauvals Road, Kelso, WA 98626.

Location: Take Exit 46 off I-5 and drive east to the first service road, then go north to the park.

Trip note: This private park provides a good stopover for travelers on I-5 looking for a spot near Kelso. The nearby Coweeman River is a highlight, along with the park's natural setting.

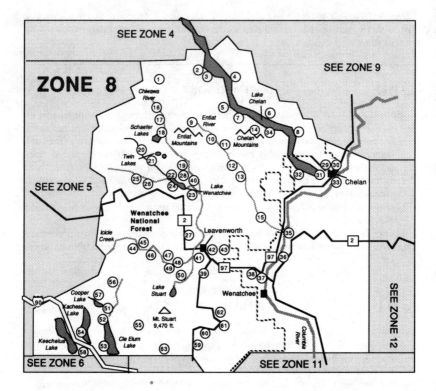

WENATCHEE

HOLDEN

Site **1**

Campsites, facilities: There are eight primitive tent sites that are accessible only by boat or ferry. Picnic tables are provided. Pit toilets and firewood are available, but there is no piped water.

Reservations, fee: No reservations necessary; no fee. Open mid-June to late-September.

Who to contact: Phone Wenatchee National Forest at 509-682-2576, or write at Chelan Ranger District, Chelan, WA 98816.

Location: Take the 8:30 a.m. ferry from Chelan, Manson or Fields Point Landing and go to Lucerne, 41 miles from the town of Chelan. (This spectacular voyage costs $18 or less for a round trip, depending on your destination. For more information call 509-682-2224). From Lucerne take the bus 12 miles west to Holden. The campground is at the end of the road.

Trip note: Getting there is half the fun, with a ferry boat and bus rides. Several trails to lakes in the Glacier Peak Wilderness are accessible from a trail next to the campground, which is set along Railroad Creek. Since this area is along the eastern slope of the Cascade Range, it is drier than the western slopes and not as heavily forested. However, there is no shortage of glacier-fed streams and lakes in the area. See a Forest Service map for details. Less than a mile from the campground is the site of the Holden Mine, which was Washington's largest gold, copper and zinc mine until it closed in 1957. Many of the buildings from the mining town have been preserved and Holden Village offers housing and meals for travelers.

LUCERNE

Site **2**

Campsites, facilities: There are eight tent sites accessible only by boat. Piped water and picnic tables are provided. Pit toilets and firewood are available, and a cafe is located within one mile. Boat docks are nearby.

Reservations, fee: No reservations necessary; no fee. Open May to late-October.

Who to contact: Phone Wenatchee National Forest at 509-682-2576, or write at Chelan Ranger District, Chelan, WA 98816.

Location: Take the 8:30 a.m. ferry from Chelan, Manson or Fields Point Landing and go to Lucerne, 41 miles from the town of Chelan. See campsite 1 for ferry information.

Trip note: This campground is set along the shore of Lake Chelan, a 55-mile long lake. It's the second deepest lake in North America, with a depth of 1500 feet. Mountains reaching to 8000 feet flank each side of the lake. See Trip Note for campsite 1 for information on Holden Mine and Village.

DOMKE LAKE

Site **3**

Campsites, facilities: There are six tent sites accessible only by boat. Picnic tables are provided. Pit toilets and firewood are available, but there is no piped water. Boat docks and rentals are nearby.

Reservations, fee: No reservations necessary; $2 fee per night. Open May to late-October.

Who to contact: Phone Wenatchee National Forest at 509-682-2576, or write at Chelan Ranger District, Chelan, WA 98816.

Location: Take the 8:30 a.m. ferry from Chelan, Manson or Fields Point Landing and get off at Lucerne, 41 miles from the town of Chelan. Hike about one mile to Domke Lake and the campground. See campsite 1 for additional ferry information.

Trip note: Little known and little used, this is a perfect jumpoff for a wilderness backpacking trip. Domke Lake is about one mile long and 1/2 of a mile wide. The trail continues past the lake into Glacier Peak Wilderness. See a Forest Service map for details.

PRINCE CREEK

Site **4**

Campsites, facilities: There are six tent sites accessible only by boat. Picnic tables are provided. Pit toilets and firewood are available, but there is no piped water. Boat docks are nearby.

Reservations, fee: No reservations necessary; $2 fee per night. Open May to mid-November.

Who to contact: Phone Wenatchee National Forest at 509-682-2576, or write at Chelan Ranger District, Chelan, WA 98816.

Location: Take the 8:30 a.m. ferry from Chelan, Manson or Fields Point Landing and get off at Prince Creek, 35 miles from the town of Chelan. See campsite 1 for additional ferry information.

Trip note: This camp is set along the shore of Lake Chelan at the mouth of Prince Creek. A trail from camp follows Prince Creek into the Lake Chelan-Sawtooth Wilderness, and then connects to a network of other trails—all of which lead to various lakes and streams. A Forest Service map details the options.

GRAHAM HARBOR CREEK

Site **5**

Campsites, facilities: There are 15 tent sites accessible only by boat. Picnic tables are provided. Pit toilets and firewood are available, but there is no piped water. Boat docks are nearby.

Reservations, fee: No reservations necessary; $2 fee per night. Open all year.

Who to contact: Phone Wenatchee National Forest at 509-682-2576, or write at Chelan Ranger District, Chelan, WA 98816.

Location: Take the 8:30 a.m. ferry from Chelan, Manson or Fields Point Landing and get off at Graham Harbor Creek, 31 miles from the town of Chelan. See campsite 1 for additional ferry information.

Trip note: This campground is set along Lake Chelan at the mouth of Graham Harbor Creek. It is one of 12 campgrounds on giant Chelan.

DEER POINT
Site 6

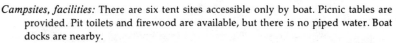

Campsites, facilities: There are six tent sites accessible only by boat. Picnic tables are provided. Pit toilets and firewood are available, but there is no piped water. Boat docks are nearby.

Reservations, fee: No reservations necessary; $2 fee per night. Open May to late-October.

Who to contact: Phone Wenatchee National Forest at 509-682-2576, or write at Chelan Ranger District, Chelan, WA 98816.

Location: Take the 8:30 a.m. ferry from Chelan, Manson or Fields Point Landing and get off at Deer Point, 22 miles from the town of Chelan. See campsite 1 for additional ferry information.

Trip note: Another little known spot set along the shore of Chelan Lake. If you want to camp on the remote east shore, this is one of three camps. The others are sites 4 and 8.

BIG CREEK
Site 7

Campsites, facilities: There are five primitive tent sites accessible only by boat. Picnic tables are provided. Pit toilets and firewood are available, but there is no piped water. Boat docks are nearby.

Reservations, fee: No reservations necessary; no fee. Open May to late-October.

Who to contact: Phone Wenatchee National Forest at 509-682-2576, or write at Chelan Ranger District, Chelan, WA 98816.

Location: Take the 8:30 a.m. ferry from Chelan, Manson or Fields Point Landing and get off at Big Creek, 27 miles from the town of Chelan. See campsite 1 for additional ferry information.

Trip note: Another in a series of camps on Chelan. If you decide to camp here or any other boat campsite during the late fall or early winter, be advised that the water level often drops, putting the docks out of reach.

MITCHELL CREEK
Site 8

Campsites, facilities: There are 10 tent sites accessible only by boat. Picnic tables are provided. Pit toilets and firewood are available, but there is no piped water. Boat docks are nearby.

Reservations, fee: No reservations necessary; $2 fee per night. Open May to late-October.

Who to contact: Phone Wenatchee National Forest at 509-682-2576, or write at Chelan Ranger District, Chelan, WA 98816.

Location: Take the 8:30 a.m. ferry from Chelan, Manson or Fields Point Landing and get off at Mitchell Creek, 15 miles from the town of Chelan.

Trip note: This campground is set along the shore of Lake Chelan. Fishing, swimming, boating, hiking and waterskiing are all options here.

COTTONWOOD
Site 9

Campsites, facilities: There are 25 tent sites. Piped water and picnic tables are provided. Pit toilets and firewood are available.

Reservations, fee: No reservations necessary; $4 fee per night. Open early-June to mid-October.

Who to contact: Phone Wenatchee National Forest at 509-784-1511, or write at Entiat Ranger District, Box 476, Entiat, WA 98822.

Location: From Entiat, drive 1 1/2 miles southwest on Highway 97, then turn northwest on County Road 371 and go 25 miles. Continue northwest on Forest Service Road 317 for 13 miles to the campground.

Trip note: At 3100-feet elevation, this campground is at a major trailhead leading into the Glacier Peak Wilderness. It is set along the Entiat River. A Forest Service map details the back country.

NORTH FORK
Site 10

Campsites, facilities: There are seven tent sites. Piped water and picnic tables are provided. Pit toilets and firewood are available.

Reservations, fee: No reservations necessary; $3 fee per night. Open mid-May to mid-November.

Who to contact: Phone Wenatchee National Forest at 509-784-1511, or write at Entiat Ranger District, Box 476, Entiat, WA 98822.

Location: From Entiat, drive 1 1/2 miles southwest on Highway 97, then turn northwest on County Road 371 and go 25 miles. Turn northwest on Forest Service Road 317 and drive 8 1/2 miles to the campground.

Trip note: One of six campgrounds nestled along the Entiat River. This one is set near the confluence of the Entiat and the North Fork of the Entiat Rivers. Entiat Falls is nearby.

SILVER FALLS
Site 11

Campsites, facilities: There are 30 tent sites and four sites for trailers or motorhomes up to 21 feet long. Piped water and picnic tables are provided. Pit toilets and firewood are available.

Reservations, fee: No reservations necessary; $5 fee per night. Open mid-May to mid-November.

Who to contact: Phone Wenatchee National Forest at 509-784-1511, or write at Entiat Ranger District, Box 476, Entiat, WA 98822.

Location: From Entiat, drive 1 1/2 miles southwest on Highway 97, then turn northwest on County Road 371 and go 25 miles. Turn northwest on Forest Service Road 317 and drive 5 1/2 miles to the campground.

Trip note: This campground is set at the confluence of Silver Creek and the Entiat River. A trail from camp leads 1/2 mile to the base of Silver Falls. An enchanted spot.

LAKE CREEK
Site 12

Campsites, facilities: There are eight tent sites. Picnic tables are provided. Pit toilets and firewood are available, but there is no piped water.

Reservations, fee: No reservations necessary; $2 fee per night. Open May to late-October.

Who to contact: Phone Wenatchee National Forest at 509-784-1511, or write at Entiat

Ranger District, Box 476, Entiat, WA 98822.

Location: From Entiat, drive 1 1/2 miles southwest on Highway 97, then turn northwest on County Road 371 and go 25 miles. Turn northwest on Forest Service Road 317 and drive three miles to the campground.

Trip note: This camp is set at the confluence of Lake Creek and the Entiat River. It is at a trail crossroads, one heads northeast up to Lake Creek Basin in the Chelan Mountains, and several others head south and west into the Entiat Mountains. See a Forest Service map for details. Campsite 13 is a nearby spot with piped water.

FOX CREEK
Site 13

Campsites, facilities: There are nine tent sites. Piped water and picnic tables are provided. Pit toilets and firewood are available.

Reservations, fee: No reservations necessary; $3 fee per night. Open May to early-November.

Who to contact: Phone Wenatchee National Forest at 509-784-1511, or write at Entiat Ranger District, Box 476, Entiat, WA 98822.

Location: From Entiat, drive 1 1/2 miles southwest on Highway 97, then turn northwest on County Road 371 and go 25 miles. Turn northwest on Forest Service Road 317 and drive two miles to campground.

Trip note: This camp is set along the Entiat River near Fox Creek. It is a good alternate to campsite 12, but without the traffic. During the winter, some of the snow-covered logging roads in the area are open for use by snowmobiles and cross-country skiers. Contact the Forest Service for details.

JUNIOR POINT
Site 14

Campsites, facilities: Although without campground facilities, this spot is frequently used as a layover campground. No toilets and no piped water are available.

Reservations, fee: No reservations necessary; $2 fee per night. Open mid-July to late-September.

Who to contact: Phone Wenatchee National Forest at 509-784-1511, or write at Entiat Ranger District, Box 476, Entiat, WA 98822.

Location: From the town of Chelan, drive three mile west on Highway 97, then turn northwest on County Road 10 and go 16 miles. Turn west on Forest Service Road 298 and go 14 miles to camping area.

Trip note: It has a view of Lake Chelan, otherwise it is difficult to comprehend why any fee at all is charged. The camp gets little use.

PINE FLAT
Site 15

Campsites, facilities: There are eight tent sites. Picnic tables are provided. Pit toilets and firewood are available, but there is no piped water.

Reservations, fee: No reservations necessary; $2 fee per night. Open mid-April to early-November.

Who to contact: Phone Wenatchee National Forest at 509-784-1511, or write at Entiat Ranger District, Box 476, Entiat, WA 98822.

Location: From Entiat, drive 1 1/2 miles southwest on Highway 97, then turn northwest on

County Route 371 and go 10 miles. Turn northwest on Forest Service Road 2710 and go 3 1/2 miles to campground.

Trip note: You get guaranteed quiet around these parts. This camp is set along the Mad River at a major backpacking trailhead that provides access to several areas in the Entiat Mountains. The trail that follows the Mad River provides shelters along the route. Contact the Forest Service for details.

PHELPS CREEK
Site **16**

Campsites, facilities: There are seven tent sites. Picnic tables are provided. Pit toilets and firewood are available, but there is no piped water.

Reservations, fee: No reservations necessary; $2 fee per night. Open mid-June to mid-October.

Who to contact: Phone Wenatchee National Forest at 509-763-3103, or write at Leavenworth Ranger District, 600 Sherbour, Leavenworth, WA 98826.

Location: From the town of Leavenworth, drive 16 miles northwest on Highway 2, turn north on Highway 207 and go four miles. Turn east on County Road 22 and go one mile, then head northwest on Forest Service Road 311 for 21 miles to the campground.

Trip note: This campground is set at the confluence of Phelps Creek and the Chiwawa River. A key trailhead for backpackers is nearby that provides access to Glacier Peak Wilderness. Advisable to obtain Forest Service map.

ATKINSON FLAT
Site **17**

Campsites, facilities: There are six primitive, undeveloped sites for tents, trailers or motorhomes up to 21 feet long. No toilets and no piped water are available.

Reservations, fee: No reservations necessary; no fee. Open mid-June to mid-October.

Who to contact: Phone Wenatchee National Forest at 509-763-3103, or write at Leavenworth Ranger District, 600 Sherbourne, Leavenworth, WA 98826.

Location: From the town of Leavenworth, drive 16 miles northwest on Highway 2, turn north on Highway 207 and go four miles. Turn east on County Road 22 and go one mile, then head northwest on Forest Service Road 311 for 15 miles to the campground.

Trip note: This is one of several "minimum maintenance" campgrounds provided by the Forest Service in this area. "Minimum maintenance" means that minimum impact camping techniques are a necessity. It is set along the Chiwawa River.

SCHAEFER CREEK
Site **18**

Campsites, facilities: There are five primitive, undeveloped sites for tents, trailers or motorhomes. Neither toilets nor piped water are available.

Reservations, fee: No reservations necessary; no fee. Open mid-June to mid-October.

Who to contact: Phone Wenatchee National Forest at 509-763-3103, or write at Leavenworth Ranger District, 600 Sherbourne, Leavenworth, WA 98826.

Location: From the town of Leavenworth, drive 16 miles northwest on Highway 2, turn north on Highway 207 and go four miles. Turn east on County Road 22 and go one mile, then head northwest on Forest Service Road 311 for 14 miles to the campground.

Trip note: Like campsite 17, this is also a "minimum maintenance" campground. It is set along the Chiwawa River and less than a mile north of Rock Creek, where two major recreation trails intersect. See a Forest Service map for details.

MEADOW CREEK

Site **19**

Campsites, facilities: There are seven primitive, undeveloped sites for tents, trailers or motorhomes. Neither toilets nor piped water are available.

Reservations, fee: No reservations necessary; no fee. Open May to late-October.

Who to contact: Phone Wenatchee National Forest at 509-763-3103, or write at Leavenworth Ranger District, 600 Sherbourne, Leavenworth, WA 98826.

Location: From the town of Leavenworth, drive 16 miles northwest on Highway 2, turn north on Highway 207 and go four miles. Turn east on County Road 22 and go one mile, then head northeast on Forest Service Road 311 for 2 1/2 miles to the campground.

Trip note: This is a "go-for-it" spot. There's nobody keeping track of you, but plenty of recreation options. This minimum maintenance campground is set near the confluence of Meadow Creek and the Chiwawa River. Both Fish Lake and Lake Wenatchee are within five miles of camp.

WHITE RIVER
FALLS

Site **20**

Campsites, facilities: There are five tent sites. Picnic tables are provided. Pit toilets and firewood are available, but there is no piped water.

Reservations, fee: No reservations necessary; $2 fee per night. Open June to mid-October.

Who to contact: Phone Wenatchee National Forest at 509-763-3103, or write at Leavenworth Ranger District, 600 Sherbourne, Leavenworth, WA 98826.

Location: From the town of Leavenworth, drive 16 miles northwest on Highway 2, then turn north on Highway 207 and go 8 1/2 miles. Head northwest on County Road 22 for one mile, then continue northwest on Forest Service Road 293 for nine miles.

Trip note: This campground is set close to the White River Falls on the White River. It is located at a major trailhead that connects to a network of hiking trails into the Glacier Peak Wilderness. Quiet and beautiful, you get your $2 worth.

NAPEEQUA

Site **21**

Campsites, facilities: There are three tent sites and two sites for trailers or motorhomes up to 31 feet long. Picnic tables are provided. Pit toilets and firewood are available, but there is no piped water.

Reservations, fee: No reservations necessary; $2 fee per night. Open mid-May to late-October.

Who to contact: Phone Wenatchee National Forest at 509-763-3103, or write at Leavenworth Ranger District, 600 Sherbourne, Leavenworth, WA 98826.

Location: From the town of Leavenworth, drive 16 miles northwest on Highway 2, then turn north on Highway 207 and go eight miles. Head northwest on County Road 22 for one mile, then continue northwest on Forest Service Road 293 for six miles and you'll arrive at the campground.

Trip note: This campground is set along the White River. A trail from camp heads east for about two miles to Twin Lakes in Glacier Peak Wilderness. Worth the hike.

Site 22
LAKE WENATCHEE
RANGER STATION

Campsites, facilities: There are eight tent sites. Piped water and picnic tables are provided. Pit toilets and firewood are available. A store and cafe are within one mile.

Reservations, fee: No reservations necessary; $2 fee per night. Open May to late-October.

Who to contact: Phone Wenatchee National Forest at 509-763-3103, or write at Leavenworth Ranger District, 600 Sherbourne, Leavenworth, WA 98826.

Location: From the town of Leavenworth, drive 16 miles northwest on Highway 2, turn north on Highway 207 and go 7 1/2 miles to the campground.

Trip note: This campground is set along the northwestern shore of Lake Wenatchee, a popular resort area. One of five camps set at this lake.

Site 23
NASON CREEK

Campsites, facilities: There are 27 tent sites and 40 sites for trailers or motorhomes up to 31 feet long. Piped water and picnic tables are provided. Flush toilets, sanitary services and a laundromat are available within one mile. Boat docks, launching facilities and rentals are nearby.

Reservations, fee: No reservations necessary; $5 fee per night. Open May to late-October.

Who to contact: Phone Wenatchee National Forest at 509-763-3103, or write at Leavenworth Ranger District, 600 Sherbourne, Leavenworth, WA 98826.

Location: From Leavenworth, drive 16 miles northwest on Highway 2, turn northeast on Highway 207 and go 3 1/2 miles. Head west on County Road 290 for 100 yards to the campground.

Trip note: This campground is on Nason Creek near Lake Wenatchee. Recreation activities include swimming, fishing and waterskiing.

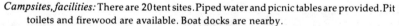

Site 24
GLACIER VIEW

Campsites, facilities: There are 20 tent sites. Piped water and picnic tables are provided. Pit toilets and firewood are available. Boat docks are nearby.

Reservations, fee: No reservations necessary; $4 fee per night. Open mid-May to mid-October.

Who to contact: Phone Wenatchee National Forest at 509-763-3103, or write at Leavenworth Ranger District, 600 Sherbourne, Leavenworth, WA 98826.

Location: From The town of Leavenworth, drive 16 miles northwest on Highway 2, turn northeast on Highway 207 and go 3 1/2 miles. Turn west on County Road 290 and go four miles, then continue west on Forest Service Road 290 for 1 1/2 miles to the campground.

Trip note: This campground is on the southwestern shore of Lake Wenatchee, one of the quieter camps on the lake.

Site 25
LAKE CREEK

Campsites, facilities: There are 12 tent sites. Piped water and picnic tables are provided. Pit toilets and firewood are available.

Reservations, fee: No reservations necessary; $3 fee per night. Open May to early-November.

Who to contact: Phone Wenatchee National Forest at 509-784-1511, or write at Leavenworth Ranger District, 600 Sherbourne, Leavenworth, WA 98826.

Location: From the town of Leavenworth, drive 16 miles northwest on Highway 2, turn north on Highway 207 and go 8 1/2 miles. Turn west on County Road 22 and go 1 1/2 miles, then continue west on Forest Service Road 283 for 10 miles to the campground.

Trip note: This camp is set along the Wenatchee River. It is a remote and primitive spot, yet has piped water. That's a perfect combination.

SODA SPRINGS
Site **26**

Campsites, facilities: There are five tent sites. Picnic tables are provided. Pit toilets and firewood are available, but there is no piped water.

Reservations, fee: No reservations necessary; $2 fee per night. Open May to late-October.

Who to contact: Phone Wenatchee National Forest at 509-763-3103, or write at Leavenworth Ranger District, 600 Sherbourne, Leavenworth, WA 98826.

Location: From the town of Leavenworth, drive 16 miles northwest on Highway 2, turn north on Highway 207 and go 8 1/2 miles. Turn west on County Road 22 and go 1 1/2 miles, then west on Forest Service Road 283 for 7 1/2 miles to the campground.

Trip note: This campground is set along the Wenatchee River. A small, quiet closer-to-civilization option to campsite 25, yet no piped water.

TUMWATER
Site **27**

Campsites, facilities: There are 80 tent sites and 80 sites for trailers or motorhomes up to 22 feet long. Piped water and picnic tables are provided. Flush toilets and firewood are available.

Reservations, fee: No reservations necessary; $6 fee per night. Open May to late-October.

Who to contact: Phone Wenatchee National Forest at 509-763-1413, or write at Leavenworth Ranger District, 600 Sherbourne, Leavenworth, WA 98826.

Location: From the town of Leavenworth, drive 10 miles northwest on Highway 2 and you'll see the campground entrance.

Trip note: This large, popular camp provides a little bit of both worlds. It is a good layover for campers cruising Highway 2. But there are also two Forest Service roads nearby, each less than a mile long, which end at trailheads that provide access to the Alpine Lakes Wilderness. If you don't like to hike, no problem. The camp is on the Wenatchee River in the Tumwater Canyon.

LAKE WENATCHEE
STATE PARK
Site **28**

Campsites, facilities: There are 197 tent sites. Piped water and picnic tables are provided. Flush toilets, sanitary services, a store, ice, showers, firewood, cafe, playground, and horse rentals are available. Some facilities are wheelchair accessible. Boat docks, launching facilities and rentals are nearby.

Reservations, fee: No reservations necessary; $6 fee per night. Open all year.

Who to contact: Phone at 509-763-3101, or write at Highway 207, Leavenworth, WA 98826.

Location: From the town of Leavenworth, drive 22 miles north on Highway 207 and you'll see the park entrance.

Trip note: This park is set in a nice spot, the drive-in sites are spaced just right, so you can expect plenty of company. The secluded campsites are near the Wenatchee River which offers opportunities for canoeing, kayaking, swimming, fishing and horseback riding.

PARADISE RESORT
Site **29**

Campsites, facilities: There are 10 tent sites and 23 drive-through sites for trailers or motorhomes. Electricity, piped water and picnic tables are provided. Flush toilets, showers, firewood and ice are available. Pets and motorbikes are permitted. Boat launching facilities and rentals are nearby.

Reservations, fee: Reservations accepted; $10 fee per night. Open mid-April to mid-October.

Who to contact: Phone at 509-687-3444, or write at Route 1, Box 202, Manson, WA 98831.

Location: From Chelan, drive seven miles west on Highway 150, then turn northwest on Wapato Lake Road and go three miles to East Lake Road.

Trip note: This campground is set along the shore of Wapato Lake about two miles from Lake Chelan. The town of Chelan offers a history museum and a downtown area with many restored buildings from the early days.

KAMEI RESORT
Site **30**

Campsites, facilities: There are 12 tent sites and 40 sites for trailers or motorhomes of any length. Electricity, piped water, sewer hookups and picnic tables are provided. Flush toilets, showers and ice are available. Pets and motorbikes are permitted. Boat docks, launching facilities and rentals are nearby.

Reservations, fee: Reservations accepted; $7 fee per night. Open late-April to August.

Who to contact: Phone at 509-687-3690, or write at Route 1, Box 238, Manson, WA 98831.

Location: From Chelan, drive seven miles west on Highway 150, then turn north on Wapato Lake Road and drive three miles to the resort.

Trip note: This resort is on Lake Wapato, about two miles from Lake Chelan. If you have an extra day, take the ferry boat ride on Lake Chelan, which is detailed in campsite 1.

LAKEVIEW PARK
Site **31**

Campsites, facilities: There are 42 drive-through sites for trailers or motorhomes of any length. Electricity, piped water and sewer hookups are provided. Flush toilets, sanitary services, showers, playground, bottled gas, a store, cafe, laundromat and ice are available. Pets are permitted. Boat docks and launching facilities are nearby.

Reservations, fee: Reservations accepted; $12 fee per night. Open April to November.

Who to contact: Phone at 509-687-3612, or write at Γ Ɔ. Box 324, Manson, WA 98831.

Location: From the town of Chelan, drive 7 1/2 miles northwest on Highway 150 and you'll see the park.

Trip note: This developed park for motorhomes and trailers is set along the shore of Lake Chelan. Nearby recreation options include an 18-hole golf course.

Site 32   LAKE CHELAN STATE PARK   ▲

Campsites, facilities: There are 134 tent sites and 17 sites for trailers or motorhomes up to 30 feet long. Picnic tables are provided. Flush toilets, sanitary services, a store, cafe, ice, playground, electricity, piped water, sewer hookups, showers and firewood are available. Some facilities are wheelchair accessible. Boat docks and launching facilities are nearby.

Reservations, fee: Reservations accepted; $6 fee per night. Open April to late-October.

Who to contact: Phone at 509-687-3710, or write at Route 1, Box 90, Chelan, WA 98816.

Location: Drive nine miles west of the city of Chelan off Highway 97. The park is on the south side of the lake.

Trip note: This is recreation headquarters for Lake Chelan. See trip notes for campsites 1-7 for some of the options available. Watersports include fishing, swimming, scuba diving and waterskiing.

Site 33   LAKESHORE TRAILER PARK AND MARINA

Campsites, facilities: There are 160 drive-through sites for trailers or motorhomes of any length. Electricity, piped water, sewer hookups and picnic tables are provided. Flush toilets, sanitary services, showers, a store, cafe, laundromat, ice, playground, bottled gas are available within one mile. Boat docks and launching facilities are nearby.

Reservations, fee: Reservations accepted; $18 fee per night. Open March to November.

Who to contact: Phone at 509-682-5031, or write at P.O. Box 1669, Chelan, WA 98816.

Location: From the center of the town of Chelan, drive one mile north on Highway 97 to Highway 50.

Trip note: This municipal park and marina on Lake Chelan serves all members of the family. Nearby recreation options include an 18-hole golf course, miniature golf course and lighted tennis courts. A visitor center is nearby.

Site 34   TWENTY-FIVE MILE CREEK STATE PARK   ▲

Campsites, facilities: There are 52 tent sites and 33 sites for trailers or motorhomes up to 60 feet long. Picnic tables are provided. Restrooms, piped water, electricity, sewer hookups and a swimming pool are available. A boat dock is nearby.

Reservations, fee: No reservations; $6 fee per night. Open early-April to late-October.

Who to contact: Phone at 509-687-3710, or write c/o Lake Chelan State Park, Route 1, Box 90, Chelan, WA 98816.

Location: Drive 18 miles north of the town of Chelan on the South Shore Road and you'll see the park at the end of the road.

Trip note: This campground is located on Twenty-Five Mile Creek near where it empties into Lake Chelan. Forest Service Road 5900, which heads west from the park accesses several trailheads leading into the Forest Service lands of the Chelan Mountains. Obtain a Wenatchee National Forest Service map for details.

Site 35
ENTIAT
CITY PARK

Campsites, facilities: There are 100 tent sites and 31 sites for trailers or motorhomes.
Electricity, piped water and picnic tables are provided. Flush toilets, sanitary services,
showers, playground, bottled gas, a store, cafe, laundromat and ice are available.
Motorbikes are permitted. Boat docks and launching facilities are nearby.

Reservations, fee: Reservations accepted; $10 fee per night. Open April to mid-September.

Who to contact: Phone at 509-784-1500, or write at P.O. Box 228, Entiat, WA 98822.

Location: Drive 16 miles north of Wenatchee on Highway 97 to the town of Entiat. The
park is set along the shore of Lake Entiat.

Trip note: Lake Entiat is actually a dammed portion of the Columbia River. Rocky Reach
Dam, located 10 miles south, is the closest to this campground. A good camping spot
for boaters, with launching facilities nearby.

Site 36
LINCOLN ROCK
STATE PARK

Campsites, facilities: There are 27 sites for trailers or motorhomes up to 25 feet long. Picnic
tables are provided. Flush toilets, sanitary services, playground, showers and firewood are available. Some facilities are wheelchair accessible. Boat docks and
launching facilities are located on Lake Entiat.

Reservations, fee: No reservations necessary; $6 fee per night. Open all year.

Who to contact: Phone at 509-884-3044, or write at Route 3, P.O. Box 3137, East Wenatchee,
WA 98801.

Location: From East Wenatchee, drive six miles north on Highway 2 and you'll see the
park.

Trip note: An option to nearby campsite 35, this park is ideal for families with motorhomes
or trailers. Set adjacent to the Rocky Reach Dam along the shore of Lake Entiat.
Watersports include swimming, boating and waterskiing.

Site 37
TOWN AND COUNTRY
TRAILER PARK

Campsites, facilities: There are 12 drive-through sites for trailers or motorhomes up to 25
feet long. Electricity, piped water, sewer hookups and picnic tables are provided.
Flush toilets, showers, ice and a swimming pool are available. Bottled gas, a store and
cafe are located within one mile. Motorbikes are permitted. Boat docks and launching
facilities are nearby.

Reservations, fee: Reservations accepted; $10 fee per night. MasterCard and Visa accepted.
Open all year.

Who to contact: Phone at 509-663-5157, or write at 2921 School Street, Wenatchee, WA
98801.

Location: From the town of Wenatchee, drive three miles west via Highways 2 and 97.

Trip note: Good layover for cross-country travelers who reach the Highway 2/97 junction.
This park is set in an urban area along the Wenatchee River. Nearby recreation
options include hiking trails, marked bike trails, a full service marina and tennis
courts.

Site 38   WENATCHEE RIVER COUNTY PARK

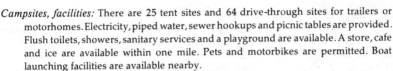

Campsites, facilities: There are 25 tent sites and 64 drive-through sites for trailers or motorhomes. Electricity, piped water, sewer hookups and picnic tables are provided. Flush toilets, showers, sanitary services and a playground are available. A store, cafe and ice are available within one mile. Pets and motorbikes are permitted. Boat launching facilities are available nearby.

Reservations, fee: No reservations necessary; $10 fee per night. Open April to late-October.

Who to contact: Phone at 509-662-2525, or write at P.O. Box 254, Monitor, WA 98836.

Location: From the town of Wenatchee, drive six miles northwest on Highway 2. The park is near the town of Monitor.

Trip note: This muncipal park is set along the Wenatchee River. The only option for tent campers in immediate area.

Site 39   BLU SHASTIN RV PARK

Campsites, facilities: There are 20 tent sites and 70 drive-through sites for trailers or motorhomes of any length. Electricity, piped water, sewer hookups and picnic tables are provided. Flush toilets, sanitary services, showers, a recreation hall, firewood, laundromat, ice, playground and a swimming pool are available. Bottled gas, a store and cafe are located within one mile. Pets and motorbikes are permitted.

Reservations, fee: Reservations accepted; $12 fee per night. MasterCard and Visa accepted. Open all year.

Who to contact: Phone at 509-548-4184, or write at 3300 Highway 97, Leavenworth, WA 98826.

Location: From the town of Leavenworth, go three miles southeast on Highway 2 to the junction with Highway 97, then go seven miles south on Highway 97 to the park.

Trip note: This park is set in a mountainous area near Penshastin Creek. Nearby recreation options include hiking trails and marked bike trails.

Site 40   MIDWAY VILLAGE GROCERY AND RV PARK

Campsites, facilities: There are 20 tent sites and 23 sites for trailers or motorhomes of any length. Electricity, piped water, sewer hookups and picnic tables are provided. Bottled gas, a store, showers, firewood, cafe, laundromat, ice and playground are available. Pets and motorbikes are permitted. Boat docks, launching facilities and rentals are nearby.

Reservations, fee: Reservations accepted; $9 fee per night. Open all year.

Who to contact: Phone at 509-763-3344, or write at 14193 Chiwawa, Leavenworth, WA 98826.

Location: From the town of Winton, drive one mile northwest on Highway 2 to Highway 207 and then go four miles north to the bridge over the Wenatchee River. Head east for one mile and you'll see the park.

Trip note: This private campground is a short distance from Lake Wenatchee State Park (campsite 28) and is set along the Wenatchee River. Nearby recreation options include waterskiing, swimming, boating, fishing, hiking and bike riding.

Site **41**
ICICLE RIVER
RANCH

Campsites, facilities: There are 30 tent sites and 41 drive-through sites for trailers or motorhomes of any length. Electricity, piped water, sewer hookups and picnic tables are provided. Flush toilets and bottled gas are available. Showers and firewood are available for an extra fee. Pets and motorbikes are permitted.

Reservations, fee: Reservations accepted; $11 fee per night. Open mid-April to late-October.

Who to contact: Phone at 509-548-5420, or write at 7310 Icicle, Leavenworth, WA 98826.

Location: Take Icicle Road south off Highway 2 in Leavenworth and drive three miles to the campground.

Trip note: One of three campgrounds in immediate area. This wooded spot is set along Icicle Creek. Nearby recreation options include an 18-hole golf course and hiking trails.

Site **42**
KOA
PINE VILLAGE

Campsites, facilities: There are 40 tent sites and 60 drive-through sites for trailers or motorhomes of any length. Picnic tables are provided. Flush toilets, sanitary services, showers, firewood, a recreation hall, store, laundromat, ice, playground, wading pool, heated swimming pool, electricity, piped water and sewer hookups are available. Bottled gas and cafe are located within one mile. Pets and motorbikes are permitted.

Reservations, fee: Reservations accepted; $14 fee per night. American Express, Master-Card and Visa accepted. Open April to November.

Who to contact: Phone at 509-548-7709, or write at Pine Village KOA, 11401 River Bend Drive, Leavenworth, WA 98826.

Location: Drive 1/2 mile east from the town of Leavenworth on Highway 2 to River Bend Drive, then go south 1/4 mile to the campground.

Trip note: This campground is set among pines with access to the Wenatchee River. Nearby recreation options include an 18-hole golf course and hiking trails.

Site **43**
CHALET
TRAILER PARK

Campsites, facilities: There are 40 tent sites and 24 sites for trailers or motorhomes of any length. Electricity, piped water, sewer hookups and picnic tables are provided. Flush toilets, sanitary services and showers are available. Bottled gas, a store, cafe, laundromat and ice are available within one mile. Pets and motorbikes are permitted.

Reservations, fee: Reservations accepted; $10 fee per night. Open May to early-October.

Who to contact: Phone at 509-548-4578, or write at 6504 NE 171st Place, Bothel, WA 98155.

Location: From the town of Leavenworth, drive 1/2 mile southeast on Highway 2 to the campground.

Trip note: This park is set along the Wenatchee River near the town of Leavenworth. Nearby recreation options include an 18-hole golf course.

BLACKPINE CREEK
Site 44   HORSECAMP

Campsites, facilities: There are nine sites for tents, trailers or motorhomes up to 21 feet long. Piped water and picnic tables are provided. Pit toilets, firewood and horse facilities are available.

Reservations, fee: No reservations necessary; $3 fee per night. Open mid-May to late-October.

Who to contact: Phone Wenatchee National Forest at 509-782-1413, or write at Leavenworth Ranger District, 600 Sherbourne, Leavenworth, WA 98826.

Location: From the town of Leavenworth, drive 1/2 mile southeast on Highway 2, then turn south on Highway 71 and drive three miles. Turn northwest on Forest Service Road 2451 and drive 15 miles to the campground.

Trip note: This campground is set on Black Pine Creek near Icicle Creek at a major trailhead leading into the Alpine Lakes Wilderness. It is one of seven rustic camp spots on the creek.

ROCK ISLAND
Site 45

Campsites, facilities: There are 19 sites for tents, trailers or motorhomes up to 21 feet long. Piped water and picnic tables are provided. Pit toilets and firewood are available.

Reservations, fee: No reservations necessary; $4 fee per night. Open May to late-October.

Who to contact: Phone Wenatchee National Forest at 509-782-1413, or write at Leavenworth Ranger District, 600 Sherbourne, Leavenworth, WA 98826.

Location: From the town of Leavenworth, drive 1/2 mile southeast on Highway 2, then turn south on Highway 71 and drive three miles. Turn northwest on Forest Service Road 2451 and drive 14 miles to campground.

Trip note: This campground is set along Icicle Creek about a mile from the trailhead accessing Alpine Lakes Wilderness.

CHATTER CREEK
Site 46

Campsites, facilities: There are 13 sites for tents, trailers or motorhomes up to 21 feet long. Piped water and picnic tables are provided. Pit toilets and firewood are available.

Reservations, fee: No reservations necessary; $4 fee per night. Open May to late-October.

Who to contact: Phone Wenatchee National Forest at 509-782-1413, or write at Leavenworth Ranger District, 600 Sherbourne, Leavenworth, WA 98826.

Location: From the town of Leavenworth, drive 1/2 mile southeast on Highway 2, then turn south on Highway 71 and drive three miles. Turn northwest on Forest Service Road 2451 and drive 12 1/2 miles to campground.

Trip note: This campground is set along Icicle Creek and Chatter Creek. Trails lead out in several directions from the camp into the Alpine Lakes Wilderness.

IDA CREEK
Site 47

Campsites, facilities: There are 10 sites for tents, trailers or motorhomes up to 21 feet long. Piped water and picnic tables are provided. Pit toilets and firewood are available.

Reservations, fee: No reservations necessary; no fee. Open May to late-October.

Who to contact: Phone Wenatchee National Forest at 509-782-1413, or write at Leavenworth Ranger District, 600 Sherbourne, Leavenworth, WA 98826.

Location: From the town of Leavenworth, drive 1/2 miles southeast on Highway 2, then turn south on Highway 71 and drive three miles. Turn northwest on Forest Service Road 2451 and drive 10 miles to campground.

Trip note: This campground is set along Icicle Creek and Ida Creek. One of several small, quiet campgrounds set along Icicle Creek.

JOHNNY CREEK
Site **48**

Campsites, facilities: There are 16 sites for tents, trailers or motorhomes up to 21 feet long. Piped water and picnic tables are provided. Pit toilets and firewood are available.

Reservations, fee: No reservations necessary; $4 fee per night. Open May to late-October.

Who to contact: Phone Wenatchee National Forest at 509-782-1413, or write at Leavenworth Ranger District, 600 Sherbourne, Leavenworth, WA 98826.

Location: From the town of Leavenworth, drive 1/2 mile southeast on Highway 2, then turn south on Highway 71 and drive three miles. Turn northwest on Forest Service Road 2451 and drive eight miles to campground.

Trip note: This campground is set along Icicle Creek and Johnny Creek.

BRIDGE CREEK
Site **49**

Campsites, facilities: There are six sites for tents, trailers or motorhomes up to 21 feet long. Piped water and picnic tables are provided. Pit toilets and firewood are available.

Reservations, fee: No reservations necessary; $4 fee per night. Open mid-April to late-October.

Who to contact: Phone Wenatchee National Forest at 509-782-1413, or write at Leavenworth Ranger District, 600 Sherbourne, Leavenworth, WA 98826.

Location: From the town of Leavenworth, drive 1/2 mile southeast on Highway 2, then turn south on Highway 71 and drive three miles. Turn northwest on Forest Service Road 2451 and drive 5 1/2 miles to campground.

Trip note: A small, quiet spot. This campground is set along Icicle Creek and Bridge Creek. About one mile south of camp at Eightmile Creek is a trail that accesses the Alpine Lakes Wilderness. See a Forest Service map for details.

EIGHTMILE
Site **50**

Campsites, facilities: There are 22 sites for tents, trailers or motorhomes up to 21 feet long. Piped water and picnic tables are provided. Pit toilets and firewood are available.

Reservations, fee: No reservations necessary; $4 fee per night. Open mid-April to late-October.

Who to contact: Phone Wenatchee National Forest at 509-782-1413, or write at Leavenworth Ranger District, 600 Sherbourne, Leavenworth, WA 98826.

Location: From the town of Leavenworth, drive 1/2 mile southeast on Highway 2, then turn south on Highway 71 and drive three miles. Turn west on Forest Service Road 2451 and drive four miles to campground.

Trip note: This campground is set along Icicle Creek and Eightmile Creek. A key trailhead for backpackers is located here that provides access for many lakes and streams in the Alpine Lakes Wilderness.

SALMON LA SAC

Site **51**

Campsites, facilities: There are 59 sites for tents, trailers or motorhomes up to 21 feet long. Piped water and picnic tables are provided. Flush toilets and firewood are available. Some facilities are wheelchair accessible.

Reservations, fee: No reservations necessary; $4 fee per night. Open late-May to late-October.

Who to contact: Phone Wenatchee National Forest at 509-674-4411, or write at Cle Elum Ranger District, West 2nd Street, Cle Elum, WA 98922.

Location: From the town of Cle Elum, drive 11 miles northwest on Highway 903, then continue northwest on County Road 903 for 10 1/2 miles to campground.

Trip note: This is an ideal base camp for backpackers and day hikers. The camp is set along the Cle Elum River at a major trailhead. Hikers can follow creeks heading off in several directions, including into the Alpine Lakes Wilderness. A Forest Service map details the possibilities.

RED MOUNTAIN

Site **52**

Campsites, facilities: There are 13 sites for tents, trailers or motorhomes up to 15 feet long. Picnic tables are provided. Pit toilets and firewood are available, but there is no piped water. Boat docks are nearby.

Reservations, fee: No reservations necessary; $2 fee per night. Open mid-May to mid-November.

Who to contact: Phone Wenatchee National Forest at 509-674-4411, or write at Cle Elum Ranger District, West 2nd Street, Cle Elum, WA 98922.

Location: From the town of Cle Elum, drive 11 miles northwest on Highway 903, then continue northwest on County Road 903 for eight miles to campground.

Trip note: An option to nearby campsite 51, with two big differences. This site has no piped water and is just a mile from Cle Elum Lake. The campground is set along the Cle Elum River, just above where it feeds into the lake.

WISH POOSH

Site **53**

Campsites, facilities: There are 10 sites for tents, trailers or motorhomes up to 21 feet long. Piped water and picnic tables are provided. Flush toilets, firewood, a cafe and ice are available. Boat docks and launching facilities are located on Cle Elum Lake.

Reservations, fee: No reservations necessary; $6 fee per night. Open mid-May to mid-November.

Who to contact: Phone Wenatchee National Forest at 509-674-4411, or write at Cle Elum Ranger District, West 2nd Street, Cle Elum, WA 98922.

Location: From the town of Cle Elum, drive 10 miles northwest on Highway 903, the turn west on Forest Service Road 112 and go about 100 yards to the campground.

Trip note: This campground is set along the shore of Cle Elum Lake, where waterskiing, fishing and swimming are among recreation possibilities.

KACHESS
Site **54**

Campsites, facilities: There are 133 tent sites and 26 sites for trailers or motorhomes up to 32 feet long. Piped water and picnic tables are provided. Restrooms, sanitary services, firewood and a store are available. Boat docks, launching facilities and rentals are located on Kachess Lake.

Reservations, fee: No reservations necessary; $6 fee per night. Open late-May to October.

Who to contact: Phone Wenatchee National Forest at 509-674-4411, or write at Cle Elum Ranger District, West 2nd Street, Cle Elum, WA 98922.

Location: From the town of Cle Elum, drive 21 miles northwest on Highway 190, then turn northeast on Forest Service Road 49 and drive 5 1/2 miles to the campground.

Trip note: This is the only campground on the shore of Kachess Lake and it is a winner. Recreation opportunities include waterskiing, fishing, hiking and bicycling. A trail from camp heads north into Alpine Lakes Wilderness. See a Forest Service map for details. The Kachess Sno-Park is about a mile south of the campground, which provides parking and access to Forest Service Roads and open areas which are ideal for snowmobiling and cross-country skiing.

BEVERLY
Site **55**

Campsites, facilities: There are 15 tent sites and three sites for trailers or motorhomes up to 21 feet long. Picnic tables are provided. Pit toilets are available, but there is no piped water.

Reservations, fee: No reservations necessary; $2 fee per night. Open June to mid-November.

Who to contact: Phone Wenatchee National Forest at 509-674-4411, or write at Cle Elum Ranger District, West 2nd Street, Cle Elum, WA 98922.

Location: From the town of Cle Elum, drive eight miles east on Highway 970, turn north on County Road 107, then go north on Forest Service Road 9737 for four miles to campground.

Trip note: This primitive campground is set along the North Fork of the Teanaway River. There are several trails near camp leading up nearby creeks and into the Alpine Lakes Wilderness.

FISH LAKE
Site **56**

Campsites, facilities: There are 10 tent sites. Picnic tables are provided. Pit toilets and firewood are available, but there is no piped water. Boat docks are nearby.

Reservations, fee: No reservations necessary; no fee. Open July to October.

Who to contact: Phone Wenatchee National Forest at 509-674-4411, or write at Cle Elum Ranger District, West 2nd Street, Cle Elum, WA 98922.

Location: From the town of Cle Elum, drive 11 miles northwest on Highway 903, then 10 1/2 miles northwest on Forest Service Road 903, and turn northeast on Forest Service Road 4330 and go 11 miles to campground.

Trip note: This campground is way out there, just a short jaunt to the Alpine Lakes Wilderness. Numerous opportunities to access trails into the backcountry. This camp is nestled along the shore of tiny Tucquala Lake, a jewel near the headwaters of Cle Elum Creek.

OWHI
Site 57

Campsites, facilities: There are 22 tent sites. Picnic tables are provided. Pit toilets and firewood are available, but there is no piped water. Boat docks and launching facilities are nearby.

Reservations, fee: No reservations necessary; $2 fee per night. Open mid-June to mid-October.

Who to contact: Phone Wenatchee National Forest at 509-674-4411, or write at Cle Elum Ranger District, West 2nd Street, Cle Elum, WA 98922.

Location: From Cle Elum go 11 miles northwest on Highway 903, then 9 1/2 miles northwest on County Road 903. Turn northwest on Forest Service Road 228 and go five miles, then north on Forest Service Road 235 for about 300 yards to campground.

Trip note: This spot has everything. Well, everything but piped water. It is located on the shore of Cooper Lake, near the boundary of Alpine Lakes Wilderness. A nearby trailhead provides access to several lakes in the Wilderness and extends to the Pacific Crest Trail. See a Forest Service map for details.

CRYSTAL SPRINGS
Site 58

Campsites, facilities: There are 20 tent sites and seven sites for trailers or motorhomes up to 21 feet long. Piped water and picnic tables are provided. Pit toilets and firewood is available. Boat docks and rentals are nearby.

Reservations, fee: No reservations necessary; $4 fee per night. Open mid-May to mid-November.

Who to contact: Phone Wenatchee National Forest at 509-674-4411, or write at Cle Elum Ranger District, West 2nd Street, Cle Elum, WA 98922.

Location: From the town of Cle Elum go 20 1/2 miles northwest on I-90, then turn northwest on Forest Service Road 212 and drive 1/2 mile to the campground.

Trip note: This campground is just off Highway 90 and a short drive from Kachess Lake and Keechelus Lake. There are boat ramps at both lakes. For winter sports, there are also several Sno-parks in the area, which provide parking and access to Forest Service roads and open areas which are available for snowmobiling and cross-country skiing. The Pacific West Ski Area is at the north end of Keechelus Lake.

MINERAL SPRINGS
Site 59

Campsites, facilities: There are 12 tent sites and seven sites for trailers or motorhomes up to 21 feet long. Piped water and picnic tables are provided. Flush toilets, showers, store, cafe, laundromat and a gas station are available.

Reservations, fee: No reservations necessary; $4 fee per night. Open mid-April to late-November.

Who to contact: Phone Wenatchee National Forest at 509-674-4411, or write at Cle Elum Ranger District, West 2nd Street, Cle Elum, WA 98922.

Location: From the town of Cle Elum, go southeast for four miles on Highway 10, then turn northeast on Highway 97 and drive 14 miles to the campground.

Trip note: This campground is set at the confluence of Medicine Creek and Swauk Creek. It is one of five campgrounds along Highway 97.

SWAUK
Site **60**

Campsites, facilities: There are 23 tent sites. Piped water and picnic tables are provided. Pit toilets and firewood are available.

Reservations, fee: No reservations necessary; $5 fee per night. Open mid-April to late-November.

Who to contact: Phone Wenatchee National Forest at 509-674-4411, or write at Cle Elum Ranger District, West 2nd Street, Cle Elum, WA 98922.

Location: From the town of Cle Elum, go southeast for four miles on Highway 10, then turn northeast on Highway 97 and drive 18 miles to the campground.

Trip note: This campground is set along Swauk Creek. It is a prime spot, particularly during winter months. About three miles east of the campground is Swauk Sno-Park, which provides a parking area and access to Forest Service Roads and open areas for snowmobiling and cross-country skiing.

TRONSEN
Site **61**

Campsites, facilities: There are 20 tent sites and 20 sites for trailers or motorhomes up to 21 feet long. Piped water and picnic tables are provided. Pit toilets and firewood are available.

Reservations, fee: No reservations necessary; $4 fee per night. Open mid-May to late-October.

Who to contact: Phone Wenatchee National Forest at 509-782-1413, or write at Leavenworth Ranger District, 600 Sherbourne, Leavenworth, WA 98826.

Location: From the town of Leavenworth, drive 4 1/2 miles southeast on Highway 2, then turn south on Highway 97 and drive 18 miles to the campground.

Trip note: This campground is set along Tronsen Creek. Like campsite 60, it's a good winter layover. About a mile away is the Swauk Sno-park, which provides parking and access to Forest Service roads and open areas for snowmobiling and cross-country skiing.

BONANZA
Site **62**

Campsites, facilities: There are five sites for tents, trailers or motorhomes up to 15 feet long. Piped water and picnic tables are provided. Pit toilets and firewood are available.

Reservations, fee: No reservations necessary; $4 fee per night. Open mid-April to late-November.

Who to contact: Phone Wenatchee National Forest at 509-782-1413, or write at Leavenworth Ranger District, 600 Sherbourne, Leavenworth, WA 98826.

Location: From the town of Leavenworth, drive 4 1/2 miles southeast on Highway 2, then turn south on Highway 97 and drive 13 miles to the campground.

Trip note: This campground is just off Highway 97 and is set along Tronsen Creek. If this camp is full, nearby options are campsites 60 and 62, which are south and north, respectively. Each site is about 10 miles from campsite 61.

INDIAN CAMP

Site **63**

Campsites, facilities: There are nine campsites for tents or small trailers. Picnic tables, fire grills and tent pads are provided. Pit toilets are available, but there is no piped water.

Reservations, fee: No reservations necessary; no fee. Open all year.

Who to contact: Phone the Department of Natural Resources at 1-800-527-3305, or write Department of Natural Resources AW-11, 1065 South Capitol Way, Olympia, WA 98504.

Location: In Cle Elum take exit 85 off I-90 and drive east on Highway 970 for seven miles. Turn left on Teanaway Road and go 7 1/2 miles, then turn left on West Fork Teanaway Road and drive 1/2 mile. Go right on Middle Fork Teanaway Road and drive four miles to the campground, which will be on your left.

Trip note: This campground is set along the Middle Fork of the Teanaway River. Bet you didn't know about it.

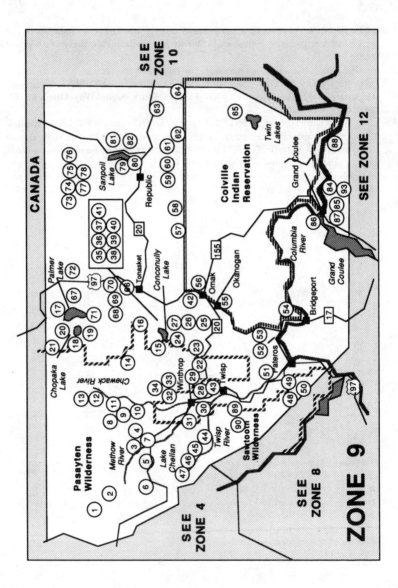

COLVILLE

HARTS PASS
Site **1**

Campsites, facilities: There are five tent sites. Picnic tables are provided. Pit toilets are available, but there is no piped water. Pets are permitted.

Reservations, fee: No reservations necessary; $3 fee per night. Open mid-July to late-September.

Who to contact: Phone Okanogan National Forest at 509-996-2266, or write at Okanogan District Ranger, Winthrop, WA 98862.

Location: From the town of Winthrop, drive 13 miles northwest on Highway 20, then continue northwest on County Road 1163 for seven miles. Go 12 1/2 miles northwest on Forest Service Road 5400 and you'll arrive at the campground. Be aware that this last stretch of road is not suitable for trailers or RVs.

Trip note: This campground is set at the edge of the Pasayten Wilderness, which offers 500 miles of trails to alpine meadows, glacier-fed lakes and streams, and along ridges to spectacular mountain heights. The ruggedness of the terrain and the fragility of the alpine meadows require that hikers obtain Wilderness Permits. Contact the District Ranger for details. The Pacific Crest Trail passes near camp, and nearby Slate Peak, at 7500 feet elevation, offers a great view of the Northern Cascade Range.

MEADOWS
Site **2**

Campsites, facilities: There are 14 tent sites. Picnic tables are provided. Pit toilets are available, but there is no piped water. Pets are permitted.

Reservations, fee: No reservations necessary; no fee. Open mid-July to late-September.

Who to contact: Phone Okanogan National Forest at 509-996-2266, or write at Okanogan District Ranger, Winthrop, WA 98862.

Location: From the town of Winthrop, drive 13 miles northwest on Highway 20, then continue northwest on County Road 1163 for seven miles. Go 12 1/2 miles northwest on Forest Service Road 5400, then turn south of Forest Service Road 500 and drive one mile to the campground.

Trip note: This campground is about one mile from campsite 1 and offers the same opportunities. It is adjacent to the Pacific Crest Trail.

RIVER BEND
Site **3**

Campsites, facilities: There are four tent sites and one site for a trailer or motorhome up to

21 feet long. Piped water and picnic tables are provided. Pit toilets are available and pets are permitted.

Reservations, fee: No reservations necessary; $3 fee per night. Open June to late-September.

Who to contact: Phone Okanogan National Forest at 509-996-2266, or write at Okanogan District Ranger, Winthrop, WA 98862.

Location: From the town of Winthrop, drive 13 miles northwest on Highway 20, then continue northwest on County Road 1163 for seven miles. Go 2 1/2 miles northwest on Forest Service Road 5400, then head west on Forest Service Road 60 and drive 1/2 mile to the campground.

Trip note: This campground is set along the Methow River about two miles from the boundary of the Pasayten Wilderness. There are several trails near camp that provide access to the Wilderness, as well as one that follows the Methow River west for about eight miles before hooking up with the Pacific Crest Trail near Azurite Peak; a Forest Service map will show you the options. If you are interested in travelling with pack animals or horses there is a Forest Service camp nearby that provides facilities. See the trip note to campsite 4 for further details.

BALLARD
Site 4   ▲

Campsites, facilities: There are six tent sites and one site for a trailer or motorhome up to 21 feet long. Piped water and picnic tables are provided. Pit toilets are available and pets are permitted.

Reservations, fee: No reservations necessary; $3 fee per night. Open June to late-September.

Who to contact: Phone Okanogan National Forest at 509-996-2266, or write at Okanogan District Ranger, Winthrop, WA 98862.

Location: From the town of Winthrop, drive 13 miles northwest on Highway 20, then continue northwest on County Road 1163 for seven miles. Go two miles northwest on Forest Service Road 5400 until you see the campground.

Trip note: This campground is set at 2600 feet elevation, about 1/2 of a mile from campsite 3. Facilities for horsepacking, including a hitch rail, truck dock and water, are available at a primitive camp less than a mile northeast of Ballard Camp.

KLIPCHUCK
Site 5   🚐

Campsites, facilities: There are 26 tent sites and 60 sites for trailers or motorhomes up to 32 feet long. Piped water and picnic tables are provided. Flush and pit toilets are available, and pets are permitted.

Reservations, fee: No reservations necessary; $5 fee per night. Open June to late-September.

Who to contact: Phone Okanogan National Forest at 509-996-2266, or write at Okanogan District Ranger, Winthrop, WA 98862.

Location: From the town of Winthrop, drive 17 miles northwest on Highway 20, then continue northwest on Forest Service Road 300 for one mile and you'll see the campground.

Trip note: This campground is set along Early Winters Creek at 3000 feet elevation. A trail from camp leads about five miles up and over Delancy Ridge to the Methow River. Another trail starts nearby on Forest Service Road 200 (Sandy Butte-Cedar Creek Road) and goes two miles up Cedar Creek to lovely Cedar Creek Falls. See a Forest Service map for details.

LONE FIR

Site **6**

Campsites, facilities: There are 28 tent sites and 13 sites for trailers or motorhomes up to 21 feet long. Piped water and picnic tables are provided. Pit toilets are available. Pets are permitted.

Reservations, fee: No reservations necessary; $5 fee per night. Open June to late-September.

Who to contact: Phone Okanogan National Forest at 509-996-2266, or write at Okanogan District Ranger, Winthrop, WA 98862.

Location: From the town of Winthrop, drive 27 miles northwest on Highway 20 and you'll see the campground.

Trip note: This campground is set at 3800 feet elevation, 800 feet higher on Early Winters Creek than campsite 5. This spot is easier to reach than campsite 5, and as a result, gets more traffic.

EARLY
Site **7** ## WINTERS

Campsites, facilities: There are seven tent sites and five sites for trailers or motorhomes up to 15 feet long. Piped water and picnic tables are provided. Pit toilets are available. Pets are permitted.

Reservations, fee: No reservations necessary; $5 fee per night. Open June to late-September.

Who to contact: Phone Okanogan National Forest at 509-996-2266, or write at Okanogan District Ranger, Winthrop, WA 98862.

Location: From the town of Winthrop, drive 16 miles northwest on Highway 20 and you'll see the campground entrance.

Trip note: This campground is set at the confluence of Early Winters Creek and the Methow River. There are several trails that follow the streams in the area. A Forest Service information center is nearby.

HONEYMOON

Site **8**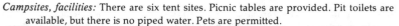

Campsites, facilities: There are six tent sites. Picnic tables are provided. Pit toilets are available, but there is no piped water. Pets are permitted.

Reservations, fee: No reservations necessary; $2 fee per night. Open June to late-September.

Who to contact: Phone Okanogan National Forest at 509-996-2266, or write at Okanogan District Ranger, Winthrop, WA 98862.

Location: From the town of Winthrop, drive 6 1/2 miles north on County Road 1213, continue north on Forest Service Road 51 for 2 1/2 miles, then turn northwest on Forest Service Road 5130 and drive nine miles to the campground.

Trip note: This campground is set at 3500 feet elevation along Eightmile Creek. If you continue north seven miles to the end of Forest Service Road 5130, you will reach a trailhead that provides access to Pasayten Wilderness. See a Forest Service map for details. As to why it is named Honeymoon Camp, well, there are some things about camping that not even this book can answer.

NICE
Site 9

Campsites, facilities: There are seven tent sites and four sites for trailers or motorhomes up to 15 feet long. Picnic tables are provided. Pit toilets are available, but there is no piped water. Pets are permitted.

Reservations, fee: No reservations; no fee. Open June to late-September.

Who to contact: Phone Okanogan National Forest at 509-996-2266, or write at Okanogan District Ranger, Winthrop, WA 98862.

Location: From the town of Winthrop, drive 6 1/2 miles north on County Road 1213, continue north on Forest Service Road 51 for three miles, then turn northwest on Forest Service Road 5130 and drive four miles to the campground.

Trip note: This campground is set along Eightmile Creek about four miles from Buck Lake.

FLAT
Site 10

Campsites, facilities: There are 12 tent sites and three sites for trailers or motorhomes up to 15 feet long. Piped water and picnic tables are provided. Pit toilets are available. Pets are permitted.

Reservations, fee: No reservations necessary; $3 fee per night. Open June to late-September.

Who to contact: Phone Okanogan National Forest at 509-996-2266, or write at Okanogan District Ranger, Winthrop, WA 98862.

Location: From the town of Winthrop, drive 6 1/2 miles north on County Road 1213, continue north on Forest Service Road 51 for three miles, then turn northwest on Forest Service Road 5130 for two miles to the campground.

Trip note: This campground is set along Eightmile Creek two miles from where it empties to the Chewack River. Buck Lake is about three miles away. This is the closest of six camps to County Road 1213.

FALLS CREEK
Site 11

Campsites, facilities: There are nine tent sites and three sites for trailers or motorhomes up to 15 feet long. Piped water and picnic tables are provided. Pit toilets are available. Pets are permitted.

Reservations, fee: No reservations necessary; $4 fee per night. Open June to late-September.

Who to contact: Phone Okanogan National Forest at 509-996-2266, or write at Okanogan District Ranger, Winthrop, WA 98862.

Location: From the town of Winthrop, drive 6 1/2 miles north on County Road 1213, continue north on Forest Service Road 5160 for five miles to the campground.

Trip note: This campground is set at the confluence of Falls Creek and the Chewack River, a quiet and pretty spot that is about a 20-minute drive out of Winthrop. Nearby campsites 12 and 13 do not have piped water, but this camp does.

CHEWACK
Site 12

Campsites, facilities: There are 10 tent sites and six sites for trailers or motorhomes up to

15 feet long. Picnic tables are provided. Pit toilets are available. There is no piped water. Pets are permitted.

Reservations, fee: No reservations; no fee. Open June to late-September.

Who to contact: Phone Okanogan National Forest at 509-996-2266, or write at Okanogan District Ranger, Winthrop, WA 98862.

Location: From the town of Winthrop, drive 6 1/2 miles north on County Road 1213, continue northeast on Forest Service Road 5160 for 8 1/2 miles to the campground.

Trip note: This campground is set along the Chewack River. A more primitive option to nearby campsite 11.

Site **13**   CAMP 4

Campsites, facilities: There are five tent sites. Picnic tables are provided. Pit toilets are available. There is no piped water. Pets are permitted.

Reservations, fee: No reservations necessary; $2 fee per night. Open June to late-September.

Who to contact: Phone Okanogan National Forest at 509-996-2266, or write at Okanogan District Ranger, Winthrop, WA 98862.

Location: From the town of Winthrop, drive 6 1/2 miles north on County Road 1213, then continue northeast on Forest Service Road 5160 for 11 miles to the campground.

Trip note: This campground is set along the Chewack River, the smallest and most primitive of three camps on the river. There are two horse and pack animal facilities five miles north of camp: one is at Lake Creek and the other at Andrews Creek. They both have corrals, hitching rails, truck docks and water for the stock. Trails leading into the Pasayten Wilderness leave from both locations. Contact the Forest Service for details.

Site **14**   TIFFANY
SPRING

Campsites, facilities: There are six tent sites and six sites for trailers or motorhomes up to 15 feet long. Picnic tables are provided. Pit toilets and firewood are available, but there is no piped water. Pets are permitted.

Reservations, fee: No reservations necessary; no fee. Open July to late-September.

Who to contact: Phone Okanogan National Forest at 509-486-2186, or write at Okanogan District Ranger, Winthrop, WA 98862.

Location: From the town of Conconully drive 1 1/2 miles southwest on County Road 2017, then turn northwest on Forest Service Road 364 and drive 21 miles. Turn northeast on Forest Service Road 370 and go 7 1/2 miles to the campground.

Trip note: This campground is set at 6800 feet elevation and is less than a mile hike from Tiffany Lake. Tiffany Mountain rises 8200 feet in the distance. No other campgrounds are in the vicinity, and it is advisable to obtain a Forest Service map of the area.

Site **15**   KERR

Campsites, facilities: There are 13 tent sites and 13 sites for trailers or motorhomes up to 21 feet long. Picnic tables are provided. Pit toilets and firewood are available, but there is no piped water. Pets are permitted. Boat docks, launching facilities and rentals are available nearby at Conconully Reservoir.

Reservations, fee: No reservations necessary; $3 fee per night. Open mid-May to mid-September.

Who to contact: Phone Okanogan National Forest at 509-486-2186, or write at Okanogan District Ranger, Winthrop, WA 98862.

Location: From the town of Conconully drive two miles northwest on County Road 2361, then go northwest on Forest Service Road 38 for two miles to the campground.

Trip note: This campground is set along Salmon Creek about four miles north of the Conconully Reservoir. One of many campgrounds located near the lake.

SUGARLOAF
Site **16**

Campsites, facilities: There are five tent sites and five sites for trailers or motorhomes up to 21 feet long. Piped water and picnic tables are provided. Pit toilets and firewood are available. Pets are permitted. Boat docks, launching facilities and rentals are nearby.

Reservations, fee: No reservations necessary; $3 fee per night. Open mid-May to mid-September.

Who to contact: Phone Okanogan National Forest at 509-486-2186, or write at Okanogan District Ranger, Winthrop, WA 98862.

Location: From the town of Conconully drive 4 1/2 miles northeast on County Road 4015 to the campground.

Trip note: At 2400 feet elevation, this campground is set along the shore of Conconully Lake. This is the smallest, most private of the camps on the lake.

PALMER
Site **17** LAKE

Campsites, facilities: There are six campsites for tents or small trailers. Picnic tables, fire grills and tent pads are provided. Pit toilets are available, but there is no piped water.

Reservations, fee: No reservations necessary; no fee. Open all year.

Who to contact: Phone the Department of Natural Resources at 1-800-527-3305, or write Department of Natural Resources AW-11, 1065 South Capitol Way, Olympia, WA 98504.

Location: Drive five miles north of the town of Tonaskey on County Route 9437, then head west to the town of Loomis on County Road 9425. From Loomis, continue north on County Road 9425 for 8 1/2 miles, keep right, and you'll find the campground at the north end of the lake.

Trip note: This campground is set along the shore of Palmer Lake, the only camp at the lake. The winter range of the deer is in the Sinlahekin Valley to the south of Palmer Lake. There are numerous migration routes in the area. Wildlife not for hunting include the endangered Bighorn sheep, cougar, Bald and Golden eagles, black and brown bear and grouse. See campsite 20 for information on fishing for Atlantic Salmon in nearby Chopaka Lake.

NORTH FORK
Site **18** NINE MILE

Campsites, facilities: There are 11 campsites for tents or small trailers. Picnic tables, fire grills and tent pads are provided. Pit toilets and piped water are available.

Reservations, fee: No reservations necessary; no fee. Open all year.

Who to contact: Phone the Department of Natural Resources at 1-800-527-3305, or write Department of Natural Resources AW-11, 1065 South Capitol Way, Olympia, WA 98504.

Location: Drive five miles north of the town of Tonaskey on County Route 9437, then head west to the town of Loomis on County Road 9425. From Loomis, continue north on County Road 9425 for two miles, then turn left on Toats Coulee Road. Go 5 1/2 miles to the lower camp. Continue 100 yards to the upper camp at the junction of OM-T-2000 and OM-T-1000. Take OM-T-1000 Road and drive 2 1/2 miles to the campground.

Trip note: This campground is set in the forest along the North Fork of Touts Coulee Creek and Nine Mile Creek. This area is frequented by the Northwestern moose. It is advisable to obtain a map that details the area from the Department of Natural Resources.

Site **19**   TOATS COULEE

Campsites, facilities: There are 12 campsites for tents or small trailers. Picnic tables, fire grills and tent pads are provided. Pit toilets are available. There is no piped water.

Reservations, fee: No reservations necessary; no fee. Open all year.

Who to contact: Phone the Department of Natural Resources at 1-800-527-3305, or write Department of Natural Resources AW-11, 1065 South Capitol Way, Olympia, WA 98504.

Location: Drive five miles north of the town of Tonaskey on County Route 9437, then head west to the town of Loomis on County Road 9425. From Loomis, continue north on County Road 9425 for two miles, then turn left on Toats Coulee Road. Go 5 1/2 miles to the lower camp. Continue 100 yards to the upper camp at the junction of OM-T-2000 and OM-T-1000.

Trip note: This wooded camp is set along the Touts Coulee Creek. Some moose are in the area. A road for snowmobile use follows the South Fork of Touts Coulee Creek and swings south then heads east along Cecil Creek. Contact the Department of Natural Resources for details. This is one of three little-known camps in the vicinity.

Site **20**   CHOPAKA LAKE   ▲

Campsites, facilities: There are 15 campsites for tents or small trailers. Picnic tables, fire grills and tent pads are provided. Pit toilets, piped water and boat launching facilities are available.

Reservations, fee: No reservations necessary; no fee. Open all year.

Who to contact: Phone the Department of Natural Resources at 1-800-527-3305, or write Department of Natural Resources AW-11, 1065 South Capitol Way, Olympia, WA 98504.

Location: Drive five miles north of the town of Tonaskey on County Route 9437, then head west to the town of Loomis on County Road 9425. From Loomis continue north on County Road 9425, for two miles, then turn left on Toats Coulee Road and go 1 1/2 miles. Turn right onto a steep, one-lane road and drive 3 1/2 miles, keep left and drive 1 1/2 miles, then turn right and drive two miles to the campground.

Trip note: This campground is set along the western shore of Chopaka Lake. The lake is stocked with Atlantic Salmon and only catch and release fly fishing with barbless hooks is allowed. A classic setting for the expert angler.

COLD SPRINGS
Site **21**

Campsites, facilities: There are 13 campsites for tents or small trailers. Picnic tables, fire grills and tent pads are provided. Pit toilets and piped water are available. Horse stalls and feeder boxes are also available.

Reservations, fee: No reservations necessary; no fee. Open all year.

Who to contact: Phone the Department of Natural Resources at 1-800-527-3305, or write Department of Natural Resources AW-11, 1065 South Capitol Way, Olympia, WA 98504.

Location: Drive five miles north of the town of Tonaskey on County Route 9437, then head west to the town of Loomis on County Road 9425. From Loomis, continue north on County Road 9425 for two miles, then turn left on Toats Coulee Road and drive 5 1/2 miles to Toats Coulee campground at the junction of OM-T-2000 and OM-T-1000. Take OM-T-1000 Road for two miles to Cold Creek Road (gravel) and turn right. Go 1/2 mile, keep right and continue for two miles. Then keep left and go two miles to the picnic area or three miles to the campground.

Trip note: There are trails here for horseback riding, hiking and snowmobiling. Little known and remote, advisable to obtain map of area to aid directions. Some moose tromp around these parts.

J.R.
Site **22**

Campsites, facilities: There are six sites for tents, trailers or motorhomes up to 15 feet long. Piped water and picnic tables are provided. Pit toilets and firewood are available. Some facilities are wheelchair accessible. Pets are permitted.

Reservations, fee: No reservations necessary; $4 fee per night. Open late-May to early-September.

Who to contact: Phone Okanogan National Forest at 509-997-2131, or write at Twisp District Ranger, Twisp, WA 98856.

Location: From the town of Twisp, drive 12 miles east on Highway 20 to the campground.

Trip note: This campground is set along Frazier Creek near the Loup Loup summit and ski area. Some of the recreation options include fishing, hunting, cross-country skiing, snowmobiling, hiking and bicycling. Good layover for travelers looking for spot on Highway 20.

LOUP LOUP
Site **23**

Campsites, facilities: There are 20 sites for tents, trailers or motorhomes up to 21 feet long. Piped water and picnic tables are provided. Pit toilets and firewood are available. Pets are permitted.

Reservations, fee: No reservations necessary; $4 fee per night. Open late-May to early-September.

Who to contact: Phone Okanogan National Forest at 509-997-2131, or write at Twisp District Ranger, Twisp, WA 98856.

Location: From the town of Twisp, drive 13 miles east on Highway 20, then turn north on Forest Service Road 42 and drive one mile to the campground.

Trip note: At 4200 feet elevation, this campground is set next to the Loup Loup ski area which has facilities for both downhill and cross-country skiing. There are trails for hiking and horseback riding. Just far enough off Highway 20 that many out-of-towners miss it.

CONCONULLY
Site 24   STATE PARK   ▲

Campsites, facilities: There are 81 tent sites. Piped water, fire grills and picnic tables are provided. Flush toilets, sanitary services, showers, firewood and a playground are available. A store, cafe, laundromat and ice are located within one mile. Pets are permitted. Boat launching facilities are nearby.

Reservations, fee: No reservations necessary; $6 fee per night. Open all year with limited winter facilities.

Who to contact: Phone at 509-826-2108, or write at Box 95, Conconully, WA 98819.

Location: From the town of Omak, drive 22 miles northwest on Highway 97 and you'll see the park entrance.

Trip note: This park is set along Conconully Reservoir, where there is a boat launch, beach access and swimming, fishing and hiking opportunities. Of special interest is the Sinlahekin Habitat Management Area which is accessible via County Route 4015. This route heads northeast along the shore of Conconully Lake on the other side of Highway 97. The road is narrow at first, but then becomes wider as you enter the Habitat Management Area.

LEADER LAKE
Site 25   🌲

Campsites, facilities: There are 16 campsites for tents or small trailers. Picnic tables, fire grills and tent pads are provided. Pit toilets are available, but there is no piped water. Some facilities are wheelchair accessible. Boat launching facilities are nearby.

Reservations, fee: No reservations necessary; no fee. Open all year.

Who to contact: Phone the Department of Natural Resources at 1-800-527-3305, or write Department of Natural Resources AW-11, 1065 South Capitol Way, Olympia, WA 98504.

Location: Take Highway 20 west from Okanogan and go 8 1/2 miles, then turn right on Leader Lake Road and drive 400 yards to the campground.

Trip note: This campground is set along the shore of Leader Lake, where trout fishing can be good in season. Just far enough off the beaten path that it gets missed by many.

ROCK CREEK
Site 26   ▲

Campsites, facilities: There are six campsites for tents or small trailers. Picnic tables, fire grills and tent pads are provided. Pit toilets and piped water are available.

Reservations, fee: No reservations necessary; no fee. Open all year.

Who to contact: Phone the Department of Natural Resources at 1-800-527-3305, or write Department of Natural Resources AW-11, 1065 South Capitol Way, Olympia, WA 98504.

Location: Take Highway 20 west from Okanogan and go 10 miles, then turn right on Loup Loup Canyon Road and drive four miles to the camp, which is on the left.

Trip note: This wooded campground is at the confluence of Rock Creek and Loup Loup

Creek. There are hiking trails in the area. Advisable to obtain map detailing area from Department of Natural Resources.

ROCK LAKES

Site **27**

Campsites, facilities: There are eight campsites for tents or small trailers. Picnic tables, fire grills and tent pads are provided. Pit toilets are available, but there is no piped water.

Reservations, fee: No reservations necessary; no fee. Open all year.

Who to contact: Phone the Department of Natural Resources at 1-800-527-3305, or write Department of Natural Resources AW-11, 1065 South Capitol Way, Olympia, WA 98504.

Location: Take Highway 20 west from Okanogan and go 10 miles, then turn right on Loup Loup Canyon Road and drive five miles. Turn left on Rock Lakes Road and go six miles then turn left and drive 300 yards to the campground.

Trip note: This campground is set in a forested area along the shore of Rock Lake. Trout fishing can be good. A good bet is to parlay a trip here with nearby campsite 25 at Leader Lake.

KOA METHOW RIVER

Site **28**

Campsites, facilities: There are 26 tent sites and 72 drive-through sites for trailers or motorhomes of any length. Piped water and picnic tables are provided. Flush toilets, electricity, firewood, sewer hookups, sanitary services, showers, a recreation hall, store, laundromat, ice, playground and swimming pool are available. Bottled gas and a cafe are located within one mile. Pets and motorbikes are permitted.

Reservations, fee: Reservations accepted; $12 fee per night. MasterCard and Visa accepted. Open mid-April to November.

Who to contact: Phone at 509-996-2258, or write at P.O. Box 305, Winthrop, WA 98862.

Location: From the town of Winthrop, drive one mile east on Highway 20 and you'll see it.

Trip note: This campground is set along the Methow River. Nearby, Liberty Bell Alpine Tours and River Rafting offers both whitewater and scenic tours on the Methow River; phone 509-996-2250 for information. Winthrop is an interesting town with many restored, turn-of-the-century buildings lining the main street, including the Shafer Museum which displays lots of old items from that era. If you would like to observe wildlife, take a short, two-mile drive southeast out of Winthrop on County Route 9129, on the east side of the Methow River. Turn east on County Route 1631 into Davis Lake, and follow the signs to the Methow River Habitat Management Area Headquarters. Depending on the time of year, you may see mule deer, porcupine, bobcat, mountain lion, snowshoe hare, black bear, red squirrel and many species of birds. However, if you are looking for something more tame, other nearby recreation options include an 18-hole golf course and tennis courts.

PINE-NEAR TRAILER PARK

Site **29**

Campsites, facilities: There are 10 tent sites and 28 drive-through sites for trailers or motorhomes of any length. Electricity, piped water, sewer hookups and picnic tables are provided. Flush toilets, sanitary services, showers, a laundromat and playground are available. A store and cafe are located within one mile. Pets and motorbikes are permitted.

Reservations, fee: Reservations accepted; $10 fee per night. Open all year.

Who to contact: Phone at 509-996-2391, or write at P.O. Box 157, Winthrop, WA 98862.

Location: Drive east of the town of Winthrop on Highway 20 on Coral and Castle and you'll see the park.

Trip note: This campground is set along the Methow River. See trip note to campsite 28 for information on the various activities available in the Winthrop area.

Site 30
BIG TWIN
LAKE CAMPGROUND

Campsites, facilities: There are 35 tent sites and 58 drive-through sites for trailers or motorhomes of any length. Electricity, piped water, sewer hookups and picnic tables are provided. Flush toilets, sanitary services, showers, firewood, a laundromat, ice and playground are available. Pets and motorbikes are permitted. Boat docks, launching facilities and rentals can be obtained on Big Twin Lake.

Reservations, fee: Reservations accepted; $10 fee per night. Open April to late-October.

Who to contact: Phone at 509-996-2650, or write at Big Twin Lake Road, Winthrop, WA 98862.

Location: From the town of Winthrop, drive three miles south on Highway 20, then turn west on Big Twin Lake Road and drive two miles to the campground.

Trip note: This campground is set along the shore of Twin Lakes. See the trip note to campsite 28 for information on the various activites available in the Winthrop area.

Site 31
ROCKING HORSE
RANCH

Campsites, facilities: There are 25 tent sites and 10 drive-through sites for trailers or motorhomes of any length. Electricity, piped water, sewer hookups and picnic tables are provided. Flush toilets, sanitary services, showers, firewood, a recreation hall and ice are available. Some facilities are wheelchair accessible. Pets and motorbikes are permitted.

Reservations, fee: Reservations accepted; $8 fee per night. Open April to late-October.

Who to contact: Phone at 509-996-2768, or write at Star Route, P.O. Box 35, Winthrop, WA 98862.

Location: From the town of Winthrop, drive nine miles northwest on Highway 20 and you'll see the entrance to the ranch.

Trip note: This ranch is set in the lovely Methow River Valley, which is flanked on both sides by national forest. There are numerous trails nearby and a horse stable at the ranch. Owen Wister, who wrote the novel, "The Virginian," lived in the nearby town of Winthrop at the turn of the century. Portions of the novel were based on his experiences in this area.

Site 32
5-Y RESORT ON
PEARRYGIN LAKE

Campsites, facilities: There are 60 drive-through sites for tents, trailers or motorhomes of any length. Electricity, piped water, sewer hookups and picnic tables are provided.

Flush toilets, showers, firewood, a laundromat and playground are available. Bottled gas, sanitary services, a store, cafe and ice are located within one mile. Pets and motorbikes are permitted. Boat docks, launching facilities and rentals are nearby.

Reservations, fee: Reservations accepted; $10 fee per night. Open April to October.

Who to contact: Phone at 509-996-2448, or write at Route 1, P.O. Box 308, Winthrop, WA 98862.

Location: From the town of Winthrop, drive two miles northeast on Pearrygin Lake Road and you'll see the resort.

Trip note: This resort is in a wooded area along the shore of Pearrygin Lake. Nearby recreation options include an 18-hole golf course, hiking trails and a riding stable. See the trip note to campsite 28 for information on other available activities in the Winthrop area.

DERRY'S RESORT
Site **33**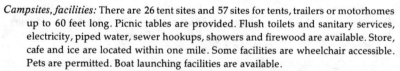

Campsites, facilities: There are 90 tent sites and 64 drive-through sites for trailers or motorhomes of any length. Electricity, piped water, sewer hookups and picnic tables are provided. Flush toilets, bottled gas, showers, firewood, sanitary services, a store, laundromat, ice and playground are available. A cafe is located within one mile. Pets and motorbikes are permitted. Boat docks, launching facilities and rentals are available on Pearrygin Lake.

Reservations, fee: Reservations accepted; $10 fee per night. Open April to mid-November.

Who to contact: Phone at 509-996-2322, or write at Route 1, P.O. Box 307, Winthrop, WA 98862.

Location: From the town of Winthrop, drive three miles northeast on Pearrygin Lake Road and you'll see the resort.

Trip note: This campground is also set along the shore of Pearrygin Lake. Nearby recreation options include an 18-hole golf course, hiking trails and a riding stable.

PEARRYGIN LAKE STATE PARK
Site **34**

Campsites, facilities: There are 26 tent sites and 57 sites for tents, trailers or motorhomes up to 60 feet long. Picnic tables are provided. Flush toilets and sanitary services, electricity, piped water, sewer hookups, showers and firewood are available. Store, cafe and ice are located within one mile. Some facilities are wheelchair accessible. Pets are permitted. Boat launching facilities are available.

Reservations, fee: Reservations accepted; $6 fee per night. Open all year with limited winter facilities.

Who to contact: Phone at 509-996-2370, or write at Route 1, Winthrop, WA 98862.

Location: From the town of Winthrop, drive five miles north on Highway 20. The park is adjacent to the highway along the shore of Pearrygin Lake.

Trip note: This park has a sandy beach and facilities for swimming, boating, fishing and hiking. In the winter there are opportunities for snowmobiling, crosscountry skiing and ice fishing. Nearby recreation options include an 18-hole golf course. One of several camps in the immediate area.

Site **35**
KOZY KABINS AND RV PARK

Campsites, facilities: There are six tent sites and 12 drive-through sites for trailers or motorhomes of any length. Electricity, piped water, sewer hookups and picnic tables are provided. Flush toilets, showers and firewood are available. Bottled gas, sanitary services, a store, cafe, laundromat and ice are located within one mile. Pets and motorbikes are permitted. Boat docks, launching facilities and rentals are nearby.

Reservations, fee: Reservations accepted; $8 fee per night. Open all year.

Who to contact: Phone at 509-826-6780, or write at P.O. Box 38, Conconully, WA 98819.

Location: From the town of Okanogan drive northwest on the Conconully Highway to the town of Conconully. The park is at the junction of "A" Avenue and Broadway.

Trip note: This park is in the town of Conconully near the lake and reservoir. Nearby recreation options include a full service marina. If you continue northeast of town on County Route 4015, the road will get a bit narrow for awhile, but it will widen again when you enter the Sinlahekin Habitat Management Area, which is managed by the Department of Game. There are some primitive campsites in this valley, especially along the shores of the lakes in the area.

Site **36**
THE OTHER PLACE

Campsites, facilities: There are 25 drive-through sites for trailers or motorhomes of any length. Electricity, piped water, sewer hookups and picnic tables are provided. Flush toilets, and showers are available. Bottled gas, sanitary services, a store, cafe, laundromat and ice are located within one mile. Pets and motorbikes are permitted. Boat docks, launching facilities and rentals are nearby.

Reservations, fee: Reservations accepted; $8 fee per night. Open mid-April to late-October.

Who to contact: Phone at 509-826-4231, or write at 310 "A" Avenue, Conconully, WA 98819.

Location: From the town of Okanogan drive northwest on the Conconully Highway to the town of Conconully. Turn east on A Avenue and drive one block to the park.

Trip note: This campground is set along the shore of Conconully Lake. See the trip note to campsite 35 for nearby recreation options and ideas.

Site **37**
JACK'S RV PARK

Campsites, facilities: There are 20 tent sites and 64 drive-through sites for trailers or motorhomes of any length. Electricity, piped water, sewer hookups and picnic tables are provided. Flush toilets, bottled gas, showers, firewood, a laundromat and swimming pool are available. Sanitary services, a store, cafe and ice are located within one mile. Pets and motorbikes are permitted. Boat docks, launching facilities and rentals are nearby.

Reservations, fee: Reservations accepted; $8 fee per night. MasterCard and Visa accepted. Open all year.

Who to contact: Phone at 509-826-0132, or write at P.O. Box 98, Conconully, WA 98819.

Location: From the town of Okanogan drive 20 miles northwest on the Conconully Highway to the town of Conconully. The park is in town.

Trip note: This park is in town, not far from Conconully Lake. Nearby recreation options include hiking trails and watersports at the lake.

Site 38 ANDY'S TRAILER PARK 🚐

Campsites, facilities: There are 38 drive-through sites for trailers or motorhomes of any length. Electricity, piped water, sewer hookups and picnic tables are provided. Flush toilets, firewood, showers, laundromat and swimming pool are available. Bottled gas, sanitary services, store, cafe and ice are located within one mile. Pets are permitted. Boat docks, launching facilities and rentals are nearby.

Reservations, fee: Reservations accepted; $8 fee per night. Open April to mid-November.

Who to contact: Phone at 509-826-0326, or write at P.O. Box 67, Conconully, WA 98819.

Location: From the town of Omak drive 18 miles northwest on the Conconully Highway and you'll find the park in the town of Conconully.

Trip note: This park is in downtown Conconully, a short distance from the lake and reservoir. Nearby recreation options include hiking trails.

Site 39 LIAR'S COVE RESORT 🚐

Campsites, facilities: There are 35 drive-through sites for trailers or motorhomes of any length. Electricity, piped water, sewer hookups and picnic tables are provided. Flush toilets, showers, laundromat and ice are available. Bottled gas, sanitary services, a store and cafe are located within one mile. Pets and motorbikes are permitted. Boat docks, launching facilities and rentals are nearby.

Reservations, fee: Reservations accepted; $10 fee per night; MasterCard and Visa accepted. Open April to early-November.

Who to contact: Phone at 509-826-1288, or write at P.O. Box 72, Conconully, WA 98819.

Location: From the town of Okanogan drive 18 miles northwest on the Conconully Highway and you'll see the park.

Trip note: This park is set along the shore of the Conconully Reservoir. Nearby recreation options include hiking trails.

Site 40 SHADY PINES RESORT 🚐

Campsites, facilities: There are five tent sites and 24 drive-through sites for trailers or motorhomes of any length. Electricity, piped water, sewer hookups and picnic tables are provided. Flush toilets, ice, showers and firewood are available. Bottled gas, sanitary services, store, cafe and laundromat are located within one mile. Pets and motorbikes are permitted. Boat launching facilities and rentals are nearby.

Reservations, fee: Reservations accepted; $11 fee per night. MasterCard and Visa accepted. Open mid-April to late-October.

Who to contact: Phone at 509-826-2287, or write at P.O. Box 44, Conconully, WA 98819.

Location: From the town of Okanogan drive 20 miles northwest on Conconully Highway, then turn west at the state park and drive one mile to the resort.

Trip note: This campground is set along the shore of the Conconully Reservoir, near the state park (campsite 24).

Site 41   FLEMMINGS RESORT AND RV PARK

Campsites, facilities: There are 11 sites for trailers or motorhomes of any length. Electricity, piped water, sewer hookups and picnic tables are provided. Flush toilets, showers and ice are available. Bottled gas, sanitary services, a store, cafe and laundromat are available within one mile. Pets and motorbikes are permitted. Boat docks, launching facilities and rentals are nearby.

Reservations, fee: Reservations accepted; $9 fee per night. Open mid-April to late-October.

Who to contact: Phone at 509-826-0813, or write at P.O. Box 131, Conconully, WA 98819.

Location: From the town of Omak, drive 17 miles northwest on the Conconully Highway and you'll see the resort.

Trip note: This resort is set along the shore of Conconully Lake. See the trip note to campsite 35 for recreation options.

Site 42   LOG CABIN TRAILER COURT

Campsites, facilities: There are 10 sites for trailers or motorhomes. Electricity, piped water and sewer hookups are provided. Flush toilets, sanitary services, showers and a laundromat are available. Bottled gas, a store, cafe and ice are located within one mile. Pets are permitted.

Reservations, fee: No reservations necessary; $8 fee per night. Open all year.

Who to contact: Phone at 509-826-4462, or write at P.O. Box 1630, Omak, WA 98841.

Location: This trailer park is located in the town of Omak, on Highway 215.

Trip note: This trailer court is located in rural Omak on the Okanogan River. Nearby recreation options include an 18-hole golf course and tennis courts.

Site 43   RIVER BEND TRAILER PARK

Campsites, facilities: There are 10 tent sites and 56 drive-through sites for trailers or motorhomes of any length. Picnic tables are provided. Flush toilets, sanitary services, firewood, a store, laundromat, ice, a playground, electricity, piped water, sewer hookups and showers are available. Pets and motorbikes are permitted.

Reservations, fee: Reservations accepted; $9 fee per night. MasterCard and Visa accepted. Open mid-April to November.

Who to contact: Phone at 509-997-3500, or write at Route 2, Box 30, Twisp, WA 98856.

Location: Drive two miles north of the town of Twisp on Highway 20 and you'll see the campground.

Trip note: This campground is set along the shore of the Methow River. The trip note for campsite 28 details the recreation possibilities available within 10 miles.

WAR CREEK
Site **44**

Campsites, facilities: There are 11 sites for tents, trailers or motorhomes up to 21 feet long. Piped water and picnic tables are provided. Pit toilets and firewood are available. Pets are permitted.

Reservations, fee: No reservations necessary; $4 fee per night. Open late-May to early-September.

Who to contact: Phone Okanogan National Forest at 509-997-2131, or write at Twisp District Ranger, Twisp, WA 98856.

Location: From the town of Twisp, drive 11 miles west on County Road 9114, then continue west on Forest Service Road 44 for 3 1/2 miles to the campground.

Trip note: This campground is set along the Twisp River near the trailhead for trail 408, which follows War Creek west up to Lake Juanita, and then to War Creek Pass at 7400 feet elevation. Backpackers can take this path down into the Lake Chelan National Recreation Area, finishing the trip at the shore of Lake Chelan at the Stehekin campground and the National Park Service outpost. It's a 15-mile trek, so contact the Forest Service for details. This area is also open in the winter for crosscountry skiing and snowmobiling.

POPLAR FLAT
Site **45**

Campsites, facilities: There are 15 tent sites and 15 sites for trailers or motorhomes up to 21 feet long. Piped water and picnic tables are provided. Pit toilets and firewood are available. Some facilities are wheelchair accessible. Pets are permitted.

Reservations, fee: No reservations necessary; $4 fee per night. Open late-May to early-September.

Who to contact: Phone Okanogan National Forest at 509-997-2131, or write at Twisp District Ranger, Twisp, WA 98856.

Location: From the town of Twisp, drive 11 miles west on County Road 9114, then head northwest on Forest Service Road 44 and drive 9 1/2 miles to the campground.

Trip note: This campground is set at 2900 feet elevation along the Twisp River. There are many trails in the area that follow streams, in some cases providing access to small lakes in the backcountry, in other cases providing access to the Lake Chelan National Recreation Area. Trail 407 is a bicycle trail. South Creek campground (Camp 46), about two miles northwest of this campground, has horse facilities. During the winter the roads are available for snowmobiling and crosscountry skiing. See a Forest Service map for details.

SOUTH CREEK
Site **46**

Campsites, facilities: There are four tent sites. Piped water and picnic tables are provided. Pit toilets and firewood are available. Pets are permitted. Horse facilities are also available.

Reservations, fee: No reservations necessary; no fee. Open late-May to early-September.

Who to contact: Phone Okanogan National Forest at 509-997-2131, or write at Twisp District Ranger, Twisp, WA 98856.

Location: From the town of Twisp, drive 11 miles west on County Road 9114, then continue west on Forest Service Road 44 for 11 miles to the campground.

Trip note: This site is small, quiet and little-known, yet with piped water and good recreation options. It is set at the confluence of the North Fork of the Twisp River and South Creek at a major trailhead that accesses Lake Chelan National Recreation Area and North Cascades National Park. See a Forest Service map for details. This area is also open in the winter for crosscountry skiing and snowmobiling.

ROADS END
Site **47**   ▲

Campsites, facilities: There are four tents sites. Piped water and picnic tables are provided. Pit toilets and firewood are available. Pets are permitted.

Reservations, fee: No reservations necessary; no fee. Open late-May to early-September.

Who to contact: Phone Okanogan National Forest at 509-997-2131, or write at Twisp District Ranger, Twisp, WA 98856.

Location: From the town of Twisp, drive 11 miles west on County Road 9114, then continue west on Forest Service Road 44 for 13 1/2 miles to the campground.

Trip note: This campground is set along the North Fork of the Twisp River at a major trailhead that provides access to the backcountry and North Cascades National Park. The trail intersects with the Pacific Crest Trail about nine miles from camp. A Forest Service map is essential. This area is also open in the winter for crosscountry skiing and snowmobiling.

ALTA LAKE
Site **48**   **STATE PARK**   ▲

Campsites, facilities: There are 164 tent sites and 16 sites for trailers or motorhomes up to 20 feet long. Picnic tables and fireplaces are provided. Flush toilets, piped water, showers, electricity, firewood and sanitary services are available. A store, cafe and ice are available within one mile. Some facilities are wheelchair accessible. Pets are permitted. Boat launching facilities are nearby.

Reservations, fee: No reservations necessary; $6 fee per night. Open all year.

Who to contact: Phone at 509-923-2473, or write at Star Route 40, Pateros, WA 98846.

Location: Take Highway 153 off Highway 97 just south of the town of Pateros and drive two miles to Alta Lake Road. Turn southwest on Alta Lake Road and drive three miles to the park.

Trip note: This state park is set among the pines along the shore of Alta Lake, where a half-mile long swimming beach and boat launch are available. Nearby recreation options include an 18-hole golf course and a riding stable.

ALTA'S WEST
Site **49**   **BEACH**

Campsites, facilities: There are 15 tent sites and 35 sites for trailers or motorhomes up to 27 feet long. Picnic tables are provided. Flush toilets, sanitary services, ice, electricity, piped water, showers and firewood are available. Pets and motorbikes are permitted. Boat docks, launching facilities and rentals are nearby.

Reservations, fee: Reservations accepted; $8 fee per night. Open all year.

Who to contact: Phone at 509-923-2863, or write at 320 112th SW, Everett, WA 98204.

Location: From the town of Pateros at the juntion of Highway 97 and 153, drive two miles northwest on Highway 153 to Alta Lake Road, turn southwest and drive three miles to the campground.

Trip note: This campground is set along the shore of Alta Lake. The lake is used for waterskiing, fishing and swimming in the summer months, and ice fishing in the winter. Snowmobiling is also permitted. There are hiking and bicycling trails nearby at the state park.

Site **50**   WHISTLIN' PINE RESORT

Campsites, facilities: There are 60 tent sites and 10 sites for trailers or motorhomes up to 30 feet long. Electricity, piped water, sewer hookups and picnic tables are provided. Flush toilets, showers, firewood and ice are available. Sanitary services are available within one mile. Pets and motorbikes are permitted. Boat docks, launching facilities and rentals are nearby.

Reservations, fee: Reservations accepted; $9 fee per night. Open April to late-October.

Who to contact: Phone at 509-923-2548, or write at P.O. Box 284, Pateros, WA 98846.

Location: From the the town of Pateros at the juntion of Highway 97 and 153, drive two miles northwest on Highway 153 to Alta Lake Road, turn southwest on Alta Lake Road and drive three miles to the resort.

Trip note: This campground is set along the shore of Alta Lake. See trip note to campsite 48 for listing of lake recreation activities.

Site **51**   OUTPOST RV PARK AND MARINA

Campsites, facilities: There are six tent sites and 20 sites for trailers or motorhomes of any length. Electricity, piped water and sewer hookups are provided. Flush toilets, bottled gas, sanitary services, a store, cafe, laundromat and ice are available. Pets and motorbikes are permitted. Boat docks and launching facilities are nearby.

Reservations, fee: Reservations accepted; $9 fee per night. MasterCard and Visa accepted. Open all year.

Who to contact: Phone at 509-923-2200, or write at P.O. Box 147, Pateros, WA 98846.

Location: This park is at the south end of the town of Pateros, which is on Highway 97.

Trip note: This park and marina is set along the shore of the Columbia River. Nearby recreation options include an 18-hole golf course, hiking trails, a riding stable and tennis courts.

Site **52**   ANGLE TRAILER COURT

Campsites, facilities: There are eight drive-through sites for trailers or motorhomes of any length. Electricity, piped water and sewer hookups are provided. Flush toilets and showers are available. Bottled gas, a store, cafe, laundromat and ice are located within one mile. Pets are permitted. Boat docks and launching facilities are nearby on the Columbia River.

Reservations, fee: Reservations accepted; $10 fee per night. Open all year.

Who to contact: Phone at 509-689-2434, or write at P.O. Box 145, Brewster, WA 98812.

Location: Drive to the town of Brewster on Highway 97, then turn southwest on 6th Avenue and drive to the trailer court.

Trip note: This trailer court is set along the shore of the Columbia River. Nearby recreation options include tennis courts.

Site 53
BREWSTER MOTEL
AND RV PARK

Campsites, facilities: There are 4 tent sites and 6 drive-through sites for trailers or motorhomes of any length. Electricity, piped water and picnic tables are provided. Flush toilets, sanitary services, showers, ice and a swimming pool are available. Sewer hookups are available for an extra fee. Bottled gas, a store, cafe and laundromat are available within one mile. Pets and motorbikes are permitted. Boat docks and launching facilities are nearby on the Columbia River.

Reservations, fee: Reservations accepted; $8 fee per night. MasterCard and Visa accepted. Open all year.

Who to contact: Phone at 509-689-2625, or write at P.O. Box 632, Brewster, WA 98812.

Location: Drive to the town of Brewster on Highway 97. The park is in town on Bridge Street.

Trip note: This park is near the Columbia River. Nearby recreation options include an 18-hole golf course, a full service marina and tennis courts.

Site 54
BRIDGEPORT
STATE PARK

Campsites, facilities: There are 28 tent sites. Piped water and picnic tables are provided. Flush toilets, showers, firewood and sanitary services are available. A store, cafe and ice are located within one mile. Pets are permitted. Boat docks and launching facilities are nearby on both the upper and lower portions of the reservoir.

Reservations, fee: No reservations necessary; $6 fee per night. Open April to late-October.

Who to contact: Phone at 509-686-7231, or write at P.O. Box 846, Bridgeport, WA 98813.

Location: Drive 21 miles south of Okanogan on Highway 97, then head southeast on Highway 17 and drive eight miles until you see the sign to turn into the park.

Trip note: This park is set along the shore of the Rufus Woods Lake, a reservoir on the Columbia River above the Chief Joseph Dam. There is beach access and a boat launch. There are also hiking trails, but the parks department warns that there are rattlesnakes in certain areas. Nearby recreation options include an 18-hole golf course.

Site 55
AMERICAN
LEGION PARK

Campsites, facilities: There are 20 sites for trailers or motorhomes of any length. Piped water and picnic tables are provided. Flush toilets and showers are available. A store, cafe, laundromat and ice are located within one mile.

Reservations, fee: No reservations necessary; $3 fee per night. Open all year.

Who to contact: Write to Okanogan City Hall, Okanogan, WA 98840.

Location: This park is located at the north end of the town of Okanogan on Highway 215.

Trip note: This city park is set along the shore of the Okanogan River. There is an historical museum in town.

Site 56 · EASTSIDE TRAILER PARK AND CAMPGROUND

Campsites, facilities: There are 50 tent sites and 68 drive-through sites for trailers or motorhomes of any length. Electricity, piped water, sewer hookups and picnic tables are provided. Flush toilets, sanitary services, showers, swimming pool and a playground are available. A store, cafe, laundromat and ice are located within one mile. Pets are permitted. Boat launching facilities are nearby.

Reservations, fee: No reservations necessary; $8 fee per night. Open April to late-October.

Who to contact: Phone at 509-826-1170, or write at P.O. Box 72, Omak, WA 98841.

Location: This campground is located just east of the town of Omak, on Highway 155 between the Okanogan River and Highway 97.

Trip note: This city park is in town, along the shore of the Okanogan River. Nearby recreation options include an 18-hole golf course.

Site 57 · CRAWFISH LAKE

Campsites, facilities: There are 22 sites for tents, trailers or motorhomes up to 31 feet long. Picnic tables are provided. Pit toilets are available, but there is no piped water. Pets are permitted. Boat docks and launching facilities are located on the lake.

Reservations, fee: No reservations necessary; $3 fee per night. Open mid-May to mid-September.

Who to contact: Phone Okanogan National Forest at 509-486-2186, or write at Tonasket District Ranger, Tonasket, WA 98855.

Location: From the town of Riverside, drive 17 1/2 miles east on County Road 9320, then head south on Forest Service Road 3612 for 1 1/2 miles. Next, turn southeast on Forest Service Road 3525 and drive 400 yards to the campground.

Trip note: This campground is set along the shore of Crawfish Lake, where fishing and waterskiing are popular. Balanced Rock Spring provides a unique water source in the area.

Site 58 · LYMAN LAKE

Campsites, facilities: There are five sites for tents, trailers or motorhomes up to 31 feet long. Picnic tables are provided. Pit toilets are available, but there is no piped water. Pets are permitted.

Reservations, fee: No reservations necessary; no fee. Open mid-May to mid-September.

Who to contact: Phone Okanogan National Forest at 509-486-2186, or write at Tonasket District Ranger, Tonasket, WA 98855.

Location: From the town of Tonasket, drive 12 1/2 miles east on Highway 20, then turn southeast on County Road 9455 and go 13 miles. Turn south on Forest Service Road 3785 and drive 2 1/2 miles, then turn northwest on Forest Service Road 358 and drive 200 yards to the campground.

Trip note: This campground is set along the shore of little Lyman Lake. Little known and little used, an idyllic setting for those wanting guaranteed quiet.

SWAN LAKE
Site 59

Campsites, facilities: There are four tent sites and 14 sites for trailers or motorhomes up to 31 feet long. Piped water, firegrills and picnic tables are provided. Firewood is available. Pets are permitted. Boat docks and launching facilities are available.

Reservations, fee: No reservations necessary; $5 fee per night. Open late-May to early-September.

Who to contact: Phone Colville National Forest at 509-775-3305, or write at Republic Ranger District, Republic, WA 99166.

Location: From the town of Republic, drive seven miles south on Highway 21, then turn southwest on Forest Service Road 53 and go eight miles to the campground.

Trip note: This campground is set along the shore of Swan Lake, elevation 3600 feet. Swimming, boating, fishing and hiking are some of the possibilities here. A good out-of-the-way spot for motorhome cruisers seeking a rustic setting.

FERRY LAKE
Site 60

Campsites, facilities: There are nine sites for tents, trailers or motorhomes up to 21 feet long. Piped water, firegrills and picnic tables are provided. Pit toilets and firewood are available. Pets are permitted. Boat docks and launching facilities are nearby.

Reservations, fee: No reservations necessary; $5 fee per night. Open June to early-September.

Who to contact: Phone Colville National Forest at 509-775-3305, or write at Republic Ranger District, Republic, WA 99166.

Location: From the town of Republic, drive seven miles south on Highway 21, then turn southwest on Forest Service Road 53 and go six miles. Turn north on Forest Service Road 5330 and drive one mile, then continue north on Forest Service Road 100 for 500 yards to the campground.

Trip note: This is one of three fishing lakes within a four-square mile area. The others are campsites 59 and 61. Most campers are not aware these three spots are available.

LONG LAKE
Site 61

Campsites, facilities: There are 12 sites for tents, trailers or motorhomes up to 21 feet long. Piped water, firegrills and picnic tables are provided. Pit toilets and firewood are available. Pets are permitted. Boat docks and launching facilities are nearby.

Reservations, fee: No reservations necessary; $5 fee per night. Open late-May to early-September.

Who to contact: Phone Colville National Forest at 509-775-3305, or write at Republic Ranger District, Republic, WA 99166.

Location: From the town of Republic, drive seven miles south on Highway 21, then turn southwest on Forest Service Road 53 and go eight miles. Turn south on Forest Service Road 400 and drive 1 1/2 miles to the campground.

Trip note: This is the third and smallest of the three lakes in this area. No motorboats allowed on the lake. Fly fishing only. Expert fishermen can get quality angling experience.

TEN MILE
Site **62**

Campsites, facilities: There are nine sites for tents, trailers or motorhomes up to 15 feet long. Piped water and picnic tables are provided. Pit toilets and firewood are available. Pets are permitted.

Reservations, fee: No reservations necessary; $5 fee per night. Open mid-May to mid-October.

Who to contact: Phone Colville National Forest at 509-775-3305, or write at Republic Ranger District, Republic, WA 99166.

Location: From the town of Republic, drive 10 miles south on Highway 21 and you'll see the campground entrance.

Trip note: This campground is set along the Sanpoil River. It is about four miles from the lakes at campsite 59, 60 and 61. A good choice is a multi-day trip, visiting each of the lakes.

KETTLE RANGE
Site **63**

Campsites, facilities: There are nine sites for tents, trailers or motorhomes up to 21 feet long. Piped water and picnic tables are provided. Pit toilets and firewood are available. Pets are permitted.

Reservations, fee: No reservations necessary; $2 fee per night. Open late-May to early-September.

Who to contact: Phone Colville National Forest at 509-738-6111, or write at Republic Ranger District, Republic, WA 99166.

Location: From the town of Republic, drive 2 1/2 miles east on Highway 21, then go east on Highway 20 for 18 miles to the campground.

Trip note: This roadside campground is located at Sherman Pass. Several trails pass through camp that provide access to various peaks and vistas in the area. No other campgrounds are in the immediate vicinity.

NE LAKE
ELLEN
Site **64**

Campsites, facilities: There are 11 sites for tents, trailers or motorhomes up to 21 feet long in this adult-only campground. Piped water and picnic tables are provided. Pit toilets and firewood are available. Pets are permitted. A boat dock is nearby.

Reservations, fee: No reservations necessary; $2 fee per night. Open late-May to early-September.

Who to contact: Phone Colville National Forest at 509-738-6111, or write at Republic Ranger District, Republic, WA 99166.

Location: From the town of Kettle Falls, drive 3 1/2 miles northwest on US 395, then head south on Highway 20 for four miles. Turn southwest on County Road 2014 and drive 4 1/2 miles, then continue southwest on Forest Service Road 2014 for 5 1/2 miles to the campground.

Trip note: Fishing and swimming are both permitted on this good-sized lake, located about three miles west of the Columbia River and the Coulee Dam National Recreation Area.

Site 65
RAINBOW
BEACH RESORT

Campsites, facilities: There are 10 tent sites and 100 drive-through sites for trailers or motorhomes of any length. Electricity, piped water, sewer hookups and picnic tables are provided. Flush toilets, bottled gas, sanitary services, a shower, firewood, recreation hall, store, cafe, laundromat, ice and playground are available. Pets and motorbikes are permitted. Boat docks, launching facilities and rentals are nearby.

Reservations, fee: Reservations required; $8 fee per night; MasterCard and Visa accepted. Open all year.

Who to contact: Phone at 509-722-5901, or write at Star Route B, Inchelium, WA 99138.

Location: From the town of Inchelium, drive 10 miles west on Bridge Creek/Twin Lakes County Road to the resort.

Trip note: This resort is set along the shore of Twin Lakes Reservoir. Nearby recreation options include hiking trails, marked bike trails, a full service marina and tennis courts. A unique chance at a quality campground set in the Colville Indian Reservation.

Site 66
RIVERVIEW MARKET
AND TRAILER COURT

Campsites, facilities: There are six sites for trailers or motorhomes of any length in this adult-only campground. Electricity, piped water, sewer hookups and picnic tables are provided. A store, cafe and ice are available. Bottled gas, sanitary services and laundromat are located within one mile.

Reservations, fee: Reservations accepted; $9 fee per night. Open all year.

Who to contact: Phone at 509-486-2491, or write at 305 West 4th Street, Tonasket, WA 98855.

Location: In the town of Tonasket, drive north on Highway 97 to 4th Street, then turn west and drive to the bridge and you'll see the trailer court.

Trip note: Nearby recreation options include marked bike trails and tennis courts. This trailer court is set along the Okanogan River.

Site 67
SUN COVE RESORT
GUEST RANCH

Campsites, facilities: There are 22 tent sites and 28 drive-through sites for trailers or motorhomes of any length. Electricity, piped water, sewer hookups and picnic tables are provided. Flush toilets, sanitary services, a recreation hall, store, cafe, laundromat, ice, playground and swimming pool are available. Showers are available for an extra fee. Pets and motorbikes are permitted. Boat docks, launching facilities and rentals are available.

Reservations, fee: Reservations accepted; $11 fee per night; MasterCard and Visa accepted. Open late-April to November.

Who to contact: Phone at 509-476-2223, or write at Route 2, Box 1294, Oroville, WA 98844.

Location: Drive eight miles north of Tonasket on Highway 97 to Ellisforde. Turn west to Wannacut Lake and follow the signs to the resort.

Trip note: This resort is set along the shore of Wannacut Lake. Nearby recreation options include hiking trails and a riding stable. A nice little spot that doesn't get much traffic.

Site 68
SPECTACLE LAKE RESORT

Campsites, facilities: There are 15 tent sites and 40 drive-through sites for trailers or motorhomes of any length. Electricity, piped water, sewer hookups and picnic tables are provided. Flush toilets, bottled gas, sanitary services, showers, store, laundromat, ice, playground and swimming pool are available. Pets and motorbikes are permitted. Boat docks, launching facilities and rentals are also available.

Reservations, fee: Reservations accepted; $9 fee per night. Open mid-April to late-November.

Who to contact: Phone at 509-223-3433, or write at 10 McCammon, Tonasket, WA 98855.

Location: From the town of Tonasket, drive 12 miles northwest on Loomis Highway and you'll see the resort.

Trip note: This resort is set along the shore of long, narrow Spectacle Lake. Nearby recreation options include swimming, fishing, hunting and horseback riding. A riding stable is nearby.

RAINBOW RESORT
Site 69

Campsites, facilities: There are 20 tent sites and 40 drive-through sites for trailers or motorhomes of any length. Electricity, piped water, sewer hookups and picnic tables are provided. Flush toilets, showers, firewood and ice are available. Pets and motorbikes are permitted. Boat docks, launching facilities and rentals are nearby.

Reservations, fee: Reservations accepted; $10 fee per night. Open April to late-October.

Who to contact: Phone at 509-223-3700, or write at 761 Loomis Highway, Tonasket, WA 98855.

Location: From the town of Tonasket, drive 14 miles northwest on Loomis Highway and you'll see the resort.

Trip note: This resort is set along the shore of Spectacle Lake. Nearby recreation options include swimming, fishing, hunting and tennis.

Site 70
SPECTACLE FALLS RESORT

Campsites, facilities: There are 10 tent sites and 28 drive-through sites for trailers or motorhomes of any length. Electricity, piped water, sewer hookups and picnic tables are provided. Flush toilets, sanitary services, showers and ice are available. Pets and motorbikes are permitted. Boat docks, launching facilities and rentals are nearby.

Reservations, fee: Reservations accepted; $9 fee per night. Open mid-April to late-October.

Who to contact: Phone at 509-223-4141, or write at 879 Loomis Highway, Tonasket, WA 98855.

Location: From the town of Tonasket, drive 15 miles northwest on Loomis Highway and you'll see the resort.

Trip note: This resort is set along the shore of Spectacle Lake. Nearby recreation options include hiking, swimming, fishing, horseback riding, and tennis. A riding stable is nearby.

STAGE STOP
Site 71   AT SULL'S RV

Campsites, facilities: There are 10 tent sites and 20 drive-through sites for trailers or motorhomes. Electricity, piped water, sewer hookups and picnic tables are provided. Bottled gas, a store, cafe, ice and playground are available. Pets and motorbikes are permitted.

Reservations, fee: Reservations accepted; $8 fee per night. Open all year.

Who to contact: Phone at 509-223-3275, or write at P.O. Box 5, Loomis, WA 98826.

Location: From the town of Tonasket, drive 20 miles northwest on Loomis Highway to the town of Loomis. The park is in town on Palmer Road.

Trip note: This campground is in rural Loomis, less than five miles from Chopaka Lake, Palmer Lake and Spectacle Lake. Nearby recreation options include hiking trails, a riding stable, a full service marina and tennis courts.

OSOOYOS
Site 72   STATE PARK

Campsites, facilities: There are 80 sites for tents, trailer, or motorhomes up to 45 feet long. Picnic tables and firegrills are provided. Flush toilets, piped water, sanitary services, a store, cafe, showers, firewood and playground are available. A laundromat and ice are located within one mile. Pets are permitted. Boat launching facilities are nearby.

Reservations, fee: No reservations necessary; $6 fee per night. Open all year.

Who to contact: Phone at 509-476-3321, or write at Route 1, P.O. Box 102 A, Oroville, WA 98844.

Location: Drive one mile north of Oroville on Highway 97 and you'll see the park.

Trip note: Many years ago, this area was the site of the annual Okanogan, which means "rendezvous," of the Indians of Washington and British Columbia. They would gather and share supplies of fish and game for the year. The park is set along the shore of Osoyoos Lake, where swimming, fishing and waterskiing are all possibilities. Lake Osooyos is a winter nesting area for geese. Nearby recreation options include an 18-hole golf course.

BONAPARTE
Site 73   LAKE RESORT

Campsites, facilities: There are 10 tent sites and 35 drive-through sites for trailers or motorhomes of any length. Electricity, piped water, sewer hookups and picnic tables are provided. Flush toilets, bottled gas, sanitary services, showers, firewood, a recreation hall, store, cafe, laundromat, ice and playground are available. Pets and motorbikes are permitted. Boat docks, launching facilities and rentals are also available.

Reservations, fee: Reservations accepted; $7 fee per night; MasterCard and Visa accepted. Open all year.

Who to contact: Phone at 509-486-2828, or write at 695 Bonaparte, Tonasket, WA 98855.

Location: From the town of Tonasket, drive 19 miles east on Highway 20 to Bonaparte Road. Turn north and drive six miles to the resort.

Trip note: This resort is set along the southeast shore of Bonaparte Lake, where fishing is popular. Nearby recreation options include hiking and hunting in the nearby Forest Service lands. In the winter, the area is open for snowmobiling and cross-country skiing.

BONAPARTE LAKE

Site **74**

Campsites, facilities: There are 25 sites for tents, trailers or motorhomes up to 31 feet long. Piped water and picnic tables are provided. Pit toilets, a store, cafe and ice are available. Sanitary services are located within one mile. Pets are permitted. Boat docks, launching facilities and rentals are also available.

Reservations, fee: No reservations necessary; $5 fee per night. Open mid-May to mid-September.

Who to contact: Phone Okanogan National Forest at 509-486-2186, or write at Tonasket District Ranger, Tonasket, WA 98855.

Location: From the town of Tonasket, drive 20 miles east on Highway 20 to Forest Service Road 32. Turn north and drive 5 1/2 miles to the campground.

Trip note: This campground is set along the southern shore of Bonaparte Lake. See the trip note for campsite 73 for lake recreation information. There are several trails nearby that provide access to Mount Bonaparte Lookout and the roadless area west of the lake. See a Forest Service map for details.

LOST LAKE

Site **75**

Campsites, facilities: There are 33 sites for tents, trailers or motorhomes up to 31 feet long. Piped water and picnic tables are provided. Pit toilets are available and pets are permitted. Boat docks and launching facilities are nearby.

Reservations, fee: No reservations necessary; $5 fee per night. Open mid-May to mid-September.

Who to contact: Phone Okanogan National Forest at 509-486-2186, or write at Tonasket District Ranger, Tonasket, WA 98855.

Location: From the town of Tonasket, drive 23 miles east on Highway 20 to Forest Service Road 33. Turn northeast and drive 10 1/2 miles, then turn northwest on Forest Service Road 50 and drive 6 1/2 miles to the campground.

Trip note: This site is set along the shore of Lost Lake where fishing, swimming, hiking, hunting and horseback riding are some of the possibilities. It is about a mile from the Big Tree Botanical Area where you can see native, old-growth trees. This area is open for snowmobiling and cross-country skiing in the winter.

BEAVER LAKE

Site **76**

Campsites, facilities: There are five sites for tents, trailers or motorhomes up to 21 feet long. Piped water and picnic tables are provided. Pit toilets are available. Pets are permitted. Boat launching facilities are nearby.

Reservations, fee: No reservations necessary; $4 fee per night. Open mid-May to mid-September.

Who to contact: Phone Okanogan National Forest at 509-486-2186, write at Tonasket District Ranger, Tonasket, WA 98855.

Location: From the town of Tonasket, drive 20 miles east on Highway 20 to Forest Service Road 32. Turn northeast and drive 11 miles, then continue northwest on Forest Service Road 3245 for three miles to the campground.

Trip note: This campground is set along the southeastern shore of long, narrow Beaver

Lake, one of several lakes in this area. Fishing, swimming, hunting and hiking are all possibilities here. See trip notes for campsites 74 and 75 for information on the other lakes.

BETH LAKE

Site **77**

Campsites, facilities: There are eight sites for tents, trailers or motorhomes up to 31 feet long. Piped water and picnic tables are provided. Pit toilets are available, and pets are permitted. Boat launching facilities are available.

Reservations, fee: No reservations necessary; $5 fee per night. Open mid-May to mid-September.

Who to contact: Phone Okanogan National Forest at 509-486-2186, or write at Tonasket District Ranger, Tonasket, WA 98855.

Location: From the town of Tonasket, drive 23 miles west on Highway 20 to County Road 4953 and turn north. Drive five miles, then continue north on Forest Service Road 32 for six miles. From there, go northwest of Forest Service Road 3245 and drive 3 1/2 miles to the campground.

Trip note: This campground is set along little Beth Lake, which is adjacent to Beaver Lake (campsite 76).

UPPER BEAVER LAKE

Site **78**

Campsites, facilities: There are five sites for tents, trailers or motorhomes up to 15 feet long. Piped water and picnic tables are provided. Pit toilets are available and pets are permitted. Boat launching facilities are nearby.

Reservations, fee: No reservations necessary; no fee. Open mid-May to mid-September.

Who to contact: Phone Okanogan National Forest at 509-486-2186, or write at Tonasket District Ranger, Tonasket, WA 98855.

Location: From the town of Tonasket, drive 20 miles east on Highway 20, then turn northeast on Forest Service Road 32 and go 11 miles. Turn northwest on Forest Service Road 3245 and drive 3 1/2 miles to the campground.

Trip note: This campground is set along the northwestern shore of Beaver Lake, near Beth Lake. See trip note to campsite 76 for further details.

TIFFANY'S RESORT

Site **79**

Campsites, facilities: There are 10 tent sites and 16 sites for trailers or motorhomes of any length. Electricity, piped water, sewer hookups and picnic tables are provided. Flush toilets, showers, firewood, a store, laundromat, ice and playground are available. Pets and motorbikes are permitted. Boat docks, launching facilities and rentals are nearby.

Reservations, fee: Reservations accepted; $8 fee per night. Open all year.

Who to contact: Phone at 509-775-3152, or write at 1026 Tiffany, Republic, WA 99166.

Location: Drive 10 miles north of the town of Republic on Highway 21, then turn north on West Curlew Lake Road and drive five miles to the resort.

Trip note: This resort is set along the western shore of Curlew Lake, where fishing can be good.

Site 80
BLACK'S
BEACH RESORT

Campsites, facilities: There are 40 tent sites and 151 drive-through sites for trailers or motorhomes of any length. Electricity, piped water, sewer hookups and picnic tables are provided. Flush toilets, bottled gas, sanitary services, showers, firewood, recreation hall, a store, cafe, laundromat, ice and playground are available. Pets and motorbikes are permitted. Boat docks, launching facilities and rentals are located nearby.

Reservations, fee: Reservations accepted; $10 fee per night. Open all year.

Who to contact: Phone at 509-775-3989, or write at 848 Blacks Beach, Republic, WA 99166.

Location: Drive north of the town of Republic on West Curlew Lake Drive and you will see the entrance to the resort on the lake.

Trip note: This is another resort set along Curlew Lake. Waterskiing, swimming and fishing are all options here.

Site 81
CURLEW LAKE
STATE PARK

Campsites, facilities: There are 64 tent sites and 18 sites for trailers or motorhomes up to 35 feet long. Picnic tables are provided. Flush toilets, sanitary services, electricity, piped water, sewer hookups, showers and firewood are available. Some facilities are wheelchair accessible. Pets are permitted. Boat launching facilities are also available.

Reservations, fee: No reservations necessary; $6 fee per night. Open April to late-October.

Who to contact: Phone at 509-775-3592, or write at 974 Curlew Lake Street, Republic, WA 99166.

Location: Drive 10 miles north of the town of Republic on Highway 21 and you'll see the park entrance.

Trip note: This park is set along the eastern shore of Curlew Lake. There is beach access, fishing, swimming, waterskiing and hiking. Nearby recreation options include an 18-hole golf course, and in the winter, snowmobiling.

Site 82
PINE POINT
RESORT

Campsites, facilities: There are 20 tent sites and 60 drive-through sites for trailers or motorhomes of any length. Electricity, piped water, sewer hookups and picnic tables are provided. Flush toilets, sanitary services, firewood, showers, a store, laundromat, ice and playground are available. Pets and motorbikes are permitted. Boat docks, launching facilities and rentals are nearby.

Reservations, fee: Reservations accepted; $8 fee per night; MasterCard and Visa accepted. Open mid-April to November.

Who to contact: Phone at 509-775-3645, or write at 1060 Pine Point, Republic, WA 99166.

Location: Drive eight miles north of the town of Republic on Highway 21, then turn northwest on Pine Point Road and drive 600 yards to the campground.

Trip note: This resort is on the southeastern shore of Curlew Lake just south of the State Park (campsite 81). Fishing, swimming, and waterskiing are all possibilities on this narrow, five-mile long lake in the heart of the gold country.

SPRING CANYON
Site **83**

Campsites, facilities: There are 87 sites for tents, trailers or self-contained motorhomes up to 26 feet long. Piped water, firegrills and picnic tables are provided. Flush toilets, sanitary services, a cafe and playground are available. Some facilities are wheelchair accessible. Pets are permitted. Boat docks and launching facilities are nearby.

Reservations, fee: No reservations necessary; $6 fee per night. Open all year.

Who to contact: Phone Coulee Dam National Recreation Area at 509-633-1360, or write at P.O. Box 37, Coulee Dam, WA 99116.

Location: Drive three miles east of the town of Grand Coulee on Highway 174 and you'll see the campground entrance.

Trip note: Fishing for bass, walleye, trout and sunfish are popular at this Franklin Roosevelt Lake. And, if you don't like to fish, try waterskiing. This campground is not far from the Grand Coulee Dam, which has a visitor center. There are also hiking trails in the area.

LAKEVIEW TERRACE
Site **84** ## MOBILE PARK

Campsites, facilities: There are 20 tent sites and 15 drive-through sites for trailers or motorhomes of any length. Electricity, piped water, sewer hookups and picnic tables are provided. Flush toilets, showers, a laundromat and playground are available. Pets and motorbikes are permitted. Boat docks, launching facilities and rentals are nearby.

Reservations, fee: Reservations accepted; $8 fee per night. Open all year.

Who to contact: Phone at 509-633-2169, or write at Highway 174, Grand Coulee, WA 99133.

Location: Drive 3 1/2 miles east of the town of Grand Coulee on Highway 174 and you'll see the park entrance.

Trip note: This resort is set near the Franklin Roosevelt Lake, which is created by the Grand Coulee Dam. See trip note for campsite 84 for water recreation options. A full service marina and tennis courts are nearby.

LEE MOTEL AND
Site **85** ## TRAILER PARK

Campsites, facilities: There are five tent sites and 28 drive-through sites for trailers or motorhomes of any length. Electricity, piped water, sewer hookups and picnic tables are provided. Flush toilets, showers and a laundromat are available. Bottled gas, a store, cafe and ice are available within one mile. Pets and motorbikes are permitted. Boat docks, launching facilities and rentals are nearby.

Reservations, fee: Reservations accepted; $10 fee per night. Open all year.

Who to contact: Phone at 509-633-1992, or write at 212 Grand Coulee, Grand Coulee, WA 99133.

Location: Drive 600 yards east of the town of Grand Coulee on Highway 174 and you'll see the park entrance.

Trip note: Set very close to the Grand Coulee Dam. Nearby recreation options include an 18-hole golf course, a full service marina and tennis courts.

Site 86
CURLEY'S TRAILER PARK

Campsites, facilities: There are 10 tent sites and 20 drive-through sites for trailers or motorhomes of any length. Electricity, piped water, sewer hookups and picnic tables are provided. Flush toilets, bottled gas, a store, cafe, laundromat and ice are available within one mile. Pets and motorbikes are permitted. Boat docks, launching facilities and rentals are nearby.

Reservations, fee: Reservations accepted; $8 fee per night. Open all year.

Who to contact: Phone at 509-633-0750, or write at P.O. Box 61, Grand Coulee, WA 99133.

Location: Drive 1/2 mile northwest of Grand Coulee on Highway 174 and you'll see the park.

Trip note: This park is set along the shore of the Grand Coulee Reservoir a short distance from the Grand Coulee Dam. Nearby recreation options include an 18-hole golf course and tennis courts.

Site 87
COULEE PLAYLAND RESORT

Campsites, facilities: There are 70 tent sites and 40 drive-through sites for trailers or motorhomes of any length. Electricity, piped water, sewer hookups and picnic tables are provided. Flush toilets, sanitary services, a store, laundromat, showers, firewood, ice and playground are available. Bottled gas and a cafe are located within one mile. Pets and motorbikes are permitted. Boat docks, launching facilities and rentals are nearby.

Reservations, fee: Reservations accepted; $10 fee per night. MasterCard and Visa accepted. Open all year.

Who to contact: Phone at 509-633-2671, or write at P.O. Box 457, Electric City, WA 99123.

Location: Drive three miles south of the town of Grand Coulee on Highway 155 to Electric City. This spot is in town.

Trip note: Nearby recreation options include hiking trails, marked bike trails, a full service marina and tennis courts.

Site 88
KELLER FERRY

Campsites, facilities: There are 50 sites for tents, trailers or motorhomes up to 16 feet long. Piped water, firegrills and picnic tables are provided. Flush toilets, sanitary services, ice and a playground are available. A cafe is located within one mile. Pets are permitted. Boat docks, launching facilities, fuel and marine dump station are also available nearby.

Reservations, fee: No reservations necessary; $6 fee per night. Open all year.

Who to contact: Phone Coulee Dam National Recreation Area at 509-633-1360, or write at P.O. Box 37, Coulee Dam, WA 99116.

Location: Drive 14 miles north of the town of Wilbur on Highway 21 and you'll see the campground.

Trip note: This campground is set along the shore of Franklin Roosevelt Lake, a large reservoir created by the Grand Coulee Dam about 15 miles west of camp. Waterskiing, fishing and swimming are all options here.

WISHING TREE
Site **89**   CAMPGROUND

Campsites, facilities: There are 10 tent sites and 12 drive-through sites for trailers or motorhomes of any length. Electricity, piped water and sewer hookups are provided. Flush toilets, sanitary services and showers are available. Bottled gas, a store, cafe, laundromat and ice are located within one mile. Motorbikes are permitted. Boat launching facilities are nearby.

Reservations, fee: Reservations accepted; $9 fee per night. MasterCard and Visa accepted. Open April to late-November.

Who to contact: Phone at 509-997-0833, or write at P.O. Box 117, Carlton, WA 98814.

Location: Take Highway 153 off Highway 97 just south of the town of Pateros and drive northwest for 26 miles to Carlton. The campground is in town on Highway 153.

Trip note: A nice, little out-of-the-way place for motorhomes. This campground is set along the Methow River. A good side trip is to explore westward up Libby Creek, a tributary to the Methow. Primitive campers might like to continue this route and seek out campsite 90.

FOGGY DEW
Site **90**

Campsites, facilities: There are 13 sites for tents, trailers or motorhomes. Picnic tables are provided. Pit toilets and firewood are available, but there is no piped water. Pets are permitted.

Reservations, fee: No reservations necessary; $3 fee per night. Open late-May to early-September.

Who to contact: Phone Okanogan National Forest at 509-997-2131, or write at Twisp District Ranger, Twisp, WA 98856.

Location: From the town of Carlton, drive four miles south on Highway 153, then continue south on County Road 1029 for one mile. Next, turn west on Forest Service Road 4340 and drive four miles to the campground.

Trip note: This campground is set at the confluence of Foggy Dew Creek and the North Fork of Gold Creek. There are several trails nearby that provide access to various backcountry lakes and streams. To get to the trailheads, just follow the Forest Service Roads near camp. Bicycles are allowed on Trails 417, 429 and 431. In the winter the area is open for both cross-country skiing and snowmobiling. See a Forest Service map for options.

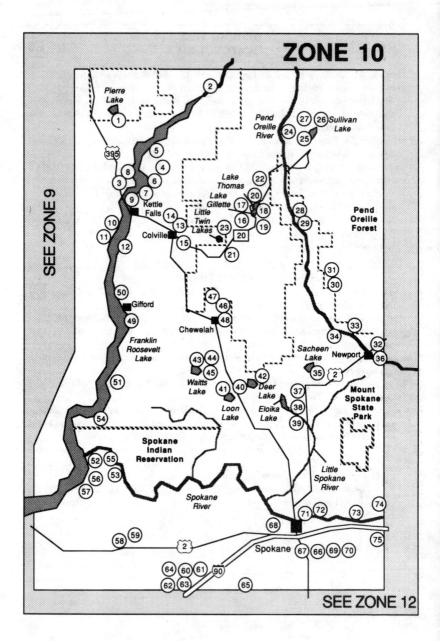

ZONE 10

SPOKANE

PIERRE LAKE
Site **1**

Campsites, facilities: There are 15 sites for tents, trailers or motorhomes up to 32 feet long. Piped water, firegrills and picnic tables are provided. Pit toilets and firewood are available. A store and ice are located within one mile. Pets are permitted. Boat docks and launching facilities are nearby.

Reservations, fee: No reservations necessary; $2 fee per night. Open late-May to early-September.

Who to contact: Phone Colville National Forest at 509-738-6111, or write at Republic Ranger Station, Republic, WA 99166.

Location: From the town of Colville, drive about 31 miles north on Highway 395 to the town of Orient. From the town of Orient, drive four miles east on County Route 1510, then turn north on County Route 1500 and drive three miles to the campground.

Trip note: This campground is set along the shore of Pierre Lake, a quiet, little-known jewel near the Canadian border. A short drive from Highway 395, yet the campgrounds get relatively little use.

SHEEP CREEK
Site **2**

Campsites, facilities: There are 11 campsites for tents or small trailers. Picnic tables, fire grills and tent pads are provided. Pit toilets, piped water and a group shelter are available.

Reservations, fee: No reservations necessary; no fee. Open all year.

Who to contact: Phone the Department of Natural Resources at 1-800-527-3305, or write Department of Natural Resources AW-11, 1065 South Capitol Way, Olympia, WA 98504.

Location: From the town of Northport, drive north on Highway 25 for one mile, then turn left on Sheep Creek Road and go four miles. Turn right into the campground.

Trip note: This campground is set in a forested area along Sheep Creek, about four miles from the Columbia River, and very close to the Canadian border. A primitive camp, yet with piped water.

WHISPERING
Site **3** PINE RV PARK

Campsites, facilities: There are 15 tent sites and 40 drive-through sites for trailers or

motorhomes of any length. Electricity, sewer hookups and picnic tables are provided. Flush toilets, sanitary services, a laundromat, playground, piped water, showers and firewood are available. Pets are permitted.

Reservations, fee: Reservations accepted; $8 fee per night. Open April to November.

Who to contact: Phone at 509-738-2593, or write at P.O. Box 778, Kettle Falls, WA 99141.

Location: From the town of Kettle Falls, drive 6 1/2 miles north on Highway 395, then turn east at the sign for the campground and drive 300 yards to the entrance.

Trip note: This campground is a good layover for Highway 395 motorhome cruisers. It is set along the shore of the Columbia River. Nearby recreation options include marked bike trails, a full service marina and tennis courts. A good sidetrip is to Colville National Forest East Portal Interpretive Area, which is less than 10 miles away. To reach it, drive south to the junction with Highway 20 and go southwest for about six miles. There's a nature trail and the Bangs Mountain Auto Tour, a five-mile drive that takes you through old-growth forest to Bangs Mountain Vista, which overlooks the Columbia River-Kettle Falls area.

WILLIAMS LAKE
Site **4**

Campsites, facilities: There are eight campsites for tents or small trailers. Picnic tables, fire grills and tent pads are provided. Pit toilets, piped water and a boat launch are available.

Reservations, fee: No reservations necessary; no fee. Open all year.

Who to contact: Phone the Department of Natural Resources at 1-800-527-3305, or write Department of Natural Resources AW-11, 1065 South Capitol Way, Olympia, WA 98504.

Location: From the town of Colville, drive west on Highway 395 for 1 1/2 miles, then head north on Williams Lake Road for 15 miles. Turn left and then immediately left again to the campground.

Trip note: With a plethora of camps set on nearby Franklin D. Roosevelt Lake, this secluded spot provides a good alternative. It is set along the shore of Williams Lake, where the trout fishing is good. In winter, ice fishing is an option.

NORTH GORGE
Site **5**

Campsites, facilities: There are 10 sites for tents, trailers or motorhomes. Piped water, firegrills and picnic tables are provided. Pit toilets are available, and pets are permitted. Boat docks and launching facilities are nearby.

Reservations, fee: No reservations necessary; no fee. Open all year.

Who to contact: Phone Coulee Dam National Recreation Area at 509-738-6266, or write at Kettle Falls Ranger District, Route 1, Box 537, Kettle Falls, WA 99141.

Location: From town of Kettle Falls, drive about 20 miles north on Highway 25 and you'll see the campground entrance.

Trip note: This is the first of many campgrounds we discovered along the shore of 130-mile long Franklin D. Roosevelt Lake, which was formed by damming the Columbia River at Coulee. Recreation options include waterskiing and swimming. There is also fishing for walleye, trout, bass and sunfish. During winter, the lake level is drawn down and a unique trip is to walk along the barren lake's edge.

EVANS

Site **6**

Campsites, facilities: There are 43 sites for tents, trailers or motorhomes up to 26 feet long. Piped water, firegrills and picnic tables are provided. Flush toilets, sanitary services and a playground are available. Pets are permitted. Boat docks and launching facilities are nearby.

Reservations, fee: No reservations necessary; $6 fee per night. Open mid-May to mid-October.

Who to contact: Phone Coulee Dam National Recreation Area at 509-738-6266, or write at Kettle Falls Ranger District, Route 1, Box 537, Kettle Falls, WA 99141.

Location: Drive eight miles north of the town of Kettle Falls on Highway 25 and you'll see the campground entrance.

Trip note: Like campsite 5, this campground is set along the shore of Franklin D. Roosevelt Lake. Fishing, swimming and waterskiing are all options here.

MARCUS ISLAND

Site **7**

Campsites, facilities: There are 24 sites for tents, trailers or motorhomes up to 20 feet long. Piped water, firegrills and picnic tables are provided. Pit toilets are available. A store is located within one mile. Pets are permitted. A boat dock is nearby.

Reservations, fee: No reservations necessary; no fee. Open all year.

Who to contact: Phone Coulee Dam National Recreation Area at 509-738-6266, or write at Kettle Falls Ranger District, Route 1, Box 537, Kettle Falls, WA 99141.

Location: Drive four miles north of the town of Kettle Falls, and you'll see the campground entrance.

Trip note: This campground is set just south of campsite 6 and is quite similar to that camp, including being nestled along the lake's edge. Waterskiing, fishing and swimming are the primary recreation options.

KAMLOOPS

Site **8**

Campsites, facilities: There are 14 primitive tent sites. Picnic tables and firegrills are provided. Pit toilets are available, but there is no piped water. Pets are permitted. Boat docks are nearby.

Reservations, fee: No reservations necessary; no fee. Open all year.

Who to contact: Phone Coulee Dam National Recreation Area at 509-738-6266, or write at Kettle Falls Ranger District, Route 1, Box 537, Kettle Falls, WA 99141.

Location: From the town of Kettle Falls, drive seven miles west and north on Highway 395 to the campground.

Trip note: This is one of the few primitive campsites of the many located along Franklin D. Roosevelt Lake. It is set at Kamloops Island, an optimum area for waterskiing and fishing. See the trip note to campsite 3 for side trip information.

KETTLE FALLS

Site **9**

Campsites, facilities: There are 75 sites for tents, trailers or motorhomes up to 26 feet long.

Piped water, firegrills and picnic tables are provided. Flush toilets, sanitary services, firewood, a cafe and playground are available. A store is available within one mile. Some facilities are wheelchair accessible. Pets are permitted. Boat docks, fuel and launching facilities are nearby.

Reservations, fee: No reservations necessary; $6 fee per night. Open all year.

Who to contact: Phone Coulee Dam National Recreation Area at 509-738-6266, or write at Kettle Falls Ranger District, Route 1, Box 537, Kettle Falls, WA 99141.

Location: Drive two miles west of the town of Kettle Falls and you'll see the campground entrance.

Trip note: This is a modern, developed campground that attracts fairly heavy use in summer months. It is set along the shore of Franklin D. Roosevelt Lake, where waterskiing, swimming and fishing are all options. In the summer there is a lifeguard on duty, and the rangers offer campfire programs in the evenings. Park Headquarters is nearby.

SHERMAN CREEK

Site **10**

Campsites, facilities: There are six tent sites at this campground which is accessible only by boat. Piped water, picnic tables, and firegrills are provided. Pit toilets and boat docks are available.

Reservations, fee: No reservations necessary; no fee. Open all year with limited winter facilities.

Who to contact: Phone Coulee Dam National Recreation Area at 509-738-6266, or write at Kettle Falls Ranger District, Route 1, Box 537, Kettle Falls, WA 99141.

Location: This campground is located opposite the town of Kettle Falls on the other side of Franklin D. Roosevelt Lake.

Trip note: This is one of the few campgrounds east of the Cascade Range that is accessible only by boat. It is located in an idyllic setting where Sherman Creek enters Franklin D. Roosevelt Lake (Columbia River). It is within the boundaries of the Sherman Creek Habitat Management Area, an 8,000-acre area that provides critical winter deer habitat and a year-around habitat for many little critters.

HAAG COVE

Site **11**

Campsites, facilities: There are 18 primitive sites for tents, trailers or motorhomes up to 26 feet long. Piped water, firegrills and picnic tables are provided. Pit toilets and boat docks are available. Pets are permitted.

Reservations, fee: No reservations necessary; no fee. Open all year.

Who to contact: Phone Coulee Dam National Recreation Area at 509-738-6266, or write at Kettle Falls Ranger District, Route 1, Box 537, Kettle Falls, WA 99141.

Location: From the town of Republic, drive 25 miles east on Highway 30, then turn south on County Road 3 and drive five miles to the campground.

Trip note: This campground is tucked away in a cove along the shore of Franklin D. Roosevelt Lake (Columbia River). A good sidetrip is to the Sherman Creek Habitat Management Area, located just north of camp. It is rugged and steep, but a good place to see and photograph wildlife.

BRADBURY BEACH
Site **12**

Campsites, facilities: There are five tent sites. Picnic tables and firegrills are provided. Pit toilets and piped water are available. Pets are permitted. Boat docks and launching facilities are nearby.

Reservations, fee: No reservations necessary; no fee. Open all year with limited winter facilities.

Who to contact: Phone Coulee Dam National Recreation Area at 509-738-6266, or write at Kettle Falls Ranger District, Route 1, Box 537, Kettle Falls, WA 99141.

Location: From the town of Kettle Falls, drive 10 miles south on Highway 25 to the campground.

Trip note: Quiet, small, pretty, yet the availability of piped water make spot a winner. It is one of the smallest camps set along Franklin Roosevelt Lake. See trip note to campsite 5 for recreation possibilities.

ROADHOUSE LODGE
Site **13**   # INCORPORATED

Campsites, facilities: There are 12 tent sites and 14 sites for trailers or motorhomes. Electricity, piped water, sewer hookups and picnic tables are provided. Flush toilets, sanitary services, showers, firewood and a cafe are available. Bottled gas, a store, laundromat and ice are located within one mile. Some facilities are wheelchair accessible. Pets and motorbikes are permitted.

Reservations, fee: Reservations accepted; $8 fee per night. MasterCard and Visa accepted. Open all year.

Who to contact: Phone at 509-684-3021, or write at Route 3, Box 16, Colville, WA 99114.

Location: This park is located in the town of Colville, 64 miles north of Spokane, on Highway 395.

Trip note: This a good layover for motorhome cruisers who want to stay in Colville. Nearby recreation options include an 18-hole golf course, hiking trails and tennis courts. The main headquarters for Colville National Forest is in town at 795 South Main Street. You can purchase a Forest Service map there for $1, which details nearby back-country roads and hiking trails.

DOUGLAS FALLS
Site **14**

Campsites, facilities: There are 18 campsites for tents or small trailers. Picnic tables, fire grills and tent pads are provided. Pit toilets and piped water are available. Some facilities are wheelchair accessible. A baseball field is nearby.

Reservations, fee: No reservations necessary; no fee. Open all year.

Who to contact: Phone the Department of Natural Resources at 1-800-527-3305, or write Department of Natural Resources AW-11, 1065 South Capitol Way, Olympia, WA 98504.

Location: Drive to the eastern edge of the town of Colville on Highway 20. Take Aladdin Road north off Highway 20 and drive two miles, then continue straight for five miles. You'll see the parking area on the left.

Trip note: This campground is set in a wooded area along Mill Creek near Douglas Falls, just outside of town. It is one of the only campgrounds in the Pacific Northwest that has a baseball field.

ROCKY LAKE
Site 15

Campsites, facilities: There are seven campsites for tents or small trailers. Picnic tables, fire grills and tent pads are provided. Pit toilets, piped water and a boat launch are available.

Reservations, fee: No reservations necessary; no fee. Open all year.

Who to contact: Phone the Department of Natural Resources at 1-800-527-3305, or write Department of Natural Resources AW-11, 1065 South Capitol Way, Olympia, WA 98504.

Location: Take Highway 20 off Highway 395 in Colville and drive six miles east, then turn right on Rocky Lake Road and go three miles and turn right again onto a one-lane gravel road. Go about 100 yards and stay left, then continue another 300 yards to the campground.

Trip note: This is not exactly paradise, but it has remarkable recreational diversity nearby. Rocky Lake is a shallow, weedy pond lined with a lot of rocks. That is where the campground is set. But if you backtrack a bit on Rocky Lake Road you'll see the entrance signs for the nearby Little Pend Oreille Habitat Management Area. This is a premium area for hiking, fishing, hunting, and photographing wildlife.

CARNEY'S BLACK
Site 16   LAKE RESORT

Campsites, facilities: There are 12 tent sites and six sites for trailers or motorhomes of any length. Piped water and picnic tables are provided. Flush toilets, sanitary services, ice, electricity, showers and firewood are available. Pets are permitted. Boat docks, launching facilities and rentals are located nearby.

Reservations, fee: Reservations accepted; $7 fee per night. Open April to late-October.

Who to contact: Phone at 509-684-2093, or write at HCR 12, Box 151, Colville, WA 99114.

Location: From the town of Colville, drive 18 miles east on Highway 20, then turn north on Black Lake Road and drive two miles to the resort.

Trip note: This resort is set along the shore of Black Lake, a narrow, one-mile long natural lake. The area is very private, with good fishing in May and June for brook trout. If you dislike roughing it, a cabin that sleeps six is available for rental for $125, and includes a boat and dock facilities. An excellent side trip is seven miles northeast to a chain of lakes, all with good fishing. See the trip note to campsite 15 for information on nearby Little Pend Oreille Habitat Management Area.

BEAVER LODGE
Site 17   INCORPORATED

Campsites, facilities: There are 25 tent sites and 25 drive-through sites for trailers or motorhomes of any length. Electricity, piped water, sewer hookups and picnic tables are provided. Flush toilets, bottled gas, showers, firewood, recreation hall, a store, cafe, ice and playground are available. Sanitary services are located within one mile. Pets and motorbikes are permitted. Boat docks, launching facilities and rentals are nearby.

Reservations, fee: Reservations accepted; $8 fee per night. MasterCard and Visa accepted. Open all year.

Who to contact: Phone at 509-684-5657, or write at P.O. Box 196, Tiger Route, Colville, WA 99114.

Location: From the town of Colville, drive 25 miles east on Highway 20 to the lodge.

Trip note: This developed camp is set along the shore of Lake Thomas, one of seven lakes in a chain. Nearby recreation options include hiking trails and marked bike trails. At the southern end of the chain of lakes, Little Pend Oreille Information Site is available. At the northern end of the chain of lakes, at Lake Leo, there is a Nordic Ski Trail during winter.

LAKE THOMAS

Site 18

Campsites, facilities: There are 15 tent sites. Piped water, firegrills and picnic tables are provided. Pit toilets and firewood are available. Sanitary services are located within one mile. Pets are permitted. Boat docks, launching facilities and rentals are nearby.

Reservations, fee: No reservations necessary; $5 fee per night. Open mid-May to mid-September.

Who to contact: Phone Colville National Forest at 509-684-4557, or write at Colville Ranger District, 795 South Main, Colville, WA 99114.

Location: Drive four miles south of Ione on Highway 31, then turn southwest on Highway 20 and drive 11 miles. Go east on County Road 200 for one mile to the campground.

Trip note: This campground is set along the shore of Lake Thomas. See trip note to campsite 17 for recreation information.

EAST GILLETTE

Site 19

Campsites, facilities: There are 30 sites for tents, trailers or motorhomes up to 31 feet long. Piped water, firegrills and picnic tables are provided. Pit toilets, sanitary services and firewood are available. A store and ice are located within one mile. Some facilities are wheelchair accessible. Pets are permitted. Boat docks, launching facilities and rentals are nearby.

Reservations, fee: No reservations necessary; $10 fee per night. Open mid-May to mid-September.

Who to contact: Phone Colville National Forest at 509-684-4557, or write at Colville Ranger District, 795 South Main, Colville, WA 99114.

Location: Drive four miles south of Ione on Highway 31, then turn southwest on Highway 20 and drive 11 miles. Go east on County Road 200 for 1/2 mile to the campground.

Trip note: This campground is set along the shore of Lake Gillette, just south of campsites 17 and 18 and part of the chain of lakes. See trip note to campsite 17 for recreation information.

LAKE LEO

Site 20

Campsites, facilities: There are eight sites for tents, trailers or motorhomes up to 15 feet long. Piped water and picnic tables are provided. Pit toilets and firewood are available. Pets are permitted. Boat docks, launching facilities and rentals are nearby.

Reservations, fee: No reservations necessary; $5 fee per night. Open mid-May to mid-September.

Who to contact: Phone Colville National Forest at 509-684-4557, or write at Colville Ranger District, 795 South Main, Colville, WA 99114.

Location: Drive four miles south of Ione on Highway 31, then turn southwest on Highway 20 and drive seven miles to the campground.

Trip note: Lake Leo is the northernmost camp on the chain of lakes. This is the quietest of the camps in the immediate vicinity. Frater and Nile lakes, both quite small, are set a mile north. In winter, there is a Nordic ski trail that starts adjacent to camp.

FLODELLE CREEK
Site **21**

Campsites, facilities: There are eight campsites for tents or small trailers. Picnic tables, fire grills and tent pads are provided. Pit toilets and piped water are available. Motorbikes are permitted.

Reservations, fee: No reservations necessary; no fee. Open all year.

Who to contact: Phone the Department of Natural Resources at 1-800-527-3305, or write Department of Natural Resources AW-11, 1065 South Capitol Way, Olympia, WA 98504.

Location: Take Highway 20 out of Colville and drive east for 20 miles. Turn right on a two-lane gravel road and go 300 yards, then go left and drive 100 yards to the campground entrance.

Trip note: This little-known campground is set along the shore of Flodelle Creek, where hiking, hunting and fishing is quite good. It is advisable to obtain a detailed map of the area from the Department of Natural Resources.

IONE TRAILER
Site **22**   PARK AND MOTEL

Campsites, facilities: There are three tent sites and 19 sites for trailers or motorhomes of any length. Electricity, piped water, sewer hookups and picnic tables are provided. Flush toilets, bottled gas, sanitary services, showers, laundromat and a playground are available. A store, cafe and ice are located within one mile. Motorbikes are permitted. Boat docks and launching facilities are nearby.

Reservations, fee: Reservations accepted; $9 fee per night. Open all year.

Who to contact: Phone at 509-442-3213, or write at P.O. Box 517, Ione, WA 99139.

Location: This park is in the town of Ione on Highway 31.

Trip note: This is a good layover for campers with motorhomes or trailers who want to stay in town. The park is set along the shore of the Pend Oreille River. Nearby recreation options include marked bike trails.

LITTLE TWIN
Site **23**   LAKES

Campsites, facilities: There are 16 sites for tents, trailers or motorhomes up to 15 feet long. Piped water, firegrills and picnic tables are provided. Pit toilets and firewood are available. Pets are permitted. Boat docks, launching facilities and rentals are located nearby.

Reservations, fee: No reservations necessary; no fee. Open mid-May to mid-September.

Who to contact: Phone Colville National Forest at 509-684-4557, or write at Colville Ranger District, 795 South Main, Colville, WA 99114.

Location: Drive 12 1/2 miles east of Colville on Highway 20, then turn northeast on County Road 4915 and drive 1 1/2 miles. Turn north on Forest Service Road 4939 and drive 4 1/2 miles to the campground.

Trip note: This campground is set along the shore of Little Twin Lakes. See the trip note to campsite 15 for side trip information.

EDGEWATER
Site 24

Campsites, facilities: There are 23 sites for tents, trailers or motorhomes up to 21 feet long. Piped water and picnic tables are provided. Pit toilets are available and pets are permitted. Boat docks and launching facilities are nearby.

Reservations, fee: No reservations necessary; $2 fee per night. Open late-May to early-September.

Who to contact: Phone Colville National Forest at 509-446-2681, or write at Sullivan Land Ranger District, Metaline Falls, WA 99153.

Location: Drive one mile south of Ione on Highway 31, then turn east on County Road 9345 for 300 yards. Turn north on County Road 3669 and go two miles, then turn west to the campground.

Trip note: This campground is set along the shore of the Pend Oreille River, about two miles downstream from the Box Canyon Dam. The camp is not far out of the town of Ione, yet has a rustic feel to it.

NOISY CREEK
Site 25

Campsites, facilities: There are 19 tent sites and eight sites for trailers or motorhomes up to 32 feet long. Piped water and picnic tables are provided. Pit toilets are available. Pets are permitted. Boat docks and launching facilities are nearby.

Reservations, fee: No reservations necessary; $5 fee per night. Open late-May to early-September.

Who to contact: Phone Colville National Forest at 509-446-2681, or write at Sullivan Land Ranger District, Metaline Falls, WA 99153.

Location: Drive one mile south of Ione on Highway 31, then turn and drive northeast on County Road 9345 for nine miles to the campground.

Trip note: This campground is situated in an idyllic setting, adjacent to where Noisy Creek pours into Sullivan Lake. Sullivan Lake is about 3 1/2 miles long and waterskiing is allowed. There is a trail from camp that heads east along Noisy Creek and then north up to Hall Mountain (elevation 6323 feet), which is Bighorn sheep country.

SULLIVAN LAKE
Site 26

Campsites, facilities: There are 35 sites for tents, trailers or motorhomes up to 32 feet long. Piped water and picnic tables are provided. Pit toilets are available. Sanitary services are located within one mile. Pets are permitted. Boat docks and launching facilities are nearby.

Reservations, fee: No reservations necessary; $5 fee per night. Open late-May to early-September.

Who to contact: Phone Colville National Forest at 509-446-2681, or write at Sullivan Land
Ranger District, Metaline Falls, WA 99153.

Location: Drive 1 1/2 miles east of Metaline Falls on Highway 31, then go east for five miles
on County Road 9345 to the campground.

Trip note: This campground is set along the north shore of Sullivan Lake. There are trails
and roads leading to backcountry areas to the northeast, all of which is detailed on a
Forest Service map.

MILL POND
Site **27**

Campsites, facilities: There are 10 sites for tents, trailers or motorhomes up to 21 feet long.
Piped water and picnic tables are provided. Pit toilets are available. Sanitary services
are located within one mile. Pets are permitted. Boat docks and launching facilities are
nearby.

Reservations, fee: No reservations necessary; $5 fee per night. Open late-May to early-
September.

Who to contact: Phone Colville National Forest at 509-446-2681, or write at Sullivan Land
Ranger District, Metaline Falls, WA 99153.

Location: Drive 1 1/2 miles northeast of Metaline Falls on Highway 31, then go east for 3 1/2
miles on County Road 9345 to the campground.

Trip note: This campground is set along the shore of a small lake just north of Lake Sullivan.
This is a good base camp for backpackers. A trail starts here and takes off into the back
country.

BLUESIDE RESORT
Site **28**

Campsites, facilities: There are 20 tent sites and 34 drive-through sites for trailers or
motorhomes of any length. Electricity, piped water, sewer hookups and picnic tables
are provided. Flush toilets, sanitary services, showers, recreation hall, a store, laundromat, ice, firewood, playground and swimming pool are available. Pets and motorbikes are permitted. Boat docks, launching facilities and rentals are nearby.

Reservations, fee: Reservations accepted; $8 fee per night. Open all year with limited
winter facilities.

Who to contact: Phone at 509-445-1327, or write at Route 2, P.O. Box 260, Usk, WA
99180.

Location: Drive 10 miles south of Tiger on Highway 20. The resort is near mileage marker
400.

Trip note: This resort is set along the shore of the Pend Oreille River. Nearby recreation
options include marked bike trails. The only other campground in the vicinity is site
29.

THE OUTPOST
Site **29**   RESORT

Campsites, facilities: There are 15 tent sites and 20 drive-through sites for trailers or
motorhomes of any length. Picnic tables are provided. Flush toilets, sanitary services,
firewood, a store, cafe, ice, playground, electricity, piped water, sewer hookups and
showers are available. Pets and motorbikes are permitted. Boat docks and launching
facilities are nearby.

Reservations, fee: Reservations accepted; $8 fee per night. Open all year with limited winter facilities.

Who to contact: Phone at 509-445-1317, or write at State Route 2, Box 145, Cusick, WA 99119.

Location: Drive 33 miles northwest of Newport on Highway 20. The resort is between mileage markers 305 and 306.

Trip note: This campground is set along the the shore of the Pend Oreille River. If you are cruising Highway 20, campsite 28 is located about five miles north, otherwise the nearest alternative is campsite 34, about a half-hour's drive to the south.

SOUTH SKOOKUM
Site **30** LAKE

Campsites, facilities: There are 15 sites for tents, trailers or motorhomes up to 21 feet long. Piped water, firegrills and picnic tables are provided. Pit toilets and firewood are available. Pets are permitted. Boat docks and launching facilities are nearby.

Reservations, fee: No reservations necessary; $5 fee per night. Open late-May to early-September.

Who to contact: Phone Colville National Forest at 509-447-3129, or write at Newport Ranger District, Newport, WA 99156.

Location: Drive 16 miles northwest of Newport on Highway 20 to the town of Usk. Take Forest Service Road 3389 northeast and drive 7 1/2 miles to the campground.

Trip note: This campground is set along the shore of South Skookum Lake, at the foot of Kings Mountain (4383 feet elevation). Waterskiing is allowed. It is one of several lakes in the immediate area. You pass Kings Lake on Road 3389 about a mile before you get to camp.

BROWNS LAKE
Site **31**

Campsites, facilities: There are 17 sites for tents, trailers or motorhomes up to 21 feet long. Piped water and picnic tables are provided. Pit toilets and firewood are available. Pets are permitted. Boat docks and launching facilities are nearby.

Reservations, fee: No reservations necessary; $5 fee per night. Open late-May to early-September.

Who to contact: Phone Colville National Forest at 509-447-3129, or write at Newport Ranger District, Newport, WA 99156.

Location: Drive 16 miles northwest of Newport on Highway 20 to the town of Usk. Take Forest Service Road 50 and go northeast for 6 1/2 miles, then turn north on Forest Service Road 5030 and go three miles to the campground.

Trip note: This campground is set along the shore of Browns Lake aobut five miles from campsite 30. In addition to those two, the only other campground in the area on the east side of the Pend Oreille River is campsite 33.

PIONEER PARK
Site **32** 🚐

Campsites, facilities: There are 12 tent sites and 13 sites for trailers or motorhomes up to 21 feet long. Piped water and picnic tables are provided. Pit toilets and firewood are available. Some facilities are wheelchair accessible. Pets are permitted. Boat docks, launching facilities and rentals are nearby.

Reservations, fee: No reservations necessary; $5 fee per night. Open late-May to early-September.

Who to contact: Phone Colville National Forest at 509-447-3129, or write at Newport Ranger District, Newport, WA 99156.

Location: Drive 1/2 miles northeast of Newport on Highway 2, then go north on County Road 9305 for two miles to the campground.

Trip note: This campground is set along the shore of Box Canyon Reservoir on the Pend Oreille River near the town of Newport. Waterskiing is allowed. A good motorhome/tent park located just inside the Washington state border. Because it is set on the east side of the river, it is more secluded than campsite 36.

SKOOKUM CREEK
Site **33**

Campsites, facilities: There are 12 campsites for tents or small trailers. Picnic tables, fire grills and tent pads are provided. Pit toilets and piped water are available.

Reservations, fee: No reservations necessary; no fee. Open all year.

Who to contact: Phone the Department of Natural Resources at 1-800-527-3305, or write Department of Natural Resources AW-11, 1065 South Capitol Way, Olympia, WA 98504.

Location: Drive 16 miles northwest of Newport on Highway 20 to the town of Usk. Go east across the bridge and turn right on LeClerc Road. Drive 2 1/2 miles then turn left and drive about 400 yards to the campground.

Trip note: This campground is in a wooded area along Skookum Creek, about a mile and a half from where it empties into the Pend Oreille River. It's a good canoeing spot, has piped water and gets little attention. You can't beat the price of admission.

DALKENA's HIDE-A-WAY RESORT
Site **34**

Campsites, facilities: There are 10 tent sites and 30 sites for trailers or motorhomes up to 30 feet long. Picnic tables are provided. Flush toilets, sanitary services, showers, a store, cafe, ice, electricity, piped water and sewer hookups are available. Pets and motorbikes are permitted. Boat docks and launching facilities are nearby.

Reservations, fee: Reservations accepted; $6 fee per night. Open all year.

Who to contact: Phone at 509-447-4174, or write at Route 1, Box 610, Newport, WA 99156.

Location: Drive 11 miles north of Newport on Highway 20 and you'll see the resort entrance.

Trip note: This resort is set along the shore of the Pend Oreille River near the town of Dalkena. A good layover for motorhome cruisers on Highway 20. Nearest option is 16 miles in Newport at campsite 36.

CIRCLE MOON
Site **35**

Campsites, facilities: There are 50 tent sites and 34 sites for trailers or motorhomes of any length. Electricity, piped water, sewer hookups and picnic tables are provided. Flush toilets, sanitary services, showers, firewood, a cafe and playground are available. Pets and motorbikes are permitted. Boat docks and launching facilities are nearby.

Reservations, fee: Reservations accepted; $7 fee per night. Open May to November.

Who to contact: Phone at 509-447-3735, or write at Route 3, Box 1038, Newport, WA 99156.

Location: Drive 12 miles southwest of Newport to the junction of Highways 195/2/211, and head northwest on Highway 211 for 4 miles to the campground.

Trip note: This campground is set along the shore of Sacheen Lake. A nice spot just a short drive off Highway 211, yet missed by most all of the out-of-staters.

Site 36   R & R CAMPGROUND AND MOTORHOME PARK   ⊟

Campsites, facilities: There are 25 tent sites and 10 sites for trailers or motorhomes of any length. Electricity, piped water, sewer hookups and picnic tables are provided. Flush toilets, sanitary services and showers are available. Bottled gas, a store, cafe, laundromat and ice are located within one mile. Pets and motorbikes are permitted.

Reservations, fee: Reservations accepted; $7 fee per night. Open mid-May to mid-October.

Who to contact: Phone at 509-447-3663, or write at P.O. Box 178, Newport, WA 99156.

Location: The campground is in Newport at the east edge of town, two blocks off Highway 2/195.

Trip note: This campground is near the Pend Oreille River, right in the town of Newport. It is a major junction for this part of the country, where Highways 2 and 20 intersect. If you want a more secluded spot, campsite 32 is about a 15-minute drive away, on the east side of the river.

Site 37   PEND OREILLE COUNTY PARK   ⊟

Campsites, facilities: There are 20 tent sites and 36 sites for trailers or motorhomes up to 34 feet long. Electricity and picnic tables are provided. Flush toilets, showers, firewood and playground are available. Piped water, sewer hookups, bottled gas, sanitary services, a store, cafe, laundromat and ice are located within one mile. Pets are permitted.

Reservations, fee: Reservations accepted; $8 fee per night. Open all year.

Who to contact: Phone at 509-292-2544, or write at Route 3, P.O. Box 718, Newport, WA 99156.

Location: Drive 14 miles southwest of the town of Newport on Highway 2 and you'll see the park entrance.

Trip note: This county park offers hiking trails, a riding stable and 444 acres of mountain woodlands. It is a good base camp for a weekend adventure, with Eloika, Trout and Sacheen Lakes all within 10 miles of the park.

Site 38   WATERS EDGE CAMPGROUND   ⊟

Campsites, facilities: There are 15 tent sites and 30 drive-through sites for trailers or motorhomes of any length. Electricity, piped water, sewer hookups and picnic tables are provided. Flush toilets, sanitary services, firewood, showers, laundromat and ice are available. Bottled gas, a store and cafe are available within one mile. Pets and motorbikes are permitted. Boat docks, launching facilities and rentals are nearby.

Reservations, fee: Reservations accepted; $9 fee per night. Open April to late-September.

Who to contact: Phone at 509-292-2111, or write at Eloika Lake, Elk, WA 99009.

Location: Drive 28 miles north of Spokane on Highway 2, then go west on Bridges Road for one mile and you'll see the campground.

Trip note: This campground is set along the shore of Eloika Lake, considered one of the better lakes for fishing in the region. Trout fishing can be excellent as soon as the ice is off the lake in spring. During the hot days of summer, crappie fishing turns on.

JERRY'S LANDING
Site 39

Campsites, facilities: There are five tent sites and 20 drive-through sites for trailers or motorhomes of any length. Picnic tables are provided. Flush toilets, sanitary services, a store, cafe, ice, electricity, piped water, sewer hookups, showers and firewood are available. Bottled gas is available within one mile. Pets and motorbikes are permitted. Boat docks, launching facilities and rentals are nearby.

Reservations, fee: Reservations accepted; $8 fee per night. Open April to November.

Who to contact: Phone at 509-292-2337, or write at Route 1, Box 147, Elk, WA 99009.

Location: Drive 23 miles north of Spokane on Highway 2, then head west on Oregon Road for one mile to the campground.

Trip note: This campground is also set along the shore of Eloika Lake. See the trip note to campsite 38 for details.

GRANITE POINT
ROCK
Site 40

Campsites, facilities: There are 68 sites for trailers or motorhomes of any length. Electricity, piped water, sewer hookups and picnic tables are provided. Flush toilets, showers, recreation hall, a store, cafe, laundromat, ice and playground are available. No pets. Bottled gas is located within one mile. Boat docks, launching facilities and rentals are nearby.

Reservations, fee: Reservations accepted; $12 fee per night. Open mid-April to mid-September.

Who to contact: Phone at 509-233-2100, or write at Route 1, Box 254, Loon Lake, WA 99148.

Location: Drive 26 miles north of Spokane on Highway 395.

Trip note: This campground is set along the shore of Loon Lake, a clear, clean, spring-fed lake. In the spring, the Mackinaw trout range from 4-30 pounds and can be taken by deepwater trolling, downriggers suggested. Easier to catch are Kokanee salmon and rainbow trout in the 12 to 14-inch class. A sprinkling of perch, sunfish and bass come out of their doldrums when the weather heats up.

SHORE ACRES
Site 41

Campsites, facilities: There are 14 tent sites and 21 drive-through sites for trailers or motorhomes up to 30 feet long. Electricity, piped water, sewer hookups and picnic tables are provided. Flush toilets, sanitary services, a store, cafe, showers, firewood, ice and a playground are available. Pets and motorbikes are permitted. Boat docks, launching facilities and rentals are nearby.

Reservations, fee: Reservations accepted; $9 fee per night. Open mid-April to late-October.

Who to contact: Phone at 509-233-2474, or write at Route 1, box 166, Loon Lake, WA 99148.

Location: Drive 30 miles north of Spokane on Highway 395, then go west on Highway 292 to the northwest edge of Loon Lake.

Trip note: Set along the shore of Loon Lake, this campground offers a long expanse of beach and is an option to campsite 40. See the trip note for campsite 40 for details about the fishing.

HANEY'S RESORT
Site **42**

Campsites, facilities: There are 27 tent sites and 62 drive-through sites for trailers or motorhomes of any length. Electricity, piped water, sewer hookups and picnic tables are provided. Flush toilets, sanitary services, a store, cafe, showers, firewood, laundromat and ice are available. Pets and motorbikes are permitted. Boat docks, launching facilities and rentals are nearby.

Reservations, fee: Reservations accepted; $12 fee per night. Open mid-April to late-October.

Who to contact: Phone at 509-233-2370, or write at Route 1, Box 502, Loon Lake, WA 99148.

Location: Drive 30 miles north of Spokane on Highway 395, then head east on Deer Lake road and drive six miles to the resort.

Trip note: Fishing and waterskiing are popular at Deer Lake. Nearby recreation options include a full service marina and a riding stable. Some groups use the camps as their own party headquarters on weekends. They even sleep an hour or two, whether they need it or not.

WINONA BEACH RESORT
Site **43**   AND RV PARK

Campsites, facilities: There are seven tent sites and 36 drive-through sites for trailers or motorhomes of any length. Electricity, piped water, sewer hookups and picnic tables are provided. Flush toilets, sanitary services, firewood, recreation hall, a store, cafe and ice are available. Bottled gas is located within one mile. Pets and motorbikes are permitted. Boat docks, launching facilities and rentals are nearby.

Reservations, fee: Reservations accepted; $12 fee per night. Open mid-April to late-October.

Who to contact: Phone at 509-937-2231, or write at Route 1, Box 29C, Valley, WA 99181.

Location: Drive 42 miles north of Spokane on Highway 395, then turn west on Waitts Lake Road and drive five miles to the resort.

Trip note: This resort is set along the shore of Waitts Lake. In the spring, the fishing for brown trout and rainbow trout can be quite good. In summer, the trout head to deeper water, and easier to catch are bluegills and perch.

TEAL'S WAITTS
Site **44**   LAKE

Campsites, facilities: There are 15 tent sites and 27 sites for trailers or motorhomes of any length. Electricity, piped water, sewer hookups and picnic tables are provided. Flush toilets, bottled gas, sanitary services, showers, recreation hall, a store, firewood, cafe, laundromat and ice are available. Pets are permitted. Boat docks, launching facilities and rentals are nearby.

Reservations, fee: Reservations required; $10 fee per night. MasterCard and Visa accepted. Open early-April to late-October.

Who to contact: Phone at 509-937-2400, or write at Route 1, Box 50, Valley, WA 99181.

Location: Drive 42 miles north of Spokane on Highway 395, then turn north on Highway 232 for 1 1/2 miles and head west on Highway 231 to Waitts Lake.

Trip note: This resort is set along the shore of Waitts Lake. See trip note to campsite 43 for information about the lake.

Site 45   SILVER BEACH RESORT

Campsites, facilities: There are 53 sites for trailers or motorhomes of any length. Electricity, piped water, sewer hookups and picnic tables are provided. Flush toilets, bottled gas, sanitary services, recreation hall, a store, showers, cafe, laundromat, ice and playground are available. Pets are permitted. Boat docks, launching facilities and rentals are nearby.

Reservations, fee: Reservations accepted; $11 fee per night. Open early-April to late-October.

Who to contact: Phone at 509-937-2811, or write at Route 1, Box 41, Valley, WA 99181.

Location: Drive 38 miles north of Spokane on Highway 395 to the Valley exit, then head west for six miles until you get to Waitts Lake. The resort is on the lake.

Trip note: This resort offers grassy sites set along the shore of Waitts Lake where fishing and waterskiing are popular. See the trip note to campsite 43 for information about the lake.

Site 46   FORTY-NINER MOTEL AND CAMPGROUND

Campsites, facilities: There are 15 tent sites and 28 drive-through sites for trailers or motorhomes of any length. Electricity, piped water, sewer hookups and picnic tables are provided. Flush toilets, sanitary services, showers, recreation hall, ice and swimming pool are available. Bottled gas, a store, cafe and laundromat are located within one mile. Pets are permitted.

Reservations, fee: Reservations accepted; $10 fee per night. MasterCard and Visa accepted. Open all year.

Who to contact: Phone at 509-935-8613, or write at P.O. Box 124, Chewelah, WA 99109.

Location: Drive 44 miles north of Spokane on Highway 395, then drive five miles east of Chewelah on County Route 2902 to the campground.

Trip note: This is in the heart of the mining country. Nearby recreation options include an 18-hole golf course, hiking trails and marked bike trails. A good deal for motorhome cruisers, with a rustic setting yet only five miles from town.

Site 47   CHEWELAH GOLF AND COUNTRY CLUB

Campsites, facilities: There are 41 drive-through sites for trailers or motorhomes of any length. Electricity, piped water, sewer hookups and picnic tables are provided. Sanitary services and a cafe are available. A laundromat is located within one mile. Pets are permitted.

Reservations, fee: Reservations required; $8 fee per night. MasterCard and Visa accepted. Open April to November.

Who to contact: Phone at 509-935-6807, or write at P.O. Box 315, Chewelah, WA 99109.

Location: Drive 44 miles north of Spokane on Highway 395 to the town of Chewelah. Then go north on Sand Canyon Road for three miles, and follow the signs to the club.

Trip note: Nearby recreation options include an 18-hole golf course, hiking trails and marked bike trails. A good sidetrip is to Waitts Lake, detailed in the trip notes to campsite 43.

Site **48**
CHEWELAH CITY PARK

Campsites, facilities: There are 50 tent sites and 40 sites for trailers or motorhomes of any length. Electricity, piped water and picnic tables are provided. Flush toilets and a playground are available. A store, cafe, laundromat and ice are located within one mile. Pets are permitted.

Reservations, fee: No reservations necessary; no fee. Open all year.

Who to contact: Write at Chewelah City Park, Chewelah, WA 99109.

Location: Drive 44 miles north of Spokane on Highway 395 to the town of Chewelah. The park is on the north edge of town.

Trip note: This is a good option to nearby campsites 46 and 47, and the price doesn't come any cheaper. It is set along Chewelah Creek. Nearby recreation options include an 18-hole golf course, marked bike trails and tennis courts.

Site **49**
GIFFORD

Campsites, facilities: There are 47 sites for tents, trailers or motorhomes up to 20 feet long. Piped water, firegrills and picnic tables are provided. Pit toilets and pets are permitted. Boat docks and launching facilities are nearby.

Reservations, fee: No reservations necessary; $6 fee per night. Open all year.

Who to contact: Phone Coulee Dam National Recreation Area at 509-633-1360, or write at P.O. Box 37, Coulee Dam, WA 99116.

Location: This campground is located about three miles south of the town of Gifford on Highway 25.

Trip note: This campground is set along the shore of Franklin D. Roosevelt Lake (Columbia River). Fishing and waterskiing are some of the recreation options here. For a more detailed description of Roosevelt Lake, see the trip notes for campsite 5.

Site **50**
CLOVER LEAF

Campsites, facilities: There are eight tent sites. Piped water, firegrills and picnic tables are provided. Pit toilets, Pets are permitted. A boat dock is available.

Reservations, fee: No reservations necessary; no fee. Open all year with limited winter facilities.

Who to contact: Phone Coulee Dam National Recreation Area at 509-633-1360, or write at P.O. Box 37, Coulee Dam, WA 99116.

Location: This campground is located about two miles south of the town of Gifford on Highway 25.

Trip note: It's free, it's small, and it's quite primitive. In this particular area of Roosevelt

Lake, water skiing is not advised, fishing is. See the trip notes for campsite 5 for recreation details.

HUNTERS PARK
Site **51**

Campsites, facilities: There are 39 sites for tents, trailers or motorhomes up to 26 feet long. Piped water, firegrills and picnic tables are provided. Flush toilets, a store and ice are available within one mile. Pets are permitted. Boat docks and launching facilities are nearby.

Reservations, fee: No reservations necessary; $6 fee per night. Open mid-May to mid-October.

Who to contact: Phone Coulee Dam National Recreation Area at 509-725-2715, or write at Fort Spokane, Star Route, Box 30, Davenport, WA 99122.

Location: This campground is located two miles west of the town of Hunters on an access road off Highway 25.

Trip note: This campground is set on a shoreline point along Roosevelt Lake (Columbia River). A good spot for swimming, fishing or waterskiing. See trip note to campsite 5.

FORT SPOKANE
Site **52**

Campsites, facilities: There are 67 sites for tents, trailers or motorhomes up to 26 feet long. Piped water, picnic tables and firegrills is provided. Flush toilets, sanitary services and a playground are available. A store and ice are located within one mile. Some facilities are wheelchair accessible. Pets are permitted. Boat docks, launching facilities and a marine dump station are nearby.

Reservations, fee: No reservations necessary; $6 fee per night. Open all year.

Who to contact: Phone Coulee Dam National Recreation Area at 509-725-2715, or write at Fort Spokane, Star Route, Box 30, Davenport, WA 99122.

Location: Drive 26 miles north of the town of Davenport on Highway 25 and you'll see the campground.

Trip note: This modern campground is set along the shore of Roosevelt Lake. A lifeguard is on duty during the summer and the rangers offer evening campfire programs. One of 16 campgrounds on 130-mile long Roosevelt Lake.

PORCUPINE BAY
Site **53**

Campsites, facilities: There are 31 sites for tents, trailers or motorhomes up to 20 feet long. Piped water, picnic tables and firegrills are provided. Flush toilets and a playground are available. Pets are permitted. Boat docks and launching facilities are nearby.

Reservations, fee: No reservations necessary; $6 fee per night. Open late-May to mid-October.

Who to contact: Phone Coulee Dam National Recreation Area at 509-725-2715, or write at Fort Spokane, Star Route, Box 30, Davenport, WA 99122.

Location: Drive 20 miles north of the town of Davenport on Highway 25, and then head north on a County Road and you'll see the campground.

Trip note: This is a good spot for campers with boats because of its proximity to a nearby dock and launch. A swimming beach is adjacent to the campground and a lifeguard is on duty during the summer months.

ENTERPRISE
Site 54

Campsites, facilities: There are 12 tent sites, and this campground is accessible only by boat. Picnic tables and firegrills are provided, but no piped water is available. Pets are permitted. Boat docks are nearby.

Reservations, fee: No reservations necessary; no fee. Open all year.

Who to contact: Phone Coulee Dam National Recreation Area at 509-725-2715, or write at Fort Spokane, Star Route, Box 30, Davenport, WA 99122.

Location: This camp is located 10 miles north of Fort Spokane and is accessible only by boat.

Trip note: This is one of the few boat-in camps anywhere east of the Cascade Range, and one of two on Roosevelt Lake. The other is at campsite 10. (Another boat-in site is campsite 55 on the Spokane River.) This is quite a pretty spot, situated adjacent to where Wilmont Creek empties into the lake.

DETILLON
Site 55

Campsites, facilities: There are 12 tent sites. Picnic tables and firegrills are provided, but no piped water is available. Pets are permitted. Boat docks and a marine dump station are nearby.

Reservations, fee: No reservations necessary; no fee. Open all year.

Who to contact: Phone Coulee Dam National Recreation Area at 509-725-2715, or write at Fort Spokane, Star Route, Box 30, Davenport, WA 99122.

Location: This camp is located six miles northeast of Fort Spokane and accessible only by boat.

Trip note: This is a secluded, primitive spot that gets very little traffic. It is set along the shore of the Spokane River, which like Roosevelt Lake, has its water backed up by the Grand Coulee Dam. Waterskiing, fishing and swimming are all options at this quiet spot.

SEVEN BAYS
Site 56 RESORT

Campsites, facilities: There are 20 tent sites and 70 drive-through sites for trailers or motorhomes of any length. Electricity, piped water, sewer hookups and picnic tables are provided. Flush toilets, bottled gas, sanitary services, showers, a store, cafe, laundromat and ice are available. Pets and motorbikes are permitted. Boat docks and launching facilities are nearby.

Reservations, fee: Reservations accepted; $8 fee per night. Open March to October.

Who to contact: Phone at 509-725-5794, or write at Route 1, Box 62L, Davenport, WA 99122.

Location: Drive five miles southwest of the town of Miles on Creston Road and you'll see the resort.

Trip note: This resort is set along the shore of Roosevelt Lake, and is an option to campsites 52 and 57. A full service marina sets this spot apart from the others.

HAWK CREEK
Site **57**

Campsites, facilities: There are 16 sites for tents or trailers and motorhomes up to 16 feet long. Picnic tables, firegrills and piped water are provided. Pit toilets are available. Pets are permitted. Boat docks and launching facilities are nearby.

Reservations, fee: No reservations necessary; no fee. Open all year.

Who to contact: Phone Coulee Dam National Recreation Area at 509-633-1360, or write at P.O. Box 37, Coulee Dam, WA 99116.

Location: This campground is located about 10 miles southwest of the town of Miles on Creston Road at the mouth of Hawk Creek.

Trip note: This is a pleasant spot set along the shore of Roosevelt Lake (Columbia River), adjacent to the mouth of Hawk Creek. It gets less use than the other campgrounds at Roosevelt Lake, but is an idyllic spot.

MICK'S EXXON
Site **58**   AND RV PARK

Campsites, facilities: There are 12 drive-through sites for trailers or motorhomes. Electricity, piped water and sewer hookups are provided. Flush toilets, bottled gas and sanitary services are available. A store, cafe, laundromat and ice are located within one mile. Pets are permitted.

Reservations, fee: Reservations accepted; $7 fee per night. MasterCard and Visa accepted. Open all year.

Who to contact: Phone at 509-725-0015, or write at P.O. Box 242, Davenport, WA 99122.

Location: The park is located in the town of Davenport on Highway 2 at the eastern edge of town.

Trip note: One of two motorhome parks in the town of Davenport. Nearby recreation options include tennis courts. This is an OK layover point for motorhome travelers on Highway 2. The nearest alternatives are on the outskirts of Spokane.

DIAMOND S MOTEL
Site **59**   AND RV PARK

Campsites, facilities: There are nine drive-through sites for trailers or motorhomes of any length. Electricity, piped water and sewer hookups are provided. Bottled gas, sanitary services, a store, cafe, laundromat and ice are available within one mile. Pets are permitted.

Reservations, fee: Reservations accepted; $7 fee per night. MasterCard and Visa accepted. Open May to November.

Who to contact: Phone at 509-725-7742, or write at P.O. Box 106, Davenport, WA 99122.

Location: The park is located in the town of Davenport on Highway 2 at the eastern edge of town.

Trip note: A good stopover site in Davenport. Nearby recreation options include tennis courts.

Site 60
WEST MEDICAL LAKE RESORT

Campsites, facilities: There are 10 tent sites and 30 sites for trailers or motorhomes. Picnic tables are provided. Flush toilets, showers, a cafe and ice are available. Electricity, piped water and sewer hookups can be obtained for an extra fee. Pets and motorbikes are permitted. Boat docks, launching facilities and rentals are nearby.

Reservations, fee: Reservations required; $6 fee per night. Open mid-April to July.

Who to contact: Phone at 509-299-3921, or write at P.O. Box 216, Medical Lake, WA 99022.

Location: Take exit 264 off Highway 90 near Medical Lake and drive 4 1/2 miles north on Sain Road, then turn west on Faucher and go 1/2 mile to the resort.

Trip note: This resort is set along the shore of Medical Lake, one of five campgrounds on the lake. A popular spot for Spokane locals making the half-hour drive. There are actually two lakes: West Medical is the larger of the two and also has the better fishing, with boat rentals available. Medical Lake is just a quarter-mile wide and a half-mile long and boating is restricted to rowboats, canoes, kayaks and sailboats. The lakes got their names from the wondrous medical powers once attributed to these waters.

Site 61
CONNIE's COVE CAMPGROUND

Campsites, facilities: There are five tent sites and 16 sites for trailers or motorhomes of any length. Electricity, piped water, sewer hookups and picnic tables are provided. Showers, flush toilets, a cafe and ice are available. Pets are permitted. Boat docks, launching facilities and rentals are nearby.

Reservations, fee: Reservations accepted; $8 fee per night. Open mid-April to late-September.

Who to contact: Phone at 509-299-3717, or write at Route 1, Box 19, Medical Lake, WA 99022.

Location: Take exit 264 off Highway 90 near Medical Lake and drive 300 feet west on Salnave Road, then turn north on Clear Lake Road and follow the signs.

Trip note: This resort is set along the shore of Medical Lake. Nearby recreation options include marked bike trails and tennis courts. See trip note to campsite 60 for more details about the lake.

Site 62
PICNIC PINES ON SILVER LAKE

Campsites, facilities: There are 10 tent sites and 29 drive-through sites for trailers or motorhomes of any length. Electricity, piped water, sewer hookups and picnic tables are provided. Flush toilets, showers, a recreation hall, store, cafe, ice and playground are available. Bottled gas and laundromat are located within one mile. Pets and motorbikes are permitted. Boat docks, launching facilities and rentals are nearby.

Reservations, fee: Reservations accepted; $8 fee per night. MasterCard and Visa accepted. Open all year.

Who to contact: Phone at 509-299-3223, or write at Route 1, Box 90-1, Medical Lake, WA 99022.

Location: Take exit 270 off Highway 90 near Spokane and drive three miles west on Medical Lake Road to the park.

Trip note: This resort is set along the shore of Medical Lake. Nearby recreation options include marked bike trails, a full service marina and tennis courts.

Site 63   BERNIE'S LAST RESORT

🚐

Campsites, facilities: There are 20 tent sites and 26 drive-through sites for trailers or motorhomes up to 32 feet long. Picnic tables are provided. Flush toilets, sanitary services, showers, a recreation hall, store, cafe, laundromat, ice, playground, bottled gas, electricity, piped water and sewer hookups are available. Pets and motorbikes are permitted. Boat docks, launching facilities and rentals are nearby.

Reservations, fee: Reservations accepted; $8 fee per night. Open mid-April to late-September.

Who to contact: Phone at 509-299-7273, or write at Route 1, Box 267, Medical Lake, WA 99022.

Location: Take exit 270 off Highway 90 near Spokane and drive three miles west on Medical Lake Road to the resort.

Trip note: This resort is set along the shore of Medical Lake and is one of five camps at the lake.

Site 64   BARBER'S RESORT

🚐

Campsites, facilities: There are 35 tent sites and 50 drive-through sites for trailers or motorhomes of any length. Electricity, piped water and picnic tables are provided. Flush toilets, bottled gas, sanitary services, showers, cafe, ice and playground are available. Pets and motorbikes are permitted. Boat docks, launching facilities and rentals are nearby.

Reservations, fee: Reservations accepted; $8 fee per night. Open mid-April to late-September.

Who to contact: Phone at 509-299-3830, or write at Route 1, Box 64, Cheney, WA 99004.

Location: Take exit 264 off Highway 90 near Cheney and drive two miles west on Salnave Road and follow the signs to the resort.

Trip note: This resort is set along the shore of Medical Lake. Nearby recreation options include marked bike trails, a riding stable and tennis courts.

Site 65   MYERS PARK AND RESORT

🚐

Campsites, facilities: There are five tent sites and 30 sites for trailers or motorhomes of any length. Electricity, piped water, sewer hookups and picnic tables are provided. Flush toilets, showers, a restaurant and lounge, ice and a playground are available. Pets and motorbikes are permitted. Boat docks, launching facilities and rentals are nearby.

Reservations, fee: Reservations accepted; $7 fee per night. Open April to late-September.

Who to contact: Phone at 509-235-6367, or write at Route 4, Box 233, Cheney, WA 99004.

Location: Take the Tyler exit off Interstate 90 near Cheney and drive to the town of Cheney. Turn right at the Farmers and Merchants Bank and drive three miles to the resort.

Trip note: This resort is set along the shore of Fish Lake, a 47-acre fishing lake that offers seasonal fishing for brook trout. Nearby recreation options include tennis courts.

Site **66**   OVERLAND STATION

Campsites, facilities: There are 40 tent sites and 32 drive-through sites for trailers or motorhomes of any length. Electricity, piped water, sewer hookups and picnic tables are provided. Flush toilets, showers, a store, cafe, laundromat, ice and playground are available. Pets and motorbikes are permitted.

Reservations, fee: Reservations accepted; $12 fee per night. Open all year.

Who to contact: Phone at 509-747-1703, or write at Route 14, Box 586, Spokane, WA 99204.

Location: Take exit 272 off Highway 90 in Spokane. The park is on the northeast corner of the intersection.

Trip note: One of seven campgrounds located in the immediate Spokane area. A number of sidetrips are available to learn the history of the area, including the Cheney Cowles Memorial Museum and the Museum of Native American Cultures. Riverfront Park is the site of the 1974 world exposition and it now offers a science center and planetarium, opera house, Japanese garden, gondola ride, carousel, ice skating rink and five-screen theatre. The closest lake with good fishing is Eloika Lake, described in the trip note to campsites 38 and 39.

Site **67**   SMOKEY TRAIL CAMPGROUND

Campsites, facilities: There are 40 tent sites and 30 drive-through sites for trailers or motorhomes up to 30 feet long. Picnic tables are provided. Flush toilets, sanitary services, showers, firewood, a store, laundromat, ice and playground are available. Electricity, piped water and sewer can be obtained for an extra fee. Pets and motorbikes are permitted.

Reservations, fee: Reservations accepted; $9 fee per night. Open mid-May to late-September.

Who to contact: Phone at 509-747-9415, or write at Rural Route 14, Box 650, Spokane, WA 99204.

Location: Take exit 272 off Highway 90 in Spokane and drive one mile east on Hallett. Then turn south on Mallon and drive 1/2 mile to the campground.

Trip note: This park is in a wooded, rural area. Nearby recreation options include an 18-hole golf course and hiking trails are nearby. See trip note to campsite 66.

Site **68**   SUNSET CAMP
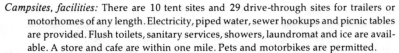

Campsites, facilities: There are 10 tent sites and 29 drive-through sites for trailers or motorhomes of any length. Electricity, piped water, sewer hookups and picnic tables are provided. Flush toilets, sanitary services, showers, laundromat and ice are available. A store and cafe are within one mile. Pets and motorbikes are permitted.

Reservations, fee: Reservations accepted; $11 fee per night. Open May to late-October.

Who to contact: Phone at 509-747-9467, or write at S 4110 Fosseen, Spokane, WA 99204.

Location: Take exit 276 (Geiger Field) off Highway 90, go five miles west of Spokane and drive to campground.

Trip note: Nearby recreation options include an 18-hole golf course and a riding stable. See the trip note to campsite 66 for information on attractions in Spokane.

TRAILER INNS
Site 69

Campsites, facilities: There are 158 drive-through sites for trailers or motorhomes of any length. Electricity, piped water, sewer hookups and picnic tables are provided. Flush toilets, bottled gas, showers, recreation hall, swimming pool, laundromat, ice and playground are available. Sanitary services, a store and cafe are within one mile. Pets and motorbikes are permitted.

Reservations, fee: Reservations accepted; $11 fee per night. MasterCard and Visa accepted. Open all year.

Who to contact: Phone at 509-535-1811, or write at 6021 East 4th Avenue, Spokane, WA 99212.

Location: Take exit 283 B off Highway 90 in Spokane and drive east on 3rd Avenue. Follow the signs to the campground.

Trip note: Nearby recreation options include an 18-hole golf course and tennis courts. See the trip note to campsite 66 for information on attractions in Spokane.

EL RANCHO MOTEL
Site 70   AND TRAILER PARK

Campsites, facilities: There are eight tent sites and eight sites for trailers or motorhomes of any length. Electricity, piped water, sewer hookups and picnic tables are provided. Flush toilets, sanitary services, showers, laundromat, ice and a swimming pool are available. Bottled gas, store and cafe are located within one mile. Pets are permitted.

Reservations, fee: Reservations accepted; $9 fee per night. American Express, MasterCard and Visa accepted. Open April to November.

Who to contact: Phone at 509-455-9400, or write at 3000 West Sunset, Spokane, WA 99204.

Location: Take the Maple Street exit off Highway 90 and drive one mile west on Business 90 to 3000 West Sunset.

Trip note: Nearby recreation options include an 18-hole golf course, hiking trails, marked bike trails and tennis courts. See the trip note for campsite 66 for information on attractions in Spokane.

NORTH VIEW MOBILE
Site 71   PARK AND CAMPGROUNDS

Campsites, facilities: There are 21 drive-through sites for trailers or motorhomes of any length. Electricity, piped water, sewer hookups and picnic tables are provided. Flush toilets, sanitary services, showers, recreation hall, bottled gas, a store, cafe, laundromat and ice are available. Pets are permitted.

Reservations, fee: Reservations accepted; $15 fee per night. Open all year.

Who to contact: Phone at 509-467-9512, or write at N 8004 Division, Spokane, WA 99208.

Location: Take Division Street north off Highway 90 in Spokane and drive 5 miles to Lincoln Street, then go east 1 block and you're there.

Trip note: Nearby recreation options include an 18-hole golf course, marked bike trails and tennis courts. See the trip note for campsite 66 for information on attractions in Spokane.

Site 72
SHADOWS MOTEL AND TRAILER PARK

Campsites, facilities: There are 20 tent sites and 60 drive-through sites for trailers or motorhomes of any length. Electricity, piped water and sewer hookups are provided. Flush toilets, sanitary services, showers and laundromat are available. Bottled gas, a store, cafe and ice are located within one mile. Pets and motorbikes are permitted.

Reservations, fee: Reservations accepted; $15 fee per night. MasterCard and Visa accepted. Open May to mid-October.

Who to contact: Phone at 509-467-6951, or write at N 9025 Division, Spokane, WA 99208.

Location: Take Division Street north off Highway 90 in Spokane and drive five miles to N 9025 Division Street.

Trip note: Nearby recreation options include an 18-hole golf course, hiking trails, marked bike trails and tennis courts. See the trip note for campsite 66 for information on attractions in Spokane.

Site 73
KOA SPOKANE

Campsites, facilities: There are 50 tent sites and 190 drive-through sites for trailers or motorhomes of any length. Piped water and picnic tables are provided. Flush toilets, sanitary services, showers, recreation hall, a store, laundromat, ice, playground and swimming pool, electricity and sewer hookups are available. A cafe is located within one mile. Pets are permitted.

Reservations, fee: Reservations accepted; $17 fee per night. MasterCard and Visa accepted. Open all year.

Who to contact: Phone at 509-924-4722, or write at 3025 Barker, Otis Orchards, WA 99027.

Location: Go 13 miles east of Spokane on Highway 90 and take exit 293. Drive north on Barker for 1 1/2 miles to the campground.

Trip note: This campground is set along the shore of the Spokane River. Nearby recreation options include an 18-hole golf course and tennis courts. See the trip note to campsite 66 for information on attractions in Spokane.

Site 74
UNITED CAMPGROUND- ALPINE MOTEL

Campsites, facilities: There are 75 tent sites and 150 drive-through sites for trailers or motorhomes of any length. Piped water and picnic tables are provided. Flush toilets, sanitary services, showers, recreation hall, a store, cafe, electricity, sewer hookups, laundromat, ice, playground and swimming pool are available. Bottled gas is available within one mile. Pets are permitted.

Reservations, fee: Reservations accepted; $12 fee per night. MasterCard and Visa accepted. Open all year.

Who to contact: Phone at 509-928-3300, or write at P.O. Box 363, Green Acres, WA 99016.

Location: Go 13 miles east of Spokane on Highway 90 and take exit 293. Drive east on Highway 290 for four miles to the campground.

Trip note: This campground is near the Spokane River, just far enough out of town to give it a good country feeling. A good sidetrip is the 10-mile drive form Newman Lake. Nearby recreation options include an 18-hole golf course, marked bike trails and tennis courts.

Site 75   SANDY BEACH RESORT

Campsites, facilities: There are 24 sites for trailers or motorhomes up to 30 feet long. Electricity, piped water, sewer hookups and picnic tables are provided. Flush toilets, showers, firewood, a store, cafe, laundromat, ice and playground are available. Pets are permitted. Boat docks, launching facilities and rentals are nearby.

Reservations, fee: Reservations accepted; $13 fee per night. Open mid-April to late-September.

Who to contact: Phone at 509-255-6222, or write at Liberty Lake, WA 99019.

Location: Drive 15 miles east of Spokane on Highway 90 to the Liberty Lake exit, then go south two miles and follow the signs to the resort.

Trip note: This park is nestled along the shore of Liberty Lake, just inside the Washington state border. Trout fishing can be particularly good in spring. Nearby recreation options include an 18-hole golf course and tennis courts.

Site 76   RIVERSIDE STATE PARK

Campsites, facilities: There are 110 sites for tents or self-contained motorhomes up to 45 feet long. Picnic tables and firegrills are provided. Flush toilets, playground, showers and firewood are available. A store, cafe and ice are available within one mile. Some facilities are wheelchair accessible. Pets are permitted. Boat launching facilities are located on the Spokane River.

Reservations, fee: No reservations necessary; $6 fee per night. Open all year.

Who to contact: Phone at 509-456-3964, or write at Riverside State Park, Spokane, WA 99205.

Location: Drive six miles northwest of Spokane on Riverside Park Drive to the jucntion with Highway 291. The park entrance is there.

Trip note: A good option for people looking for a more rural alternative to the camps set on the outskirts of Spokane. This large state park provides an interpretive center, riding stable, and trails for hiking, horseback riding, and Off-Road Vehicles. Nearby recreation options include an 18-hole golf course.

Site 77   LONG LAKE CAMP AND PICNIC AREA

Campsites, facilities: There are seven campsites for tents or small trailers. Picnic tables, fire grills and tent pads are provided. Pit toilets and piped water are available.

Reservations, fee: No reservations necessary; no fee. Open all year.

Who to contact: Phone the Department of Natural Resources at 1-800-527-3305, or write Department of Natural Resources AW-11, 1065 South Capitol Way, Olympia, WA 98504.

Location: Drive 21 miles west of Spokane on Highway 2 to Reardan. Go north on Highway 231 for 14 miles, then turn right on Long Lake Dam Road. Drive five miles and turn right into the campground.

Trip note: This is a secret spot that Spokaners should take advantage of. It's about a 45-

minute drive out of Spokane and you get a small, quiet spot set along the Spokane River. It comes free.

MOUNT SPOKANE
STATE PARK

Site **78**

Campsites, facilities: There are 12 tent sites. Piped water and picnic tables are provided. Flush toilets and a cafe are available. Laundromat is located within one mile. Pets are permitted.

Reservations, fee: No reservations necessary; $6 fee per night. Open all year with limited winter facilities.

Who to contact: Phone at 509-456-4169, or write at Route 1, Box 336, Mead, WA 99021.

Location: This park is located 30 miles northeast of Spokane on Highway 206.

Trip note: A prime hideaway on the slopes of 5878-foot Mt. Spokane. Mt. Kit Carson (5180 feet) sits alongside as its little brother. Nearby recreation options include marked hiking trails, a riding stable and tennis courts. One of the better short trips available out of Spokane.

DRAGOON CREEK

Site **79**

Campsites, facilities: There are 27 campsites for tents or small trailers. Picnic tables, fire grills and tent pads are provided. Pit toilets and piped water are available. Some of the facilities are wheelchair accessible.

Reservations, fee: No reservations necessary; no fee. Open all year.

Who to contact: Phone the Department of Natural Resources at 1-800-527-3305, or write Department of Natural Resources AW-11, 1065 South Capitol Way, Olympia, WA 98504.

Location: From the junction of Highways 2/395 in Spokane, drive north on Highway 395 for 10 miles. Turn left on Dragoon Creek Road and drive 1/2 mile to the campground entrance.

Trip note: Out of towners just plain don't know about this one. This site is not far from Highway 395, but quiet and rustic along Dragoon Creek, a tributary to the Little Spokane River. The Department of Natural Resources offers a map that details the area.

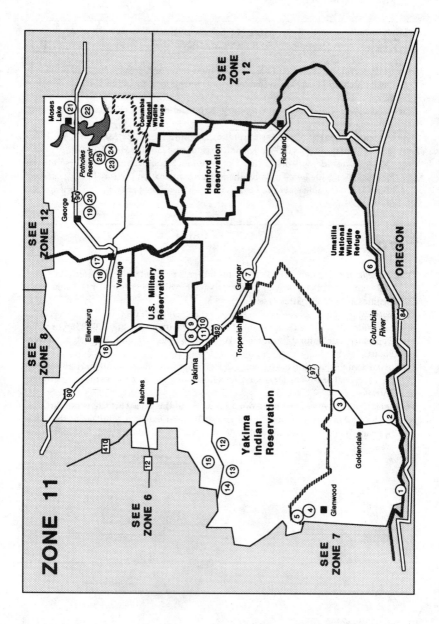

YAKIMA

Site 1
HORSETHIEF LAKE
STATE PARK
▲

Campsites, facilities: There are 12 sites for tents or self-contained motorhomes up to 30 feet long. Piped water, firegrills and picnic tables are provided. Flush toilets, showers, firewood and sanitary services are available. A store and cafe are located within one mile. Some facilities are wheelchair accessible. Pets are permitted. Boat launching facilities are located on both the lake and the river.

Reservations, fee: No reservations necessary; $6 fee per night. Open April to late-October.

Who to contact: Phone at 509-767-1159, or write at Route 677, P.O. Box 27 A, Goldendale, WA 98620.

Location: From the town of Goldendale, drive 28 miles west on Highway 14 to the park.

Trip note: A good spot to camp if you are driving along the Columbia River Highway. This state park is set along the shore of Horsethief Lake adjacent to the Dalles Dam. There are hiking trails and access both to the lake and the Columbia River. Only non-powered boats are allowed, and fishing is for trout and bass. See trip note to campsite 2 for information on other recreation options in the area.

Site 2
MARYHILL
STATE PARK
☐

Campsites, facilities: There are 50 sites with full hookups for trailers or motorhomes up to 50 feet long. Picnic tables are provided. Flush toilets, sanitary services, a store and cafe are available. Electricity, piped water, sewer hookups, showers and firewood can be obtained for an extra fee. Some facilities are wheelchair accessible. Pets are permitted. Boat docks and launching facilities are nearby.

Reservations, fee: No reservations necessary; $6 fee per night. Open all year.

Who to contact: Phone at 509-773-5007, or write at Route 677, P.O. Box 27 A, Goldendale, WA 98620.

Location: From the town of Goldendale, drive 12 miles south on Highway 97 to the park.

Trip note: This park is set along the Columbia River and the recreation opportunities include fishing, waterskiing and windsurfing. The climate here is very pleasant from March through mid-November. There are two interesting spots near the town of Maryhill, one is a replica of Stonehenge which is located on a bluff overlooking the Columbia River, and the other is the Maryhill Museum (phone 509-773-3733 for details). A great side trip is 30 miles northwest, to the Klickitat Habitat Management

Area. It is run by the Department of Game and has some primitive camping spots and a boat launch along the Klickitat River, where you can enjoy boating, fishing, hunting or observing wildlife. To get there drive 11 miles west of Goldendale on Highway 142, then continue northwest on Glendale Road for five miles and look for the headquarters on your left. The public areas beyond the wildlife refuge headquarters are easier to get to. Another treat at the refuge is Stinson Flat, a good steelhead fishing spot.

Site 3   BROOKS MEMORIAL STATE PARK   ◣

Campsites, facilities: There are 22 tent sites and 23 sites with full hookups for trailers or motorhomes up to 50 feet long. Picnic tables and firegrills are provided. Flush toilets, sanitary services and a playground are available. Electricity, piped water, sewer hookups, showers and firewood can be obtained for an extra fee. Ice is located within one mile. Some facilities are wheelchair accessible. Pets are permitted.

Reservations, fee: No reservations necessary; $6 fee per night. Open all year with limited winter facilities.

Who to contact: Phone at 509-773-4611, or write at Route 1, Box 136, Goldendale, WA 98620.

Location: From the town of Goldendale, drive 15 miles northeast on Highway 97 to the park.

Trip note: There is only one other campground (site 2) within 25 miles. This forested park is set at nearly 3000 feet elevation. There are several miles of hiking trails and a 1 1/2 mile long nature trail. A unique side trip is for bird watching at Toppenish National Wildlife Refuge, 28 miles north of the park via Highway 97; phone the refuge at 509-865-2405 for details. If you like star gazing, the Goldendale Observatory is located just one mile north of the town of Goldendale. It houses one of the largest telescopes in the world available for public use; phone 509-773-3141 for hours of operation.

Site 4   BIRD CREEK   ▲

Campsites, facilities: There are eight campsites for tents or small trailers. Picnic tables, fire grills and tent pads are provided. Pit toilets are available, but there is no piped water.

Reservations, fee: No reservations necessary; no fee. Open all year.

Who to contact: Phone the Department of Natural Resources at 1-800-527-3305, or write Department of Natural Resources AW-11, 1065 South Capitol Way, Olympia, WA 98504.

Location: Drive 34 miles west of the town of Goldendale to Glenwood. From the post office in Glenwood, drive 300 yards west then turn right on Bird Creek Road and drive one mile. Turn left, then right on a dirt road and drive one mile. Stay left on K-3000 Road and drive 300 yards, cross a gravel road, stay right for the next two miles, and then turn right into the campground.

Trip note: This campground is set in a forested area along Bird Creek, one of two camps in the immediate area. (The other is campsite 5, also a primitive site.) This spot is just east of the Mount Adams Wilderness area. See the trip note for campsite 2 for information on the nearby Klickitat Habitat Management Area.

ISLAND CAMP

Site **5**

Campsites, facilities: There are six campsites for tents or small trailers. Picnic tables, fire grills and tent pads are provided. Pit toilets are available, but there is no piped water.

Reservations, fee: No reservations necessary; no fee. Open all year.

Who to contact: Phone the Department of Natural Resources at 1-800-527-3305, or write Department of Natural Resources AW-11, 1065 South Capitol Way, Olympia, WA 98504.

Location: Drive 34 miles west of the town of Goldendale to Glenwood. From the post office in Glenwood, drive 300 yards west then turn right on Bird Creek Road and drive one mile. Turn left, then right on a dirt road and drive one mile. Stay left on K-3000 Road and drive 300 yards, cross a gravel road, stay right for the next two miles, go past the Bird Creek camp entrance, and continue on K-3000 Road for 1 1/2 miles. Stay right for 1 1/2 miles then turn right into the campground.

Trip note: This campground is set in a forested area along Bird Creek. There are lava tubes and blow holes nearby. In the winter the roads are used for snowmobiling. See the trip note to campsite 2 for information on boating and fishing in the nearby Klickitat Habitat Management Area.

CROW BUTTE
STATE PARK

Site **6**

Campsites, facilities: There are 50 sites for trailers or motorhomes up to 50 feet long. Electricity, piped water, sewer hookups, firegrills and picnic tables are provided. Flush toilets, showers and sanitary services are available. Some facilities are wheelchair accessible. Boat launching facilities are nearby.

Reservations, fee: No reservations necessary; $6 fee per night. Open all year with limited winter facilities.

Who to contact: Phone at 509-875-2644, or write at P.O. Box 277, Paterson, WA 99345.

Location: From the town of McNary Dam, drive 14 miles west on Highway 14 to the park.

Trip note: This state park is set along the Columbia River, the only campground in a 25-mile radius. Recreation options include waterskiing, fishing, swimming and hiking. The Umatilla National Wildlife Refuge is adjacent to the park and allows fishing and hunting in specified areas.

GRANGER MOBILE VILLA
AND RV PARK

Site **7**

Campsites, facilities: There are 45 tent sites and 45 drive-through sites for trailers or motorhomes of any length. Electricity, piped water and sewer hookups are provided. Flush toilets, sanitary services, showers and a laundromat are available. Bottled gas, a store, cafe and ice are located within one mile. Pets and motorbikes are permitted.

Reservations, fee: Reservations accepted; $10 fee per night. Open all year.

Who to contact: Phone at 509-854-1300, or write at P.O. Box 695, Granger, WA 98932.

Location: Drive 25 miles south of Yakima on Highway 82 to the town of Granger. Take the Highway 223 exit in Granger, and you'll see the park.

Trip note: This park is near the Yakima River. A unique side trip can be made to the

Toppenish Wildlife Refuge, which is particularly good for bird watching. It is 15 miles away, south of the town of Toppenish on Highway 97. Call for information at 509-865-2405.

KOA YAKIMA
Site **8**

Campsites, facilities: There are 40 tent sites and 77 drive-through sites for trailers or motorhomes of any length. Picnic tables are provided. Flush toilets, bottled gas, sanitary services, showers, a recreation hall, store, laundromat, ice, playground, electricity, piped water, sewer hookups and firewood are available. A cafe is located within one mile. Pets and motorbikes are permitted. Boat rentals, including paddle-boats, are available.

Reservations, fee: Reservations accepted; $12 fee per night. Open all year.

Who to contact: Phone at 509-248-5882, or write at 1500 Keyes Road, Yakima, WA 98901.

Location: Take the Highway 24 exit off Highway 82 in Yakima and drive 1/2 mile east. Turn north on Keys Road and drive 300 yards to the campground.

Trip note: This campground offers well-maintained, shaded sites, set along the Yakima River. Some points of interest in Yakima are the Yakima Valley Museum and the Yakima Trolley Lines which offer rides on restored trolley cars originally built in 1906. Indian Rock Paintings State Park is five miles west of Yakima on Highway 12. Nearby recreation options include an 18-hole golf course, hiking trails, marked bike trails and tennis courts.

CIRCLE H
RV RANCH
Site **9**

Campsites, facilities: There are 25 tent sites and 36 drive-through sites for trailers or motorhomes of any length. Electricity, piped water, sewer hookups and picnic tables are provided. Flush toilets, showers, a recreation hall, laundromat, playground and swimming pool are available. Bottled gas, sanitary services, a store, cafe and ice are located within one mile. Pets and motorbikes are permitted.

Reservations, fee: Reservations accepted; $11 fee per night. MasterCard and Visa accepted. Open all year.

Who to contact: Phone at 509-457-3683, or write at 1107 South 18th Street, Yakima, WA 98901.

Location: Take exit 34 off Highway 82 in Yakima and drive 300 yards west to 18th Street. Turn north and drive 300 yards to the park.

Trip note: Nearby recreation options include an 18-hole golf course, hiking trails, marked bike trails and a riding stable. See trip note to campsite 8 for information on points of interest in Yakima.

TRAILER INN RV PARK
AND RECREATION CENTER
Site **10**

Campsites, facilities: There are 101 drive-through sites for trailers or motorhomes of any length. Electricity, piped water, sewer hookups and picnic tables are provided. Flush toilets, bottled gas, sanitary services, showers, a recreation hall, laundromat, ice, swimming pool, whirlpool, sauna and playground are available. A store and cafe are located within one mile. Pets are permitted.

Reservations, fee: Reservations accepted; $13 fee per night. MasterCard and Visa accepted. Open all year.

Who to contact: Phone at 509-452-9561, or write at 1610 North 1st Street, Yakima, WA 98901.

Location: Take exit 31 off Highway 82 in Yakima and drive three blocks south on North 1st Street to the park.

Trip note: Nearby recreation options include an 18-hole golf course, hiking trails, marked bike trails and tennis courts. See trip note for campsite 8 for information on some of the points of interest in Yakima.

Site 11   YAKIMA SPORTSMEN'S STATE PARK

Campsites, facilities: There are 28 tent sites and 36 drive-through sites for trailers or motorhomes of any length. Picnic tables are provided. Flush toilets, sanitary services and a playground are available. Electricity, piped water, sewer hookups, showers and firewood can be obtained for an extra fee. A store, cafe and ice are available within one mile. Pets are permitted.

Reservations, fee: No reservations necessary; $6 fee per night. Open all year.

Who to contact: Phone at 509-575-2774, or write at Route 9, P.O. Box 498, Yakima, WA 98901.

Location: Take Highway 82 east out of Yakima and drive one mile to the park.

Trip note: This park is set along the Yakima River. There is also a pond in the park for children to fish in. Nearby recreation options include an 18-hole golf course and hiking trails. See trip note to campsite 8 for information on other points of interest in Yakima.

Site 12   AHTANUM CAMP

Campsites, facilities: There are 11 campsites for tents or small trailers. Picnic tables, fire grills and tent pads are provided. Pit toilets and piped water are available.

Reservations, fee: No reservations necessary; no fee. Open all year.

Who to contact: Phone the Department of Natural Resources at 1-800-527-3305, or write Department of Natural Resources AW-11, 1065 South Capitol Way, Olympia, WA 98504.

Location: Drive two miles south of Yakima on Highway 82 to Union Gap. Go west on Ahtanum Road to Tampico. Continue west on A-2000 Road (middle fork) and drive 9 1/2 miles to the campground, which will be on the left.

Trip note: This campground is set along Ahtanum Creek, one of four primitive campsites in a 10-mile vicinity. A good side trip is to continue driving on A-2000 Road for 14 miles, where you will reach the Darland Mountain viewpoint at 6900 feet elevation. The road gets very steep near the lookout and is not suitable for motorhomes or trailers. In the winter, this area offers 60 miles of groomed trails for snowmobilers. A snow shelter with firewood is provided at campsite 13. Contact the Department of Natural Resources for a map.

Site 13   TREE PHONES

Campsites, facilities: There are 14 campsites for tents or small trailers. Picnic tables, fire grills and tent pads are provided. Pit toilets are available, but there is no piped water. Motorbikes are permitted. Saddlestock facilities are also available.

Reservations, fee: No reservations necessary; no fee. Open all year.

Who to contact: Phone the Department of Natural Resources at 1-800-527-3305, or write Department of Natural Resources AW-11, 1065 South Capitol Way, Olympia, WA 98504.

Location: Drive two miles south of Yakima on Highway 82 to Union Gap. Go west on Ahtanum Road to Tampico. Continue west on A-2000 Road (middle fork) and drive 15 miles, then go left and drive 100 yards to the campground.

Trip note: This forested campground is set along the Middle Fork of Ahtanum Creek. The nearby trails are used by motorbike riders, hikers and horseback riders. During summer months, there are beautiful wildflower displays. See trip note to campsite 12 for snowmobiling information.

CLOVER FLATS
Site **14**

Campsites, facilities: There are nine campsites for tents or small trailers. Picnic tables, fire grills and tent pads are provided. Pit toilets and piped water are available.

Reservations, fee: No reservations necessary; no fee. Open all year.

Who to contact: Phone the Department of Natural Resources at 1-800-527-3305, or write Department of Natural Resources AW-11, 1065 South Capitol Way, Olympia, WA 98504.

Location: Drive two miles south of Yakima on Highway 82 to Union Gap. Go west on Ahtanum Road to Tampico. Continue west on A-2000 Road (middle fork).

Trip note: This campground is in the sub-alpine zone on the slope of Darland Mountain, which peaks at 6982 feet. There are trails that connect this area with Goat Rocks Wilderness, six miles to the west. Contact the Department of Natural Resources or Wenatchee National Forest for details. See the trip note for campsite 12 for information on winter snowmobiling.

SNOW CABIN
Site **15**

Campsites, facilities: There are eight campsites for tents or small trailers. Picnic tables, fire grills and tent pads are provided. Pit toilets are available, but there is no piped water. Saddlestock facilities are available.

Reservations, fee: No reservations necessary; no fee. Open all year.

Who to contact: Phone the Department of Natural Resources at 1-800-527-3305, or write Department of Natural Resources AW-11, 1065 South Capitol Way, Olympia, WA 98504.

Location: Drive two miles south of Yakima on Highway 82 to Union Gap. Go west on Ahtanum Road to Tampico. Continue west on A-2000 Road (middle fork) and drive 10 miles to Ahtanum Camp. From there, take the North Fork Ahtanum Road (A-3000) and drive 4 1/2 miles. Keep left and drive 2 1/2 miles to the campground, which will be on your left.

Trip note: The most remote of four area campgrounds, this spot is set in a wooded area along the North Fork of the Ahtanum Creek. Green Lake is about two miles from camp and is accessible by car. See trip note to campsite 12 for information on winter snowmobiling.

KOA ELLENBERG
Site **16**

Campsites, facilities: There are 50 tent sites and 100 drive-through sites for trailers or motorhomes of any length. Piped water and picnic tables are provided. Flush toilets, sanitary services, showers, a recreation hall, store, laundromat, ice, playground, wading pool and swimming pool are available. Electricity and sewer hookups can be obtained for an extra fee. Bottled gas and a cafe are located within one mile. Pets and motorbikes are permitted.

Reservations, fee: Reservations accepted; $12 fee per night. MasterCard and Visa accepted. Open April to November.

Who to contact: Phone at 509-925-9319, or write at Route 1, P.O. Box 252, Ellensburg, WA 98926.

Location: Take exit 106 off Highway 90 near Ellenburg and you'll see the campground.

Trip note: This is the only campground in a 25-mile radius. It offers well-maintained, shaded campsites along the Yakima River. The Kittitas County Historical Museum is in town at 3rd and Pine Streets. Nearby recreation options include an 18-hole golf course and tennis courts.

GINKGO/WANAPUM STATE PARK
Site **17**

Campsites, facilities: There are 50 sites for trailers or motorhomes up to 60 feet long. Picnic tables and firegrills are provided. Flush toilets are provided and electricity, piped water, sewer hookups, showers and firewood are available for an extra fee. Some facilities are wheelchair accessible. Pets are permitted. Boat docks and launching facilities are nearby.

Reservations, fee: No reservations necessary; $6 fee per night. Open all year.

Who to contact: Write at Ginkgo/Wanapum State Park, Vantage, WA 98950.

Location: Drive 29 miles east of the town of Ellensburg on Highway 90, then take the Vantage exit and drive south to the park.

Trip note: This state park is set along the Columbia River and Wanapum Lake. It is the site of an ancient petrified forest and there is an interpretive center and trail. Recreation options include hiking, swimming, boating, waterskiing and fishing.

KOA VANTAGE
Site **18**

Campsites, facilities: There are 25 tent sites and 100 sites for trailers or motorhomes of any length. Picnic tables are provided. Flush toilets, bottled gas, sanitary services, showers, a recreation hall, laundromat, ice, playground, swimming pool, sauna and whirlpool are available. Electricity, piped water and sewer hookups can be obtained for an extra fee. Store and cafe are located within one mile. Pets and motorbikes are permitted. Boat docks and launching facilities are nearby.

Reservations, fee: Reservations accepted; $10 fee per night. MasterCard and Visa accepted. Open all year.

Who to contact: Phone at 509-856-2230, or write at P.O. Box 36, Vantage, WA 98950.

Location: Drive 29 miles east of the town of Ellensburg on Highway 90 to the town of Vantage, then take exit 136 and drive north for 1/2 mile to park.

Trip note: This campground offers pleasant, grassy sites overlooking the Columbia River, a short distance from the state park (see campsite 17). This is the only campground in the immediate area that provides space for tent camping. The next closest is 12 miles away at campsite 12 in George.

Site 19   GEORGE EXXON   🚗

Campsites, facilities: There are 10 drive-through sites for trailers or motorhomes of any length. Electricity, piped water and sewer hookups are provided. Sanitary services, store and ice are available. Bottled gas and cafe are located within one mile. Pets are permitted. Boat launching facilities are nearby.

Reservations, fee: Reservations accepted; $5 fee per night. MasterCard and Visa accepted. Open all year.

Who to contact: Phone at 509-785-4511, or write at P.O. Box 5098, George, WA 98824.

Location: Drive 41 miles east of the town of Ellensburg on Highway 90 to the town of George. Take exit 149 and drive 300 yards southwest to the park.

Trip note: This roadside park is in a desert-like area. A good side trip is taking the county road south out of town and visiting the sand dunes north of Frenchman Hills Lake.

Site 20   SHADY TREE
RV PARK   🚗

Campsites, facilities: There are five tent sites and 44 drive-through sites for trailers or motorhomes of any length. Electricity, piped water, sewer hookups and picnic tables are provided. Flush toilets, showers and a laundromat are available. Sanitary services are located within one mile. Pets and motorbikes are permitted.

Reservations, fee: Reservations accepted; $10 fee per night. Open all year.

Who to contact: Phone at 509-785-2851, or write at P.O. Box 5306, George, WA 98824.

Location: Drive 41 miles east of the town of Ellensburg on Highway 90 to the town of George. Go to the intersection of Highways 281 and 283 and you'll see the park.

Trip note: This is an oasis in this desert-like area. A good side trip is to Frenchman Hills Lakes, a desolate area bordered by sand dunes.

Site 21   BIG SUN
RESORT   🚗

Campsites, facilities: There are 10 tent sites and 50 drive-through sites for trailers or motorhomes of any length. Electricity, piped water, sewer hookups and picnic tables are provided. Flush toilets, a recreation hall, laundromat, ice and playground are available. Showers can be obtained for an extra fee. Bottled gas, sanitary services, a store and cafe are located within one mile. Pets and motorbikes are permitted. Boat docks, launching facilities and rentals are nearby.

Reservations, fee: Reservations accepted; $10 fee per night. Open all year.

Who to contact: Phone at 509-765-8294, or write at 2300 West Marina, Moses Lake, WA 98837.

Location: Take exit 176 off Highway 90 in Moses Lake and drive 1/2 mile on Broadway to Burress Avenue. Turn west on Burress and go one block to the park.

Trip note: This park is a short distance from Moses Lake State Park, which is open for day-use only. You will find shady picnic spots with tables and firegrills, beach access and moorage floats. Waterskiing is allowed on the lake.

Site **22**   WILLOWS TRAILER VILLAGE

Campsites, facilities: There are 20 tent sites and 64 drive-through sites for trailers or motorhomes of any length. Electricity, piped water, sewer hookups and picnic tables are provided. Flush toilets, bottled gas, showers, a store, laundromat and ice are available. Pets and motorbikes are permitted.

Reservations, fee: Reservations accepted; $10 fee per night. Open all year.

Who to contact: Phone at 509-765-7531, or write at Route 3, P.O. Box 53, Moses Lake, WA 98837.

Location: Take exit 179 off Highway 90 in Moses Lake and drive 2 1/2 miles south on Highway 17, then go 300 yards southwest on O'Sullivan Dam Road to the park.

Trip note: This is one of four campgrounds set in the area. See the trip note to campsites 21 and 24 for information on recreation spots in this area.

Site **23**   MAR-DON RESORT

Campsites, facilities: There are 160 drive-through sites for tents, trailers or motorhomes of any length. Electricity, piped water, sewer hookups and picnic tables are provided. Flush toilets, bottled gas, sanitary services, showers, a recreation hall, store, laundromat, ice and playground are available. Pets and motorbikes are permitted. Boat docks, rentals and launching facilities are nearby.

Reservations, fee: No reservations necessary; $12 fee per night. American Express, MasterCard and Visa accepted. Open all year.

Who to contact: Phone at 509-765-5061, or write at 800 O'Sullivan, Othello, WA 99344.

Location: Take exit 179 off Highway 90 in Moses Lake and drive 1 1/2 miles south on Highway 17, then head south on O'Sullivan Dam Road and drive about 15 miles to the west end of the dam. From there you'll see the resort.

Trip note: See trip note to campsite 24 for information on the area. Nearby recreation options include hiking trails and marked bike trails.

Site **24**   FISH HAVEN RESORT

Campsites, facilities: There are 40 tent sites and 90 drive-through sites for trailers or motorhomes of any length. Electricity, piped water and sewer hookups are provided. Flush toilets, showers, a store, firewood and ice are available. Bottled gas, sanitary services and a cafe are located within one mile. Pets and motorbikes are permitted. Boat launching facilities are nearby.

Reservations, fee: No reservations necessary; $10 fee per night. Open March to late-October.

Who to contact: Phone at 509-346-2366, or write at 691 O'Sullivan Dam Road, Othello, WA 99344.

Location: Take exit 179 off Highway 90 in Moses Lake and drive 1 1/2 miles south on Highway 17, then turn southwest on O'Sullivan Road and drive about 14 miles to 691 O'Sullivan Dam Road.

Trip note: This park is set along the Potholes Reservoir, a unique lake formed in a desert area by the O'Sullivan Dam. The area get very little rainfall. The nearby Columbia Wildlife Refuge is populated with many types of birds and is used most heavily as a wintering range from November through January. The numerous sloughs and small lakes formed by seepage from the reservoir provide the best fishing spots.

Site **25**

POTHOLES
STATE PARK

Campsites, facilities: There are 66 tent sites and 60 sites for trailers or motorhomes up to 25 feet long. Picnic tables and firegrills are provided. Flush toilets, sanitary services, a store and playground are available. Electricity, piped water, sewer hookups, showers and firewood can be obtained for an extra fee. Some facilities are wheelchair accessible. Pets are permitted. Boat launching facilities and rentals are nearby.

Reservations, fee: No reservations necessary; $6 fee per night. Open all year.

Who to contact: Phone at 509-765-7271, or write at Royal Star Route, Othello, WA 99344.

Location: Drive 24 miles southwest of Moses Lake on Highway 170.

Trip note: See the trip note for campsite 24 for a description of this unique area. Water-skiing, fishing, and hiking are some of the options here. A side trip to the Columbia Wildlife Refuge is recommended.

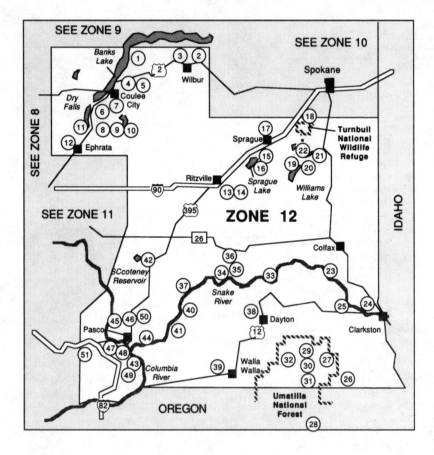

SOUTHEASTERN PLAINS

Site 1
STEAMBOAT ROCK STATE PARK

Campsites, facilities: There are 100 sites for trailers or motorhomes up to 60 feet long. Picnic tables are provided. Flush toilets, a cafe and playground are available. Electricity, piped water, sewer hookups and showers can be obtained for an extra fee. Some facilities are wheelchair accessible. Pets are permitted. Boat launching facilities are nearby.

Reservations, fee: Reservations accepted; $6 fee per night. Open all year with limited winter facilities.

Who to contact: Phone at 509-633-1304, or write at P.O. Box 352, Electric City, WA 99123.

Location: Drive eight miles south of Grand Coulee on Highway 155.

Trip note: This state park is set along the shores of Banks Lake, a reservoir a few miles down from the Grand Coulee Dam. There is a swimming beach, and fishing and waterskiing are popular. Horse trails are available in nearby Northrup Canyon. During the winter, the park is used by snowmobilers, cross-country skiers and ice fishermen.

Site 2
BELLS TRAILER PARK

Campsites, facilities: There are two tent sites and 10 sites for trailers or motorhomes of any length. Electricity, piped water, sewer hookups and picnic tables are provided. Showers, flush toilets, a laundromat and ice are available. Bottled gas, sanitary services, a store and cafe are located within one mile. Pets and motorbikes are permitted.

Reservations, fee: Reservations accepted; $8 fee per night. Open all year.

Who to contact: Phone at 509-647-5888, or write at Route 1, Box 75, Wilbur, WA 99185.

Location: This park is located in eastern edge of Wilbur on Highway 2.

Trip note: This private park is in the small town of Wilbur, about 20 miles south of the Grand Coulee Dam. Nearby recreation options include an 18-hole golf course and tennis courts. A good side trip is to take Highway 21 north for 20 minutes to Roosevelt Lake.

Site 3
WILBUR CAMPGROUND AND MOTEL

Campsites, facilities: There are 20 tent sites and 20 sites for trailers or motorhomes of any

length. Piped water, sewer hookups and picnic tables are provided. Flush toilets, sanitary services, electricity and showers are available. Bottled gas, a store, cafe, laundromat and ice are located within one mile. Pets and motorbikes are permitted.

Reservations, fee: Reservations accepted; $7 fee per night. Open mid-March to mid-November.

Who to contact: Phone at 509-647-5608, or write at P.O. Box 538, Wilbur, WA 99185.

Location: This park is located on the west side of the town of Wilbur on Highway 2.

Trip note: The camp is an option to campsite 2 and has the same recreational possibilities.

BLUE TOP
Site **4**   **TRAILER PARK**

Campsites, facilities: There are seven sites for trailers or motorhomes of any length. Electricity, piped water and sewer hookups are provided. Bottled gas, sanitary services, a store, cafe, laundromat and ice are available within one mile. Pets are permitted. Boat docks and launching facilities are nearby.

Reservations, fee: Reservations accepted; $7 fee per night. MasterCard and Visa accepted. Open all year.

Who to contact: Phone at 509-632-5596, or write at P.O. Box 836, Coulee City, WA 99115.

Location: This park is located in the town of Coulee City. Drive there on Highway 2, then turn south on 4th Street and drive 300 yards to Walnut Street. You'll see the park.

Trip note: One of two campgrounds in the immediate area, the other is campsite 5. Both are located at the southern end of Banks Lake, near Dry Falls Dam. Nearby recreation options include hiking trails, marked bike trails, a riding stable and tennis courts. Several side trips are possible from here. Dry Falls is four miles southwest, just off Highway 17, where you will find the remnants of a huge, 3 1/2-mile wide waterfall from the last ice age, and an interpretive center that describes its history. Summer Falls State Park, located seven miles south of town, is known for a big set of waterfalls. Another option are the mineral waters at Soap Lake, 26 miles to the south on Highway 17.

COULEE
Site **5**   **CITY PARK**   ▲

Campsites, facilities: There are 75 tent sites and 34 drive-through sites for trailers or motorhomes up to 24 feet long. Electricity, piped water, sewer hookups and picnic tables are provided. Flush toilets, sanitary services, showers and a playground are available. Bottled gas, firewood, a store, cafe, laundromat and ice are located within one mile. Boat docks and launching facilities are nearby.

Reservations, fee: No reservations necessary; $7 fee per night. Open mid-April to October.

Who to contact: Phone at 509-632-5331, or write at P.O. Box 398, Coulee City, WA 99115.

Location: This park is located in the town of Coulee City, on Highway 2.

Trip note: This park is set along the south shore of 30-mile-long Banks Lake, where boating, fishing and waterskiing are popular. Nearby recreation options include an 18-hole golf course. See trip note to campsite 4 for more details on the area.

Site **6**
SUN LAKES
STATE PARK

Campsites, facilities: There are 191 tent sites and 18 sites for trailers or motorhomes up to 50 feet long. Picnic tables are provided. Flush toilets, sanitary services, a cafe, laundromat, ice, swimming pool, electricity, piped water, sewer hookups, showers and firewood are available. A store is located within one mile. Some facilities are wheelchair accessible. Pets are permitted. Boat docks, launching facilities and rentals are nearby.

Reservations, fee: No reservations necessary; $6 fee per night. Open all year.

Who to contact: Phone at 509-632-5583, or write at Star Route 1, P.O. Box 136, Coulee City, WA 99115.

Location: Drive seven miles southwest of Coulee City on Highway 17 and you'll find the park.

Trip note: Sun Lakes State Park is set along the shore of Park Lake, which is used primarily by boaters and waterskiers. The Lake Lenore Caves can be reached by a trail at the north end of the lake. Dry Falls and the interpretive center are also within the park boundaries. See trip note for campsite 4 for description of Dry Falls. Nearby recreation options include an 18-hole golf course, hiking trails and a riding stable.

Site **7**
SUN LAKES
PARK RESORT

Campsites, facilities: There are 112 drive-through sites for trailers or motorhomes of any length. Electricity, piped water, sewer hookups and picnic tables are provided. Flush toilets, bottled gas, sanitary services, a store, showers, firewood, a cafe, laundromat, ice, playground and swimming pool are available. Pets are permitted. Boat docks, launching facilities and rentals are nearby.

Reservations, fee: Reservations accepted; $12 fee per night. MasterCard and Visa accepted. Open mid-April to November.

Who to contact: Phone at 509-632-5291, or write at Star Route 1, P.O. Box 141, Coulee City, WA 99115.

Location: Drive seven miles southwest of Coulee City on Highway 17 and you'll come to the park.

Trip note: This is the concession that operates within Sun Lakes State Park. See trip note for campsite 6.

Site **8**
BLUE LAKE RESORT
AND RV PARK
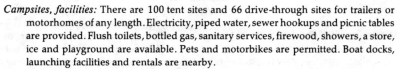

Campsites, facilities: There are 100 tent sites and 66 drive-through sites for trailers or motorhomes of any length. Electricity, piped water, sewer hookups and picnic tables are provided. Flush toilets, bottled gas, sanitary services, firewood, showers, a store, ice and playground are available. Pets and motorbikes are permitted. Boat docks, launching facilities and rentals are nearby.

Reservations, fee: Reservations accepted; $8 fee per night. Open April to October.

Who to contact: Phone at 509-632-5364, or write at Star Route 1, P.O. Box 158, Coulee City, WA 99115.

Location: Drive 11 miles southwest of Coulee City on Highway 17 and you'll come to the park.

Trip note: This park is set along the shore of Blue Lake between Sun Lakes and Lake Lenore Caves State Parks. See trip note for campsite 6.

Site 9   LAURENT'S SUN VILLAGE RESORT

Campsites, facilities: There are six tent sites and 105 drive-through sites for trailers or motorhomes of any length. Electricity, piped water, sewer hookups and picnic tables are provided. Flush toilets, bottled gas, sanitary services, a store, a cafe, laundromat, ice and playground are available. Showers and firewood can be obtained for an extra fee. Pets and motorbikes are permitted. Boat docks, launching facilities and rentals are nearby.

Reservations, fee: Reservations accepted; $10 fee per night. MasterCard and Visa accepted. Open mid-April to October.

Who to contact: Phone at 509-632-5664, or write at Star Route 1, P.O. Box 151, Coulee City, WA 99115.

Location: Drive 10 miles southwest of Coulee City on Highway 17 to Blue Lake. Head east for 1/2 mile. The resort is at the north end of the lake.

Trip note: Like campsite 8, this campground is set along the shore of Blue Lake. See trip note to campsite 6 for information on the nearby state parks and other recreation options.

Site 10   COULEE LODGE RESORT

Campsites, facilities: There are 14 tent sites and 30 drive-through sites for trailers or motorhomes of any length. Electricity, piped water, sewer hookups and picnic tables are provided. Flush toilets, bottled gas, sanitary services, a store, showers, firewood, laundromat and ice are available. Cafe is located within one mile. Some facilities are wheelchair accessible. Pets and motorbikes are permitted. Boat docks, launching facilities and rentals are nearby.

Reservations, fee: Reservations accepted; $9 fee per night. MasterCard and Visa accepted. Open mid-April to October.

Who to contact: Phone at 509-632-5565, or write at Star Route 1, P.O. Box 156, Coulee City, WA 99115.

Location: Drive 10 miles southwest of Coulee City on Highway 17 to Blue Lake. The resort is at the north end of the lake.

Trip note: One of five camps in the general area, one of three in the immediate vicinity. See trip note to campsite 8 for details.

Site 11   SMOKIAM RV PARK

Campsites, facilities: There are 20 tent sites and 50 drive-through sites for trailers or motorhomes. Electricity, piped water, sewer hookups and picnic tables are provided. Flush toilets, sanitary services and showers are available. Bottled gas, a store, a cafe, laundromat and ice are located within one mile. Pets and motorbikes are permitted.

Reservations, fee: Reservations accepted; $7 fee per night. Open March to early-November.

Who to contact: Phone at 509-246-1366, or write at P.O. Box 591, Soap Lake, WA 98851.

Location: Drive 25 miles southwest of Coulee City on Highway 17 to the town of Soap

Lake. The park is at the north end of town.

Trip note: Smokiam is the Indian word for "healing waters" and is the name the Indians gave to what is now called Soap Lake. Nearby recreation options include hot mineral baths, an 18-hole golf course, hiking trails, marked bike trails and tennis courts.

OASIS PARK
Site **12**

Campsites, facilities: There are 38 tent sites and 66 drive-through sites for trailers or motorhomes of any length. Picnic tables are provided. Flush toilets, bottled gas, sanitary services, a store, laundromat, ice and swimming pool are available. Electricity, piped water, sewer hookups and showers can be obtained for an extra fee. A cafe is located within one mile. Pets and motorbikes are permitted.

Reservations, fee: Reservations accepted; $7 fee per night. MasterCard and Visa accepted. Open all year.

Who to contact: Phone at 509-754-5102, or write at Route 2, 5103 Highway 28, Ephrata, WA 98823.

Location: This park is located 1 1/2 miles south of the town of Ephrata on Highway 28.

Trip note: This can be a warm, arid area in the summer, but fortunately, this park offers shaded sites. There are two fishing ponds, one has bass and crappie, while the other is for kids. Nearby recreation options include an 18-hole golf course. See trip note for campsite 11 for information on mineral baths seven miles north of this park.

COTTAGE MOTEL AND TRAILER PARK
Site **13**

Campsites, facilities: There are 26 drive-through sites for trailers or motorhomes of any length. Electricity, piped water and sewer hookups are provided. Flush toilets, sanitary services and showers are available. Bottled gas, a store, a cafe, laundromat and ice are located within one mile. Pets and motorbikes are permitted.

Reservations, fee: Reservations accepted; $10 fee per night. Open all year.

Who to contact: Phone at 509-659-0721, or write at 508 East First, Ritzville, WA 99169.

Location: Drive on Interstate 90 to the town of Ritzville. Take exit 220 and drive to 508 East First Street on the eastern edge of town.

Trip note: This is one of two parks in Ritzville, set in the middle of the Washington plains country. The other is campsite 14. This park is 56 miles from Spokane. Nearby recreation options include an 18-hole golf course.

COMFORT INN MOTEL AND RV PARK
Site **14**

Campsites, facilities: There are 30 drive-through sites for tents, trailers or motorhomes of any length. Electricity, piped water, sewer hookups and picnic tables are provided. Flush toilets, sanitary services, showers, laundromat, ice, playground and swimming pool are available. Bottled gas, a store and cafe are located within one mile. Pets and motorbikes are permitted.

Reservations, fee: Reservations accepted; $12 fee per night. American Express, Master-Card and Visa accepted. Open March to late-October.

Who to contact: Phone at 509-659-1007, or write at 1405 Smitty's Boulevard, Ritzville, WA 99169.

Location: Drive on Interstate 90 to the town of Ritzville. Take exit 221 and you'll see the motel one-half block off the freeway.

Trip note: If all you have is a tent, well, this is the only site in a radius of 25 miles in all directions. The nearest fishing is at Sprague Lake, 30 miles north on Highway 395. Burroughs Historial Museum is a possible sidetrip in town. Nearby recreation options include an 18-hole golf course and tennis courts.

Site 15   BOB LEE CAMPGROUND

Campsites, facilities: There are 25 tent sites and 30 drive-through sites for trailers or motorhomes. Electricity, piped water, sewer hookups and picnic tables are provided. Flush toilets, sanitary services, showers, firewood, ice, a playground and swimming pool are available. Pets and motorbikes are permitted. Boat docks, launching facilities and rentals are nearby.

Reservations, fee: Reservations accepted; $9 fee per night. Open mid-April to October.

Who to contact: Phone at 509-257-2332, or write at Route 1, Box 41, Sprague, WA 99032.

Location: Take exit 231 off Interstate 90 in the town of Sprague. Head east on Keystone and follow the signs to the campground.

Trip note: This campground is set along the shore of Sprague Lake. The fishing is best in May and June for rainbow trout, with some bass in spring and fall. Because there is an abundance of natural feed in the lake, the fish reach larger sizes here than in neighboring lakes. In late July through August, a fair algae bloom is a turnoff for swimmers and water skiers.

Site 16   SPRAGUE LAKE RESORT

Campsites, facilities: There are 50 tent sites and 30 drive-through sites for trailers or motorhomes of any length. Electricity, piped water, sewer hookups and picnic tables are provided. Flush toilets, sanitary services, a store, laundromat, showers, ice and playground are available. Pets are permitted. Boat docks, launching facilities and rentals are nearby.

Reservations, fee: Reservations accepted; $9 fee per night. Open April to mid-October.

Who to contact: Phone at 509-257-2864, or write at Route 1, Box 5, Sprague, WA 99032.

Location: Get off Interstate 90 at the Sprague exit for the business center. Follow the signs and drive two miles to the resort.

Trip note: This campground is set along the shore of Sprague Lake, about 35 miles from Spokane. See trip note to campsite 15.

Site 17   LAST ROUNDUP MOTEL AND RV PARK

Campsites, facilities: There are 15 tent sites and 15 drive-through sites for trailers or motorhomes. Electricity, piped water, sewer hookups and picnic tables are provided. Flush toilets, showers, a laundromat and ice are available. Bottled gas, sanitary services, a store and cafe are located within one mile. Pets and motorbikes are permitted.

Reservations, fee: Reservations accepted; $7 fee per night. MasterCard and Visa accepted. Open all year.

Who to contact: Phone at 509-257-2583, or write at Route 1, Box C-1, Sprague, WA 99032.

Location: Take exit 245 off Interstate 90 in Sprague and drive 1/2 mile south on Highway 23.

Trip note: The camp is set just on the outskirts of the town of Sprague. The best game in town is at nearby Sprague Lake. See trip note to campsite 15 for information on Sprague Lake.

Site 18
PEACEFUL PINES CAMPGROUND

Campsites, facilities: There are 20 tent sites and 18 sites for trailers or motorhomes of any length. Electricity, piped water, sewer hookups and picnic tables are provided. Flush toilets, sanitary services and showers are available. Store, a cafe, a laundromat and ice are located within one mile. Pets and motorbikes are permitted.

Reservations, fee: Reservations accepted; $8 fee per night. Open all year.

Who to contact: Phone at 509-235-4966, or write at Route 1, Box 350, Cheney, WA 99004.

Location: Drive nine miles southwest of Spokane on Interstate 90. Take the Highway 904 exit to Chaney. Drive one mile southwest of Chaney on Highway 904 and you'll see the campground.

Trip note: This campground is a short distance from Turnbull National Wildlife Refuge, an expanse of marsh and pine that is a significant stopover point for migratory birds on the Pacific Flyway. You can pick up a map and bird checklist at the refuge headquarters. A prime spot, only a 45-minute drive out of Spokane, yet relatively few know of it.

Site 19
WILLIAMS LAKE RESORT

Campsites, facilities: There are 12 tent sites and 60 sites for trailers or motorhomes of any length. Electricity, piped water and picnic tables are provided. Flush toilets, bottled gas, sanitary services, firewood, a store, a cafe, ice and playground are available. Pets and motorbikes are permitted. Boat docks, launching facilities and rentals are nearby.

Reservations, fee: Reservations accepted; $9 fee per night. Open mid-April to late-September.

Who to contact: Phone at 509-235-2391, or write at Route 1, Box 284, Cheney, WA 99004.

Location: Drive 11 1/2 miles south of the town of Cheney on Cheney Road, then head north on Williams Lake Road and drive 3 1/2 miles to the campground.

Trip note: This resort is set along the shore of Williams Lake. The lake is just under three miles long and is popular for swimming and water skiing. It is also one of the top fishing lakes in the region for rainbow and cutthroat trout. The lake is bordered in some areas by rocky cliffs. See trip note to campsite 18 for information on nearby Turnbull National Wildlife Refuge.

Site 20
LEWIS BROTHERS RESORT

Campsites, facilities: There are 25 tent sites and 62 sites for trailers or motorhomes of any

length. Electricity, piped water, sewer hookups and picnic tables are provided. Flush toilets, bottled gas, sanitary services, a store, a cafe, showers, laundromat, ice and playground are available. Pets and motorbikes are permitted. Boat docks, launching facilities and rentals are nearby.

Reservations, fee: Reservations accepted; $8 fee per night. Open mid-April to late-September.

Who to contact: Phone at 509-235-2341, or write at Route 3, Box 330, Cheney, WA 99004.

Location: Drive 12 miles south of the town of Cheney on Williams Lake Road and follow the signs to the resort.

Trip note: This resort is set along the shore of Williams Lake, a more developed option to campsite 19.

Site **21**   BUNKERS RESORT

Campsites, facilities: There are 35 drive-through sites for trailers or motorhomes of any length. Electricity, piped water and picnic tables are provided. Flush toilets, bottled gas, sanitary services, recreation hall, a store, a cafe and ice are available. Pets are permitted. Boat docks, launching facilities and rentals are nearby.

Reservations, fee: Reservations accepted; $8 fee per night. MasterCard and Visa accepted. Open mid-April to October.

Who to contact: Phone at 509-235-5212, or write at Route 1, Box 270, Cheney, WA 99004.

Location: Drive 14 miles south of the town of Cheney and follow the signs to the resort.

Trip note: This campground is set along the shore of Williams Lake. See the trip note to campsite 19 for information on the lake and trip note to campsite 18 for information on nearby Turnbull National Wildlife Refuge.

Site **22**   RICHARD'S RESORT

Campsites, facilities: There are 20 tent sites and 25 drive-through sites for trailers or motorhomes up to 30 feet long. Electricity, piped water and picnic tables are provided. Flush toilets, bottled gas, sanitary services, a store, a cafe, ice and playground are available. Pets are permitted. Boat docks, launching facilities and rentals are nearby.

Reservations, fee: Reservations accepted; $8 fee per night. Open March to late-October.

Who to contact: Phone at 509-235-2331, or write at Route 3, Box 3328, Cheney, WA 99004.

Location: Drive 15 miles south of the town of Cheney and follow the signs to Badger Lake.

Trip note: This resort is set along the shore of Badger Lake. See trip note to campsite 18 for information on nearby Turnbull National Wildlife Refuge.

Site **23**   WAWAWAI COUNTY PARK

Campsites, facilities: There are nine drive-through sites for tents, trailers or motorhomes up to 24 feet long. Picnic tables are provided. Playground is available. Some facilities are wheelchair accessible. Pets are permitted. Boat docks and launching facilities are nearby.

Reservations, fee: No reservations necessary; $4 fee per night. Open all year.
Who to contact: Phone at 509-397-4304, or write at Room 3, ONB Building, Colfax, WA 99111.
Location: Drive 16 miles southwest of the town of Pullman on Wawawai Road.
Trip note: This park is on the north shore of the Snake River, upstream from Lower Granite Dam. The campground is hidden at the end of obscure Wawawai Road. Swimming, fishing and hiking are all options here. It can get quite hot in the summer.

Site 24   NOBLE'S MOBILE HOME PARK

Campsites, facilities: There are 10 sites for trailers or motorhomes of any length. Electricity, piped water and sewer hookups are provided. Sanitary services and laundromat are available. Bottled gas, a store, a cafe and ice are located within one mile. Pets are permitted. Boat docks, launching facilities and rentals are nearby.
Reservations, fee: Reservations accepted; $5 fee per night. Open all year.
Who to contact: Phone at 509-758-7031, or write at 1432 Tenth Street, Clarkston, WA 99403.
Location: Drive one mile south of Highway 12 in the town of Clarkston to 10th Street. The park is at 1432 10th Street.
Trip note: This camp is set just inside the Washington state border. Nearby recreation options include swimming, fishing and boating on the Snake River. There is also an 18-hole golf course and tennis courts. There are outfitters in Clarkston that will take you sightseeing up the Grand Canyon of the Snake River. Call the Chamber of Commerce at 509-758-7712 for details.

Site 25   CHIEF TIMOTHY STATE PARK

Campsites, facilities: There are 68 sites for tents, trailers or motorhomes up to 60 feet long. Picnic tables and firegrills are provided. Flush toilets, sanitary services and a playground are available. Electricity, piped water, sewer hookups, showers and firewood can be obtained for an extra fee. Some facilities are wheelchair accessible. Pets are permitted. Boat docks and launching facilities are nearby.
Reservations, fee: No reservations necessary; $6 fee per night. Open all year.
Who to contact: Phone at 509-758-9580, or write at Highway 12, Clarkston, WA 99403.
Location: Drive eight miles southwest of the town of Clarkston on Highway 12 to the park.
Trip note: This unique state park is set on a bridged island in the Snake River. It offers all watersports, docks for boat campers, a beach area and an interpretive center. It is one of three camps in a 30-mile circle.

Site 26   FIELDS SPRING STATE PARK

Campsites, facilities: There are 24 sites for tents or self-contained trailers or motorhomes. Piped water, picnic tables and firegrills are provided. Flush toilets, sanitary services and a playground are available. Showers and firewood can be obtained for an extra fee. A store, a cafe and ice are located within one mile. Some facilities are wheelchair accessible. Pets are permitted.
Reservations, fee: No reservations necessary; $6 fee per night. Open all year.

Who to contact: Phone at 509-256-3332, or write at Box 86, Anatone, WA 99401.

Location: Drive 4 1/2 miles south of the town of Anatone on Highway 129.

Trip note: Just about nobody knows about this spot, and it's a good one, tucked away in the southeast corner of the state. This park is noted for its variety of bird life and wildflowers. A hiking trail leads up to Puffer Butte at 4500 feet elevation, which offers a panoramic view of the Snake River Canyon, Idaho, Oregon, Washington and the Wallowa Mountains. Two day-use areas with boat launches managed by the Department of Game are within about 25 miles of the park. One is called the Snake River Access, 22 1/2 miles south of the town of Asotin on Snake River Road; the other is the Grand Ronde River Access, 24 miles south of Asotin on the same road. During the winter, this state park is open for snowmobiling and crosscountry skiing.

WICKIUP
Site **27**

Campsites, facilities: There are eight sites for tents, trailers or motorhomes up to 15 feet long. Picnic tables are provided. Pit toilets are available, but there is no piped water. Pets are permitted.

Reservations, fee: No reservations necessary; $2 fee per night. Open mid-June to late-October.

Who to contact: Phone Umatilla National Forest at 509-843-1891, or write at Umatilla Ranger Station, Asotin, WA 99402.

Location: Drive 24 miles southwest of the town of Asotin on County Route 105, then head southwest on Forest Service Road 4300 for seven miles to the campground.

Trip note: This is a primitive Forest Service campground that gets very little camper pressure. It is a good jumpoff for summer backpacking trips or a fall hunting trip. A Forest Service map details back country roads and trails.

GODMAN
Site **28**

Campsites, facilities: There are four sites for tents, trailers or motorhomes up to 15 feet long. Picnic tables are provided. Pit toilets and firewood are available, but there is no piped water. Pets are permitted.

Reservations, fee: No reservations necessary; $2 fee per night. Open mid-June to late-October.

Who to contact: Phone Umatilla National Forest at 509-843-1891, or write at Umatilla Ranger Station, Asotin, WA 99402.

Location: Drive 14 miles southeast of the town of Dayton on County Route 118, then head south on Forest Service Road 46 for 11 miles to the campground.

Trip note: A tiny, little-known spot that borders a wilderness area. There are several trails nearby that provide access to the Wenaha-Tucannon Wilderness for hikers and horseback riders. In the winter the trails and roads are used for snowmobiling.

ALDER THICKET
Site **29**

Campsites, facilities: There are four sites for tents, trailers or motorhomes up to 15 feet long. Picnic tables are provided. Pit toilets and firewood are available, but there is no piped water. Pets are permitted.

Reservations, fee: No reservations necessary; $2 fee per night. Open mid-May to mid-November.

Who to contact: Phone Umatilla National Forest at 509-843-1891, or write at Umatilla Ranger Station, Pomeroy, WA 99347.

Location: Drive nine miles south of Pomeroy on Highway 128, then head south on County Road 107 and drive eight miles. Turn south on Forest Service Road 40 and drive 3 1/2 miles to the campground.

Trip note: This is probably the first time you've heard of this spot. Hardly anybody knows about it, including people who live relatively nearby in Walla Walla. It is prime base camp for a back country hiking adventure in summer, or a hunting jumpoff point in the fall. A National Forest map details the possibilities.

TEAL SPRINGS
Site **30**

Campsites, facilities: There are five sites for tents, trailers or motorhomes up to 15 feet long. Piped water and picnic tables are provided. Pit toilets and firewood are available. Pets are permitted.

Reservations, fee: No reservations necessary; $2 fee per night. Open June to mid-November.

Who to contact: Phone Umatilla National Forest at 509-843-1891, or write at Umatilla Ranger Station, Pomeroy, WA 99347.

Location: Drive nine miles south of Pomeroy on Highway 128 and then head south on County Road 107 and drive 7 1/2 miles. Turn south on Forest Service Road 200 and drive nine miles to the campground.

Trip note: One of several small, primitive camps in the area. This one has piped water, a valuable asset. A National Forest map details the back country roads, trails and streams.

BIG SPRINGS
Site **31**

Campsites, facilities: There are six tent sites. Picnic tables are provided. Pit toilets and firewood are available, but there is no piped water. Pets are permitted.

Reservations, fee: No reservations necessary; $2 fee per night. Open mid-May to mid-November.

Who to contact: Phone Umatilla National Forest at 509-843-1891, or write at Umatilla Ranger Station, Pomeroy, WA 99347.

Location: Drive 15 miles southeast of the town of Pomeroy on Highway 128, then head south on County Road 191 for 3 1/2 miles. Go five miles southwest on Forest Service Road 42000 to the campground.

Trip note: A more primitive, remote option to campsite 30. In the fall, it is used primarily by hunters. In the summer, it is a possible base camp for a backpacking trip. It's advisable to obtain a Forest Service map of the area.

TUCANNON
Site **32**

Campsites, facilities: There are 15 sites for tents, trailers or motorhomes up to 15 feet long. Picnic tables are provided. Pit toilets and firewood are available, but there is no piped water. Pets are permitted.

Reservations, fee: No reservations necessary; $2 fee per night. Open May to late-November.

Who to contact: Phone Umatilla National Forest at 509-843-1891, or write at Umatilla Ranger Station, Pomeroy, WA 99347.

Location: Drive 17 miles southwest of Pomeroy on County Road 101, then head southwest on Forest Service Road 47 for four miles. Turn south on Forest Service Road 160 and drive 200 yards to the campground.

Trip note: A back country camp in Umatilla National Forest. For people willing to rough it, this is the place. There is plenty of hiking, fishing and hunting all in a rugged setting.

Site 33
CENTRAL FERRY STATE PARK

Campsites, facilities: There are 60 sites for trailers or motorhomes up to 45 feet long. Picnic tables are provided. Flush toilets, sanitary services, a store, cafe, electricity, piped water, sewer hookups, showers and firewood are available. Some facilities are wheelchair accessible. Pets are permitted. Boat docks, launching facilities and a fishing pier are nearby.

Reservations, fee: No reservations necessary; $6 fee per night. Open all year.

Who to contact: Phone at 509-549-3551, or write at Route 3, Box 99, Pomeroy, WA 99347.

Location: This park is located 34 miles southwest of the town of Colfax, via Highways 26 and 127.

Trip note: This is the only campground in a 20-mile circle. It is set along the shore of the Snake River and has a beach. Waterskiing, boating, swimming, and fishing for bass and catfish are all options here.

Site 34
LYON'S FERRY STATE PARK

Campsites, facilities: There are 52 sites for tents, self-contained trailers or motorhomes. Picnic tables and firegrills are provided. Flush toilets, sanitary services, showers and firewood are available. Some facilities are wheelchair accessible. Pets are permitted. Boat docks and launching facilities are nearby.

Reservations, fee: No reservations necessary; $6 fee per night. Open April to late-September.

Who to contact: Phone at 509-646-3252, or write at P.O. Box 217, Starbuck, WA 99359.

Location: This park is located 39 miles west of the town of Pomeroy via Highways 12 and 261.

Trip note: This state park is set at the confluence of the Snake and Palouse Rivers. Fishing, hiking, swimming, waterskiing and boating are all options here. A riding stable is nearby.

Site 35
LYONS FERRY MARINA

Campsites, facilities: There are 25 tent sites and 18 sites for trailers or motorhomes of any length. Picnic tables are provided. Flush toilets, showers, a store, a cafe, laundromat, ice, electricity, piped water and sewer hookups are available. Sanitary services are available within one mile. Pets are permitted. Boat docks and launching facilities are nearby.

Reservations, fee: No reservations necessary; $6 fee per night. Open all year with limited winter facilities.

Who to contact: Phone Corps of Engineers at 509-399-2387, or write at P.O. Box 387, Starbuck, WA 99359.

Location: This park and marina is located 37 miles west of the town of Pomeroy via Highways 12 and 261.

Trip note: The highlight here is eight miles of shoreline access to the Snake River. Unique elements include a 200-foot gorge, basalt bluffs and lava terraces.

Site 36   PALOUSE FALLS STATE PARK

Campsites, facilities: There are 10 primitive campsites for tents, self-contained trailers or motorhomes up to 40 feet long. Picnic tables and firegrills are provided. Pit toilets are available.

Reservations, fee: No reservations necessary; $6 fee per night. Open April to late-September.

Who to contact: Phone at 509-646-3252, or write at Route 3, P.O. Box 99, Pomeroy WA 99347.

Location: This park is located 45 miles west of the town of Pomeroy via Highways 12 and 261.

Trip note: This state park is set at the confluence of the Snake and Palouse Rivers, just enough off the beaten path to be missed by many. Spectacular 190-foot Palouse Falls is worth the trip. A riding stable is nearby.

Site 37   WINDUST

Campsites, facilities: There are 10 primitive tent sites and 10 sites for trailers or motor-homes. Picnic tables and firegrills are provided. Flush toilets and a playground are available. Pets and motorbikes are permitted. Boat docks and launching facilities are nearby.

Reservations, fee: No reservations necessary; no fee. Open all year.

Who to contact: Phone Corps of Engineers at 509-399-2387, or write at P.O. Box 387, Starbuck, WA 99359.

Location: Drive 30 miles northeast of the town of Pasco on Pasco-Kahlotus Road, then head south on Burr Canyon Road for five miles to the campground.

Trip note: This is the only game in town, with no other campgrounds within a 20-mile circle. This campground is set along the shore of Sacajawea Lake near the Lower Monumental Dam on the Snake River. Swimming and fishing are popular.

Site 38   RIVERVIEW TRAVEL TRAILER PARK

Campsites, facilities: There are 10 tent sites and 30 sites for trailers or motorhomes of any length. Electricity, piped water, sewer hookups and picnic tables are provided. Flush toilets, bottled gas, showers, a laundromat and ice are available. A store and cafe are located within one mile. Pets are permitted.

Reservations, fee: Reservations accepted; $10 fee per night. Open April to mid-October.

Who to contact: Phone at 509-382-2064, or write at Route 2, P.O. Box 238, Dayton, WA 99328.

Location: Drive 12 miles north of the town of Dayton on Interstate 12 and you'll see the park entrance.

Trip note: This trailer park is set in a rural area along the Tucannon River. A good side trip is to take Highway 261 north to Palouse Falls State Park. See trip note for campsite 36.

Site 39   LEWIS AND CLARK TRAIL STATE PARK

Campsites, facilities: There are 49 sites for tents or self-enclosed trailers or motorhomes up to 28 feet long. Picnic tables and firegrills are provided. Flush toilets, showers, firewood and sanitary services are available. A store, cafe and ice are located within one mile. Pets are permitted.

Reservations, fee: No reservations necessary; $6 fee per night. Open all year.

Who to contact: Phone at 509-337-6457, or write at Route 1, P.O. Box 90, Dayton, WA 99328.

Location: Drive five miles west of the town of Dayton on Interstate 12 and you'll see the park entrance.

Trip note: If it's getting late and you need a spot, you'd better pick this one. There are no other campgrounds within 20 miles. It is not a bad choice, set along the original Lewis and Clark Trail. During the summer, the rangers offer campfire programs where they share the details of this site's history.

Site 40   FORT WALLA WALLA PARK

Campsites, facilities: There are 49 tent sites and 24 drive-through sites for trailers or motorhomes up to 34 feet long. Piped water and picnic tables are provided. Flush toilets, sanitary services and a playground are available. Electricity, showers and firewood can be obtained for an extra fee. Bottled gas, a store, a cafe, laundromat and ice are located within one mile. Pets are permitted.

Reservations, fee: Reservations accepted; $8 fee per night. Open April to October including limited and some off-season weekends.

Who to contact: Phone at 509-525-3700, or write at Route 5, Box 33-D, Walla Walla, WA 99362.

Location: This part is on the western edge of Walla Walla on Dalles Military Road.

Trip note: How about spending a night in Walla Walla? Well, this is the one spot to consider. The nearest campground (campsite 30) is some 30 miles away. This 200-acre city park has nature and bike trails. A large museum complex adjoins the park. Nearby recreation options include an 18-hole golf course and tennis courts.

Site 41   FISHHOOK PARK

Campsites, facilities: There are 35 tent sites and 41 drive-through sites for trailers or motorhomes of any length. Picnic tables and firegrills are provided. Flush toilets, sanitary services, showers and a playground are available. Some facilities are wheelchair accessible. Pets are permitted. Boat docks and launching facilities are nearby.

Reservations, fee: No reservations necessary; $7 fee per night. Open April to late-September.

Who to contact: Phone Corps of Engineers at 509-547-7781, or write at P.O. Box 2427, Tri-

Cities, WA 99302.

Location: Drive four miles southeast of the town of Pasco on Interstate 395, then go 15 miles northeast on Highway 124. Turn northwest on Page Road and drive four miles to the park.

Trip note: If you are driving along Highway 124 and you need a spot for the night, make the turn on Page Road and check out this park. It is set along the Snake River and has a beach. Fishing, swimming and waterskiing are all options here.

CHARBONNEAU PARK
Site 42   ▲

Campsites, facilities: There are 69 drive-through sites for tents, trailers or motorhomes of any length. Picnic tables and firegrills are provided. Flush toilets, sanitary services, showers, playground, electricity, piped water and sewer hookups are available. Some facilities are wheelchair accessible. Pets are permitted. Boat docks, launching facilities and marine dump station are nearby.

Reservations, fee: No reservations necessary; $8 fee per night. Open all year.

Who to contact: Phone Corps of Engineers at 509-547-7781, or write at P.O. Box 2427, Tri-Cities, WA 99302.

Location: Drive four miles southeast of the town of Pasco on Interstate 395, then go eight miles northeast on Highway 124. Turn north on Sun Harbor Road and drive two miles to the park.

Trip note: This campground is set along the shore of the Snake River, just below Ice Harbor Dam. It has a good swimming beach. Fishing, hunting, swimming and waterskiing are options here.

SCOOTENEY PARK
Site 43   ⊟

Campsites, facilities: There are 21 drive-through sites for trailers or motorhomes of any length. Picnic tables are provided. Flush toilets, showers and playground are available. Pets are permitted. Boat docks and launching facilities are nearby.

Reservations, fee: No reservations necessary; $2 fee per night. Open April to November.

Who to contact: Phone at 509-545-3514, or write at Courthouse, Pasco, WA 99301.

Location: Drive 24 miles north of Pasco on Interstate 395 to the town of Mesa, then go north on Highway 17 for seven miles to the park.

Trip note: This county park is set along the shore of the Scooteney Reservoir, a waterskiing and swimming lake. There are no other campgrounds in the area.

McNARY HABITAT
Site 44   MANAGEMENT AREA   ⛊

Campsites, facilities: There are 24 primitive sites for tents, trailers or motorhomes. No piped water is available. Boat launching facilities are nearby.

Reservations, fee: No reservations necessary; no fee. Open all year.

Who to contact: Phone Department of Game at 509-456-4082, or write at North 8702 Division Street, Spokane, WA 99218.

Location: Drive 10 miles southeast of Pasco on Interstate 395. The area is located between the Snake and the Walla Walla Rivers.

Trip note: A premium spot yet only a 10-minute drive out of Pasco. This area adjoins the McNary National Wildlife Refuge, accessible by foot or horseback. Seven miles of stream frontage along the Columbia River is accessible. Fishing on the adjacent wildlife refuge is good for bass, bluegill, bullhead and carp, and some hunting is allowed in season.

HOOD PARK
Site **45**

Campsites, facilities: There are 69 drive-through sites for tents, trailers or motorhomes of any length. Piped water, firegrills and picnic tables are provided. Flush toilets, sanitary services, showers, electricity and a playground are available. A cafe is available within one mile. Some facilities are wheelchair accessible. Pets are permitted. Boat docks and launching facilities are nearby.

Reservations, fee: No reservations necessary; $8 fee per night. Open April to late-October.

Who to contact: Phone Corps of Engineers at 509-547-7781, or write at P.O. Box 2427, Tri-Cities, WA 99302.

Location: Drive four miles southeast of the town of Pasco on Interstate 395, then head northeast.

Trip note: A more developed, nearby alternative to campsite 44. This park has beach access for swimming and river access for waterskiing. Other recreation options include volleyball and horseshoes. McNary Wildlife Refuge and Sacajawea State Park are nearby.

GREENTREE
RV PARK
Site **46**

Campsites, facilities: There are 70 sites for trailers or motorhomes of any length. Electricity, piped water and sewer hookups are provided. A laundromat and showers are available. Bottled gas, a store, a cafe and ice are located within one mile. Pets and motorbikes are permitted. Boat docks, launching facilities and rentals are nearby.

Reservations, fee: Reservations accepted; $10 fee per night. Open all year.

Who to contact: Phone at 509-547-6220, or write at 2103 North Fifth Avenue, #69, Pasco, WA 99301.

Location: This park is located in Pasco. To get there, take exit 13 off Interstate 182 and you'll see it on the southwest corner.

Trip note: This park is in urban Pasco. Nearby recreation options include an 18-hole golf course, hiking trails, a full service marina and tennis courts. The Franklin County Historical Museum, which is located in town, and the Sacajawea State Park Museum and Interpretive Center, located three miles southeast of town, both offer extensive collections of Indian artifacts.

ARROWHEAD
RV PARK
Site **47**

Campsites, facilities: There are 20 tent sites and 70 drive-through sites for trailers or motorhomes of any length. Electricity, piped water, sewer hookups and picnic tables are provided. Flush toilets, showers, laundromat and ice are available. A store and cafe are located within one mile. Pets and motorbikes are permitted.

Reservations, fee: Reservations accepted; $13 fee per night. Open all year.

Who to contact: Phone at 509-545-8206, or write at 3120 Commercial, Pasco, WA 99301.

Location: This park is located at the east edge of Pasco at 3120 Commercial Street.

Trip note: An OK layover spot in Pasco. See the trip note to campsite 46 for information on Pasco. Nearby recreation options include an 18-hole golf course, a full service marina and tennis courts.

Site **48**
COLUMBIA PARK
CAMPGROUND

Campsites, facilities: There are 22 tent sites and 18 drive-through sites for trailers or motorhomes. Electricity, piped water and picnic tables are provided. Flush toilets, sanitary services, ice and a playground are available. Showers and firewood can be obtained for an extra fee. A store and cafe are located within one mile. Pets and motorbikes are permitted. Boat docks and launching facilities are nearby.

Reservations, fee: Reservations accepted; $8 fee per night. Open mid-April to mid-October.

Who to contact: Phone at 509-783-3711, or write at 6601 SE Columbia, Richland, WA 99352.

Location: This campground is located between Richland and Kennewick. Take the Columbia Center exit north off Interstate 12, and drive one mile east to the campground.

Trip note: The campground is set on the Columbia River, adjacent to Columbia Park. Nearby recreation options include waterskiing on the Columbia River, an 18-hole golf course, hiking trails, marked bike trails and tennis courts. The sun can feel like a branding iron during the summer out here.

Site **49**
DESERT GOLD
RV PARK

Campsites, facilities: There are 84 drive-through sites for trailers or motorhomes of any length in this adult only campground. Electricity, piped water, sewer hookups and picnic tables are provided. Flush toilets, showers, sanitary services, a store, laundromat, ice and swimming pool are available. Bottled gas and a cafe are located within one mile. Pets are permitted. Boat docks and launching facilities are nearby on the Columbia River.

Reservations, fee: Reservations accepted; $10 fee per night. American Express, Master-Card and Visa accepted. Open all year with limited winter facilities.

Who to contact: Phone at 509-627-1000, or write at 611 SE Columbia Drive, Richland, WA 99352.

Location: This park is located in the the town of Richland. Take Columbia Drive west for 300 yards to 611 Columbia Drive SE.

Trip note: This is a nice motorhome park set about a mile from the Columbia River. Nearby recreation options include an 18-hole golf course, hiking trails, a full service marina, tennis courts or a visit to the Department of Energy public information center at the Hanford Science Center.

Site **50**
TRAILER
CITY PARK

Campsites, facilities: There are 100 sites for trailers or motorhomes of any length. Electricity, piped water and sewer hookups are provided. Laundromat and swimming pool are available. Bottled gas, a store, a cafe and ice are located within one mile. Boat docks and launching facilities are nearby.

Reservations, fee: Reservations accepted; $12 fee per night. Open all year.

Who to contact: Phone at 509-783-2513, or write at 7120 W Bonnie, Kennewick, WA 99336.

Location: This park is located in the town of Kennewick. To get there take The Columbia Center Boulevard exit off Highway 12 and go south. Follow the signs.

Trip note: This urban park is near a number of recreation options including an 18-hole golf course, a state park and museum (see trip note to campsite 46), a wildlife refuge (campsite 44), and a full service marina.

Site 51   RIVIERA TRAILER VILLAGE

Campsites, facilities: There are six sites for trailers or motorhomes of any length. Electricity, piped water and sewer hookups are provided. Flush toilets, showers, a recreation hall, laundromat and swimming pool are available. Bottled gas, a store, a cafe and ice are located within one mile. Pets are permitted. Boat docks and launching facilities are nearby.

Reservations, fee: Reservations accepted; $6 fee per night. Open all year.

Who to contact: Phone at 509-547-3521, or write at Lot 90 Riviera, Pasco, WA 99301.

Location: Take the Court Street exit off Interstate 395 in Pasco, turn left on Road 34 and drive to the park.

Trip note: This small motorhome park is located just a half mile from the Columbia River and provides easy access to the highway. See the trip note to campsite 46 for information on some of the sights in Pasco. Nearby recreation options include an 18-hole golf course, marked bike trails, a full service marina and tennis courts.

Site 52   BEACH RV PARK

Campsites, facilities: There are six tent sites and 38 drive-through sites for trailers or motorhomes of any length. Electricity, piped water, sewer hookups and picnic tables are provided. Flush toilets, showers, a laundromat and ice are available. Bottled gas, sanitary services, a store and cafe are located within one mile. Pets and motorbikes are permitted. Boat launching facilities are nearby.

Reservations, fee: Reservations accepted; $13 fee per night. Open all year.

Who to contact: Phone at 509-588-5959, or write at Route 2, Box 2094 C, Benton City, WA 99320.

Location: Take the Benton City exit off Interstate 82 and drive one block north, then turn west on Abby Street to the park.

Trip note: If you are heading west on Highway 182 and it is getting late, you'd best stop here. There is nowhere else to stop for a long stretch. This park is set along the shore of the Yakima River. Nearby recreation options include an 18-hole golf course, a full service marina and tennis courts.

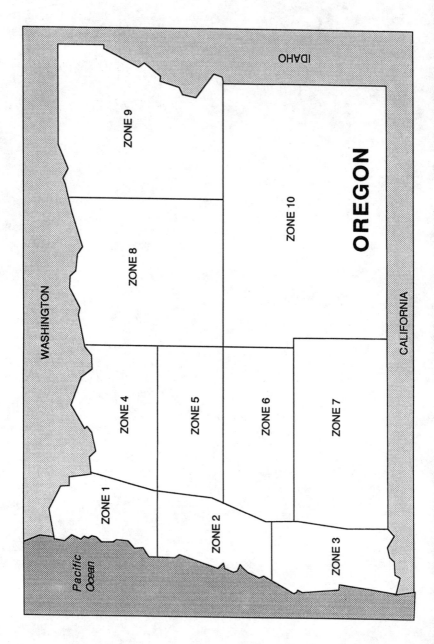

GUIDE TO OREGON CAMPING AREAS

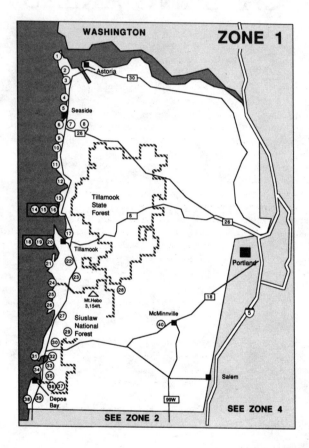

TILLAMOOK

Site 1
FORT STEVENS
STATE PARK

Campsites, facilities: There are 260 tent sites, 343 sites for trailers or motorhomes of any length, and a special camping area for hikers and bicyclists. Electricity, piped water, sewer hookups and picnic tables are provided. Flush toilets, Sanitary services, showers, firewood, a laundromat and playground are available. Some facilities are wheelchair accessible. Pets are permitted. Boat docks and launching facilities are nearby.

Reservations, fee: Reservations accepted; $8 fee per night. Open all year.

Who to contact: Phone at 503-861-1671, or write at Hammond, OR 97121.

Location: From Astoria, cross the Klaskanine River west on Highway 30. Take the Hammond exit and drive four miles to the park.

Trip note: This is a classic spot, set at the northern tip of Oregon, right where the Columbia River enters the Pacific Ocean. This large state park offers five miles of ocean frontage, three miles of Columbia River frontage and several small lakes. Fishing is best out at the point, swimming is best in the small lakes. The park has bike paths, eight miles of hiking trails and the trailhead for the Oregon Coast Trail.

Site 2
KAMPERS WEST
CAMPGROUND

Campsites, facilities: There are 50 tent sites and 200 drive-through sites for trailers or motorhomes of any length. Electricity, piped water and picnic tables are provided. Flush toilets, bottled gas, sanitary services, showers, a laundromat and ice are available. A store and cafe are located within one mile. Pets and motorbikes are permitted.

Reservations, fee: Reservations accepted; $7 fee per night. Open May to October.

Who to contact: Phone at 503-861-1814, or write at 1140 NW Warrenton Drive, Warrenton, OR 97146.

Location: From Gearhart, take US 101 north to Warrenton Drive exit. Go north on Warrenton Drive to the park, located at 1140 NW Warrenton Drive.

Trip note: Located just four miles from Fort Stevens State Park. This is a privately run site and offers full RV services. Nearby recreation options include an 18-hole golf course, hiking trails, marked bike trails and a riding stable.

Site 3   NEACOXIE LAKE TRAILER PARK

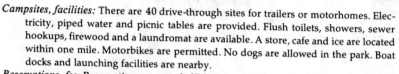

Campsites, facilities: There are 40 drive-through sites for trailers or motorhomes. Electricity, piped water and picnic tables are provided. Flush toilets, showers, sewer hookups, firewood and a laundromat are available. A store, cafe and ice are located within one mile. Motorbikes are permitted. No dogs are allowed in the park. Boat docks and launching facilities are nearby.

Reservations, fee: Reservations accepted; $7 fee per night. Open all year.

Who to contact: Phone at 503-861-3921, or write at P.O. Box 776, Warrenton, OR 97146.

Location: From Warrenton, drive four miles south on US 101. At Sunset Beach Road, drive west for 1/2 mile to the park.

Trip note: This campground is set along the shore of Neacoxie Lake, but is also just a half mile from the ocean. The lake is 3 1/2 miles long and is stocked with trout and a stable perch population. Nearby recreation options include an 18-hole golf course and a riding stable.

Site 4   BUD'S CAMPGROUND

Campsites, facilities: There are 25 sites for trailers or motorhomes of any length. Electricity, piped water, sewer hookups and picnic tables are provided. Flush toilets, showers, a store, laundromat and ice are available. Bottled gas and cafe are located within one mile. Pets and motorbikes are permitted. Boat docks, launching facilities and rentals are nearby.

Reservations, fee: Reservations accepted; $7 fee per night. Open all year.

Who to contact: Phone at 503-738-6855, or write at P.O. Box 2525,, Gearhart, OR 97138.

Location: From Gearhart, drive one mile north on US 101 and you'll see the campground entrance.

Trip note: This private campground is set along the ocean, about four miles north of the town of Seaside (see trip notes to campsites 5 and 6). Nearby recreation options include an 18-hole golf course, hiking trails and a riding stable.

Site 5   PINE COVE RV PARK

Campsites, facilities: There are 23 tent sites and 21 sites for trailers or motorhomes of any length. Electricity, piped water and sewer hookups are provided. Flush toilets, showers, a laundromat, firewood and playground are available. A store, cafe and ice are located within one mile. Pets are permitted.

Reservations, fee: Reservations accepted; $12 fee per night. MasterCard and Visa accepted. Open all year.

Who to contact: Phone at 503-738-5243, or write at 2481 Highway 101 N, Seaside, OR 97138.

Location: Take US 101 to Seaside. Go north about one mile past Seaside on US 101. The park is located at 2481 Highway 101 North.

Trip note: This park and motel is set among the pines about a mile from the town of Seaside. It is a good spot for fishing, both in the ocean and in the two rivers that run through town, where you can fish from the bridges. Crabbing is good on calm spring days in the ocean. Nearby recreation options include an 18-hole golf course and hiking trails. See trip note for campsite 6 for more information about Seaside.

Site **6**
VENICE
RV PARK

Campsites, facilities: There are 26 drive-through sites for trailers or motorhomes of any length. Electricity, piped water, sewer hookups and picnic tables are provided. Flush toilets, bottled gas, showers, a laundromat and ice are available. A store and cafe are located within one mile. Pets are permitted.

Reservations, fee: Reservations accepted; $12 fee per night. Open all year.

Who to contact: Phone at 503-738-8851, or write at 1032-24th Avenue, Seaside, OR 97138.

Location: Take US 101 to the north end of the town of Seaside, turn on 24th Avenue and drive to the campground at 1032-24th Avenue.

Trip note: This park is set along the Neawanna River, one of two rivers that run through the town of Seaside. Seaside offers beautiful ocean beaches for fishing and surfing, moped and bike rentals, shops and a theatre. The city has provided swings and volleyball nets on the beach. An 18-hole golf course is available nearby.

Site **7**
RIVERSIDE LAKE RV
AND TRAILER PARK

Campsites, facilities: There are eight tent sites and 37 drive-through sites for trailers or motorhomes of any length. Electricity, piped water and picnic tables are provided. Flush toilets, showers, firewood, a laundromat and ice are available. Sewer hookups can be obtained for an extra fee. Bottled gas, sanitary services, a store and cafe are located within one mile. Pets and motorbikes are permitted. Boat launching facilities are nearby.

Reservations, fee: Reservations accepted; $9 fee per night. Open all year.

Who to contact: Phone at 503-738-6779, or write at Hamlet Route, Box 255, Seaside, OR 97138.

Location: From Seaside, go 1 1/2 miles south on US 101, then follow the signs to the park. It is just north of the junction of Highway 26 and US 101.

Trip note: This park is set along the shore of the Necanicum River, which attracts a steelhead run every winter. It is low during the summer but provides many pools for swimming, and boating is allowed. There is a small scenic lake in the campground that attracts wildlife. No swimming or boating is allowed in the lake, but it is stocked with trout, a program that began in 1988. Nearby recreation options include an 18-hole golf course and a riding stable.

Site **8**
SADDLE MOUNTAIN
STATE PARK

Campsites, facilities: There are nine primitive tent sites. Picnic tables are provided. Flush toilets and firewood are available. Pets are permitted.

Reservations, fee: No reservations necessary; $6 fee per night. Open mid-April to late-October.

Who to contact: Phone at 503-861-1671, or write at Cannon Beach, OR 97110.

Location: From Cannon Beach, go nine miles east on US 26, then eight miles northeast on the entrance road to the park.

Trip note: This is a good alternative to the many beach front parks in Zone 3. A three-mile trail climbs to the top of Saddle Mountain, a great lookout on clear days. This park is a real find for the naturalist interested in rare and unusual varieties of plants, many of which have evolved along the slopes of this isolated mountain.

Site 9   RV RESORT AT CANNON BEACH

Campsites, facilities: There are 100 drive-through sites for trailers or motorhomes of any length. Electricity, piped water, sewer hookups and picnic tables are provided. Flush toilets, bottled gas, showers, firewood, recreation hall, a store, cafe, laundromat, ice, playground and swimming pool are available. Pets are permitted.

Reservations, fee: Reservations accepted; $20 fee per night. American Express, Master-Card and Visa accepted. Open all year.

Who to contact: Phone at 503-436-2231, or write at P.O. Box 219, Cannon Beach, OR 97110.

Location: Driving north on Highway 101, take the third exit for Cannon Beach and you'll see the signs for the resort.

Trip note: This private resort is located about seven blocks from one of the nicest beaches in the region. From Cannon Beach you can walk for miles in either direction. Just two miles north is Ecola State Park. Nearby recreation options include marked bike trails, a riding stable and tennis courts.

Site 10   WRIGHT'S FOR CAMPING

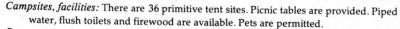

Campsites, facilities: There are 10 tent sites and eight sites for trailers or motorhomes. Electricity and piped water are provided. Flush toilets, bottled gas and showers are available. A store, cafe, laundromat and ice are available within one mile. Pets and motorbikes are permitted.

Reservations, fee: Reservations accepted; $7 fee per night. Open late-June to early-September.

Who to contact: Phone at 503-436-2347, or write at P.O. Box 213, Cannon Beach, OR 97110.

Location: From the town of Cannon Beach, take US 101 south for one mile and follow signs to the campground.

Trip note: This camp provides a more rustic setting than some of the more developed motorhome parks in the region. It is set close to the ocean and vast beachs of the area. Nearby recreation options include hiking trails and marked bike trails.

Site 11   OSWALD WEST STATE PARK

Campsites, facilities: There are 36 primitive tent sites. Picnic tables are provided. Piped water, flush toilets and firewood are available. Pets are permitted.

Reservations, fee: No reservations necessary; $5 fee per night. Open mid-March to late-October.

Who to contact: Phone at 503-368-5943, or write at 8300 3rd Street, Nehalem, OR 97130.

Location: This park is located 10 miles south of the town of Cannon Beach on US 101.

Trip note: This state park is set along a dramatic section of the Oregon Coast, with rugged cliffs rising high above the ocean. This is not beach-walking territory, but the park does offer 15 miles of hiking trails, including the Oregon Coast Trail, a small beach, and several fishing streams.

Site 12 — NEHALEM BAY STATE PARK

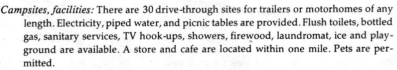

Campsites, facilities: There are 292 sites for trailers or motorhomes of any length, and a special camping area for hikers and bicyclists. Electricity, piped water and picnic tables are provided. Flush toilets, sanitary services, showers, firewood and a laundromat are available. Some facilities are wheelchair accessible. Pets are permitted. Boat launching facilities are located nearby on Nehalem Bay.

Reservations, fee: No reservations necessary; $7 fee per night. Open mid-April to late-October.

Who to contact: Phone at 503-368-5943, or write at 8300 3rd Street, Nehalem, OR 97131.

Location: From Cannon Beach, drive 17 miles south on US 101 to Nehalem, then head west on the entrance road for 1 1/2 miles to the park.

Trip note: This state park is located on a sandy point that separates the Pacific Ocean and Nehalem Bay. It offers six miles of beach frontage. The Oregon Coast Trail passes through the park.

Site 13 — JETTY FISHERY RV PARK

Campsites, facilities: There are six tent sites and 30 drive-through sites for trailers or motorhomes of any length. Electricity, piped water and picnic tables are provided. Flush toilets, bottled gas, firewood, a store, showers, cafe and ice are available. Pets are permitted. Boat docks, launching facilities and rentals are nearby.

Reservations, fee: Reservations accepted; $7 fee per night. MasterCard and Visa accepted. Open all year.

Who to contact: Phone at 503-368-5746, or write at 27550 Highway 101 North, Rockaway, OR 97136.

Location: From Rockaway, drive three miles north on US 101 and you will see the park entrance.

Trip note: This small park is located at the base of a mile-long jetty, which extends out into Nehalem Bay and the ocean. Fishing and crabbing are good off the jetty, but sometimes the snags bite good too. There is a small beach on the bay side of the jetty, a popular spot for kids. For boaters, a full-service marina is nearby.

Site 14 — SHOREWOOD TRAVEL TRAILER VILLAGE

Campsites, facilities: There are 30 drive-through sites for trailers or motorhomes of any length. Electricity, piped water, and picnic tables are provided. Flush toilets, bottled gas, sanitary services, TV hook-ups, showers, firewood, laundromat, ice and playground are available. A store and cafe are located within one mile. Pets are permitted.

Reservations, fee: Reservations accepted; $9 fee per night. Open all year.

Who to contact: Phone at 503-355-2278, or write at 17600 Ocean Boulevard, Rockaway, OR 97136.

Location: From Rockaway, travel two miles south on US 101, then west on Watesco Road to Pacific. Go south on Pacific, then west on Third, and south on Ocean Boulevard to the trailer park.

Trip note: This park is set along a beach that is ideal for surf fishing for perch or beach-combing during low tides. A good side trip is the 1 1/2-mile hike to Tillamook Bay jetty. An 18-hole golf course is located a short drive from the park.

Site 15   BARVIEW JETTY COUNTY PARK   ▲

Campsites, facilities: There are 200 tent sites and 40 drive-through sites for trailers or motorhomes of any length. Electricity, piped water, sewer hookups and picnic tables are provided. Flush toilets, sanitary services, showers and a playground are available. Bottled gas, a store, cafe and ice are located within one mile. Pets are permitted.

Reservations, fee: Reservations accepted; $9 fee per night. Open all year.

Who to contact: Phone at 503-322-3522, or write at PO Box 633, Garibaldi, OR 97118.

Location: From the town of Garibaldi, go two miles north on US 101, then 1/4 mile west to campground.

Trip note: This park is near the beach, yet set in a wooded area. Nearby recreation options include an 18-hole golf course, hiking trails, bike trails and a full service marina.

Site 16   BIAK BY THE SEA TRAILER COURT   🚍

Campsites, facilities: There are three tent sites and 45 drive-through sites for trailers or motorhomes of any length. Electricity, piped water and sewer hookups are provided. Flush toilets, showers and a laundromat are available. Bottled gas, a store, cafe and ice are located within one mile. Pets and motorbikes are permitted. Boat docks, launching facilities and rentals are nearby.

Reservations, fee: Reservations accepted; $7 fee per night; MasterCard and Visa accepted. Open all year.

Who to contact: Phone at 503-322-3200, or write at Box 507, Garibaldi, OR 97118.

Location: This trailer park is located at the northern edge of the town of Garibaldi on Fisherman's Wharf.

Trip note: This park is set along the shore of Tillamook Bay, where deep sea fishing, crabbing, clamming, surf fishing, scuba diving and beachcombing make it a prime retreat. The nearby town of Tillamook offers a cheese factory and a historical museum. A good side trip is to Cape Meares State Park, where you can hike through a national wildlife preserve and see where the seabirds nest along the cliffs.

Site 17   PACIFIC CAMPGROUND AND OVERNIGHT TRAILER PARK   🚍

Campsites, facilities: There are 20 tent sites and 28 drive-through sites for trailers or motorhomes of any length. Electricity, piped water, sewer hookups and picnic tables are provided. Flush toilets, bottled gas, showers, firewood and ice are available. A store and cafe are located within one mile. Pets and motorbikes are permitted.

Reservations, fee: Reservations accepted; $9 fee per night. Open all year.

Who to contact: Phone at 503-842-5201, or write at 1950 Suppress North, Tillamook, OR 97141.

Location: From Tillamook, drive 2 1/2 miles north on US 101 and you'll see the campground entrance.

Trip note: This campground is set at the southern end of Tillamook Bay, not far from the Wilson River. The Tillamook Cheese Factory is just south of the park, and an 18-hole golf course is also nearby. See the trip note to campsite 16 for more information about the area.

Site **18**
HAPPY CAMP
RESORT

Campsites, facilities: There are 30 tent sites and 40 drive-through sites for trailers or motorhomes of any length. Electricity, piped water and picnic tables are provided. Flush toilets, bottled gas, sanitary services, showers, firewood, a store, sewer hook-ups, cafe, laundromat, ice and playground are available. Pets are permitted. Boat docks, launching facilities and rentals are nearby.

Reservations, fee: Reservations accepted; $7 fee per night. Open all year.

Who to contact: Phone at 503-842-4012, or write at Box 52, Netarts, OR 97143.

Location: From Tillamook, drive seven miles west on Netarts Highway and you'll see the campground entrance.

Trip note: Netarts Bay offers sheltered waters, perfect for small boaters to take advantage of excellent crabbing. Shoreliners can discover good crabbing and fair perch fishing. Crabbing gear, boat rentals, and crab cooking are available. The camp is set along the shore of Netarts Bay, a short drive from Cape Lookout State Park (campsite 21) and Cape Meares State Park and National Wildlife Refuge (campsite 16).

Site **19**
BIG SPRUCE
TRAILER PARK

Campsites, facilities: There are 23 drive-through sites for trailers or motorhomes of any length. Electricity, piped water, sewer hookups and picnic tables are provided. Flush toilets, bottled gas, showers and laundromat are available. Store, cafe and ice are located within one mile. Pets are permitted. Boat docks and launching facilities are nearby.

Reservations, fee: Reservations accepted; $9 fee per night. Open all year.

Who to contact: Phone at 503-842-7443, or write at 4850 Netarts Highway, Tillamook, OR 97141.

Location: From Tillamook, go 6 1/2 miles west on Cape Lookout-Netarts Highway.

Trip note: This trailer park is one block from the boat launch on Netarts Bay. See trip note to campsite 18 for details on the fishing here.

Site **20**
BAY SHORE
RV PARK

Campsites, facilities: There are five tent sites and 54 drive-through sites for trailers or motorhomes of any length. Electricity, piped water, sewer hookups and picnic tables are provided. Flush toilets, bottled gas, showers, firewood, a recreation hall, laundromat and ice are available. A store and cafe are located within one mile. Pets are permitted. Boat docks, launching facilities and rentals are nearby.

Reservations, fee: Reservations accepted; $9 fee per night. MasterCard and Visa accepted. Open all year.

Who to contact: Phone at 503-842-7774, or write at P.O. Box 218, Netarts, OR 97413.

Location: From US 101 in the town of Tillamook, go six miles west on Cape-Lookout-Netarts Highway and you will see the park entrance.

Trip note: One of three camps set on the east shore of Netarts Bay. See the trip note to campsite 18 for more information about the fishing here.

Site **21**
CAPE LOOKOUT
STATE PARK

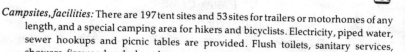

Campsites, facilities: There are 197 tent sites and 53 sites for trailers or motorhomes of any length, and a special camping area for hikers and bicyclists. Electricity, piped water, sewer hookups and picnic tables are provided. Flush toilets, sanitary services, showers, firewood and a laundromat are available. A cafe is located within one mile. Some facilities are wheelchair accessible. Pets are permitted.

Reservations, fee: Reservations accepted; $8 fee per night. Open all year.

Who to contact: Phone at 503-842-4981, or write at 13000 Whiskey Creek Road West, Tillamook, OR 97141.

Location: From Tillamook, travel 11 miles southwest on Netarts Road and you'll see the park entrance.

Trip note: This is unique park that offers a variety of walks. One trail leads out along a ridge to headlands high above the ocean. Another walk will take you out through a variety of estuarine habitats along the five-mile sand spit that extends between the ocean and Netarts Bay.

Site **22**
KOA TILLAMOOK

Campsites, facilities: There are 12 tent sites and 71 drive-through sites for trailers or motorhomes of any length. Piped water and picnic tables are provided. Flush toilets, bottled gas, sanitary services, showers, firewood, recreation hall, electricity, sewer hookups, a store, laundromat, ice and playground are available. Pets are permitted.

Reservations, fee: Reservations accepted; $10 fee per night. MasterCard and Visa accepted. Open all year.

Who to contact: Phone at 503-842-4779, or write at 11880 Highway 101 South, Tillamook, OR 97141.

Location: From Tillamook, drive six miles south on Highway 101 and you'll see the campground entrance.

Trip note: This campground is set along the Tillamook River. Boat launching facilities are available nearby.

Site **23**
CAMPER COVE
PARK

Campsites, facilities: There are two tent sites and 15 drive-through sites for trailers or motorhomes up to 31 feet long. Electricity, piped water, sewer hookups and picnic tables are provided. Flush toilets, bottled gas, sanitary services, showers, firewood, a recreation hall, laundromat and ice are available. Pets are permitted.

Reservations, fee: Reservations accepted; $10 fee per night. Open April to late-February.

Who to contact: Phone at 503-398-5334, or write at Box 42, Beaver, OR 97108.

Location: From Beaver, go 2 1/2 miles north on US 101 and you will see the park entrance.

Trip note: This small, wooded campground is set along Beaver Creek, set far enough off the highway to provide quiet. The park can be used as a base camp for fishermen, with steelhead and salmon fishing in season in the nearby Nestucca River.

SAND BEACH
Site 24

Campsites, facilities: There are 101 sites for tents, trailers or motorhomes up to 30 feet long. Picnic tables and firegrills are provided. Piped water, flush toilets and sanitary services are available. Pets are permitted. Boat docks are nearby.

Reservations, fee: No reservations necessary; $7 fee per night. Open mid-May to early-September.

Who to contact: Phone Siuslaw National Forest at 503-392-3161, or write at Hebo Ranger District, Hebo, OR 97122.

Location: From Pacific City, travel 1/4 mile west on County Road 536, then head north on County Road 535 for 8 1/4 miles, turn west on County Road 503 and drive one mile, and turn southwest on Forest Service Road S3001 and drive 1 3/4 miles to the campground.

Trip note: This area is known for its large sand dunes, which are open to off-road vehicles. The campground is set along the shore of Sand Lake, which is actually more like an estuary—the ocean is just around the bend.

CAPE KIWANDA
RV PARK
Site 25

Campsites, facilities: There are 20 tent sites and 130 drive-through sites for trailers or motorhomes of any length. Electricity, piped water, sewer hookups and picnic tables are provided. Flush toilets, sanitary services, showers, firewood, a recreation hall, laundromat and playground are available. Bottled gas, a store, cafe and ice are located within one mile. Pets and motorbikes are permitted. Boat docks, launching facilities and rentals are nearby.

Reservations, fee: Reservations accepted; $9 fee per night. Open all year.

Who to contact: Phone at 503-965-6230, or write at Box 129, Pacific City, OR 97135.

Location: In Pacific City, drive three miles west on Pacific City Loop Road, then cross the bridge and travel one mile north and you'll see the park entrance.

Trip note: This park is set along the ocean, a short distance from Cape Kiwanda State Park, which is open for day-use only. There is a boat launch there and hiking trails that lead out to the cape. A recreation option is four miles south at Nestucca Spit, where there is another day-use park. The point extends about three miles and is a good spot for birdwatching.

RAINES RESORT
AND RV PARK
Site 26

Campsites, facilities: There are five tent sites and 12 sites for trailers or motorhomes of any length. Electricity, piped water, sewer hookups and picnic tables are provided. Flush toilets, sanitary services, showers, a store and laundromat are available. Bottled gas, a cafe and ice are located within one mile. Pets and motorbikes are permitted. Boat docks, launching facilities and rentals are nearby.

Reservations, fee: Reservations accepted; $8 fee per night. MasterCard and Visa accepted. Open all year.

Who to contact: Phone at 503-965-6371, or write at P.O. Box 399, Pacific City, OR 97135.

Location: From Pacific City, drive 1 1/2 miles north on Brooten Road, then one block west on Woods Bridge and you'll see the campground entrance.

Trip note: This campground is set along the Nestucca River, which attracts a king salmon run from late August through Thanksgiving. Nearby recreation options include a full service marina.

HEBO LAKE
Site **27**

Campsites, facilities: There are 16 tent sites and six sites for trailers or motorhomes up to 16 feet long. Picnic tables and firegrills are provided. Piped water, vault toilets and firewood are available. A store, cafe and ice are located within five miles. Pets are permitted. Boat docks are nearby.

Reservations, fee: No reservations necessary; $4 fee per night. Open mid-April to mid-October.

Who to contact: Phone Siuslaw National Forest at 503-392-3161, or write at Hebo Ranger District, Hebo, OR 97122.

Location: From Hebo, drive one mile north on US 101, then three miles southeast on Highway 22 to Forest Service Road 14. From there, go east for five miles to the campground.

Trip note: This Forest Service campground is set along the shore of little Hebo Lake. This is a secluded campground where the campsites are nestled under trees. There is a shaded group area with tables and a large barbeque. A nearby trail leads eight miles to South Lake in the backcountry.

ROCKY BEND
Site **28**

Campsites, facilities: There are seven tent sites. Picnic tables and firegrills are provided. Vault toilets and piped water are available. Pets are permitted.

Reservations, fee: No reservations necessary; no fee. Open mid-April to mid-October.

Who to contact: Phone Siuslaw National Forest at 503-392-3161, or write at Hebo Ranger District, Hebo, OR 97122.

Location: Just north of Beaver, turn east on County Road 858 and drive 15 1/2 miles to the campground.

Trip note: This campground is set along the Nestucca River, a little-known, secluded spot that provides a guarantee for peace and quiet.

CASTLE ROCK
Site **29**

Campsites, facilities: There are four sites for trailers or motorhomes up to 16 feet long. Picnic tables are provided and pit toilets are available, but there is no piped water.

Reservations, fee: No reservations necessary; no fee. Open all year.

Who to contact: Phone Siuslaw National Forest at 503-392-3161, or write at Hebo Ranger District, Hebo, OR 97122.

Location: This campground is located about four miles south of the town of Hebo on Highway 22.

Trip note: This tiny spot provides an alternative for motorhome drivers to the large beachfront RV parks popular on the Oregon coast. It is set along Three Rivers.

NESKOWIN CREEK

Site 30

Campsites, facilities: There are 12 primitive tent sites. Picnic tables and firegrills are provided. Pit toilets are available, but there is no piped water. Pets are permitted.
Reservations, fee: No reservations necessary; no fee. Open mid-April to mid-October.
Who to contact: Phone Siuslaw National Forest at 503-392-3161, or write at Hebo Ranger District, Hebo, OR 97122.
Location: From the town of Neskowin, go 1 1/2 miles south on US 101, then 4 1/2 miles southeast on County Road 12. From there, travel about 100 yards west on Forest Service Road 12131 and you'll see the campground.
Trip note: This campground is set along Neskowin Creek, in the Cascade Head Scenic Area, a rustic setting. If you take Forest Service Road 1861 west from camp for five miles, you will come to a trailhead which provides hiking access west to the coast. See a Forest Service map for details.

KOA LINCOLN CREEK

Site 31

Campsites, facilities: There are 41 tent sites and 45 drive-through sites for trailers or motorhomes of any length. Picnic tables are provided. Flush toilets, bottled gas, sanitary services, showers, firewood, recreation hall, a store, cafe, laundromat, ice and playground are available. Electricity, piped water, sewer, and cable TV hookups are available for an extra fee. Pets and motorbikes are permitted. Boat launching facilities are nearby.
Reservations, fee: Reservations required; $8 fee per night. MasterCard and Visa accepted. Open all year.
Who to contact: Phone at 503-994-2961, or write at Park Lane, Route 2, Box 255, Otis, OR 97368.
Location: From Lincoln City, go 1 1/4 mile north on US 101, then one mile east on East Devil's Lake Road and you're there.
Trip note: This area offers opportunity for beachcombing, tidepooling and fishing along a seven-mile stretch of beach. Two stops to consider if you're going into Lincoln City for supplies: the Premier Market, which has smoked salmon, and the Colonial Bakery, for the best pastries west of Paris. Nearby recreation options include an 18-hole golf course and tennis courts.

DEVIL'S LAKE STATE PARK

Site 32

Campsites, facilities: There are 68 tent sites and 32 sites for trailers or motorhomes of any length. Electricity, piped water, sewer hookups and picnic tables are provided. Flush toilets, showers, firewood, a store, cafe, laundromat and ice are available. Some facilities are wheelchair accessible. Pets are permitted. Boat docks and launching facilities are nearby.
Reservations, fee: Reservations accepted; $8 fee per night. Open mid-April to late-October.
Who to contact: Phone at 503-994-2002, or write at 1542 Northeast 6th,, Lincoln City, OR 97367.
Location: This park is in Lincoln City, just off US 101.

Trip note: A take-your-pick deal. At Devil's Lake, you can swim, fish or water ski. An alternative is to head west and explore the seven miles of beaches. Lincoln City also has a number of art and craft galleries in town.

Site 33
TREE N' SEA
TRAILER PARK

Campsites, facilities: There are seven sites for trailers or motorhomes of any length. Electricity, piped water and sewer hookups are provided. Flush toilets and showers are available. A store, cafe and laundromat are available within one mile. Pets are permitted.

Reservations, fee: Reservations accepted; $10 fee per night. Open all year.

Who to contact: Phone at 503-996-3801, or write at 1015 South 51st Street, Lincoln City, OR 97367.

Location: In Lincoln City, turn west off of US 101 onto Southwest 51st Street and drive one block to the park.

Trip note: This park is set along the ocean in the town of Lincoln City. See the trip notes to campsites 31 and 32 for recreation options.

Site 34
COYOTE ROCK
RV PARK

Campsites, facilities: There are eight tent sites and 50 sites for trailers or motorhomes of any length. Electricity, piped water, sewer hookups and picnic tables are provided. Flush toilets, bottled gas, showers, ice and a playground are available. Firewood is available for an extra fee. Pets are permitted. Boat docks, launching facilities and rentals are nearby.

Reservations, fee: Reservations accepted; $10 fee per night. MasterCard and Visa accepted. Open all year.

Who to contact: Phone at 503-996-3436, or write at Kernville Box 299, Lincoln City, OR 97367.

Location: From Lincoln City, travel two miles south on US 101, then two miles east on Highway 229 and you will see the park entrance.

Trip note: This park is set along the shore of the Siletz River, about two miles from where it pours into Siletz Bay. Nearby recreation options include marked bike trails.

Site 35
SPORTSMAN'S LANDING
RV PARK

Campsites, facilities: There are 30 sites for trailers or motorhomes of any length. Electricity, piped water and sewer hookups are provided. Flush toilets, bottled gas, sanitary services, showers, a store, cafe, laundromat, ice and playground are available. Pets are permitted. Boat docks, launching facilities and rentals are nearby.

Reservations, fee: Reservations accepted; $7 fee per night; MasterCard and Visa accepted. Open all year.

Who to contact: Phone at 503-996-4225, or write at Kernville Route, Lincoln City, OR 97367.

Location: From Lincoln City, go two miles south on US 101, then four miles east on Highway 229 and you'll see the park entrance.

Trip note: This area offers a number of back country trips. The park is set along the shore of the Siletz River—and if you head farther east on Highway 229, you will discover several Forest Service Roads that lead into the Siuslaw National Forest and provide access to a number of creeks. See a Forest Service map for details.

HOLIDAY HILLS

Site **36**

Campsites, facilities: There are 22 sites for trailers or motorhomes of any length. Electricity, piped water, sewer hookups and picnic tables are provided. Flush toilets, sanitary services, showers, laundromat and a playground are available. Bottled gas, a store, cafe and ice are located within one mile. Pets and motorbikes are permitted.
Reservations, fee: Reservations accepted; $11 fee per night. Open all year.
Who to contact: Phone at 503-764-2430, or write at HC63, Box 77, Depoe Bay, OR 97341.
Location: From Depoe Bay, travel four miles north on US 101 and you will see the entrance.
Trip note: A prime side trip is to Fogerty Creek State Park, just two miles away. It offers beach access, wooded hiking trails and fishing in Fogerty Creek. An 18-hole golf course is nearby.

SEA AND SAND
OVERNIGHT PARK

Site **37**

Campsites, facilities: There are 85 drive-through sites for trailers or motorhomes of any length. Electricity, piped water, sewer hookups and picnic tables are provided. Flush toilets, showers, sanitary services, firewood and laundromat are available. Store, cafe and ice are located within one mile. Pets are permitted.
Reservations, fee: Reservations accepted; $13 fee per night. Open all year.
Who to contact: Phone at 503-764-2313, or write at HC63, Box 79, Depoe Bay, OR 97341.
Location: From Depoe Bay, drive four miles north on US 101 and you'll see the campground entrance.
Trip note: Beachcombing is popular at this park, set near the ocean near Gleneden Beach on Siletz Bay. The Siltetz River and numerous small creeks are in the area.

BOILER BAY
TRAILER PARK

Site **38**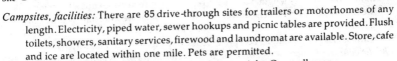

Campsites, facilities: There are 12 drive-through sites for trailers or motorhomes of any length. Electricity, piped water, sewer hookups and picnic tables are provided. Flush toilets, showers, a laundromat and playground are available. Bottled gas, sanitary services, a store, cafe and ice are located within one mile. Pets and motorbikes are permitted. Boat docks, launching facilities and rentals are nearby.
Reservations, fee: No reservations necessary; $7 fee per night. Open all year.
Who to contact: Phone at 503-765-2548, or write at HC 63 Box 7, Depoe Bay, OR 97341.
Location: From Depoe Bay, drive 1 1/2 miles north on US 101 and you will see the park entrance.
Trip note: This camp is set near a local landmark, the Boiler Bay Wayside—where the water spouts through the blowholes and over the road during storms or high tides. Fogerty Creek State Park is also nearby. Nearby recreation options include marked bike trails and a full-service marina.

Site 39

HOLIDAY
RV PARK

Campsites, facilities: There are 110 drive-through sites for trailers or motorhomes of any length. Electricity, piped water, sewer hookups and picnic tables are provided. Flush toilets, bottled gas, showers, recreation hall, a store, cafe, laundromat, ice, playground and swimming pool are available. Pets are permitted.

Reservations, fee: Reservations accepted; $14 fee per night. MasterCard and Visa accepted. Open all year.

Who to contact: Phone at 503-765-2302, or write at P.O. Box 433, Depoe Bay, OR 97341.

Location: This park is located on US 101 at the north edge of town in Depoe Bay.

Trip note: This is a scenic stretch of coastline and some of the prime side trips include Depoe State Park and Depoe Creek. Nearby recreation options include an 18-hole golf course, tennis courts and a public aquarium.

Site 40

MULKEY O
RV PARK

Campsites, facilities: There are 50 tent sites and 27 drive-through sites for trailers or motorhomes of any length. Electricity, piped water, sewer hookups and picnic tables are provided. Flush toilets, showers and a laundromat are available. Pets and motorbikes are permitted.

Reservations, fee: Reservations accepted; $8 fee per night. Open all year.

Who to contact: Phone at 503-472-2475, or write at 13901 Southwest Highway 18, McMinnville, OR 97128.

Location: From McMinnville, travel 3 1/2 miles southwest on Highway 18 and you will see the park entrance.

Trip note: If you are in the area and looking for a camping spot, you had best stop here — there are no other campgrounds within 30 miles. This wooded park is set near the South Yamhill River. Nearby recreation options include an 18-hole golf course, tennis courts and the Western Deer Park and Arboretum, which has a playground.

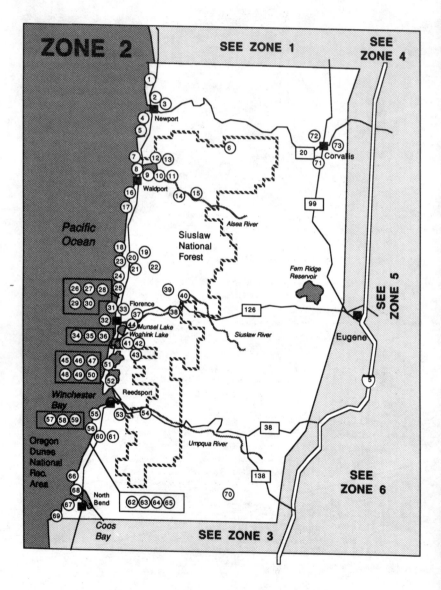

UMPQUA

BEVERLY BEACH
STATE PARK

Campsites, facilities: There are 152 tent sites, 127 sites for trailers or motorhomes of any
   length, and a special camping area reserved for hikers and bicyclists. Picnic tables and
   firegrills are provided. Piped water, flush toilets, showers, sanitary dump facilities,
   electricity, water and sewer hookups are available. There is a cafe in the park. Some
   facilities are wheelchair accessible. Pets and motorbikes are permitted.
Reservations, fee: Reservations accepted; $8 fee per night. Open all year.
Who to contact: Phone at 503-265-7655, or write at Star Route North, Box 684, Newport,
   OR 97365.
Location: From Newport, go seven miles north on US 101 and you'll see the park
   entrance.
Trip note: This beautiful campground is set in a wooded, grassy area on the east side of US
   101; like magic, you walk through a tunnel under the roadway and emerge on the
   beach. Just a mile to the north is a small, day-use state park called Devil's Punchbowl,
   so-called because of the the unusual bowl-shaped rock formation which has caverns
   under it where the waves rumble about. For some great ocean views, head north one
   more mile to the Otter Crest Wayside.

AGATE BEACH TRAILER
AND RV PARK

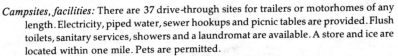

Campsites, facilities: There are 37 drive-through sites for trailers or motorhomes of any
   length. Electricity, piped water, sewer hookups and picnic tables are provided. Flush
   toilets, sanitary services, showers and a laundromat are available. A store and ice are
   located within one mile. Pets are permitted.
Reservations, fee: Reservations accepted; $10 fee per night. Open all year.
Who to contact: Phone at 503-265-7670, or write at 6138 North Coast Highway, Newport,
   OR 97365.
Location: In Newport, off US 101 at the north end of town.
Trip note: This park is a short distance from Agate Beach Wayside, a small state park with
   beach access. Agate hunting can be good. Sometimes the agates are covered by a layer
   of sand and you have to dig a bit. But other times wave action will clear the sand,
   unveiling the agates at low tides.

Site 3
HARBOR VILLAGE
RV PARK

Campsites, facilities: There are 140 sites for trailers or motorhomes of any length. Electricity, piped water, sewer hookups and picnic tables are provided. Flush toilets, showers, a laundromat and ice are available. Bottled gas, a store and cafe are located within one mile. Boat docks, launching facilities and rentals are nearby.

Reservations, fee: Reservations accepted; $9 fee per night. MasterCard and Visa accepted. Open all year.

Who to contact: Phone at 503-265-5088, or write at 923 Southeast Bay Boulevard, Box 6, Newport, OR 97365.

Location: From Newport, go east 1/2 mile on US 20, then 1/2 mile south on John Moore Road to the bay, and turn left and you'll see the entrance to the trailer park.

Trip note: This park is set right along the shore of Yaquina Bay. See the trip note to campsite 4 for information on attractions in the town of Newport. Nearby recreation options include an 18-hole golf course, hiking trails and a full service marina.

Site 4
SOUTH BEACH MARINA
AND RV PARK

Campsites, facilities: There are 38 sites for trailers or motorhomes. Electricity, piped water and sewer hookups are provided. Flush toilets, showers, a store, cafe, laundromat, ice and playground are available. Pets and motorbikes are permitted. Boat docks and launching facilities are nearby.

Reservations, fee: Reservations accepted; $10 fee per night. MasterCard and Visa accepted. Open all year.

Who to contact: Phone at 503-867-3321, or write at P.O. Box 1343, Newport, OR 97365.

Location: From Newport, travel 1/4 mile south on US 101, then 1/2 mile east on Marine Science Drive and you'll see the park entrance.

Trip note: This park is set along the shore of Yaquina Bay, near the town of Newport, a resort which offers a variety of attractions. Among them are ocean fishing, a museum and aquarium at the nearby Hatfield Marine Science Center, the Undersea Garden, the Waxworks, Ripley's Believe It or Not and the Lincoln County Historical Society Museum. Nearby recreation options include an 18-hole golf course, hiking trails, a full service marina and tennis courts.

Site 5
SOUTH BEACH
STATE PARK

Campsites, facilities: There are 257 sites for trailers or motorhomes up to 54 feet long, and a special camping area for hikers and bicyclists. Firegrills and picnic tables are provided. Electricity, water hookups, flush toilets, sanitary services, showers, firewood and a laundromat are available. Some facilities are wheelchair accessible. Pets are permitted.

Reservations, fee: Reservations accepted; $7 fee per night. Open mid-April to late-October.

Who to contact: Phone at 503-867-7451, or write at Box 1350, Newport, OR 97365.

Location: From Newport, go south on US 101 for two miles and you'll see the park entrance.

Trip note: This park is set along the beach and offers opportunities for hiking, beachcombing and fishing. The Oregon Coast Trail goes through the park and there is a primitive hike-in campground available. See the trip note to campsite 4 for information on attractions in Newport.

BIG ELK

Site **6**

Campsites, facilities: There are 10 campsites for tents, trailers or motorhomes up to 20 feet long. Picnic tables and firegrills are provided, and piped water and vault toilets are available. Pets are permitted.

Reservations, fee: No reservations necessary; $3 fee per night. Open all year.

Who to contact: Phone at 503-487-5811, or write at Siuslaw National Forest, Alsea Ranger District, Alsea, OR 97324.

Location: From the town of Philomath, just west of Corvallis, drive 15 1/2 miles west on Highway 20, then turn south on County Route 547 and drive eight miles to the town of Harlan. From there, take County Route 538 west for 1 1/2 miles to the campground entrance.

Trip note: This out-of-the-way spot is just an hour's drive from Corvallis. It is set along Elk Creek. A National Forest map details the back country roads and trails in the area.

SEAL ROCKS
TRAILER COVE

Site **7**

Campsites, facilities: There are 26 drive-through sites for trailers or motorhomes of any length. Electricity, piped water, sewer hookups and picnic tables are provided. Flush toilets, sanitary services and showers are available. Firewood, a store, a cafe and ice are located within one mile.

Reservations, fee: No reservations necessary; $10 fee per night. Open all year.

Who to contact: Phone at 503-563-3955, or write at Box 71, Seal Rock, OR 97376.

Location: From the town of Seal Rock, travel 1/4 mile south on US 101 and you'll see the park entrance.

Trip note: This trailer park is set along the rugged coastline near Seal Rock State Park, which is open for day-use only. There you can see seals, sea lions and a variety of birds.

ALSEA BAY
TRAILER PARK

Site **8**

Campsites, facilities: There are 50 drive-through sites for trailers or motorhomes of any length. Electricity, piped water and sewer hookups are provided. Flush toilets, showers and a recreation hall are available. Bottled gas, sanitary services, a store, cafe, laundromat and ice are located within one mile. Pets are permitted. Boat docks, launching facilities and rentals are nearby.

Reservations, fee: Reservations accepted; $10 fee per night. Open all year.

Who to contact: Phone at 503-563-2250, or write at P.O. Box 397, Waldport, OR 97394.

Location: This park is located in the rural town of Waldport off US 101 near the north end of Alsea Bay Bridge.

Trip note: This area is a favorite for fishermen because Alsea Bay has sandy as well as rocky shorelines. The crabbing and clamming can also be quite good. Ona Beach State Park is about five mile north on US 101 and offers additional fishing opportunities and a boat ramp along Beaver Creek. It is open for day-use only. Other nearby recreation options include hiking trails, marked bike trails and a marina.

Site 9   CHINOOK TRAILER PARK

Campsites, facilities: There are 15 sites for trailers or motorhomes of any length in this adults-only campground. Electricity, piped water and sewer hookups are provided. Flush toilets, showers and a laundromat are available. Bottled gas, a store, cafe and ice are located within one mile. Pets and motorbikes are permitted. Boat docks are nearby.

Reservations, fee: Reservations accepted; $10 fee per night. Open all year.

Who to contact: Phone at 503-563-3485, or write at 3700 Highway 34, Waldport, OR 97394.

Location: From Waldport, travel 3 1/2 miles east on Highway 34 and you'll see the entrance.

Trip note: This trailer park is set along the shore of the Alsea River. For more information on the area, see the trip note for campsite 8.

Site 10   DRIFT CREEK LANDING

Campsites, facilities: There are 60 drive-through sites for trailers or motorhomes of any length. Electricity, piped water and sewer hookups are provided. Flush toilets, bottled gas, showers, a recreation hall, store, cafe and laundromat are available. Pets are permitted. Boat docks, launching facilities and rentals are nearby.

Reservations, fee: Reservations accepted; $9 fee per night. Open all year.

Who to contact: Phone at 503-563-3610, or write at 3850 Highway 34, Waldport, OR 97394.

Location: From Waldport, travel 3 1/2 miles east on Highway 34 and you'll see the campground.

Trip note: This campground is set along the shore of the Alsea River. An 18-hole golf course is located nearby. For more information on the area, see the trip note for campsite 8.

Site 11   FISHIN' HOLE TRAILER PARK

Campsites, facilities: There are five tent sites and 33 sites for trailers or motorhomes of any length. Electricity, piped water, sewer hookups and picnic tables are provided. Flush toilets, showers, a store, cafe and laundromat are available. Bottled gas is located within one mile. Pets are permitted. Boat docks, launching facilities and rentals are nearby.

Reservations, fee: Reservations accepted; $10 fee per night. Open all year.

Who to contact: Phone at 503-563-3401, or write at 3900 Highway 34, Waldport, OR 97394.

Location: Drive four miles east of Waldport on Highway 34 and you'll see the entrance.

Trip note: This is one of several campgrounds set along the shore of the Alsea River here. For information on the area, see the trip note to campsite 8.

Site **12**   TAYLOR'S LANDING

Campsites, facilities: There are six tent sites and 28 sites for trailers or motorhomes of any length. Electricity, piped water, sewer hookups and picnic tables are provided. Flush toilets, bottled gas, showers, a cafe and laundromat are available. Pets and motorbikes are permitted. Boat docks, launching facilities and rentals are nearby.

Reservations, fee: Reservations accepted; $10 fee per night. MasterCard and Visa accepted. Open all year.

Who to contact: Phone at 503-528-3388, or write at 4250 Highway 34, Waldport, OR 97394.

Location: From Waldport, go seven miles east on Highway 34 and look for the entrance.

Trip note: This campground is set along the Alsea River. For more information on the area, see the trip notes to campsite 8 and 13.

Site **13**   KOZY KOVE MARINA

Campsites, facilities: There are 15 tent sites and 27 sites for trailers or motorhomes of any length. Electricity, piped water, sewer hookups and picnic tables are provided. Flush toilets, bottled gas, sanitary services, showers, a store, cafe, laundromat and ice are available. Pets and motorbikes are permitted. Boat docks, launching facilities and rentals are nearby.

Reservations, fee: Reservations accepted; $12 fee per night. MasterCard and Visa accepted. Open all year.

Who to contact: Phone at 503-528-3251, or write at 4800 Highway 34, Waldport, OR 97394.

Location: From Waldport, drive 9 1/2 miles east on Highway 34 and you'll see the entrance.

Trip note: This campground is set along the Alsea River about 10 miles from the town of Waldport. Nearby Forest Service roads provide access to the various creeks and streams in the surrounding mountains. Consult a Siuslaw National Forest map for details.

Site **14**   CANAL CREEK

Campsites, facilities: There are seven campsites for tents and 10 sites for tents, trailers or motorhomes. Picnic tables and firegrills are provided, and piped water and vault toilets are available. A picnic shelter is also available.

Reservations, fee: No reservations; $5 fee per night. Open all year.

Who to contact: Phone at 503-563-3211, or write at Siuslaw National Forest, Waldport Ranger District, Waldport, OR 97394.

Location: Drive about seven miles east of the town of Waldport on Highway 34 to Forest Service Road 3462, then turn south and go three miles to the campground.

Trip note: This pleasant little campground is off the beaten path, in a large wooded, open area along Canal Creek. The climate here is relatively mild, with 13 degrees Fahrenheit being the coldest winter temperature recorded in recent years. On the other hand, there is the rain . . . lots of it.

BLACKBERRY

Site **15**

Campsites, facilities: There are 32 sites for tents, trailers or motorhomes. Picnic tables and firegrills are provided, and piped water and flush toilets are available. There is no firewood. A boat ramp and launching facilities are nearby.

Reservations, fee: No reservations; $5 fee per night. Open from May through September.

Who to contact: Phone at 503-487-5811, or write at Siuslaw National Forest, Alsea Ranger District, Alsea, OR 97324.

Location: From the town of Waldport, drive about 15 miles east on Highway 34 to the campground entrance. From the town of Alsea, drive 22 miles west on Highway 34 to the campground.

Trip note: This is a good base camp for a fishing trip on the Alsea River. The Forest Service has provided boat launches and picnic areas at several spots along this stretch of river. Often there will be an unofficial "camp host," who can provide inside information on nearby recreational opportunities.

BEACHSIDE
STATE PARK

Site **16**

Campsites, facilities: There are 60 tent sites and 20 sites for trailers or motorhomes up to 30 feet long. Electricity, piped water and picnic tables are provided. Flush toilets, sanitary services, showers, firewood and a laundromat are available. Some facilities are wheelchair accessible. Pets are permitted.

Reservations, fee: Reservations accepted; $7 fee per night. Open mid-April to late-October.

Who to contact: Phone at 503-563-3023, or write at Box 1350, Newport, OR 97365.

Location: From Waldport, travel four miles south on US 101 and you'll see the park entrance.

Trip note: This state park offers a half-mile long beach and is not far from Alsea Bay and the Alsea River. See the trip note to campsites 8 and 13 for more information on the fishing opportunities in the area.

TILLICUM BEACH

Site **17**

Campsites, facilities: There are 57 sites for tents, trailers or motorhomes up to 32 feet long. Picnic tables and firegrills are provided. Flush toilets, piped water and a store are available. Pets are permitted. Boat docks, launching facilities and rentals are nearby.

Reservations, fee: No reservations necessary; $6 fee per night. Open all year.

Who to contact: Phone at 503-563-3211, or write at Siuslaw National Forest, Waldport Ranger District, Waldport, OR 97394.

Location: Drive 4 1/2 miles south of Waldport on US 101 and you'll see the campground entrance.

Trip note: This campground is set along the ocean, just south of Beachside State Park. Nearby Forest Service roads provide access to streams in the mountains east of the beach area. A Forest Service map details the possibilities. In the summer, rangers offer campfire programs.

CAPE PERPETUA
Site 18

Campsites, facilities: There are 37 sites for tents, trailers or motorhomes up to 22 feet long. Picnic tables and firegrills are provided. Flush toilets, piped water and sanitary services are available. Pets are permitted. Boat docks and launching facilities are nearby.

Reservations, fee: No reservations necessary; $6 fee per night. Open mid-May to late-September.

Who to contact: Phone at 503-563-3211, or write at Cape Perpetua Visitor Center, P.O. Box 274, Yachats, OR 97498.

Location: From Yachats, go three miles south on US 101 and you'll see the entrance.

Trip note: This Forest Service campground is set along Cape Creek in the Cape Perpetua Scenic Area. The Visitor Information Center here provides hiking and driving maps to guide you through this spectacular area. Maps also highlight the tidepool and picnic areas. The coastal cliffs can be perfect for whale watching from December through March. Neptune State Park is just south and offers additional rugged coastline vistas.

TENMILE CREEK
Site 19

Campsites, facilities: There are four sites for tents, small trailers or motorhomes. Firegrills and picnic tables are provided. Vault toilets are available, but there is no piped water.

Reservations, fee: No reservations necessary; no fee. Open all year.

Who to contact: Phone at 503-563-3211, or write at Siuslaw National Forest, Waldport Ranger District, Waldport, OR 97394.

Location: Drive 4 1/2 miles south of Cape Perpetua on US 101. Turn east on Forest Service Road 56 for 5 1/2 miles and you'll see the campground entrance.

Trip note: This small, secluded spot is only 15, 20 minutes from the highway, yet remains a virtual secret. A map of Siuslaw National Forest details the surrounding back country. Bring your own drinking water or a water filter.

ROCK CREEK
Site 20

Campsites, facilities: There are seven tent sites and nine sites for tents, trailers or motorhomes up to 22 feet long. Firegrills and picnic tables are provided. Flush toilets and piped water are available. Pets are permitted.

Reservations, fee: No reservations necessary; $4 fee per night. Open late-May to mid-September.

Who to contact: Phone at 503-563-3211, or write at Suislaw National Forest, Waldport Ranger District, Waldport, OR 97394.

Location: Drive 10 miles south of Yachats on US 101 and you'll see the campground entrance on your left.

Trip note: This little out-of-the-way campground is set along Rock Creek, just 1/4-mile from the ocean. A premium spot for coast highway travelers.

Site 21
LANHAM
BIKE CAMP

Campsites, facilities: There are 10 primitive tent sites at this bike-in/hike-in campground. Picnic tables and firegrills are provided, and vault toilets are available. There is no piped drinking water.

Reservations, fee: No reservations necessary; no fee. Open all year.

Who to contact: Phone at 503-563-3211, or write at Suislaw National Forest, Waldport Ranger District, Waldport, OR 97394.

Location: Drive 10 miles south of Yachats on US 101 to the Rock Creek campground and hike in from there.

Trip note: This is an ideal and popular layover spot for bikers working their way along the coast highway. And you can't beat the price.

Site 22
BIG CREEK

Campsites, facilities: There are four sites for tents, trailers or motorhomes up to 16 feet long. Firegrills and picnic tables are provided. Vault toilets are available, but there is no piped water. Pets are permitted.

Reservations, fee: No reservations necessary; no fee. Open late-May to mid-September.

Who to contact: Phone at 503-563-3211, or write at Suislaw National Forest, Waldport Ranger District, Waldport, OR 97394.

Location: Drive 10 miles south of Yachats on US 101, then turn east on Forest Service Road 57 and drive eight miles (narrow, winding road) to the campground.

Trip note: This is a little-known jewel that is ideal for people who want to get away from the crowd and don't mind a primitive setting. It is set along Big Creek, where you arrive after driving on a narrow, winding road. Bring a water filter or your own water supply.

Site 23
SEA PERCH

Campsites, facilities: There are 10 drive-through sites for tents, trailers or motorhomes of any length. Electricity, piped water, sewer hookups and picnic tables are provided. Flush toilets, bottled gas, sanitary services, showers, firewood, recreation hall, a store, cafe, laundromat, ice and playground are available. Pets and motorbikes are permitted.

Reservations, fee: Reservations accepted; $10 fee per night. MasterCard and Visa accepted. Open all year.

Who to contact: Phone at 503-547-3505, or write at 95480 Highway 101, Yachats, OR 97498.

Location: From Yachats, go 6 1/2 miles south on US 101 to mile marker 171.

Trip note: This is one of the most scenic areas of the Oregon coast and Sea Perch Camp is set right in the middle of it. A private camp, it is set just south of Cape Perpetua. For more information, see trip note for campsite 18.

Site **24**
CARL G. WASHBURNE
STATE PARK

Campsites, facilities: There are eight tent sites and 58 sites for trailers or motorhomes up to
45 feet long. Electricity, piped water, sewer hookups and picnic tables are provided.
Flush toilets, showers, firewood and a laundromat are available. Pets are permitted.

Reservations, fee: No reservations necessary; $8 fee per night. Open all year.

Who to contact: Phone at 503-238-7488, or write at Florence, OR 97439.

Location: From Florence, drive 14 miles north on US 101, then one mile west on the park
entrance road.

Trip note: This park is located in a unique area with a variety of exciting trips. Short hikes
lead from the campground to a two-mile long beach and extensive tide pools along
the base of the cliffs. The inland sections of this park are frequented by elk, which are
commonly spotted by campers. Just three miles south of the park are the Sea Lion
Caves, where an elevator is provided to take visitors down into the cavern to provide
an insider's view to the life of a sea lion.

Site **25**
ALDER LAKE

Campsites, facilities: There are 22 sites for tents, trailers or motorhomes up to 30 feet long.
Picnic tables and firegrills are provided. Flush toilets and piped water are available.
Pets are permitted. Boat docks, launching facilities and rentals are nearby.

Reservations, fee: No reservations necessary; $6 fee per night. Open mid-May to mid-
September.

Who to contact: Phone at 503-271-3611, or write at Oregon Dunes National Recreation
Area, 855 Highway Avenue, Reedsport, OR 97467.

Location: From Florence, drive seven miles north on US 101, then 1/4 mile west on Forest
Service Road 792 and you'll see the campground.

Trip note: This campground is set near three lakes, Alder Lake (quite small), Sutton Lake
(larger), and Mercer Lake (largest). A boat launch is available at Sutton Lake. An
option is exploring the expansive sand dunes in the area by foot. No off-road-vehicle
access here. See trip note for campsite 31 for other information on the area.

Site **26**
DUNE LAKE

Campsites, facilities: There are 17 sites for tents, trailers or motorhomes up to 22 feet long.
Picnic tables and firegrills are provided. Flush toilets and piped water are available.
Pets are permitted. Boat docks, launching facilities and rentals are nearby.

Reservations, fee: No reservations necessary; $6 fee per night. Open mid-April to
October.

Who to contact: Phone at 503-271-3611, or write at Oregon Dunes National Recreation
Area, 855 Highway Avenue, Reedsport, OR 97467.

Location: From Florence, go south on US 101 for seven miles, then 1/4 mile west on Forest
Service Road 792 to the campground.

Trip note: This campground is adjacent to campsite 25, Alder Lake.

Site 27
SUTTON CREEK/ B LOOP

Campsites, facilities: There are 31 sites for tents, trailers or motorhomes up to 22 feet long. Picnic tables and firegrills are provided. Flush toilets and piped water are available. Pets are permitted. Boat docks and launching facilities are nearby.

Reservations, fee: No reservations necessary; $6 fee per night. Open all year.

Who to contact: Phone at 503-271-3611, or write at Oregon Dunes National Recreation Area, 855 Highway Avenue, Reedsport, OR 97467.

Location: From the town of Florence, drive six miles north on US 101, then 1 1/2 miles northwest on Forest Service Road 794. From there, go 1/4 mile northeast on Forest Service Road 793 and you'll see the campground entrance.

Trip note: Campsites 27 and 28 are located adjacent to each other on Sutton Creek, not far from Sutton Lake. Swimming and fishing are both popular. A hiking trail leads from camp out to the dunes. There is no off-road-vehicle access here. See trip note to campsite 29 for further side trip suggestions.

Site 28
SUTTON CREEK/ C LOOP

Campsites, facilities: There are 18 sites for tents, trailers or motorhomes up to 22 feet long. Picnic tables and firegrills are provided. Flush toilets and piped water are available. Pets are permitted. Boat docks and launching facilities are nearby.

Reservations, fee: No reservations necessary; $6 fee per night. Open from June through Labor Day weekend.

Who to contact: Phone at 503-271-3611, or write at Oregon Dunes National Recreation Area, 855 Highway Avenue, Reedsport, OR 97467.

Location: From the town of Florence, go six miles north on US 101, then 1 1/2 miles northwest on Forest Service Road 794. From there, go 1/4 mile northeast on Forest Service Road 793 and you'll see the campground entrance.

Trip note: See trip note to campsite 27, which is set adjacent to campsite 28.

Site 29
SUTTON LAKE/ D-LOOP

Campsites, facilities: There are 13 sites for tents, trailers or motorhomes up to 16 feet long. Picnic tables and firegrills are provided. Flush toilets and piped water are available. Pets are permitted. Boat docks and launching facilities are nearby.

Reservations, fee: No reservations necessary; $6 fee per night. Open June to early-September.

Who to contact: Phone at 503-271-3611, or write the Oregon Dunes National Recreation Area at 855 Highway Avenue, Reedsport, OR 97467.

Location: Travel six miles north of Florence on US 101, then 1 1/2 miles northwest on Forest Service Road 794. From there go 3/4 mile northeast on Forest Service Road 793 and you'll see the campground.

Trip note: Fishing, boating, swimming and hiking to the beach area are the most popular activities, and insiders know of a one-of-a-kind opportunity nearby. Visit Darlington State Park, just a mile to the south, where you can watch a unique insect-eating plant—the cobra lilly—do its stuff.

Site 30
SUTTON LAKE/
E-LOOP

Campsites, facilities: There are 17 sites for tents, trailers or motorhomes up to 16 feet long. Picnic tables and firegrills are provided. Flush toilets and piped water are available. Pets are permitted. Boat docks and launching facilities are nearby.

Reservations, fee: No reservations necessary; $6 fee per night. Open July to early-September.

Who to contact: Phone at 503-271-3611, or write the Oregon Dunes National Recreation Area at 855 Highway Avenue, Reedsport, OR 97467.

Location: From Florence, go six miles north on US 101, then 1 1/2 miles northwest on Forest Service Road 794. From there, go 3/4 mile northeast on Forest Service Road 793 and you'll see the campground.

Trip note: For information, see the trip note to campsite 29.

Site 31
LANE COUNTY HARBOR
VISTA PARK

Campsites, facilities: There are 27 sites for tents, trailers or motorhomes up to 32 feet long. Picnic tables are provided. Flush toilets, sanitary services, showers, piped water and a playground are available. Pets and motorbikes are permitted.

Reservations, fee: No reservations necessary; $6 fee per night. Open all year, but facilities are limited during the winter.

Who to contact: Phone at 503-997-8721, or write at P.O. Box 700, Florence, OR 97439.

Location: From the town of Florence, travel three miles north on Rhodendron Drive, then take Harbor Vista Road to 87658 Harbor Vista Road.

Trip note: This county park is set out among the dunes near the entrance to the harbor and offers a great lookout point from the observation deck. There are a number of side trips available, including Darlington State Park (see trip note to campsite 29), Jessie M. Honeyman Memorial State Park (see trip note for campsite 43), and the Indian Forest, just four miles north of the town of Florence. Florence also has displays of Indian dwellings and crafts.

Site 32
RHODODENDRON
TRAILER PARK

Campsites, facilities: There are 18 drive-through sites for trailers or motorhomes of any length. Electricity, piped water and sewer hookups are provided. Flush toilets, showers and a laundromat are available. Bottled gas, a store, cafe and ice are located within one mile. Pets are permitted. Boat docks are nearby.

Reservations, fee: Reservations accepted; $9 fee per night. Open all year.

Who to contact: Phone at 503-997-2206, or write at 87735 Highway 101, Florence, OR 97439.

Location: From Florence, go three miles north on US 101 and you'll see the park.

Trip note: See the trip note to campsite 31 for side trip possibilities. Nearby recreation options include an 18-hole golf course, a riding stable and tennis courts.

Site 33

MERCER LAKE
RESORT

Campsites, facilities: There are 15 drive-through sites for trailers or motorhomes of any length. Electricity, piped water, sewer hookups and picnic tables are provided. Flush toilets, bottled gas, sanitary services, showers, a store, laundromat, ice and playground are available. Pets are permitted. Boat docks, launching facilities and rentals are nearby.

Reservations, fee: Reservations accepted; $8 fee per night. MasterCard and Visa accepted. Open all year.

Who to contact: Phone at 503-997-3633, or write at 88875 Bay Berry, Florence, OR 97439.

Location: From Florence, go five miles north on US 101, then one mile east on Mercer Lake Road. Go north on Resort Road to the campground.

Trip note: This resort is set along the shore of Mercer Lake, one of a number of lakes that have formed among the ancient dunes in this area.

Site 34

WAYSIDE MOBILE
AND RV PARK

Campsites, facilities: There are 22 sites for trailers or motorhomes of any length. Electricity, piped water, sewer hookups and picnic tables are provided. Flush toilets, sanitary services, showers and laundromat are available. Bottled gas, a store, cafe and ice are located within one mile. Pets are permitted. Boat launching facilities are nearby.

Reservations, fee: Reservations accepted; $10 fee per night. Open all year.

Who to contact: Phone at 503-997-6451, or write at 3760 Highway 101 North, Florence, OR 97439.

Location: In Florence, from the junction of Highway 126 and US 101, travel 1 3/4 miles north on US 101 to the park.

Trip note: See the trip notes to campsites 31 and 36 for side trip ideas. Nearby recreation options include an 18-hole golf course, a riding stable and tennis courts.

Site 35

KOA FLORENCE
DUNES CAMPGROUND

Campsites, facilities: There are 25 tent sites and 100 drive-through sites for trailers or motorhomes of any length. Piped water and picnic tables are provided. Flush toilets, sanitary services, showers, a store, laundromat, ice, playground, electricity, sewer hookups and firewood are available for an extra fee. Bottled gas is located within one mile. Pets and motorbikes are permitted. Boat docks and launching facilities are nearby.

Reservations, fee: Reservations accepted; $9 fee per night. MasterCard and Visa accepted. Open all year.

Who to contact: Phone at 503-997-6431, or write at 87115 Rhododendron, Florence, OR 97439.

Location: Drive 1 1/2 miles north of Florence on US 101, then go one mile west on 35th Street and one block north on Rhododendron Drive.

Trip note: Nearby recreation options include an 18-hole golf course and a full service marina.

Site **36** | PORT OF SIUSLAW
RV AND MARINA

Campsites, facilities: There are 20 tent sites and 78 sites for trailers or motorhomes of any length. Electricity, piped water, sewer hookups and picnic tables are provided. Flush toilets, bottled gas, sanitary services, showers, firewood, a recreation hall, a store, laundromat and ice are available. A cafe is located within one mile. Pets are permitted. Boat docks and launching facilities are nearby.

Reservations, fee: Reservations accepted; $9 fee per night. Open all year.

Who to contact: Phone at 503-997-3040, or write at P.O. Box 1638, Florence, OR 97439.

Location: In Florence, turn off US 101 and go about 1/2 mile east on First Street to Harbor Street and you'll see the marina.

Trip note: This resort is set along the Siuslaw River in the town of Florence. Fishermen with boats will find the support pilings for the Highway 101 Bridge good spots for perch and flounder fishing.

Site **37** | MID-WAY MARINA
AND RV PARK

Campsites, facilities: There are five tent sites and 40 sites for trailers or motorhomes up to 26 feet long. Electricity, piped water, sewer hookups and picnic tables are provided. Flush toilets, bottled gas, showers, a recreation hall, a store, cafe, laundromat and ice are available. Pets and motorbikes are permitted. Boat docks, launching facilities and rentals are located nearby.

Reservations, fee: Reservations accepted; $9 fee per night. Open all year.

Who to contact: Phone at 503-997-3031, or write at 07790 Highway 126, Florence, OR 97439.

Location: From Florence, travel 5 1/2 miles east on Highway 126 and you'll see the entrance to the park.

Trip note: This rural park is set along the shore of the Siuslaw River mid-way between Florence and Mapleton, and offers boat rentals and facilities. Fishing can be excellent in season, but it's advisable to phone for the latest report.

Site **38** | ARCHIE
KNOWLES

Campsites, facilities: There are nine sites for tents, trailers or motorhomes up to 16 feet long. Picnic tables and firegrills are provided. Flush toilets and piped water are available. Pets are permitted.

Reservations, fee: No reservations necessary; $4 fee per night. Open May to early-September.

Who to contact: Phone at 503-268-4473, or write at Siuslaw National Forest, Mapleton Ranger District, Mapleton, OR 97453.

Location: From Mapleton, go three miles east on Highway 126 and you'll see the campground entrance.

Trip note: This little campground is set along Knowles Creek about three miles from the Siuslaw River. A more rustic alternative to campsite 37.

Site 39   NORTH FORK SIUSLAW

Campsites, facilities: There are five tent sites. Picnic tables and firegrills are provided. Pit toilets are available, but there is no piped water. Pets are permitted.

Reservations, fee: No reservations necessary; $4 fee per night. Open July to early-September.

Who to contact: Phone at 503-268-4473, or write at Siuslaw National Forest, Mapleton Ranger District, Mapleton, OR 97453.

Location: From Florence, drive one mile east on Highway 36, then 13 1/2 miles northeast on County Route 5070 and you'll see the campground.

Trip note: Little known and little used, this can be the ideal hideaway. It is set along the North Fork of the Siuslaw River—a dirt road opposite camp follows Wilhelm Creek for about two miles. See a Forest Service map for other trip possibilities.

Site 40   MAPLE LAKE TRAILER PARK-MARINA

Campsites, facilities: There are five tent sites and 41 drive-through sites for trailers or motorhomes of any length. Electricity, piped water and sewer hookups are provided. Flush toilets, bottled gas, sanitary services and showers are available. A store, cafe and ice are located within one mile. Pets and motorbikes are permitted. Boat docks and launching facilities are nearby.

Reservations, fee: Reservations accepted; $7 fee per night. Open all year.

Who to contact: Phone at 503-268-4822, or write at 10730 Highway 126, Mapleton, OR 97453.

Location: This park is located in Mapleton on Highway 126.

Trip note: This park is set along the shore of the Siuslaw River in Mapleton. There are boat rentals and hiking trails nearby. The general area is surrounded by Siuslaw National Forest land. A Forest Service map details nearby back country trip ideas.

Site 41   LAKESHORE TRAILER PARK

Campsites, facilities: There are 25 drive-through sites for trailers or motorhomes of any length. Electricity, piped water and sewer hookups are provided. Flush toilets, showers, a store and laundromat are available. A cafe is located within one mile. Pets are permitted. Boat docks are nearby.

Reservations, fee: Reservations accepted; $8 fee per night. Open all year.

Who to contact: Phone at 503-997-2741, or write at 83763 Highway 101, Florence, OR 97439.

Location: From Florence, go four miles south on US 101 and you'll see the park.

Trip note: A prime area for vacationers. This park is set along the shore of Woahink Lake, a popular spot to fish for trout, perch, catfish, crappie, bluegill and bass. It is adjacent to Honeyman Memorial State Park and the Oregon Dunes Recreation Area. Off-road-vehicle access to the dunes can be found four miles northeast of the park. Hiking trails through the dunes can be found at Honeyman State Park. If you set out across the dunes off the trail, note your path—people going off trail commonly get lost out here.

Site 42   SILTCOOS LAKE RESORT MOTEL

Campsites, facilities: There are two tent sites and six drive-through sites for trailers or motorhomes up to 32 feet long. Electricity, piped water, sewer hookups and picnic tables are provided. Flush toilets, showers, a recreation hall and playground are available. Bottled gas, a store, cafe, laundromat and ice are located within one mile. Pets and motorbikes are permitted. Boat docks, launching facilities and rentals are nearby.

Reservations, fee: Reservations accepted; $10 fee per night. MasterCard and Visa accepted. Open all year.

Who to contact: Phone at 503-997-3741, or write at Box 36, Westlake, OR 97493.

Location: From Florence, go six miles south on US 101, then 1/4 mile east on Westlake turnoff and you'll see the motel.

Trip note: This resort is set along the Siltcoos River adjacent to Siltcoos Lake—a large lake with many inlets, ideal for fishing. Just across the highway, you will find off-road vehicle and hiking access to the Oregon Dunes National Recreation Area.

Site 43   DARLINGS RESORT

Campsites, facilities: There are 10 sites for trailers or motorhomes of any length. Electricity, piped water, sewer hookups and picnic tables are provided. Flush toilets, showers, firewood, a store, cafe and laundromat are available. Pets are permitted. Boat docks, launching facilities and rentals are nearby.

Reservations, fee: Reservations accepted; $8 fee per night. Open all year.

Who to contact: Phone at 503-997-2741, or write at 4879 Darling Loop, Florence, OR 97439.

Location: From Florence, go five miles south on US 101, then 1/2 mile east on North Beach Road to the resort.

Trip note: This park is set in a rural area along the north shore of Siltcoos Lake, adjacent to the extensive Oregon Dunes National Recreation Area. An access point to the dunes for hikers and off-road-vehicles is just across the highway. A full service marina is at the lake.

Site 44   JESSIE M. HONEYMAN MEMORIAL STATE PARK

Campsites, facilities: There are 241 tent sites, 141 sites for trailers or motorhomes up to 55 feet long, and a special camping area for hikers and bicyclists. Electricity, piped water, sewer hookups and picnic tables are provided. Flush toilets, sanitary services, showers, firewood and laundromat are available. Some facilities are wheelchair accessible. Pets are permitted. Boat docks and launching facilities are nearby.

Reservations, fee: Reservations accepted; $8 fee per night. Open all year.

Who to contact: Phone at 503-997-3851, or write at 84505 Highway 101, Florence, OR 97439.

Location: From Florence drive three miles south on US 101 and you'll see the park entrance.

Trip note: This is a popular state park set along the shore of Cleowax Lake and adjacent to the dunes of the Oregon Dunes National Recreation Area. Many good hiking trails are available in the park. For off-road-vehicle access to the dunes, head about three miles north on the main highway. Boating, fishing and swimmng are popular at either of the two lakes within the park.

DRIFTWOOD
Site **45**
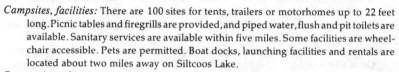

Campsites, facilities: There are 100 sites for tents, trailers or motorhomes up to 22 feet long. Picnic tables and firegrills are provided, and piped water, flush and pit toilets are available. Sanitary services are available within five miles. Some facilities are wheelchair accessible. Pets are permitted. Boat docks, launching facilities and rentals are located about two miles away on Siltcoos Lake.

Reservations, fee: No reservations necessary; $4 fee per night. Open all year.

Who to contact: Phone at 503-271-3611, or write Oregon Dunes National Recreation Area, 855 Highway Avenue, Reedsport, OR 97467.

Location: From Florence, go seven miles south on US 101, then 1 1/2 miles west on Forest Service Road 1078 and you'll see the campground.

Trip note: This campground is set near the ocean in the Oregon Dunes National Recreation Area and has off-road-vehicle access. Several small lakes, the Siltcoos River and Siltcoos Lake are nearby.

LAGOON
Site **46**

Campsites, facilities: There are 51 sites for tents, trailers or motorhomes up to 22 feet long. Picnic tables and firegrills are provided, and piped water, flush and pit toilets are available. Sanitary services are located within five miles. Pets are permitted. Boat docks, launching facilities and rentals are nearby on Siltcoos Lake.

Reservations, fee: No reservations necessary; $6 fee per night. Open June to late-September.

Who to contact: Phone at 503-271-3611, or write Oregon Dunes National Recreation Area, 855 Highway Avenue, Reedsport, OR 97467.

Location: From Florence, go seven miles south on US 101, then 1 1/3 miles west on Forest Service Road 1076 and you're there.

Trip note: This is one of several campgrounds in this area. This one is set along the lagoon about one mile from Siltcoos Lake. There are hiking trails nearby and off-road-vehicle access about one-half of a mile away at Driftwood Campground.

TYEE
Site **47**
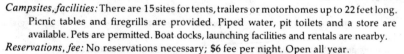

Campsites, facilities: There are 15 sites for tents, trailers or motorhomes up to 22 feet long. Picnic tables and firegrills are provided. Piped water, pit toilets and a store are available. Pets are permitted. Boat docks, launching facilities and rentals are nearby.

Reservations, fee: No reservations necessary; $6 fee per night. Open all year.

Who to contact: Phone at 503-271-3611, or write Oregon Dunes National Recreation Area, 855 Highway Avenue, Reedsport, OR 97467.

Location: From Florence, go six miles south on US 101, then 100 yards southeast on Forest Service Road 1068 and you'll see the campground.

Trip note: This campground is set along the shore of Siltcoos Lake, an option to nearby campsites 45 and 46. Swimming, fishing and waterskiing are permitted at the lake. Off-road-vehicle access to the dunes is available from campsite 45 and there are hiking trails.

WAXMYRTLE
Site 48

Campsites, facilities: There are 53 sites for tents, trailers or motorhomes up to 22 feet long. Picnic tables and firegrills are provided. Piped water and flush toilets are available. Pets are permitted. Boat docks, launching facilities and rentals are nearby on Siltcoos Lake.

Reservations, fee: No reservations necessary; $6 fee per night. Open June to late-September.

Who to contact: Phone at 503-271-3611, or write Oregon Dunes National Recreation Area, 855 Highway Avenue, Reedsport, OR 97467.

Location: From Florence, travel seven miles south on US 101, then 1 1/4 miles west on Forest Service Road 1078 and you'll see the campground on your left.

Trip note: One of four camps in the immediate vicinity. It is set adjacent to campsite 46 and less than a mile from campsite 45, which has off-road-vehicle access to the dunes. The campground is set near the lagoon, about a mile from Siltcoos Lake, a good-sized lake with boating facilities where waterskiing, fishing and swimming are permitted. There are hiking trails in the area.

LODGEPOLE
Site 49

Campsites, facilities: There are three sites for tents, trailers or motorhomes up to 16 feet long. Picnic tables and firegrills are provided, and piped water and pit toilets are available. Pets are permitted. Boat docks, launching facilities and rentals are nearby on Siltcoos Lake.

Reservations, fee: No reservations necessary; $4 fee per night. Open June to late-September.

Who to contact: Phone at 503-271-3611, or write Oregon Dunes National Recreation Area, 855 Highway Avenue, Reedsport, OR 97467.

Location: From Florence, travel seven miles south on US 101, then turn west on Forest Service Road 1078 and you'll see the campground.

Trip note: This is the smallest, most private and fastest camp to fill in the Siltcoos Lake area. This campground is set along the Siltcoos River and offers good fishing. It is within a mile of the previous four camps. Campsite 45 has off-road-vehicle access to the dunes. Siltcoos Lake has complete boating facilities.

CARTER LAKE
Site 50

Campsites, facilities: There are 22 sites for tents, trailers or motorhomes up to 22 feet long. Picnic tables and firegrills are provided, and piped water and pit toilets are available. Pets are permitted. Boat docks, launching facilities and rentals are nearby.

Reservations, fee: No reservations necessary; $6 fee per night. Open all year.

Who to contact: Phone at 503-271-3611, or write Oregon Dunes National Recreation Area, 855 Highway Avenue, Reedsport, OR 97467.

Location: From Florence, drive 8 1/2 miles south on US 101, then 200 yards west on Forest Service Road 1086 and you're there.

Trip note: This campground is set along the north shore of Carter Lake. Boating, swimming and fishing are permitted on this long, narrow lake, which is set among dunes overgrown with vegetation. Hiking is allowed in the dunes, but there is no off-road-vehicle access here. If you want ORV access then head north one mile to Forest

Service Road 1076, turn west and drive 1 1/4 miles to Driftwood Campground (campsite 45).

Site 51   TAHKENITCH LANDING

Campsites, facilities: There are about 15 sites for tents, trailers or motorhomes up to 22 feet long. Picnic tables are provided and pit toilets are available. There is no drinking water, however there is water nearby at Tahkenitch Lake Campground (campsite 52). Pets are permitted. Boat launching facilities are available about 500 yards north of the campground.

Reservations, fee: No reservations necessary; $2 fee per night. Open June to late-September.

Who to contact: Phone at 503-271-3611, or write Oregon Dunes National Recreation Area, 855 Highway Avenue, Reedsport, OR 97467.

Location: From the town of Reedsport, drive seven miles north on US 101 and you'll see the campground on the east side of the road.

Trip note: This camp overlooks Tahkenitch Lake and has easy access for fishing or swimming. The camp area is actually an open piece of land with picnic tables, a do-it-yourself proposition.

Site 52   TAHKENITCH LAKE

Campsites, facilities: There are 35 sites for tents, trailers or motorhomes up to 22 feet long. Picnic tables and firegrills are provided. Piped water, and flush and pit toilets are available. Pets are permitted. Boat docks and launching facilities are on the lake.

Reservations, fee: No reservations necessary; $6 fee per night. Open June to late-September.

Who to contact: Phone at 503-271-3611, or write Oregon Dunes National Recreation Area, 855 Highway Avenue, Reedsport, OR 97467.

Location: From Reedsport, travel seven miles north on US 101, then 100 yards west on Forest Service Road 1090 and you're there.

Trip note: This campground is set in a wooded area near the shore of Tahkenitch Lake, a reservoir which offers numerous coves and backwater areas for fishing and swimming. There is a hiking trail nearby that goes through the dunes out to the beach. If this camp is filled, campsite 51 provides nearby space.

Site 53   COHO MARINA & RV PARK

Campsites, facilities: There are 49 drive-through sites for trailers or motorhomes of any length. Electricity, piped water, sewer hookups and picnic tables are provided. Flush toilets, bottled gas, sanitary services, showers, a store and ice are available. Cafe and laundromat are located within one mile. Pets are permitted. Boat docks and launching facilities are nearby.

Reservations, fee: Reservations accepted; $10 fee per night. MasterCard and Visa accepted. Open all year.

Who to contact: Phone at 503-271-4676, or write at 1580 Winchester, Reedsport, OR 97467.

Location: This park is located in the town of Reedsport off US 101.

Trip note: This park is set along the shore of the Umpqua River in the town of Reedsport, an area that attracts great fishing in season.

ECHO RESORT MOTEL & RV PARK

Site **54**

Campsites, facilities: There are 14 tent sites and 28 sites for trailers or motorhomes of any length. Electricity, piped water, sewer hookups and picnic tables are provided. Flush toilets, showers, firewood, a store and ice are available. Pets are permitted. Boat docks and launching facilities are nearby.

Reservations, fee: Reservations accepted; $8 fee per night. Open all year.

Who to contact: Phone at 503-271-2025, or write at Route 4, Box 27, Reedsport, OR 97467.

Location: From Reedsport, drive 7 1/2 miles east on Highway 38 and you'll see the park.

Trip note: This wooded park is set along the Umpqua River near an elk preserve. Fishing for salmon and steelhead can be outstanding in season. In summer months, cruising Highway 38 is one of the prettiest drives in the Western U.S.

UMPQUA LIGHTHOUSE STATE PARK

Site **55**

Campsites, facilities: There are 41 tent sites and 22 sites for trailers or motorhomes up to 44 feet long. Electricity, piped water, sewer hookups and picnic tables are provided. Flush toilets, showers, firewood and a laundromat are available. Pets are permitted. Boat docks and launching facilities are on the Umpqua River.

Reservations, fee: No reservations necessary; $8 fee per night. Open mid-April to late-October.

Who to contact: Phone at 503-271-4118, or write at Box 94, Winchester Bay, OR 97467.

Location: Drive six miles south of the town of Reedsport on US 101 and you'll see the park entrance.

Trip note: This park is set near the mouth of the Umpqua River, a unique area where the dunes are as high as 500 feet. Hiking trails lead out from the park south into Umpqua Dunes Scenic Area. The park offers over two miles of beach access on the ocean and 1/2 mile along the Umpqua River.

WILLIAM M. TUGMAN STATE PARK

Site **56**

Campsites, facilities: There are 115 sites for trailers or motorhomes up to 50 feet long, and a special camping area for hikers and bicyclists. Electricity, piped water and picnic tables are provided. Flush toilets, sanitary services, showers, firewood and a laundromat are available. Some facilities are wheelchair accessible. Pets are permitted. Boat docks and launching facilities are nearby.

Reservations, fee: No reservations necessary; $8 fee per night. Open mid-April to late-October.

Who to contact: Phone at 503-271-4118, or write c/o Umpqua Lighthouse State Park, P.O. Box 94, Winchester Bay, OR 97467.

Location: From Reedsport, travel eight miles south on US 101 and you'll see the park entrance.

Trip note: This campground is set along the shore of Eel Lake, which offers almost five miles of shoreline for swimming and trout fishing. There is a boat ramp, but there is a

10-mph speed limit for boats. Across the highway is the Oregon Dunes National Recreation Area.

Site 57
SURFWOOD CAMPGROUND & RV PARK

Campsites, facilities: There are 22 tent sites and 141 drive-through sites for trailers or motorhomes. Electricity, piped water, sewer hookups and picnic tables are provided. Flush toilets, sanitary services, showers, firewood, a store, cafe, laundromat, ice, playground and swimming pool are available. Pets and motorbikes are permitted. Boat docks and launching facilities are nearby.

Reservations, fee: Reservations accepted; $8 fee per night. Open all year.

Who to contact: Phone at 503-271-4020, or write at HC 4, Box 268, Reedsport, OR 97467.

Location: Travel 1/2 mile north of Winchester Bay on US 101 and you'll see the park entrance.

Trip note: The pull-through sites are separated by shrubs, which helps privacy. This park is a half-mile drive from the marina at Winchester Bay. Fishing is the focal point, but there are other possibilities in the area. There are many trails nearby, leading west across the dunes to the ocean and east to lakes in wooded areas. Some 10 miles east, an elk reserve is located adjacent to Highway 38.

Site 58
UMPQUA BEACH RESORT

Campsites, facilities: There are 50 drive-through sites for trailers or motorhomes of any length. Electricity, piped water, sewer hookups and picnic tables are provided. Flush toilets, bottled gas, showers, a store, cafe, laundromat and ice are available. Sanitary services are located within one mile. Pets and motorbikes are permitted. Boat docks and launching facilities are nearby.

Reservations, fee: Reservations accepted; $10 fee per night. MasterCard and Visa accepted. Open all year.

Who to contact: Phone at 503-271-3443, or write at HC 4, Box 242, Reedsport, OR 97467.

Location: Take the Windy Cove exit off US 101 near Winchester Bay and drive 1 1/2 miles west to the resort.

Trip note: This resort is set on the shore of Winchester Bay in a fishing village near the mouth of the Umpqua River. For details on nearby recreation options, see the trip note to campsite 57.

Site 59
WINDY COVE COUNTY PARK

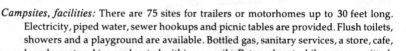

Campsites, facilities: There are 75 sites for trailers or motorhomes up to 30 feet long. Electricity, piped water, sewer hookups and picnic tables are provided. Flush toilets, showers and a playground are available. Bottled gas, sanitary services, a store, cafe, laundromat and ice are located within one mile. Pets and motorbikes are permitted. Boat docks, launching facilities and rentals are nearby.

Reservations, fee: No reservations necessary; $9 fee per night. Open all year.

Who to contact: Phone at 503-271-4138, or write at P.O. Box 265, Winchester Bay, OR 97467.

Location: Drive south of Reedsport on Highway 101 to Winchester Bay and take the Windy Cove exit to the park.

Trip note: This county park is set on the ocean and offers boat rentals and fishing equipment. Nearby recreation options include an 18-hole golf course and tennis courts.

Site 60   NORTH LAKE RESORT & MARINA

Campsites, facilities: There are 92 drive-through sites for trailers or motorhomes of any length. Picnic tables are provided. Flush toilets, bottled gas, sanitary services, showers, firewood, a store, ice, playground, electricity, piped water and sewer hookups are available. A cafe and laundromat are located within one mile. Pets are permitted. Boat docks, launching facilities and rentals are nearby.

Reservations, fee: Reservations accepted; $8 fee per night. MasterCard and Visa accepted. Open all year.

Who to contact: Phone at 503-759-3515, or write at 2090 North Lake Avenue, Lakeside, OR 97449.

Location: Take Lakeside exit off US 101, then go 3/4 miles east to North Lake Avenue and 1/2 mile east to the resort.

Trip note: This resort is set along the shore of Tenmile Lake, which has a full service marina.

Site 61   SEADRIFT MOTEL & CAMPGROUND

Campsites, facilities: There are 45 drive-through sites for trailers or motorhomes of any length. Picnic tables are provided. Flush toilets, bottled gas, sanitary services, showers and a playground are available. A store, cafe and laundromat are located within one mile. Pets are permitted. Boat docks, launching facilities and rentals are nearby.

Reservations, fee: Reservations accepted; $9 fee per night. MasterCard and Visa accepted. Open all year.

Who to contact: Phone at 503-759-3102, or write at Box 331, Lakeside, OR 97449.

Location: Go 1/4 mile north of the Northern Lakes exit on US 101 in Lakeside and you'll see the campground entrance.

Trip note: This spot is set near Tenmile Lake, a popular spot for bass fishing, swimming and waterskiing. Hiking trails through the Umpqua Dunes Scenic Area are accessible from Forest Service campgrounds located nearby on the west side of US 101.

Site 62   NORTH EEL CREEK

Campsites, facilities: There are 52 sites for tents, trailers or motorhomes up to 22 feet long. Picnic tables and firegrills are provided. Piped water, and flush and pit toilets are available. Pets are permitted. Boat docks, launching facilities and rentals are nearby.

Reservations, fee: No reservations necessary; $6 fee per night. Open June to late-September.

Who to contact: Phone Oregon Dunes National Recreation Area at 503-271-3611, or write at 855 Highway Avenue, Reedsport, OR 97467.

Location: From Reedsport, travel 12 miles southwest on US 101 and you'll see the campground entrance on your right.

Trip note: This campground is set along Eel Creek, near both Eel Lake and Tenmile Lake.

Waterskiing is allowed at Tenmile Lake, but not at Eel Lake. There are trails nearby that access the Umpqua Dunes Scenic Area. Access for off-road-vehicles is available at campsite 65.

MID EEL
Site **63**

Campsites, facilities: There are 27 sites for tents, trailers or motorhomes up to 16 feet long. Picnic tables and firegrills are provided. Flush toilets and piped water are available. Pets are permitted. Boat docks, launching facilities and rentals are nearby.

Reservations, fee: No reservations necessary; $6 fee per night. Open June to late-September.

Who to contact: Phone Oregon Dunes National Recreation Area at 503-271-3611, or write at 855 Highway Avenue, Reedsport, OR 97467.

Location: From Reedsport, go 12 miles southwest on US 101, then about 100 yards west on Forest Service Road 1093.

Trip note: This campground is set very near campsite 62 and offers the same opportunities.

SOUTH EEL
Site **64**   CREEK

Campsites, facilities: There are three tent sites and 10 sites for tents, trailers or motorhomes up to 22 feet long. Picnic tables and firegrills are provided. Flush toilets and piped water are available. A store, cafe, laundromat and ice are located within a mile. Pets are permitted. Boat docks, launching facilities and rentals are nearby.

Reservations, fee: Reservations required; $6 fee per night. Open June to late-September.

Who to contact: Phone Oregon Dunes National Recreation Area at 503-271-3611, or write at 855 Highway Avenue, Reedsport, OR 97467.

Location: From Reedsport, go 13 miles southwest on US 101, then 100 yards southwest on Forest Service Road 1090.

Trip note: This campground is set a short distance from campsite 62. See trip note for recreation details.

SPINREEL
Site **65**

Campsites, facilities: There are 25 sites for tents, trailers or motorhomes up to 22 feet long. Picnic tables and firegrills are provided, and pit toilets are available. There is no drinking water. Firewood, a store and a laundromat are available. Pets are permitted. Boat docks, launching facilities and rentals are located on Tenmile Lake.

Reservations, fee: No reservations necessary, no fee. Open all year. Note: The Forest Service has plans to provide piped water, in which case a small nightly fee will be charged.

Who to contact: Phone Oregon Dunes National Recreation Area at 503-271-3611, or write at 855 Highway Avenue, North Bend, OR 97459.

Location: From North Bend, go eight miles northwest on US 101, and you'll see a sign directing you to Spinreel Campground. Drive one mile northwest on a County Road to the campground.

Trip note: This campground is set at the outlet of Tenmile Lake, in the Oregon Dunes National Recreation Area. Boating facilities are located near the camp. There are hiking trails and off-road-vehicle access to the dunes.

BLUEBILL LAKE

Site **66**

Campsites, facilities: There are 18 sites for tents, trailers or motorhomes up to 22 feet long. Picnic tables and firegrills are provided. Flush toilets and piped water are available. Pets are permitted. Boat docks and launching facilities are nearby.

Reservations, fee: No reservations necessary; $6 fee per night. Open all year.

Who to contact: Phone Oregon Dunes National Recreation Area at 503-271-3611, or write at 855 Highway Avenue, Reedsport, OR 97467.

Location: From North Bend, travel 2 1/2 miles north on US 101, then 3/4 mile west on County Road 609. From there, go 2 1/2 miles northwest on Forest Service Road 1099 and you'll see the campground entrance.

Trip note: This campground gets very little camper pressure. It is set next to little Bluebill Lake, so small it dries up during the summer. It is a short distance from Horsefall Lake, which is surrounded by private property. If you continue west on the Forest Service Road you will come to a picnicking and parking area near the beach that has off-road-vehicle access to the dunes.

KELLEY'S
RV PARK

Site **67**

Campsites, facilities: There are 38 drive-through sites for trailers or motorhomes of any length. Electricity, piped water, sewer hookups and picnic tables are provided. Flush toilets, sanitary services, a laundromat and ice are available. Bottled gas, a store and cafe are within one mile. Pets are permitted. Boat docks and launching facilities are nearby.

Reservations, fee: Reservations accepted; $8 fee per night. MasterCard and Visa accepted. Open all year.

Who to contact: Phone at 503-888-6531, or write at 555 South Empire Boulevard, Coos Bay, OR 97420.

Location: In Coos Bay take the Charleston exit off US 101 and go 4 1/2 miles to 555 South Empire Boulevard.

Trip note: This RV park is in the town of Coos Bay, well-known for its salmon, deep sea fishing and lumber. Nearby recreation options include a full service marina.

HORSEFALL
STAGING

Site **68**

Campsites, facilities: There are 125 sites for trailers or motorhomes of any length. Pit toilets are available, but there is no drinking water so bring your own. Pets are permitted.

Reservations, fee: No reservations necessary; $4 fee per night. Open all year.

Who to contact: Phone Oregon Dunes National Recreation Area at 503-271-3611, or write at 855 Highway Avenue, Reedsport, OR 97467.

Location: Drive north out of North Bend on US 101. About two-thirds of the way across the bridge, there is a causeway to the left called Jordon Cove Road. Take Jordon Cove Road and drive past the paper mill, then bear right on Forest Service Road 1099 and you'll see the campground entrance.

Trip note: This campground is actually a nice, large paved area for parking motorhomes. It is the staging area for off-road-vehicle access into the southern section of Oregon Dunes National Recreation Area.

Site 69   SUNSET BAY STATE PARK

Campsites, facilities: There are 108 tent sites and 29 sites for trailers or motorhomes up to 47 feet long. Electricity, piped water, sewer hookups and picnic tables are provided. Flush toilets, showers, firewood and a laundromat are available. A cafe is located within one mile. Some facilities are wheelchair accessible. Pets are permitted.

Reservations, fee: Reservations accepted; $8 fee per night. Open mid-April to late-October.

Who to contact: Phone at 503-888-4902, or write at 13030 Cape Argo Highway, Coos Bay, OR 97420.

Location: From Coos Bay, travel 12 miles southwest on the Cape Argo Highway and you'll see the park entrance.

Trip note: This campground is set near Sunset Bay, which is a small, enclosed and well-protected bay with a nice beach for swimming.

Site 70   TYEE

Campsites, facilities: There are 10 sites for tents, trailers or motorhomes. Piped water, firegrills and picnic tables are provided. Pit toilets and firewood are available. A store is located within one mile. Pets are permitted.

Reservations, fee: No reservations necessary; $5 fee per night. Open May to late-October.

Who to contact: Phone at 503-672-4491, or write at 777 NW Garden Valley Boulevard, Roseburg, OR 97470.

Location: From Sutherlin, go 12 miles northwest on Highway 138 and you'll see the campground entrance.

Trip note: Here is a classic spot, set along the Umpqua River with great fishing in season, yet very few people know of it. It is managed by the Bureau of Land Management, which rarely publicizes its campgrounds.

Site 71   WILLIAMETTE CITY PARK

Campsites, facilities: There are 25 sites for tents, trailers or motorhomes of any length. Vault toilets, piped water, a covered outdoor kitchen area, picnic tables and a small playground are available. Bottled gas, a store, cafe, laundromat and ice are within one mile. There is a dump station at the Texaco on 9th Street in the center of town, three miles away. Pets and motorbikes are permitted. Boat docks and launching facilities are located two miles away.

Reservations, fee: No reservations necessary; $4 fee per night. Open April to late-October.

Who to contact: Phone at 503-757-6918, or write at Corvallis Department of Parks and Recreation, P.O. Box 1083, Corvallis, OR 97339.

Location: From Corvalis, go one mile south on Highway 99W, then go 1/2 mile east on SE Goodnight Road to the park.

Trip note: This 40-acre city park is set along the banks of the Willamette River, just outside

Corvallis. The camping area is actually a large clearing near the entrance to the park, which has been left in its natural state. There are trails leading down to the river, and the bird watching is good here. Trout fishing can be a winner on the Willamette.

CORVALLIS
Site **72**   **MOTORHOME PARK**

Campsites, facilities: There are 13 sites for trailers or motorhomes. Electricity, piped water and sewer hookups are provided. Flush toilets, showers, a store, cafe, laundromat and ice are available. Bottled gas and sanitary services are located within one mile. Pets and motorbikes are permitted.

Reservations, fee: Reservations accepted; $10 fee per night. Open all year.

Who to contact: Phone at 503-752-2334, or write at 200 Northwest 53rd Street, Corvallis, OR 97330.

Location: From Corvallis, go 2 1/2 miles west on US 20/ Highway 34, then turn north on 53rd Street and travel 1 1/4 mile to the park.

Trip note: This is a decent layover spot on your way to and from the coast. Nearby recreation options include an 18-hole golf course, hiking trails and a riding stable.

SOUTH CORVALLIS
Site **73**   **TRAILER COURT**

Campsites, facilities: There are 12 sites for trailers or motorhomes of any length. Electricity, piped water and sewer hookups are provided. Flush toilets, showers and a laundromat are available. Bottled gas, a store, cafe and ice are located within one mile. Pets are permitted.

Reservations, fee: Reservations accepted; $8 fee per night. Open all year.

Who to contact: Phone at 503-753-3334, or write at 245 Southwest Twin Oak, Corvallis, OR 97330.

Location: From Corvallis, drive south on Highway 99W one block south of the bridge. The trailer court is located one block west of there.

Trip note: This park is in Corvallis, home of Oregon State University. Nearby recreation options include an 18-hole golf course, hiking trails, a riding stable and tennis courts.

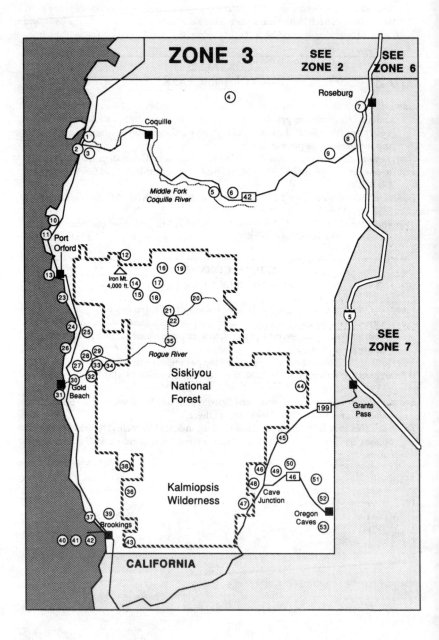

SISKIYOU

BULLARDS BEACH
Site 1

Campsites, facilities: There are 92 tent sites and 100 sites for trailers or motorhomes up to 55 feet long. A special camping area is reserved for hikers and bicyclists. Electricity, piped water, sewer hookups, picnic tables and firegrills are provided. Flush toilets, sanitary services, showers, firewood, a store, cafe, laundromat and a loading ramp for horses are available. Some facilities are wheelchair accessible. Pets are permitted. Boat docks and launching facilities are located in the park on the Coquille River.

Reservations, fee: No reservations necessary; $8 fee per night. Open all year.

Who to contact: Phone at 503-347-2209, or write at P.O. Box 25, Bandon, OR 97411.

Location: Drive north of the town of Bandon on US 101 for about one mile and you'll see the park entrance on the west side of the road.

Trip note: The Coquille River is the centerpiece for this park. It offers good fishing in season, both for boaters and bankers, with four miles of shore access. If fishing isn't your thing, the park has several hiking trails.

DRIFTWOOD SHORES RV PARK
Site 2

Campsites, facilities: There are 40 drive-through sites for trailers or motorhomes of any length. Electricity, piped water and sewer hookups are provided. Flush toilets, sanitary services, showers, a store, cafe, laundromat and ice are available. Bottled gas is located within one mile. Pets are permitted. Boat docks and launching facilities are nearby.

Reservations, fee: Reservations accepted; $8 fee per night. Open all year.

Who to contact: Phone at 503-347-4122, or write at 935 East 2nd Street, Bandon, OR 97411.

Location: From US 101 in Bandon, take Highway 42S and travel one block south and you'll see the park entrance.

Trip note: This is an in-town motorhome park that can be a base point for many adventures. Rockhounds will enjoy beachcombing, with agates and other semi-precious stones hidden along the beaches. Kids will enjoy the West Coast Game Park Walk-Thru Safari petting zoo seven miles south of town, and Bandon State Park, which is four miles south of town and offers a good wading spot in the creek at the north end of the park. Nearby recreation opportunites include an 18-hole golf course, riding stable and tennis courts.

BLUE JAY CAMPGROUND

Site **3**

Campsites, facilities: There are 19 tent sites and 22 sites for trailers or motorhomes up to 30 feet long. Electricity, piped water and picnic tables are provided. Flush toilets, bottled gas, sanitary services, showers, firewood, a store, cafe, laundromat, ice and playground are available. Pets and motorbikes are permitted. Boat launching facilities are nearby.

Reservations, fee: Reservations accepted; $7 fee per night. Open all year.

Who to contact: Phone at 503-347-3258, or write at P.O. Box 281, Bandon, OR 97411.

Location: Drive two miles south of the town of Bandon on US 101, then go 1/2 mile west on Beach Loop Road and you'll see the campground entrance.

Trip note: The trip note for campsite 2 offers sidetrip information in Bandon. This park is near the beach and close to an 18-hole golf course and hiking trails.

PARK CREEK

Site **4**

Campsites, facilities: There are 12 sites for tents, small trailers or campervans. Picnic tables and firegrills are provided, and pit toilets are available. There is no water. Pets are permitted.

Reservations, fee: No reservations necessary; no fee. Open all year.

Who to contact: Phone at 503-269-5880, or write the Bureau of Land Management at 333 4th Street, Coos Bay, OR 97420.

Location: Follow Middle Canyon Road east from Coquille for 24 miles to the campground.

Trip note: You want to be by yourself? You came to the right place. This pretty little campground is set along Park Creek out in the middle of nowhere.

REMOTE CAMPGROUND

Site **5**

Campsites, facilities: There are 17 sites for trailers or motorhomes of any length. Electricity, piped water, sewer hookups and picnic tables are provided. Showers, a store and laundromat are available. Pets and motorbikes are permitted.

Reservations, fee: Reservations accepted; $9 fee per night. Open all year.

Who to contact: Phone at 503-572-5105, or write at Box 13, Highway 42, Remote, OR 97468.

Location: This campground is located east of the town of Remote on Highway 42.

Trip note: This is a good layover for the motorhome cruiser heading between Roseburg and Coos Bay. It is a quiet, pretty spot, set along the Middle Fork of the Coquille River.

BEAR CREEK

Site **6**

Campsites, facilities: There are nine tent sites and eight sites for trailers or motorhomes up to 16 feet long. Picnic tables and firegrills are provided, and pit toilets and piped water are available. Pets are permitted.

Reservations, fee: No reservations necessary; no fee. Open all year.

Who to contact: Phone at 503-269-5880, or write the Bureau of Land Management at 333
South 4th Street, Coos Bay, OR 97420.

Location: From Coquille, go 26 miles southeast on Highway 42 to the campground.

Trip note: The spot is a rustic camping option to campsite 5, and the price is right. It is set
along Bear Creek near where it empties into the Middle Fork of the Coquille River.
Nice little spot.

Site 7   JOHN P. AMACHER COUNTY PARK

Campsites, facilities: There are 40 sites for trailers or motorhomes up to 30 feet long.
Electricity, piped water, sewer hookups and picnic tables are provided. Flush toilets,
showers, firewood and a playground are available. Bottled gas, a store, cafe, laundromat and ice are located within one mile. Pets and motorbikes are permitted. Boat
launching facilities are nearby.

Reservations, fee: No reservations necessary; $9 fee per night. Open all year.

Who to contact: Phone at 503-672-4901, or write at P.O. Box 800, Winchester, OR
97495.

Location: This campground is five miles north of the town of Roseburg.

Trip note: This is a prime layover spot for I-5 motorhome cruisers. It is a wooded county
park set along the banks of the Umpqua River, just enough off the beaten track to be
missed by most out-of-towners. Nearby recreation options include an 18-hole golf
course and tennis courts.

Site 8   SAFARI WILDLIFE RV PARK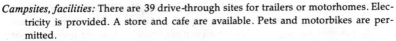

Campsites, facilities: There are 39 drive-through sites for trailers or motorhomes. Electricity is provided. A store and cafe are available. Pets and motorbikes are permitted.

Reservations, fee: No reservations necessary; $5 fee per night. Open all year.

Who to contact: Phone at 503-679-6761, or write at P.O. Box 1600, Winston, OR 97496.

Location: In Winston, take exit 119 off I-5 and continue 3 1/2 miles southwest on Highway
42 to the park.

Trip note: This park is adjacent to the Wildlife Safari Park in Winston (near Roseburg),
which offers a walk through and a petting zoo. Nearby recreation options include an
18-hole golf course, hiking trails and marked bike trails.

Site 9   TWIN RIVERS VACATION PARK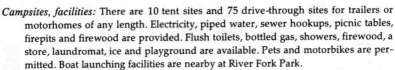

Campsites, facilities: There are 10 tent sites and 75 drive-through sites for trailers or
motorhomes of any length. Electricity, piped water, sewer hookups, picnic tables,
firepits and firewood are provided. Flush toilets, bottled gas, showers, firewood, a
store, laundromat, ice and playground are available. Pets and motorbikes are permitted. Boat launching facilities are nearby at River Fork Park.

Reservations, fee: Reservations accepted; $12.50 fee per night. Open all year.

Who to contact: Phone at 503-673-3811, or write at 433 River Forks Park, Roseburg, OR
97470.

Location: Near Roseburg, take exit 125 off I-5 and follow it five miles west to Old Garden
Valley Road, then turn south for 1 1/2 miles to the campground.

Trip note: The country park is set next to River Fork Park, a 100-acre day-use park, situated where the North and South Forks of the Umpqua River meet. In season, salmon and steelhead migrate through here. It has a playground for children including a fort, teepees, totem poles and wading pool.

Site 10   KOA PINE SPRINGS

Campsites, facilities: There are 46 tent sites and 24 drive-through sites for trailers or motorhomes of any length. Picnic tables are provided. Flush toilets, bottled gas, sanitary services, showers, firewood, a recreation hall, a store, cafe, laundromat, ice, playground, electricity, piped water and sewer hookups are available. Pets and motorbikes are permitted.

Reservations, fee: Reservations accepted; $9 fee per night. MasterCard and Visa accepted. Open all year.

Who to contact: Phone at 503-348-2358, or write at 46612 Highway 101, Langlois, OR 97450.

Location: This campground is located about 10 miles north of Port Orford on US 101.

Trip note: This spot is often considered as just a layover camp, but it offers large, secluded sites set among big trees and coastal ferns. It is minutes away from Elk River and Sixes River, where the fishing can be good. Camp Blanco State Park is just a few miles away.

Site 11   CAPE BLANCO STATE PARK

Campsites, facilities: There are 58 sites for tents, trailers or motorhomes up to 40 feet long. A special camping area is reserved for hikers and bicyclists. Picnic tables, piped water, electrical hook-ups and firegrills are provided. Firewood, flush toilets, showers, a laundromat and sanitary disposal station are available. Pets are permitted. Some facilities are wheelchair accessible.

Reservations, fee: No reservations necessary; $7 fee per night. Open mid-April to late-September.

Who to contact: Phone at 503-332-2971, or write at P.O. Box 299, Sixes, OR 97476.

Location: Travel four miles north of Port Orford on US 101, then head northwest on the road to the park and drive five miles to the campground.

Trip note: This large park is named for the white chalk ("blanco") appearance of the seacliffs, which rise 200 feet above the ocean. Sea lions inhabit the offshore rocks, and there are trails and a road that leads to the black-sand beach below the cliffs. There is good access to the Sixes River, which travels for over two miles through the meadows and forests of the park. Of historical interest are the lighthouse and Hughes House Museum, both located within the park.

Site 12   SIXES RIVER

Campsites, facilities: There are 19 sites for tents, trailers or motorhomes up to 16 feet long. Picnic tables and firegrills are provided, and pit toilets are available. There is no piped water. Pets are permitted.

Reservations, fee: No reservations necessary; no fee. Open all year.

Who to contact: Phone at 503-269-5880, or write the Bureau of Land Management at 333

South 4th Street, Coos Bay, OR 97420.

Location: Drive on US 101 to town of Sixes, then head east on Highway 184 for 11 1/2 miles to the campground. The last half mile is unpaved.

Trip note: This is a primitive, secluded campground for people who want quiet and a free, rustic spot. It is set along the banks of Sixes River.

PORT ORFORD
Site 13 — TRAILER VILLAGE

Campsites, facilities: There are seven tent sites and 49 drive-through sites for trailers or motorhomes of any length. Electricity, piped water, sewer hookups and picnic tables are provided. Flush toilets, bottled gas, sanitary services, showers, recreation hall, a store, cafe, laundromat and ice are available. Pets and motorbikes are permitted. Boat docks and launching facilities are nearby.

Reservations, fee: Reservations accepted; $9 fee per night. Open all year.

Who to contact: Phone at 503-332-1041, or write at P.O. Box 697, Port Orford, OR 97465.

Location: In the town of Port Orford, drive one block east on Madrona Avenue, then 1/2 mile north on Port Orford Loop.

Trip note: This is a friendly, Mom-and-Pop campground in Port Orford, where the hosts make you feel at home. An informal group campfire and happy hour is scheduled each evening. There is a small gazebo where you can get coffee in the morning and a patio where you can sit. Fishing is good during the fall and winter on the nearby Elk and Sixes Rivers, and the campground has a smokehouse, freezer and cleaning table.

BUTLER BAR
Site 14

Campsites, facilities: There are 16 sites for tents, trailers or motorhomes up to 16 feet long. Picnic tables and firegrills are provided. Piped water, pit toilets and firewood are available. Pets are permitted.

Reservations, fee: No reservations necessary; $2 fee per night. Open late-May to late-September.

Who to contact: Phone Siskiyou National Forest at 503-439-3011, or write at Powers Ranger District, Port Orford, OR 97465.

Location: From Port Orford, go three miles north on US 101, then 7 1/2 miles southeast on County Road 208. From there, take Forest Service Road 325 southeast and drive 11 miles to the campground. The road is paved all the way to the campground.

Trip note: This campground is set back from the shore of the Elk River and is surrounded by old growth forest, with some reforested areas nearby. Across the river is the Grassy Knob Wilderness Area, but it has no trails and is too rugged to hike. Elk River has native trout and steelhead in the winter.

LAIRD LAKE
Site 15

Campsites, facilities: There are five tent sites. Picnic tables and firegrills are provided, and pit toilets and firewood are available. There is no water. Pets are permitted.

Reservations, fee: No reservations necessary; no fee. Open late-May to late-September.

Who to contact: Phone Siskiyou National Forest at 503-439-3011, or write at Powers

Ranger District, Powers, OR 97466.

Location: From Port Orford, go three miles north on US 101, then 7 1/2 miles southeast on County Road 208. From there, take Forest Service Road 325 southeast and drive 15 1/2 miles to the campground. The road is paved all the way to the campground.

Trip note: This secluded campground is set along the shore of Laird Lake in a very private and scenic spot. Most campers have no idea that such a spot is available here.

MYRTLE GROVE
Site **16**

Campsites, facilities: There are eight tent sites and four sites for trailers or motorhomes. Picnic tables and firegrills are provided. Pit toilets and firewood are available. There is no water. Pets are permitted.

Reservations, fee: No reservations necessary; no fee. Open late-May to late-September.

Who to contact: Phone Siskiyou National Forest at 503-439-3011, or write at Powers Ranger District, Powers, OR 97466.

Location: From Powers, take State Highway 242 for 4 1/4 miles, then go 4 1/2 miles south on Forest Service Road 33, and you'll see the campground. The road is paved all the way to the campground.

Trip note: This Forest Service campground is set along the South Fork of the Coquille River, a little downstream from campsite 7, in similar surroundings. A few miles away is the Big Tree Recreation Site, where there is a huge Port Orford Cedar. A prime hike can be made on a trail that runs adjacent to Elk Creek.

DAPHNE GROVE
Site **17**

Campsites, facilities: There are 17 sites for tents, trailers or motorhomes up to 15 feet long. Picnic tables and firegrills are provided. Pit toilets, piped water and firewood are available. Pets are permitted.

Reservations, fee: No reservations necessary; $4 fee per night. Open late-May to late-September.

Who to contact: Phone Siskiyou National Forest at 503-439-3011, or write at Powers Ranger District, Powers, OR 97466.

Location: From the town of Powers, go 4 1/2 miles southeast on State Highway 242, then 10 1/2 miles south on Forest Service Road 33, and you'll see the campground entrance. The road is paved all the way to the campground.

Trip note: A prime spot far enough out of the way that it attracts little use. It is set along the South Fork of the Coquille River and is surrounded by old growth Douglas Fir and Cedar.

ROCK CREEK
Site **18**

Campsites, facilities: There are six tent sites and two sites for trailers or motorhomes. Picnic tables and firegrills are provided, and pit toilets and firewood are available. There is no piped water. Pets are permitted.

Reservations, fee: No reservations necessary; $2 fee per night. Open late-May to late-September.

Who to contact: Phone Siskiyou National Forest at 503-439-3011, or write at Powers Ranger District, Powers, OR 97466.

Location: From Powers, go 4 1/2 miles on State Highway 242 to Forest Service Road 33. Go south on Forest Service Road 33 for 13 miles, then 1 1/2 miles southwest on Forest Service Road 3347 to the campground. The road is paved all the way.

Trip note: This little-known camp is set along Rock Creek, just upstream from its confluence with the South Fork of the Coquille River. It is surrounded by old growth forest and some reforested areas. One good side trip here is the one-mile climb to Azalea Lake, which is stocked with trout. There are some hike-in campsites at the lake, but there is no piped drinking water. In July, the Azalea blooms can be spectacular.

SQUAW LAKE

Site **19**

Campsites, facilities: There are seven sites for tents, trailers or motorhomes. Picnic tables and firegrills are provided. Pit toilets, piped water and firewood are available. Pets are permitted.

Reservations, fee: No reservations necessary; $2 fee per night. Open late-May to late-September.

Who to contact: Phone Siskiyou National Forest at 503-439-3011, or write at Powers Ranger District, Powers, OR 97466.

Location: Take State Highway 242 southeast from Powers for 4 1/2 miles. At Forest Service Road 33 go south for 12 1/2 miles, then southeast on Forest Service Road 3348 for 4 1/2 miles. Turn and head east on Forest Service Road 3342 for one mile and you'll see the campground. The road is paved all but the last 1/2 mile.

Trip note: This campground is set along the shore of five-acre Squaw Lake, set in rich, old-growth forest. The trailheads for Panther Ridge Trail and Coquille River Falls Trail are a 10-minute drive from the campground. It is strongly advised to obtain a Forest Service map, which details the back country roads and trails.

TUCKER FLAT

Site **20**

Campsites, facilities: There are 10 primitive tent sites. Picnic tables and firegrills are provided. Piped water, pit toilets and firewood are available. Pets are permitted.

Reservations, fee: No reservations necessary; no fee. Open May to late-October.

Who to contact: Phone at 503-779-2351, or write the Bureau of Land Management at 3040 Biddle Road, Medford, OR 97501.

Location: Travel 20 miles west of Glendale on Cow Creek Road, then five miles southwest on Marial Road to the campground.

Trip note: This campground is set in the Zane Grey Bureau of Land Management tract, covering 18,460 acres. The Rogue River passes through the tract, and the Rogue River Trail is alongside for 26 miles. This is rugged country, with steep canyons and many small waterfalls. There is a riding stable nearby.

FOSTER BAR

Site **21**

Campsites, facilities: There are 10 sites for tents, trailers or motorhomes up to 16 feet long. Fire rings and picnic tables are provided. Pit toilets and firewood are available, but there is no drinking water. Pets are permitted. Boat launching facilities are available.

Reservations, fee: No reservations necessary; $2 fee per night. Open March to late-September.

Who to contact: Phone Siskiyou National Forest at 503-247-6651, or write Gold Beach
Ranger District, P.O. Box 548, 1225 South Ellensburg, Gold Beach, OR 97444.

Location: From Gold Beach, take Jerry Flat Road east for 30 miles to the turn-off to Agness.
Turn right on Illahe-Agness Road and drive three miles to the campground.

Trip note: This campground is located on the banks of the Rogue River, a popular put-in
spot for the eight-mile inner tube ride to the town of Agness. Life jackets are mandatory because of rough rapids. A day permit is required from the Forest Service in
order to put a boat into the water here. People also fish off the river bar. Campsites 22
and 35 provide nearby options.

ILLAHE

Site **22**

Campsites, facilities: There are 23 sites for tents, trailers or motorhomes up to 21 feet long.
Piped water, fire rings and picnic tables are provided. Flush toilets and firewood are
available. A store is located within five miles. Pets are permitted. Boat docks are
nearby at Foster Bar campground (campsite 13).

Reservations, fee: No reservations necessary; no fee. Open mid-May to mid-October.

Who to contact: Phone Siskiyou National Forest at 503-247-6651, or write Gold Beach
Ranger District, P.O. Box 548, 1225 South Ellensburg, Gold Beach, OR 97444.

Location: From Agness, travel five miles north on County Road 375 and you'll see the
campground entrance.

Trip note: This campground is quiet and isolated, yet boating and fishing opportunities are
just a mile away at campsite 21.

HUMBUG MOUNTAIN STATE PARK

Site **23**

Campsites, facilities: There are 75 tent sites and 30 sites for trailers or motorhomes up to 45
feet long. A special camping area is reserved for hikers and bicyclists. Electricity,
piped water, sewer hookups, firegrills and picnic tables are provided. Flush toilets,
showers, firewood and a laundromat are available. Pets are permitted.

Reservations, fee: No reservations necessary; $8 fee per night. Open mid-April to late-
October.

Who to contact: Phone at 503-332-6774, or write at Port Orford, OR 97465.

Location: From Port Orford, go six miles south on US 101 and you'll see the park
entrance.

Trip note: This park is named after the mountain that towers almost 2000 feet above the
nearby coastline. A three-mile trail leads to its peak. This is a special place, with both
the Pacific Ocean and nearby Bush Creek accessible. You can fish in either.

ARIZONA BEACH CAMPGROUND

Site **24**

Campsites, facilities: There are 31 tent sites and 96 drive-through sites for trailers or
motorhomes of any length. Electricity, piped water, sewer hookups and picnic tables
are provided. Flush toilets, bottled gas, sanitary services, showers, firewood, a recreation hall, a store, laundromat, ice and playground are available. Pets and motorbikes
are permitted.

Reservations, fee: Reservations accepted; $12 fee per night. MasterCard and Visa accepted.
Open all year.

Who to contact: Phone at 503-332-6491, or write at P.O. Box 621, Gold Beach, OR 97444.

Location: Drive 15 miles north of Gold Beach on US 101 and you'll see the campground.

Trip note: This pleasant campground offers grassy, tree-lined sites set along a half mile of ocean beach frontage. A creek runs through the campground and people swim at the mouth of it in the summer. The elk and deer roam nearby. An 11-unit motel is available for campers who need some cleanup time.

Site 25   HONEYBEAR CAMPGROUND

Campsites, facilities: There are 20 tent sites and 58 drive-through sites for trailers or motorhomes of any length. Picnic tables are provided. Flush toilets, electricity, piped water, cable TV, sanitary services, showers, firewood, recreation hall, a store, laundromat, ice and playground are available. Pets and motorbikes are permitted.

Reservations, fee: Reservations accepted; $9 fee per night. MasterCard and Visa accepted. Open May to late-October.

Who to contact: Phone at 503-247-2765, or write at P.O. Box 97, Ophir, OR 97464.

Location: From Gold Beach, go nine miles north on US 101 to Ophir Road. The campground is two miles north on Ophir Road.

Trip note: This campground offers wooded sites with ocean views. The owners have built a huge, authentic chalet which contains a German deli, a recreation area, and a big dance floor. Six nights a week during the summer, they hold dances with live music provided by a European band.

Site 26   NESIKA BEACH TRAILER PARK

Campsites, facilities: There are 10 tent sites and 27 drive-through sites for trailers or motorhomes of any length. Electricity, piped water, sewer hookups and picnic tables are provided. Flush toilets, sanitary services, showers, a store, cafe, laundromat and ice are available. Pets and motorbikes are permitted.

Reservations, fee: Reservations accepted; $8 fee per night. Open all year.

Who to contact: Phone at 503-247-6077, or write at 32887 Nesika Road, Gold Beach, OR 97444.

Location: Take US 101 seven miles north of Gold Beach to Nesika Road. From there, go 1/2 mile west on Nesika Road to the campground.

Trip note: This campground is next to Neskika Beach, a good layover spot for Highway 101 cruisers. An 18-hole golf course is available nearby.

Site 27   FOUR SEASONS RV RESORT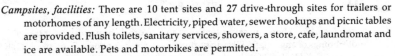

Campsites, facilities: There are 45 drive-through sites for trailers or motorhomes up to 35 feet long. Electricity, piped water, sewer hookups and picnic tables are provided. Flush toilets, bottled gas, sanitary services, showers, firewood, a recreation hall, store, laundromat and ice are available. Pets and motorbikes are permitted. Boat docks and launching facilities are nearby.

Reservations, fee: Reservations accepted; $12 fee per night. Open all year.

Who to contact: Phone at 503-247-7959, or write at 96526 North Bank Rogue, Gold Beach, OR 97444.

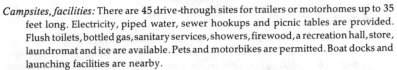

Location: Drive one mile north of Gold Beach on US 101, then three miles northeast on Rogue River Road. From there, follow the signs on North Bank Rogue Road to the campground.

Trip note: This resort is set along the shore of the Rogue River. Nearby recreation options include an 18-hole golf course, a riding stable, and boat trips on the wild and scenic Rogue—on anything from a raft to a jet boat.

Site 28   KIMBALL CREEK BEND

Campsites, facilities: There are eight tent sites and 56 drive-through sites for trailers or motorhomes of any length. Electricity, piped water, sewer hookups and picnic tables are provided. Flush toilets, bottled gas, sanitary services, showers, recreation hall, a store, cafe, laundromat, ice and playground are available. Pets are permitted. Boat docks and launching facilities are nearby.

Reservations, fee: Reservations accepted; $11 fee per night. MasterCard and Visa accepted. Open all year.

Who to contact: Phone at 503-247-7580, or write at 32051 Watson, Gold Beach, OR 97444.

Location: From Gold Beach, go one mile north on US 101, then 3 1/2 miles northeast on Rogue River Road to North Bank Rogue Road and head 4 1/2 miles southeast to the campground.

Trip note: This campground is set along the scenic Rogue River, just far enough from the coast to provide quiet and its own distinct character. Nearby recreation options include an 18-hole golf course, hiking trails and boating facilities.

Site 29   LUCKY LODGE RV PARK

Campsites, facilities: There are seven tent sites and 36 drive-through sites for trailers or motorhomes of any length. Electricity, piped water, sewer hookups and picnic tables are provided. Flush toilets, bottled gas, sanitary services, showers, firewood, recreation hall and laundromat are available. Pets and motorbikes are permitted. Boat docks and rentals are nearby.

Reservations, fee: Reservations accepted; $8 fee per night. Open all year.

Who to contact: Phone at 503-247-7618, or write at 32040 Watson Lane, Gold Beach, OR 97444.

Location: Go one mile north of Gold Beach on US 101. At Rogue River Road, go northeast 3 1/2 miles to North Bank Rogue Road and follow it 4 1/2 miles to the park.

Trip note: Nearby recreation options include hiking trails and a riding stable.

Site 30   INDIAN CREEK RECREATION PARK

Campsites, facilities: There are 25 tent sites and 100 drive-through sites for trailers or motorhomes of any length. Electricity, piped water, sewer hookups and picnic tables are provided. Flush toilets, showers, firewood, a recreation hall, store, sauna, cafe, laundromat, ice and playground are available. Bottled gas is located within one mile. Pets and motorbikes are permitted. Boat docks, launching facilities and rentals are nearby.

Reservations, fee: Reservations accepted; $12 fee per night. MasterCard and Visa accepted. Open all year.

Who to contact: Phone at 503-247-7704, or write at 94680 Jerry's Flat, Gold Beach, OR 97444.

Location: Look for Jerry's Flat Road in Gold Beach, drive 1/2 mile down the road and you'll find the campground.

Trip note: This campground is set along the Rogue River on the outskirts of the town of Gold Beach. Nearby recreation options include a riding stable and boat trips on the Rogue.

Site 31   SANDY CAMP RV

Campsites, facilities: There are 50 tent sites and 36 drive-through sites for trailers or motorhomes of any length. Electricity, piped water, sewer hookups and picnic tables are provided. Flush toilets, showers, firewood and ice are available. Bottled gas, sanitary services, a store, cafe and laundromat are located within one mile. Pets and motorbikes are permitted. Boat docks, launching facilities and rentals are nearby.

Reservations, fee: Reservations accepted; $9 fee per night. MasterCard and Visa accepted. Open April to mid-October.

Who to contact: Phone at 503-247-2301, or write at P.O. Box 455, Gold Beach, OR 97444.

Location: This park is in the town of Gold Beach, at the south jetty of the Port of Gold Beach.

Trip note: This park is set right on the ocean. Nearby recreation options include beachcombing, marked bike trails and boating facilities.

Site 32   ANGLERS TRAILER VILLAGE

Campsites, facilities: There are 36 drive-through sites for trailers or motorhomes of any length. Electricity, piped water and sewer hookups are provided. Flush toilets, showers, a recreation hall, store, laundromat and ice are available. Pets and motorbikes are permitted.

Reservations, fee: Reservations accepted; $7 fee per night. Open all year.

Who to contact: Phone at 503-247-7922, or write at 95706 Jerry's Flat, Gold Beach, OR 97444.

Location: In Gold Beach, turn east at the south end of Rogue River Bridge, then go 3 1/2 miles north on Jerry's Flat Road to the campground.

Trip note: One of seven campgrounds set along the lower Rogue River.

Site 33   LOBSTER CREEK

Campsites, facilities: There are five sites for tents, trailers or motorhomes up to 21 feet long. Piped water, fire rings and picnic tables are provided. Flush toilets are available. Pets are permitted. A boat launch is also available.

Reservations, fee: No reservations necessary; no fee. Open April to late-October.

Who to contact: Phone Siskiyou National Forest at 503-247-6651, or write Gold Beach Ranger District, P.O. Box 548, 1225 South Ellensburg, Gold Beach, Beach, OR 97444.

Location: From Gold Beach, take County Road 375 for 4 1/2 miles northeast, then go 5 1/2 miles northeast on Forest Service Road 33 to the campground.

Trip note: This tiny, little-known campground is set on a riverbar along the Rogue River, about a 15-minute drive from Gold Beach. Good base camp for a fishing trip.

Site 34   QUOSATANA

Campsites, facilities: There are 44 sites for tents, trailers or motorhomes up to 32 feet long. Piped water, firegrills and picnic tables are provided. Flush toilets, firewood, and a sanitary disposal station are available. Pets are permitted. A boat ramp is available.

Reservations, fee: No reservations necessary; $5 fee per night. Open April to late-October.

Who to contact: Phone Siskiyou National Forest at 503-247-6651, or write Gold Beach Ranger District, P.O. Box 548, 1225 South Ellensburg, Gold Beach, Beach, OR 97444.

Location: From Gold Beach, go 4 1/2 miles northeast on County Road 595, then 10 miles northeast on Forest Service Road 33 to the campground.

Trip note: This campground is set along the banks of the Rogue, upriver from much smaller campsite 33. A good base camp for a Rogue River fishing trip.

Site 35   COUGAR LANE CAMPGROUND

Campsites, facilities: There are five tent sites and 91 drive-through sites for trailers or motorhomes of any length. Electricity, piped water, sewer hookups and picnic tables are provided. Flush toilets, bottled gas, sanitary services, showers and a laundromat are available. A store, cafe and ice are located within one mile. Pets and motorbikes are permitted. Boat launching facilities are nearby.

Reservations, fee: Reservations accepted; $10 fee per night. MasterCard and Visa accepted. Open all year.

Who to contact: Phone at 503-247-2813, or write at 04215 Agness Road, Agness, OR 97406.

Location: From Gold Beach, drive 28 miles east on Jerry's Flat Road and you'll see the entrance to the campground.

Trip note: This is a destination campground set along the scenic Rogue River, in the middle of the Siskiyou National Forest. Fishing is the main focus here. Boating is sharply limited with the nearest pullout 12 miles downstream. It is advisable to obtain a Forest Service map, which details the back country.

Site 36   LOEB STATE PARK

Campsites, facilities: There are 53 sites for trailers or motorhomes up to 50 feet long, and a special camping area for hikers and bicyclists. Electricity, piped water and picnic tables are provided. Flush toilets and firewood are available. Pets are permitted.

Reservations, fee: No reservations necessary; $7 fee per night. Open mid-April to late-October.

Who to contact: Phone at 503-469-2021, or write c/o Harris Beach State Park, 1655 Highway 101, Brookings, OR 97415.

Location: From the town of Brookings, drive eight miles northeast on a county road that goes along the Chetco River and you'll see the entrance to the park.

Trip note: This park is located in a canyon formed by the Chetco River, and is adjacent to Siskiyou National Forest. There are hiking trails in the forest. A Forest Service map details trailheads.

Site 37   HARRIS BEACH STATE PARK

Campsites, facilities: There are 66 tent sites and 85 sites for trailers or motorhomes up to 50 feet long. A special camping area for hikers and bicyclists. Picnic tables and firegrills are provided. Electricity, piped water, sewer hookups, flush toilets, sanitary services, showers, firewood and a laundromat are available. Some facilities are wheelchair accessible. Pets are permitted.

Reservations, fee: Reservations accepted; $8 fee per night. Open all year.

Who to contact: Phone at 503-469-2021, or write at 1655 Highway 101, Brookings, OR 97415.

Location: Drive two miles north of Brookings on US 101 and you'll see the park entrance.

Trip note: This state park is set along the beach. Goat Rock, a migratory bird sanctuary is just offshore. There are numerous trout streams in the area. For details, pick up a Siskiyou Forest Service map in Brookings at 555 Fifth Street. In fall and winter, the nearby Chetco River attracts good runs of salmon and steelhead, respectively.

Site 38   LITTLE REDWOOD

Campsites, facilities: There are 16 sites for tents, trailers or motorhomes up to 16 feet long. Picnic tables and firegrills are provided, and pit toilets and firewood are available. Pets are permitted.

Reservations, fee: No reservations necessary; $4 fee per night. Open late-May to mid-September.

Who to contact: Phone Siskiyou National Forest at 503-469-2196, or write Chetco Ranger District, P.O. Box 730, Brookings, OR 97415.

Location: Go south for 1/2 mile on US 101 from Brookings to County Road 784, then turn northeast on County Road 784 and continue 7 1/2 miles. At Forest Service Road 376, turn northeast and drive six miles to the campground.

Trip note: This campground is set among old growth fir trees near the bank of the Chetco River. The primary watersport here is swimming in the summer, although there is some fishing for trout. In winter months, this is a prime base camp for a steelhead trip. The camp is also on the main western access route to the Kalmiopsis Wilderness, which is about 20 miles away. If this and nearby campsite 39 are full, the Forest Service offers a number of small, alternative sites. If you are stuck, call them for details.

Site 39   RIVER BEND RV PARK

Campsites, facilities: There are eight tent sites and 120 drive-through sites for trailers or motorhomes of any length. Electricity, piped water, sewer hookups and picnic tables are provided. Flush toilets, bottled gas, sanitary services, showers, a recreation hall with exercise equipment, a store, cafe, laundromat, cable RV, ice and playground are available. Pets and motorbikes are permitted. Boat launching facilities are also available.

Reservations, fee: Reservations accepted; $10 fee per night. Open all year.

Who to contact: Phone at 503-469-3356, or write at 98203 South Bank Chetco, Brookings, OR 97415.

Location: In Brookings, drive 1 1/2 miles east on Chetco River Road and follow the signs to the park.

Trip note: This campground is set along the banks of the Chetco River and offers complete fishing services including guided salmon and steelhead trips on the Chetco in fall and winter. Deep sea trips for salmon or rockfish are available in the summer. Bait, tackle and a free fishing class for campers is offered. There is a beach for sunbathing and swimming.

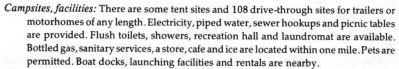

Site **40**   CHETCO RV PARK

Campsites, facilities: There are 119 drive-through sites for trailers or motorhomes of any length. Electricity, piped water, sewer hookups and picnic tables are provided. Flush toilets, bottled gas, sanitary services, showers, a recreation hall, store, cafe, laundromat and ice are available. Pets are permitted. Boat docks, launching facilities and rentals are nearby.

Reservations, fee: Reservations accepted; $11 fee per night. MasterCard and Visa accepted. Open all year.

Who to contact: Phone at 503-469-3863, or write at P.O. Box 760, Brookings, OR 97415.

Location: In Brookings, go one mile south of Chetco River Bridge on US 101 and you'll see the park entrance.

Trip note: This park is near both the Chetco River, known for its winter steelhead run, and the beach. Whale watching time is good from January through May. Nature trails are a good side trip, located a short drive up the river road.

Site **41**   DRIFTWOOD TT RETREAT

Campsites, facilities: There are some tent sites and 108 drive-through sites for trailers or motorhomes of any length. Electricity, piped water, sewer hookups and picnic tables are provided. Flush toilets, showers, recreation hall and laundromat are available. Bottled gas, sanitary services, a store, cafe and ice are located within one mile. Pets are permitted. Boat docks, launching facilities and rentals are nearby.

Reservations, fee: Reservations accepted; $9 fee per night. Open all year.

Who to contact: Phone at 503-469-3213, or write at Box 2066, Harbor, OR 97415.

Location: Go to the south end of Chetco River Bridge in Brookings, then follow Lower Harbor Road to camp.

Trip note: This park is set along the beach near the mouth of the Chetco River. Nearby recreation options include bike trails, hiking trails and a full service marina.

Site **42**   SEA BIRD RV

Campsites, facilities: There are 60 drive-through sites for trailers or motorhomes of any length. Electricity, piped water, sewer hookups and picnic tables are provided. Flush toilets, bottled gas, sanitary services, showers, a recreation hall, store, cafe, laundromat and ice are available. Pets and motorbikes are permitted. Boat docks, launching facilities and rentals are nearby.

Reservations, fee: Reservations accepted; $8 fee per night. Open all year.

Who to contact: Phone at 503-469-3512, or write at P.O. Box 1026, Brookings, OR 97415.

Location: In Brookings, drive 1/4 mile south of Chetco River Bridge on US 101 and you'll see the park entrance.

Trip note: This is one of several campgrounds set along the beach here. Nearby recreation options include marked bike trails, a full service marina and tennis courts.

WINCHUCK
Site 43

Campsites, facilities: There are five tent sites and eight sites for trailers or motorhomes up to 16 feet long. Picnic tables and firegrills are provided, and pit toilets, piped water and firewood are available. Pets are permitted.

Reservations, fee: No reservations necessary; $4 fee per night. Open late-May to mid-September.

Who to contact: Phone Siskiyou National Forest at 503-469-2196, or write Chetco Ranger District, P.O. Box 730, Brookings, OR 97415.

Location: From Brookings, go 5 1/2 miles south on US 101, then six miles east on County Road 896. From there, take Forest Service Road 3907 and go one mile east to the campground.

Trip note: This forested campground is set along the banks of the Winchuck River, an out-of-the-way stream that out-of-towners don't have a clue about. It's quiet, remote and not that far from the coast, although it feels like it.

BIG PINE
Site 44

Campsites, facilities: There are 14 tent sites. Picnic tables and firegrills are provided, and pit toilets and firewood are available. There is no piped water. Pets are permitted.

Reservations, fee: No reservations necessary; $2 fee per night. Open late-May to mid-September.

Who to contact: Phone Siskiyou National Forest at 503-476-3830, or write Galice Ranger District, P.O. Box 1131, Grants Pass, OR 97526.

Location: Go 3 1/2 miles north of Grants Pass on I-5, then turn northwest on County Road 2-6 and drive 12 1/2 miles. At Forest Service Road 355 head southwest for 12 3/4 miles to the campground.

Trip note: This little campground is in an isolated area west of Grants Pass, set in a valley of old-growth pine and douglas fir. A small creek is about one mile from camp. It is advisable to obtain a National Forest map.

THE LAST RESORT
Site 45

Campsites, facilities: There are 18 tent sites and 25 sites for trailers or motorhomes of any length. Electricity, piped water, sewer hookups and picnic tables are provided. Flush toilets, bottled gas, sanitary services, showers, firewood, a recreation hall, store, cafe, laundromat, ice and playground are available. Pets and motorbikes are permitted.

Boat docks, launching facilities and rentals are nearby.

Reservations, fee: Reservations accepted; $9 fee per night. Open all year.

Who to contact: Phone at 503-597-4989, or write at 2700 Lake Shore Drive, Selma, OR 97538.

Location: Near Selma, take the Lake Selmac exit off US 199, then go two miles east on Lake Selmac Road to the resort.

Trip note: This resort is set along the shore of Lake Selmac. A golf course is nearby. A unique tour is available at Oregon Caves National Monument, about 30 miles away. To get there, drive 20 miles east of the town of Cave Junction on Highway 46. This road gets narrow near the end and is not recommended for trailers. A 75-minute guided tour is available. The caves are a long, winding trail through a series of amazing caverns. Dress warm, it can be cold and clammy.

Site 46   KERBY TRAILER PARK AND CAMPGROUND

Campsites, facilities: There are 10 tent sites and 14 drive-through sites for trailers or motorhomes of any length. Electricity, piped water, sewer hookups and picnic tables are provided. Flush toilets, bottled gas, showers and a laundromat are available. A store and ice are located within one mile. Pets and motorbikes are permitted.

Reservations, fee: Reservations accepted; $7 fee per night. Open all year.

Who to contact: Phone at 503-592-2897, or write at 24542 Redwood Highway, Kerby, OR 97531.

Location: This campground is about 400 yards south of Kerby on US 199.

Trip note: This small campground is set near the Illinois River, a good stream during the summer for swimming. See the trip note to campsite 45 for side trip information. Other recreation options include an 18-hole golf course, hiking trails and tennis courts.

Site 47   SHADY ACRES

Campsites, facilities: There are four tent sites and 16 drive-through sites for trailers or motorhomes of any length. Electricity, piped water, sewer hookups and picnic tables are provided. Flush toilets, bottled gas, sanitary services, showers and firewood are available. A store, cafe, laundromat and ice are located within one mile. Pets and motorbikes are permitted.

Reservations, fee: Reservations accepted; $7 fee per night. Open all year.

Who to contact: Phone at 503-592-3702, or write at 27550 Redwood Highway, Cave Junction, OR 97523.

Location: From Cave Junction, go one mile south on US 199 and you'll see the entrance.

Trip note: This park is set in a forested area on the banks of the Illinois River. See the trip note to campsite 45 for information on Oregon Caves National Monument.

Site 48   TRAILS END RV PARK & CAMPGROUND

Campsites, facilities: There are 25 tent sites and 16 drive-through sites for trailers or motorhomes of any length. Electricity, piped water, sewer hookups and picnic tables are provided. Flush toilets, bottled gas, sanitary services, showers and a playground are available. A store, cafe, laundromat and ice are located within one mile. Pets and motorbikes are permitted.

Reservations, fee: Reservations accepted; $10 fee per night. Open all year.

Who to contact: Phone at 503-592-3354, or write at 336 Burch Drive, Cave Junction, OR 97523.

Location: Go south on US 199 from Cave Junction for 2 1/2 miles, then turn west on Burch Drive and travel about 400 yards to the campground entrance.

Trip note: This campground is set along the Illinois River, about 20 miles from Oregon Caves National Monument. See trip note to campsite 45 for details. The Kerbyville Historical Museum is two miles south of Caves Junction. Nearby recreation options include hiking trails, bike trails and a riding stable.

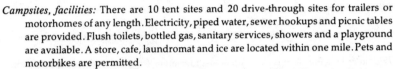

Site **49**
CAVES HIGHWAY TRAILER PARK

Campsites, facilities: There are 10 tent sites and 20 drive-through sites for trailers or motorhomes of any length. Electricity, piped water, sewer hookups and picnic tables are provided. Flush toilets, bottled gas, sanitary services, showers and a playground are available. A store, cafe, laundromat and ice are located within one mile. Pets and motorbikes are permitted.

Reservations, fee: Reservations accepted; $10 fee per night. Open all year.

Who to contact: Phone at 503-592-3338, or write at 977 Caves Highway, Cave Junction, OR 97523.

Location: From Cave Junction, off US 199, take Highway 46 one mile east to the campground.

Trip note: See the trip note to campsite 45 for additional information on the nearby Oregon Caves National Monument. Nearby recreation options include an 18-hole golf course, hiking trails, marked bike trails and tennis courts.

Site **50**
WOODLAND ECHOES RESORT

Campsites, facilities: There are 20 drive-through sites for trailers or motorhomes of any length. Picnic tables are provided. Flush toilets, showers, firewood, a cafe and ice are available. Pets are permitted.

Reservations, fee: Reservations accepted; $6 fee per night. MasterCard and Visa accepted. Open all year.

Who to contact: Phone at 503-592-3406, or write at 7901 Caves Highway, Cave Junction, OR 97523.

Location: From Cave Junction, take Highway 46 east for eight miles.

Trip note: See the trip note to campsite 45 for information about the nearby Oregon Caves National Monument.

Site **51**
GRAYBACK

Campsites, facilities: There are 35 sites for tents, trailers or motorhomes up to 22 feet long. Picnic tables and firegrills are provided. Flush toilets and piped water are available. Pets are permitted.

Reservations, fee: No reservations necessary; $4 fee per night. Open May through September.

Who to contact: Phone Siskiyou National Forest at 503-592-2166, or write to Illinois Valley

Ranger District at P.O. Box 389, Cave Junction, OR 97523.

Location: From Cave Junction, go 12 miles east on Highway 46.

Trip note: This wooded campground is set along the banks of Sucker Creek, about ten miles from Oregon Caves National Monument. It is a good spot to camp if you're planning to visit the caves.

CAVE CREEK
Site **52**

Campsites, facilities: There are 18 tent sites. Piped water, pit toilets, picnic tables are provided. Firewood is available. Showers are located within five miles. Pets are permitted.

Reservations, fee: No reservations necessary; $4 fee per night. Open June to mid-September.

Who to contact: Phone Siskiyou National Forest at 503-592-2166, or write Illinois Valley Ranger District at P.O. Box 389, Cave Junction, OR 97523.

Location: Take Highway 46 east of Cave Junction for 16 miles, then go one mile south on Forest Service Road 4032.

Trip note: This Forest Service camp is just four miles from the Oregon Caves National Monument—no campground is closer. See the trip note to campsite 45 for details on the Oregon Caves. The camp is set along Cave Creek, a small creek with some trout fishing opportunities. There are many hiking trails in the area.

BOLAN LAKE
Site **53**

Campsites, facilities: There are 22 sites for tents, trailers or motorhomes up to 16 feet long. Picnic tables and firegrills are provided. Pit toilets and firewood are available, but there is no piped water. Pets are permitted. Boat docks and launching facilities are nearby.

Reservations, fee: No reservations necessary; $2 fee per night. Open July to November.

Who to contact: Phone Siskiyou National Forest at 503-592-2166, or write Illinois Valley Ranger District at P.O. Box 389, Cave Junction, OR 97523.

Location: From Cave Junction, take County Road 12 eight miles southeast, then go 14 miles southeast on County Road 4007. Located at Forest Service Road 408.

Trip note: This campground is set along the shore of 15-acre Bolan Lake. Very few out-of-towners know about this spot. A trail leads from the lake up to a lookout point and ties into miles of other trails. See a Forest Service map for more information.

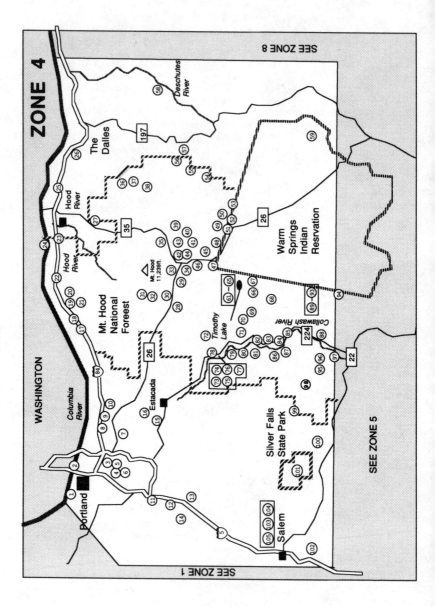

MOUNT HOOD

Site 1
JANTZEN BEACH
RV PARK

Campsites, facilities: There are 164 drive-through sites for trailers or motorhomes of any length. Electricity, piped water, sewer hookups and picnic tables are provided. Flush toilets, bottled gas, showers, a recreation hall, store, cafe, laundromat, ice, playground and swimming pool are available. Pets are permitted. Boat docks, launching facilities and rentals are nearby.

Reservations, fee: Reservations accepted; $14 fee per night. MasterCard and Visa accepted. Open all year.

Who to contact: Phone at 503-289-7626, or write at 1503 North Hayden Island, Portland, OR 97217.

Location: Take I-5 about four miles north of Portland and look for the Jantzen Beach exit, then go 1/2 mile west on Hayden Island Drive.

Trip note: This motorhome campground is set near the banks of the Columbia River on the outskirts of Portland. Nearby recreation options include an 18-hole golf course, a riding stable and tennis courts.

Site 2
PORTLAND MOBILE
HOME PARK

Campsites, facilities: There are 100 drive-through sites for trailers or motorhomes of any length. Electricity, piped water and sewer hookups are provided. Flush toilets, bottled gas, sanitary services, showers, a store, cafe, laundromat and ice are available. Pets are permitted.

Reservations, fee: Reservations accepted; $14 fee per night. Open all year.

Who to contact: Phone at 503-285-1617, or write at 9000 Northeast Union, Portland, OR 97211.

Location: This campground is in Portland at exit 307 off I-5. Follow Northeast Union Avenue for 1 1/2 miles south to the campground.

Trip note: Many recreation opportunities are available in the Portland area. Numerous marinas on the Willamette and Columbia rivers offer boat trips and rentals, and the city parks and nearby state parks (503-238-7488) offer hiking, bicycling and horseback riding possibilities. The Columbia River Highway along Route 30 is a scenic drive. If golf is your game, Portland has 18 public golf courses. The winter ski areas at Mount Hood are an hour's drive away.

Site 3   LAWN ACRES MOBILE & RV PARK

Campsites, facilities: There are 20 drive-through sites for trailers or motorhomes of any length. Electricity, piped water and sewer hookups are provided. Flush toilets, showers and a laundromat are available. Bottled gas, a store, cafe and ice are located within one mile. Pets are permitted.

Reservations, fee: Reservations accepted; $9 fee per night. Open all year.

Who to contact: Phone at 503-654-5739, or write at 11421 Southeast 82nd Street, Portland, OR 97266.

Location: In Portland off I-205, drive west on Sunnyside, then 1/2 mile north on 82nd Avenue.

Trip note: This is a Portland-based motorhome park in a wooded setting. See the trip note to campsite 2 for information about the recreation possibilities in Portland.

Site 4   FIR GROVE RV & TRAILER PARK

Campsites, facilities: There are five tent sites and 25 sites for trailers or motorhomes of any length. Electricity, piped water and sewer hookups are provided. Flush toilets, showers and ice are available. Bottled gas, sanitary services, a store, cafe and playground are located within one mile. Pets and motorbikes are permitted.

Reservations, fee: Reservations accepted; $12 fee per night. MasterCard and Visa accepted. Open all year.

Who to contact: Phone at 503-252-9993, or write at 5541 Northeast 72nd, Portland, OR 97218.

Location: In Portland off I-205, go about 400 yards northeast on Columbia Boulevard, then one mile west on Northeast Killingsworth and you'll see the park entrance.

Trip note: This park is set near the banks of the Columbia River in the outskirts of Portland. See the trip note to campsite 2 for information about the nearby recreation opportunities.

Site 5   SOUTH GATE MOBILEHOME & RV PARK

Campsites, facilities: There are 24 sites for trailers or motorhomes of any length in this adult only campground. Electricity, piped water and sewer hookups are provided. Flush toilets, showers and a laundromat are available. Bottled gas, sanitary services, a store, cafe and ice are located within one mile. Motorbikes are permitted.

Reservations, fee: No reservations necessary; $7 fee per night. Open all year.

Who to contact: Phone at 503-775-0456, or write at 7911 Southeast 82nd, Portland, OR 97266.

Location: In Portland off I-205, take the Foster exit and go 1/2 mile west to 82nd Avenue. The park is one mile south.

Trip note: Motorhome campers can use this for a base of operations for a Portland vacation. See the trip note to campsite 2 for information about the recreation possibilities in the area.

Site 6
TALL FIRS RV & MOBILE HOME PARK

Campsites, facilities: There are six sites for trailers or motorhomes of any length. Electricity, piped water and sewer hookups are provided. Flush toilets, showers and a laundromat are available. Bottled gas, a store, cafe and ice are located within one mile. Pets are permitted.

Reservations, fee: No reservations necessary; $12 fee per night. Open all year.

Who to contact: Phone at 503-761-8210, or write at 15656 Southeast Division, Portland, OR 97236.

Location: Take the Division Street exit off I-205 in Portland and go east on Southeast Division.

Trip note: This small RV park is located in Portland. See the trip note for campsite 2 for information about the recreation possibilities in the area.

Site 7
BELL ACRES MOBILE ESTATES

Campsites, facilities: There are 12 drive-through sites for trailers or motorhomes of any length in this adult only campground. Electricity, piped water and sewer hookups are provided. Flush toilets, showers, a recreation hall and laundromat are available. Bottled gas, sanitary services, a store, cafe and ice are located within one mile. Pets are permitted.

Reservations, fee: Reservations accepted; $12 fee per night. Open all year.

Who to contact: Phone at 503-665-4774, or write at 2980 Northeast Division, Gresham, OR 97030.

Location: Take East Hogan Road off US 26 in Gresham and travel 1/2 mile north, then go 1/2 mile east on Northeast Division.

Trip note: This is an option for motorhome campers in Portland. See the trip note for campsite 2 for information on recreation opportunities in the area.

Site 8
CROWN POINT RV PARK

Campsites, facilities: There are 15 drive-through sites for trailers or motorhomes of any length. Electricity, piped water and picnic tables are provided. Flush toilets, bottled gas, sanitary services, showers, a store, laundromat and ice are available. Pets are permitted.

Reservations, fee: Reservations accepted; $11 fee per night. Open April to late-October.

Who to contact: Phone at 503-695-5207, or write at 37035 Northeast Benfield, Corbett, OR 97019.

Location: Take I-84 east from Portland to exit 22 near Troutdale, then take Highway 30 southeast about 400 yards to the park.

Trip note: This little park is located near the Columbia River along scenic Highway 30. Crown Point State Park is nearby and is open during the days. It offers views of the Columbia River Gorge and the historical Vista House, a memorial built in 1918 to honor Oregon's pioneers.

Site 9
ROLLING HILLS
MOBILE TERRACE

Campsites, facilities: There are 101 drive-through sites for trailers or motorhomes of any length. Electricity, piped water, sewer hookups and picnic tables are provided. Flush toilets, bottled gas, showers, recreation hall, laundromat and swimming pool are available. A store, cafe and ice are located within one mile. Pets are permitted.

Reservations, fee: Reservations accepted; $14 fee per night. Open all year.

Who to contact: Phone at 503-666-7282, or write at 20145 Northeast Sandy, Troutdale, OR 97060.

Location: From Troutdale, take I-84 West to Sandy Boulevard exit, then go 3/4 mile west on Sandy Boulevard to the motorhome park.

Trip note: A full-service layover spot set about 10 miles east of Portland near the Columbia River. Nearby recreation options include an 18-hole golf course, a full service marina and tennis courts.

Site 10
MULTNOMAH COUNTY
CAMPGROUND/OXBOW

Campsites, facilities: There are 45 sites for tents, trailers or motorhomes up to 35 feet long. Picnic tables are provided, and piped water, pit toilets, firewood and a playground are available. Boat launching facilities are nearby.

Reservations, fee: No reservations necessary; $6 fee per night. Open all year.

Who to contact: Phone at 503-663-4708, or write at 3010 Southeast Oxbow, Gresham, OR 97030.

Location: In Gresham, take Southeast Division four miles east, then continue east four miles on Oxbow Parkway to the park.

Trip note: This 1000-acre park is set along the Sandy River, a short distance for the Columbia Gorge, and has been designated as a natural preservation area. Fishing, swimming and non-motored boating are permitted here.

Site 11
TRAILER PARK
OF PORTLAND

Campsites, facilities: There are 100 drive-through sites for trailers or motorhomes of any length. Electricity, piped water, sewer hookups and picnic tables are provided. Flush toilets, sanitary services, showers, laundromat and playground are available. Bottled gas, a store, cafe and ice are located within one mile. Pets and motorbikes are permitted.

Reservations, fee: Reservations accepted; $13 fee per night. MasterCard and Visa accepted. Open all year.

Who to contact: Phone at 503-692-0225, or write at 6645 Southwest Nyberg Road, Tualatin, OR 97062.

Location: Take I-5 south from Portland to Tualatin, then take exit 289 and follow Highway 212 east for about 1/4 mile to the park.

Trip note: This park is set just south of Portland. See the trip note for campsite 2 for information about the recreation possibilities in the area.

Site **12**
FOUR-U
MOBILE PARK

Campsites, facilities: There are nine sites for trailers or motorhomes of any length. Electricity, piped water and sewer hookups are provided. Flush toilets, sanitary services, showers and laundromat are available. A store, cafe and ice are located within one mile. Pets are permitted.

Reservations, fee: Reservations accepted; $10 fee per night. Open all year.

Who to contact: Phone at 503-639-3350, or write at 18030 Southwest Lower Boones, Portland, OR 97223.

Location: Go 11 miles south of Portland on I-5, take exit 290, then go west to Lower Boones Ferry Road.

Trip note: An option for motorhome campers visiting the Portland area who want a base camp outside the city. Nearby recreation options include an 18-hole golf course and marked bike trails.

Site **13**
ISBERG
RV PARK

Campsites, facilities: There are 84 drive-through sites for trailers or motorhomes of any length. Electricity, piped water and sewer hookups are provided. Flush toilets, bottled gas, sanitary services, showers, recreation hall, a store, cafe, laundromat and ice are available. Pets are permitted.

Reservations, fee: Reservations accepted; $12 fee per night. MasterCard and Visa accepted. Open all year.

Who to contact: Phone at 503-678-2646, or write at 21599 Dolores Northeast, Aurora, OR 97002.

Location: Take I-5 north for about seven miles from the town of Woodburn, then take exit 278 at Aurora and go about 200 yards to the park.

Trip note: This motorhome campground is in a rural area just off the main highway and offers a recreation room, a jogging trail and a pitch-and-putt golf course.

Site **14**
CHAMPOEG
STATE PARK

Campsites, facilities: There are 48 sites for trailers or motorhomes up to 30 feet long. Electricity, piped water and picnic tables are provided. Flush toilets, sanitary services, showers, firewood and laundromat are available. Some facilities are wheelchair accessible. Pets are permitted. Boat docking facilities are nearby.

Reservations, fee: No reservations necessary; $7 fee per night. Open all year with limited winter facilities.

Who to contact: Phone at 503-678-1251, or write at 7679 Champoeg Road NE, Saint Paul, OR 97137.

Location: Take the Champoeg-Aurora exit off I-5 between Salem and Portland and drive eight miles west to the park.

Trip note: This state park is set along the banks of the Willamette River and offers an interpretive center, a botanical garden featuring native plants, and hiking and bike paths.

Site 15   MILO MCIVER
STATE PARK

Campsites, facilities: There are 44 sites for trailers or motorhomes of any length. Electricity, piped water and picnic tables are provided. Flush toilets, sanitary services, showers, firewood and laundromat are available. Some of the facilities are wheelchair accessible. Pets are permitted. Boat launching facilities are nearby.

Reservations, fee: No reservations necessary; $7 fee per night. Open mid-April to late-October.

Who to contact: Phone at 503-630-7150, or write at 24101 South Entrance Road, Estacada, OR 97023.

Location: This state park is located five miles north of Estacada just off Highway 211.

Trip note: This park is not far from the Portland area, yet far enough off the beaten track to provide a feel of separation from the metropolitan area. It is set along the banks of the Collawash River and has a boat ramp. Trails for hiking and horseback riding, and a group picnic area are also accessible.

Site 16   NORTH FORK
EAGLE CREEK

Campsites, facilities: There are 18 tent sites and five drive-through sites for trailers or motorhomes up to 20 feet long. Picnic tables are provided, and piped water and pit toilets are available. Pets are permitted.

Reservations, fee: No reservations necessary; $4 fee per night. Open mid-May to late-September.

Who to contact: Phone the Bureau of Land Management at 503-399-5646, or write at Box 3227, Salem, OR 97302.

Location: Take US 26 southeast from Portland 28 miles, then turn south on Firwood Road and continue five miles to the campground.

Trip note: This campground is set along the North Fork of Eagle Creek. A more primitive option to nearby campsite 15. Known by few from outside the area.

Site 17   AINSWORTH
STATE PARK

Campsites, facilities: There are 45 sites for trailers or motorhomes of any length. Electricity, piped water, sewer hookups and picnic tables are provided. Flush toilets, showers, firewood and a laundromat are available. Pets are permitted.

Reservations, fee: No reservations necessary; $8 fee per night. Open mid-April to late-October.

Who to contact: Phone at 503-695-2301, or write at Bonneville, OR 97014.

Location: Travel 37 miles east of Portland on Highway 30 to the park.

Trip note: This state park is set along the scenic Columbia Gorge. A two-mile section of the Columbia Gorge Trail connects this park with John Yeon State Park, which is open during the day. Fishermen should take a look at the Bonneville Fish Hatchery, where a giant sturgeon provides a unique sight.

EAGLE CREEK
Site **18**

Campsites, facilities: There are 19 sites for tents, trailers or motorhomes up to 22 feet long. Picnic tables and firegrills are provided. Piped water, flush toilets, sanitary services and firewood are available. Pets are permitted. Boat docks and launching facilities are nearby.

Reservations, fee: No reservations necessary; $5 fee per night. Open mid-May to October. Reservations required for groups.

Who to contact: Phone Columbia Gorge Ranger District at 503-695-2276, or write at Mt. Hood National Forest, 31520 SE Woodard Road, Troutdale, OR 97060.

Location: This campground is located two miles east of the town of Bonneville off Highway 84.

Trip note: A good base camp for a hiking trip. The Eagle Creek Trail leaves the campground and goes 14 miles to Waddam Lake, where it intersects with the Pacific Crest Trail. There is a primitive campground at the 7 1/2-mile point. The upper seven miles of the trail passes through the Cascade Range wilderness.

HERMAN
Site **19** ## HORSE CAMP

Campsites, facilities: There are seven sites for tents, trailers or motorhomes up to 31 feet long. Piped water, firegrills and picnic tables are provided, and stock handling facilities are available. Sanitary services, showers, a store, cafe, laundromat and ice are nearby. Some facilities are wheelchair accessible. Pets are permitted.

Reservations, fee: No reservations necessary; no fee. Open mid-May to October.

Who to contact: Phone Columbia Gorge Ranger District at 503-695-2276, or write Mount Hood National Forest, 31520 SE Woodard Road, Troutdale, OR 97060.

Location: Located about 1 1/2 miles east of the town of Cascade Locks.

Trip note: This campground is located about 1/2 mile from Herman Creek, not far from the Pacific Crest Trail. One of three campgrounds in the immediate area.

KOA CASCADE
Site **20** ## LOCKS

Campsites, facilities: There are 25 tent sites and 74 drive-through sites for trailers or motorhomes of any length. Electricity, piped water, sewer hookups and picnic tables are provided. Flush toilets, bottled gas, sanitary services, showers, firewood, recreation hall, a store, laundromat, ice, playground and a heated swimming pool are available. A cafe is located within one mile. Pets and motorbikes are permitted.

Reservations, fee: Reservations accepted; $12 fee per night. MasterCard and Visa accepted. Open all year.

Who to contact: Phone at 503-374-8668, or write at Star Route Box 660, Cascade Locks, OR 97014.

Location: Turn off I-84 in Cascade Locks and travel two miles east on Forest Lane to the campground.

Trip note: A good layover for motorhome campers touring the Columbia River corridor. Nearby recreation options include bike trails, hiking trails and tennis courts. The 200-acre Cascade Locks and Marine Park is nearby and offers everything from museums to boat trips.

CASCADE LOCKS
MARINE PARK
Site **21**

Campsites, facilities: There are 10 tent sites and 30 drive-through sites for trailers or motorhomes of any length. Picnic tables are provided. Flush toilets, sanitary services, showers and a playground are available. Bottled gas, a store, cafe, laundromat and ice are located within one mile. Pets and motorbikes are permitted. Boat docks and launching facilities are nearby.

Reservations, fee: No reservations necessary; $7 fee per night. Open all year.

Who to contact: Phone at 503-374-8619, or write at P.O. Box 307, Cascade Locks, OR 97014.

Location: In Cascade Locks, take exit 42 off I-84 and follow it 1/2 mile east to the park.

Trip note: This riverfront park covers 200 acres and offers a museum and boatrides. Nearby recreation options include hiking trails and tennis courts.

WYETH
Site **22**

Campsites, facilities: There are 20 sites for tents, trailers or motorhomes up to 32 feet long. Firegrills and picnic tables are provided, and piped water and flush toilets are available. Pets are permitted.

Reservations, fee: No reservations necessary; $7 fee per night. Open mid-May to October.

Who to contact: Phone Columbia Gorge Ranger District at 503-695-2276, or write Mount Hood National Forest, 31520 SE Woodard Road, Troutdale, OR 97060.

Location: Travel seven miles east of the town of Cascade Locks on I-84 to the Wyeth exit, then go 1/2 mile on a county road and you'll see the campground entrance.

Trip note: A good layover spot for Columbia River corridor cruisers. It is set along Gordon Creek, near the Columbia.

TUCKER PARK
Site **23**

Campsites, facilities: There are five tent sites and 29 sites for tents, trailers or motorhomes of any length. Picnic tables are provided, and electricity, piped water, flush toilets, showers, firewood and a playground are available. A store, cafe, laundromat and ice are located within one mile. Pets and motorbikes are permitted.

Reservations, fee: Reservations accepted; $8 fee per night. Open April to November.

Who to contact: Phone at 503-386-4477, or write at 2440 Dee Highway, Hood River, OR 97031.

Location: From the town of Hood River travel four miles south on State Route 281 to the park.

Trip note: This county park is set along the banks of the Hood River. It's just far enough out of the way to be missed by most of the tourist traffic.

VIENTO
STATE PARK
Site **24**

Campsites, facilities: There are five tent sites and 58 sites for trailers or motorhomes up to 30 feet long. Electricity, piped water and picnic tables are provided. Flush toilets, showers, firewood and a laundromat are available. Pets are permitted.

Reservations, fee: No reservations necessary; $7 fee per night. Open mid-April to late-October.

Who to contact: Phone at 503-295-2215, or write at Hood River, OR 97031.

Location: Travel eight miles west on I-84 from Hood River and you'll see the park entrance.

Trip note: This park is set along the Columbia River Gorge and offers scenic hiking trails. A picturesque drive is along old Highway 30, which skirts the Columbia River.

Site **25**   MEMALOOSE STATE PARK

Campsites, facilities: There are 67 tent sites and 43 sites for trailers or motorhomes of any length. Electricity, piped water, sewer hookups and picnic tables are provided. Flush toilets, sanitary services, showers and firewood are available. Some facilities are wheelchair accessible. Pets and motorbikes are permitted.

Reservations, fee: No reservations necessary; $8 fee per night. Open mid-April to late-October.

Who to contact: Phone at 503-478-3336, or write at 5th & Washington, Dalles, OR 97058.

Location: From The Dalles, go 11 miles west on I-84 and you'll see the turn-off. Access is available travelling westbound only.

Trip note: This park is set along the scenic Columbia River Gorge. A prime layover spot for campers cruising the Oregon/Washington border.

Site **26**   LONE PINE TRAVEL PARK

Campsites, facilities: There are 10 tent sites and 22 drive-through sites for trailers or motorhomes of any length. Electricity, piped water and sewer hookups are provided. Flush toilets, showers, a cafe, laundromat, ice and playground are available. Bottled gas and sanitary services are located within one mile. Pets are permitted. Boat docks and launching facilities are nearby.

Reservations, fee: Reservations accepted; $12 fee per night. MasterCard and Visa accepted. Open all year.

Who to contact: Phone at 503-296-9133, or write at 335 US 197, The Dalles, OR 97058.

Location: Near The Dalles, take exit 87 off I-84 to US 197 and follow it to the park.

Trip note: This area gets hot weather and occasional winds shooting the river canyon during summer months. Nearby recreation options include an 18-hole golf course and tennis courts.

Site **27**   TOLL BRIDGE PARK

Campsites, facilities: There are 18 tent sites and 20 sites for trailers or motorhomes up to 20 feet long. Electricity, piped water, sewer hookups and picnic tables are provided. Flush toilets, sanitary services, showers, firewood, a recreation hall and playground are available. Bottled gas, a store, cafe, laundromat and ice are located within one mile. Pets and motorbikes are permitted.

Reservations, fee: Reservations accepted; $8 fee per night. Open April to November, and some off-season weekends.

Who to contact: Phone at 503-352-6300, or write at 7360 Toll Bridge, Parkdale, OR 97041.

Location: Travel on Highway 35 south from Hood River for 18 miles. One mile south of the town of Mount Hood, go 1/4 mile southwest on a county road to 7360 Toll Bridge Road.

Trip note: This 100-acre county park is set along the East Fork of the Hood River and offers bike trails, hiking trails and tennis courts. The Mt. Hood Wilderness area is located southwest of the park.

GREEN CANYON
Site 28   ◭

Campsites, facilities: There are 15 sites for tents, trailers or motorhomes up to 31 feet long. Picnic tables and firegrills are provided, and pit toilets, firewood and piped water are available. A store, cafe and ice are located within five miles. Some facilities are wheelchair accessible. Pets are permitted.

Reservations, fee: No reservations necessary; $5 fee per night. Open May to late-September.

Who to contact: Phone Zig Zag Ranger District at 503-666-0704, or write at 70220 East Highway 35, ZigZag, OR 97049.

Location: Just north of Zig Zag on Highway 26, take Forest Service Road 2618 and drive 4 1/2 miles south to the campground.

Trip note: A winner that few out-of-towners know about. It is set along the banks of the Salmon River. There is a long trail nearby that parallels the Salmon River past several waterfalls. See a Forest Service map for details.

CAMP CREEK
Site 29   ◭

Campsites, facilities: There are 30 sites for tents, trailers or motorhomes up to 22 feet long. Piped water, firegrills and picnic tables are provided. Flush toilets and firewood are available. Pets are permitted.

Reservations, fee: No reservations necessary; $3 fee per night. Open late-May to late-September.

Who to contact: Phone Zig Zag Ranger District at 503-666-0704, or write at 70220 East Highway 35, ZigZag, OR 97049.

Location: Travel southeast on Highway 26 from Rhododendron about three miles to camp.

Trip note: This campground is set along Camp Creek, not far from the Zigzag River.

TOLL GATE
Site 30   ▣

Campsites, facilities: There are 23 tent sites and nine sites for trailers or motorhomes up to 22 feet long. Picnic tables and firegrills are provided, and pit toilets and firewood are available. There is no piped water. Pets are permitted.

Reservations, fee: No reservations necessary; $4 fee per night. Open late-May to late-September.

Who to contact: Phone Zig Zag Ranger District at 503-666-0704, or write at 70220 East Highway 35, ZigZag, OR 97049.

Location: This campground is about 2 1/2 miles southeast of the town of ZigZag on Highway 26.

Trip note: This campground is set along the banks of the Zigzag River near the town of Rhododendron, the most primitive of the three camps in the immediate vicinity. The Mount Hood Wilderness is nearby and there are numerous trails in the area.

MCNEIL
Site **31**

Campsites, facilities: There are 34 tent sites and 34 sites for trailers or motorhomes up to 22 feet long. Picnic tables are provided. Firewood is available. There is no piped water. Pets are permitted.

Reservations, fee: No reservations necessary; $3 fee per night. Open May to late-September.

Who to contact: Phone Zig Zag Ranger District at 503-666-0704, or write at 70220 East Highway 35, ZigZag, OR 97049.

Location: From Zigzag go 4 1/2 miles northeast on County Route 18, then 1/2 mile northeast on Forest Service Road 17. The camp is about 200 yards east on Forest Service Road 1825.

Trip note: This campground is set along the Clear Fork of the Sandy River near the western border of the Mount Hood Wilderness area. Several trails nearby provide access to the Wilderness backcountry. See a Forest Service map for options.

RILEY HORSE
Site **32** CAMP

Campsites, facilities: There are 14 sites for tents, trailers or motorhomes up to 22 feet long. Piped water, firegrills and picnic tables are provided. Firewood and facilities for horses are available. Pets are permitted.

Reservations, fee: No reservations necessary; $3 fee per night. Open May to late-September.

Who to contact: Phone Zig Zag Ranger District at 503-666-0704, or write at 70220 East Highway 35, ZigZag, OR 97049.

Location: Take County Route 18 northeast of ZigZag for four miles, then go one mile east on Forest Service Road 1825. The campground is about 100 yards south on Forest Service Road 382.

Trip note: This campground is just across the road from campsite 31 and offers the same opportunities, except that this camp provides stock handling facilities.

ALPINE
Site **33**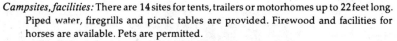

Campsites, facilities: There are seven tent sites and three sites for trailers or motorhomes up to 22 feet long. Piped water, firegrills and picnic tables are provided. Firewood is available. Pets are permitted.

Reservations, fee: No reservations necessary; $3 fee per night. Open July to late-September.

Who to contact: Phone Zig Zag Ranger District at 503-666-0704, or write at 70220 East Highway 35, ZigZag, OR 97049.

Location: From Government Camp, take Highway 50 northeast 4 1/2 miles to the campground.

Trip note: This small, quiet campground is adjacent to the Mt. Hood ski area on the south slopes of Mt. Hood. The Pacific Crest Trail passes very close to camp and there are several trails nearby that offer access to the Mt. Hood Wilderness area.

STILL CREEK
Site **34**

Campsites, facilities: There are 27 sites for tents, trailers or motorhomes up to 30 feet long. Picnic tables and firegrills are provided, and pit toilets and piped water are available. Firewood is available. Pets are permitted.

Reservations, fee: No reservations necessary; $3 fee per night. Open mid-June to late-September.

Who to contact: Phone Zig Zag Ranger District at 503-666-0704, or write at 70220 East Highway 35, ZigZag, OR 97049.

Location: From Government Camp, go one mile east on US 26, then 500 yards south on Forest Service Road 2650.

Trip note: This primitive camp is set near the junction of Highways 26 and 35, located along Still Creek where it pours off the south slope of Mt. Hood.

ROBINHOOD
Site **35**

Campsites, facilities: There are 24 tent sites and 24 sites for trailers or motorhomes up to 16 feet long. Piped water and picnic tables are provided. Firewood is available. Pets are permitted. Boat docks are available nearby.

Reservations, fee: No reservations necessary; $4 fee per night. Open mid-May to early-September.

Who to contact: Phone Ranger District at 503-666-0701, or write at Mount Hood National Forest at 2955 NW Division Street, Gresham, OR 97030.

Location: From Parkdale, go three miles southeast on Highway P28, then 12 miles south on Highway 35 to the campground.

Trip note: This campground is set along the East Fork of the Hood River, at the base of Mt. Hood. A trail from camp follows the river north for about four miles to Sherwood Campground. From there, it joins a network of trails that provide access to the Mt. Hood Wilderness.

KNEBAL SPRINGS
Site **36**

Campsites, facilities: There are six sites for tents, trailers or motorhomes up to 21 feet long. Picnic tables and firegrills are provided, and pit toilets and firewood are available. There is no piped water. Horse loading and tending facilities. Pets are permitted.

Reservations, fee: No reservations necessary; $2 fee per night. Open July to early-September.

Who to contact: Phone Barlow Ranger District at 503-467-2291, or write Mount Hood National Forest at P.O. Box 67, Dufur, OR 97021.

Location: Go 12 miles southwest of Dufur on County Road 1 and continue west on Forest Service Road 44. At Forest Service Road 4430 travel four miles north, then go southwest on Forest Service Road 1720 for one mile to the campground.

Trip note: This is in a semi-primitive area near Knebal Springs, an ephemeral water. A trail from camp provides access to a network of other trails in the area. A Forest Service map is advised.

EIGHT MILE
Site **37**   ## CROSSING

Campsites, facilities: There are 14 sites for tents, trailers or motorhomes up to 16 feet long. Picnic tables and firegrills are provided. Pit toilets, piped water and firewood are available. Pets are permitted.

Reservations, fee: No reservations necessary; $4 fee per night. Open June to mid-October.

Who to contact: Phone Barlow Ranger District at 503-467-2291, or write Mount Hood National Forest at P.O. Box 67, Dufur, OR 97021.

Location: Go 12 miles southwest of Dufur on County Road 1 and continue west on Forest Service Road 44. At Forest Service Road 4430 travel north for 1/2 mile to the campground.

Trip note: This campground is set along Eight Mile Creek and gets little camping pressure. Some trails are in the area. See a Forest Service map for options.

PEBBLE FORD
Site **38**

Campsites, facilities: There are five sites for tents, trailers or motorhomes up to 15 feet long. Picnic tables and firegrills are provided, and pit toilets and firewood are available. There is no piped water. Pets are permitted.

Reservations, fee: No reservations necessary; $2 fee per night. Open July to early-September.

Who to contact: Phone Barlow Ranger District at 503-467-2291, or write Mount Hood National Forest at P.O. Box 67, Dufur, OR 97021.

Location: From Dufur, go 12 miles southwest on County Road 1, then five miles west on Forest Service Road 44. Turn south on Forest Service Road 131 and travel 1/2 mile and you'll see the campground.

Trip note: This is just a little camping spot by the side of the gravel Forest Service road. Small, primitive and quiet.

BADGER LAKE
Site **39**

Campsites, facilities: This small campground is only accessible by 4-wheel drive vehicles. Picnic tables and firegrills are provided, and pit toilets are available. There is no piped water. Pets are permitted.

Reservations, fee: No reservations necessary; no fee. Open July to early-September.

Who to contact: Phone Barlow Ranger District at 503-467-2291, or write Mount Hood National Forest at P.O. Box 67, Dufur, OR 97021.

Location: From the town of Mount Hood travel 19 miles south on Highway 35, then take a left onto Forest Service Road 3550 and drive 3 1/2 miles to Forest Service Road 3530. Turn left and drive one mile to Camp Windy. From there go two miles on Forest Service Road 4860, then make a hairpin left on Forest Service Road 140 and drive four miles to the lake. The last two miles require a 4-wheel drive vehicle.

Trip note: This high country campground is set along the shore of Badger Lake. Boating is permitted. It is adjacent to the Badger-Jordan Wilderness area and numerous trails provide access to the backcountry. A Forest Service map details the back country roads and trails.

BONNEY MEADOWS
Site 40

Campsites, facilities: There are six sites for tents, trailers or motorhomes up to 21 feet long. Picnic tables and firegrills are provided, and pit toilets are available. There is no piped water. Firewood is also available. Pets are permitted.

Reservations, fee: No reservations necessary; $4 fee per night. Open July to early-September.

Who to contact: Phone Barlow Ranger District at 503-467-2291, or write Mount Hood National Forest at P.O. Box 67, Dufur, OR 97021.

Location: From town of Tygh Valley on Highway 197, head west to Wamic. From Wamic, go six miles west on County Road 226, then continue south and west on Forest Service Road 48 for 14 miles. Next, go two miles north on Forest Service Road 4890, then continue four miles north on Forest Service Road 4891 to the campground.

Trip note: This is a high-elevation, primitive campground set on the east side of the Cascade Range. As a result, there is little water in the area. Several trails are available, one of which travels 1 1/2 miles up to a group of small lakes. See a Forest Service map for details.

BARLOW CROSSING
Site 41

Campsites, facilities: There are five sites for tents, trailers or motorhomes up to 15 feet long. Picnic tables and firegrills are provided, and pit toilets and firewood are available. There is no piped water. Pets are permitted.

Reservations, fee: No reservations necessary; no fee. Open mid-May to mid-September.

Who to contact: Phone Bear Springs Ranger District at 503-328-6211, or write Mount Hood National Forest at Route 1, Box 65, Maupin, OR 97037.

Location: Take US 26 two miles east of Government Camp, then six miles east on Highway 35. The camp is located nine miles south on Forest Service Road 48.

Trip note: This small roadside campground is set along Barlow Creek and is not known by many folks.

BARLOW CREEK
Site 42

Campsites, facilities: There are five sites for tents, trailers or motorhomes up to 16 feet long. Picnic tables and firegrills are provided. Firewood and pit toilets are available, but there is no piped water. Pets are permitted.

Reservations, fee: No reservations necessary; no fee. Open May to October.

Who to contact: Phone Bear Springs Ranger District at 503-328-6211, or write Mount Hood National Forest at Route 1, Box 65, Maupin, OR 97037.

Location: Go two miles east of Government Camp on US 26, then go 4 1/2 miles east on Highway 35. From there, go four miles southeast on Forest Service Road 3530.

Trip note: This campground is set along Barlow Creek on Old Barlow Road, which was the wagon trail for early settlers in this area. One of several primitive Forest Service camps in the immediate vicinity.

GRINDSTONE
Site **43**

Campsites, facilities: There are four sites for tents, trailers or motorhomes up to 16 feet
   long. Picnic tables and firegrills are provided. Firewood and pit toilets are available,
   but there is no piped water. Pets are permitted.

Reservations, fee: No reservations necessary; no fee. Open May to October.

Who to contact: Phone Bear Springs Ranger District at 503-328-6211, or write Mount Hood
   National Forest at Route 1, Box 65, Maupin, OR 97037.

Location: Drive two miles east of Government Camp on US 26, then go 4 1/2 miles east on
   Highway 35. From there, go two miles southeast on Forest Service Road 3530.

Trip note: This tiny campground is set a few miles upstream on Barlow Creek from
   campsite 42, on Old Barlow Road. A little known and little used spot.

DEVIL'S HALF
Site **44**   ACRE MEADOW

Campsites, facilities: There are six sites for tents, trailers or motorhomes up to 16 feet long.
   Picnic tables and firegrills are provided. Firewood and pit toilets are available. There
   is no piped water. Pets are permitted.

Reservations, fee: No reservations necessary; no fee. Open May to October.

Who to contact: Phone Bear Springs Ranger District at 503-328-6211, or write Mount Hood
   National Forest at Route 1, Box 65, Maupin, OR 97037.

Location: Go two miles east of Government Camp on US 26, then go 4 1/2 miles east on
   Highway 35. From there, go one mile southeast on Forest Service Road 3530.

Trip note: This campground is set a few miles upstream on Barlow Creek from campsite 43,
   which was the wagon trail for early settlers to this area. Several hiking trails are
   nearby, including the Pacific Crest Trail, which provide access to some small lakes in
   the area.

FROG LAKE
Site **45**

Campsites, facilities: There are 33 sites for tents, trailers or motorhomes up to 16 feet long.
   Piped water and picnic tables are provided, and pit toilets and firewood are available.
   Pets are permitted. Boat docks and launching facilities are nearby. No motorized
   boats allowed.

Reservations, fee: No reservations necessary; $6 fee per night. Open mid-June to
   October.

Who to contact: Phone Bear Springs Ranger District at 503-328-6211, or write Mount Hood
   National Forest at Route 1, Box 65, Maupin, OR 97037.

Location: From Government Camp, go seven miles southeast on US 26, then one mile
   southeast on Forest Service Road 2610. The camp is about 500 yards south on Forest
   Service Road 230.

Trip note: A classic spot in the Cascade Range. This campground is set on the shore of little
   Frog Lake, a short distance from the Pacific Crest Trail. Several other trails lead to
   nearby lakes.

Site 46
TRILLIUM LAKE

Campsites, facilities: There are 30 sites for tents, trailers or motorhomes up to 30 feet long. Picnic tables and firegrills are provided, and pit toilets and piped water are available. Pets are permitted. Some of the facilities are wheelchair accessible. Boat docks and launching facilities are available on the lake, but no motors are permitted.

Reservations, fee: No reservations necessary; $6 fee per night. Open late-May to late-September.

Who to contact: Phone Zig Zag Ranger District at 503-666-0704, or write at 70220 East Highway 35, ZigZag, OR 97049.

Location: Take US 26 two miles southeast of Government Camp, then go south on Forest Service Road 2656 for 1 1/4 miles to the campground.

Trip note: This campground is set along the shores of Trillium Lake, which is about 1/2 mile long and 1/4 mile wide. A good lake for canoes and rafts.

Site 47
CLEAR LAKE

Campsites, facilities: There are 28 sites for tents, trailers or motorhomes up to 22 feet long. Picnic tables and firegrills are provided, and piped water, pit toilets and firewood are available. Pets are permitted. Boat docks and launching facilities are nearby. Motorboats are allowed and there is no speed limit.

Reservations, fee: No reservations necessary; $4 fee per night. Open late-May to early-September.

Who to contact: Phone Bear Springs Ranger District at 503-822-3381, or write Mount Hood National Forest at Route 1, Box 65, Maupin, OR 97037.

Location: Travel nine miles southeast of Government Camp on US 26, then go one mile south on Forest Service Road 449.

Trip note: This campground is set along the shore of Clear Lake, a spot favored by fishermen, swimmers and windsurfers. A nearby trail heads north from the lake and provides access to the Pacific Crest Trail and Frog Lake.

Site 48
WHITE RIVER STATION

Campsites, facilities: There are five sites for tents, trailers or motorhomes up to 16 feet long. Picnic tables and firegrills are provided, and pit toilets and firewood are available, but no piped water is available. Pets are permitted.

Reservations, fee: No reservations necessary; no fee. Open May to October.

Who to contact: Phone Bear Springs Ranger District at 503-328-6211, or write Mount Hood National Forest at Route 1, Box 65, Maupin, OR 97037.

Location: Take US 26 two miles east of Government Camp, then go two miles east on Highway 35. Turn south on Forest Service Route 46 and travel nine miles southeast, and then turn south and drive one mile on Forest Service Road 3530.

Trip note: This tiny campground is set along the White River on Old Barlow Road, an original wagon trail used by early settlers. One of several small, secluded camps in the area.

FOREST CREEK

Site **49**

Campsites, facilities: There are five sites for tents, trailers or motorhomes up to 22 feet long. Picnic tables and firegrills are provided, and pit toilets and piped water are available. Pets are permitted.

Reservations, fee: No reservations necessary; $2 fee per night. Open July to early-September.

Who to contact: Phone Barlow Ranger District at 503-467-2291, or write Mount Hood National Forest at P.O. Box 67, Dufur, OR 97021.

Location: From town of Tygh Valley on Highway 197, head west to Wamic. Take County Route 226 six miles west of Wamic, then go 12 1/2 miles southwest on Forest Service Road 48. From there go one mile southeast on Forest Service Road 4885, then south for 1/4 mile on Forest Service Road 3530 to the campground.

Trip note: This is a very old camp set along Forest Creek on the original Barlow Trail. Early settlers used to camp here. You cross a small bridge to reach the camp.

KEEPS MILL

Site **50**

Campsites, facilities: There are five sites for tents. The road to the campground is not good for trailers. Picnic tables and firegrills are provided, and pit toilets and firewood are available. There is no piped water. Pets are permitted.

Reservations, fee: No reservations necessary; no fee. Open May to October.

Who to contact: Phone Bear Springs Ranger District at 503-328-6211, or write Mt. Hood National Forest at Route 1, Box 65, Maupin, OR 97037.

Location: Take County Route 226 six miles west of Wamic, then go 12 1/2 miles southwest on Forest Service Road 48. From there go three miles southeast on Forest Service Road 4885, then turn right and drive 1/4 mile to the campground.

Trip note: This campground is located at the confluence of Clear Creek and the White River. Hiking trails are in the area. A map of Mt. Hood National Forest details the back roads and trails, and is strongly advised.

CLEAR CREEK

Site **51**

Campsites, facilities: There are six sites for tents, trailers or motorhomes up to 16 feet long. Picnic tables and firegrills are provided, and pit toilets and firewood are available. There is no piped water. Pets are permitted.

Reservations, fee: No reservations necessary; no fee. Open May to October.

Who to contact: Phone Bear Springs Ranger District at 503-328-6211, or write Mt. Hood National Forest at Route 1, Box 65, Maupin, OR 97037.

Location: Drive 28 miles west of Maupin on Highway 216, then three miles north on Forest Service Road 2130. The camp is located about 1/2 mile east on Forest Service Road 260.

Trip note: This campground is set along the banks of Clear Creek. A secluded, little-known camp in Mt. Hood National Forest. A Forest Service map details recreational options.

BEAR SPRINGS
Site **52**

Campsites, facilities: There are 21 sites for tents, trailers or motorhomes up to 16 feet long. Electricity, piped water, fire grills and picnic tables are provided. Pit toilets and firewood are available. Pets are permitted.

Reservations, fee: No reservations necessary; $4 fee per night. Open June to October.

Who to contact: Phone Bear Springs Ranger District at 503-328-6211, or write Mt. Hood National Forest at Route 1, Box 65, Maupin, OR 97037.

Location: Coming from the northwest on Highway 26, turn east on Highway 216 just before entering Warm Springs Indian Reservation. Continue on Highway 216 for five miles and look for the campground on the right side.

Trip note: This campground is set along the banks of Indian Creek, just far enough east of Highway 26 to be missed by the highway cruisers.

MCCUBBINS GULCH
Site **53**

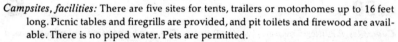

Campsites, facilities: There are five sites for tents, trailers or motorhomes up to 16 feet long. Picnic tables and firegrills are provided, and pit toilets and firewood are available. There is no piped water. Pets are permitted.

Reservations, fee: No reservations necessary; no fee. Open May to October.

Who to contact: Phone Bear Springs Ranger District at 503-328-6211, or write Mount Hood National Forest at Route 1, Box 65, Maupin, OR 97037.

Location: Coming from the northwest on Highway 26, turn east on Highway 216 just before entering Warm Springs Indian Reservation. Continue on Highway 216 for six miles, then make a sharp left onto Forest Service Road 2110 and continue for 1 1/2 miles. Look for the campground entrance on the right side.

Trip note: This is a small and primitive camp that gets little attention from travelers.

ROCK CREEK RESERVOIR
Site **54**

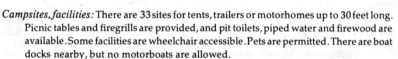

Campsites, facilities: There are 33 sites for tents, trailers or motorhomes up to 30 feet long. Picnic tables and firegrills are provided, and pit toilets, piped water and firewood are available. Some facilities are wheelchair accessible. Pets are permitted. There are boat docks nearby, but no motorboats are allowed.

Reservations, fee: No reservations necessary; $6 fee per night. Open late-April to early-October.

Who to contact: Phone Barlow Ranger District at 503-467-2291, or write Mount Hood National Forest, P.O. Box 67, Defur, OR 97021.

Location: Travel west on County Route 226 for six miles out of Wamic, then go one mile southwest on Forest Service Road 48. The campground is located about 200 yards west on Forest Service Road 4820.

Trip note: This campground is set along the shore of Rock Creek Reservoir. A loop trail is nearby.

Site **55**
BONNEY CROSSING

Campsites, facilities: There are eight sites for tents, trailers or motorhomes. Picnic tables and firegrills are provided. Pit toilets and firewood are available. There is no piped water. Pets are permitted. Boat docks are nearby.

Reservations, fee: No reservations necessary; $4 fee per night. Open late-April to mid-October.

Who to contact: Phone Barlow Ranger District at 503-467-2291, or write Mount Hood National Forest at P.O. Box 67, Dufur, OR 97021.

Location: Drive six miles west of Wamic on County Road 226, then one mile west on Forest Service Road 48. From there, go 200 yards west on Forest Service Road 4810 to the campground.

Trip note: This campground is set along Badger Creek and is the trailhead for the Badger Creek Trail, which provides access to the Badger Creek Wilderness. See a Forest Service map for details.

Site **56**
CASCADE HYLANDS RESORT

Campsites, facilities: There are 35 tent sites and 75 sites for trailers or motorhomes. Electricity, piped water, sewer hookups and picnic tables are provided. Flush toilets, bottled gas, sanitary services, showers, firewood, a store, cafe, laundromat and ice are available. Pets and motorbikes are permitted. Boat docks, launching facilities and rentals are nearby.

Reservations, fee: Reservations accepted; $10 fee per night. MasterCard and Visa accepted. Open all year.

Who to contact: Phone at 503-544-2271, or write at 34 No. Mariposa Drive, Wamic, OR 97063.

Location: Take the Tygh Valley Road exit off US 197, then go 4 1/2 miles west on Wamic Road to Pine Hollow Reservoir Road, follow it 3 1/2 miles north to the resort.

Trip note: This resort is set along the shore of Pine Hollow Reservoir. It's the best game in town for motorhome campers.

Site **57**
WASCO COUNTY FAIRGROUNDS

Campsites, facilities: There are 50 tent sites and 150 drive-through sites for trailers or motorhomes of any length. Electricity, piped water and picnic tables are provided. Flush toilets, sanitary services and showers are available. A store, cafe and ice are located within one mile. Pets are permitted.

Reservations, fee: Reservations accepted; $5 fee per night. Open all year.

Who to contact: Phone at 503-483-2288, or write at Route 1, Box 93, Tygh Valley, OR 97063.

Location: Take US 197 south from Maupin, at Tygh Valley Road go southwest for about 500 yards. The campground is located on Fairgrounds Road.

Trip note: This county campground is set near the confluence of Badger Creek and Tygh Creek. Nearby recreation options include hiking trails, marked bike trails and tennis courts.

BEAVERTAIL
Site **58**

Campsites, facilities: There are 21 tent sites and 18 drive-through sites for trailers or motorhomes up to 20 feet long. Picnic tables and firegrills are provided, and piped water and vault toilets are available. Pets are permitted. Boat launching facilities are nearby.

Reservations, fee: No reservations necessary; $2 fee per night. Open all year.

Who to contact: Phone at 503-447-4115, or write the Bureau of Land Management at P.O. Box 550, Prineville, OR 97754.

Location: This campground is located 17 miles northeast of Maupin along the Deschutes River Road.

Trip note: This isolated campground is set along the banks of the Deschutes River on BLM land. The Deschutes is one of the classic trout streams in the Pacific Northest.

KAH-NEE-TA
Site **59**   RESORT

Campsites, facilities: There are 90 drive-through sites for trailers or motorhomes of any length. Electricity, piped water and sewer hookups are provided. Flush toilets, bottled gas, sanitary services, showers, a cafe, laundromat, ice, playground and swimming pool are available. Pets and motorbikes are permitted.

Reservations, fee: Reservations accepted; $10 fee per night. American Express, Master-Card and Visa accepted. Open all year.

Who to contact: Phone at 800-831-0100, or write at Warm Springs, OR 97761.

Location: From Warm Springs drive 11 miles northeast on the county road to Kah-Nee-Ta.

Trip note: This is the only public camp on the east side of the Warm Springs Indian Reservation—with no other camps within 30 miles. Nearby recreation options include an 18-hole golf course, hiking trails, a riding stable and tennis courts.

LITTLE CRATER
Site **60**

Campsites, facilities: There are 16 sites for tents, trailers or motorhomes up to 16 feet long. Picnic tables and firegrills are provided, and pit toilets, piped water and firewood are available. Pets are permitted.

Reservations, fee: No reservations necessary; $4 fee per night. Open June to October.

Who to contact: Phone Bear Springs Ranger District at 503-328-6211, or write Mount Hood National Forest at Route 1, Box 65, Maupin, OR 97037.

Location: Travel 15 miles southeast from the town of Government Camp on Highway 26, then go six miles south on Highway 42. From there, go 2 1/2 miles northwest on Forest Service Road 58 to the campground.

Trip note: This camp is next to Crater Creek and scenic little Crater Lake. It's also alongside the Pacific Crest Trail about a mile from Timothy Lake. See the trip note to campsite 61 for more information about Timothy Lake.

GONE CREEK

Site 61

Campsites, facilities: There are 50 sites for tents, trailers or motorhomes up to 31 feet long. Piped water, firegrills and picnic tables are provided. Pit toilets and firewood are available. Pets are permitted. Boat docks are nearby.

Reservations, fee: No reservations necessary; $6 fee per night. Open mid-May to mid-September.

Who to contact: Phone Bear Springs Ranger District at 503-328-6211, or write Mount Hood National Forest at Route 1, Box 65, Maupin, OR 97037.

Location: Take US 26 southeast of Government Camp for 15 miles, then go eight miles south on Forest Service Road 42. The campground is about 500 yards west on Forest Service Road 57.

Trip note: This campground is set along the shore of Timothy Lake at 3200 feet elevation, one of five camps at the lake. Timothy Lake provides good fishing for brook trout, cutthroat trout, rainbow trout and kokanee salmon. Boats with motors are allowed, but a 10-mph speed limit keeps it quiet. Several trails are in the area, including the Pacific Crest Trail, which provide access to several small mountain lakes.

HOODVIEW

Site 62

Campsites, facilities: There are 43 sites for tents, trailers or motorhomes up to 31 feet long. Picnic tables and firegrills are provided, and piped water, pit toilets and firewood are available. Pets are permitted. Boat docks are nearby.

Reservations, fee: No reservations necessary; $6 fee per night. Open mid-May to mid-September.

Who to contact: Phone Bear Springs Ranger District at 503-328-6211, or write Mount Hood National Forest at Route 1, Box 65, Maupin, OR 97037.

Location: Follow the directions to campsite 62, but on Forest Service Road 57 continue for another mile to the campground.

Trip note: This site is also set along the shore of Timothy Lake. See trip note for campsite 61 for details.

OAK FORK

Site 63

Campsites, facilities: There are 47 sites for tents, trailers or motorhomes up to 22 feet long. Picnic tables and firegrills are provided, and piped water, pit toilets and firewood are available. Pets are permitted. Boat docks and launching facilities are nearby.

Reservations, fee: No reservations necessary; $6 fee per night. Open June to October.

Who to contact: Phone Bear Springs Ranger District at 503-328-6211, or write Mt. Hood National Forest at Route 1, Box 65, Maupin, OR 97037.

Location: Take US 26 southeast from Government Camp for 15 miles, then go eight miles south on Forest Service Road 42 and three miles west on Forest Service Road 57.

Trip note: This camp is set along the shore of Timothy Lake. See trip note for campsite 61 for details.

Site 64 PINE POINT

Campsites, facilities: There are 25 sites for tents, trailers or motorhomes up to 31 feet long: 10 single sites, 10 double sites and five group campsites. Picnic tables and firegrills are provided, and piped water, pit toilets and firewood are available. Pets are permitted. Boat docks and launching facilities are nearby.

Reservations, fee: No reservations necessary; fees range from $6, $10 to $20, depending on type of campsite. Open late-May to mid-September.

Who to contact: Phone Bear Springs Ranger District at 503-328-6211, or write Mt. Hood National Forest at Route 1, Box 65, Maupin, OR 97037.

Location: From Government Camp, go 15 miles southeast on US 26, then eight miles south on Forest Service Road 42. The camp is located five miles west on Forest Service Road 57.

Trip note: One of five camps on Timothy Lake. See trip note to campsite 61 for details.

Site 65 MEDITATION POINT

Campsites, facilities: There are four tent sites accessible by trail or by boat. Picnic tables and firegrills are provided, and pit toilets and firewood are available. There is no piped water. Pets are permitted. Boat docks and launching facilities are nearby.

Reservations, fee: No reservations necessary; no fee. Open late-May to mid-September.

Who to contact: Phone Bear Springs Ranger District at 503-328-6211, or write Mt. Hood National Forest at Route 1, Box 65, Maupin, OR 97037.

Location: From Government Camp, go 15 miles southeast on US 26, then eight miles south on Forest Service Road 42. Park at Pine Point campground, located five miles west on Forest Service Road 57, and hike one mile or take a boat to the north shore of the lake.

Trip note: Accessible only by foot or boat, this offers a more secluded location along Timothy Lake than campsites 61-64. See trip note to campsite 61 for details about the lake.

Site 66 CLACKAMAS LAKE

Campsites, facilities: There are 47 sites for tents, trailers or motorhomes up to 16 feet long. Piped water, firegrills and picnic tables are provided. Pit toilets and firewood are available. Pets are permitted. Boat docks and launching facilities are nearby.

Reservations, fee: No reservations necessary; $4 fee per night. Open June to October.

Who to contact: Phone Bear Springs Ranger District at 503-328-6211, or write Mt. Hood National Forest at Route 1, Box 65, Maupin, OR 97037.

Location: Take US 26 southeast of Government Camp 15 miles, then go eight miles south on Forest Service Road 42 and the camp is about 500 yards east on Forest Service Road 4270.

Trip note: Clackamas Lake is small and shallow, but not far from the Clackamus River. The Pacific Crest Trail passes nearby and Timothy Lake is little more than a one-mile hike from camp. See the trip note to campsite 61 for information on Timothy Lake.

| Site **67** | JOE GRAHAM
HORSE CAMP | |

Campsites, facilities: There are 14 sites for tents, trailers or motorhomes up to 31 feet long. Picnic tables, and firegrills are provided. Piped water, pit toilets and firewood are available. Pets are permitted.

Reservations, fee: Reservations accepted; $5 fee per night. Open mid-May to mid-September.

Who to contact: Phone Bear Springs Ranger District at 503-328-6211, or write Mt. Hood National Forest at Route 1, Box 65, Maupin, OR 97037.

Location: From Government Camp, go 15 miles southeast on Highway 26, then eight miles south on Forest Service Road 42.

Trip note: This campround is set just north of tiny Clackamus Lake and is the only campground in the area that allows horses. See the trip notes for campsites 66 for additional information. Timothy Lake (campsite 61) provides a nearby alternative to the northwest.

| Site **68** | SUMMIT LAKE | |

Campsites, facilities: There are six tent sites. Firegrills and picnic tables are provided, and pit toilets and firewood are available. There is no piped water. Pets are permitted. Boat docks are nearby, but no motorboats are allowed.

Reservations, fee: No reservations necessary; no fee. Open late-May to October.

Who to contact: Phone Bear Springs Ranger District at 503-328-6211, or write Mt. Hood National Forest at Route 1, Box 65, Maupin, OR 97037.

Location: Take Highway 26 southeast out of Government Camp about 15 miles, then go 13 miles south on Forest Service Road 42. Head west on Forest Service Road 141 (a dirt road) for one mile to the campground.

Trip note: An idyllic setting in a remote area along the western slopes of the Cascade Range. This camp is located on the shore of little Summit Lake. Primitive, but a jewel.

| Site **69** | SHELLROCK
CREEK | |

Campsites, facilities: There are five sites for tents, trailers or motorhomes. Picnic tables and firegrills are provided, and pit toilets are available. There is no piped water. Pets are permitted.

Reservations, fee: No reservations necessary; no fee. Open mid-June to early-September.

Who to contact: Phone Clackamus Ranger District at 503-630-4256, or write Mt. Hood National Forest, 61431 East Highway 224, Estacada, OR 97023.

Location: From Government Camp, go 15 miles southeast on US 26, then eight miles south on Forest Service Road 42, and turn west on Forest Service Road 57. Drive 15 miles to Forest Service Road 58. The campground is one mile south on Forest Service Road 58.

Trip note: This quiet little campground is at a nice spot on Shellrock Creek, good for "sneak fishing" for trout. Advisable to obtain Forest Service map, which details back country roads and trails.

HARRIET LAKE
Site **70**

Campsites, facilities: There are 13 sites for tents, trailers or motorhomes up to 31 feet long. Picnic tables and firegrills are provided, and piped water and vault toilets are available. Some facilities are wheelchair accessible. Pets are permitted. Boat docks and launching facilities are located on the lake. No horses are allowed in the campground.

Reservations, fee: No reservations necessary; $5 fee per night. Open late-April to late-September.

Who to contact: Phone Clackamus Ranger District at 503-630-4256, or write Mt. Hood National Forest, 61431 East Highway 224, Estacada, OR 97023.

Location: From Government Camp, go 15 miles southeast on US 26, then eight miles south on Forest Service Road 42. Turn west on Forest Service Road 57 and drive 15 miles to Forest Service Road 58. Drive one mile south on Forest Service Road 58, then west on Forest Service Road 4630 for two miles to the campground.

Trip note: This little lake has been formed by a dam on the Oak Grove Fork of the Clackamus River, and is a popular spot during the summer. Rowboats and boats with small motors are permitted. The lake can provide good fishing for a variety of trout, including brown, brook, rainbow and cutthroat trout.

HIDEAWAY
Site **71** LAKE

Campsites, facilities: There are nine sites for tents, small trailers or camper vans. Picnic tables and firegrills are provided, and pit toilets and piped water are available. Pets are permitted.

Reservations, fee: No reservations necessary; $4 fee per night. Open mid-June to late-September.

Who to contact: Phone Clackamus Ranger District at 503-630-4256, or write Mt. Hood National Forest, 61431 East Highway 224, Estacada, OR 97023.

Location: From Estacada, go 27 miles southeast on Highway 224, then 7 1/2 miles east on Forest Service Road 57. From there, take Forest Service Road 58, and travel three miles north to Forest Service Road 5830, turn northwest and drive 5 1/2 miles to the campground.

Trip note: A jewel of a spot. This small, deep lake is set at 3800 feet elevation, with the campsites separate and set around the lake. An 8 1/2-mile loop trail begins at the north end of the lake which goes past a number of lakes in the Rock Lakes Basin, all of which support populations of rainbow and brook trout. If you don't want to make the whole trip in a day, you can camp overnight at Serene Lake. See a Forest Service map for directions.

HIGH ROCK
Site **72** SPRINGS

Campsites, facilities: There are six tent sites. Picnic tables and firegrills are provided, and pit toilets are available. There is no piped water. Pets are permitted.

Reservations, fee: No reservations necessary; no fee. Open mid-June to late-September.

Who to contact: Phone Clackamus Ranger District at 503-630-4256, or write Mt. Hood National Forest, 61431 East Highway 224, Estacada, OR 97023.

Location: Take Highway 224 southeast of Escatada for 27 miles, then go 7 1/2 miles east on Forest Service Road 57. Turn northeast on Forest Service Road 58 and travel 10 1/2 miles to the campground.

Trip note: This small, remote campground is adjacent to High Rock. A half-mile climb offers a tremendous view of the surrounding area, including Mt. Hood. About four miles east of camp are trails that lead to some of the fishing lakes in Rock Lakes Basin. In August and September, ripe huckleberries are available in the area.

LAZY BEND
Site **73** ▲

Campsites, facilities: There are 13 sites for tents, trailers or motorhomes up to 22 feet long. Picnic tables and fireplaces are provided. Piped water and flush toilets are available. A sanitary dump station is within five miles at Carter Bridge campground. Pets are permitted.

Reservations, fee: No reservations necessary; $5 fee per night. Open late-April through Labor Day.

Who to contact: Phone Estacada Ranger District at 503-630-6861, or write Mt. Hood National Forest at 200 SW Club House Drive, Escatada, OR 97023.

Location: From Escatada, go 10 1/2 miles southeast on Highway 224 to the campground.

Trip note: This campground is set along the banks of the Clackamus River, near the large North Fork Reservoir. Far enough off the highway to provide a secluded, primitive feel.

FISH CREEK
Site **74** ▲

Campsites, facilities: There are 25 sites for tents, trailers or motorhomes. Picnic tables and firegrills are provided, and vault toilets, pump water, and firewood are available. Pets are permitted.

Reservations, fee: No reservations necessary; $5 fee per night. Open late-May to early-September.

Who to contact: Phone Estacada Ranger District at 503-630-6861, or write Mt. Hood National Forest at 200 SW Club House Drive, Escatada, OR 97023.

Location: From Escatada, go 15 1/2 miles southeast on Highway 224 and you'll see the campground.

Trip note: This campground is set along the banks of the Clackamus River, not far from the Clackamus River Trail. There is an amphitheatre near camp. Not far from North Fork Reservoir.

ARMSTRONG
Site **75**

Campsites, facilities: There are 12 sites for tents, trailers or motorhomes up to 30 feet long. Picnic tables and fire rings are provided, and vault toilets, piped water and firewood are available. Some facilities are wheelchair accessible. Pets are permitted.

Reservations, fee: No reservations necessary; $5 fee per night. Open late-May to early-September.

Who to contact: Phone Estacada Ranger District at 503-630-6861, or write Mt. Hood National Forest at 200 SW Club House Drive, Escatada, OR 97023.

Location: Go 15 miles southeast of Escatada on Highway 224 and you'll see the campground entrance.

Trip note: This campground is set along the banks of the Clackamus River and offers good fishing access. One of four camps in immediate area.

CARTER BRIDGE
Site **76**

Campsites, facilities: There are 19 sites for tents, trailers or motorhomes up to 30 feet long. Picnic tables and fireplaces are provided, and vault toilets, piped water, a sanitary dump station and firewood are available. Some facilities are wheelchair accessible. Pets are permitted.

Reservations, fee: No reservations necessary; $5 fee per night. Open all year.

Who to contact: Phone Estacada Ranger District at 503-630-6861, or write Mt. Hood National Forest at 200 SW Club House Drive, Escatada, OR 97023.

Location: Go 15 miles southeast of Escatada on Highway 224 and you'll see the campground.

Trip note: This campground is set along the banks of the Clackamus River.

LOCKABY
Site **77**

Campsites, facilities: There are 30 sites for tents, trailers or motorhomes up to 16 feet long. Picnic tables and fireplaces are provided, and vault toilets, pump water and firewood are available. Pets are permitted.

Reservations, fee: No reservations necessary; $5 fee per night. Open late-May to early-September.

Who to contact: Phone Estacada Ranger District at 503-630-6861, or write Mt. Hood National Forest at 200 SW Club House Drive, Escatada, OR 97023.

Location: From Escatada, go 15 miles southeast on Highway 224.

Trip note: This campground is set along the banks of the Clackamus River. One of many campgrounds set on or near Highway 224 in the area.

ROARING RIVER
Site **78**

Campsites, facilities: There are 14 sites for tents, trailers or motorhomes up to 16 feet long. Picnic tables and fireplaces are provided, and vault toilets, pump water, and firewood are available. Pets are permitted.

Reservations, fee: No reservations necessary; $2 fee per night. Open mid-May to mid-September.

Who to contact: Phone Estacada Ranger District at 503-822-3317, or write Mt. Hood National Forest at 200 SW Club House Drive, Escatada, OR 97023.

Location: Drive 18 miles south of Estacada on Highway 224 to the campground.

Trip note: This campground is set along the banks of the Roaring River and provides access to the Dry Ridge Trail, and several other trails into the adjacent roadless area. See a Forest Service map for details.

SUNSTRIP

Site **79**

Campsites, facilities: There are nine sites for tents, trailers or motorhomes up to 15 feet long. Picnic tables and fireplaces are provided, and vault toilets, pump water and firewood are available. Pets are permitted.

Reservations, fee: No reservations necessary; $5 fee per night. Open late-May to early-September.

Who to contact: Phone Estacada Ranger District at 503-630-6861, or write Mt. Hood National Forest at 200 SW Club House Drive, Escatada, OR 97023.

Location: Take Highway 224 southeast from Escatada about 18 miles to the campground.

Trip note: This campground is set along the banks of the Clackamus River and offers fishing and rafting access. One of 15 campgrounds set along the Highway 224 corridor.

INDIAN HENRY

Site **80**

Campsites, facilities: There are 88 sites for tents, trailers or motorhomes up to 22 feet long. Picnic tables and firegrills are provided, and flush toilets, sanitary dump station, piped water and firewood are available. Some facilities are wheelchair accessible. Pets are permitted.

Reservations, fee: Reservations accepted; $6 fee per night. Open late-May to early-September.

Who to contact: Phone Estacada Ranger District at 503-630-6861, or write Mt. Hood Ranger District at 200 SW Club House Drive, Escatada, OR 97023.

Location: From Escatada, take Highway 224 southeast for 23 miles, then go 1/2 mile southeast on Forest Service Road 53.

Trip note: This campground is set along the banks of the Clackamus River and offers a trail that can be traveled on by wheelchair. Group campsites and an amphitheater are available. The Clackamus River Trail is nearby.

ALDER FLAT

Site **81**

Campsites, facilities: There are six tent sites at this hike-in campground. Picnic tables and firegrills are provided, and pit toilets are available. There is no piped water. Pets are permitted.

Reservations, fee: No reservations necessary; no fee. Open late-April to late-September.

Who to contact: Phone Clackamus Ranager District at 503-630-4256, or write Mt. Hood National Forest at 61431 East Highway 224, Estacada, OR 97023.

Location: Take Highway 224 southeast from Estacada for 26 miles to the Ripplebrook Ranger Station. Parking for the camp is about 1/2 mile west of the Ranger Station. Hike one mile to the campground.

Trip note: This secluded hike-in campground is set along the banks of the Clackamus River. If you want peace and quiet, and don't mind the short walk to get it, this is the spot. Be sure to pack out what you brought in.

RIPPLEBROOK
Site **82**

Campsites, facilities: There are 13 sites for trailers or motorhomes up to 16 feet long. Picnic tables and firegrills are provided, and pit toilets and piped water are available. Pets are permitted, but horses are not allowed in campground.

Reservations, fee: No reservations necessary; $5 fee per night. Open late-April to late-September.

Who to contact: Phone Clackamus Ranger District at 503-630-4256, or write Mt. Hood National Forest, 61431 East Highway 224, Estacada, OR 97023.

Location: Travel 26 1/2 miles southeast of Escatada on Highway 224 and you'll see the campground entrance.

Trip note: This campground is set along the banks of the Oak Grove Fork of the Clackamus River. There is a four-mile foot trail from camp that follows the river south to Riverside campground, a nice walk in beautiful country.

RAINBOW
Site **83**

Campsites, facilities: There are 17 sites for tents, trailers or motorhomes up to 16 feet long. Piped water, firegrills and picnic tables are provided, and pit toilets are available. Pets are permitted.

Reservations, fee: No reservations necessary; $5 fee per night. Open late-April to late-September.

Who to contact: Phone Clackamus Ranger District at 503-630-4256, or write Mt. Hood National Forest at 61431 East Highway 224, Escatada, OR 97023.

Location: From Escatada, go 27 miles southeast on Highway 224 to Forest Service Road 46. The camp is about 100 yards south on Forest Service Road 46.

Trip note: This campground is set along the banks of the Oak Grove Fork of the Clackamus River not far from when it empties into the Clackamus River. Nearby Ripplebrook campground provides an option.

RIVERSIDE
Site **84**

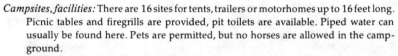

Campsites, facilities: There are 16 sites for tents, trailers or motorhomes up to 16 feet long. Picnic tables and firegrills are provided, pit toilets are available. Piped water can usually be found here. Pets are permitted, but no horses are allowed in the campground.

Reservations, fee: No reservations necessary; $5 fee per night. Open mid-May to late-September.

Who to contact: Phone Clackamus Ranger District at 503-854-3366, or write Mt. Hood National Forest, 61431 East Highway 224, Estacada, OR 97023.

Location: Take Highway 224 southeast of Escatada 27 miles, then go 2 1/2 miles south on Forest Service Road 46 to the campground.

Trip note: This campground is set along the banks of the Clackamus River. A trail worth hiking leaves camp and follows the river for four miles north to Ripplebrook campground.

RIVERFORD

Site **85**

Campsites, facilities: There are 10 sites for tents, trailers or motorhomes up to 16 feet long. Picnic tables and firegrills are provided, and pit toilets are available. There is no piped water except at nearby Two Rivers Picnic Area. Pets are permitted.

Reservations, fee: No reservations necessary; no fee. Open late-April to late-September.

Who to contact: Phone Clackamus Ranger District at 503-630-4256, or write Mt. Hood National Forest, 61431 East Highway 224, Estacada, OR 97023.

Location: From Escatada, go 27 miles southeast on Highway 224, then 3 1/2 miles south on Forest Service Road 46 to the campground.

Trip note: This campground is set at the confluence of the Clackamus and the Collawash Rivers. Some nice swimming spots are available, but use care; some areas are rocky, swift and treacherous.

RAAB

Site **86**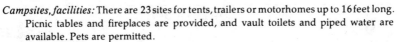

Campsites, facilities: There are 27 sites for tents, trailers or motorhomes up to 22 feet long. Picnic tables and firegrills are provided, and pit toilets are available. Piped water can be found a half-mile away at Two Rivers Picnic Area. Pets are permitted.

Reservations, fee: No reservations necessary; no fee. Open late-May to early-September.

Who to contact: Phone Clackamus Ranger District at 503-630-4256 or write Mt. Hood National Forest at 61431 East Highway 224, Escatada, OR 97023.

Location: Take Highway 224 southeast of Escatada 27 miles, then go four miles south on Forest Service Road 46 to the campground.

Trip note: This campground is set along the banks of the Collawash River, about a mile from its confluence with the Clackamus River.

KINGFISHER

Site **87**

Campsites, facilities: There are 23 sites for tents, trailers or motorhomes up to 16 feet long. Picnic tables and fireplaces are provided, and vault toilets and piped water are available. Pets are permitted.

Reservations, fee: No reservations necessary; $5 fee per night. Open late-May to early-September.

Who to contact: Phone Estacada Ranger District at 503-630-6861, or write at Mt. Hood National Forest, 200 SW Club House Drive, Estacada, OR 97023.

Location: Take Highway 224 out of Estacada and go 26 miles southeast to Forest Service Road 46. Go 3 1/2 miles south on Forest Service Road 46, three miles south on Forest Service Road 63, then one mile west on Forest Service Road 70 to the campground.

Trip note: This campground is set along the banks of the Hot Springs Fork of the Collawash River, about three miles from Bagby Hot Springs, a Forest Service day-use area. It is an easy 1 1/2-mile hike to the hot springs from the day-use area.

ROUND LAKE

Site **88**

Campsites, facilities: There are six tent sites at this hike-in campground. Picnic tables and firegrills are provided, and pit toilets are available. There is no piped water. Pets are permitted.

Reservations, fee: No reservations necessary; $3 fee per night. Open mid-June to late-September.

Who to contact: Phone Clackamus Ranager District at 503-630-4256, or write Mt. Hood National Forest at 61431 East Highway 224, Escatada, OR 97023.

Location: From Escatada, go 27 miles southeast on Highway 224, then 3 1/2 miles south on Forest Service Road 46. Get on Forest Service Road 63 and go southeast for 12 1/2 miles, then continue southeast on Forest Service Road 6370 for 6 3/4 miles until you get to the campground parking area. Hike 1/2 mile to the campground.

Trip note: This is an idyllic spot, beautiful and secluded, set at the edge of Round Lake. Well worth figuring out the maze of Forest Service roads and then making the half-mile hike. Don't be discouraged by the cleared areas as you hike to the lake.

CAMP TEN
 Site **89**

Campsites, facilities: There are eight sites for tents, trailers or motorhomes up to 16 feet long. Picnic tables and firegrills are provided, and pit toilets are available. There is no piped water. Pets are permitted. A store is nearby that sells fishing tackle and other supplies. Boat docks, launching facilities and rentals are nearby.

Reservations, fee: No reservations necessary; no fee. Open mid-June to late-September.

Who to contact: Phone Clackamus Ranger District at 503-630-4256, or write Mt. Hood National Forest, 61431 East Highway 224, Estacada, OR 97023.

Location: Take Highway 224 southeast of Escatada for 27 miles, then go south on Forest Service Road 46 for about 22 miles. From there, travel on Forest Service Road 4690 southeast for 8 1/4 miles. When you reach Forest Service Road 4220, head south for six miles to the campground.

Trip note: This is one of several campgrounds set along the shore of Olallie Lake, a popular area. Boats without motors, such as canoes, kayaks and rafts, are permitted on the lake. Numerous smaller lakes in the area can be reached from trails nearby. A Forest Service map details the possibilities.

LOWER LAKE
Site **90**

Campsites, facilities: There are nine tent sites. Picnic tables and firegrills are provided, and pit toilets are available. There is no piped water. Pets are permitted. Boat docks, launching facilities and rentals are nearby at Olallie Lake.

Reservations, fee: No reservations necessary; no fee. Open mid-June to late-September.

Who to contact: Phone Clackamus Ranger District at 503-630-4256, or write Mt. Hood National Forest, 61431 East Highway 224, Estacada, OR 97023.

Location: Take Highway 224 southeast of Escatada for 27 miles, then go south on Forest Service Road 46 for about 22 miles. From there, travel on Forest Service Road 4690 southeast for 8 1/2 miles. When you reach Forest Service Road 4220, head south for 4 1/2 miles to the parking area. Hike 1/2 mile to the campground.

Trip note: This sunny, open campground is set along the shore of Lower Lake, a small, deep lake used for fishing and swimming. It is a short distance from Olallie Lake and near a network of trails that provide access to other nearby lakes. It is strongly advised to obtain a Forest Service map, which details the back country roads and trails.

Site **91**　　OLALLIE MEADOWS

Campsites, facilities: There are seven sites for tents, trailers or motorhomes up to 16 feet
long. Picnic tables and firegrills are provided, and pit toilets are available. There is no
piped water. Pets are permitted. Boat docks, launching facilities and rentals are
located about three miles away on Olallie Lake.

Reservations, fee: No reservations necessary; no fee. Open mid-June to late-September.

Who to contact: Phone Clackamus Ranger District at 503-630-4256, or write Mt. Hood
National Forest, 61431 East Highway 224, Estacada, OR 97023.

Location: Take Highway 224 southeast of Escatada for 27 miles, then go south on Forest
Service Road 46 for about 22 miles. From there, travel on Forest Service Road 4690
southeast for 8 1/4 miles. When you reach Forest Service Road 4220, head south for 1
1/2 miles to the campground.

Trip note: This campground is set at 4500 feet elevation, in a large, peaceful meadow about
three miles from Olallie Lake. The Pacific Crest Trail passes very close to camp.
Horses are permitted only at specified campsites. Contact the Forest Service for
details.

Site **92**　　PAUL DENNIS

Campsites, facilities: There are 15 sites for tents or small campers (trailers are not recommended) and three hike-in tentsites. Picnic tables and firegrills are provided, and pit
toilets are available. There is no piped water. A store and ice are nearby. Pets are
permitted. Boat docks, launching facilities and rentals are located on Olallie Lake.

Reservations, fee: No reservations necessary; no fee. Open mid-June to late-September.

Who to contact: Phone Clackamus Ranger District at 503-630-4256, or write Mount Hood
National Forest, 61431 East Highway 224, Estacada, OR 97023.

Location: Take Highway 224 southeast of Escatada for 27 miles, then go south on Forest
Service Road 46 for about 22 miles. From there, travel on Forest Service Road 4690
southeast for 8 1/4 miles. When you reach Forest Service Road 4220, head south for 6
1/4 miles to the campground.

Trip note: This campground is set along the north shore of Olallie Lake. From here you can
see the reflection of Mount Jefferson (10,497 feet). Boats with motors are not permitted on the lake. Numerous smaller lakes in the area can be reached from nearby
trails. Advisable to obtain a Forest Service map.

Site **93**　　PENINSULA

Campsites, facilities: There are 35 sites for tents, trailers or motorhomes up to 22 feet long,
and six walk-in tentsites. Picnic tables and firegrills are provided, and pit toilets and
piped water are available. Some facilities are wheelchair accessible. Pets are permitted. Boat docks, launching facilities and rentals are nearby.

Reservations, fee: No reservations necessary; $5 fee per night. Open mid-June to late-
September.

Who to contact: Phone Clackamus Ranger District at 503-630-4256, or write Mount Hood
National Forest, 61431 East Highway 224, Estacada, OR 97023.

Location: Take Highway 224 southeast of Escatada for 27 miles, then go south on Forest

Service Road 46 for about 22 miles. From there, travel on Forest Service Road 4690 southeast for 8 1/4 miles. When you reach Forest Service Road 4220, head south for 6 1/2 miles to the campground.

Trip note: This is the largest of several campgrounds set along the shore of Olallie Lake. The amphitheatre is near camp, and during the summer, rangers present campfire programs. Boats without motors are permitted on the lake. Numerous smaller lakes in the area can be reached from trails nearby.

Site 94   BREITENBUSH LAKE

Campsites, facilities: There are 20 sites for tents, trailers or motorhomes. Picnic tables and firegrills are provided, and pit toilets are available. There is no piped water. A store and ice are located within five miles. Pets are permitted. Boat docks, launching facilities and rentals are nearby.

Reservations, fee: No reservations necessary; $3 fee per night. Open mid-June to late-September.

Who to contact: Phone Clackamus Ranger District at 503-630-4256, or write Mt. Hood National Forest, 61431 East Highway 224, Estacada, OR 97023.

Location: From Escatada, drive 27 miles southeast on Highway 224, then 28 1/2 miles south on Forest Service Road 46, then turn east on Forest Service Road 4220 and drive 8 1/2 miles to the lake. Be aware that the access road to the lake is not maintained and can be pretty rough. A vehicle with clearance can help.

Trip note: This lakeside campground is set at 5500-feet elevation on the western border of the Warm Springs Indian Reservation. Breitenbush is a large lake, which borders on the Jefferson Wilderness area. Numerous trails provide access to other lakes in the area, and horses are allowed in areas specified by the Forest Service. Ripe huckleberries can be found in the area in late August and September.

Site 95   BREITENBUSH

Campsites, facilities: There are two tent sites and 28 sites for trailers or motorhomes up to 16 feet long (longer trailers may have difficulty parking and turning). Picnic tables and firegrills are provided, and piped water, vault toilets and a store are available. Some of the facilities are wheelchair accessible. Pets are permitted.

Reservations, fee: No reservations necessary; $5 fee per night. Open all year, but facilities are limited in winter.

Who to contact: Phone Detroit Ranger District at 503-854-3366, or write Willamette National Forest, State Highway 22, Detroit, OR 97360.

Location: From Detroit, travel 10 miles north on Forest Service Road 46 (Breitenbush Road) to the campground.

Trip note: This campground is set along the Breitenbush River and has fishing access available. South Breitenbush Gorge National Recreation Trail is three miles away. It is detailed on a map of Willamette National Forest.

Site 96   CLEATOR BEND

Campsites, facilities: There are nine sites for tents, trailers or motorhomes up to 16 feet long. Picnic tables and firegrills are provided, and piped water and vault toilets are available. Pets are permitted.

Reservations, fee: No reservations necessary; $3 fee per night. Open mid-May to late-September.

Who to contact: Phone Detroit Ranger District at 503-854-3366, or write Willamette National Forest, State Highway 22, Detroit, OR 97360.

Location: From Detroit, travel nine miles northeast on Forest Service Road 46 (Breitenbush Road) to the campground.

Trip note: This camp is set quite close to campsite 95. See trip note for recreation options.

HUMBUG

Site **97**

Campsites, facilities: There are 22 sites for tents, trailers or motorhomes up to 22 feet long. Picnic tables and firegrills are provided, and piped water and vault toilets are available. Pets are permitted.

Reservations, fee: No reservations necessary; $5 fee per night. Open mid-April to late-September.

Who to contact: Phone Detroit Ranger District at 509-854-3366, or write Willamette National Forest, State Highway 22, Detroit, OR 97360.

Location: From Detroit, travel five miles northeast on Forest Service Road 46 (Breitenbush Road) to the campground.

Trip note: This campground is set along the bank of Breitenbush River about four miles from where it empties into Detroit Lake (See Zone 5). Fishing and hiking are popular here.

ELK LAKE

Site **98**

Campsites, facilities: There are 12 tent sites. Picnic tables and firegrills are provided, and vault toilets are available. There is no piped water. Pets are permitted. Boat docks and launching facilities are nearby.

Reservations, fee: No reservations necessary; no fee. Open July to mid-September.

Who to contact: Phone Detroit Ranger District at 503-854-3366, or write Willamette National Forest, State Highway 22, Detroit, OR 97360.

Location: From the town of Detroit, travel 4 1/2 miles north on Forest Service Road 46 (Breitenbush Road), then ten miles north on Forest Service Road 2209 (Elkhorn-Elk Lake Road) to the campground. The road is rough.

Trip note: This remote campground is set along the shore of Elk Lake, where boating, fishing and swimming can be quite good in summer months. Several trails are nearby that provide access to the Bull of the Wood Wilderness.

SHADY COVE

Site **99**

Campsites, facilities: There are 11 tent sites. Picnic table and firegrills are provided and vault toilets are available. There is no piped water. Pets are permitted.

Reservations, fee: No reservations necessary; no fee. Open mid-May to late-September.

Who to contact: Phone Detroit Ranger District at 509-854-3366, or write Willamette National Forest, State Highway 22, Detroit, OR 97360.

Location: From the town of Mehama, travel 19 miles northeast on Little North Santiam

Road to the campground.

Trip note: This campground is set where Battle and Cedar Creeks meet to form the Little North Santiam River. A classic spot in the Cascades.

Site **100**   ELKHORN VALLEY

Campsites, facilities: There are 16 sites for tents, trailers or motorhomes up to 18 feet long. Picnic tables and firegrills are provided, and pit toilets and piped water are available. Pets are permitted.

Reservations, fee: No reservations necessary; $4 fee per night. Open mid-May to late-November.

Who to contact: Phone the Bureau of Land Management at 503-399-5646, or write at Box 3227, Salem, OR 97302.

Location: This campground is located 25 miles east of Salem on Highway 22, then nine miles northeast on Elkhorn Road to the campground.

Trip note: This campground is set along Elkhorn Creek, not far from the North Fork of the Santiam River. An option to campsite 99, which is located about 10 miles to the east on the same road.

Site **101**   SILVER FALLS STATE PARK

Campsites, facilities: There are 53 tent sites and nine sites for trailers or motorhomes up to 35 feet long. Electricity, piped water and picnic tables are provided. Flush toilets, sanitary services, showers, firewood, a laundromat and playground are available. Some facilities are wheelchair accessible. Pets are permitted.

Reservations, fee: No reservations necessary; $7 fee per night. Open mid-April to early-October.

Who to contact: Phone at 503-873-8681, or write at 20024 Silver Falls Highway, Sublimity, OR 97385.

Location: Take the Salem exit off I-5 to Highway 22 and proceed southeast five miles, then go east 15 miles on Highway 214 to the park.

Trip note: This is Oregon's largest state park, covering more than 8000 acres. Numerous trails are available here, including some that meander past waterfalls over 100 feet high in the moist forest of Silver Creek Canyon. A stable is located near the park entrance.

Site **102**   FOREST GLEN RV PARK

Campsites, facilities: There are 100 drive-through sites for tents, trailers or motorhomes of any length. Electricity, piped water, sewer hookups and picnic tables are provided. Flush toilets, bottled gas, sanitary services, showers, a recreation hall, laundromat, ice and swimming pool are available. A cafe is within one mile. Pets and motorbikes are permitted.

Reservations, fee: Reservations accepted; $10 fee per night. Open all year.

Who to contact: Phone at 503-363-7616, or write at 8372 Enchanted Way, Turner, OR 97392.

Location: From Salem, travel seven miles south on I-5 to exit 248, then 1/2 mile south on Enchanted Way.

Trip note: This is a good layover for motorhome travelers on Interstate 5. It is just south of Salem. Nearby recreation options include an 18-hole golf course, tennis courts, and the Enchanted Forest, a kids' tour with statues of storybook characters.

Site **103**   SALEM TRAILER
                         PARK VILLAGE

Campsites, facilities: There are 22 sites for trailers or motorhomes of any length in this adults-only campground. Electricity, piped water and sewer hookups are provided. Flush toilets, showers and a laundromat are available. Bottled gas, a store, cafe and ice are located within one mile.
Reservations, fee: No reservations necessary; $10 fee per night. Open all year.
Who to contact: Phone at 503-393-7424, or write at 4733 Portland Northeast, Salem, OR 97305.
Location: In Salem, take Highway 99E 1/2 mile east to the park.
Trip note: This park is set in the city of Salem, Oregon's state capital. Several museums and parks are located in town, and the Williamette River flows nearby. Other recreation options include an 18-hole golf course, marked bike trails and a full service marina.

Site **104**   CENTER STREET
                         MOBILE PARK

Campsites, facilities: There are 11 sites for trailers or motorhomes up to 27 feet long. Electricity, piped water and sewer hookups are provided. Laundromat is available. Bottled gas, a store, cafe and ice are located within one mile.
Reservations, fee: No reservations necessary; a small fee is charged. Open all year.
Who to contact: Phone at 503-363-2684, or write at 4155 Center, Salem, OR 97301.
Location: Take the Market Street exit off I-5 at Salem and drive east for 1/4 mile to Lancaster, then turn south and travel one mile to Center Street. Head east and drive to 4155 Center Street.
Trip note: This park is in the center of Salem. See the trip note for campsite 103 for information on Salem. An 18-hole golf course is nearby.

Site **105**   KOA SALEM

Campsites, facilities: There are 30 tent sites and 190 drive-through sites for trailers or motorhomes of any length. Picnic tables are provided. Flush toilets, bottled gas, sanitary services, showers, a recreation hall, store, laundromat, ice, playground, electricity, piped water and sewer hookups are available. A cafe is located within one mile. Pets and motorbikes are permitted.
Reservations, fee: Reservations accepted; $8 fee per night. MasterCard and Visa accepted. Open all year.
Who to contact: Phone at 503-581-6736, or write at 1595 Lancaster Drive Southeast, Salem, OR 97301.
Location: Take the 253 exit off Highway 22 in Salem and drive to Lancaster Drive, then turn south and drive to 1595 Lancaster Drive.
Trip note: This park is just off Interstate 5 in Salem (see trip note for campsite 103). Nearby recreation options include an 18-hole golf course, hiking trails, a riding stable and tennis courts.

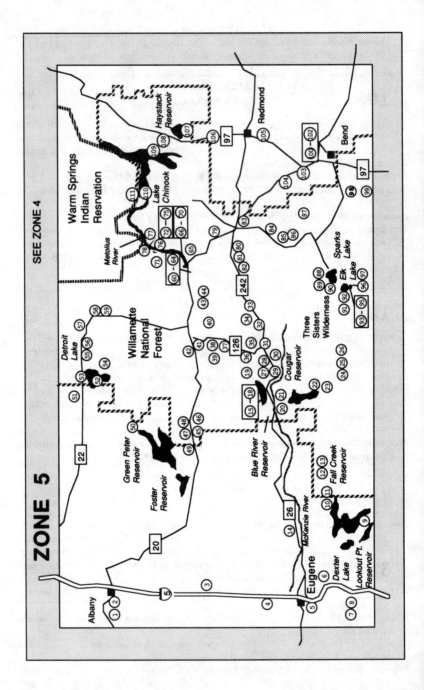

WILLAMETTE

Site 1
ALBANY TRAILER PARK

Campsites, facilities: There are 13 drive-through sites for trailers or motorhomes of any length. Electricity, piped water and sewer hookups are provided. Flush toilets, showers, a store, laundromat and ice are available. Sanitary services are located within one mile. Pets are permitted.

Reservations, fee: Reservations accepted; $9 fee per night. Open all year.

Who to contact: Phone at 503-928-8532, or write at 1197 Century Drive, Albany, OR 97321.

Location: This camp is located in the town of Albany at 1197 Century Drive.

Trip note: Albany is located at the confluence of the Willamette and the Calapooia Rivers. Nearby recreation options include a golf course and tennis courts.

Site 2
THE VILLAGE ESTATE

Campsites, facilities: There are 13 drive-through sites for trailers or motorhomes of any length. Electricity, piped water and sewer hookups are provided. Flush toilets and showers are available. Sanitary services, a store, cafe, laundromat and ice are within one mile. Pets are permitted.

Reservations, fee: Reservations accepted; $6 fee per night. Open all year.

Who to contact: Phone at 503-926-3383, or write at 3246 Salem Avenue, Albany, OR 97321.

Location: This motorhome park is located in the town of Albany just off I-5.

Trip note: This is an option to campsite 1, also located in Albany. An okay layover spot for motorhome campers traveling Interstate 5.

Site 3
DIAMOND HILL RV PARK

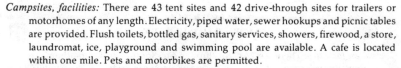

Campsites, facilities: There are 43 tent sites and 42 drive-through sites for trailers or motorhomes of any length. Electricity, piped water, sewer hookups and picnic tables are provided. Flush toilets, bottled gas, sanitary services, showers, firewood, a store, laundromat, ice, playground and swimming pool are available. A cafe is located within one mile. Pets and motorbikes are permitted.

Reservations, fee: Reservations accepted; $10 fee per night. MasterCard and Visa accepted. Open all year.

Who to contact: Phone at 503-995-8050, or write at 32917 Diamond Hill, Harrisburg, OR 97446.

Location: Drive 15 miles north of Eugene on I-5, then take exit 209 and the campground is about one block away.

Trip note: This private campground is located in the center of the Willamette Valley, just off the highway. No other campgrounds are in the area. Campsite 4 is the closest, about 10 miles to the south.

KOA EUGENE

Site **4**

Campsites, facilities: There are 30 tent sites and 114 drive-through sites for trailers or motorhomes of any length. Electricity, piped water, sewer hookups and picnic tables are provided. Flush toilets, bottled gas, sanitary services, showers, a recreation hall, store, laundromat, ice and playground are available. A cafe is located within one mile. Pets and motorbikes are permitted.

Reservations, fee: Reservations accepted; $13 fee per night. MasterCard and Visa accepted. Open all year.

Who to contact: Phone at 503-343-4832, or write at Route 2, Box 353, Eugene, OR 97401.

Location: Go seven miles north of Eugene on I-5, take the Coburg exit and go 400 yards west to the campground.

Trip note: Eugene is one of Oregon's major cities, but offers many riverside parks and hiking opportunities. Both the Willamette and McKenzie rivers run right through town. The McKenzie, in particular, provides good trout fishing. Nearby recreation options include a golf course and tennis courts.

EUGENE MOBILE VILLAGE

Site **5**

Campsites, facilities: There are 30 drive-through sites for trailers or motorhomes of any length. Electricity, piped water and sewer hookups are provided. Flush toilets, sanitary services, showers, a recreation hall, laundromat and playground are available. Bottled gas, a store, cafe and ice are located within one mile. Pets are permitted.

Reservations, fee: Reservations accepted; $9 fee per night. MasterCard and Visa accepted. Open all year.

Who to contact: Phone at 503-747-2257, or write at 4750 Franklin, Eugene, OR 97403.

Location: In Eugene, take exit 189 off I-5, then go one mile on Franklin Blvd to the park.

Trip note: This motorhome park is in Eugene near the Willamette River (see trip note for campsite 4). Nearby recreation options include a golf course, bike paths, a full service marina and tennis courts.

CHALET VILLAGE MOBILE HOME PARK

Site **6**

Campsites, facilities: There are 24 drive-through sites for trailers or motorhomes of any length. Electricity, piped water and sewer hookups are provided. Flush toilets, sanitary services, showers, a recreation hall and swimming pool are available. Bottled gas, a store, cafe, laundromat and ice are within one mile. Pets are permitted.

Reservations, fee: Reservations accepted; $10 fee per night. Open all year.

Who to contact: Phone at 503-747-8311, or write at 205 South 54th Street, Springfield, OR 97478.

Location: Take I-5 to the town of Springfield then go east to the park, which is located in town.

Trip note: The town of Springfield is set on the outskirts of Eugene, close to both the Willamette River and McKenzie River. Highway 126 heading east borders the McKenzie, known for good trout fishing and rafting opportunities.

Site 7   KOA SHERWOOD FOREST

Campsites, facilities: There are 40 tent sites and 100 drive-through sites for trailers or motorhomes of any length. Electricity, piped water, sewer hookups and picnic tables are provided. Flush toilets, sanitary services, showers, a recreation hall, store, laundromat, ice, playground and swimming pool are available. Bottled gas and a cafe are within one mile. Pets and motorbikes are permitted.

Reservations, fee: Reservations accepted; $9 fee per night. MasterCard and Visa accepted. Open all year.

Who to contact: Phone at 503-895-4110, or write at 298 East Oregon, Creswell, OR 97426.

Location: Travel on I-5 to the town of Creswell and go west on Oregon Avenue for 1/2 block to the campground.

Trip note: This is a fairly good layover spot for motorhome travelers heading north on Interstate 5. It is 10 miles before hitting Eugene. Nearby recreation options include a golf course, a riding stable and tennis courts.

Site 8   TAYLOR'S TRAVEL PARK

Campsites, facilities: There are 10 tent sites and 24 drive-through sites for trailers or motorhomes of any length. Electricity, piped water, sewer hookups and picnic tables are provided. Flush toilets, sanitary services, showers and playground are available. Bottled gas, a store, cafe, laundromat and ice are within one mile. Pets and motorbikes are permitted.

Reservations, fee: Reservations accepted; $8 fee per night. Open all year.

Who to contact: Phone at 503-895-4715, or write at 82149 Davisson, Creswell, OR 97426.

Location: Travel on I-5 to the town of Creswell, then go 1/4 mile west on Oregon Avenue and 1 1/4 mile south on Highway 99 to Davisson Road. From there, go 1/2 mile south to the park.

Trip note: An option to nearby campsite 7. This wooded campground is set near the Willamette River. Nearby recreation options include a golf course, bike paths and a full service marina.

Site 9   WINBERRY ▲

Campsites, facilities: There are six sites for tents, trailers or motorhomes up to 16 feet long. Picnic tables and firegrills are provided, and piped water, vault toilets and firewood are available. Pets are permitted.

Reservations, fee: No reservations necessary; $2 fee per night. Open all year.

Who to contact: Phone the Lowell Ranger District at 503-937-2129, or write at Willamette

National Forest, Lowell, OR 97452.
Location: From Lowell, go two miles north on County Route 6220, then six miles southeast on County Route 6245 (Winberry Road). Continue 3 1/2 miles on Forest Service Road 191 to the campground.

Trip note: This campground is located at the confluence of Winberry Creek and North Blanket Creek. A little inside knowledge: On the map, Lookout Point Reservoir appears about three miles away, but to get there you have to drive nine miles to the town of Lowell at the north end of the reservoir. Elijah Barstow State Park which is open for day-use is about five miles southwest of Lowell on Highway 58. Hiking and horseback riding trails are located there.

DOLLY VARDEN
Site **10**

Campsites, facilities: There are two tent sites and four sites for tents, trailers or motorhomes up to 16 feet long. Picnic tables and firegrills are provided, and vault toilets and firewood are available. There is no piped water. Pets are permitted.

Reservations, fee: No reservations necessary; no fee. Open May to mid-September.

Who to contact: Phone the Lowell Ranger District at 503-937-2129, or write at Willamette National Forest, Lowell, OR 97452.

Location: From Lowell, go two miles north on County Route 6220, then 10 miles east on County Route 6240 and Forest Service Road 18 (Fall Creek Road) to the campground.

Trip note: This campground is adjacent to Fall Creek and is at the lower trailhead for the scenic, 14-mile Fall Creek National Recreation Trail. Primitive campsites are located along this trail, which follows the creek and ranges between 960 to 1385 feet elevation for the length of the trail.

BIG POOL
Site **11**

Campsites, facilities: There are three tent sites and two sites for tents, trailers or motorhomes up to 16 feet long. Picnic tables and firegrills are provided, and vault toilets, piped water and firewood are available. Pets are permitted.

Reservations, fee: No reservations necessary; $3 fee per night. Open May to mid-September.

Who to contact: Phone the Lowell Ranger District at 503-937-2129, or write at Willamette National Forest, Lowell, OR 97452.

Location: From Lowell, drive two miles north on County Route 6220, then 10 miles east on County Route 6240 and 1 1/2 miles on Forest Service Road 181 (Fall Creek Road) to the campground.

Trip note: This campground is set along Fall Creek at about 1000 feet elevation. The scenic Fall Creek National Recreation Trail passes camp on the other side of the creek. See trip note for campsite 10.

BEDROCK
Site **12**

Campsites, facilities: There are 20 sites for tents, trailers or motorhomes up to 22 feet long. Picnic tables and firegrills are provided, and vault toilets, piped water and firewood are available. Pets are permitted.

Reservations, fee: No reservations necessary; $3 fee per night. Open May to late-October.

Who to contact: Phone the Lowell Ranger District at 503-937-2129, or write at Willamette National Forest, Lowell, OR 97452.

Location: From Lowell, drive two miles north on County Route 6220, then 10 miles east on County Route 6240 and four miles on Forest Service Road 18 (Fall Creek Road) to the campground.

Trip note: This campground is set along the banks of Bedrock Creek near its confluence with Fall Creek. It is one of the access points for the scenic Fall Creek National Recreation Trail. See the trip note for campsite 10 for trail information. It is also adjacent to the Jones Trail, which heads north for about six miles before joining a forest service road.

PUMA CREEK
Site 13 ▲

Campsites, facilities: There are 11 sites for tents, trailers or motorhomes up to 16 feet long. Picnic tables and firegrills are provided, and vault toilets, piped water and firewood are available. Pets are permitted.

Reservations, fee: No reservations necessary; $3 fee per night. Open May to late-October.

Who to contact: Phone the Lowell Ranger District at 503-937-2129, or write at Willamette National Forest, Lowell, OR 97452.

Location: From Lowell, travel two miles north on County Route 6220, then 10 miles east on County Route 6240 and 6 1/2 miles east on Forest Service Road 18 (Fall Creek Road) to the campground.

Trip note: This campground is set along the banks of Fall Creek, across the creek from the Fall Creek National Recreation Trail. This is one of four camps in the immediate area.

VIDA-LEA
Site 14   MOBILE LODGE 🚐

Campsites, facilities: There are two tent sites and five drive-through sites for trailers or motorhomes of any length in this adult only campground. Electricity, piped water and sewer hookups are provided. Flush toilets, sanitary services, showers and a laundromat are available. Motorbikes are permitted. Boat docks and launching facilities are nearby.

Reservations, fee: Reservations accepted; $8 fee per night. Open all year.

Who to contact: Phone at 503-896-3898, or write at 44221 McKenzie Highway, Leaburg, OR 97489.

Location: From Leaburg, go three miles east on Highway 126 to the park.

Trip note: This private resort is set along the banks of the scenic McKenzie River. Ben and Kay Dorris State Park, which is open for day-use, is about six mile east of the campground on Highway 126 and is also set along the McKenzie River. Nearby recreation options include a golf course, hiking trails and bike paths.

LAZY DAYS
Site 15

Campsites, facilities: There are 18 drive-through sites for trailers or motorhomes of any length. Electricity, piped water, sewer hookups and picnic tables are provided. Flush toilets, bottled gas, showers, firewood and a laundromat are available. Pets are permitted. Boat launching facilities are nearby.

Reservations, fee: Reservations accepted; $8 fee per night. Open all year.

Who to contact: Phone at 503-822-3889, or write at 52511 McKenzie, Blue River, OR 97413.

Location: Go 1 1/2 miles east on Highway 126 from Blue River.

Trip note: This motorhome park is set along the banks of the McKenzie River, not far from Blue River Reservoir. This lake covers about 1400 acres and offers opportunities for fishing, swimming and waterskiing. A golf course is fairly close.

Site 16   MCKENZIE RIVER TRAILER COURT

Campsites, facilities: There are 10 tent sites and six sites for trailers or motorhomes of any length. Electricity, piped water, sewer hookups and picnic tables are provided. Flush toilets, showers and a laundromat are available. Bottled gas, a store, cafe and ice are within one mile. Pets and motorbikes are permitted.

Reservations, fee: Reservations accepted; $11 fee per night. Open all year.

Who to contact: Phone at 503-822-6067, or write at 52508 McKenzie, Blue River, OR 97413.

Location: Take Highway 126 east from Blue River for 1 1/2 miles.

Trip note: This campground is set along the banks of the McKenzie River, not far from Blue River Reservoir. See the trip note for campsite 15 for recreation options.

Site 17   MAPLE LEAF RV PARK

Campsites, facilities: There are three tent sites and 27 drive-through sites for trailers or motorhomes of any length. Electricity, piped water, sewer hookups and picnic tables are provided. Flush toilets, bottled gas, showers, firewood and a laundromat are available. Pets are permitted.

Reservations, fee: Reservations accepted; $10 fee per night. Open all year.

Who to contact: Phone at 503-822-3912, or write at 52970 McKenzie, Blue River, OR 97413.

Location: Take Highway 126 east from Blue River 2 1/2 miles and watch for signs.

Trip note: This wooded campground is set near the McKenzie River, not far from Blue River Reservoir. See the trip note for campsite 15.

Site 18   DELTA

Campsites, facilities: There are 39 sites for tents, trailers or motorhomes up to 21 feet long. Picnic tables and firegrills are provided, and piped water, vault toilets and firewood are available. Some facilities are wheelchair accessible. Pets are permitted.

Reservations, fee: No reservations necessary; $5 - $7 fee per night. Open all year.

Who to contact: Phone Blue River Ranger District at 503-822-3317, or write at Willamette National Forest, Blue River, OR 97413.

Location: From Blue River travel five miles east to Forest Service Road 400 (Delta Road) and go one mile to the campground.

Trip note: This popular campground is set along the banks of the McKenzie River in a stand of old-growth Douglas Fir. Blue River Reservoir and Cougar Lake are nearby, both of which offer trout fishing, waterskiing, and swimming.

MONA

Site **19**

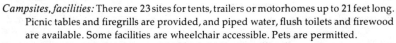

Campsites, facilities: There are 23 sites for tents, trailers or motorhomes up to 21 feet long. Picnic tables and firegrills are provided, and piped water, flush toilets and firewood are available. Some facilities are wheelchair accessible. Pets are permitted.

Reservations, fee: No reservations necessary; $6 fee per night. Open all year.

Who to contact: Phone Blue River Ranger District at 503-822-3317, or write at Willamette National Forest, Blue River, OR 97413.

Location: From Blue River, travel about four miles east on Highway 126, then head north on Forest Service Road 15 for three miles to the campground.

Trip note: This campground is set along the banks of the Blue River near where it enters Blue River Reservoir. There is a boat ramp across the river from the campground. After launching, boat campers can ground their boats near their campsites.

RAINBOW MOBILE
HOME & RV PARK

Site **20**

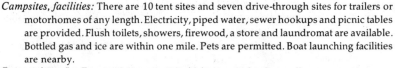

Campsites, facilities: There are 10 tent sites and seven drive-through sites for trailers or motorhomes of any length. Electricity, piped water, sewer hookups and picnic tables are provided. Flush toilets, showers, firewood, a store and laundromat are available. Bottled gas and ice are within one mile. Pets are permitted. Boat launching facilities are nearby.

Reservations, fee: Reservations accepted; $8 fee per night. Open all year.

Who to contact: Phone at 503-822-3928, or write at 54665 McKenzie, Blue River, OR 97413.

Location: From Blue River, travel six miles east on Highway 126, then 1/2 mile southeast on McKenzie River Drive.

Trip note: This campground is set along the banks of the South Fork of the McKenzie River, not far from Cougar Lake. See the trip note to campsite 21 for recreation options.

PATIO TRAILER
COURT

Site **21**

Campsites, facilities: There are 66 sites for trailers or motorhomes of any length in this adult-only campground. Electricity, piped water, sewer hookups and picnic tables are provided. Flush toilets, bottled gas, sanitary services, showers, firewood, a recreation hall and laundromat are available. A store, cafe and ice are within one mile. Pets are permitted.

Reservations, fee: Reservations accepted; $10 fee per night. Open all year.

Who to contact: Phone at 503-822-3596, or write at 55636 McKenzie, Blue River, OR 97413.

Location: Go six miles east on Highway 126 from Blue River, then go two miles south on McKenzie River Drive.

Trip note: This motorhome park is set near the banks of the South Fork of the McKenzie River, not far from Cougar Lake, which offers opportunities for fishing, swimming and waterskiing. Nearby recreation options include a golf course, hiking trails and bike paths.

SLIDE CREEK
Site **22**

Campsites, facilities: There are 16 sites for tents, trailers or motorhomes. Picnic tables and firegrills are provided, and piped water, vault toilets and firewood are available. Pets are permitted. A boat ramp is nearby.

Reservations, fee: No reservations necessary; $3 fee per night. Open mid-May to mid-September.

Who to contact: Phone Blue River Ranger District at 503-822-3317, or write at Willamette National Forest, Blue River, OR 97413.

Location: Take US 126 east of Blue River for 3 1/2 miles, then travel south on Forest Service Road 19 (Aufderheide Drive) for three miles. Take the Eastside Road 500 along the east side of Cougar Reservoir about nine miles to the campground.

Trip note: This campground is set along the banks of Cougar Lake, which cover about 1300 acres and offers opportunities for fishing and swimming. Set west of Olallie Mountain near the Three Sisters Wilderness.

FRENCH PETE
Site **23**

Campsites, facilities: There are 17 sites for tents, trailers or motorhomes. Picnic tables and firegrills are provided, and piped water, vault toilets and firewood are available. Some facilities are wheelchair accessible. Pets are permitted.

Reservations, fee: No reservations necessary; $5 fee per night. Open mid-May to mid-September.

Who to contact: Phone Blue River Ranger District at 503-822-3317, or write at Willamette National Forest, Blue River, OR 97413.

Location: Take US 126 east of Blue River for 3 1/2 miles, then go south on Forest Service Road 19 (Aufderheide Drive) for 12 miles to the campground.

Trip note: This quiet, wooded campground is set along the banks of the South Fork of the McKenzie River and French Pete Creek. There is a trail across the road from the campground that provides access to the Three Sisters Wilderness. Three more primitive camps (campsites 24-26) are a few miles southeast on the same road.

HOMESTEAD
Site **24**

Campsites, facilities: There are seven sites for tents, trailers or motorhomes. Picnic tables and firegrills are provided, and vault toilets and firewood are available. There is no piped water. Pets are permitted.

Reservations, fee: No reservations necessary; no fee. Open mid-May to mid-September.

Who to contact: Phone Blue River Ranger District at 503-822-3317, or write at Willamette National Forest, Blue River, OR 97413.

Location: Take US 126 east of Blue River for 3 1/2 miles, then go south on Forest Service Road 19 (Aufderheide Drive) for 19 miles to the campground.

Trip note: This quiet little campground is set along the banks of the South Fork of the McKenzie River. Little-known and it is free. Campsite 26 is nearby and has piped water.

TWIN SPRINGS

Site **25**

Campsites, facilities: There are five sites for tents, trailers or motorhomes. Picnic tables and firegrills are provided, and vault toilets and firewood are available. There is no piped water. Pets are permitted.

Reservations, fee: No reservations necessary; no fee. Open mid-May to mid-September.

Who to contact: Phone Blue River Ranger District at 503-822-3317, or write at Willamette National Forest, Blue River, OR 97413.

Location: Take US 126 east of Blue River for 3 1/2 miles, then go south on Forest Service Road 19 (Aufderheide Drive) for 21 miles to the campground.

Trip note: This pretty little campground is set along the banks of the South Fork of the McKenzie River.

FRISSELL
Site **26**   CROSSING

Campsites, facilities: There are 12 sites for tents, trailers or motorhomes. Picnic tables and firegrills are provided, and piped water, vault toilets and firewood are available. Pets are permitted.

Reservations, fee: No reservations necessary; $3 fee per night. Open mid-May to mid-September.

Who to contact: Phone Blue River Ranger District at 503-822-3317, or write at Willamette National Forest, Blue River, OR 97413.

Location: Take US 126 east of Blue River for 3 1/2 miles, then go south on Forest Service Road 19 (Aufderheide Drive) for 23 miles to the campground.

Trip note: This campground is at 2600 feet elevation and is set along the banks of the South Fork of the McKenzie River, adjacent to a trailhead that provides access to the backcountry of the Three Sisters Wilderness. This is the only camp in the immediate area that provides piped water.

MCKENZIE BRIDGE
Site **27**

Campsites, facilities: There are 20 sites for tents, trailers or motorhomes up to 22 feet long. Picnic tables and firegrills are provided, and vault toilets, piped water and firewood are available. Pets are permitted.

Reservations, fee: No reservations necessary; $4 fee per night. Open late-May to early-September.

Who to contact: Phone McKenzie Ranger District at 503-822-3381, or write at Willamette National Forest, McKenzie Bridge, OR 97413.

Location: From the town of McKenzie Bridge, travel one mile west on Highway 126 to the campground.

Trip note: This campground is set along the banks of the McKenzie River, near the town of McKenzie Bridge. Good evening fly fishing for trout during summer on this stretch of river.

Site 28
HORSE CREEK
GROUP CAMP

Campsites, facilities: There are eight tent sites and 13 sites for trailers or motorhomes up to 21 feet long. Picnic tables and firegrills are provided, and piped water, vault toilets and firewood are available. Pets are permitted.

Reservations, fee: Reservations required; $30 fee per night. Open all year.

Who to contact: Phone McKenzie Ranger District at 503-822-3381, or write at Willamette National Forest, McKenzie Bridge, OR 97413.

Location: From the town of McKenzie Bridge on Highway 126, turn south on Horse Creek Road and drive three miles to the campground.

Trip note: This campground is reserved for groups. It is set along the banks of Horse Creek, near the town of McKenzie Bridge.

Site 29
THE HUB
TRAILER PARK

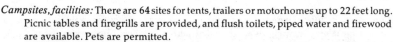

Campsites, facilities: There are 36 drive-through sites for trailers or motorhomes of any length. Electricity, piped water, sewer hookups and picnic tables are provided. Flush toilets, bottled gas, sanitary services, showers, a recreation hall and laundromat are available. A store, cafe and ice are within one mile. Pets are permitted.

Reservations, fee: Reservations accepted; $9 fee per night. MasterCard and Visa accepted. Open all year.

Who to contact: Phone at 503-822-3514, or write at 56642 McKenzie Highway, McKenzie Bridge, OR 97413.

Location: This camp is located in the town of McKenzie Bridge on the south side of US 126.

Trip note: This motorhome park is set near the banks of the McKenzie River. The Forest Service office is available in the town of McKenzie Bridge and provides information on many of the recreation options in the area.

Site 30
PARADISE CREEK

Campsites, facilities: There are 64 sites for tents, trailers or motorhomes up to 22 feet long. Picnic tables and firegrills are provided, and flush toilets, piped water and firewood are available. Pets are permitted.

Reservations, fee: No reservations necessary; $8 fee per night. Open late-May to early-September.

Who to contact: Phone McKenzie Ranger District at 503-822-3381, or write at Willamette National Forest, McKenzie Bridge, OR 97413.

Location: Travel on Highway 126 east of McKenzie Bridge 3 1/2 miles.

Trip note: This campground is set along the banks of the McKenzie River. You get easy access via the highway, yet a rustic, streamside setting. Trout fishing can be good.

Site 31
LIMBERLOST

Campsites, facilities: There are four tent sites and 10 sites for tents, trailers or motorhomes. Picnic tables and firegrills are provided, and vault toilets and firewood are available.

There is no piped water. Pets are permitted.

Reservations, fee: No reservations necessary; no fee. Open late-May to early-September.

Who to contact: Phone McKenzie Ranger District at 503-822-3381, or write at Willamette National Forest, McKenzie Bridge, OR 97413.

Location: Take Highway 126 four miles east of McKenzie Bridge, then go 1/2 mile on Highway 242 to the camp.

Trip note: This little campground is set along Lost Creek about two miles from where it empties into the McKenzie River. Hidden and secluded, a good base camp for a trout fishing trip.

ALDER SPRINGS
Site **32**

Campsites, facilities: There are seven tent sites. Picnic tables and firegrills are provided, and vault toilets, piped water and firewood are available. Pets are permitted.

Reservations, fee: No reservations necessary; $2 fee per night. Open late-May to early-September.

Who to contact: Phone McKenzie Ranger District at 503-822-3381, or write at Willamette National Forest, McKenzie Bridge, OR 97413.

Location: Travel east on Highway 126 for seven miles east of McKenzie Bridge to Highway 242, then head east on Highway 242 for eight miles to the campground.

Trip note: This remote campground is set at 3600 feet elevation and offers good hiking possibilities. A map of Willamette National Forest details the nearby back roads and trails.

FROG CAMP
Site **33**

Campsites, facilities: There are six tent sites. Picnic tables and firegrills are provided, and pit toilets and firewood are available. There is no piped water. Pets are permitted.

Reservations, fee: No reservations necessary; no fee. Open late-June to early-September.

Who to contact: Phone McKenzie Ranger District at 503-822-3381, or write at Willamette National Forest, McKenzie Bridge, OR 97413.

Location: Travel east on Highway 126 for seven miles east of McKenzie Bridge to Highway 242, then head east on Highway 242 for 12 miles to the campground on your right.

Trip note: This remote campground is set at 4800 feet elevation adjacent to a trail that heads up and intersects with the Pacific Crest Trail about four miles from camp. Campsite 34, which is nearby, provides a hike-in, lakeside option.

SCOTT LAKE
Site **34**

Campsites, facilities: There are 20 tent sites. Picnic tables and firegrills are provided, and pit toilets and firewood are available. There is no piped water. Pets are permitted. Boat docks are located nearby.

Reservations, fee: No reservations necessary; no fee. Open late-June to early-September.

Who to contact: Phone McKenzie Ranger District at 503-822-3381, or write at Willamette National Forest, McKenzie Bridge, OR 97413.

Location: Travel east on Highway 126 for seven miles east of McKenzie Bridge to Highway 242, then head east on Highway 242 for 14 1/2 miles to Forest Service Road 1532 and turn left to the campground.

Trip note: This campground offers hike-in sites set around Scott Lake, elevation 4800 feet. Non-motorized boats are allowed on the lake, and there are trails leading out from camp that provide access to several small lakes in the Mount Washington Wilderness.

Site 35   BELKNAP WOODS RESORT

Campsites, facilities: There are six tent sites and 36 sites for trailers or motorhomes of any length. Electricity, piped water, sewer hookups and picnic tables are provided. Flush toilets, showers, laundromat and swimming pool are available. Pets and motorbikes are permitted.

Reservations, fee: Reservations accepted; $8 fee per night. MasterCard and Visa accepted. Open April to late-October.

Who to contact: Phone at 503-822-3535, or write at Box 1, McKenzie Bridge, OR 97413.

Location: This camp is located in Belknap Springs on Belknap Springs Road.

Trip note: This campground is set along the banks of the McKenzie River. Nearby recreation options include hot springs, hiking trails and bike paths. One in a series of campgrounds on the slopes of the Cascade Range along a 20-mile stretch of Highway 126.

Site 36   OLALLIE

Campsites, facilities: There are 17 sites for tents, trailers or motorhomes up to 22 feet long. Picnic tables and firegrills are provided, and vault toilets, piped water and firewood are available. Pets are permitted.

Reservations, fee: No reservations necessary; $3 fee per night. Open late-May to early-September.

Who to contact: Phone McKenzie Ranger District at 503-822-3381, or write at Willamette National Forest, McKenzie Bridge, OR 97413.

Location: Travel 11 miles northeast of McKenzie Bridge on Highway 126 to the camp.

Trip note: This campground is set along the banks of the McKenzie River and offers opportunities for boating, fishing and hiking. You get easy access from Highway 126, and also a jumpoff point into Willamette National Forest. Forest Service map details back roads and trails.

Site 37   TRAIL BRIDGE

Campsites, facilities: There are 24 sites for tents, trailers or motorhomes. Picnic tables and firegrills are provided, and piped water, vault toilets and firewood are available. Pets are permitted. Boat docks are nearby.

Reservations, fee: No reservations necessary; $4 fee per night. Open late-May to early-September.

Who to contact: Phone McKenzie Ranger District at 503-822-3381, or write at Willamette National Forest, McKenzie Bridge, OR 97413.

Location: Drive on Highway 126 northeast of McKenzie Bridge for 13 miles, then turn southwest at the turn-off at the north end of Trailbridge Reservoir and go 200 yards to the campground.

Trip note: This campground is set along the shore of Trailbridge Reservoir, where boating, fishing and hiking are recreation options. An exceptional spot for car campers.

LAKES END
Site 38

Campsites, facilities: There are 17 tent sites at this campground which is only accessible by boat. Picnic tables and firegrills are provided, and vault toilets and firewood are available. There is no piped water. Pets are permitted. Boat docks are nearby.

Reservations, fee: No reservations necessary; no fee. Open late-May to early-September.

Who to contact: Phone McKenzie Ranger District at 503-822-3381, or write at Willamette National Forest, McKenzie Bridge, OR 97413.

Location: Drive northeast from the town of McKenzie Bridge on Highway 126 for 13 miles, then go three miles north on Forest Service Road 1477 to the boat ramp. Travel by boat for another two miles to the north end of Smith Reservoir where the campground is located.

Trip note: This secluded boat-in campground is set along the shore of Smith Reservoir. One of the few boat-in campgrounds in the entire state. No cars, no traffic and the fishing can be good.

ICE CAP
Site 39   CREEK

Campsites, facilities: There are eight tent sites and 14 sites for tents, trailers or motorhomes up to 16 feet long. Picnic tables and firegrills are provided, and piped water, flush toilets and firewood are available. Pets are permitted. Boat docks, launching facilities and rentals are nearby.

Reservations, fee: No reservations necessary; $5 fee per night. Open late-May to early-September.

Who to contact: Phone McKenzie Ranger District at 503-822-3381, or write at Willamette National Forest, McKenzie Bridge, OR 97413.

Location: Drive on Highway 126 north of the town of McKenzie Bridge for 19 miles, then go 200 yards southwest on the entrance road to the campground.

Trip note: This campground is set along the shore of Carmen Reservoir, which was created by a dam on the McKenzie River. The McKenzie River National Recreation Trail passes by camp, and Koosah Falls and Sahalie Falls are nearby.

COLDWATER
Site 40   COVE

Campsites, facilities: There are 35 sites for tents, trailers or motorhomes up to 22 feet long. Picnic tables and firegrills are provided, and piped water, vault toilets, firewood, a store and a cafe are available. Pets are permitted. Some facilities are wheelchair accessible. Boat docks, launching facilities and rentals are nearby.

Reservations, fee: No reservations necessary; $4 fee per night. Open late-May to early-September.

Who to contact: Phone McKenzie Ranger District at 503-822-3381, or write at Willamette National Forest, McKenzie Bridge, OR 97413.

Location: Take Highway 126 north of McKenzie Bridge for 14 miles, then go east on Forest Service Road 1372 to the campground.

Trip note: This campground is set along the south shore of Clear Lake. This spring-fed lake is formed by a natural lava dam and is the source of the McKenzie River. The northern section of the McKenzie River National Recreation Trail passes by camp.

FISH LAKE
Site **41**

Campsites, facilities: There are eight sites for tents, trailers or motorhomes up to 16 feet long. Picnic tables and firegrills are provided, and piped water, pit toilets and firewood are available. Pets are permitted.

Reservations, fee: No reservations necessary; no fee. Open late-June to early-September.

Who to contact: Phone McKenzie Ranger District at 503-822-3381, or write at Willamette National Forest, Sisters, OR 97759.

Location: Travel on Highway 126 north of the town of McKenzie Bridge for 23 miles, then go 200 yards southwest on the entrance road to the campground.

Trip note: This campground is set along the shore of Fish Lake, which is something of a paradox since it usually dries up at the end of the summer. An interpretive display is set up at the guard station nearby. Across the road is a trail that follows the Old Santiam Wagon Road and the northern trailhead for the McKenzie River National Recreation Trail. The Clear Lake picnic area is two miles south off Highway 126.

LOST PRAIRIE
Site **42**

Campsites, facilities: There are six tent sites and four sites for trailers or motorhomes up to 22 feet long. Picnic tables and firegrills are provided, and piped water, vault toilets and firewood are available. Some facilities are wheelchair accessible. Pets are permitted.

Reservations, fee: No reservations necessary; $4 fee per night. Open mid-April to mid-November.

Who to contact: Phone Sweet Home Ranger District at 503-367-5168, or write at Willamette National Forest, Sweet Home, OR 97386.

Location: From Albany, drive east on US 20 40 miles to the camp. From Highway 126, turn west at the U.S. 20 junction and look for the camp on the north side of the road.

Trip note: This campground is set along the banks of Hackleman Creek at 3300 feet elevation. An option to nearby campsite 41.

BIG LAKE
Site **43**

Campsites, facilities: There are 21 sites for tents, trailers or motorhomes up to 16 feet long. Picnic tables and firegrills are provided, and piped water, vault toilets and firewood are available. Pets are permitted. Boat docks and launching facilities are nearby.

Reservations, fee: No reservations necessary; $8 fee per night. Open late-June to early-September.

Who to contact: Phone McKenzie Ranger District at 503-822-3381, or write at Willamette National Forest, Sisters, OR 97759.

Location: From the town of Sisters, go 21 miles west on Highway 20, then 3 1/2 miles south on Forest Service Road 2690.

Trip note: This is a jewel of a spot set on the north shore of Big Lake at 4650 feet elevation. Fishing, swimming, waterskiing and hiking make it attractive. One of the better hikes is a five-mile loop trail that heads out from the south shore of the lake and cuts past a few small lakes before returning.

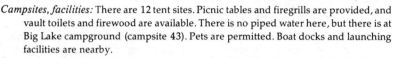

Site **44**

BIG LAKE WEST

Campsites, facilities: There are 12 tent sites. Picnic tables and firegrills are provided, and vault toilets and firewood are available. There is no piped water here, but there is at Big Lake campground (campsite 43). Pets are permitted. Boat docks and launching facilities are nearby.

Reservations, fee: No reservations necessary; no fee. Open late-June to early-September.

Who to contact: Phone McKenzie Ranger District at 503-822-3381, or write at Willamette National Forest, Sisters, OR 97759.

Location: Take Highway 20 west from Sisters for 21 miles, then 4 1/2 miles south on Forest Service Road 2690, then hike a short distance to the campground.

Trip note: This camp is set along the western shore of Big Lake and is a primitive option to campsite 43.

 Site **45**

HOUSE ROCK

Campsites, facilities: There are 17 tent sites. Picnic tables and firegrills are provided, and vault toilets and piped water are available. Pets are permitted.

Reservations, fee: No reservations necessary; $4 fee per night. Open mid-April to mid-November.

Who to contact: Phone Sweet Home Ranger District at 509-367-5168, or write at Willamette National Forest, Sweet Home, OR 97386.

Location: From Sweet Home, travel 26 1/2 miles east on US 20, then follow Forest Service Road 2044 southeast for a short distance to the campground.

Trip note: This campground is set where Sheep Creek and Squaw Creek meet to form the Santiam River. Trout fishing can be good, particularly during summer evenings. Camp elevation is 1600 feet.

Site **46**

FERNVIEW

Campsites, facilities: There are 11 sites for tents, trailers or motorhomes up to 22 feet long. Picnic tables and firegrills are provided, and piped water and vault toilets are available. Pets are permitted.

Reservations, fee: No reservations necessary; $3 fee per night. Open mid-April to mid-November.

Who to contact: Phone Sweet Home Ranger District at 509-367-5168, or write at Willamette National Forest, Sweet Home, OR 97386.

Location: From Sweet Home, go 23 miles east on US 20 to the campground.

Trip note: This campground is set at the confluence of Boulder Creek and the Santiam River. A three-mile trail connects this campground with Trout Creek (campsite 47).

Site **47**

TROUT CREEK

Campsites, facilities: There are 24 sites for tents, trailers or motorhomes up to 22 feet long.

Picnic tables and firegrills are provided, and piped water and vault toilets are available. Pets are permitted.

Reservations, fee: No reservations necessary; $5 fee per night. Open mid-April to mid-November.

Who to contact: Phone Sweet Home Ranger District at 509-367-5168, or write at Willamette National Forest, Sweet Home, OR 97386.

Location: Travel 18 1/2 miles east of Sweet Home on US 20 to the campground.

Trip note: This campground is set along the banks of the Santiam River, about seven miles east of the town of Cascadia. It is at the foot of the Menagerie Wilderness. Fishing and swimming are some of the possibilities here. A nearby trail travels east for about three miles to Fernview Campground (campsite 46).

YUKWAH
Site **48**

Campsites, facilities: There are 20 sites for tents, trailers or motorhomes up to 31 feet long. Picnic tables and firegrills are provided, and piped water and vault toilets are available. Pets are permitted.

Reservations, fee: No reservations necessary; $4 fee per night. Open all year.

Who to contact: Phone Sweet Home Ranger District at 509-367-5168, or write at Willamette National Forest, Sweet Home, OR 97386.

Location: Travel 19 miles east of Sweet Home on US 20 to the campground.

Trip note: This campground is adjacent to campsite 47 and offers the same recreation possibilities.

CASCADIA
Site **49**   STATE PARK   ▲

Campsites, facilities: There are 26 sites for tents, trailers or motorhomes up to 35 feet long. Picnic tables and firegrills are provided, and piped water, flush toilets and firewood are available. A store is located within one mile. Some facilities are wheelchair accessible. Pets are permitted.

Reservations, fee: No reservations necessary; $5 fee per night. Open mid-April to late-October.

Who to contact: Phone at 503-343-7812, or write at P.O. Box 736, Cascadia, OR 97329.

Location: Travel 14 miles east of Sweet Home on US 20 to the park.

Trip note: This 258-acre park is set along the banks of the Santiam River.

YELLOW BOTTOM
Site **50**   ▲

Campsites, facilities: There are 12 tent sites and 10 drive-through sites for trailers or motorhomes up to 20 feet long. Picnic tables and firegrills are provided, and piped water and vault toilets are available. Pets are permitted.

Reservations, fee: No reservations necessary; $4 fee per night. Open mid-May to late-November.

Who to contact: Phone at 503-399-5646, or write the Bureau of Land Management at Box 3227, Salem, OR 97302.

Location: From Sweet Home, go 21 miles northeast on Quartzville Road.

Trip note: This campground is set along the banks of Quartzville Creek, always missed by

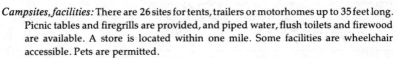

out-of-town visitors. It is located on the edge of Willamette National Forest and the Middle Santiam Wilderness.

Site 51
DETROIT LAKE
STATE PARK

Campsites, facilities: There are 139 tent sites and 176 sites for trailers or motorhomes of any length. Firegrills and picnic tables are provided, and flush toilets, showers, electricity, piped water, sewer hookups, firewood and a laundromat are available. Pets are permitted. Boat docks and launching facilities are nearby.

Reservations, fee: Reservations accepted; $8 fee per night. Open mid-April to late-October.

Who to contact: Phone at 503-854-3346, or write at Box 549, Detroit, OR 97342.

Location: From the town of Detroit, travel two miles west on Highway 22 to the park.

Trip note: This campground is set along the shore of Detroit Lake at 1600 feet elevation. Fishing, swimming and waterskiing are permitted. The lake is very crowded on the opening day of trout season in late April. Heavily stocked.

Site 52
PIETY ISLAND

Campsites, facilities: There are 12 tent sites on this island campground which is accessible by boat only. Picnic tables and firegrills are provided, and pit toilets are available. Pets are permitted. Boat docks, launching facilities and rentals are nearby.

Reservations, fee: No reservations necessary; no fee. Open May to late-September.

Who to contact: Phone Detroit Ranger District at 509-854-3366, or write at Willamette National Forest, State Highway 22, Detroit, OR 97460.

Location: This campground is located in the middle of Detroit Lake one mile southwest of the town of Detroit.

Trip note: If you want to get away from the crowds at Detroit Lake State Park, this camp provides that possibility for boaters. Other campgrounds along the shore have piped water available.

Site 53
UPPER ARM

Campsites, facilities: There are three tent sites and two sites for trailers or motorhomes up to 16 feet long. Firegrills and picnic tables are provided, and pit toilets are available. There is no piped water. Pets are permitted. Boat docks, launching facilities and rentals are nearby.

Reservations, fee: No reservations necessary; no fee. Open mid-April to late-December.

Who to contact: Phone Detroit Ranger District at 509-854-3366, or write at Willamette National Forest, State Highway 22, Detroit, OR 97460.

Location: From the town of Detroit, travel one mile northeast on Forest Service Road 46 (Breitenbush Road) to the campground.

Trip note: This little campground is set along the shore of the narrow upper arm of Detroit Lake, close to where Breitenbush River empties into it. The smallest and most primitive camp in the area.

SOUTHSHORE
Site **54**

Campsites, facilities: There are eight tent sites and 22 sites for trailers or motorhomes up to
   22 feet long. Fire grills and picnic tables are provided, and vault toilets and piped
   water are available. Some facilities are wheelchair accessible. Pets are permitted. Boat
   launching facilities are nearby.

Reservations, fee: No reservations necessary; $5 fee per night. Open mid-April to late-
   September.

Who to contact: Phone Detroit Ranger District at 509-854-3366, or write at Willamette
   National Forest, State Highway 22, Detroit, OR 97460.

Location: Drive 2 1/2 miles southeast of Detroit on Highway 22, then four miles west on
   Forest Service Road 10 (Blow Out Road) to the campground.

Trip note: This campground is set along the south shore of Detroit Lake, where fishing,
   swimming and waterskiing are some of the recreation options. This is a popular place,
   particularly in late April when the trout season opens. The Stahlman Point Trailhead
   is about 2 1/2 miles from camp.

HOOVER
Site **55**

Campsites, facilities: There are two tent sites and 35 sites for tents, trailers or motorhomes
   up to 22 feet long. Picnic tables and firegrills are provided. Flush toilets and piped
   water are available. Some facilities are wheelchair accessible. Pets are permitted. Boat
   docks, launching facilities and rentals are nearby.

Reservations, fee: No reservations necessary; $5 fee per night. Open mid-April to mid-
   October.

Who to contact: Phone Detroit Ranger District at 503-854-3356, or write at Willamette
   National Forest, State Highway 22, Detroit, OR 97460.

Location: From Detroit, drive 2 1/2 miles southeast on Highway 22, then one mile
   northwest on Forest Service Road 10 (Blow Out Road) to the campground.

Trip note: This campground is along the eastern arm of Detroit Lake, near the mouth of the
   Santiam River. See the trip note to campsite 54 for recreation details.

HOOVER
Site **56**   GROUP CAMP

Campsites, facilities: There are seven sites for tents, trailers or motorhomes up to 15 feet
   long. Piped water and picnic tables are provided, and piped water, vault toilets and a
   group picnic shelter are available. Pets are permitted. Boat docks, launching facilities
   and rentals are nearby.

Reservations, fee: Reservations required; fee depends on group size. Open mid-April to
   mid-October.

Who to contact: Phone Detroit Ranger District at 503-854-3366, or write at Willamette
   National Forest, State Highway 22, Detroit, OR 97460.

Location: From Detroit, drive 2 1/2 miles southwest on Highway 22, then 1/2 mile
   northwest on Forest Service Road 10 (Blow Out Road) to the campground.

Trip note: See the trip notes to campsites 54 and 55, which are also set at Detroit Lake.

Site **57**
WHISPERING FALLS

Campsites, facilities: There are 12 sites for tents, trailers or motorhomes up to 22 feet long. Picnic tables and firegrills are provided, and piped water and vault toilets are available. A cafe is nearby. Pets are permitted.

Reservations, fee: No reservations necessary; $5 fee per night. Open mid-April to late-September.

Who to contact: Phone Detroit Ranger District at 509-854-3366, or write at Willamette National Forest, State Highway 22, Idanha, OR 97360.

Location: From Detroit, drive eight miles east on Highway 22 to the campground.

Trip note: This popular campground is set along the banks of the Santiam River. If the campsites at Detroit Lake are crowded, this provides a more secluded option. It's about a 10-minute drive from the lake.

Site **58**
RIVERSIDE

Campsites, facilities: There are 37 sites for tents, trailers or motorhomes up to 21 feet long. Picnic tables and firegrills are provided, and piped water and vault toilets are available. Pets are permitted.

Reservations, fee: No reservations necessary; $5 fee per night. Open late-April to late-September.

Who to contact: Phone Detroit Ranger District at 503-630-4256, or write at Willamette National Forest, State Highway 22, Idanha, OR 97360.

Location: From Detroit, travel 14 miles southeast on Highway 22 to the campground.

Trip note: This campground is set along the banks of the Santiam River. The Mt. Jefferson Wilderness is located directly to the east in Willamette National Forest.

Site **59**
MARION FORKS

Campsites, facilities: There are eight sites for tents, trailers or motorhomes up to 22 feet long. Picnic tables and firegrills are provided, and vault toilets and piped water are available. Pets are permitted.

Reservations, fee: No reservations necessary; $5 fee per night. Open mid-May to mid-September.

Who to contact: Phone Detroit Ranger District at 509-854-3366, or write at Willamette National Forest, State Highway 22, Idanha, OR 97360.

Location: From Detroit, travel 16 miles southeast on Highway 22 to the campground.

Trip note: This campground is set at the confluence of Marion Creek and the Santiam River, adjacent to a Forest Service Ranger Station. A possible side trip is touring the nearby state fish hatchery.

Site **60**
BLUE LAKE RESORT

Campsites, facilities: There are 40 sites for tents, trailers or motorhomes of any length. Picnic tables and firegrills are provided, and electricity, piped water, sewer hookups, flush toilets, bottled gas, sanitary disposal station, showers, firewood, a store, cafe, ice and playground are available. Pets are permitted. Boat docks, launching facilities and rentals are nearby.

Reservations, fee: Reservations accepted; $10 fee per night. MasterCard and Visa accepted. Open all year.

Who to contact: Phone at 503-595-6671, or write at Star Route, Sisters, OR 97759.

Location: From Sisters, travel 13 miles northwest on Highway 126, then 2 1/2 miles west on Suttle Lake Forest Highway.

Trip note: This 200-acre resort is set along the shore of Suttle Lake, one of five camps along the lake. Recreation options include fishing, swimming, hiking, bicycling and horseback riding.

SOUTH SHORE
Site **61**

Campsites, facilities: There are 39 sites for tents, trailers or motorhomes up to 22 feet long. Picnic tables and firegrills are provided, and piped water and vault toilets are available. Pets are permitted. Boat docks, launching facilities and rentals are nearby.

Reservations, fee: No reservations necessary; $6 fee per night. Open mid-April to late-September.

Who to contact: Phone Sisters Ranger District at 503-549-2111 or write Deschutes National Forest, Sisters, OR 97759.

Location: Travel 14 miles northwest of the town of Sisters on Highway 126 to Suttle Lake Forest Road and head west to the campground.

Trip note: This campground is located on the south shore of Suttle Lake, at 3400 feet elevation. Rental boats and fishing supplies are available at the nearby resort. Waterskiing is permitted on the lake. A loop trail goes around the lake. A stable and horseback riding rentals are nearby.

LINK CREEK
Site **62**

Campsites, facilities: There are 33 sites for tents, trailers or motorhomes up to 22 feet long. Picnic tables and firegrills are provided, and piped water and vault toilets are available. Pets are permitted. Boat docks, launching facilities and rentals are nearby.

Reservations, fee: No reservations necessary; $6 fee per night. Open mid-April to late-September.

Who to contact: Phone Sisters Ranger District at 503-549-2111 or write Deschutes National Forest, Sisters, OR 97759.

Location: Travel 14 miles northwest of the town of Sisters on Highway 126 to Suttle Lake Forest Road and head west to the campground.

Trip note: This campground is located at the west end of Suttle Lake. See the trip note for campsite 61 for recreation details.

BLUE BAY
Site **63**

Campsites, facilities: There are 25 sites for tents, trailers or motorhomes up to 22 feet long. Picnic tables and firegrills are provided, and piped water and vault toilets are available. Pets are permitted. Boat docks, launching facilities and rentals are nearby.

Reservations, fee: No reservations necessary; $6 fee per night. Open mid-April to late-September.

Who to contact: Phone Sisters Ranger District at 503-549-2111 or write Deschutes National
    Forest, Sisters, OR 97759.
Location: Travel 14 miles northwest of the town of Sisters on Highway 126 to Suttle Lake
    Forest Road and head west to the campground.
Trip note: This campground is set along the south shore of Suttle Lake. See the trip note for
    to campsite 61 for recreation details.

SCOUT LAKE
Site 64

Campsites, facilities: There are 13 sites for tents, trailers or motorhomes up to 22 feet long.
    Picnic tables and firegrills are provided, and vault toilets and piped water are avail-
    able. Pets are permitted.
Reservations, fee: No reservations necessary; $5 fee per night. Open mid-April to late-
    September.
Who to contact: Phone Sisters Ranger District at 503-549-2111 or write Deschutes National
    Forest, Sisters, OR 97759.
Location: Travel 14 miles northwest of the town of Sisters on Highway 126 to Suttle Lake
    Forest Road and head west, then turn and go south of Suttle Lake on Forest Service
    Road 2066 for a short distance to the campground.
Trip note: This campground is set about 1/4 mile from Suttle Lake along the shore of little
    Scout Lake. It is a good area for swimming and hiking. This campground is available
    for groups, but reservations need to be made in advance. Call the ranger district
    for details.

RIVERSIDE
Site 65

Campsites, facilities: There are 19 sites for tents, trailers or motorhomes up to 21 feet long.
    Picnic tables and firegrills are provided, and vault toilets and piped water are avail-
    able. Pets are permitted.
Reservations, fee: No reservations necessary; no fee. Open mid-April to mid-October.
Who to contact: Phone Sisters Ranger District at 503-549-2111 or write Deschutes National
    Forest, Sisters, OR 97759.
Location: From the store in Camp Sherman, go two miles south on Forest Service Road
    900 to the campground.
Trip note: This campground is set along the banks of the Metolius River, less than a mile
    from Metolius Springs at the base of Black Butte. It is just enough off the highway to be
    missed by most others.

CAMP SHERMAN
Site 66

Campsites, facilities: There are 15 sites for tents, trailers or motorhomes up to 22 feet long.
    Picnic tables and firegrills are provided, and vault toilets and piped water are avail-
    able. Pets are permitted.
Reservations, fee: No reservations necessary; $6 fee per night. Open May to October.
Who to contact: Phone Sisters Ranger Station at 503-549-2111, or write Deschutes
    National Forest, Sisters, OR 97759.
Location: From the store in Camp Sherman, travel 1/2 mile north on Forest Service Road
    113 to the campground.

Trip note: This campground is set along the banks of the Metolius River, where you can fish for wild trout. This place is for expert fly fishermen seeking a quality angling experience. Advisable to obtain a map of Deschutes National Forest, which details back roads, trails, and streams. This is one of five camps in the immediate area.

ALLINGHAM

Site **67**

Campsites, facilities: There are 10 sites for tents, trailers or motorhomes up to 22 feet long. Picnic tables and firegrills are provided, and vault toilets and piped water are available. Pets are permitted.

Reservations, fee: No reservations necessary; $6 fee per night. Open May to October.

Who to contact: Phone Sisters Ranger Station at 503-549-2111, or write Deschutes National Forest, Sisters, OR 97759.

Location: From the store in Camp Sherman, travel one mile north to the campground.

Trip note: This campground is set along the banks of the Metolius River, one of five camps in the immediate area. See trip note to campsite 66.

SMILING RIVER

Site **68**

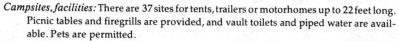

Campsites, facilities: There are 37 sites for tents, trailers or motorhomes up to 22 feet long. Picnic tables and firegrills are provided, and vault toilets and piped water are available. Pets are permitted.

Reservations, fee: No reservations necessary; $6 fee per night. Open May to October.

Who to contact: Phone Sisters Ranger Station at 503-549-2111, or write Deschutes National Forest, Sisters, OR 97759.

Location: From the store in Camp Sherman, travel one mile north to the campground.

Trip note: This campground is set along the banks of the Metolius River. See trip note to campsite 66.

PINE REST

Site **69**

Campsites, facilities: There are eight tent sites. Picnic tables and firegrills are provided, and vault toilets and piped water are available. Pets are permitted.

Reservations, fee: No reservations necessary; $6 fee per night. Open May to October.

Who to contact: Phone Sisters Ranger Station at 503-549-2111, or write Deschutes National Forest, Sisters, OR 97759.

Location: From the store in Camp Sherman, travel 1 1/2 miles north to the campground.

Trip note: This campground is set along the banks of the Metolius River. See trip note to campsite 66.

GORGE

Site **70**

Campsites, facilities: There are 18 sites for tents, trailers or motorhomes up to 22 feet long. Picnic tables and firegrills are provided, and vault toilets and piped water are available. Pets are permitted.

Reservations, fee: No reservations necessary; $6 fee per night. Open May to October.

Who to contact: Phone Sisters Ranger Station at 503-549-2111, or write Deschutes
National Forest, Sisters, OR 97759.

Location: From the store in Camp Sherman, travel two miles north to the campground.

Trip note: This campground is set along the banks of the Metolius River. See trip note to
campsite 66.

JACK CREEK
Site 71

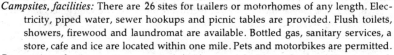

Campsites, facilities: There are 11 sites for tents, trailers or motorhomes up to 15 feet long.
Picnic tables and firegrills are provided, and vault toilets are available. There is no
piped water. Pets are permitted.

Reservations, fee: No reservations necessary; no fee. Open mid-April to mid-October.

Who to contact: Phone Sisters Ranger Station at 503-549-2111, or write Deschutes
National Forest, Sisters, OR 97759.

Location: This campground is located five miles northwest of Camp Sherman via Forest
Service Roads 12 and 1230.

Trip note: This campground is set along the banks of the Jack Creek where fishing and
hiking are recreation options. A trail passes a mile east of camp that travels nine miles
south to Black Butte, or many miles north and west into the Mount Jefferson
Wilderness. A more primitive option to the other camps in the area.

BLACK BUTTE
MOTEL & RV PARK
Site 72

Campsites, facilities: There are 26 sites for trailers or motorhomes of any length. Electricity, piped water, sewer hookups and picnic tables are provided. Flush toilets,
showers, firewood and laundromat are available. Bottled gas, sanitary services, a
store, cafe and ice are located within one mile. Pets and motorbikes are permitted.

Reservations, fee: Reservations accepted; $11 fee per night. MasterCard and Visa accepted.
Open all year.

Who to contact: Phone at 503-595-6514, or write at HCR 97736, Box 1250, Camp Sherman,
OR 97730.

Location: From Camp Sherman, travel five miles north on Forest Service Road 14 to the
park.

Trip note: This motorhome park is set along the banks of the Metolius River. See trip notes
to campsites 66 and 71.

COLD SPRINGS
RESORT/RV PARK
Site 73

Campsites, facilities: There are 11 sites for trailers or motorhomes of any length. Electricity, piped water and sewer hookups are provided. Bottled gas, a store, cafe,
laundromat and ice are located within one mile. Pets and motorbikes are permitted.

Reservations, fee: Reservations accepted; $12 fee per night. Open mid-April to mid-
October.

Who to contact: Phone at 503-595-6271, or write at HCR, Box 1270, Camp Sherman, OR
97730.

Location: From Camp Sherman, travel five miles on Forest Service Road 14 to the
park.

Trip note: This wooded motorhome park is fairly close to the Metolius River. Nearby recreation options include a golf course, hiking trails, a riding stable and tennis courts.

Site **74**   METOLIUS
                            RIVER RESORT   🚐

Campsites, facilities: There are 10 drive-through sites for trailers or motorhomes of any length. Electricity, piped water, sewer hookups and picnic tables are provided. Flush toilets, bottled gas, showers, a cafe and ice are available. A store and laundromat are located within one mile. Pets are permitted.

Reservations, fee: Reservations accepted; $10 fee per night. MasterCard and Visa accepted. Open all year.

Who to contact: Phone at 503-595-6281, or write at Star Route Box 1210, Camp Sherman, OR 97730.

Location: From Camp Sherman, travel five miles north on Forest Service Road 14 to the resort.

Trip note: This motorhome resort is set near the banks of the Metolius River. Nearby recreation options include a golf course and hiking trails. Trout fishing can be good on the Metolius.

Site **75**   ALLEN SPRINGS   🚐

Campsites, facilities: There are four tent sites and 13 sites for tents, trailers or motorhomes up to 22 feet long. Picnic tables and firegrills are provided, and vault toilets and piped water are available. A store, cafe, laundromat and ice are located within five miles. Pets are permitted.

Reservations, fee: No reservations necessary; $6 fee per night. Open May to October.

Who to contact: Phone Sisters Ranger Station at 503-549-2111, or write Deschutes National Forest, Sisters, OR 97759.

Location: From Camp Sherman, travel five miles north on Forest Service Road 14 to the campground.

Trip note: This campground is set along the banks of the Metolius River, where fishing and hiking can be good. The Wizard Falls Fish Hatchery is about a mile away, a good side trip.

Site **76**   PIONEER FORD   ▲

Campsites, facilities: There are two tent sites and 18 sites for tents, trailers or motorhomes up to 22 feet long. Piped water and firegrills are provided, and piped water, vault toilets and firewood are available. Pets are permitted.

Reservations, fee: No reservations necessary; $6 fee per night. Open May to October.

Who to contact: Phone Sisters Ranger Station at 503-549-2111, or write Deschutes National Forest, Sisters, OR 97759.

Location: From Camp Sherman, travel seven miles north on Forest Service Road 14 to the campground.

Trip note: This campground is set along the banks of the Metolius River. See trip notes to campsites 66 and 71 for recreation options.

LOWER BRIDGE
Site **77**

Campsites, facilities: There are 12 sites for tents, trailers or motorhomes up to 22 feet long. Picnic tables and firegrills are provided, and vault toilets and piped water are available. Pets are permitted.

Reservations, fee: No reservations necessary; $6 fee per night. Open May to October.

Who to contact: Phone Sisters Ranger Station at 503-549-2111, or write Deschutes National Forest, Sisters, OR 97759.

Location: From Camp Sherman, travel nine miles north on Forest Service Road 14 to the entrance road to the campground. The last 1/2 mile is on a dirt road.

Trip note: This campground is set along the banks of the Metolius River. See trip notes to campsites 66 and 71 for details about the area.

SHEEP SPRINGS
Site **78** HORSE CAMP

Campsites, facilities: There are 11 sites for tents, trailers or motorhomes up to 15 feet long. Piped water and firegrills are provided, and piped water, vault toilets and box stalls for horses are available.

Reservations, fee: Reservations required; fee depends on size of group. Open late-May to mid-September.

Who to contact: Phone Sisters Ranger Station at 503-549-2111, or write Deschutes National Forest, Sisters, OR 97759.

Location: Travel four miles north of Camp Sherman on Forest Service Road 1420, then one mile north on Forest Service Road 12. From there, drive 1 1/2 miles northwest on Forest Service Road 1230 to the campground.

Trip note: This equestrian camp is located near the trailhead for the Metolius-Windigo Horse Trail, which heads northeast into the Mount Jefferson Wilderness and south to Black Butte. Contact the Forest Service for details and maps of back country.

INDIAN FORD
Site **79**

Campsites, facilities: There are 25 sites for tents, trailers or motorhomes up to 22 feet long. Picnic tables and firegrills are provided, and vault toilets and piped water are available. Pets are permitted.

Reservations, fee: No reservations necessary; $6 fee per night. Open May to October.

Who to contact: Phone Sisters Ranger Station at 503-549-2111, or write Deschutes National Forest, Sisters, OR 97759.

Location: From the town of Sisters travel five miles northwest on US 20 to the campground.

Trip note: This campground is set along the banks of Squaw Creek. Stream fishing for trout can be good in the area. On the north side of nearby Black Butte is the spring which feeds the Metolius River. This can be a particularly good spot to fly fish for trout.

COLD SPRINGS
Site **80**

Campsites, facilities: There are 23 sites for tents, trailers or motorhomes up to 22 feet long.

Picnic tables and firegrills are provided, and vault toilets and piped water are available. Pets are permitted.

Reservations, fee: No reservations necessary; $5 fee per night. Open May to October.

Who to contact: Phone Sisters Ranger Station at 503-549-2111, or write Deschutes National Forest, Sisters, OR 97759.

Location: From the town of Sisters, travel five miles west on Highway 242 to the campground.

Trip note: This wooded campground is set at 3400 feet elevation, at the source of little Trout Creek. A trail passes near camp and extends for miles, both north and south. It is just far enough off the main drag to be missed by many campers.

WHISPERING PINE
Site 81

Campsites, facilities: There are six primitive tent sites. Picnic tables and firegrills are provided, and pit toilets are available. There is no piped water. Pets are permitted.

Reservations, fee: No reservations necessary; no fee. Open June to September.

Who to contact: Phone Sisters Ranger Station at 503-549-2111, or write Deschutes National Forest, Sisters, OR 97759.

Location: From the town of Sisters, travel 11 miles southwest via Highway 242 and Forest Service Road 1018 to the campground.

Trip note: This wooded campground is set at 4400 feet elevation near Trout Creek Swamp. A primitive alternative to campsite 80, near McKenzie Pass.

LAVA CAMP
Site 82   LAKE

Campsites, facilities: There are two tent sites and 10 sites for tents, trailers or motorhomes up to 22 feet long. Picnic tables and firegrills are provided, and pit toilets are available. There is no piped water. Pets are permitted.

Reservations, fee: No reservations necessary; no fee. Open June to September.

Who to contact: Phone Sisters Ranger Station at 503-549-2111, or write Deschutes National Forest, Sisters, OR 97759.

Location: From the town of Sisters travel 17 miles west on Highway 242 to the campground.

Trip note: This wooded campground is set at 5200 feet elevation in the McKenzie Pass, not far from the Pacific Crest Trail. Other trails provide hiking possibilities as well. A map of Deschutes National Forest details back roads, trails and streams.

CIRCLE 5
Site 83   TRAILER PARK

Campsites, facilities: There are three tent sites and 22 drive-through sites for trailers or motorhomes of any length. Electricity, piped water, sewer hookups and picnic tables are provided. Flush toilets, bottled gas, sanitary services, showers and laundromat are available. A store, cafe and ice are located within one mile. Pets are permitted.

Reservations, fee: Reservations accepted; $10 fee per night. Open all year.

Who to contact: Phone at 503-549-3861, or write at P.O. Box 1360, Sisters, OR 97759.

Location: From Sisters, go 1/2 mile southeast on US 20 and you'll see the park entrance.

Trip note: This motorhome camp is just outside the town of Sisters. Nearby recreation options include a riding stable and tennis courts.

Site **84** BLACK PINE SPRING

Campsites, facilities: There are five sites for tents, trailers or motorhomes up to 15 feet long. Picnic tables and firegrills are provided, and pit toilets are available. There is no piped water. Pets are permitted.

Reservations, fee: No reservations necessary; no fee. Open mid-June to mid-October.

Who to contact: Phone Sisters Ranger District at 503-549-2111, or write Deschutes National Forest, Sisters, OR 97759.

Location: Go nine miles south of Sisters on Forest Service Road 16.

Trip note: This primitive, remote campground is set at 4400 feet elevation. Three Creeks Lakes are about nine miles south on Forest Service Road 16. A small, quiet spot. If it is full, campsites 85 and 86 provide options.

Site **85** THREE CREEKS LAKE

Campsites, facilities: There are 10 sites for tents, trailers or motorhomes up to 16 feet long. Picnic tables and firegrills are provided, and pit toilets are available. There is no piped water. Pets are permitted. Boat docks, launching facilities and rentals are nearby. Boats with motors are not permitted.

Reservations, fee: No reservations necessary; $4 fee per night. Open mid-June to mid-September.

Who to contact: Phone Sisters Ranger District at 503-549-2111, or write Deschutes National Forest, Sisters, OR 97759.

Location: From the town of Sisters, travel 18 miles south on Forest Service Road 16 to the campground.

Trip note: This wooded campground is set along the shore of Three Creeks Lake. Fishing, swimming, hiking and non-motorized boating are the highlights. A pretty spot.

Site **86** DRIFTWOOD

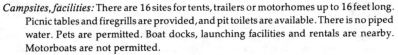

Campsites, facilities: There are 16 sites for tents, trailers or motorhomes up to 16 feet long. Picnic tables and firegrills are provided, and pit toilets are available. There is no piped water. Pets are permitted. Boat docks, launching facilities and rentals are nearby. Motorboats are not permitted.

Reservations, fee: No reservations necessary; $4 fee per night. Open mid-June to mid-September.

Who to contact: Phone Sisters Ranger District at 503-549-2111, or write Deschutes National Forest, Sisters, OR 97759.

Location: From the town of Sisters, travel 18 miles south on Forest Service Road 16 to the campground.

Trip note: This wooded campground is set along the shore of Three Creeks Lake. A nice spot, hidden from outsiders. Fishing, swimming, hiking and non-motorized boating are some of the recreation options.

TUMALO FALLS

Site **87**

Campsites, facilities: There are four tent sites. Picnic tables and firegrills are provided, and vault toilets are available. There is no piped water. Pets are permitted.

Reservations, fee: No reservations necessary; no fee. Open July to October.

Who to contact: Phone Bend Ranger District at 503-388-5664, or write Deschutes National Forest, 1230 NE Third Street, Bend, OR 97701.

Location: From Bend, travel 16 miles west on Forest Service Roads 4601 and 4603 to the campground.

Trip note: This secluded campground is set at 5000 feet elevation along the banks of beautiful Tumalo Creek. Tumalo Falls, a 97-foot waterfall, is a short distance from camp. The area surrounding the creek and camp was involved in a major fire in the 1970s, and young trees and vegetation is getting re-established. There are many trails in the area. Advisable to obtain Forest Service map, which details roads in the outback.

TODD LAKE

Site **88**

Campsites, facilities: There are four tent sites. Picnic tables and firegrills are provided, and vault toilets are available. There is no piped water. Pets are permitted.

Reservations, fee: No reservations necessary; no fee. Open July to October.

Who to contact: Phone Bend Ranger District at 503-388-5664, or write Deschutes National Forest, 1230 NE Third Street, Bend, OR 97701.

Location: From Bend, go 25 miles west on County Route 46, then about one mile north on the Forest Service entrance road. It is a short hike to the campground.

Trip note: This small campground is set along the shore of an alpine lake at 6200 feet elevation. It is popular for canoeing, and offers great views. One of the numerous campsites in the area that offer a pristine mountain experience, yet can be reached by car.

DEVILS LAKE

Site **89**

Campsites, facilities: There are nine tent sites. Picnic tables and firegrills are provided, and vault toilets are available. There is no piped water. Pets are permitted. Boat docks are nearby.

Reservations, fee: No reservations necessary; no fee. Open July to October.

Who to contact: Phone Bend Ranger District at 503-388-5664, or write Deschutes National Forest, 1230 NE Third Street, Bend, OR 97701.

Location: From Bend, travel 27 miles west on Cascade Lakes Highway (Highway 46). Walk 200 yards to the campground.

Trip note: This walk-in campground is set along the shore of a scenic alpine lake with water that is an aqua-jade color. Devil's Lake is a popular rafting and canoeing spot, and there are several trailheads that lead from the lake into the wilderness.

SODA CREEK

Site **90**

Campsites, facilities: There are four tent sites and eight sites for tents, trailers or motorhomes up to 22 feet long. Picnic tables and firegrills are provided, and vault toilets are
available. There is no piped water. Pets are permitted. Boat docks are nearby.

Reservations, fee: No reservations necessary; no fee. Open July to October.

Who to contact: Phone Bend Ranger District at 503-388-5664, or write Deschutes National
Forest, 1230 NE Third Street, Bend, OR 97701.

Location: From Bend, go 25 miles southwest on County Route 46, then about 100 yards
south on Forest Service Road 400.

Trip note: This campground is located on the road to Sparks Lake, nestled between two
meadows in a pastoral setting. Fishing and boating, particularly canoeing, are ideal
here.

MALLARD MARSH

Site **91**

Campsites, facilities: There are 15 sites for tents, trailers or motorhomes up to 22 feet long.
Picnic tables and firegrills are provided, and vault toilets are available. There is no
piped water. Pets are permitted. Boat docks, launching facilities and rentals are
nearby.

Reservations, fee: No reservations necessary; no fee. Open late-May to late-September.

Who to contact: Phone Bend Ranger District at 503-388-5664, or write Deschutes National
Forest, 1230 NE Third Street, Bend, OR 97701.

Location: From Bend, go 31 miles southwest on Highway 46, then two miles southeast on
Forest Service Road 470 to the camp.

Trip note: This campground is set along the shore of Hosmer Lake, which is stocked with
Atlantic Salmon and reserved for fly-fishing only. It is a quiet campground and the
lake is ideal for canoeing. A pristine, quality angling experience.

SOUTH

Site **92**

Campsites, facilities: There are 23 sites for tents, trailers or motorhomes up to 22 feet long.
Picnic tables and firegrills are provided, and vault toilets are available. There is no
piped water. Pets are permitted. Boat docks, launching facilities and rentals are
nearby.

Reservations, fee: No reservations necessary; no fee. Open late-May to late-September.

Who to contact: Phone Bend Ranger District at 503-388-5664, or write Deschutes National
Forest, 1230 NE Third Street, Bend, OR 97701.

Location: From Bend, go 31 miles southwest on County Route 46, then three miles
southeast on Forest Service Road 470 to the campround.

Trip note: This campground is set along the shore of Hosmer Lake. See the trip note to
campsite 91 for recreation details.

POINT

Site **93**

Campsites, facilities: There are nine sites for tents, trailers or motorhomes up to 22 feet long, but be advised the sites are uneven and difficult for motorhomes. Picnic tables and firegrills are provided, and vault toilets and piped water are available. Pets are permitted. Boat docks, launching facilities and rentals are nearby.

Reservations, fee: No reservations necessary; $6 fee per night. Open late-May to late-September.

Who to contact: Phone Bend Ranger District at 503-388-5664, or write Deschutes National Forest, 1230 NE Third Street, Bend, OR 97701.

Location: From Bend, travel 33 miles southwest on County Route 46 to the campground entrance.

Trip note: This hidden campground is set along the shore of Elk Lake. Fishing can be good here, same goes for hiking. A map of Deschutes National Forest details the trails.

Site 94   ELK LAKE

Campsites, facilities: There are 22 sites for tents, trailers or motorhomes up to 22 feet long, but be advised the sites are uneven and difficult for motorhomes. Picnic tables and firegrills are provided, and vault toilets and piped water are available. Pets are permitted. Boat docks, launching facilities and rentals are nearby.

Reservations, fee: No reservations necessary; $6 fee per night. Open June to October.

Who to contact: Phone Bend Ranger District at 503-388-5664, or write Deschutes National Forest, 1230 NE Third Street, Bend, OR 97701.

Location: From Bend, travel 33 miles southwest on County Route 46 to Elk Lake. The campground is on the southwest side of the lake.

Trip note: This campground is set along the shore of Elk Lake, adjacent to a private resort. See the trip note to campsite 93 for recreation options.

Site 95   LITTLE FAWN GROUP CAMP

Campsites, facilities: There are four tent sites and 27 sites for tents, trailers or motorhomes up to 22 feet long. Picnic tables and firegrills are provided, and vault toilets are available. There is no piped water. Pets are permitted. Boat docks, launching facilities and rentals are nearby on the southwest shore of the lake.

Reservations, fee: Reservations required; fee depends on group's size. Open June to October.

Who to contact: Phone Bend Ranger District at 503-388-5664, or write Deschutes National Forest, 1230 NE Third Street, Bend, OR 97701.

Location: Go 31 miles southwest of Bend on Highway 46, then two miles southeast on Forest Service Road 470. The campground is on the east side of Elk Lake.

Trip note: This campground is set along the eastern shore of Elk Lake. You can choose between sites on the lake's edge, or nestled nearby in forest. At a lake inlet, there is a play area for children. See the trip note to campsite 93 for recreation options.

Site 96   LAVA LAKE

Campsites, facilities: There are 45 sites for tents, trailers or motorhomes up to 22 feet long. Picnic tables and firegrills are provided, and vault toilets, piped water and sanitary disposal services are available. Pets are permitted. Boat docks, launching facilities and rentals are nearby.

Reservations, fee: No reservations necessary; $6 fee per night. Open June to October.

Who to contact: Phone Bend Ranger District at 503-388-5664, or write Deschutes National Forest, 1230 NE Third Street, Bend, OR 97701.

Location: From Bend, travel 38 miles southwest on Highway 46 to the entrance to Lava Lake. The campground is on the lake.

Trip note: This well-designed campground is set along the shore of pretty Lava Lake, with Mount Bachelor and the Three Sisters in the background. A classic picture. Boating and fishing are popular here.

LITTLE LAVA LAKE
Site **97**

Campsites, facilities: There are 14 sites for tents, trailers or motorhomes up to 22 feet long. Picnic tables and firegrills are provided, and vault toilets and piped water are available. Pets are permitted. Boat docks, launching facilities and rentals are nearby.

Reservations, fee: No reservations necessary; no fee. Open June to late-September.

Who to contact: Phone Bend Ranger District at 503-388-5664, or write Deschutes National Forest, 1230 NE Third Street, Bend, OR 97701.

Location: From Bend, travel 38 miles southwest on Highway 46 to the entrance to Lava Lakes. The campground is on Little Lava Lake.

Trip note: The campsites at this popular campground are not well marked, but the camping area is near the lakeshore. Boating, fishing, swimming and hiking are some of the recreation options.

DILLON FALLS
Site **98**

Campsites, facilities: There are seven sites for tents, trailers or motorhomes up to 30 feet long. Picnic tables and firegrills are provided, and vault toilets are available. There is no piped water. Pets are permitted.

Reservations, fee: No reservations necessary; no fee. Open May to October.

Who to contact: Phone Bend Ranger Station at 503-388-5664, or write Deschutes National Forest, 1230 NE Third Street, Bend, OR 97701.

Location: From Bend, travel 6 1/2 miles southwest on Highway 46, then drive three miles south on Forest Service Road 41. The camp is one mile further south on Forest Service Road 700.

Trip note: This campground is set in a deep gorge along the banks of the Deschutes River. It gets heavy day use because it is a take-out point for rafters and drift boaters. (Boaters should beware of Dillon Falls, located downstream). Some good day walks are available on trails along the river. They are detailed on a Forest Service map.

BESSON CAMP
Site **99**

Campsites, facilities: There are three sites for tents, trailers or motorhomes up to 16 feet long. Picnic tables and firegrills are provided, and a pit toilet is available. There is no piped water. Pets are permitted. A boat launch is nearby.

Reservations, fee: No reservations necessary; no fee. Open May to October.

Who to contact: Phone Bend Ranger Station at 503-388-5664, or write Deschutes National Forest, 1230 NE Third Street, Bend, OR 97701.

Location: From Bend, travel 14 1/2 miles south on Highway 97, then 4 1/2 miles west on

Sun River-Spring River Road (Forest Service Road 40). The camp is 1/2 mile further north on Forest Service Road 41.

Trip note: This secluded and unknown little spot is set along the bank of the Deschutes River. It has a boat launch and good trout fishing.

Site **100**   BEND KEYSTONE RV PARK

Campsites, facilities: There are 18 sites for trailers or motorhomes of any length. Electricity, piped water and sewer hookups are provided. Flush toilets, showers and a laundromat are available. Bottled gas, sanitary services, a store, cafe and ice are located within one mile. Pets are permitted.

Reservations, fee: Reservations accepted; $10 fee per night. Open all year.

Who to contact: Phone at 503-382-2335, or write at 305 Northeast Burnside, Bend, OR 97701.

Location: Travel 1/2 mile south of the junction off Highway 97 and Highway 20 in Bend. You'll see the turn-off for the park.

Trip note: Bend is a popular spot to use as a home base. The 100-mile Deschutes Forest Highway Loop connects here. Several state parks are within an hour's drive and several city-managed parks provide access to the Deschutes River. Good side trips include the Oregon High Desert Museum, just six miles south of Bend on Highway 97. Just a few miles further is the Lava River Cave and the Lava Butte Geological Area.

Site **101**   CROWN VILLA RV PARK

Campsites, facilities: There are 106 drive-through sites for trailers or motorhomes of any length. Electricity, piped water, sewer hookups and picnic tables are provided. Flush toilets, showers, cable television, a laundromat, bottled gas, ice, sanitary disposal station and a playground are available. A store and a cafe are located within one mile. Pets are permitted.

Reservations, fee: Reservations accepted; $13 fee per night. Visa/Mastercard accepted. Open all year.

Who to contact: Phone at 503-388-1131, or write at 60801 Brosterhous, Bend, OR 97702.

Location: Travel two miles south of Bend on US 97, then head east on Brosterhous Road to 60801 Brosterhous Road.

Trip note: This motorhome park offers large, grassy sites. Nearby recreation options include horseback riding and golf. See the trip note to campsite 100 for additional recreation information.

Site **102**   LOWE'S RV AND TRAILER PARK

Campsites, facilities: There are 10 tent sites and 35 drive-through sites for trailers or motorhomes of any length. Electricity, piped water, picnic tables and sewer hookups are provided. Flush toilets, showers and a laundromat are available. Bottled gas, sanitary services, a store, cafe and ice are located within one mile. Pets are permitted.

Reservations, fee: Reservations accepted; $10 fee per night. Open all year.

Who to contact: Phone at 503-382-6206, or write at 61415 South Highway 97, Bend, OR
  97701.
Location: Travel 1/2 mile south of Bend on US 97 and you'll see the trailer park
  entrance.
Trip note: This park is set near the Deschutes River. Nearby recreation options include a
  golf course, a stable, bike paths and tennis courts. See the trip note to campsite 100 for
  additional recreation information.

KOA BEND
Site **103**

Campsites, facilities: There are 40 tent sites and 74 drive-through sites for trailers or
  motorhomes of any length. Piped water and picnic tables are provided. Electricity,
  sewer hookups, flush toilets, showers, a laundromat, store, cafe, ice, firewood, playground, swimming pool, recreation room, bottled gas and sanitary disposal station
  are available. Pets are permitted.
Reservations, fee: Reservations accepted; $11 fee per night. Visa/Mastercard accepted.
  Open all year.
Who to contact: Phone at 503-382-7728, or write at 63615 North Highway 97, Bend, OR
  97701.
Location: Travel two miles north of Bend on US 97 and you'll see the campground
  entrance.
Trip note: Nearby recreation options include a golf course, hiking trails, bike paths and
  tennis courts. See the trip note to campsite 100 for additional recreation infor-
  mation.

TUMALO
Site **104**   STATE PARK

Campsites, facilities: There are 68 tent sites and 20 sites for trailers or motorhomes up to 35
  feet long. Electricity, piped water, sewer hookups, firegrills and picnic tables are
  provided. Flush toilets, showers, firewood, a laundromat and playground are available. A store, cafe and ice are located within one mile. Pets are permitted.
Reservations, fee: No reservations necessary; $8 fee per night. Open mid-April to late-
  October.
Who to contact: Phone at 503-382-2601, or write Tumalo State Park, Bend, OR 97701.
Location: From Bend, go five miles northwest on US 20, then one mile west on the
  entrance road to the park.
Trip note: This campground is set along the banks of the Deschutes River. Trout fishing can
  be good. See the trip note to campsite 100 for recreation information about the
  area.

DESERT TERRACE
Site **105**   MOBILE ESTATES

Campsites, facilities: There are 20 drive-through sites for trailers or motorhomes of any
  length. Electricity, piped water, sewer hookups and picnic tables are provided. Flush
  toilets, showers and a laundromat are available. Pets are permitted.
Reservations, fee: Reservations accepted; $10 fee per night. Open all year.
Who to contact: Phone at 503-548-2546, or write at 5063 South Highway 97, Redmond, OR
  97756.

Location: Travel three miles south of Redmond on US 97 and you'll see the entrance.

Trip note: Nearby recreation options include a golf course, hiking trails, bike paths, tennis courts and Petersen's Rock Gardens. This motorhome park is centrally located to many recreation opportunities. See the trip notes to campsites 100 and 108 for more details.

Site **106**   CROOKED RIVER RANCH RV PARK

Campsites, facilities: There are 40 tent sites and 94 drive-through sites for trailers or motorhomes of any length. Electricity, piped water and sewer hookups are provided. Flush toilets, sanitary services, showers, a store, cafe, laundromat, ice, playground and swimming pool are available. Pets and motorbikes are permitted.

Reservations, fee: Reservations accepted; $10 fee per night. Open mid-March to late-October.

Who to contact: Phone at 503-923-1441, or write at P.O. Box 1262, Crooked River, OR 97760.

Location: Drive five miles north of Redmond on US 97, then west at Terribone and follow the signs.

Trip note: This campground is a short distance from Smith Rock State Park, which offers unique and colorful volcanic formations overlooking the Crooked River Canyon. To the north is Lake Billy Chinook, which offers fishing for bass and panfish, and waterskiing. Nearby recreation options include a golf course and tennis courts.

Site **107**   HAYSTACK LAKE

Campsites, facilities: There are 24 sites for tents, trailers or motorhomes up to 22 feet long. Picnic tables and firegrills are provided, and flush toilets, piped water and firewood are available. A store, cafe and ice are located within five miles. Pets are permitted. Boat docks, launching facilities and rentals are nearby.

Reservations, fee: No reservations necessary; $5 fee per night. Open April to November.

Who to contact: Phone Madras Ranger Station at 503-447-4120, or write Ochocho National Forest, Madras, OR 97741.

Location: Drive on US 97 for nine miles south of Madras, then three miles southeast on County Route 6, then 1/2 mile north on Forest Service Road 1275.

Trip note: This campground is set along the shore of Haystack Reservoir, where waterskiing, swimming and fishing are some of the recreation options. Camping and fishing crowds are relatively light.

Site **108**   KOA MADRAS

Campsites, facilities: There are 21 tent sites and 68 drive-through sites for trailers or motorhomes of any length. Electricity, piped water, sewer hookups and picnic tables are provided. Flush toilets, bottled gas, sanitary services, showers, firewood, a recreation hall, a store, cafe, laundromat, ice, playground and swimming pool are available. Pets and motorbikes are permitted. Boat docks and launching facilities are nearby.

Reservations, fee: Reservations accepted; $9 fee per night. MasterCard and Visa accepted. Open March to late-November.

Who to contact: Phone at 503-546-3073, or write at 2435 Southwest Jericho Lane, Culver, OR 97734.

Location: Travel nine miles south of Madras on US 97, then 1/2 mile east on Jericho Lane to the campground.

Trip note: This campground is about three miles from Lake Billy Chinook, a steep-sided reservoir formed where Crooked River, Metolius River, Deschutes River and Squaw Creek merge. Like much of the country east of the Cascades, it is a high desert area.

Site 109   COVE PALISADES STATE PARK   ▲ 🚐

Campsites, facilities: There are 94 tent sites and 178 sites for trailers or motorhomes of any length. Electricity, piped water, sewer hookups and picnic tables are provided. Flush toilets, sanitary services, showers, firewood, a store, cafe, laundromat and ice are available. Some facilities are wheelchair accessible. Pets are permitted. Boat docks, launching facilities and rentals are nearby.

Reservations, fee: Reservations accepted; $8 fee per night. Open mid-April to late-October.

Who to contact: Phone at 503-546-3412, or write at Route 1, Box 60 CP, Culver, OR 97734.

Location: From Madras drive nine miles south on US 97 to Culver, then head west for five miles to the Park.

Trip note: This park is set along the shore of Lake Billy Chinook. See the trip note to camps 106 and 108 for recreation details.

Site 110   PERRY SOUTH   ▲

Campsites, facilities: There are four tent sites and 59 sites for tents, trailers or motorhomes up to 22 feet long. Picnic tables and firegrills are provided, and piped water and vault toilets are available. Pets are permitted. Boat docks and launching facilities are nearby.

Reservations, fee: No reservations necessary; $3 fee per night. Open May to October.

Who to contact: Phone Sisters Ranger District at 503-549-2111, or write Deschutes National Forest, P.O. Box 249, Sisters, OR 97759.

Location: From the town of Culver, drive 25 miles west and north on County Route 64 to the campground entrance.

Trip note: This campground is set near the shore of the Metolius Arm of Lake Billy Chinook. See the trip note to campsites 106 and 108 for recreation details. This camp borders the Warm Springs Indian Reservation.

Site 111   MONTY

Campsites, facilities: There are 45 sites for tents, trailers or motorhomes up to 22 feet long. Picnic tables and firegrills are provided, and piped water, firewood and vault toilets are available. Pets are permitted. Boat docks and launching facilities are nearby.

Reservations, fee: No reservations necessary; $3 fee per night. Open May to October.

Who to contact: Phone Sisters Ranger District at 503-549-2111, or write Deschutes National Forest, P.O. Box 249, Sisters, OR 97734.

Location: From the town of Culver, drive 30 miles west and north on County Route 64 to the campground entrance.

Trip note: This remote campground is set along the banks of the Metolius River near where it empties into Lake Billy Chinook. Trout fishing can be good. Located just outside Warm Springs Indian Reservation.

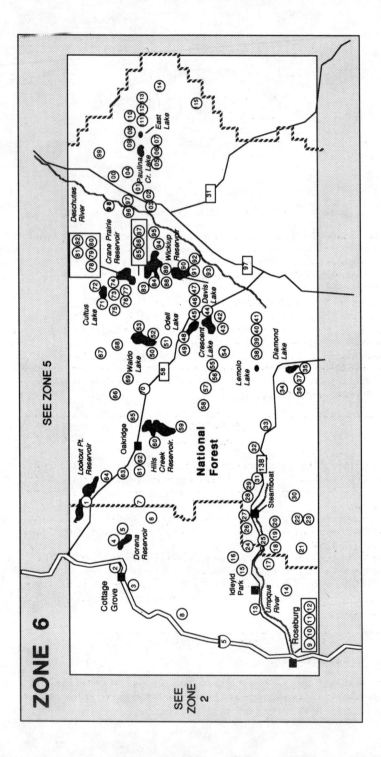

CASCADE

Site 1
DEXTER SHORES
MOTORHOME & RV PARK

🚐

Campsites, facilities: There are 10 sites for trailers or motorhomes. Electricity, piped water, sewer hookups and picnic tables are provided. Flush toilets, sanitary services, showers, firewood, a laundromat and playground are available. Bottled gas, a cafe and ice are within one mile. Pets and motorbikes are permitted. Boat docks and launching facilities are nearby.

Reservations, fee: Reservations accepted; $9 fee per night. Open all year.

Who to contact: Phone at 503-937-3711, or write at P.O. Box 70, Dexter, OR 97431.

Location: Travel west on Highway 58 about 18 miles from the town of Oakridge, then go southeast on Dexter Road about one mile to the park.

Trip note: If you are traveling on Interstate 5, this motorhome park is well worth the 15-minute drive out of Springfield. It is set near the shore of Lookout Point Reservoir, where fishing and boating are permitted. Swimming and waterskiing are allowed on nearby Dexter and Fall Creek Lakes.

Site 2
FRONTIER
VILLAGE

🚐

Campsites, facilities: There are six drive-through sites for trailers or motorhomes up to 30 feet long. Electricity, piped water and sewer hookups are provided. Flush toilets, showers and a laundromat are available. Bottled gas, a store, a cafe and ice are within one mile.

Reservations, fee: Reservations accepted; $6 fee per night. Open all year.

Who to contact: Phone at 503-942-3266, or write at 1557 Pacific Highway North, Cottage Grove, OR 97424.

Location: This campground is located in the north end of the town of Cottage Grove.

Trip note: The town of Cottage Grove is noted for the numerous recreation opportunities available along the Willamette and Row Rivers, which pass on either side of town. Dorena Reservoir is a short drive to the east. Nearby recreation options include a golf course and bike paths.

Site 3
PINE MEADOWS

🔺

Campsites, facilities: There are 93 sites for tents, trailers or motorhomes of any length. Picnic tables and firegrills are provided. Flush toilets, sanitary services, showers and a playground are available. Pets and motorbikes are permitted. Boat docks and launching facilities are nearby.

Reservations, fee: No reservations necessary; $6 fee per night. Open Memorial Day to Labor Day.

Who to contact: Phone Corps of Engineers at 503-942-5631, or write Army Corps of Engineers Recreation Information, Cottage Grove, OR 97424.

Location: Travel south of the town of Cottage Grove on I-5, take exit 170, then go 3 1/2 miles south on London Road to the campground.

Trip note: This campground is set near the banks of Cottage Grove Reservoir, where boating, fishing and swimming are among the recreation options available. It's an easy hop from I-5, but a lot of vacationers don't realize it.

SCHWARZ PARK

Site **4**

Campsites, facilities: There are 155 tent sites and 35 drive-through sites for trailers or motorhomes of any length. Picnic tables and firegrills are provided. Flush toilets, sanitary services and showers are available. A store is within one mile. Pets and motorbikes are permitted. Boat docks and launching facilities are nearby.

Reservations, fee: No reservations necessary; no fee. Open mid-May to late-September.

Who to contact: Phone Corps of Engineers at 503-942-5631, or write Army Corps of Engineers Recreation Information, Cottage Grove, OR 97424.

Location: Take exit 174 off I-5 in the town of Cottage Grove, then go four miles east on Row Road to the campground entrance road.

Trip note: This large campground is set along the shore of Dorena Lake, a reservoir where fishing, swimming and boating are among the recreation options available.

BAKER BAY
COUNTY PARK

Site **5**

Campsites, facilities: There are 34 sites for trailers or motorhomes up to 20 feet long. Picnic tables and firegrills are provided. Piped water and sanitary services are available. A store is located within one mile. Pets and motorbikes are permitted. Boat docks and launching facilities are nearby.

Reservations, fee: No reservations necessary; $3 fee per night. Open late-April to late-October.

Who to contact: Phone at 503-942-7669, or write Lane County Recreation Department, Eugene, OR 97401.

Location: Take exit 174 of I-5 in the town of Cottage Grove, then travel eight miles east on Row Road to the campground.

Trip note: This campground is set along the shore of Dorena Lake, a reservoir where fishing, waterskiing, canoeing, swimming and boating are among the recreation options available.

SHARPS CREEK

Site **6**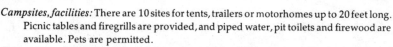

Campsites, facilities: There are 10 sites for tents, trailers or motorhomes up to 20 feet long. Picnic tables and firegrills are provided, and piped water, pit toilets and firewood are available. Pets are permitted.

Reservations, fee: No reservations necessary; no fee. Open all year.

Who to contact: Phone at 503-687-6651, or write the Bureau of Land Management at P.O. Box 10266, Eugene, OR 97440.

Location: Take exit 174 off I-5 at Cottage Grove, then travel 18 miles east on Row River Road and four miles south on Sharps Creek Road to the campground.

Trip note: This campground is set along the bank of Sharps Creek. Like nearby campsite 7, this is just far enough off the beaten path to be missed by most campers.

RUJADA
Site **7**

Campsites, facilities: There are eight sites for tents, trailers or motorhomes up to 22 feet long. Picnic tables and firegrills are provided, and vault toilets and piped water are available. Pets are permitted.

Reservations, fee: No reservations necessary; no fee. Open late-May to late-September.

Who to contact: Phone Cottage Grove Ranger District at 503-942-5591, or write Umpqua National Forest, P.O. Box 38, Culp Creek, OR 97424.

Location: From Cottage Grove, drive east past Dorena Drive to Culp Creek. Travel on County Route 2400 east out of Culp Creek for four miles, then go two miles northeast on Forest Service Road 17 to the campground.

Trip note: This campground is set along the banks of Layng Creek, about two miles upstream from its confluence with Row River. A small, hidden spot—free and with piped water. A rare combination.

PASS CREEK
COUNTY PARK
Site **8**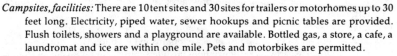

Campsites, facilities: There are 10 tent sites and 30 sites for trailers or motorhomes up to 30 feet long. Electricity, piped water, sewer hookups and picnic tables are provided. Flush toilets, showers and a playground are available. Bottled gas, a store, a cafe, a laundromat and ice are within one mile. Pets and motorbikes are permitted.

Reservations, fee: No reservations necessary; $9 fee per night. Open all year.

Who to contact: Phone at 503-942-3281, or write at P.O. Box 87, Curtin, OR 97428.

Location: From Roseburg, travel 35 miles north on I-5, then take exit 163 and drive to the park.

Trip note: A decent layover spot for travelers on Interstate 5—there are no other campgrounds within 25 miles in any direction.

DOUGLAS COUNTY
FAIRGROUNDS RV
Site **9**

Campsites, facilities: There are 50 sites for trailers or motorhomes of any length. Electricity, piped water and picnic tables are provided. Flush toilets, sanitary services, showers and a playground are available. A store, a cafe, a laundromat and ice are located within one mile. Pets are permitted.

Reservations, fee: No reservations necessary; $6 fee per night. Open all year.

Who to contact: Phone at 503-440-4500, or write at P.O. Box 1550, Roseburg, OR 97470.

Location: Take exit 123 off I-5 in Roseburg and follow the signs.

Trip note: This county park is near the Umpqua River, one of Oregon's prettiest rivers. It can get good fishing in season. Nearby recreation options include a golf course, bike paths and tennis courts.

Site 10   ALAMEDA AVENUE TRAILER PARK

Campsites, facilities: There are 35 sites for trailers or motorhomes up to 30 feet long. Electricity, piped water and sewer hookups are provided. Flush toilets, sanitary services, showers and a laundromat are available. Bottled gas, a store, a cafe and ice are located within one mile. Pets and motorbikes are permitted.

Reservations, fee: Reservations accepted; $9 fee per night. Open all year.

Who to contact: Phone at 503-672-2348, or write at 581 Northeast Alameda, Roseburg, OR 97470.

Location: In Roseburg, take the Garden Valley exit off I-5 and travel east to Business Route 99. From there, go 1/4 mile north to Northeast Alameda Avenue.

Trip note: One of four parks in Roseburg. This park is near the Umpqua River, which flows right through town. Nearby recreation options include a golf course, bike paths and tennis courts.

Site 11   NEBO TRAILER PARK

Campsites, facilities: There are 20 drive-through sites for trailers or motorhomes of any length. Electricity, piped water and sewer hookups are provided. Flush toilets, sanitary services, showers, a laundromat and ice are available. Bottled gas, a store and a cafe are within one mile. Pets are permitted.

Reservations, fee: Reservations accepted; $10 fee per night. Open all year.

Who to contact: Phone at 503-673-4108, or write at 2071 Northeast Stephens, Roseburg, OR 97470.

Location: In Roseburg, take exit 125 and go northeast to Stephens Street.

Trip note: An option for motorhome campers stopping in Roseburg. This park is near the Umpqua River. Nearby recreation options include a golf course, bike paths and tennis courts.

Site 12   TWIN RIVERS VACATION PARK

Campsites, facilities: There are 11 tent sites and 72 drive-through sites for trailers or motorhomes of any length. Electricity, piped water, sewer hookups and picnic tables are provided. Flush toilets, bottled gas, showers, firewood, a store, laundromat, ice and playground are available. Pets and motorbikes are permitted. Boat launching facilities are nearby.

Reservations, fee: Reservations accepted; $11 fee per night. Open all year.

Who to contact: Phone at 503-673-3811, or write at 433 River Forks Park, Roseburg, OR 97470.

Location: In Roseburg, take exit 125 off I-5 and travel five miles west to Old Garden Valley Road. The park is 1 1/2 miles south.

Trip note: The only campground in Roseburg with tent sites as well as motorhome sites. This wooded campground is near the Umpqua River. Nearby recreation options include a golf course, a county park and bike paths.

WHISTLER'S BEND

Site **13**

Campsites, facilities: There are 24 sites for tents, trailers or motorhomes up to 30 feet long. Picnic tables and firegrills are provided, and piped water, flush toilets, showers and a playground are available. Pets and motorbikes are permitted. Boat launching facilities are nearby.

Reservations, fee: No reservations necessary; $6 fee per night. Open all year.

Who to contact: Phone at 503-673-4863, or write at P.O. Box 800, Winchester, OR 97495.

Location: From Roseburg, travel 15 miles east on Highway 138 to the park.

Trip note: This county park is set along the bank of the North Umpqua River. It can be an idyllic spot, and is just a 20-minute drive from Interstate 5, yet gets little pressure from outsiders.

CAVITT CREEK FALLS

Site **14**

Campsites, facilities: There are eight sites for trailers or motorhomes up to 20 feet long. Picnic tables and firegrills are provided, and pit toilets, piped water and firewood are available. Pets are permitted.

Reservations, fee: No reservations necessary; $5 fee per night. Open May to late-October.

Who to contact: Phone the Bureau of Land Management at 503-672-4491, or write at 777 NW Garden Valley Boulevard, Roseburg, OR 97470.

Location: From Roseburg drive 18 times east on Highway 138 to Glide. From the town of Glide, travel seven miles southeast on Little River Road, then three miles south on Cavitt Creek Road to the campground.

Trip note: This campground is set along the bank of Cavitt Creek about three miles from its confluence with Little River. If you want to get deeper into the woods, campsites 18-21 provide options farther down the same road.

ROCK CREEK

Site **15**

Campsites, facilities: There are 17 sites for tents, trailers or motorhomes up to 18 feet long. Picnic tables and firegrills are provided, and vault toilets, piped water and firewood are available. Pets are permitted.

Reservations, fee: No reservations necessary; $5 fee per night. Open May to late-October.

Who to contact: Phone the Bureau of Land Management at 503-672-4491, or write at 777 NW Garden Valley Boulevard, Roseburg, OR 97470.

Location: From Roseburg, drive 18 miles east on Highway 138 to Glide. From the town of Glide, travel 12 miles northeast on Rock Creek Road to the campground.

Trip note: This campground is set along the bank of Rock Creek, a relatively obscure spot.

MILL POND

Site **16**

Campsites, facilities: There are 12 sites for tents, trailers or motorhomes up to 20 feet long.

Picnic tables and firegrills are provided, and vault toilets, piped water, firewood and a group shelter are available. Some facilities are wheelchair accessible. Pets are permitted.

Reservations, fee: No reservations necessary; $5 fee per night. Open May to late-October.

Who to contact: Phone the Bureau of Land Management at 503-672-4491, or write at 777 NW Garden Valley Boulevard, Roseburg, OR 97470.

Location: From Roseburg, drive 18 miles east on Highway 138 to Glide. From the town of Glide, travel 10 miles northeast on Rock Creek Road to the campground.

Trip note: This campground is set along the banks of Rock Creek. It is the first camp you will see along Rock Creek Road.

SUSAN CREEK
Site 17

Campsites, facilities: There are 33 sites for trailers or motorhomes up to 20 feet long. Picnic tables and firegrills are provided, and flush toilets, piped water and firewood are available. Some facilities are wheelchair accessible. Pets are permitted.

Reservations, fee: No reservations necessary; $6 fee per night. Open May to late-October.

Who to contact: Phone the Bureau of Land Management at 503-672-4491, or write at 777 NW Garden Valley Boulevard, Roseburg, OR 97470.

Location: From Roseburg, travel 33 miles east on Highway 138 to the campground.

Trip note: This popular campground is set along the banks of the North Umpqua River. A good base camp for a fishing trip.

WOLF CREEK
GROUP CAMP
Site 18

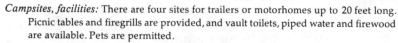

Campsites, facilities: There are five sites for tents, trailers or motorhomes up to 16 feet long. Picnic tables and firegrills are provided, and vault toilets and piped water are available. Some facilities are wheelchair accessible. Pets are permitted.

Reservations, fee: No reservations necessary; fee depends on size of group. Open mid-May to late-October.

Who to contact: Phone the North Umpqua Ranger District at 503-496-3532, or write Umpqua National Forest at Glide, OR 97443.

Location: From Roseburg, drive 18 miles east on Highway 138 to Glide. From the town of Glide, travel 11 1/2 miles southeast on County Route 17 to the campground.

Trip note: This campground is set along the banks of the Little River, near the Wolf Creek Civilian Conservation Center. If you want to get deeper into the Cascade's interior, campsites 22 and 23, about 15 miles east, are two choices.

EMILE CREEK
Site 19

Campsites, facilities: There are four sites for trailers or motorhomes up to 20 feet long. Picnic tables and firegrills are provided, and vault toilets, piped water and firewood are available. Pets are permitted.

Reservations, fee: No reservations necessary; no fee. Open May to late-October.

Who to contact: Phone the Bureau of Land Management at 503-672-4491, or write at 777 NW Garden Valley Boulevard, Roseburg, OR 97470.

Location: From Roseburg, drive 18 miles east on Highway 138 to Glide. From the town of
Glide, travel 14 miles southeast on County Route 17 to the campground.

Trip note: This little-used campground is set along the banks of the Little River, not far from
campsites 17, 18, and 20.

Site **20** COOLWATER ▲

Campsites, facilities: There are seven sites for tents, trailers or motorhomes up to 16 feet
long. Picnic tables and firegrills are provided, and vault toilets and piped water are
available. Pets are permitted.

Reservations, fee: No reservations necessary; $3 fee per night. Open mid-May to late-
October.

Who to contact: Phone the North Umpqua Ranger District at 503-496-3532, or write
Umpqua National Forest at Glide, OR 97443.

Location: From Roseburg, drive 18 miles east on Highway 138. From the town of Glide,
travel 15 1/2 miles southeast on County Route 17 to the campground.

Trip note: This campground gets little use and is set along the banks of the Little River. A
fairly remote setting, yet not a long drive out of Roseburg.

Site **21** WHITE CREEK ▲

Campsites, facilities: There are five sites for tents, trailers or motorhomes up to 31 feet
long. Picnic tables and firegrills are provided, and vault toilets and piped water are
available. Pets are permitted.

Reservations, fee: No reservations necessary; no fee. Open mid-May to late-September.

Who to contact: Phone the North Umpqua Ranger District at 503-496-3532, or write
Umpqua National Forest in Glide, OR 97443.

Location: From Roseburg, drive 18 miles east on Highway 138 to Glide. From Glide, go 16
1/2 miles east on County Route 17. The campground is 1/2 mile east on Forest
Service Road 2792.

Trip note: This campground is set at the confluence of White Creek and Little River. Hiking
and fishing are two of the recreation options here. The price is right—it's free.

Site **22** HEMLOCK LAKE ▲

Campsites, facilities: There are 17 sites for tents, trailers or motorhomes up to 22 feet long.
Picnic tables and firegrills are provided, and vault toilets and piped water are available. Pets are permitted. Boat docks and launching facilities are nearby. No motors are
permitted on the lake.

Reservations, fee: No reservations necessary; $3 fee per night. Open June to late-
October.

Who to contact: Phone the North Umpqua Ranger District at 503-496-3532, or write
Umpqua National Forest at Glide, OR 97443.

Location: From Roseburg, drive 18 miles east on Highway 138 to Glide. Travel on County
Route 17 east from Glide for 16 1/2 miles, then go 15 1/2 miles east on Forest Service
Road 27.

Trip note: This is little known, but a jewel of a spot. For starters, it is set along the shore of
Hemlock Lake. An eight-mile loop trail called the Yellow Jacket Loop is just south of

the campground. Another trail leaves camp and heads north for about three miles to Lake in the Woods Campground. From there it is just a short hike to either Hemlock Falls or Yakso Falls.

Site **23**   LAKE IN THE WOODS   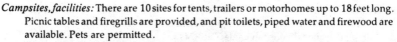

Campsites, facilities: There are nine sites for tents, trailers or motorhomes up to 16 feet long. Picnic tables and firegrills are provided, and vault toilets and piped water are available. Pets are permitted.

Reservations, fee: No reservations necessary; $3 fee per night. Open June to late-October.

Who to contact: Phone the North Umpqua Ranger District at 503-496-3532, or write Umpqua National Forest at Glide, OR 97443.

Location: From Roseburg, drive 18 miles east on Highway 138 to the town of Glide. Travel on County Route 17 east from Glide for 16 1/2 miles, then go 11 miles east on Forest Service Road 27.

Trip note: This campground is set along the shore of little Lake in the woods. There are several good hikes available. One leaves camp and heads south for about three miles to Hemlock Lake Campground. Two other nearby trails provide short, scenic hikes to either Hemlock Falls or Yakso Falls.

Site **24**   SCAREDMAN CREEK   ▲

Campsites, facilities: There are 10 sites for tents, trailers or motorhomes up to 18 feet long. Picnic tables and firegrills are provided, and pit toilets, piped water and firewood are available. Pets are permitted.

Reservations, fee: No reservations necessary; no fee. Open May to late-October.

Who to contact: Phone the Bureau of Land Management at 503-672-4491, or write at 777 NW Garden Valley Boulevard, Roseburg, OR 97470.

Location: From Roseburg, drive 39 miles east on Highway 138 to the town of Steamboat. From the town of Steamboat, go three miles north on Canton Creek Road to the campground.

Trip note: This campground is set along the banks of Canton Creek. A small camp that is virtually unknown to out-of-towners.

Site **25**   ISLAND   ▲

Campsites, facilities: There are sites for tents, trailers or motorhomes up to 22 feet long. Picnic tables and firegrills are provided, and piped water, vault toilets, and firewood are available. Pets are permitted.

Reservations, fee: No reservations necessary; $3 fee per night. Open mid-May to late-October.

Who to contact: Phone the North Umpqua Ranger District at 503-496-3532, or write Umpqua National Forest at Idleyld Park, OR 97447.

Location: From Roseburg, drive 40 east on Highway 138. The campground is set just off the highway along the Umpqua River.

Trip note: This campground is set along the banks of the Umpqua River at a spot popular for both fishing and rafting. Nearby campsites 26 and 27 provide a more primitive setting.

CANTON CREEK
Site **26**

Campsites, facilities: There are 12 sites for tents, trailers or motorhomes up to 16 feet long. Picnic tables and firegrills are provided, and piped water and vault toilets are available. Pets are permitted.

Reservations, fee: No reservations necessary; $4 fee per night. Open mid-May to late-October.

Who to contact: Phone the North Umpqua Ranager District at 503-496-3532, or write Umpqua National Forest at Idleyld Park, OR 97447.

Location: From Roseburg, drive east on Highway 138 to Steamboat, then go 400 yards northeast on Forest Service Road 232 to the campground.

Trip note: This campground is set at the confluence of Canton and Steamboat Creeks, less than a mile from the Umpqua River. This site gets little use.

STEAMBOAT FALLS
Site **27**

Campsites, facilities: There are 11 sites for tents, trailers or motorhomes up to 21 feet long. Picnic tables and firegrills are provided, and piped water and vault toilets are available. Pets are permitted.

Reservations, fee: No reservations necessary; no fee. Open June to December.

Who to contact: Phone the North Umpqua Ranager District at 503-496-3532, or write Umpqua National Forest at Idleyld Park, OR 97447.

Location: From Roseburg, drive east on Highway 138 to Steamboat, then go six miles northeast on Forest Service Road 38. The camp is 1/2 mile on Forest Service Road 3810.

Trip note: This campground is set along the banks of Steamboat Creek, near Steamboat Falls and a fish ladder which provides passage for both steelhead and salmon on their migratory upstream journey.

APPLE CREEK GROUP CAMP
Site **28**

Campsites, facilities: There are eight group sites for tents, trailers or motorhomes up to 21 feet long. Picnic tables and firegrills are provided, and vault toilets are available. There is no piped water. Pets are permitted. Boat docks are nearby.

Reservations, fee: No reservations necessary; no fee. Open mid-May to late-October.

Who to contact: Phone North Umpqua Ranger District at 503-496-3532, or write Umpqua National Forest, Glide, OR 97443.

Location: From Roseburg, travel east on Highway 138, continuing 23 miles past Idleyld Park. It is located adjacent to the highway.

Trip note: This campground is set along the banks of the Umpqua River, at a popular spot for rafting and fishing.

Site 29 HORSESHOE BEND

Campsites, facilities: There are 34 sites for tents, trailers or motorhomes up to 22 feet long. Picnic tables and firegrills are provided, and piped water, flush toilets, sanitary disposal station, a laundromat, store and firewood are available. Some facilities are wheelchair accessible. Pets are permitted. Boat docks and launching facilities are nearby.

Reservations, fee: No reservations necessary; $6 fee per night. Open mid-May to late-September.

Who to contact: Phone the North Umpqua Ranager District at 503-496-3532, or write Umpqua National Forest at Idleyld Park, OR 97447.

Location: From Roseburg, travel east from the town of Glide on Highway 138 for 48 miles, then follow Forest Service Road 2615 a short distance to the campground.

Trip note: This campground is set in the middle of a big bend in the Umpqua River. Rafting and fishing are both popular pastimes here.

Site 30 TWIN LAKES

Campsites, facilities: There are six tent sites. Picnic tables and firegrills are provided, and vault toilets are available. There is no piped water. Pets are permitted. Boat docks are nearby.

Reservations, fee: No reservations necessary; no fee. Open mid-June to late-October.

Who to contact: Phone North Umpqua Ranger District at 503-496-3532, or write Umpqua National Forest, Glide, OR 97443.

Location: From Roseburg, drive 51 miles east on Highway 138, then 10 miles south on Forest Service Road 4770.

Trip note: This remote campground is set along the shore of Big Twin Lake at 4800 feet elevation. A nearby trail leads 2 1/2 miles up Twin Lakes Mountain to 5600 feet, a nice hike.

Site 31 BOULDER FLAT

Campsites, facilities: There are 10 sites for tents, trailers or motorhomes up to 22 feet long. Picnic tables and firegrills are provided, and piped water and vault toilets are available. Sanitary disposal services, a store, laundromat and ice are located within five miles. Pets are permitted. Boat docks are nearby.

Reservations, fee: No reservations necessary; $3 fee per night. Open May to February.

Who to contact: Phone the Diamond Lake Ranger District at 503-498-2531, or write the Umpqua National Forest at HC 60, Box 101, Idleyld Park, OR 97447.

Location: From Roseburg, drive 54 miles east on Highway 138 to the campground.

Trip note: This campground is set along the banks of the Umpqua River at the confluence of Boulder Creek. A trail follows Boulder Creek north from camp for 10 1/2 miles through the Boulder Creek Wilderness, with elevation gain from 2000 to 5400 feet. A good thumper for backpackers.

Site 32 TOKETEE LAKE

Campsites, facilities: There are 33 sites for tents, trailers or motorhomes up to 22 feet long. Picnic tables and firegrills are provided, and piped water and vault toilets are available. Pets are permitted. Boat docks and launching facilities are nearby.

Reservations, fee: No reservations necessary; $3 fee per night. Open mid-April to late-October.

Who to contact: Phone the Diamond Lake Ranger District at 503-498-2531, or write the Umpqua National Forest at HC 60, Box 101, Idleyld Park, OR 97447.

Location: From Roseburg, drive about 60 miles east on Highway 138, then one mile on Forest Service Road 34 to the campground.

Trip note: This campground is set along the shore of Toketee Lake. The North Umpqua Trail passes near camp and continues north along the River for many miles. A 2 1/2-mile walk north of camp along this trail will get you to the Umpqua Hot Springs.

Site 33 WHITEHORSE FALLS

Campsites, facilities: There are five tent sites. Picnic tables and firegrills are provided, and vault toilets are available. There is no piped water is available. Pets are permitted.

Reservations, fee: No reservations necessary; no fee. Open June to late-October.

Who to contact: Phone the Diamond Lake Ranger District at 503-498-2531, or write the Umpqua National Forest at HC 60, Box 101, Idleyld Park, OR 97447.

Location: From Roseburg, travel 65 miles east on Highway 138 to the campground.

Trip note: This campground is set along the Clearwater River, one of the coldest streams in Umpqua National Forest. A small camp in a primitive setting—yet adjacent to the highway.

Site 34 CLEARWATER FALLS

Campsites, facilities: There are eight tent sites and four sites for trailers or motorhomes up to 16 feet long. Picnic tables and firegrills are provided, and piped water and vault toilets are available. Pets are permitted.

Reservations, fee: No reservations necessary; $3 fee per night. Open mid-May to late-October.

Who to contact: Phone the Diamond Lake Ranger District at 503-498-2531, or write the Umpqua National Forest at HC 60, Box 101, Idleyld Park, OR 97447.

Location: From Roseburg, drive on Highway 138 for 73 miles. At Forest Service Road 4785 head south to the campground.

Trip note: This campground is set along the banks of the Clearwater River. An attraction here is a cascading section of stream called Clearwater Falls.

Site 35 BROKEN ARROW

Campsites, facilities: There are 142 sites for tents, trailers or motorhomes up to 30 feet long. Picnic tables and firegrills are provided, and flush toilets and piped water are available. Pets are permitted. Boat docks, launching facilities and rentals are nearby.

Reservations, fee: No reservations necessary; $4 fee per night. Open late-May to mid-September.

Who to contact: Phone the Diamond Lake Ranger District at 503-498-2531, or write the Umpqua National Forest at HC 60, Box 101, Idleyld Park, OR 97447.

Location: From Roseburg, drive 78 miles east on Highway 138. Turn off on Forest Service Road 4795 to the campground.

Trip note: This campground is set at 5200 feet elevation near the south shore of Diamond Lake, the largest natural lake in Umpqua National Forest. Boating, fishing, swimming, hiking and bicyling are among the options here. Diamond Lake is adjacent to Mount Thielsen Wilderness, Crater Lake National Park and Mount Bailey, all of which offer a variety of recreation opportunities year-around. Diamond Lake is quite popular with anglers, with good trout trolling, particularly in early summer.

DIAMOND LAKE
Site **36**

Campsites, facilities: There are 160 sites for tents, trailers or motorhomes up to 22 feet long. Picnic tables and firegrills are provided, and flush toilets, piped water and firewood are available. Pets are permitted. Boat docks, launching facilities and rentals are nearby.

Reservations, fee: No reservations necessary; $6 fee per night. Open mid-May to late-October.

Who to contact: Phone the Diamond Lake Ranger District at 503-498-2531, or write the Umpqua National Forest at HC 60, Box 101, Idleyld Park, OR 97447.

Location: From Roseburg, drive 80 miles east on Highway 138. From there, go two miles south on Forest Service Road 4795 to the campground.

Trip note: This campground is set along the east shore of Diamond Lake. See the trip note for campsite 35 for recreation information.

THIELSEN VIEW
Site **37**

Campsites, facilities: There are 60 sites for tents, trailers or motorhomes up to 30 feet long. Picnic tables and firegrills are provided, and piped water and vault toilets are available. Pets are permitted. Boat docks, launching facilities and rentals are nearby.

Reservations, fee: No reservations necessary; $5 fee per night. Open late-May to late-September.

Who to contact: Phone the Diamond Lake Ranger District at 503-498-2531, or write the Umpqua National Forest at HC 60, Box 101, Idleyld Park, OR 97447.

Location: From Roseburg, drive on Highway 138 east for about 80 miles, then go south on Forest Service Road 4795 to the campground.

Trip note: This campground is set along the east shore of Diamond Lake. See the trip note to campsite 35 for information on recreation opportunities.

EAST LEMOLO
Site **38**

Campsites, facilities: There are six sites for tents, trailers or motorhomes up to 22 feet long. Picnic tables and firegrills are provided, and piped water and vault toilets are available. Pets are permitted. Boat docks, launching facilities and rentals are nearby.

Reservations, fee: No reservations necessary; $3 fee per night. Open mid-May to late-October.

Who to contact: Phone the Diamond Lake Ranger District at 503-498-2531, or write the Umpqua National Forest at HC 60, Box 101, Idleyld Park, OR 97447.

Location: From Roseburg, travel 80 miles east on Highway 138, then three miles north on Forest Service Road 2610. The park is located about two miles east on Forest Service Road 400.

Trip note: This campground is set along the east shore of Lemolo Lake, where boating and fishing are some of the recreation possibilities. Boats with motors are allowed. The North Umpqua River and adjacent trail are just beyond the north shore of the lake. If you hike for two miles northwest of the lake, you can reach spectacular Lemolo Falls.

INLET
Site **39**

Campsites, facilities: There are 13 sites for tents, trailers or motorhomes up to 22 feet long. Picnic tables and firegrills are provided, and vault toilets and piped water are available. Pets are permitted. Boat docks, launching facilities and rentals are nearby.

Reservations, fee: No reservations necessary; $3 fee per night. Open mid-May to late-October.

Who to contact: Phone the Diamond Lake Ranger District at 503-498-2531, or write the Umpqua National Forest at HC 60, Box 101, Idleyld Park, OR 97447.

Location: From Roseburg, drive 80 miles east on Highway 138, then three miles north on Forest Service Road 2610. The camp is about three miles east on Forest Service Road 400.

Trip note: This campground is set along the eastern inlet of Lemolo Lake. See the trip note to campsite 38 for recreation details.

POOLE CREEK
Site **40**

Campsites, facilities: There are 25 sites for tents, trailers or motorhomes up to 22 feet long. Picnic tables and firegrills are provided, and piped water and vault toilets are available. Pets are permitted. Boat docks, launching facilities and rentals are nearby.

Reservations, fee: No reservations necessary; $5 fee per night. Open mid-May to late-October.

Who to contact: Phone the Diamond Lake Ranger District at 503-498-2531, or write the Umpqua National Forest at HC 60, Box 101, Idleyld Park, OR 97447.

Location: From Roseburg, drive 80 miles east of Glide on Highway 138, then four miles north on Forest Service Road 2610 to the campground.

Trip note: This campground is set along the western shore of Lemolo Lake, not far from Lemolo Lake Resort which is open for recreation year-around.

LEMOLO
Site **41** ### LAKE RESORT

Campsites, facilities: There are five tent sites and 32 drive-through sites for trailers or motorhomes of any length. Electricity, piped water, sewer hookups and picnic tables are provided. Flush toilets, bottled gas, sanitary disposal services, showers, a store, a cafe, a laundromat and ice are available. Pets and motorbikes are permitted. Boat docks, launching facilities and rentals are nearby.

Reservations, fee: Reservations accepted; $8 fee per night. MasterCard and Visa accepted. Open all year.

Who to contact: Phone at 503-552-7060, or write at HC60, Box 79B, Idleyld Park, OR 97447.

Location: From Diamond Lake, go west on Highway 138 for 10 1/2 miles, then go five miles north on Lemolo Lake Road to the resort.

Trip note: This resort is set along the west shore of Lemolo Lake and offers recreation opportunities year-around.

Site 42   CONTORTA POINT

Campsites, facilities: There are nine sites for tents, trailers or motorhomes up to 22 feet long. Picnic tables and firegrills are provided, and piped water, vault toilets and firewood are available. Pets are permitted. Boat docks and launching facilities are located a mile away at Spring Campground (Site 43).

Reservations, fee: No reservations necessary; $4 fee per night. Open June to late-September.

Who to contact: Phone Crescent Ranger District at 503-433-2234, or write Deschutes National Forest at Crescent, OR 97733.

Location: From Eugene, drive southeast on Highway 58 to Crescent Lake. The turnoff is just past Odell Lake. Then drive 11 miles southwest on Forest Service Road 60, then one mile on Forest Service Road 60280.

Trip note: This campground is set along the south shore of Crescent Lake, where swimming, boating and waterskiing are among the summer pastimes. A number of trails from nearby Spring Campground (Site 43) provide access to lakes in the Diamond Peak Wilderness. A parking area for snowmobiles and cross-country skiers is at the north end of the lake.

Site 43   SPRING

Campsites, facilities: There are 68 sites for tents, trailers or motorhomes up to 22 feet long. Picnic tables and firegrills are provided, and piped water, vault toilets and firewood are available. Pets are permitted. Boat docks are nearby.

Reservations, fee: No reservations necessary; $5 fee per night. Open June to late-October.

Who to contact: Phone Crescent Ranger District at 503-433-2234, or write Deschutes National Forest, Crescent, OR 97733.

Location: From Eugene, drive southeast on Highway 58 to Crescent Lake. Drive eight miles west on Forest Service Road 60 from the town of Crescent Lake, then turn northeast on the entrance road to the campground.

Trip note: This campground is set along the south shore of Crescent Lake.

Site 44   CRESCENT LAKE

Campsites, facilities: There are 44 sites for tents, trailers or motorhomes up to 21 feet long. Picnic tables and firegrills are provided, and piped water, vault toilets and firewood are available. Pets are permitted. Boat docks, launching facilities and rentals are nearby.

Reservations, fee: No reservations necessary; $6 fee per night. Open mid-May to late-October.

Who to contact: Phone Crescent Ranger District at 503-433-2234, or write Deschutes National Forest, Crescent, OR 97733.

Location: From Eugene, drive southeast on Highway 58 to Crescent Lake. From the town of Crescent Lake, go three miles southwest on Forest Service Road 60 to the campground.

Trip note: This campground is set along the north shore of Crescent Lake. A trail from the campground heads into the Diamond Peak Wilderness and also branches north to Odell Lake.

Site **45**   ### ODELL TRAILER PARK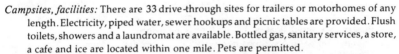

Campsites, facilities: There are 33 drive-through sites for trailers or motorhomes of any length. Electricity, piped water, sewer hookups and picnic tables are provided. Flush toilets, showers and a laundromat are available. Bottled gas, sanitary services, a store, a cafe and ice are located within one mile. Pets are permitted.

Reservations, fee: Reservations accepted; $11 fee per night. MasterCard and Visa accepted. Open May to October.

Who to contact: Phone at 503-433-2411, or write at Box 91, Crescent Lake, OR 97425.

Location: From Eugene, drive southeast on Highway 58 to Crescent Lake. In Crescent Lake, take the Crescent Lake Road exit off Highway 58. The park is at the junction.

Trip note: This motorhome park is centrally located between Crescent and Odell Lakes, both of which offer good boating and fishing. There are good hiking trails in the backcountry of nearby Diamond Peak Wilderness.

Site **46**   ### ODELL CREEK   ▲

Campsites, facilities: There are 22 sites for tents, trailers or motorhomes up to 22 feet long. Picnic tables and firegrills are provided, and piped water, vault toilets and firewood are available. Pets are permitted. Boat docks, launching facilities and rentals are nearby.

Reservations, fee: No reservations necessary; $4 fee per night. Open mid-May to late-September.

Who to contact: Phone Crescent Ranger District at 503-433-2234, or write Deschutes National Forest, Crescent, OR 97733.

Location: From Eugene, drive southeast on Highway 58 to Crescent Lake. Go 1 1/2 miles northwest of Crescent Lake junction on Highway 58, then go 400 yards southwest on Forest Service Road 5811 to the campground.

Trip note: This campground is set along the south shore of Odell Lake, where you can fish, swim and hike. A trail from camp heads southwest into the Diamond Peak Wilderness and provides access to several small lakes in the backcountry.

Site **47**   ### SUNSET COVE   ▲

Campsites, facilities: There are 27 sites for tents, trailers or motorhomes up to 22 feet long. Picnic tables and firegrills are provided, and piped water, vault toilets and firewood

are available. Pets are permitted. Boat docks, launching facilities and rentals are
nearby.

Reservations, fee: No reservations necessary; $5 fee per night. Open mid-May to mid-
October.

Who to contact: Phone Crescent Ranger District at 503-433-2234, or write Deschutes
National Forest, Crescent, OR 97733.

Location: From junction of Highway 58 and Crescent Lake Road, go 2 1/2 miles northwest
on Highway 58 to the campground.

Trip note: This campground is set along the southeast shore of Odell Lake.

Site 48   PRINCESS CREEK

Campsites, facilities: There are 46 sites for tents, trailers or motorhomes up to 22 feet long.
Picnic tables and firegrills are provided, and piped water, vault toilets and firewood
are available. Showers, a store, a laundromat and ice are available within five miles.
Pets are permitted. Boat docks and rentals are nearby.

Reservations, fee: No reservations necessary; $6 fee per night. Open mid-May to late-
October.

Who to contact: Phone Crescent Ranger District at 503-433-2234, or write Deschutes
National Forest, Crescent, OR 97733.

Location: Go 5 1/2 miles northwest of the junction of Crescent Lake Road on Highway 58
to the campground.

Trip note: This campground is set along the east shore of Odell Lake. See the trip note to
campsite 46 for recreation details.

Site 49   TRAPPER CREEK

Campsites, facilities: There are 32 sites for tents, trailers or motorhomes up to 22 feet long.
Picnic tables and firegrills are provided, and piped water, vault toilets and firewood
are available. A store, a laundromat and ice are within five miles. Pets are permitted.
Boat docks and rentals are nearby.

Reservations, fee: No reservations necessary; $6 fee per night. Open mid-May to late-
October.

Who to contact: Phone Crescent Ranger District at 503-433-2234, or write Deschutes
National Forest, Crescent, OR 97733.

Location: Go 5 1/2 miles northwest of the junction of Crescent Lake Road on Highway 58
to the campground.

Trip note: This campground is set along the east shore of Odell Lake. See the trip note to
campsite 46 for recreation details.

Site 50   SHELTER COVE RESORT

Campsites, facilities: There are 10 tent sites and 70 drive-through sites for trailers or
motorhomes up to 30 feet long. Electricity and picnic tables are provided. Flush
toilets, showers, a store, cafe and ice are available. Pets are permitted. Boat docks,
launching facilities and rentals are nearby.

Reservations, fee: No reservations necessary; $8 fee per night. MasterCard and Visa
accepted. Open late-April to mid-October.

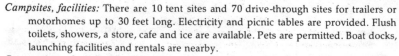

Who to contact: Phone at 503-433-2548, or write at Cascade Summit, OR 97425.

Location: From Eugene, drive southeast on Highway 58 to Odell Lake. Take the West Odell Road turn off Highway 58 at the north end of Odell Lake, then drive 2 1/2 miles south on West Odell Road to the campground.

Trip note: This private resort is set along the north shore of Odell Lake.

GOLD LAKE
Site **51**

Campsites, facilities: There are 25 sites for tents, trailers or motorhomes up to 16 feet long. Picnic tables and firegrills are provided, and piped water, vault toilets and pets are permitted. Boat docks and launching facilities are nearby.

Reservations, fee: No reservations necessary; $5 fee per night. Open June to late-September.

Who to contact: Phone Oakridge Ranger District at 503-782-2291, or write Willamette National Forest, 48458 Highway 58, Oakridge, OR 97463.

Location: From Eugene, drive 61 miles southeast on Highway 58, then two miles northeast on Forest Service Road 500 to the campground.

Trip note: This campground is set along the shore of Gold Lake, where fishing, swimming and boats without motors are permitted. The campground is set along a trail that provides access to numerous small lakes to the west and Waldo Lake to the north.

SHADOW BAY
Site **52**

Campsites, facilities: There are 92 sites for tents, trailers or motorhomes up to 22 feet long. Picnic tables and firegrills are provided, and piped water, vault toilets and pets are permitted. Boat docks and launching facilities are nearby.

Reservations, fee: No reservations necessary; $6 fee per night. Open June to late-September.

Who to contact: Phone Oakridge Ranger District at 503-782-2291, or write Willamette National Forest, 46375 Highway 58, Westfir, OR 97492.

Location: From Eugene, travel 59 miles southeast on Highway 58, then 5 1/2 miles north on Forest Service Road 5897, then two miles west on Forest Service Road 5896 to the campground.

Trip note: The camp is set at 5400 feet elevation, tucked away along the southeast shore of Waldo Lake. For hikers, a trail circles the lake and intersects several other trails that provide access to many small backcountry lakes.

NORTH WALDO
Site **53**

Campsites, facilities: There are 58 sites for tents, trailers or motorhomes up to 22 feet long. Picnic tables and firegrills are provided, and piped water, vault toilets and pets are permitted. Boat docks and launching facilities are nearby.

Reservations, fee: No reservations necessary; $6 fee per night. Open June to late-September.

Who to contact: Phone Oakridge Ranger District at 503-782-2291, or write Willamette National Forest, 46375 Highway 58, Westfir, OR 97492.

Location: From Eugene, travel 59 miles southeast on Highway 58, then 10 1/2 miles north on Forest Service Road 5897, then two miles west on Forest Service Road 5898 to the entrance road to the campground.

Trip note: See trip note to campsite 52.

TIMPANOGAS

Site **54**

Campsites, facilities: There are 10 sites for tents, trailers or motorhomes up to 21 feet long. Picnic tables and firegrills are provided, and piped water, vault toilets and firewood are available. Pets are permitted. Boat docks are nearby. Only boats without motors permitted.

Reservations, fee: No reservations necessary; no fee. Open mid-June to mid-October.

Who to contact: Phone Rigdon Ranger District at 503-782-2283, or write Willamette National Forest, 49098 Salmon Creek Road, Oakridge, OR 97463.

Location: From Eugene, travel 38 miles southeast on Highway 58, two miles past Oakridge, then 1/2 mile on County Route 360. The camp is 38 miles southeast on Forest Service Road 21.

Trip note: This remote campground is set along the shore of little Timpanogas Lake, in the Cascades National Recreation Area. A trailhead adjacent to camp provides access into the backcountry. There is a hike-in campground about two miles away at Indigo Lake that has five primitive sites and pit toilets. It is accessible from a trailhead here.

INDIGO SPRINGS

Site **55**

Campsites, facilities: There are four sites for tents, trailers or motorhomes up to 16 feet long. Picnic tables and firegrills are provided and vault toilets and firewood are available. There is no piped water. Pets are permitted.

Reservations, fee: No reservations necessary; no fee. Open mid-April to mid-November.

Who to contact: Phone Rigdon Ranger District at 503-782-2283, or write Willamette National Forest, 49098 Salmon Creek Road, Oakridge, OR 97463.

Location: From Eugene, drive southeast on Highway 58 two miles past the town of Oakridge, then 1/2 mile on County Route 360. From there, go 29 miles southeast on Forest Service Road 21. The camp is on the left.

Trip note: This campground sets along the bank of Indigo Creek, not far from its confluence with the Middle Fork of the Willamette River. It gets it name from several large springs in the area.

SACANDAGA

Site **56**

Campsites, facilities: There are 20 sites for tents, trailers or motorhomes up to 21 feet long. Picnic tables and firegrills are provided and vault toilets and firewood are available. There is no piped water. Pets are permitted.

Reservations, fee: No reservations necessary; no fee. Open mid-April to mid-November.

Who to contact: Phone Rigdon Ranger District at 503-782-2283, or write Willamette National Forest, 49098 Salmon Creek Road, Oakridge, OR 97463.

Location: From Eugene, drive southeast on Highway 58 two miles past the town of Oakridge, then 1/2 mile on County Route 360. From there, go 25 miles southeast on Forest Service Road 21. The camp is on the right.

Trip note: This primitive campground sits on a bluff overlooking the Willamette River. It's adjacent to historic Rigdon Meadows, site of a stage coach station in the pioneer days.

CAMPERS FLAT
Site **57**

Campsites, facilities: There are five sites for tents, trailers or motorhomes up to 21 feet long. Picnic tables and firegrills are provided, and piped water, vault toilets and firewood are available. Pets are permitted.

Reservations, fee: No reservations necessary; no fee. Open mid-April to mid-November.

Who to contact: Phone Rigdon Ranger District at 503-782-2283, or write Willamette National Forest, 49098 Salmon Creek Road, Oakridge, OR 97463.

Location: From Eugene drive southeast on Highway 58 two miles past Oakridge, then 1/2 mile on County Route 360. The camp is 20 miles south on Forest Service Road 21.

Trip note: This campground is set along the Middle Fork of the Willamette River.

SECRET
Site **58**

Campsites, facilities: There are six sites for tents, trailers or motorhomes up to 15 feet long. Picnic table and firegrill are provided, and vault toilets are available, but there is no piped water. Pets are permitted.

Reservations, fee: No reservations necessary; no fee. Open mid-April to mid-November.

Who to contact: Phone Rigdon Ranger District at 503-782-2283, or write Willamette National Forest, 49098 Salmon Creek Road, Oakridge, OR 97463.

Location: From Eugene drive southeast on Highway 58 two miles past the town of Oakridge, then 1/2 mile on County Route 360. From there, go 18 miles south on Forest Service Road 21.

Trip note: This campground is set along the Middle Fork of the Willamette River. Attracts few people, despite nice setting. Nobody seems to know about it.

SAND PRAIRIE
Site **59**

Campsites, facilities: There are 20 sites for tents, trailers or motorhomes up to 22 feet long. Picnic tables and firegrill are provided, and flush toilets and piped water are available. Some of the facilities are wheelchair accessible. Pets are permitted. A boat launch is nearby on Hills Creek Reservoir.

Reservations, fee: No reservations necessary; $7 fee per night. Open mid-April to mid-November.

Who to contact: Phone Rigdon Ranger District at 503-782-2283, or write Willamette National Forest, 49098 Salmon Creek Road, Oakridge, OR 97463.

Location: From Eugene, drive southeast on Highway 58 two miles past the town of Oakridge, then 1/2 mile on County Route 360. From there, go 11 miles south on Forest Service Road 21.

Trip note: This peaceful campground is set in a forest of old-growth trees along the Middle Fork of the Willamette River, just south of Hills Creek Lake. It is at the trailhead for the Middle Fork Trail, a 40-mile trail to be completed in the early 1990's.

PACKARD CREEK
Site **60**

Campsites, facilities: There are 33 sites for tents, trailers or motorhomes up to 30 feet long. Picnic tables and firegrills are provided, and piped water, vault toilets and firewood are available. Some facilities are wheelchair accessible. Pets are permitted. Boat docks and launching facilities are nearby.

Reservations, fee: No reservations necessary; $7 fee per night. Open mid-April to mid-November.

Who to contact: Phone Rigdon Ranger District at 503-782-2283, or write Willamette National Forest, 49098 Salmon Creek Road, Oakridge, OR 97463.

Location: From Eugene, drive southeast on Highway 58 two miles past the town of Oakridge, then 1/2 mile southeast on County Route 360. The camp is five miles south on Forest Service Road 21.

Trip note: This campground is set at 1600 feet elevation along the west shore of Hills Creek Lake, a 2900-acre reservoir where fishing and boating are popular. No boats with motors are permitted on the Larison Cove arm of the lake.

FERRIN
Site **61**

Campsites, facilities: There are seven sites for tents, trailers or motorhomes. Picnic tables and firegrills are provided, and vault toilets are available. There is no piped water. Pets are permitted.

Reservations, fee: No reservations necessary; no fee. Open late-April to mid-October.

Who to contact: Phone Oakridge Ranger District at 503-782-2291, or write Willamette National Forest, 46375 Highway 58, Westfir, OR 97492.

Location: From Eugene, drive 35 miles southeast on Highway 58 and you'll see the campground. It is located two miles west of Oakridge.

Trip note: This campground is set along the banks of the Middle Fork of the Willamette River, not far from the town of Oakridge. A free spot to lay out your sleeping bag for the night.

DECEPTION CREEK MOBILE PARK
Site **62**

Campsites, facilities: There are 15 sites for trailers or motorhomes of any length. Electricity, piped water and sewer hookups are provided. Flush toilets, sanitary services, showers, a laundromat and ice are available.

Reservations, fee: Reservations accepted; $10 fee per night. MasterCard and Visa accepted. Open all year.

Who to contact: Phone at 503-782-2602, or write at 46372 Highway 58, Westfir, OR 97492.

Location: From Eugene, drive 33 miles southeast on Highway 58. The camp is located three miles west of Oakridge.

Trip note: This motorhome park is set along the Middle Fork of the Willamette River, between the towns of Oakridge and Hemlock.

SHADY DELL

Site **63**

Campsites, facilities: There are nine sites for tents, trailers or motorhomes up to 15 feet long. Picnic tables and firegrills are provided, and piped water, vault toilets and firewood are available. Sanitary services, a cafe and laundromat are available within five miles. Some of the facilities are wheelchair accessible. Pets are permitted. Boat docks and launching facilities are nearby at the south end of Lookout Point Lake.

Reservations, fee: No reservations necessary; $3 fee per night. Open May to late-October.

Who to contact: Phone Lowell Ranger District at 503-937-2129, or write Willamette National Forest, Lowell, OR 97452.

Location: From Eugene, drive 33 miles southeast on Highway 58. The camp is located five miles west of Oakridge.

Trip note: This campground is set along the banks of the Middle Fork of the Willamette River, not far from Lookout Point Lake, a long narrow reservoir that sits adjacent to Highway 58.

BLACK CANYON

Site **64**

Campsites, facilities: There are 72 sites for tents, trailers or motorhomes up to 22 feet long. Picnic tables and firegrills are provided, and piped water, vault toilets and firewood are available. Sanitary services, a cafe and laundromat are within five miles. Some of the facilities are wheelchair accessible. Pets are permitted. Boat docks and launching facilities are nearby at the south end of Lookout Point Lake.

Reservations, fee: No reservations necessary; $5 fee per night. Open May to late-October.

Who to contact: Phone Lowell Ranger District at 503-937-2129, or write Willamette National Forest, Lowell, OR 97452.

Location: From Eugene, drive 30 miles southeast on Highway 58. The camp is located six miles west of Oakridge.

Trip note: This campground is set along the banks of the Middle Fork of the Willamette River, not far from Lookout Point Lake, where fishing and boating are popular.

SALMON CREEK FALLS

Site **65**

Campsites, facilities: There are 12 tent sites and six sites for trailers or motorhomes up to 16 feet long. Piped water and picnic tables are provided. Some facilities are wheelchair accessible. A store, a cafe, laundromat and ice are available within five miles. Pets are permitted.

Reservations, fee: No reservations necessary; $5 fee per night. Open late-April to mid-October.

Who to contact: Phone Lowell Ranger District at 503-937-2129, or write Willamette National Forest, Lowell, OR 97452.

Location: From Eugene, drive southeast on Highway 58 to Oakridge, then 3 1/2 miles northeast on Forest Service Road 24 (Salmon Creek Road) to the campground.

Trip note: This campground is set along the bank of Salmon Creek. It is just enough off Highway 58 that this one gets missed by most campers.

KIAHANIE

Site **66**

Campsites, facilities: There are 20 sites for tents, trailers or motorhomes up to 16 feet long. Picnic tables and firegrills are provided, and piped water, vault toilets and firewood are available. Pets are permitted.

Reservations, fee: No reservations necessary; $3 fee per night. Open late-April to mid-October.

Who to contact: Phone Oakridge Ranger District at 503-782-2291, or write Willamette National Forest, 46375 Highway 58, Westfir, OR 97492.

Location: From Eugene, drive southeast on Highway 58 to Oakridge, then go two miles to the town of Westfir. Then head 19 miles northeast on Forest Service Road 19 to the campground.

Trip note: This remote campground is set along the North Fork of the Middle Fork of the Willamette River. You want quiet, you came to the right place. An even more remote campground is farther north on Forest Service Road 19 at campsite 67.

BOX CANYON
HORSE CAMP

Site **67**

Campsites, facilities: There are 13 campsites which allow horse and rider to camp close together. Picnic tables, firegrills and corrals are provided, and firewood, a manure disposal site and vault toilets are available. There is no piped water. Pets are permitted.

Reservations, fee: No reservations necessary; no fee. Open mid-May to mid-September.

Who to contact: Phone Blue River Ranger District at 503-822-3317, or write Willamette National Forest, Blue River, OR 97413.

Location: Take US 126 east from Blue River for 3 1/2 miles, then go 30 miles south on Forest Service Road 19 (Aufderheide Forest Drive).

Trip note: Only 80 miles from Eugene, this unique and secluded campground offers trails into several wilderness areas, including Chucksney Mountain Trail, Crossing-Way Trail and Grasshopper Trail. Good base camp for a backpacking trip.

SKOOKUM CREEK

Site **68**

Campsites, facilities: There are eight tent sites. Picnic tables and firegrills are provided, and firewood, piped water and vault toilets are available. Pets are permitted.

Reservations, fee: No reservations necessary; no fee. Open mid-May to mid-September.

Who to contact: Phone Blue River Ranger District at 503-822-3317, or write Willamette National Forest, Blue River, OR 97413.

Location: Take US 126 east from Blue River for 3 1/2 miles, then go 30 miles south on Forest Service Road 19 (Aufderheide Forest Drive) to Box Canyon. From there, drive south for three miles on Forest Service Road 1957 to the campground.

Trip note: This remote campground is set near the border of the Three Sisters Wilderness. A trailhead at camp provides access to numerous lakes and other trails in the backcountry. Primitive, little-known spot.

BLAIR LAKE

Site **69**

Campsites, facilities: There are nine tent sites. Picnic tables and firegrills are provided, and piped water, firewood and vault toilets are available. Pets are permitted. Boat docks are nearby.

Reservations, fee: No reservations necessary; $4 fee per night. Open June to mid-October.

Who to contact: Phone Oakridge Ranger District at 503-782-2291, or write Willamette National Forest, 46375 Highway 58, Westfir, OR 97492.

Location: From the town Oakridge on Highway 58, travel one mile east on County Route 149 eight miles northeast on Forest Service Road 24. From there, go seven miles on Forest Service Road 1934.

Trip note: This campground is set at 4800 feet elevation along the shore of little Blair Lake. Boats without motors are permitted and fishing can be good.

BLUE POOL

Site **70**

Campsites, facilities: There are 22 sites for tents, trailers or motorhomes up to 16 feet long. Picnic tables and firegrills are provided, and piped water and vault toilets are available. Pets are permitted.

Reservations, fee: No reservations necessary; $5 fee per night. Open late-April to mid-October.

Who to contact: Phone Oakridge Ranger District at 503-782-2291, or write Willamette National Forest, 46375 Highway 58, Westfir, OR 97492.

Location: From Eugene, drive 45 miles southeast on Highway 58 to the campground.

Trip note: This campground is set along the Middle Fork of the Willamette River, at 2000 feet elevation. Easy access, a decent layover spot.

WEST CULTUS

Site **71**

Campsites, facilities: There are 15 tent sites that are accessible by boat or on foot. Picnic tables and firegrills are provided, and vault toilets are available. There is no piped water. Pets are permitted. Boat docks, launching facilities and rentals are nearby.

Reservations, fee: No reservations necessary; no fee. Open June to late-September.

Who to contact: Phone Bend Ranger District at 503-388-5664, or write Deschutes National Forest, 1230 NE Third, Bend, OR 97701.

Location: From the town of La Pine, travel 2 1/2 miles north on US 97, then turn west on County Route 46 and drive 10 miles to County Route 42 and continue west for another 10 miles. Turn north on County Route 46 (Cascade Lakes Highway) and drive six mile to Forest Service Road 4635 and turn left and drive 1 1/2 miles to the parking area.

Trip note: This campground is set at 4700 feet elevation, along the west shore of Cultus Lake. It is accessible by trail or boat only—it's about three miles from the parking area to the campground. A good spot for waterskiing, fishing and swimming. Trails branch out from the campground and provide access to numerous small backcountry lakes.

CULTUS LAKE
Site **72**

Campsites, facilities: There are 54 sites for tents, trailers or motorhomes up to 22 feet long. Picnic tables and firegrills are provided, and piped water and vault toilets are available. Pets are permitted. Boat docks, launching facilities and rentals are nearby.

Reservations, fee: No reservations necessary; $6 fee per night. Open June to October.

Who to contact: Phone Bend Ranger District at 503-388-5664, or write Deschutes National Forest, 1230 NE Third, Bend, OR 97701.

Location: From the town of La Pine, travel 2 1/2 miles north on US 97, then turn west on County Route 46 and drive 10 miles to County Route 42 and continue west for another 10 miles. Turn north on County Route 46 (Cascade Lakes Highway) and drive seven miles to the campground entrance.

Trip note: This campground is along the east shore of Cultus Lake, not far from a resort. It is a popular spot for windsurfing, waterskiing, swimming, fishing and hiking.

LITTLE CULTUS
Site **73** LAKE

Campsites, facilities: There are 10 sites for tents, trailers or motorhomes up to 22 feet long. Picnic tables and firegrills are provided, and piped water and vault toilets are available. Pets are permitted. Boat docks, launching facilities and rentals are nearby.

Reservations, fee: No reservations necessary; no fee. Open late-May to late-September.

Who to contact: Phone Bend Ranger District at 503-388-5664, or write Deschutes National Forest, 1230 NE Third, Bend, OR 97701.

Location: From the town of La Pine, travel 2 1/2 miles north on US 97, then turn west on County Route 46 and drive 10 miles to County Route 42 and continue for west for another 10 miles. Turn north on County Route 46 (Cascade Lakes Highway) and drive four miles to the campground entrance on Forest Service Road 4630.

Trip note: This campground is set along the shore of Little Cultus Lake; the campsites are not clearly marked. A popular spot for swimming, fishing, boating (speed restricted), and hiking. Nearby trails access numerous backcountry lakes, and the Pacific Crest Trail passes about six miles west of camp.

CULTUS CORRAL
Site **74** GROUP CAMP

Campsites, facilities: There are 25 sites for tents, trailers or motorhomes of any length. Picnic tables and firegrills are provided and vault toilets and a corral are available. There is no piped water. Pets are permitted. Boat docks, launching facilities and rentals are nearby.

Reservations, fee: Reservations accepted; no fee. Open June to October.

Who to contact: Phone Bend Ranger District at 503-388-5664, or write Deschutes National Forest, 1230 NE Third, Bend, OR 97701.

Location: From the town of La Pine, travel 2 1/2 miles north on US 97, then turn west on County Route 46 and drive 10 miles to County Route 42 and continue west for another 10 miles. Turn north on County Route 46 (Cascade Lakes Highway) and drive seven miles to Forest Service Road 4635, the entrance road to the campground.

Trip note: This campground is about one mile from Cultus lake, near many trails that provide access to backcountry lakes. The Pacific Crest Trail passes about 10 miles from camp. A good base camp for backpacking trip.

Site 75 — IRISH AND TAYLOR

Campsites, facilities: There are five tent sites. Picnic tables and firegrills are provided, and pit toilets are available. There is no piped water. Pets are permitted. Boat docks, launching facilities and rentals are nearby.

Reservations, fee: No reservations necessary; no fee. Open mid-June to mid-September.

Who to contact: Phone Bend Ranger District at 503-388-5664, or write Deschutes National Forest, 1230 NE Third, Bend, OR 97701.

Location: From Bend, go 43 miles southwest on Highway 46 (Cascade Lakes Highway), then 3 1/2 miles southwest on Forest Service Road 4630. The camp is 6 1/2 miles west on Forest Service Road 600 (a rough road but worth the ride).

Trip note: This remote campground is set between two small lakes, about a mile from the Pacific Crest Trail. Other nearby trails provide access into the backcountry. Little known, beautiful and free.

Site 76 — QUINN RIVER

Campsites, facilities: There are 41 sites for tents, trailers or motorhomes up to 30 feet long. Picnic tables and firegrills are provided, and piped water and vault toilets are available. Pets are permitted. Boat docks are nearby.

Reservations, fee: No reservations necessary; $6 fee per night. Open late-April to mid-October.

Who to contact: Phone Bend Ranger District at 503-388-5664, or write Deschutes National Forest, 1230 NE Third, Bend, OR 97701.

Location: From the town of La Pine, travel 2 1/2 miles north on US 97, then turn west on County Route 46 and drive 10 miles to County Route 42 and continue west for another 10 miles. Turn north on County Route 46 (Cascade Lakes Highway) and drive four miles to the campground.

Trip note: This campground is set along the western shore of Crane Prairie Reservoir, a popular spot for anglers. A large parking lot is available for boats and trailers.

Site 77 — ROCK CREEK

Campsites, facilities: There are 32 sites for tents, trailers or motorhomes up to 22 feet long. Picnic tables and firegrills are provided, and piped water, a fish cleaning station and vault toilets are available. Pets are permitted. Boat docks and launching facilities are nearby.

Reservations, fee: No reservations necessary; $6 fee per night. Open mid-May to mid-October.

Who to contact: Phone Bend Ranger District at 503-388-5664, or write Deschutes National Forest, 1230 NE Third, Bend, OR 97701.

Location: From the town of La Pine, travel 2 1/2 miles north on US 97, then turn west on County Route 46 and drive 10 miles to County Route 42 and continue west for another 10 miles. Turn north on County Route 46 (Cascade Lakes Highway) and drive three miles to the campground.

Trip note: This campground is set along the west shore of Crane Prairie Reservoir. An option to campsite 76.

COW MEADOW
Site **78**

Campsites, facilities: There are 16 sites for tents, trailers or motorhomes up to 16 feet long. Picnic tables and firegrills are provided, and vault toilets are available. There is no piped water. Pets are permitted. Boat docks are nearby.

Reservations, fee: No reservations necessary; no fee. Open May to mid-October.

Who to contact: Phone Bend Ranger District at 503-388-5664, or write Deschutes National Forest, 1230 NE Third, Bend, OR 97701.

Location: From the town of La Pine, travel 2 1/2 miles north on US 97, then turn west on County Route 46 and drive 10 miles to County Route 42 and continue west for another 10 miles. Turn north on County Route 46 (Cascade Lakes Highway) and drive seven miles to the campground entrance road on the right. (Note: the entrance road is muddy at times.)

Trip note: This campground is set along the Deschutes River near the north end of Crane Prairie Reservoir. A pretty spot and the price is right.

CRANE PRAIRIE
Site **79**

Campsites, facilities: This campground will reopen in 1989 with 142 campsites for tents, trailers or motorhomes. Picnic tables and firegrills are provided, and piped water and vault toilets are available. Pets are permitted. Boat docks, launching facilities and rentals are nearby.

Reservations, fee: No reservations necessary; $2 fee per night. Open May to October.

Who to contact: Phone Bend Ranger District at 503-388-5664, or write Deschutes National Forest, 1230 NE Third, Bend, OR 97701.

Location: Take Highway 46 southwest from Bend 48 miles, then go 10 miles south on Forest Service Road 4270 to the campground.

Trip note: This campground is set along the north shore of Crane Prairie Reservoir.

CRANE PRAIRIE
Site **80**   RESORT

Campsites, facilities: There are 20 sites for trailers or motorhomes. Electricity, piped water, sewer hookups and picnic tables are provided. Bottled gas, firewood, a store and ice are available. Pets are permitted. Boat docks, launching facilities and rentals are nearby.

Reservations, fee: Reservations accepted; $10 fee per night. MasterCard and Visa accepted. Open late-April to mid-October.

Who to contact: Phone at 503-385-2173, or write at P.O. Box 322, La Pine, OR 97739.

Location: From Bend, travel 48 miles southwest on Highway 46 (Cascade Lakes Highway) to Forest Service Road 4270 and drive seven miles to the resort entrance.

Trip note: This resort is set along the north shore of popular Crane Prairie Reservoir, a good spot for canoeing and fishing. No waterskiing permitted.

MILE
Site **81**

Campsites, facilities: There are eight sites for tents, trailers or motorhomes up to 22 feet long. Picnic tables and firegrills are provided, vault toilets are available. There is no piped water. Pets are permitted.

Reservations, fee: No reservations necessary; no fee. Open late-May to late-September.

Who to contact: Phone Bend Ranger District at 503-388-5664, or write Deschutes National Forest, 1230 NE Third, Bend, OR 97701.

Location: From Bend, travel 40 miles southwest on Highway 46 (Cascade Lakes Highway) to the campground.

Trip note: This quiet campground is set along the banks of the headwaters of the Deschutes River. A quiet, primitive spot.

DESCHUTES BRIDGE
Site **82**

Campsites, facilities: There are 15 sites for tents, trailers or motorhomes up to 22 feet long. Picnic tables and firegrills are provided, and piped water and vault toilets are available. Pets are permitted.

Reservations, fee: No reservations necessary; $5 fee per night. Open June to October.

Who to contact: Phone Bend Ranger District at 503-388-5664, or write Deschutes National Forest, 1230 NE Third, Bend, OR 97701.

Location: From Bend, travel 41 miles southwest on Highway 46 (Cascade Lakes Highway) to the campground.

Trip note: This wooded campground is set along the banks of the Deschutes River.

WEST SOUTH TWIN
Site **83**

Campsites, facilities: There are 24 sites for trailers or motorhomes up to 22 feet long. Picnic tables and firegrills are provided, and piped water and flush toilets are available. Pets are permitted. Boat docks, launching facilities and rentals are nearby.

Reservations, fee: No reservations necessary; $6 fee per night. Open mid-May to mid-October.

Who to contact: Phone Bend Ranger District at 503-388-5664, or write Deschutes National Forest, 1230 NE Third, Bend, OR 97701.

Location: From La Pine, travel 2 1/2 miles northeast on US 97, then 10 miles west on County Route 43. From there, go five miles west on County Route 42 and 1 1/2 miles on Forest Service Road 4260.

Trip note: This campground is set along the western shore of South Twin Lake, a major access point to the Wickiup Reservoir. A popular fishing spot, with very good kokanee salmon fishing.

GULL POINT
Site **84**

Campsites, facilities: There are 80 sites for tents, trailers or motorhomes up to 30 feet long. Picnic tables and firegrills are provided, and piped water, sanitary dump station and vault toilets are available. Pets are permitted. Boat docks, launching facilities and rentals are nearby.

Reservations, fee: No reservations necessary; $6 fee per night. Open May to October.

Who to contact: Phone Bend Ranger District at 503-388-5664, or write Deschutes National Forest, 1230 NE Third, Bend, OR 97701.

Location: From La Pine, travel 2 1/2 miles northeast on US 97, then 10 miles west on County Route 43. Continue another 5 1/2 miles west on County Route 42 to Forest Service Road 4260, turn south and drive to the campground.

Trip note: This campground is set along the north shore of Wickiup Reservoir. Good fishing for kokanee salmon.

Site 85   NORTH TWIN LAKE

Campsites, facilities: There are 10 sites for tents, trailers or motorhomes up to 22 feet long. Picnic tables and firegrills are provided, and vault toilets are available. There is no piped water. Pets are permitted. Boat docks, launching facilities and rentals are nearby.

Reservations, fee: No reservations necessary; $3 fee per night. Open June to late-September.

Who to contact: Phone Bend Ranger District at 503-388-5664, or write Deschutes National Forest, 1230 NE Third, Bend, OR 97701.

Location: From La Pine, travel 2 1/2 miles northeast on US 97, then 10 miles west on County Route 43. Continue another 5 1/2 miles west on County Route 42 to Forest Service Road 4260, turn south and drive 1/2 mile to the campground.

Trip note: This campground is set along the shore of North Twin Lake. A popular weekend spot for families.

Site 86   SHEEP BRIDGE

Campsites, facilities: There are 17 sites for tents, trailers or motorhomes up to 22 feet long. Picnic tables and firegrills are provided, and piped water and vault toilets are available. Pets are permitted.

Reservations, fee: No reservations necessary; no fee. Open May to mid-October.

Who to contact: Phone Bend Ranger District at 503-388-5664, or write Deschutes National Forest, 1230 NE Third, Bend, OR 97701.

Location: From La Pine, travel 2 1/2 miles north on US 97, then go 10 miles west of La Pine on County Route 43, and five miles west on County Route 42. The camp is 1/2 mile west on County Route 4260.

Trip note: This campground is set along the channel north of Wickiup Reservoir. This is an open, treeless area that is dusty in summer and with minimal privacy year around.

Site 87   SOUTH TWIN LAKE

Campsites, facilities: There are 21 sites for tents, trailers or motorhomes up to 22 feet long. Picnic tables and firegrills are provided, and piped water and flush toilets are available. Pets are permitted. Boat docks, launching facilities and rentals are nearby.

Reservations, fee: No reservations necessary; $6 fee per night. Open May to mid-October.

Who to contact: Phone Bend Ranger District at 503-388-5664, or write Deschutes National Forest, 1230 NE Third, Bend, OR 97701.

Location: From La Pine, travel 2 1/2 miles northeast on US 97, then 10 miles west on County Route 43. Continue another 5 1/2 miles west on County Route 42 to Forest Service Road 4260, turn south and drive 1 1/2 miles to the campground.

Trip note: This campground is set along the shore of South Twin Lake, a popular spot for swimming and fishing.

Site 88 — NORTH DAVIS CREEK

Campsites, facilities: There are 17 sites for tents, trailers or motorhomes up to 22 feet long. Picnic tables and firegrills are provided, and piped water and vault toilets are available. Pets are permitted. Boat docks and launching facilities are nearby.

Reservations, fee: No reservations necessary; $5 fee per night. Open May to late-October.

Who to contact: Phone Bend Ranger District at 503-388-5664, or write Deschutes National Forest, 1230 NE Third, Bend, OR 97701.

Location: From La Pine, travel 2 1/2 miles north on US 97, then 10 miles west on County Route 43. The camp is 10 miles west on County Route 42 and four miles south on County Route 46.

Trip note: This campground is set along a western channel of Wickiup Reservoir. The area was logged in 1987 because of pine beetle investation. In late summer, the reservoir level tends to drop.

Site 89 — RESERVOIR

Campsites, facilities: There are 28 sites for tents, trailers or motorhomes up to 22 feet long. Picnic tables and firegrills are provided, and piped water and vault toilets are available. Pets are permitted. Boat docks are nearby.

Reservations, fee: No reservations necessary; $4 fee per night. Open May to late-October.

Who to contact: Phone Bend Ranger District at 503-388-5664, or write Deschutes National Forest, 1230 NE Third, Bend, OR 97701.

Location: Travel 10 miles west of La Pine on County Route 43, then 10 miles west on County Route 42. From there, the camp is nine miles south on County Route 46.

Trip note: This campground is set along the south shore of Wickiup Reservoir, where the kokanee salmon fishing is good. This camp is best early in the summer, before the lake level drops. Because of pine beetle infestation, the area was logged in 1987.

Site 90 — LAVA FLOW

Campsites, facilities: There are 12 sites for tents, trailers or motorhomes up to 22 feet long. Picnic tables and firegrills are provided, and vault toilets and firewood are available. There is no piped water. Pets are permitted. Boat docks are nearby.

Reservations, fee: No reservations necessary; no fee. Open late-May to late-October.

Who to contact: Phone Crescent Ranger District at 503-433-2234, or write at Deschutes National Forest, Crescent, OR 97733.

Location: From the town of Crescent (a small town on Highway 97), travel nine miles west

on County Route 61, then nine miles north on Forest Service Road 46. The camp is
located two miles north on Forest Service Road 850.

Trip note: This campground is set along the east shore of Davis Lake. It is a very shallow
lake that provides good duck hunting during the fall. During early summer, there is
some fishing.

Site 91   EAST DAVIS LAKE

Campsites, facilities: There are 33 sites for tents, trailers or motorhomes up to 22 feet long.
Picnic tables and firegrills are provided. Piped water, firewood and vault toilets are
available. Pets are permitted. Boat docks and launching facilities are nearby.

Reservations, fee: No reservations necessary; $4 fee per night. Open mid-May to late-
October.

Who to contact: Phone Crescent Ranger District at 503-433-2234, or write at Deschutes
National Forest, Crescent, OR 97733.

Location: From Crescent, a small town on Highway 97, travel nine miles west on County
Route 61, then 6 1/2 miles north on Forest Service Road 46. The camp is 1 1/2 mile
west on Forest Service Road 46855.

Trip note: This campground is set along the south shore of Davis Lake.

Site 92   WEST DAVIS LAKE

Campsites, facilities: There are 25 sites for tents, trailers or motorhomes up to 22 feet long.
Picnic tables and firegrills are provided, and piped water, firewood and vault toilets
are available. Pets are permitted. Boat docks are nearby.

Reservations, fee: No reservations necessary; $4 fee per night. Open mid-May to late-
October.

Who to contact: Phone Crescent Ranger District at 503-433-2234, or write at Deschutes
National Forest, Crescent Lake, OR 97425.

Location: From the small town of Crescent (located on Highway 87), drive nine miles west
on County Route 61, then three miles north on Forest Service Road 46. The camp is
four miles on Forest Service Road 4660.

Trip note: This campground is set along the south shore of Davis Lake.

Site 93   CRESCENT CREEK

Campsites, facilities: There are 10 sites for tents, trailers or motorhomes up to 22 feet long.
Picnic tables and firegrills are provided. Piped water, firewood and vault toilets are
available. Pets are permitted.

Reservations, fee: No reservations necessary; $3 fee per night. Open May to late-October.

Who to contact: Phone Crescent Ranger District at 503-433-2234, or write at Deschutes
National Forest, Crescent, OR 97733.

Location: From the town of Crescent (a small town on Highway 97), travel eight miles west
on County Route 61 to the campground.

Trip note: This is one of the Cascades classic hidden campgrounds. It is set along the banks
of Crescent Creek at 4500 feet elevation.

WICKIUP BUTTE
Site **94**

Campsites, facilities: There are five sites for tents, trailers or motorhomes up to 22 feet long. Picnic tables and firegrills are provided. Piped water and vault toilets are available. Pets are permitted. Boat docks and launching facilities are nearby.

Reservations, fee: No reservations necessary; $4 fee per night. Open May to late-October.

Who to contact: Phone Bend Ranger District at 503-388-5664, or write Deschutes National Forest, 1230 NE Third, La Pin 97701, OR 97739.

Location: From La Pine, go 2 1/2 miles northeast on US 97, then seven miles west on County Route 43. The camp is located another seven miles west on Forest Service Road 44.

Trip note: This campground is set along the southeast shore of Wickiup Reservoir. This is one of the better camps on the lake, because of logging in other areas. Kokanee salmon fishing is good during early summer.

BULL BEND
Site **95**

Campsites, facilities: There are 12 sites for tents, trailers or motorhomes. Picnic tables and firegrills are provided, and vault toilets are available. There is no piped water. Pets are permitted.

Reservations, fee: No reservations necessary; no fee. Open April to October.

Who to contact: Phone Bend Ranger District at 503-388-5664, or write Deschutes National Forest, 1230 NE Third Street, Bend, OR 97701.

Location: From the town of La Pine, travel 2 1/2 miles northeast on US 97, then ten miles west on County Route 43. The camp is 1 1/2 miles southwest on Forest Service Road 4370.

Trip note: This campground is set on the inside of a major bend of the Deschutes River. A mini float trip can be made by starting from the upstream end of camp, floating around the bend, then taking out at the downstream end of camp.

FALL RIVER
Site **96**

Campsites, facilities: There are nine sites for tents, trailers or motorhomes up to 22 feet long. Picnic tables and firegrills are provided, and vault toilets are available. There is no piped water. Pets are permitted.

Reservations, fee: No reservations necessary; no fee. Open June to mid-October.

Who to contact: Phone Bend Ranger District at 503-388-5664, or write Deschutes National Forest, 1230 NE Third, Bend, OR 97701.

Location: From Bend, travel 15 miles south on US 97, then 15 miles southwest on County Route 42 to the campground.

Trip note: This campground is set along Fall River. Fishing is restricted to artificials only. Check regulations for other restrictions.

PRINGLE FALLS
Site **97**

Campsites, facilities: There are seven sites for tents, trailers or motorhomes up to 22 feet long. Picnic tables and firegrills are provided, and vault toilets are available. There is no piped water. Pets are permitted.

Reservations, fee: No reservations necessary; no fee. Open April to October.

Who to contact: Phone Bend Ranger District at 503-388-5664, or write Deschutes National Forest, 1230 NE Third, Bend, OR 97701.

Location: From the town of La Pine, travel 2 1/2 miles northeast on US 97, then seven miles west on County Route 43. The camp is about 1/2 mile northeast on Forest Service Road 4360.

Trip note: This campground is set along the Deschutes River fairly close to Pringle Falls. It is a popular canoe launching point.

Site 98   LAPINE STATE PARK

Campsites, facilities: There are 145 sites for trailers or motorhomes of any length. Electricity, piped water, sewer hookups and picnic tables are provided. Flush toilets, sanitary services, showers, firewood and laundromat are available. Some facilities are wheelchair accessible. Pets are permitted.

Reservations, fee: No reservations necessary; $8 fee per night. Open mid-April to late-October.

Who to contact: Phone at 503-536-2428, or write at P.O. Box 5309, Bend, OR 97708.

Location: From the town of La Pine, travel eight miles north on US 97, then go three miles west on the entrance road to the park.

Trip note: This state park is set along the banks of the Deschutes River. Trout fishing and canoeing possibilities are very good.

Site 99   SWAMP WELLS HORSE CAMP

Campsites, facilities: There are five primitive sites for tents, trailers or motorhomes up to 22 feet long. Picnic tables and firegrills are provided, and firewood and vault toilets are available. There is no piped water. Pets are permitted.

Reservations, fee: No reservations necessary; no fee. Open April to late-November.

Who to contact: Phone Fort Rock Ranger District at 503-388-5674, or write Deschutes National Forest, 1230 NE Third Street, Bend, OR 97701.

Location: From Bend, travel 1 1/2 miles south on US 97, then six miles east on Forest Service Road 18. The camp is five miles south on Forest Service Road 1810, then three miles southeast on 1816. You'll be traveling on a dirt road that is well marked.

Trip note: After looking at the zone map, this campground may appear to be quite remote, but it is in an area that has been heavily logged. It is a good place for horseback riding and the trails that go south re-enter the forested areas. Nearby are the Arnold Ice Caves, a system of lava tubes that are fun to explore. A Forest Service map details trail options.

Site 100   BIG RIVER

Campsites, facilities: There are two tent sites and 13 sites for tents, trailers or motorhomes up to 22 feet long. Picnic tables and firegrills are provided. Piped water and vault toilets are available. Pets are permitted. Boat docks and launching facilities are nearby.

Reservations, fee: No reservations necessary; no fee. Open April to October.

Who to contact: Phone Bend Ranger District at 503-388-5664, or write Deschutes National Forest, 1230 NE Third, Bend, OR 97701.

Location: From Bend, go 16 1/2 miles south on US 97, then five miles southwest on County Route 42.

Trip note: This is a nice spot along the banks of the Deschutes River in a nice location. Rafting, fishing and boats with motors are permitted. Access is easy.

Site 101 ALLEN'S RIVERVIEW TRAILER PARK

Campsites, facilities: There are 20 sites for tents, trailers or motorhomes of any length. Electricity, piped water, sewer hookups and picnic tables are provided. Flush toilets, bottled gas, showers, firewood, a recreation hall and laundromat are available. Pets are permitted.

Reservations, fee: Reservations accepted; $9 fee per night. Open all year.

Who to contact: Phone at 503-536-2382, or write at 52731 Huntington Road, La Pine, OR 97739.

Location: Travel 2 1/2 miles north of La Pine on US 97, then one mile west at Wickiup Junction. The camp is one mile north on Huntington Road.

Trip note: This campground is set along the bank of the Little Deschutes River. It is missed by a lot of highway travelers; they just plain don't know about it.

Site 102 HIGHLANDER MOTEL & TRAILER PARK

Campsites, facilities: There are 20 drive-through sites for trailers or motorhomes up to 35 feet long. Electricity, piped water and sewer hookups are provided. Flush toilets, bottled gas, sanitary services, showers, a store, a cafe and ice are available. Laundromat is located within one mile. Pets and motorbikes are permitted.

Reservations, fee: Reservations accepted; $6 fee per night. MasterCard and Visa accepted. Open all year.

Who to contact: Phone at 503-536-2131, or write at P.O. Box 322, La Pine, OR 97739.

Location: This campground is located in the town of La Pine at the north edge of town.

Trip note: This campground is near the Little Deschutes River. A golf course and tennis courts are nearby.

Site 103 FAR-E-NUF RV PARK

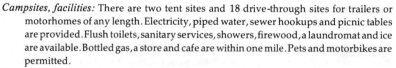

Campsites, facilities: There are two tent sites and 18 drive-through sites for trailers or motorhomes of any length. Electricity, piped water, sewer hookups and picnic tables are provided. Flush toilets, sanitary services, showers, firewood, a laundromat and ice are available. Bottled gas, a store and cafe are within one mile. Pets and motorbikes are permitted.

Reservations, fee: Reservations accepted; $9 fee per night. Open April to mid-October.

Who to contact: Phone at 503-536-2265, or write at 52158 Elderberry Lane, La Pine, OR 97739.

Location: From La Pine, go 2 1/2 miles north on US 97, then 2 1/2 miles west at Wickiup Junction. The camp is 1/2 mile south on Pine Forest and 400 yards east on Wright Avenue.

Trip note: So you thought you came far enough, eh? If you want a spot in a privately-run motorhome park near the bank of the Little Deschutes River, you found it.

Site **104** MCKAY CROSSING

Campsites, facilities: There are 10 sites for tents, trailers or motorhomes up to 22 feet long. Picnic tables and firegrills are provided, and vault toilets are available. There is no piped water. Pets are permitted.

Reservations, fee: No reservations necessary; no fee. Open June to late-October.

Who to contact: Phone Fort Rock Ranger District at 503-388-5674, or write Deschutes National Forest, 1230 NE Third Street, Bend, OR 97701.

Location: From the town of La Pine, travel five miles north on US 97, then three miles southeast on County Route 21. The camp is two miles east on Forest Service Road 2120.

Trip note: This campground is set along the bank of Paulina Creek. A nearby trail travels east for six miles to Paulina Lake (also reachable by car, see campsite 105).

Site **105** PAULINA LAKE

Campsites, facilities: There are 71 sites for trailers or motorhomes up to 30 feet long. Picnic tables and firegrills are provided, and piped water, flush toilets, showers and a laundromat are located within five miles. No piped water is available. Pets are permitted. Boat docks, launching facilities and rentals are nearby.

Reservations, fee: No reservations necessary; $6 fee per night. Open late-May to late-October.

Who to contact: Phone Fort Rock Ranger District at 503-388-5674, or write Deschutes National Forest, 1230 NE Third Street, Bend, OR 97701.

Location: Travel five miles north of La Pine on US 97, then go 13 miles east on County Route 21.

Trip note: This campground is set along the south shore of Paulina Lake, at 6300 feet elevation. The recreation options here include boating, sailing, fishing and hiking. Nearby trails provide access to the remains of volcanic activity, including craters and obsidian flows.

Site **106** CHIEF PAULINA HORSE CAMP

Campsites, facilities: There are 14 sites for tents, trailers or motorhomes up to 30 feet long. Picnic tables and firegrills are provided, and piped water and vault toilets are available. Pets are permitted. Boat docks and rentals are nearby.

Reservations, fee: Reservations required; fee depending on size of group. Open late-May to late-October.

Who to contact: Phone Fort Rock Ranger District at 503-388-5674, or write Deschutes National Forest, 1230 NE Third Street, Bend, OR 97701.

Location: From La Pine, travel five miles north on US 97, then go 15 miles east on County Route 21.

Trip note: This campground is set near the south shore of Paulina Lake. Horse trails and a vista point are nearby. See the trip note to campsite 105 for additional recreation information.

LITTLE CRATER
Site **107**   ▲

Campsites, facilities: There are 51 sites for tents, trailers or motorhomes up to 30 feet long. Picnic tables and firegrills are provided, and piped water and vault toilets are available. Pets are permitted. Boat docks, launching facilities and rentals are available nearby.

Reservations, fee: No reservations necessary; $6 fee per night. Open late-May to late-October.

Who to contact: Phone Fort Rock Ranger District at 503-386-5674, or write Deschutes National Forest, 1230 NE Third Street, Bend, OR 97701.

Location: From the town of La Pine, travel five miles north on US 97, then 15 miles east on County Route 21.

Trip note: This campground is set along the east shore of Paulina Lake, near Newberry Crater. See the trip note to campsite 105 for additional recreation information.

NORTH COVE
Site **108**   ▲

Campsites, facilities: There are 66 tent sites. Piped water and picnic tables are provided. Firewood is available. Showers and laundromat are located within five miles. Pets are permitted. Boat docks, launching facilities and rentals are nearby.

Reservations, fee: No reservations necessary; $4 fee per night. Open mid-May to late-October.

Who to contact: Phone Fort Rock Ranger District at 503-388-5674, or write Deschutes National Forest, 1230 NE Third Street, Bend, OR 97701.

Location: Go nine miles north of La Pine on US 97, then go 13 miles east on County Route 21. Park and hike 1 1/2 miles to campground on north shore of Paulina Lake.

Trip note: See the trip note to campsite 105 for additional recreation information.

WARM SPRINGS
Site **109**   🌲

Campsites, facilities: There are nine tent sites. Picnic tables are provided. Firewood is available. A laundromat is located within five miles. No piped water is available. Pets are permitted. Boat docks, launching facilities and rentals are nearby.

Reservations, fee: No reservations necessary; no fee. Open mid-May to late-October.

Who to contact: Phone Fort Rock Ranger District at 503-388-5674, or write Deschutes National Forest, 1230 NE Third Street, Bend, OR 97701.

Location: From the town of La Pine, travel five miles north on US 97, then 16 miles east on County Route 21. Park and hike 1/2 mile to the campground on the northeast shore of Paulina Lake.

Trip note: See the trip note to campsite 105 for additional recreation information about Paulina Lake.

CINDER HILL
Site **110**   ▲

Campsites, facilities: There are 109 sites for tents, trailers or motorhomes up to 30 feet long. Picnic tables and firegrills are provided, and piped water and vault toilets are available. Pets are permitted. Boat docks, launching facilities and rentals are nearby.

Reservations, fee: No reservations necessary; $6 fee per night. Open late-May to late-October.

Who to contact: Phone Fort Rock Ranger District at 503-388-5674, or write Deschutes National Forest, 1230 NE Third Street, Bend, OR 97701.

Location: From the town of La Pine, travel five miles north on US 97, then 18 miles east on County Route 21.

Trip note: This campground is set along the northeast shore of East Lake, elevation 6400 feet. Boating, fishing and hiking are among the recreation options here.

EAST LAKE
Site **111**

Campsites, facilities: There are 29 sites for tents, trailers or motorhomes up to 30 feet long. Picnic tables and firegrills are provided, and piped water and vault toilets are available. Pets are permitted. Boat docks, launching facilities and rentals are nearby.

Reservations, fee: No reservations necessary; $6 fee per night. Open late-May to late-October.

Who to contact: Phone Fort Rock Ranger District at 503-388-5674, or write Deschutes National Forest, 1230 NE Third Street, Bend, OR 97701.

Location: From the town of La Pine, travel five miles north on US 97, then 17 miles east on County Route 21.

Trip note: This campground is set along the south shore of East Lake. Boating and fishing are popular here, and hiking trails provide access to signs of former volcanic activity in the area.

HOT SPRINGS
Site **112**

Campsites, facilities: There are 43 sites for tents, trailers or motorhomes up to 30 feet long. Picnic tables and firegrills are provided, and piped water, firewood and vault toilets are available. Pets are permitted. Boat docks, launching facilities and rentals are nearby.

Reservations, fee: No reservations necessary; $6 fee per night. Open late-May to late-October.

Who to contact: Phone Fort Rock Ranger District at 503-388-5674, or write Deschutes National Forest, 1230 NE Third Street, Bend, OR 97701.

Location: Travel five miles north of La Pine on US 97, then 17 1/2 miles east on County Route 21.

Trip note: This campground is set along the south shore of East Lake. See the trip note to campsite 111 for additional recreation information.

EAST LAKE RESORT
& RV PARK
Site **113**

Campsites, facilities: There are 10 tent sites and 38 drive-through sites for trailers or motorhomes of any length. Electricity, piped water, sewer hookups and picnic tables are provided. Flush toilets, bottled gas, sanitary services, showers, firewood, a store, a cafe, laundromat, ice and playground are available. Pets and motorbikes are permitted. Boat launching facilities and rentals are nearby.

Reservations, fee: Reservations accepted; $10 fee per night. Open mid-May to mid-October.

Who to contact: Phone at 503-536-2230, or write at P.O. Box 95, La Pine, OR 97739.

Location: From the town of La Pine, travel six miles north on US 97, then 18 miles east on East Lake/Paulina Lake Road.

Trip note: This resort is set along the east shore of East Lake.

CHINA HAT
Site 114

Campsites, facilities: There are 14 sites for tents, trailers or motorhomes up to 30 feet long. Picnic tables and firegrills are provided, and vault toilets are available There is no piped water. Pets are permitted.

Reservations, fee: No reservations necessary; no fee. Open May to late-October.

Who to contact: Phone Fort Rock Ranger District at 503-388-5674, or write Deschutes National Forest, 1230 NE Third Street, Bend, OR 97701.

Location: From La Pine, drive east on Forest Service Road 22 for about 30 miles, then north on Forest Service Road 18.

Trip note: This remote campground is set at 5100 feet elevation. Hunters use it as a base camp in the fall. A rugged and primitive setting.

CABIN LAKE
Site 115

Campsites, facilities: There are 14 sites for tents, trailers or motorhomes up to 30 feet long. Picnic tables and firegrills are provided, and vault toilets are available. There is no piped water. Pets are permitted.

Reservations, fee: No reservations necessary; no fee. Open mid-May to late-October.

Who to contact: Phone Fort Rock Ranger District at 503-388-5674, or write Deschutes National Forest, 1230 NE Third Street, Bend, OR 97701.

Location: From La Pine drive about 30 miles east on Forest Service Road 22, then south on Forest Service Road 18 for six miles.

Trip note: This remote campground is set at 4500 feet elevation. Adjacent to the campground is an 80-year old bird blind; a great place to watch birds.

LITTLE DESCHUTES
Site 116

Campsites, facilities: There are six sites for tents, trailers or motorhomes up to 22 feet long. Picnic tables and firegrills are provided, and piped water, firewood and vault toilets are available. Pets are permitted.

Reservations, fee: No reservations necessary; no fee. Open May to late-September.

Who to contact: Phone the Crescent Ranger District at 503-433-2234, or write Deschutes National Forest, P.O. Box 208, Crescent, OR 97733.

Location: Travel 10 miles south of Crescent on US 97, then four miles northwest on Highway 58.

Trip note: This is a good spot for trout fishing. It is small, set along the stream, with piped water available. That makes it a good spot for camping.

CORRAL SPRING
Site **117**

Campsites, facilities: There are seven sites for tents, trailers, or motorhomes up to 22 feet long. Picnic tables and firegrills are provided, and firewood and vault toilets are available. There is no piped water. A store, cafe, laundromat and ice are available within five miles. Pets are permitted.

Reservations, fee: No reservations necessary; no fee. Open mid-May to late October.

Who to contact: Phone Chemult Ranger Station at 503-365-2229, or write at Winema National Forest, P.O. Box 150, Chemult, OR 97731.

Location: From the town of Chemult, travel 2 1/2 miles north on US 97, then go two miles west on Forest Service Road 9774.

Trip note: This campground is set next to Corral Spring. Not much out here and that's just what some people who have been cruising Highway 97 want.

DIGIT POINT
Site **118**

Campsites, facilities: There are 64 sites for tents, trailers or motorhomes up to 30 feet long. Picnic tables and firegrills are provided, and piped water, firewood, a sanitary disposal station and vault toilets are available. Pets are permitted. Boat docks and launching facilities are available nearby.

Reservations, fee: No reservations necessary; $5 fee per night. Open mid-June to October.

Who to contact: Phone Chemult Ranger Station at 503-365-2229, or write to Winema National Forest, P.O. Box 150, Chemult, OR 97731.

Location: From the town of Chemult, travel one mile north on US 97 and then 12 miles west on Forest Service Road 2731.

Trip note: This campground is set along the shore of Miller Lake, a popular spot for boating, fishing, swimming and waterskiing. Nearby trails provide access to backcountry lakes and the Pacific Crest Trail passes one mile from camp.

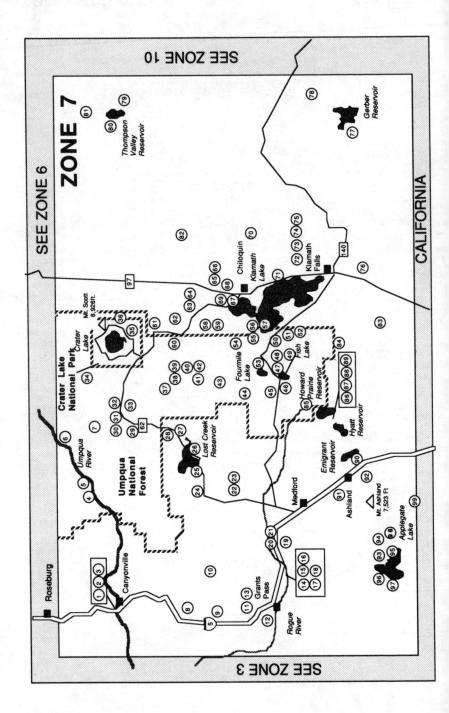

CRATER LAKE

Site 1   STANTON PARK

Campsites, facilities: There are 20 tent sites and 20 sites for trailers or motorhomes up to 30 feet long. Electricity, piped water, sewer hookups and picnic tables are provided. Flush toilets, showers and a playground are available. Bottled gas, sanitary disposal services, a store, cafe, laundromat and ice are located within one mile. Pets and motorbikes are permitted. A boat launch is nearby.

Reservations, fee: No reservations necessary; $9 fee per night. Open all year.

Who to contact: Phone at 503-839-4483, or write at Canyonville, OR 97417.

Location: Take exit 99 off I-5 in Canyonville (follow the sign), then drive one mile north on the frontage road to the campground.

Trip note: This campground is set along the banks of the South Umpqua River. It is an all-season spot, with a good beach for swimming in the summer, good steelhead fishing in the winter, and wild grape picking in the fall.

Site 2   EVERGREEN MOTEL & TRAILER PARK

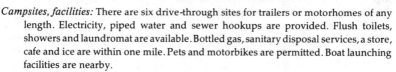

Campsites, facilities: There are six drive-through sites for trailers or motorhomes of any length. Electricity, piped water and sewer hookups are provided. Flush toilets, showers and laundromat are available. Bottled gas, sanitary disposal services, a store, cafe and ice are within one mile. Pets and motorbikes are permitted. Boat launching facilities are nearby.

Reservations, fee: Reservations accepted; $7 fee per night. MasterCard and Visa accepted. Open all year.

Who to contact: Phone at 503-839-6304, or write at HC 2 No. 8, Canyonville, OR 97417.

Location: In Canyonville, take exit 99 off I-5 and drive about 400 yards south.

Trip note: This motorhome park is set near the South Umpqua River, a good layover for cruisers touring Interstate 5. Nearby recreation options include bike paths and tennis courts.

Site 3   SURPRISE VALLEY MOBILE VILLAGE

Campsites, facilities: There are 15 tent sites and 25 drive-through sites for trailers or motorhomes of any length. Electricity, piped water, sewer hookups and picnic tables are provided. Flush toilets, showers and a laundromat are available. Pets are permitted.

Reservations, fee: No reservations necessary; $10 fee per night. Open all year.

Who to contact: Phone at 503-839-8181, or write at P.O. Box 909, Canyonville, OR 97417.

Location: From Canyonville, go three miles north on I-5 to exit 102, then one mile east on Gazley Road.

Trip note: This motorhome park is set near the South Umpqua River. Nearby recreation options include bike paths. One of three camps in the area. For a more remote setting, campsites 4-6 are the answer.

DUMONT CREEK
Site **4**

Campsites, facilities: There are five sites for tents, trailers or motorhomes up to 16 feet long. Picnic tables and firegrills are provided, and vault toilets are available. There is no piped water. Pets are permitted.

Reservations, fee: No reservations necessary; no fee. Open late-May to late-October.

Who to contact: Phone Tiller Ranger District at 503-825-3201, or write at Route 2, Box 1, Tiller, OR 97484.

Location: Go 23 miles north of Shady Cove on Highway 227, then six miles northeast on County Route 46. The camp is 5 1/2 miles northeast on Forest Service Road 28.

Trip note: This campground is set along the banks of the South Umpqua River. Quiet, primitive and remote.

BOULDER CREEK
Site **5**

Campsites, facilities: There are eight sites for tents, trailers or motorhomes up to 15 feet long. Picnic tables and firegrills are provided, and vault toilets are available. There is no piped water. Pets are permitted.

Reservations, fee: No reservations necessary; no fee. Open late-May to late-October.

Who to contact: Phone Tiller Ranger District at 503-825-3201, or write at Route 2, Box 1, Tiller, OR 97484.

Location: From Shady Cove, go 23 miles north on Highway 227, turn east on County Route 46 for six miles and the camp is seven miles northeast on Forest Service Road 28.

Trip note: This campground is set along the banks of the South Umpqua River.

CAMP COMFORT
Site **6**

Campsites, facilities: There are eight sites for tents, trailers or motorhomes up to 15 feet long. Picnic tables and firegrills are provided, and vault toilets are available. There is no piped water. Pets are permitted.

Reservations, fee: No reservations necessary; no fee. Open late-May to late-October.

Who to contact: Phone Tiller Ranger District at 503-825-3201, or write at Route 2, Box 1, Tiller, OR 97484.

Location: From Shady Cove, travel 23 miles north on Highway 227, turn east on County Route 46 for six miles and the camp is seven miles northeast on Forest Service Road 28.

Trip note: This campground is set along the banks of the South Umpqua River, deep in the Umpqua National Forest. Trailheads providing access to the Rogue-Umpqua Divide

Wilderness can be found at the ends of Forest Service Roads west of camp.

COVER
Site **7**

Campsites, facilities: There are seven sites for tents, trailers or motorhomes up to 16 feet long. Picnic tables and firegrills are provided, and vault toilets are available. There is no piped water. Pets are permitted.

Reservations, fee: No reservations necessary; no fee. Open late-May to late-October.

Who to contact: Phone Tiller Ranger District at 503-825-3201, or write at Route 2, Box 1, Tiller, OR 97484.

Location: From Canyonville, drive east on Highway 227 to Tiller. From Tiller, go east on Highway 227 for 300 yards, then northeast on County Route 46 for six miles. The camp is 12 miles east on Forest Service Road 29.

Trip note: This campground is set along the banks of Jackson Creek. If you want quiet, you came to the right place. Just about nobody knows about this one.

MEADOW WOOD RV
RESORT & CAMPGROUND
Site **8**

Campsites, facilities: There are 20 tent sites and 63 drive-through sites for trailers or motorhomes of any length. Electricity, piped water and picnic tables are provided. Flush toilets, bottled gas, sanitary disposal services, showers, firewood, recreation hall, a store, laundromat, ice, playground and swimming pool are available. Pets and motorbikes are permitted.

Reservations, fee: Reservations accepted; $12 fee per night. MasterCard and Visa accepted. Open March to late-October.

Who to contact: Phone at 503-832-2959, or write at 862 Autumn Lane, Glendale, OR 97442.

Location: Take exit 86 off I-5 in Glendale, then drive three miles south on the frontage road and about 400 yards east on Barton Road. The camp is one mile south.

Trip note: A good option for motorhome campers looking for a spot along Interstate 5. All amenities provided.

JOE CREEK WATERFALL
RV PARK
Site **9**

Campsites, facilities: There are 21 tent sites and 28 drive-through sites for trailers or motorhomes of any length. Electricity, piped water, sewer hookups and picnic tables are provided. Flush toilets, bottled gas, sanitary disposal services, showers, firewood, recreation hall, a store, cafe, laundromat and ice are available. Pets and motorbikes are permitted.

Reservations, fee: Reservations accepted; $10 fee per night. MasterCard and Visa accepted. Open all year.

Who to contact: Phone at 503-474-0250, or write at P.O. Box 5510, Grants pass, OR 97527.

Location: Go 10 miles north on I-5 from Grants Pass. Take exit 66 and go 400 yards north on Jump. Follow the signs to the campground.

Trip note: This wooded campground is set along Joe Creek. Hiking trails and bike paths are nearby. Just far enough out of Grants Pass to provide a feeling of separation.

Site 10
ELDERBERRY FLAT

Campsites, facilities: There are 10 primitive tent sites. Picnic tables and firegrills are provided, and firewood and pit toilets are available. There is no piped water. Pets are permitted.

Reservations, fee: No reservations necessary; no fee. Open late-May to late-October.

Who to contact: Phone the Bureau of Land Management at 503-776-3744, or write at 3040 Biddle Road, Medford, OR 97501.

Location: From the town of Gold Hill, take Highway 234 northeast to Meadows, then go 12 miles northwest on Meadows. From there, go eight miles north on Fork Evans Road to the campground.

Trip note: This campground is set along the banks of Evans Creek. Virtually unknown, yet about a 30-minute drive from Interstate 5.

Site 11
GRANTS PASS OVERNITERS

Campsites, facilities: There are 40 tent sites and 63 drive-through sites for trailers or motorhomes of any length. Electricity, piped water, sewer hookups and picnic tables are provided. Flush toilets, bottled gas, showers, laundromat, ice and a swimming pool are available. A store is located within one mile. Pets and motorbikes are permitted.

Reservations, fee: Reservations accepted; $12 fee per night. Open all year.

Who to contact: Phone at 503-479-7289, or write at 5941 Highland, Grants Pass, OR 97526.

Location: From Grants Pass, go three miles north on I-5 to exit 61E, then go north on the frontage road to the park.

Trip note: This wooded park is set in a rural area, just outside Grants Pass, one of several in the area.

Site 12
BEND O' THE RIVER RV PARK

Campsites, facilities: There are five tent sites and 20 drive-through sites for trailers or motorhomes of any length. Electricity, piped water, sewer hookups and picnic tables are provided. Flush toilets, sanitary disposal services, showers, firewood, a store, cafe, laundromat and ice are available. Pets and motorbikes are permitted.

Reservations, fee: Reservations accepted; $9 fee per night. Open all year.

Who to contact: Phone at 503-479-2547, or write at 7501 Lower River, Grants Pass, OR 97526.

Location: Take exit 58 off I-5 in Grant's Pass, then go south on 6th Street to G Street. The park is located seven miles west on Upper River Road.

Trip note: This campground is set along the banks of the Rogue River. A pretty spot, it is far enough out of Grants Pass to provide its own unique feel, apart from the city.

Site 13
ROGUE VALLEY OVERNITERS

Campsites, facilities: There are two tent sites and 26 drive-through sites for trailers or motorhomes of any length. Electricity, piped water and sewer hookups are provided. Flush toilets, sanitary disposal services, showers and laundromat are available. Bottled gas, a store, cafe and ice are available within one mile. Pets and motorbikes are permitted.

Reservations, fee: Reservations accepted; $11 fee per night. Open all year.

Who to contact: Phone at 503-479-2208, or write at 1806 Northwest 6th Street, Grants Pass, OR 97526.

Location: Take exit 58 off I-5 in Grants Pass, then follow 6th Street south for about 400 yards.

Trip note: This park is just off the freeway in Grants Pass, the jump-off point for trips down the Rogue River. This part of Oregon can surprise visitors with the summer heat in late June and early July.

Site 14   CIRCLE W CAMPGROUND

Campsites, facilities: There are seven tent sites and 25 drive-through sites for trailers or motorhomes of any length. Electricity, piped water, sewer hookups and picnic tables are provided. Flush toilets, sanitary disposal services, showers, a store, laundromat, ice and playground are available. Bottled gas and a cafe are located within one mile. Pets are permitted. Boat docks are nearby.

Reservations, fee: Reservations accepted; $9 fee per night. Open mid-March to mid-November.

Who to contact: Phone at 503-582-1686, or write at 8110 Rogue River, Grants Pass, OR 97527.

Location: Take the Rogue River exit off I-5, then go one mile west on Highway 99.

Trip note: This campground is set along the Rogue River. Nearby recreation options include chartered boat trips down the Rogue River, a golf course and tennis courts.

Site 15   HAVE A NICE DAY CAMPGROUND

Campsites, facilities: There are 16 tent sites and 30 drive-through sites for trailers or motorhomes of any length. Electricity, piped water, sewer hookups and picnic tables are provided. Flush toilets, bottled gas, sanitary disposal services, showers, laundromat, ice and playground are available. A store and cafe are located within one mile. Pets and motorbikes are permitted. Boat docks and launching facilities are nearby.

Reservations, fee: Reservations accepted; $10 fee per night. Open all year with limited winter facilities.

Who to contact: Phone at 503-582-1421, or write at 7275 Rogue River Highway, Grants pass, OR 97527.

Location: Take exit 48 off I-5, go across the river, then travel 1 1/2 miles west on Highway 99.

Trip note: This campground is set along the Rogue River. All the amenities available.

Site 16   LESCLARE RV PARK & CAMPGROUND

Campsites, facilities: There are 10 tent sites and 38 sites for trailers or motorhomes of any length. Electricity, piped water, sewer hookups and picnic tables are provided. Flush toilets, sanitary disposal services, showers, a store, laundromat and ice are available.

A cafe is located within one mile. Pets are permitted.

Reservations, fee: Reservations accepted; $11 fee per night. MasterCard and Visa accepted. Open all year.

Who to contact: Phone at 503-479-0046, or write at 2956 Rogue River, Grants pass, OR 97527.

Location: In Grants Pass, go south on 6th Street to Highway 99, then go two miles southeast on 99.

Trip note: This wooded campground is set along the Rogue River. Jet boats offer chartered trips down the Rogue. A golf course is nearby.

Site 17   RIVERFRONT TRAILER PARK

Campsites, facilities: There is one tent site and 20 sites for trailers or motorhomes of any length. Electricity, piped water, sewer hookups and picnic tables are provided. Flush toilets, sanitary disposal services, showers, a laundromat and ice are available. Bottled gas, a store and cafe are located within one mile. Pets and motorbikes are permitted. Boat docks and launching facilities are nearby.

Reservations, fee: Reservations accepted; $10 fee per night. Open all year.

Who to contact: Phone at 503-582-0985, or write at 7060 Rogue River, Grants Pass, OR 97527.

Location: From Rogue River, take Highway 99 two miles west to the park.

Trip note: This campground is set along the Rogue River, near the same recreation opportunities as campsite 16.

Site 18   WHISPERING PINES RV PARK

Campsites, facilities: There are five tent sites and 11 sites for trailers or motorhomes up to 35 feet long. Electricity, piped water, sewer hookups and picnic tables are provided. Flush toilets, showers and laundromat are available. Bottled gas, sanitary disposal services, a store, cafe and ice are located within one mile. Pets and motorbikes are permitted. Boat docks are nearby.

Reservations, fee: Reservations accepted; $9 fee per night. Open all year.

Who to contact: Phone at 503-582-4020, or write at Box 49, Rogue River, OR 97537.

Location: Take exit 48 off I-5 in Rogue River, then go one block south and one block west.

Trip note: This campground is set along the Rogue River, and nearby recreation options include chartered boat trips down the Rogue River, a golf course, bike paths and tennis courts.

Site 19   VALLEY OF THE ROGUE STATE PARK

Campsites, facilities: There are 77 tent sites and 97 sites for trailers or motorhomes up to 40 feet long. Electricity, piped water, sewer hookups and picnic tables are provided. Flush toilets, sanitary disposal services, showers, firewood, a laundromat, a meeting hall and group campsites are available. A cafe is located within one mile. Some facilities are wheelchair accessible. Pets are permitted. Boat launching facilities are nearby.

Reservations, fee: No reservations necessary; $8 fee per night. Open all year with limited winter facilities.

Who to contact: Phone at 503-582-1118, or write at Rogue River, OR 97537.

Location: From Grants Pass, travel 12 miles east on I-5 to the turn-off for the park.

Trip note: This state park is set along the banks of the Rogue River. Recreation options include swimming and boating. A popular spot, often filled near capacity during summer months.

Site 20   KOA GOLD'N ROGUE

Campsites, facilities: There are 30 tent sites and 45 drive-through sites for trailers or motorhomes of any length. Electricity, piped water, sewer hookups and picnic tables are provided. Flush toilets, bottled gas, sanitary disposal services, showers, firewood, a recreation hall, a store, laundromat, ice, playground and swimming pool are available. A cafe is located within one mile. Pets and motorbikes are permitted. Boat launching facilities are nearby.

Reservations, fee: Reservations accepted; $13 fee per night. MasterCard and Visa accepted. Open early-January to late-October.

Who to contact: Phone at 503-855-7710, or write at P.O. Box 320, Gold Hill, OR 97525.

Location: In Gold Hill off I-5, take South Gold Hill exit and go 400 yards to Blackwell Road. The camp is about another 400 yards south.

Trip note: This campground is set along the banks of the Rogue River, near a golf course, bike paths, tennis courts and the Oregon Vortex. One of many camps located between Gold Hill and Grants Pass.

Site 21   LAZY ACRES RV

Campsites, facilities: There are 20 drive-through sites for trailers or motorhomes of any length. Electricity, piped water, sewer hookups and picnic tables are provided. Flush toilets, bottled gas, ice and a playground are available. A store, cafe and laundromat are located within one mile. Pets and motorbikes are permitted. Boat docks are nearby.

Reservations, fee: No reservations necessary; $10 fee per night. MasterCard and Visa accepted. Open all year.

Who to contact: Phone at 503-855-7000, or write at 1550 2nd Ave, Gold Hill, OR 97525.

Location: In Gold Hill, take the South Gold Hill exit and go one mile west across the river.

Trip note: This wooded campground is set along the Rogue River, and offers the same recreation options as campsite 20.

Site 22   FLY-CASTERS CAMPGROUND & TRAILER PARK

Campsites, facilities: There are 30 sites for trailers or motorhomes of any length. Electricity, piped water, sewer hookups and picnic tables are provided. Flush toilets, bottled gas, showers and a laundromat are available. A store, cafe and ice are located within one mile. Pets are permitted. Boat launching facilities are nearby.

Reservations, fee: Reservations accepted; $8 fee per night. Open all year.

Who to contact: Phone at 503-878-2749, or write at P.O. Box 1170, Shady Cove, OR 97539.

Location: From Medford, drive north on Highway 62 for 23 miles and you will see the camp along the highway. It is set 2 3/4 miles south of the junction of Highway 62 and 227.

Trip note: This is a good base camp for motorhome drivers that want to fish or hike. It is set along the banks of the Rogue River. The county park in Shady Cove offers picnic facilities and a boat ramp. Lost Creek Lake is about a 15-minute drive to the northeast.

Site 23   SHADY TRAILS RV PARK & CAMPGROUND

Campsites, facilities: There are 27 tent sites and 48 drive-through sites for trailers or motorhomes of any length. Electricity, piped water, sewer hookups and picnic tables are provided. Flush toilets, bottled gas, sanitary disposal services, showers, a store, ice and playground are available. A cafe is located within one mile. Pets and motorbikes are permitted. Boat launching facilities are nearby.

Reservations, fee: Reservations accepted; $10 fee per night. Open all year.

Who to contact: Phone at 503-878-2206, or write at Box 1299, Shady Cove, OR 97539.

Location: From Medford, drive 23 miles north on Highway 62.

Trip note: This park is along the banks of the Rogue River.

Site 24   BOB'S RV CAMPGROUND

Campsites, facilities: There are 10 tent sites and 37 drive-through sites for trailers or motorhomes of any length. Electricity, piped water, sewer hookups and picnic tables are provided. Flush toilets, bottled gas, sanitary disposal services, showers, a laundromat, ice and playground are available. A store and cafe are located within one mile. Pets and motorbikes are permitted. Boat docks and launching facilities are nearby.

Reservations, fee: Reservations accepted; $9 fee per night. Open all year.

Who to contact: Phone at 503-878-2400, or write at 27301 Highway 62, Trail, OR 97541.

Location: From Medford, drive north on Highway 62. From the junction of Highways 62 and 227, continue east for three miles to the campground.

Trip note: This campground is set along the Rogue River about six miles from Lost Creek Lake, where boat ramps and picnic areas are available for day-use.

Site 25   ROGUE ELK COUNTY PARK

Campsites, facilities: There are 20 sites for trailers or motorhomes up to 15 feet long. Picnic tables and firegrills are provided, and piped water and vault toilets are available. Pets are permitted.

Reservations, fee: No reservations necessary; $8 fee per night. Open July to late-October.

Who to contact: Phone at Jackson County Department of Parks and Recreation at 916-465-2241, or write at 10 South Oakdale, Medford, OR 97501.

Location: Drive 27 miles northeast of Medford on Highway 62 to the campground.

Trip note: This campground is set along the Rogue River about five miles from Lost Creek Lake. Boat ramps and picnic areas are available at the lake.

Site 26
JOSEPH STEWART
STATE PARK

Campsites, facilities: There are 50 tent sites and 151 sites for trailers or motorhomes up to 40 feet long. Electricity, sewer hookups and picnic tables are provided. Flush toilets, sanitary disposal services, showers, firewood and playground are available. Some facilities are wheelchair accessible. Pets are permitted. Boat launching facilities are nearby.

Reservations, fee: No reservations necessary; $7 fee per night. Open all year.

Who to contact: Phone at 503-560-3334, or write at 35251 Highway 62, Trail, OR 97541.

Location: from Medford, go 34 miles northeast on Highway 62.

Trip note: This state park is set along the shore of Lost Creek Lake, a reservoir with a marina, beach, and boat rentals. Eight miles of hiking trails and bike paths are available through the park. A nice spot that gets attention from Oregonians in the area, but is missed by most others.

Site 27
MILL CREEK

Campsites, facilities: There are eight sites for tents, trailers or motorhomes up to 22 feet long. Picnic tables and firegrills are provided, and vault toilets are available. There is no piped water. Pets are permitted.

Reservations, fee: No reservations necessary; no fee. Open all year.

Who to contact: Phone the Prospect Ranger Station at 503-560-3623, or write Rogue River National Forest at Prospect, OR 97536.

Location: From Medford, travel 37 miles northeast on Highway 62, then one mile east on Forest Service Road 30.

Trip note: This campground is set along the bank of Mill Creek about two miles from the Upper Rogue River. One in a series of remote, primitive camps near Highway 62 that is missed by out-of-towners.

Site 28
RIVER BRIDGE

Campsites, facilities: There are six sites for tents, trailers or motorhomes up to 22 feet long. Picnic tables and firegrills are provided, and vault toilets are available. There is no piped water. Pets are permitted.

Reservations, fee: No reservations necessary; no fee. Open late-May to early-September.

Who to contact: Phone the Prospect Ranger Station at 503-560-3623, or write Rogue River National Forest at Prospect, OR 97536.

Location: From Medford, travel 39 miles northeast on Highway 62, then one mile north on Forest Service Road 6210.

Trip note: This campground is set along the bank of the Upper Rogue River. The Upper Rogue River Trail passes camp and follows the river for many miles to the Pacific Crest Trail in Crater Lake National Park. Good spot to start the hike.

Site 29
NATURAL BRIDGE

Campsites, facilities: There are 21 sites for tents, trailers or motorhomes up to 22 feet long.

Picnic tables and firegrills are provided, and vault toilets are available. There is no piped water. Pets are permitted.

Reservations, fee: No reservations necessary; no fee. Open late-May to early-September.

Who to contact: Phone the Prospect Ranger Station at 503-560-3623, or write Rogue River National Forest at Prospect, OR 97536.

Location: From Medford, travel 45 miles north on Highway 62, then one mile west on Forest Service Road 300.

Trip note: The Upper Rogue River runs underground at this spot. The Upper Rogue River Trail passes camp and follows the river for many miles to the Pacific Crest Trail in Crater Lake National Park.

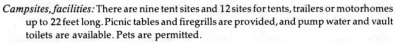

ABBOTT CREEK
Site 30

Campsites, facilities: There are nine tent sites and 12 sites for tents, trailers or motorhomes up to 22 feet long. Picnic tables and firegrills are provided, and pump water and vault toilets are available. Pets are permitted.

Reservations, fee: No reservations necessary; $3 fee per night. Open late-May to late-October.

Who to contact: Phone the Prospect Ranger Station at 503-560-3623, or write Rogue River National Forest at Prospect, OR 97536.

Location: From Medford, travel 42 miles northeast on Highway 62, then 3 1/2 miles northwest on Forest Service Road 68.

Trip Note: This campground is set at the confluence of Abbott and Woodruff Creeks about two miles from the Upper Rogue River. One of the few backwoods camps in the area that provides piped water.

UNION CREEK
Site 31

Campsites, facilities: There are 72 sites for tents, trailers or motorhomes up to 16 feet long. Picnic tables and firegrills are provided, and piped water and pit toilets are available. Pets are permitted.

Reservations, fee: No reservations necessary; $4 fee per night. Open late-May to early-September.

Who to contact: Phone the Prospect Ranger Station at 503-560-3623, or write Rogue River National Forest at Prospect, OR 97536.

Location: From Medford, travel 46 miles north of Prospect on Highway 62.

Trip note: This campground is a more developed than nearby campsites 27-29. It is set along the bank of Union Creek where it joins others to form the Upper Rogue River. The Upper Rogue River Trail passes near camp.

FAREWELL BEND
Site 32

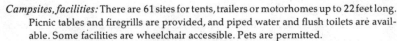

Campsites, facilities: There are 61 sites for tents, trailers or motorhomes up to 22 feet long. Picnic tables and firegrills are provided, and piped water and flush toilets are available. Some facilities are wheelchair accessible. Pets are permitted.

Reservations, fee: No reservations necessary; $6 fee per night. Open late-May to early-September.

Who to contact: Phone the Prospect Ranger Station at 503-560-3623, or write Rogue River

National Forest at Prospect, OR 97536.

Location: From Medford, travel 46 1/2 miles north on Highway 62.

Trip note: This campground is set along the bank of Upper Rogue River near the Rogue Gorge. The Upper Rogue River Trail passes near camp. It attracts a lot of campers who have visited Crater Lake.

Site 33   HUCKLEBERRY MOUNTAIN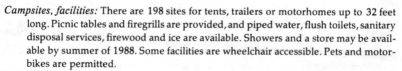

Campsites, facilities: There are 15 sites for tents, trailers or motorhomes up to 21 feet long. Picnic tables and firegrills are provided, and pump water and vault toilets are available. Pets are permitted.

Reservations, fee: No reservations necessary; no fee. Open July to late-October.

Who to contact: Phone the Prospect Ranger Station at 503-560-3623, or write Rogue River National Forest at Prospect, OR 97536.

Location: Travel 35 miles northeast of Medford to Prospect. From there continue 17 1/2 miles northeast of Prospect on Highway 62, then four miles south on Forest Service Road 60.

Trip note: This campground is set at 5400 feet elevation, about 15 miles from the entrance to Crater Lake National Park. It is a prime hideaway for people who have visited Crater Lake, just far enough off the highway to get missed by most travelers.

Site 34   HAMAKER

Campsites, facilities: There are 10 sites for tents, trailers or motorhomes up to 15 feet long. Picnic tables and firegrills are provided, and pumped water and vault toilets are available. Pets are permitted.

Reservations, fee: No reservations necessary; $4 fee per night. Open late-June to early-September.

Who to contact: Phone Prospect Ranger Station at 503-560-3623, or write at Rogue River National Forest, Prospect, OR 97536.

Location: From Medford, travel 47 miles northeast on Highway 62, then 11 miles north on Highway 230. Continue 600 yards east on Forest Service Road 6530.

Trip note: This campground is set at 4000 feet elevation along Hamaker Creek. The Upper Rogue River passes near camp. A prime little spot for Crater Lake visitors.

Site 35   MAZAMA

Campsites, facilities: There are 198 sites for tents, trailers or motorhomes up to 32 feet long. Picnic tables and firegrills are provided, and piped water, flush toilets, sanitary disposal services, firewood and ice are available. Showers and a store may be available by summer of 1988. Some facilities are wheelchair accessible. Pets and motorbikes are permitted.

Reservations, fee: No reservations necessary; $6 fee per night. Open early-July to late-September.

Who to contact: Phone Crater Lake National Park at 503-594-2511, or write at P.O. Box 7, Crater Lake, OR 97604.

Location: From Klamath Falls, go 22 miles north on US 97, then 30 miles northwest on Highway 62.

Trip note: This campground is set adjacent to the ranger station at Annie Springs. The Pacific Crest Trail passes near camp. The only trail access down to Crater Lake is at Cleetwood Cove. Some of the park facilities are open in the winter for cross-country skiing along the unplowed roadways. Winter access to the park is available only from the west on Highway 62 to Rim Village. One of two campgrounds at Crater Lake.

LOST CREEK
Site 36

Campsites, facilities: There are 12 sites for tents, trailers or small motorhomes. There is also one group site, available by reservation. Picnic tables and firegrills are provided, and piped water and flush toilets are available. Pets and motorbikes are permitted.

Reservations, fee: No reservations necessary; no fee. Open early-July to late-September.

Who to contact: Phone Crater Lake National Park at 503-594-2211, or write at P.O. Box 7, Crater Lake, OR 97604.

Location: From Klamath Falls, go 22 miles north on US 97, then 30 miles northwest on Highway 62 to Annie Springs junction. Travel around the lake on Rim Drive until the road to the Pinnacles, turn left and drive five miles to the campground.

Trip note: In good weather, this is a prime spot in Crater Lake National Park—you avoid most of the crowd, which is driving the rim road. This primitive campground is set near little Lost Creek, and the pinnacles, a series of craggy spires. The only trail access down to Crater Lake is at Cleetwood Cove. Some of the park facilities are open in the winter for cross-country skiing along the unplowed roadways. Winter access to the park is available only from the west on Highway 62 to Rim Village.

IMNAHA
Site 37

Campsites, facilities: There are four sites for tents, trailers or motorhomes up to 15 feet long. Picnic tables and firegrills are provided, and vault toilets are available. There is no piped water. Pets are permitted.

Reservations, fee: No reservations necessary; no fee. Open all year.

Who to contact: Phone Prospect Ranger Station at 503-865-3581, or write at Rogue River National Forest, Prospect, OR 97536.

Location: From Medford, travel 35 miles northeast on Highway 62 to Prospect, then 12 miles east on Forest Service Road 37 to the campground.

Trip note: This campground is set along Imnaha Creek. Trailheads at the ends of nearby Forest Service roads lead east into the Sky Lakes Wilderness. Good base camp for a wilderness trip.

SOUTH FORK
Site 38

Campsites, facilities: There are six sites for tents, trailers or motorhomes up to 15 feet long. Picnic tables and firegrills are provided, and vault toilets are available. There is no piped water. Pets are permitted.

Reservations, fee: No reservations necessary; no fee. Open all year.

Who to contact: Phone Prospect Ranger Station at 503-865-3581, or write at Rogue River National Forest, Prospect, OR 97536.

Location: From Medford, travel 15 miles north on Highway 62, then 32 miles east on Forest Service Road 34.

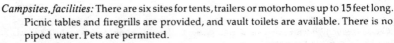

Trip note: This campground is set along the South Fork of the Rogue River. To the east, trails at the end of nearby Forest Service roads provide access to the Sky Lakes Wilderness. A map of Rogue River National Forest details all back roads, trails and waters.

BIG BEN
Site 39

Campsites, facilities: There are two sites for tents, trailers or motorhomes up to 15 feet long. Picnic tables and firegrills are provided, and vault toilets are available. There is no piped water. Pets are permitted.

Reservations, fee: No reservations necessary; no fee. Open all year.

Who to contact: Phone Prospect Ranger Station at 503-865-3581, or write at Rogue River National Forest, Prospect, OR 97536.

Location: From Medford, travel 15 miles northeast on Highway 62, then 33 miles east on Forest Service Road 34. Drive south one mile on Forest Service Road 37 to the campground.

Trip note: This is one of the tiniest official campgrounds in the Western U.S. Even then, it gets little use. It is set along Big Ben Creek near its confluence with the South Fork of the Rogue River. Nearby trails at the ends of nearby Forest Service Roads provide access to the Sky Lakes Wilderness to the east.

PARKER MEADOWS
Site 40

Campsites, facilities: There are eight sites for tents, trailers or motorhomes up to 15 feet long. Picnic tables and firegrills are provided and firewood, pumped water and vault toilets are available. Pets are permitted.

Reservations, fee: No reservations necessary; no fee. Open mid-June to late-September.

Who to contact: Phone Butte Falls Ranger Station at 503-865-3581, or write at P.O. Box 227, Butte Falls, OR 97522.

Location: From Medford, travel 14 miles northeast on Highway 62, then 18 miles east to Butte Falls. Go 10 miles southeast of Butte Falls on County Route 30, then 11 miles northeast on Forest Service Road 37.

Trip note: This campground is set at 5000 feet elevation along the bank of Parker Creek. Nearby at the ends of Forest Service roads are trailheads that provide access to the Sky Lakes Wilderness. A nice spot, complete with water.

SNOWSHOE
Site 41

Campsites, facilities: There are six sites for tents, trailers or motorhomes. Picnic tables and firegrills are provided, and pumped water and vault toilets are available. Pets are permitted.

Reservations, fee: No reservations necessary; no fee. Open all year.

Who to contact: Phone Butte Falls Ranger Station at 503-865-3581, or write at P.O. Box 227, Butte Falls, OR 97522.

Location: From Medford, travel 14 miles northeast on Highway 62, then 18 miles east to Butte Falls. Travel nine miles southeast of Butte Falls on County Route 30, then five miles northeast on Forest Service Road 3065.

Trip note: This campground is set at 400 feet elevation near Snowshoe Butte. A nice, secluded spot that is missed by many.

FOURBIT FORD
Site **42**

Campsites, facilities: There are seven sites for tents, trailers or motorhomes. Picnic tables and firegrills are provided, and pumped water and vault toilets are available. A store, cafe and ice are located within five miles. Pets are permitted. Boat docks, launching facilities and rentals are nearby.

Reservations, fee: No reservations necessary; $3 fee per night. Open late-May to late-September.

Who to contact: Phone Butte Falls Ranger Station at 503-865-3581, or write at Rogue River National Forest, P.O. Box 227, Butte Falls, OR 97522.

Location: From Medford, travel 14 miles northeast on Highway 62, then 18 miles east to Butte Falls. From Butte Falls, travel nine miles southeast on County Route 30, then one mile northeast on Forest Service Road 3065.

Trip note: This campground is set along Fourbit Creek. One in a series of hidden spots tucked away near County Route 30.

WHISKEY SPRINGS
Site **43**   ## A AND B

Campsites, facilities: There are 36 sites for tents, trailers or motorhomes up to 16 feet long. Picnic tables and firegrills are provided, and piped water and vault toilets are available. Pets are permitted. Boat docks, launching facilities and rentals are nearby.

Reservations, fee: No reservations necessary; $4 fee per night. Open late-May to early-September.

Who to contact: Phone Butte Falls Ranger Station at 503-482-3333, or write at P.O. Box 227, Butte Falls, OR 97522.

Location: From Medford, travel 14 miles northeast on Highway 62, then 18 miles east to Butte Falls. From Butte Falls, travel nine miles southeast on County Route 30, then 300 yards on Forest Service Road 3317.

Trip note: This campground is set at Whiskey Springs, near Fourbit Creek. A nature trail is nearby. One of the larger, more developed backwoods Forest Service camps in the area.

WILLOW LAKE
Site **44**   ## RESORT

Campsites, facilities: There are 35 tent sites and 45 drive-through sites for trailers or motorhomes up to 30 feet long. Electricity, piped water, sewer hookups and picnic tables are provided. Flush toilets, sanitary disposal services, showers, firewood, a store, cafe, laundromat, ice and playground are available. Pets and motorbikes are permitted. Boat docks, launching facilities and rentals are nearby.

Reservations, fee: Reservations accepted; $8 fee per night. MasterCard and Visa accepted. Open all year.

Who to contact: Phone at 503-865-3229, or write at 7800 Fish Lake, Butte Falls, OR 97533.

Location: Take I-5 to Highway 62 in Medford, travel 14 miles on Highway 62, then 25 miles east on Butte Falls Highway. From there, go two miles southeast on Willow Lake Road.

Trip note: This campground is set along the shore of Willow Lake. Nearby recreation options include hiking trails and a small marina.

WILLOW PRAIRIE
Site **45**

Campsites, facilities: There are nine sites for tents, trailers or motorhomes up to 15 feet long. Picnic tables and firegrills are provided, and piped water and vault toilets are available. A store, a cafe and ice are located within five miles. Pets are permitted. Boat docks, launching facilities and rentals are nearby.

Reservations, fee: No reservations necessary; $3 fee per night. Open late-May to late-September.

Who to contact: Phone Butte Falls Ranger Station at 503-865-3581, or write at P.O. Box 227, Butte Falls, OR 97522.

Location: From Medford, travel 31 1/2 miles east on Highway 140, then 1 1/2 miles north on Forest Service Road 37. The camp is one mile west on Forest Service Road 3738.

Trip note: A map of Rogue River National Forest details the back roads and can help you get here. The campground is set near the origin of the west branch of Willow Creek. Fish Lake is four miles south.

NORTH FORK
Site **46**

Campsites, facilities: There are seven tent sites. Picnic tables and firegrills are provided, and vault toilets are available. There is no piped water. Pets are permitted. Boat docks, launching facilities and rentals are nearby.

Reservations, fee: No reservations necessary; no fee. Open late-May to early-September.

Who to contact: Phone the Ashland Ranger Station at 503-482-3333, or write at Rogue River National Forest, 2200 Highway 66, Ashland, OR 97520.

Location: From Medford, travel 31 1/2 miles east on County Route 140, then 1/2 mile south on Forest Service Road 3706.

Trip note: Here is a small campground that is close to the highway, close to Fish Lake, yet is missed by out of towners. Why? Because it is on a Forest Service road, where motorhomes fear to tread.

FISH LAKE
Site **47**

Campsites, facilities: There are 10 tent sites and 11 sites for trailers or motorhomes up to 22 feet long. Picnic tables and firegrills are provided, and piped water, flush toilets, a store, a cafe and ice are available. Pets are permitted. Boat docks, launching facilities and rentals are nearby.

Reservations, fee: No reservations necessary; $6 fee per night. Open July to late-October.

Who to contact: Phone the Ashland Ranger Station at 503-742-7511, or write at Rogue River National Forest, 2200 Highway 66, Ashland, OR 97520.

Location: From Medford, travel 33 miles east on Highway 140.

Trip note: This campground is set along the north shore of Fish Lake. Recreation options include boating, fishing, hiking and bicycling. If this is full, campsites 48 and 49 provide options.

DOE POINT
Site **48**

Campsites, facilities: There are 25 sites for tents, trailers or motorhomes up to 22 feet long. Picnic tables and firegrills are provided, and piped water, flush toilets, a store, a cafe and ice are available. Pets are permitted. Boat docks, launching facilities and rentals are nearby.

Reservations, fee: No reservations necessary; $6 fee per night. Open July to late-October.

Who to contact: Phone the Ashland Ranger Station at 503-742-7511, or write at Rogue River National Forest, 2200 Highway 66, Ashland, OR 97520.

Location: From Medford, travel 33 miles east on Highway 140.

Trip note: This campground is set along the north shore of Fish Lake. Recreation options include boating, fishing, hiking and bicycling.

FISH LAKE
Site **49** RESORT

Campsites, facilities: There are 25 tent sites and 50 sites for trailers or motorhomes up to 30 feet long. Electricity, piped water, sewer hookups and picnic tables are provided. Flush toilets, bottled gas, sanitary disposal services, showers, a recreation hall, a store, cafe, laundromat and ice are available. Pets and motorbikes are permitted. Boat docks, launching facilities and rentals are nearby.

Reservations, fee: Reservations accepted; $9 fee per night. MasterCard and Visa accepted. Open May to mid-October.

Who to contact: Phone at 503-949-8500, or write at Box 40, Medford, OR 97501.

Location: Drive five miles north of Medford on Highway 62, then 30 miles east on Highway 140. The camp is 1/2 mile south on Fish Lake Road.

Trip note: This campground is set along Fish Lake, where hiking, bicycling, fishing and boating are some of the options. The largest of three camps at Fish Lake.

LAKE OF THE
Site **50** WOODS RESORT

Campsites, facilities: There are 30 sites for trailers or motorhomes up to 32 feet long. Electricity, piped water, sewer hookups and picnic tables are provided. Flush toilets, showers, a store, cafe, laundromat and ice are available. Sanitary disposal services are located within one mile. Pets are permitted. Boat docks, launching facilities and rentals are nearby.

Reservations, fee: Reservations accepted; $8 fee per night. MasterCard and Visa accepted. Open early-May to November.

Who to contact: Phone at 503-949-8300, or write at 950 Harriman, Klamath Falls, OR 97601.

Location: From Klamath Falls, travel northwest on Highway 140 for 35 miles, then one mile south on Lake of the Woods Road. The resort is west on Rainbow Bay Road.

Trip note: This campground is set along the shore of Lake of the Woods, a popular spot for boating and fishing. A trail leads east from the resort and provides access to numerous lakes in the Mountain Lakes Wilderness.

ASPEN POINT

Site **51**

Campsites, facilities: There are 61 sites for tents, trailers or motorhomes up to 22 feet long. Picnic tables and firegrills are provided, and piped water, flush toilets and showers are available. Pets are permitted. Boat docks, launching facilities and rentals are nearby.

Reservations, fee: No reservations necessary; $6 fee per night. Open late-May to late-September.

Who to contact: Phone Klamath Ranger District at 503-883-6824, or write at Winema National Forest, 1936 California Avenue, Klamath Falls, OR 97601.

Location: Travel 32 1/2 miles northwest of Klamath Falls on Highway 140, then 1/2 mile south on Forest Service Road 3704. The camp is 100 yards west on Forest Service Road 3704.

Trip note: This campground is set along the shore of Lake of the Woods.

SUNSET

Site **52**

Campsites, facilities: There are 67 sites for tents, trailers or motorhomes up to 22 feet long. Picnic tables and firegrills are provided, and piped water, firewood and flush toilets are available. Some facilities are wheelchair accessible. Pets are permitted. Boat docks, launching facilities and rentals are nearby.

Reservations, fee: No reservations necessary; $6 fee per night. Open June to mid-September.

Who to contact: Phone Klamath Ranger District at 503-883-6824, or write at Winema National Forest, 1936 California Avenue, Klamath Falls, OR 97601.

Location: From Klamath Falls, travel 31 miles northwest on Highway 140, then 2 1/2 miles southwest on County Route 533. The camp is 1/2 mile west on Forest Service Road 3738.

Trip note: This campground is set along the shore of Lake of the Woods.

FOURMILE LAKE

Site **53**

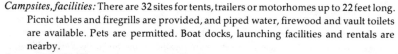

Campsites, facilities: There are 32 sites for tents, trailers or motorhomes up to 22 feet long. Picnic tables and firegrills are provided, and piped water, firewood and vault toilets are available. Pets are permitted. Boat docks, launching facilities and rentals are nearby.

Reservations, fee: No reservations necessary; $3 fee per night. Open June to late-September.

Who to contact: Phone Klamath Ranger District at 503-883-6824, or write at Winema National Forest, 1936 California Avenue, Klamath Falls, OR 97601.

Location: From Klamath Falls, travel 33 miles northwest on Highway 140, then three miles north on Forest Service Road 3661.

Trip note: This campground is set along the shore of Fourmile Lake, the only camp at the lake. There are several trails nearby that provide access to Sky Lakes Wilderness. The Pacific Crest Trail passes about two miles from camp.

COLD SPRINGS
Site **54**

Campsites, facilities: There are two tent sites. Picnic tables and firegrills are provided, and pit toilets are available. There is no piped water. Pets are permitted. Boat docks, launching facilities and rentals are nearby.

Reservations, fee: No reservations necessary; no fee. Open June to late-September.

Who to contact: Phone Klamath Ranger District at 503-883-6824, or write at Winema National Forest, 1936 California Avenue, Klamath Falls, OR 97601.

Location: From Klamath Falls, travel 28 miles northwest on Highway 140, then north on Forest Service Road 3651 for 11 miles to the end of the road. The last 1 1/2 miles is on a dirt or gravel road.

Trip note: This campground is set near the source of one of the tributaries to Lost Creek and at a trailhead that provides access to numerous lakes in Sky Lakes Wilderness. The Pacific Crest Trail passes about two miles from camp. Used primarily as a jumpoff point for backpackers.

ODESSA
Site **55**

Campsites, facilities: There are six tent sites. Picnic tables and firegrills are provided, and firewood and vault toilets are available. There is no piped water. Pets are permitted. Boat docks, launching facilities and rentals are nearby.

Reservations, fee: No reservations necessary; no fee. Open mid-May to late-September.

Who to contact: Phone Klamath Ranger District at 503-883-6824, or write at Winema National Forest, 1936 California Avenue, Klamath Falls, OR 97601.

Location: From Klamath Falls, travel 21 1/2 miles northwest on Highway 140, then one mile northeast on Forest Service Road 3639.

Trip note: This campground is set along Odessa Creek, near the shore of Upper Klamath Lake. Boating and fishing are allowed, but no waterskiing. This lake can provide excellent fishing for rainbow trout on both flies and Rapalas.

HARRIMAN SPRINGS
Site **56** RESORT & MARINA

Campsites, facilities: There are six tent sites and 17 drive-through sites for trailers or motorhomes. Electricity, piped water, sewer hookups and picnic tables are provided. Flush toilets, showers, firewood, cafe, laundromat and ice are available. Bottled gas, sanitary disposal services and a store are located within one mile. Pets and motorbikes are permitted. Boat docks, launching facilities and rentals are nearby.

Reservations, fee: Reservations accepted; $7 fee per night. Open April to late-October.

Who to contact: Phone at 503-356-2323, or write at Harriman Route, Box 79, Klamath Falls, OR 97601.

Location: Travel 27 miles northwest of Klamath Falls on Highway 140, then two miles north on Rocky Point Road.

Trip note: This resort is set along the shore of Pelican Bay at the north end of Upper Klamath Lake, adjacent to the Upper Klamath National Wildlife Refuge. Trout fishing is good, ideal from a canoe.

Site 57 — ROCKY POINT RESORT

Campsites, facilities: There are five tent sites and 28 drive-through sites for trailers or motorhomes of any length. Electricity, piped water, sewer hookups and picnic tables are provided. Flush toilets, bottled gas, sanitary disposal services, showers, firewood, recreation hall, a store, cafe, laundromat, ice and playground are available. Pets are permitted. Boat docks, launching facilities and rentals are nearby.

Reservations, fee: Reservations accepted; $10 fee per night. Open April to mid-November.

Who to contact: Phone at 503-356-2287, or write at Harriman Route, Box 92, Klamath Falls, OR 97601.

Location: From Klamath Falls, travel 27 miles northwest on Highway 140, then three miles north on Rocky Point Road.

Trip note: See the trip note for campsite 56.

Site 58 — FORT CREEK RESORT

Campsites, facilities: There are 10 tent sites and 18 sites for trailers or motorhomes of any length. Electricity, piped water, sewer hookups and picnic tables are provided. Flush toilets, showers, recreation hall, laundromat and swimming pool are available. Bottled gas, a store, cafe and ice are located within one mile. Pets and motorbikes are permitted.

Reservations, fee: Reservations accepted; $10 fee per night. Open mid-May to October.

Who to contact: Phone at 503-381-2207, or write at Box 457, Fort Klamath, OR 97626.

Location: From Klamath Falls, travel 21 miles north on Highway 97, then 12 1/2 miles north on Highway 62. The campground is just before Fort Klamath on Highway 62.

Trip note: This campground is set along the banks of Wood River, just outside of Fort Klamath, the origin of numerous military campaigns in the late 1800s against the Modoc Indians.

Site 59 — FORT KLAMATH LODGE & RV PARK

Campsites, facilities: There are five tent sites and 11 sites for trailers or motorhomes of any length. Electricity, piped water, sewer hookups and picnic tables are provided. Flush toilets, bottled gas, showers and laundromat are available. A store and ice are located within one mile. Pets and motorbikes are permitted.

Reservations, fee: Reservations accepted; $10 fee per night. MasterCard and Visa accepted. Open all year.

Who to contact: Phone at 503-381-2234, or write at P.O. Box 428, Fort Klamath, OR 97626.

Location: From Klamath Falls, travel 21 miles north on Highway 97, then 14 1/2 miles north on Highway 62. The campground is 1 1/2 miles northwest of the town of Fort Klamath.

Trip note: See the trip note for campsite 58.

Site 60 SEVENMILE MARSH

Campsites, facilities: There are two tent sites. Picnic tables and firegrills are provided, and firewood and pit toilets are available. There is no piped water. Pets are permitted.

Reservations, fee: No reservations necessary; no fee. Open mid-May to late-September.

Who to contact: Phone Klamath Ranger District at 503-883-6824, or write at Winema National Forest, 1936 California Avenue, Klamath Falls, OR 97601.

Location: From Klamath Falls, travel 21 miles north on Highway 97, then 13 miles north on Highway 62 to the town of Fort Klamath. From there, drive west on County Route 1419 for three miles, then six miles northwest on Forest Service Road 3334.

Trip note: This campground is set near Seven miles Marsh, at a trailhead that provides access to Sky Lakes Wilderness. The Pacific Crest Trail passes 1 1/2 miles from camp. This tiny camp is used primarily as a jumpoff point for backpackers.

Site 61 CRATER LAKE CAMP & RV PARK

Campsites, facilities: There are 50 tent sites and 36 drive-through sites for trailers or motorhomes of any length. Electricity, piped water, sewer hookups and picnic tables are provided. Flush toilets, showers, firewood, a store, a laundromat, ice and a playground are available. Pets and motorbikes are permitted.

Reservations, fee: Reservations accepted; $8 fee per night. MasterCard and Visa accepted. Open mid-May to October.

Who to contact: Phone at 503-381-2275, or write at Box 485, Fort Klamath, OR 97626.

Location: From Klamath Falls, travel 21 miles north on Highway 97, then 19 miles north on Highway 62 to the campground.

Trip note: This campground is located near the south entrance to Crater Lake National Park. It gets heavy traffic during the summer months.

Site 62 JACKSON F. KIMBALL STATE PARK

Campsites, facilities: There are 10 primitive sites for tents, trailers or motorhomes up to 15 feet long. Picnic tables and firegrills are provided, and firewood and vault toilets are available. There is no piped water. Pets are permitted.

Reservations, fee: No reservations necessary; $5 fee per night. Open mid-April to late-October.

Who to contact: Phone at 503-783-2471, or write at Chiloquin, OR 97624.

Location: From Klamath Falls, travel 21 miles north on Highway 97, then 13 miles north on Highway 62 to the town of Fort Klamath. From there, drive three miles north on Highway 232.

Trip note: This campground is set near the Wood River. Another nice spot just far enough off the main drag that most tourists don't have a clue about it.

Site 63 SPRING CREEK

Campsites, facilities: There are two tent sites and 24 sites for trailers or motorhomes up to 30 feet long. Picnic tables and firegrills are provided, and piped water, firewood and vault toilets are available. Pets are permitted.

Reservations, fee: No reservations necessary; $3 fee per night. Open late-May to mid-October.

Who to contact: Phone Chiloquin Ranger District at 503-783-2221, or write Winema National Forest at P.O. Box 357, Chiloquin, OR 97624.

Location: Travel eight miles north of Chiloquin on US 97, then 3 1/2 miles west on Forest Service Road 3302.

Trip note: This campground is set along the bank of Spring Creek. One of the few secluded motorhome campgrounds in the Western United States.

Site **64** WILLIAMSON RIVER

Campsites, facilities: There are eight tent sites and two sites for trailers or motorhomes up to 30 feet long. Picnic tables and firegrills are provided, and piped water and vault toilets are available. A restaurant is located within five miles. Pets are permitted.

Reservations, fee: No reservations necessary; $4 fee per night. Open June to late-October.

Who to contact: Phone Chiloquin Ranger District at 503-783-2221, or write Winema National Forest at P.O. Box 357, Chiloquin, OR 97624.

Location: From Chiloquin, travel 5 1/2 miles north on US 97, then one mile northeast on Forest Service Road 3412.

Trip note: This campground is set along the banks of the Williamson River. A map of Winema National Forest details the back roads and trails.

Site **65** WALT'S COZY CAMP

Campsites, facilities: There are 20 tent sites and 34 drive-through sites for trailers or motorhomes of any length. Electricity, piped water, sewer hookups and picnic tables are provided. Flush toilets, bottled gas, showers and firewood are available. A store, cafe, laundromat and ice are available located one mile. Pets and motorbikes are permitted.

Reservations, fee: Reservations accepted; $8 fee per night. Open April to early-November.

Who to contact: Phone at 503-783-2537, or write at P.O. Box 243, Chiloquin, OR 97624.

Location: From the town of Chiloquin, travel three miles north on US 97.

Trip note: This campground is set along the banks of the Williamson River, near Collier State Park. One of three camps in the immediate area. For a more remote setting, campsites 70 and 82 are available to the east.

Site **66** COLLIER MEMORIAL STATE PARK

Campsites, facilities: There are 18 tent sites and 50 sites for trailers or motorhomes of any length. Electricity, piped water, sewer hookups and picnic tables are provided. Flush toilets, sanitary disposal services, showers, firewood, a laundromat and playground are available. Some facilities are wheelchair accessible. Pets are permitted.

Reservations, fee: No reservations necessary; $8 fee per night. Open mid-April to late-October.

Who to contact: Phone at 503-783-2471, or write at Chiloquin, OR 97624.

Location: From Klamath Falls, travel 30 miles north on US 97.

Trip note: This campground is set at the confluence of Spring Creek and the Williamson River. A nature trail and a museum are available.

Site 67
NEPTUNE PARK RESORT

Campsites, facilities: There are 15 tent sites and 18 sites for trailers or motorhomes of any length. Electricity, piped water, sewer hookups and picnic tables are provided. Flush toilets, bottled gas, showers, a store and ice are available. Pets and motorbikes are permitted. Boat docks, launching facilities and rentals are available nearby.

Reservations, fee: Reservations accepted; $10 fee per night. MasterCard and Visa accepted. Open April to December.

Who to contact: Phone at 503-782-2489, or write at HC 30, Box 115, Chiloquin, OR 97624.

Location: From the town of Chiloquin, travel west at the Modoc Point sign and go four miles north. From there, follow the signs.

Trip note: This campground is set along the lake shore.

Site 68
WATERWHEEL CAMPGROUND & RV PARK

Campsites, facilities: There are 20 tent sites and 24 drive-through sites for trailers or motorhomes of any length. Electricity, piped water, sewer hookups and picnic tables are provided. Flush toilets, bottled gas, sanitary disposal services, showers, firewood, a store, laundromat, ice and playground are available. Cafe is available within one mile. Pets and motorbikes are permitted. Boat docks and launching facilities are nearby.

Reservations, fee: Reservations accepted; $11 fee per night. MasterCard and Visa accepted. Open all year.

Who to contact: Phone at 503-783-2738, or write at HC 30, Box 91, Chiloquin, OR 97624.

Location: From the town of Chiloquin, travel 1/4 mile south on US 97.

Trip note: This rural campground is set along the banks of the Williamson River. Hiking trails are nearby. Okay layover spot.

Site 69
WILLIAMSON RIVER RESORT

Campsites, facilities: There are eight sites for trailers or motorhomes of any length. Electricity, piped water and picnic tables are provided. Bottled gas, sanitary disposal services, a store and ice are available. A cafe is located within one mile. Pets are permitted. Boat docks, launching facilities and rentals are nearby.

Reservations, fee: Reservations accepted; $6 fee per night. MasterCard and Visa accepted. Open all year.

Who to contact: Phone at 503-783-2071, or write at HC 30, Box 78, Chiloquin, OR 97624.

Location: From the town of Chiloquin, travel 5 1/2 miles on Modoc Point Road.

Trip note: This resort is set along the banks of the Williamson River.

Site 70 POTTER'S TRAILER PARK

Campsites, facilities: There are 17 tent sites and 23 drive-through sites for trailers or motorhomes of any length. Electricity, piped water, sewer hookups and picnic tables are provided. Flush toilets, bottled gas, showers, firewood, a recreation hall, a store, cafe, laundromat and ice are available. Pets and motorbikes are permitted.

Reservations, fee: Reservations accepted; $8 fee per night. Open all year with limited winter facilities.

Who to contact: Phone at 503-783-2253, or write at Star Route 2, Chiloquin, OR 97624.

Location: Go 12 miles east of Chiloquin on Sprague River Highway.

Trip note: This campground is set along the banks of the Sprague River. For the most part, the area east of Klamath Lake doesn't get much attention. But if you want to check out a relatively nearby spot that is out in booger country, check campsite 82.

Site 71 HAGELSTEIN PARK

Campsites, facilities: There are five tent sites and five sites for trailers or motorhomes of any length. Picnic tables and firegrills are provided, and piped water and flush toilets are available. Pets are permitted. Boat docks and launching facilities are nearby.

Reservations, fee: No reservations necessary; no fee. Open April to late-November.

Who to contact: Phone at 503-882-2501, or write at County Parks Department, Klamath Falls, OR 97601.

Location: From the town of Klamath Falls, travel nine miles north on US 97.

Trip note: This county park is set along the shore of Upper Klamath Lake. This is the only campground along the eastern shore of the lake. The others are on the northwest end (campsites 55-57) or the southern end (campsites 72-75). Trout fishing can be superb here.

Site 72 KOA KLAMATH FALLS

Campsites, facilities: There are 18 tent sites and 73 drive-through sites for trailers or motorhomes of any length. Electricity, piped water, sewer hookups and picnic tables are provided. Flush toilets, bottled gas, sanitary disposal services, showers, recreation hall, a store, laundromat, ice, playground and swimming pool are available. A cafe is within one mile. Pets and motorbikes are permitted. Boat docks and launching facilities are nearby.

Reservations, fee: Reservations accepted; $10 fee per night. MasterCard and Visa accepted. Open all year with limited winter facilities.

Who to contact: Phone at 503-884-4644, or write at 3435 Shasta Way, Klamath Falls, OR 97601.

Location: From the town of Klamath Falls, travel 1 1/2 miles northwest on US 97, then one block west on Shasta Way.

Trip note: This campground is set along the shore of Upper Klamath Lake, near the marina. Hiking trails and tennis courts are nearby.

Site **73**   MALLARD CAMPGROUND

Campsites, facilities: There are 10 tent sites and 43 drive-through sites for trailers or motorhomes of any length. Electricity, piped water, sewer hookups and picnic tables are provided. Flush toilets, showers, a recreation hall, laundromat, ice and swimming pool are available. Bottled gas, a store and cafe are located within one mile. Pets and motorbikes are permitted.

Reservations, fee: Reservations accepted; $10 fee per night. MasterCard and Visa accepted. Open all year with limited winter facilities.

Who to contact: Phone at 503-882-0482, or write at Route 5, Box 1348, Klamath Falls, OR 97601.

Location: From the town of Klamath falls, travel 3 1/2 miles north on US 97.

Trip note: This campground is near Hanks Marsh on the southeast shore of Upper Klamath Lake. Nearby recreation options include a golf course, bike paths and a marina.

Site **74**   NORTH HILLS MOBILE PARK

Campsites, facilities: There are 15 sites for trailers or motorhomes of any length. Electricity, piped water and sewer hookups are provided. A laundromat and a swimming pool are available. Bottled gas, a store, cafe and ice are within one mile. Pets are permitted.

Reservations, fee: Reservations accepted; $6 fee per night. Open all year with limited winter facilities.

Who to contact: Phone at 503-884-9068, or write at 3611 Highway 97N, Klamath Falls, OR 97601.

Location: Travel two miles north of Klamath Falls on US 97.

Trip note: This park is near Upper Klamath Lake. A golf course, hiking trails, a marina and tennis courts are nearby.

Site **75**   WISEMAN'S MOBILE COURT & RV

Campsites, facilities: There are eight tent sites and 12 sites for trailers or motorhomes of any length. Electricity, piped water and sewer hookups are provided. Flush toilets, sanitary disposal services, showers and a laundromat are available. Bottled gas is located within one mile. Pets are permitted.

Reservations, fee: Reservations accepted; $9 fee per night. Open all year.

Who to contact: Phone at 503-882-4081, or write at 6800 South 6th, Klamath Falls, OR 97603.

Location: Take Highway 140 east from Klamath Falls for 4 1/2 miles.

Trip note: This park is set along the banks of a river.

Site **76**   TINGLEY LAKE ESTATES

Campsites, facilities: There are six tent sites and 10 drive-through sites for trailers or motorhomes of any length. Electricity, piped water, sewer hookups and picnic tables are provided. Flush toilets, sanitary disposal services, showers, a laundromat and playground are available. A store, cafe and ice are located within one mile. Pets and motorbikes are permitted. Boat docks are nearby.

Reservations, fee: Reservations accepted; $8 fee per night. Open all year.

Who to contact: Phone at 503-882-8386, or write at 11800 Tingley, Klamath Falls, OR 07603.

Location: From Klamath Falls, go seven miles southwest on US 97, then two miles east on Old Midland Rd. The camp is 1/2 mile west on Tingley Road.

Trip note: This private-operated park provides a layover spot for travelers heading into Oregon on Highway 97.

GERBER RESERVOIR

Site **77**

Campsites, facilities: There are 50 sites for tents, trailers or motorhomes up to 30 feet long. Picnic tables and firegrills are provided, and piped water, firewood and vault toilets are available. Pets are permitted. Boat launching facilities are nearby.

Reservations, fee: No reservations necessary; $2 fee per night. Open mid-May to mid-October.

Who to contact: Phone at 503-947-2177, or write the Bureau of Land Management at P.O. Box 151, Lakeview, OR 97630.

Location: From Klamath Falls, travel 19 miles east on Highway 140, then drive southeast for about 17 miles to the turn-off for the Lake and go 11 miles northeast on Gerber Road.

Trip note: This campground is set at 4800 feet elevation along the west shore of Gerber Reservoir. Just about nobody has heard of Gerber Reservoir, set out in the middle of nowhere. And that's just how they like it.

LOFTON
RESERVOIR

Site **78**

Campsites, facilities: There are 10 tent sites and seven sites for trailers or motorhomes up to 22 feet long. Picnic tables and firegrills are provided, and piped water and vault toilets are available. Pets are permitted. Boat docks and launching facilities are nearby.

Reservations, fee: No reservations necessary; $4 fee per night. Open June to late-October.

Who to contact: Phone the Bly Ranger District at 503-353-2427, or write at Fremont National Forest, Bly, OR 97622.

Location: Drive 54 miles east of Klamath Falls on Highway 14 to the town of Bly. From Bly, continue 13 miles southeast on Highway 140, then seven miles south on Forest Service Road 3715. From there, go 1 1/2 miles northeast on Forest Service Road 3715A.

Trip note: This remote campground is set along the shore of little Lofton Lake. Numerous other lakes are nearby and are accessible by Forest Service Roads. This area marks the beginning of the Southeast Basin, a dry, sandy area that extends to Idaho.

EAST BAY

Site **79**

Campsites, facilities: There are 19 sites for tents, trailers or motorhomes. Picnic tables and firegrills are provided, and firewood, piped water and vault toilets are available. Pets are permitted. Boat docks and launching facilities are nearby.

Reservations, fee: No reservations necessary; $4 fee per night. Open mid-May to late-October.

Who to contact: Phone Silver Lake Ranger District at 503-576-2107, or write Fremont National Forest, Silver Lake, OR 97638.

Location: From the town of Silver Lake, go 1/2 mile west on Highway 31, then 13 miles south on Forest Service Road 2823. From there, go 1 1/2 miles west on Forest Service Road 2823D.

Trip note: This campground is set along the east shore of Thompson Reservoir. It is a long way from home, and you'd best bring all your supplies with you. Campsite 81 is a more primitive setting along a stream.

Site 80   THOMPSON RESERVOIR

Campsites, facilities: There are 16 tent sites and six sites for trailers or motorhomes up to 22 feet long. Picnic tables and firegrills are provided, and piped water, firewood, and vault toilets are available. Pets are permitted. Boat docks and launching facilities are nearby.

Reservations, fee: No reservations necessary; $4 fee per night. Open mid-May to late-October.

Who to contact: Phone Silver Lake Ranger District at 503-576-2107, or write Fremont National Forest, Silver Lake, OR 97638.

Location: From the town of Silver Lake, travel one mile west on Highway 31, then 14 miles south on Forest Service Road 288. The camp is one mile east on Forest Service Road 3024.

Trip note: This campground is set along the north shore of Thompson Reservoir. Fishing and boating permitted. See trip note to campsite 79 for options.

Site 81   SILVER CREEK MARSH

Campsites, facilities: There are five tent sites. Picnic tables and firegrills are provided, and piped water, firewood and vault toilets are available. Pets are permitted.

Reservations, fee: No reservations necessary; $4 fee per night. Open mid-May to late-October.

Who to contact: Phone Silver Lake Ranger District at 503-576-2107, or write Fremont National Forest, Silver Lake, OR 97638.

Location: From the town of Silver Lake, travel one mile west on Highway 31, then 10 miles south on Forest Service Road 288. The camp is 200 yards southwest on Forest Service Road 2919.

Trip note: This campground is set adjacent to Silver Creek Marsh near Silver Creek. A small, quiet spot that gets little attention.

Site 82   HEAD OF THE RIVER

Campsites, facilities: There are six sites for tents, trailers or motorhomes up to 30 feet long. Picnic tables and firegrills are provided, and firewood and vault toilets are available. There is no piped water. Pets are permitted.

Reservations, fee: No reservations necessary; no fee. Open June to mid-October.

Who to contact: Phone Chiloquin Ranger District at 503-783-2221, or write Winema National Forest at P.O. Box 357, Chiloquin, OR 97624.

Location: From Chiloquin, go five miles north east on County Route 858, then 27 miles northeast on County Route 600. The camp is one mile north on Forest Service Road 3037.

Trip note: This campground is set along the headwaters of the Williamson River. Just about nobody knows about this one. A small, lonely spot.

TOPSY
Site **83**

Campsites, facilities: There are 12 sites for trailers or motorhomes. Picnic tables and firegrills are provided, and pit toilets and firewood are available. There is no piped water. Pets are permitted. Boat launching facilities are nearby.

Reservations, fee: No reservations necessary; no fee. Open April to late-October.

Who to contact: Phone at 503-776-3774, or write the Bureau of Land Management at 3040 Biddle Road, Medford, OR 97504.

Location: From Klamath Falls, travel 17 miles west on Highway 66 then one mile south on Topsy County Road.

Trip note: This campground is set along the upper Klamath River. This is a good spot for trout fishing and a top river for rafters -- experts only. Scout Class IV and V white-water at Caldera, Satan's Gate, Hell's Corner and Three Rocks.

SURVEYOR
Site **84**

Campsites, facilities: There are eight primitive sites for tents, trailers or motorhomes up to 20 feet long. Picnic tables and firegrills are provided, and piped water, firewood and vault toilets are available. Pets are permitted.

Reservations, fee: No reservations necessary; no fee. Open June to late-October.

Who to contact: Phone at 503-776-3744, or write the Bureau of Land Managment at 3040 Biddle Road, Medford, OR 97504.

Location: From Ashland, travel 20 miles east on Dead Indian Road, then 10 miles east on the route to Keno.

Trip note: This campground is set at 5200 feet elevation. It is an obscure little spot near Spencer Creek.

DALEY CREEK
Site **85**

Campsites, facilities: There are five tent sites. Picnic tables and firegrills are provided, and piped water, firewood and vault toilets are available. Pets are permitted.

Reservations, fee: No reservations necessary; no fee. Open late-May to early-September.

Who to contact: Phone Ashland Ranger District at 503-482-3333, or write Rogue River National Forest, 2200 Highway 66, Ashland, OR 97520.

Location: Go 25 miles northeast of Ashland on County Route 364, then 1 1/2 miles north on Forest Service Road 3706.

Trip note: This campground is set along the banks of Daley Creek. It is a primitive and free alternative to camping at nearby and more developed Fish Lake (campsites 47-49) or Hyatt Lake/Howard Prairie Reservoir (campsites 86-89).

CAMPER'S COVE
Site **86**

Campsites, facilities: There are 25 drive-through sites for trailers or motorhomes up to 30 feet long. Electricity, piped water, sewer hookups and picnic tables are provided. Flush toilets, bottled gas, showers, firewood, a store, cafe and ice are available. Pets are permitted. Boat docks are nearby.

Reservations, fee: Reservations accepted; $8 fee per night. MasterCard and Visa accepted. Open April to late-October.

Who to contact: Phone at 503-482-1201, or write at P.O. Box 222, Ashland, OR 97520.

Location: Travel 18 miles east of Ashland on Highway 66, then three miles northeast on Hyatt Lake Road. The camp is 2 1/2 miles on Hyatt Prairie Road.

Trip note: This campground is set along the shore of Hyatt Lake. The Pacific Crest Trail passes about one mile away.

HOWARD PRAIRIE LAKE RESORT
Site **87**

Campsites, facilities: There are 155 tent sites and 285 sites for trailers or motorhomes of any length. Electricity, piped water, sewer hookups and picnic tables are provided. Flush toilets, bottled gas, sanitary disposal services, showers, firewood, a store, cafe, laundromat and ice are available. Pets are permitted. Boat docks, launching facilities and rentals are nearby.

Reservations, fee: No reservations necessary; $5 fee per night. MasterCard and Visa accepted. Open mid-April to late-October.

Who to contact: Phone at 503-773-3619, or write at P.O. Box 4709, Medford, OR 97501.

Location: From Ashland, take Highway 66 east to Dead Indian Road, go 19 miles east to Howard Prairie Road and drive five miles south to the reservoir.

Trip note: This wooded campground is set along the shore of Howard Prairie Lake, where hiking, swimming, fishing and boating are among the recreation options. This is one of the largest campgrounds within more than a hundred miles.

HYATT LAKE RESORT
Site **88**

Campsites, facilities: There are 20 tent sites and 55 drive-through sites for trailers or motorhomes of any length. Electricity, piped water, sewer hookups and picnic tables are provided. Flush toilets, bottled gas, sanitary disposal services, showers, a store, cafe, laundromat, ice and playground are available. Pets and motorbikes are permitted. Boat docks, launching facilities and rentals are nearby.

Reservations, fee: Reservations accepted; $7 fee per night. MasterCard and Visa accepted. Open April to November.

Who to contact: Phone at 503-482-0525, or write at P.O. Box 447, Ashland, OR 97520.

Location: Go 18 miles east of Ashland on Highway 66, then three miles northeast on Hyatt Lake Road. The camp is one mile on Hyatt Prairie Road.

Trip note: This campground is set along the shore of Hyatt Lake, where hiking, fishing and swimming are some of the recreation options. A downscaled option to the resort at adjacent Howard Prairie Reservoir.

Site 89

EAST SHORE HYATT LAKE

Campsites, facilities: There are 30 sites for trailers or motorhomes of any length. Picnic tables and firegrills are provided, and firewood and vault toilets are available. Sanitary disposal services, a store, cafe and ice are within one mile. Pets and motorbikes are permitted.

Reservations, fee: No reservations necessary; $2 fee per night. Open May to mid-October.

Who to contact: Phone at 503-776-3744, or write the Bureau of Land Management at 3040 Biddle Road, Medford, OR 97504.

Location: From Ashland, go 20 miles east on Highway 66, then go five miles north on East Hyatt Lake Road. There are two campgrounds.

Trip note: These campgrounds are set along the east shore of Hyatt Lake. Nearby recreation options include a marina and a stable.

Site 90

KOA GLENYAN

Campsites, facilities: There are 30 tent sites and 38 drive-through sites for trailers or motorhomes of any length. Electricity, piped water, sewer hookups and picnic tables are provided. Flush toilets, bottled gas, sanitary disposal services, showers, firewood, recreation hall, a store, cafe, laundromat, ice, playground and swimming pool are available. Pets and motorbikes are permitted.

Reservations, fee: Reservations accepted; $10 fee per night. MasterCard and Visa accepted. Open late-February to late-October.

Who to contact: Phone at 503-482-4138, or write at 5310 Highway 66, Ashland, OR 97520.

Location: Travel 3 1/2 miles east on Highway 66 from Ashland.

Trip note: This campground offers shady sites near Emigrant Lake. Nearby recreation options include a golf course, hiking trails, bike paths and tennis courts. An easy jump from Interstate 5 at Ashland.

Site 91

JACKSON HOT SPRINGS

Campsites, facilities: There are 30 tent sites and 20 drive-through sites for trailers or motorhomes of any length. Electricity, piped water, sewer hookups and picnic tables are provided. Flush toilets, showers, a cafe, laundromat, ice and swimming pool are available. Bottled gas is located within one mile. Pets are permitted.

Reservations, fee: No reservations necessary; $9 fee per night. Open all year.

Who to contact: Phone at 503-482-3776, or write at 2253 Highway 99N, Ashland, OR 97520.

Location: Near Ashland, take exit 19 off I-5, and travel west for one mile to the stoplight, then turn right and drive 500 feet.

Trip note: This campground has mineral hot springs that empty into a swimming pool, not a hot pool (76 degrees). Hot mineral baths are available in private rooms. Nearby recreation options include a golf course, hiking trails, bike paths and tennis courts.

MOUNT ASHLAND

Site **92**

Campsites, facilities: There are eight sites for tents, trailers or motorhomes up to 15 feet long. Picnic tables and firegrills are provided, and vault toilets are available. There is no piped water is available. Pets are permitted.

Reservations, fee: No reservations necessary; no fee. Open July to late-October.

Who to contact: Phone Ashland Ranger District at 503-482-3333, or write Rogue River National Forest, 2200 Highway 66, Ashland, OR 97520.

Location: From Ashland, travel 12 miles south on I-5 to County Route 993. Take 993 west one mile, then Forest Service Road 20 for nine miles to the campground.

Trip note: This campground is set at 6000 feet elevation along the Pacific Crest Trail. On clear days, there are great lookouts, particularly to the south where California's 14,000-foot Mt. Shasta is an awesome sight.

FLUMET FLAT

Site **93**

Campsites, facilities: There are 23 sites for tents, trailers or motorhomes up to 21 feet long. Picnic tables and firegrills are provided, and piped water, flush toilets, showers, a store, cafe, laundromat and ice are available. Some facilities are wheelchair accessible. Pets are permitted.

Reservations, fee: Reservations required; $5 fee per night. Open late-May to early-September.

Who to contact: Phone Star Ranger District at 503-899-1812, or write Rogue River National Forest at 6941 Upper Applegate Road, Jacksonville, OR 97530.

Location: From Jacksonville, travel eight miles southwest on Highway 238, nine miles southwest on County Route 10 and one mile southwest on Forest Service Road 1095.

Trip note: This campground is set along the banks of the Applegate River about six miles north of Applegate Reservoir. A nature trail is nearby. Campsites 95-97 provide lakeshore camping, but get more people.

BEAVER SULPHUR

Site **94**

Campsites, facilities: There are three sites for tents, trailers or motorhomes. Picnic tables and firegrills are provided, and vault toilets are available. There is no piped water. Pets are permitted. Boat docks and launching facilities are nearby.

Reservations, fee: No reservations necessary; no fee. Open June to September.

Who to contact: Phone Star Ranger District at 503-899-1812, or write Rogue River National Forest at 6941 Upper Applegate Road, Jacksonville, OR 97530.

Location: From Jacksonville, travel eight miles southwest on Highway 238, nine miles southwest on County Route 10 and three miles east on Forest Service Road 20.

Trip note: This campground is set along the banks of Beaver Creek, about seven miles from Applegate Lake. Tiny and hidden.

FRENCH GULCH
Site **95**

Campsites, facilities: There are nine sites for tents, trailers or motorhomes up to 15 feet long. Picnic tables and firegrills are provided, and piped water and vault toilets are available. Some facilities are wheelchair accessible. Pets are permitted. Boat docks and launching facilities are nearby.

Reservations, fee: No reservations necessary; $3 fee per night. Open late-May to early-September.

Who to contact: Phone Star Ranger District at 503-899-1812, or write Rogue River National Forest at 6941 Upper Applegate Road, Jacksonville, OR 97530.

Location: From Jacksonville, travel eight miles southwest on Highway 238, then 14 miles southwest on County Route 10. From there go 1 1/2 miles east on Forest Service Road 1075.

Trip note: This campground is set along the shore of Applegate Reservoir. A popular summer fishing spot for Ashland anglers.

CARBERRY
Site **96**

Campsites, facilities: There are five sites for tents, trailers or motorhomes. Picnic tables and firegrills are provided, and vault toilets are available. There is no piped water. Pets are permitted. Boat docks and launching facilities are nearby.

Reservations, fee: No reservations necessary; no fee. Open June to September.

Who to contact: Phone Star Ranger District at 503-899-1812, or write Rogue River National Forest at 6941 Upper Applegate Road, Jacksonville, OR 97530.

Location: Go eight miles southwest on Highway 238, then 14 miles south on County Route 10.

Trip note: This campground is set along the southwest shore of Applegate Reservoir. A smaller and more primitive option to nearby campsite 95.

WATKINS
Site **97**

Campsites, facilities: There are 14 sites for tents, trailers or motorhomes. Picnic tables and firegrills are provided, and piped water and vault toilets are available. Pets are permitted. Boat docks and launching facilities are nearby.

Reservations, fee: No reservations necessary; $2 fee per night. Open June to September.

Who to contact: Phone Star Ranger District at 503-899-1812, or write Rogue River National Forest at 6941 Upper Applegate Road, Jacksonville, OR 97530.

Location: From Jacksonville, go eight miles southwest on Highway 238, then 14 miles southwest on County Route 10.

Trip note: This campground is set along the southwest shore of Applegate Reservoir.

SQUAW LAKES
Site **98**

Campsites, facilities: There are 11 sites for tents, trailers or motorhomes. Picnic tables and firegrills are provided, and piped water and vault toilets are available. Pets are permitted. Boat docks are nearby.

Reservations, fee: Reservations required; $2 fee per night. Open early-July to early-September.

Who to contact: Phone Star Ranger District at 503-899-1812, or write Rogue River National Forest at 6941 Upper Applegate Road, Jacksonville, OR 97530.

Location: Travel eight miles southwest of Jacksonville on Highway 238, then 14 miles southwest on County Route 10. The camp is eight miles southeast on Forest Service Road 1075.

Trip note: This campground is set along the shore of little Squaw Lakes. Numerous trails are in the area. A more intimate setting than at the larger Applegate Lake to the west.

WRANGLE

Site **99**

Campsites, facilities: There are five sites for tents, trailers or motorhomes up to 15 feet long. Picnic tables and firegrills are provided, and piped water, community kitchen and vault toilets are available. Pets are permitted.

Reservations, fee: No reservations necessary; no fee. Open early-June to late-October.

Who to contact: Phone Star Ranger District at 503-899-1812, or write Rogue River National Forest at 6941 Upper Applegate Road, Jacksonville, OR 97530.

Location: From Ashland, travel three miles north on Highway 99 to the town of Talent, then drive south on Forest Service Road 22 for 17 miles until it ends at Forest Service Road 20. Head east on 20 for 4 1/2 miles. The entrance road to the campground is on the right.

Trip note: This campground is set at the headwaters of Wrangle Creek in the Siskiyou Mountains. The Pacific Crest Trail passes near camp. A map of Rogue River National Forest details hiking trails and streams, as well as back country roads.

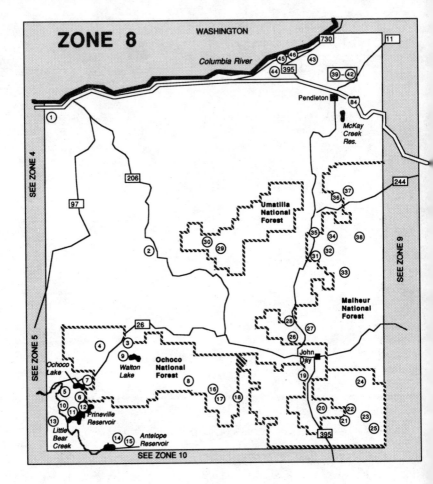

ZONE EIGHT

COLUMBIA

Site 1
DESCHUTES RIVER STATE RECREATION AREA

Campsites, facilities: There are 34 sites for tents, trailers or motorhomes up to 30 feet long. Picnic tables and firegrills are provided, and piped water and flush toilets are available. Pets are permitted.

Reservations, fee: No reservations necessary; $7 fee per night. Open mid-April to late-October.

Who to contact: Phone at 503-739-2322, or write at Star Route Box 29, Wasco, OR 97065.

Location: Travel 12 miles east on I-84 from The Dalles, then go five miles southeast on Highway 206.

Trip note: This park is set along the Deschutes River at the mouth of the Columbia River. Across the river is a small day-use state park called Heritage Landing, which has a boat ramp and restroom facilities. The Corps of Engineers offer a free train ride and tour of the dam at the Dalles during the summer. A bonus is good rafting and steelhead fishing possibilities here in season. For 25 miles upstream, the river is mostly inaccessible by car. A hiking trail from camp goes up the west bank into that area.

Site 2
SHELTON WAYSIDE

Campsites, facilities: There are 43 sites for tents, trailers or motorhomes up to 30 feet long. Picnic tables and firegrills are provided, and piped water, firewood and vault toilets are available. Pets are permitted.

Reservations, fee: No reservations necessary; $6 fee per night. Open mid-April to late-October.

Who to contact: Phone at 503-575-2773, or write Clyde Holiday State Park at P.O. Box 9, Canyon City, OR 97820.

Location: Go 10 miles southeast of Fossil on Highway 19.

Trip note: This is a good layover if you are stuck in the area with no place to camp for the night; there are no campgrounds on major roadways for an hour's drive in any direction. The closest options are primitive sites (campsites 29 & 30), accessible by Forest Service roads.

Site 3
OCHOCO DIVIDE

Campsites, facilities: There are 28 sites for tents, trailers or motorhomes up to 22 feet long.

Picnic tables and firegrills are provided, and firewood and vault toilets are available. There is no piped water. Pets are permitted.

Reservations, fee: No reservations necessary; $3 fee per night. Open mid-May to mid-October.

Who to contact: Phone Big Summit Ranger District at 503-447-3845, or write Ochoco National Forest at 2321 East Third, Prineville, OR 97754.

Location: From Prineville, go 31 miles northeast on US 26, then 100 yards southeast on Forest Service Road 550.

Trip note: This campground is set at 4700 feet elevation along the banks of Marks Creek near the Ochoco Divide. A pretty and primitive camp near the highway.

WILDCAT

Site **4**

Campsites, facilities: There are 17 sites for tents, trailers or motorhomes up to 30 feet long. Picnic tables and firegrills are provided, and piped water, firewood and vault toilets are available. Pets are permitted.

Reservations, fee: No reservations necessary; $4 fee per night. Open mid-April to late-October.

Who to contact: Phone the Prineville Ranger District at 503-447-3825, or write at P.O. Box 255, Mitchell Star Route, Prineville, OR 97754.

Location: From the town of Prineville, travel nine miles east on US 26, then nine miles northeast on County Route 122. The camp is two miles on Forest Service Road 33.

Trip note: This campground is set along the East Fork of Mill Creek at a trailhead that provides access into the Mill Creek Wilderness. A little-known spot, except by backpackers with local knowledge.

CRYSTAL CORRAL
RV PARK

Site **5**

Campsites, facilities: There are 20 tent sites and 22 drive-through sites for trailers or motorhomes of any length. Electricity, piped water and sewer hookups are provided. Flush toilets, bottled gas, showers, a store, cafe, laundromat and ice are available. Pets and motorbikes are permitted. Boat docks, launching facilities and rentals are nearby.

Reservations, fee: Reservations accepted; $7 fee per night. Open all year.

Who to contact: Phone at 503-447-5932, or write at HC 69, Box 91, Prineville, OR 97754.

Location: Travel eight miles east of Prineville on US 26.

Trip note: This motorhome park is not far from Ochoco Lake State Park. Campsites 6 and 7 are located along the lake. For a primitive option, see campsite 12.

LAKESHORE
MOTOR PARK

Site **6**

Campsites, facilities: There are 21 tent sites and 43 drive-through sites for trailers or motorhomes up to 35 feet long. Electricity, piped water, sewer hookups and picnic tables are provided. Flush toilets, bottled gas, sanitary disposal services, showers, firewood, a recreation hall, a store, laundromat, ice and playground are available. A cafe is located within one mile. Pets are permitted. Boat docks, launching facilities and rentals are nearby.

Reservations, fee: Reservations accepted; $10 fee per night. MasterCard and Visa accepted. Open all year.

Who to contact: Phone at 503-447-5398, or write at 108 MS Route, Prineville, OR 97754.

Location: From Prineville, travel nine miles east on US 26.

Trip note: This campground is set along the shore of Ochoco Reservoir. Fishing and boating are popular here.

Site 7   OCHOCO LAKE STATE PARK

Campsites, facilities: There are 22 sites for tents, trailers or motorhomes up to 30 feet long. Picnic tables and firegrills are provided, and piped water, firewood and flush toilets are available. Pets are permitted. Boat launching facilities are nearby.

Reservations, fee: No reservations necessary; $7 fee per night. Open mid-April to late-October.

Who to contact: Phone at 503-575-2773, or write Clyde Holiday State Park at P.O. Box 9, Canyon City, OR 97820.

Location: Travel seven miles east of Prineville on US 26.

Trip note: This is one of the nicer camps along Highway 26 in eastern Oregon. A state park, it is set along the shore adjacent to Ochoco Reservoir, where boating and fishing are popular pastimes.

Site 8   DEEP CREEK

Campsites, facilities: There are six sites for tents, trailers or motorhomes up to 22 feet long. Picnic tables and firegrills are provided, and piped water, firewood and vault toilets are available. Pets are permitted.

Reservations, fee: No reservations necessary; no fee. Open June to mid-October.

Who to contact: Phone Big Summit Ranger District at 503-447-3845, or write Ochoco National Forest at 2321 East Third, Prineville, OR 97754.

Location: From the town of Prineville, travel 16 1/2 miles east on US 26, then 8 1/2 miles northeast on County Route 22. The camp is 23 1/2 miles southeast on Forest Service Road 42.

Trip note: This camp is small and gets little use, but it is set at a nice spot—the confluence of Deep Creek and the North Fork of the Crooked River.

Site 9   WALTON LAKE

Campsites, facilities: There are 23 sites for tents, trailers or motorhomes up to 22 feet long. Picnic tables and firegrills are provided, and piped water, firewood and vault toilets are available. Pets are permitted. Boat docks and launching facilities are nearby.

Reservations, fee: No reservations necessary; $5 fee per night. Open June to late-September.

Who to contact: Phone Big Summit Ranger District at 503-447-3845, or write Ochoco National Forest at 2321 East Third, Prineville, OR 97754.

Location: Travel 16 1/2 miles east of Prineville on US 26, then 8 1/2 miles northeast on County Route 123. The camp is six miles northeast on Forest Service Road 22.

Trip note: This campground is set along the shore of Walton Lake. Fishing and swimming is popular and boats without motors are allowed. Hikers can explore a nearby trail that leads south to Round Mountain.

Site 10
DUNN ROVIN
RV PARK

Campsites, facilities: There are 25 drive-through sites for trailers or motorhomes of any length. Electricity, piped water, sewer hookups and picnic tables are provided. Flush toilets, showers, a laundromat and playground are available. Pets and motorbikes are permitted.

Reservations, fee: Reservations accepted; $7 fee per night. Open all year.

Who to contact: Phone at 503-447-3632, or write at 600 Davis Road, Prineville, OR 97754.

Location: From Prineville, travel one mile east on US 26, then one mile south on Combs Flat Road. From there, go 1 1/2 mile south on Prineville Reservoir Road, and 6 1/2 miles on Davis Road.

Trip note: This motorhome park is set fairly close to Prineville Reservoir.

Site 11
PRINEVILLE
RESERVOIR RESORT

Campsites, facilities: There are 75 drive-through sites for trailers or motorhomes of any length. Electricity, piped water and picnic tables are provided. Flush toilets, bottled gas, sanitary disposal services, showers, firewood, a store, cafe, laundromat and ice are available. Pets are permitted. Boat docks, launching facilities and rentals are nearby.

Reservations, fee: Reservations accepted; $10 fee per night. MasterCard and Visa accepted. Open mid-March to mid-October.

Who to contact: Phone at 503-447-7468, or write at 1300 PLR, Prineville, OR 97754.

Location: Travel on US 26 for one mile east of Prineville, then go one mile south on Combs Flat Road. The camp is 18 miles south on Prineville Reservoir Road.

Trip note: This resort is set along the shore of the Prineville Reservoir, a good spot for watersports and fishing.

Site 12
PRINEVILLE
RESERVOIR

Campsites, facilities: There are 48 tent sites and 22 sites for trailers or motorhomes of any length. Electricity, piped water, sewer hookups and picnic tables are provided. Flush toilets, showers, firewood and a laundromat are available. A cafe is located within one mile. Pets are permitted. Boat docks and launching facilities are nearby.

Reservations, fee: Reservations accepted; $8 fee per night. Open mid-April to late-October.

Who to contact: Phone at 503-447-4363, or write at Box 1050, Prineville, OR 97754.

Location: From the town of Prineville, travel one mile east on US 26, then go one mile south on Combs Flat Road. Travel 16 miles southeast on Prineville Reservoir Road to the reservoir.

Trip note: This state park is set along the shore of the Prineville Reservoir. Swimming, boating, fishing and waterskiing are among the options available here. This is one of two campgrounds on the lake; the other is campsite 11 (motorhomes only). Campsite 13 provides another option, set on the Crooked River below the Prineville Dam.

Site **13**   LOWER CROOKED RIVER

Campsites, facilities: There are 30 tent sites. Picnic tables and firegrills are provided, and piped water and vault toilets are available. Pets are permitted.

Reservations, fee: No reservations necessary; no fee. Open late-April to December.

Who to contact: Phone the Bureau of Land Management at 503-447-4115, or write at P.O. Box 550, Prineville, OR 97754.

Location: From the town of Prineville, travel 16 miles south on Highway 27.

Trip note: This campground is set along the banks of the Crooked River, just below the Prineville Dam.

Site **14**   ANTELOPE RESERVOIR

Campsites, facilities: There are 24 sites for tents, trailers or motorhomes up to 30 feet long. Picnic tables and firegrills are provided, and piped water, firewood and vault toilets are available. Pets are permitted. Boat docks and launching facilities are nearby.

Reservations, fee: No reservations necessary; $3 fee per night. Open late-April to late-October.

Who to contact: Phone the Prineville Ranger District at 503-447-3825, or write at P.O. Box 255, Mitchell Star Route, Prineville, OR 97754.

Location: From Prineville, travel 29 miles southeast on Highway 380, then 11 miles south on Forest Service Road 17. The camp is 300 yards east on Forest Service Road 17.

Trip note: This campground is set along the west shore of Antelope Reservoir. Fishing can be good and boating with motors is permitted. A good lake for canoes.

Site **15**   WILEY FLAT

Campsites, facilities: There are five sites for tents, trailers or motorhomes up to 30 feet long. Picnic tables and firegrills are provided, and piped water, firewood and vault toilets are available. Pets are permitted.

Reservations, fee: No reservations necessary; $2 fee per night. Open mid-June to late-October.

Who to contact: Phone the Prineville Ranger District at 503-447-3825, or write at P.O. Box 255, Mitchell Star Route, Prineville, OR 97754.

Location: Go 34 miles southeast of Prineville on Highway 380, then 10 miles southeast on Forest Service Road 16. The camp is one mile west on Forest Service Road 16.

Trip note: This campground is set along Wiley Creek. A nice, hidden spot, with minimal crowds and piped water. A map of Ochoco National Forest details nearby hiking trails and access roads. Campsite 17 provides a nearby but more primitive alternative.

Site **16**   WOLF CREEK

Campsites, facilities: There are 17 sites for tents, trailers or motorhomes up to 22 feet long. Picnic tables and firegrills are provided, and piped water, firewood and vault toilets are available. Pets are permitted.

Reservations, fee: No reservations necessary; no fee. Open mid-April to late-October.

Who to contact: Phone Paulina Ranger District at 503-477-3713, or write Ochoco National Forest at 6015 Paulina Star Route, Paulina, OR 97751.

Location: Travel 3 1/2 miles east of the town of Paulina on County Route 380, then 6 1/2 miles north on County Route 113. The camp is 1 1/2 miles north on Forest Service Road 142.

Trip note: This campground is set along the banks of Wolf Creek, a nice stream that runs through Ochoco National Forest. A quality spot.

SUGAR CREEK

Site **17**

Campsites, facilities: There are 10 sites for tents, trailers or motorhomes up to 21 feet long. Picnic tables and firegrills are provided, and firewood and vault toilets are available. There is no piped water. Pets are permitted.

Reservations, fee: No reservations necessary; no fee. Open mid-April to late-October.

Who to contact: Phone Paulina Ranger District at 503-477-3713, or write Ochoco National Forest at 6015 Paulina Star Route, Paulina, OR 97751.

Location: From Paulina, go 3 1/2 miles east on County Route 380, then 6 1/2 miles north on County Route 113. The camp is two miles east on Forest Service Road 158.

Trip note: This campground is set along the banks of Sugar Creek. It is one of three primitive camps in the outback of the Ochoco National Forest. The others are campsites 16 and 18. All are small and remote.

FRAZIER

Site **18**

Campsites, facilities: There are 12 sites for tents, trailers or motorhomes up to 21 feet long. Picnic tables and firegrills are provided, and firewood and vault toilets are available. There is no piped water. Pets are permitted.

Reservations, fee: No reservations necessary; no fee. Open mid-May to late-October.

Who to contact: Phone Paulina Ranger District at 503-477-3713, or write Ochoco National Forest at 6015 Paulina Star Route, Paulina, OR 97751.

Location: From the town of Paulina, travel 3 1/2 miles east on County Route 380, then two miles north on County Route 113. The camp is 10 miles east on County Route 135 and six miles on Forest Service Road 158.

Trip note: This campground is set along the banks of Frazier Creek. There are some dirt roads adjacent to camp that are good for mountain biking. Advisable to obtain map of Ochoco National Forest.

STARR

Site **19**

Campsites, facilities: There are 12 tent sites and nine sites for trailers or motorhomes up to 16 feet long. Picnic tables and firegrills are provided, and firewood and vault toilets are available. There is no piped water. Pets are permitted.

Reservations, fee: No reservations necessary; no fee. Open early-May to November.

Who to contact: Phone Malheur National Forest at 503-575-1731, or write at 139 NE Dayton Street, John Day, OR 97845.

Location: From the town of John Day travel 15 miles south on US 395.

Trip note: This is a good layover for travelers on Highway 395. It is set adjacent to Starr Springs, near an area that is popular in the winter for skiing.

WICKIUP

Site **20**

Campsites, facilities: There are seven sites for tents, trailers or motorhomes up to 16 feet long. Picnic tables and firegrills are provided, and piped water, firewood and vault toilets are available. Pets are permitted.

Reservations, fee: No reservations necessary; $4 fee per night. Open early-May to November.

Who to contact: Phone Malheur National Forest at 503-575-1731, or write at 139 NE Dayton, John Day, OR 97845.

Location: Travel 10 miles south of John Day on US 395 and eight miles southeast on Forest Service Road 1541.

Trip note: This campground is set along the bank of Wickiup Creek.

PARISH CABIN

Site **21**

Campsites, facilities: There are 17 sites for tents, trailers or motorhomes up to 22 feet long. Picnic tables and firegrills are provided, and piped water and vault toilets are available. Pets are permitted.

Reservations, fee: No reservations necessary; $4 fee per night. Open mid-May to late-November.

Who to contact: Phone Malheur National Forest at 503-575-1731, or write at 139 NE Dayton, John Day, OR 97845.

Location: From the town of John Day, travel 10 miles south on US 395, then 16 miles southeast on Forest Service Road 15 to the campground.

Trip note: This campground is set along the bank of Bear Creek.

CANYON MEADOWS

Site **22**

Campsites, facilities: There are 19 sites for tents, trailers or motorhomes up to 16 feet long. Picnic tables and firegrills are provided, and piped water, firewood and vault toilets are available. Pets are permitted. Boat docks and launching facilities are nearby.

Reservations, fee: No reservations necessary; $4 fee per night. Open mid-May to late-October.

Who to contact: Phone Malheur National Forest at 503-575-1731, or write at 139 NE Dayton, John Day, OR 97845.

Location: From John Day, go south on US 395 for 10 miles, then nine miles southeast on Forest Service Road 1541. The camp is five miles northeast on Forest Service Road 1520.

Trip note: This campground is set along the shore of Canyon Meadows Reservoir, where non-motorized boating, fishing and hiking are recreation options.

INDIAN SPRINGS

Site **23**

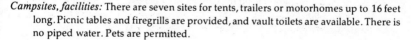

Campsites, facilities: There are seven sites for tents, trailers or motorhomes up to 16 feet long. Picnic tables and firegrills are provided, and vault toilets are available. There is no piped water. Pets are permitted.

Reservations, fee: No reservations necessary, $4 fee per night. Open all year.

Who to contact: Phone Malheur National Forest at 503-575-1731, or write at 139 NE Dayton Street, John Day, OR 97845.

Location: From John Day, travel 10 miles south on Highway 395, then east on Forest Service Road 15 for about 15 miles to Forest Service Road 16. Turn left and go 2 1/2 miles, then turn left on Forest Service Road 1640 and go seven miles north (gravel then dirt road).

Trip note: This campground is set at Indian Springs, a pretty spot near Bear Creek. A side trip option is driving the 77-mile loop around Strawberry Mountain Wilderness. A map of Malheur National Forest details the back roads. Backpackers and hikers will find many trailheads along the Forest Service roads.

STRAWBERRY

Site **24**

Campsites, facilities: There are 11 sites for tents, trailers or motorhomes up to 16 feet long. Picnic tables and firegrills are provided, and piped water and vault toilets are available. Pets are permitted.

Reservations, fee: No reservations necessary; $4 fee per night. Open June to mid-October.

Who to contact: Phone Malheur National Forest at 503-820-3311, or write at 139 NE Dayton, John Day, OR 97845.

Location: From the town of John Day, travel 13 miles east, then go 8 1/2 miles south on County Route 60, then 2 1/2 miles south on Forest Service Road 6001.

Trip note: This campground is set along the bank of Strawberry Creek. Nearby trails provide access into the Strawberry Mountain Wilderness, to Strawberry Lake and Strawberry Falls. It is a pretty area. There are two other campgrounds, Slide Creek and McNaughton Spring, that are along the entrance road to Strawberry. They have camping facilities, but no piped water. No fee is charged.

BIG CREEK

Site **25**

Campsites, facilities: There are 14 sites for tents, trailers or motorhomes up to 16 feet long. Picnic tables and firegrills are provided, and piped water and vault toilets are available. Pets are permitted.

Reservations, fee: No reservations necessary; no fee. Open mid-May to mid-November.

Who to contact: Phone Malheur National Forest at 503-820-3311, or write at 139 NE Dayton, John Day, OR 97845.

Location: From the town of John Day, travel 11 miles south on US 395, then southeast on Forest Service Road 15 for 16 miles, then eight miles east on Forest Service Road 16, and 1/2 mile north on Forest Service Road 815.

Trip note: This campground is set along the bank of Big Creek. Trails at the end of nearby Forest Service Roads provide accesss into Strawberry Mountain Wilderness.

CLYDE HOLLIDAY
WAYSIDE

Site **26**

Campsites, facilities: There are 30 sites for trailers or motorhomes of any length. Electricity, picnic tables and firegrills are provided, and piped water, firewood, sanitary disposal services, showers and flush toilets are available. Some facilities are wheelchair accessible. Pets are permitted.

Reservations, fee: No reservations necessary; $7 fee per night. Open mid-April to late-October.

Who to contact: Phone at 503-575-2773, or write at 511 Hillcrest Road, John Day, OR 97845.

Location: Travel seven miles west of the town of John Day on US 26.

Trip note: This roadside campground is set near the John Day River. Of special interest in the town of John Day is Kam Wah Chung, a Chinese Herbalist's office from the 1880's that is now a museum administered by the State Parks Department.

MAGONE LAKE
Site **27**

Campsites, facilities: There are 16 sites for tents, trailers or motorhomes up to 16 feet long. Picnic tables and firegrills are provided, and piped water, firewood and vault toilets are available. Pets are permitted. Boat docks and launching facilities are nearby.

Reservations, fee: No reservations necessary; $4 fee per night. Open mid-May to November.

Who to contact: Phone Malheur National Forest at 503-575-2110, or write 139 NE Dayton Street, John Day, OR 97845.

Location: From the town of John Day, travel eight miles west, then go nine miles north on US 395, then eight miles northeast on Forest Service Road 36. The camp is two miles north on Forest Service Road 1219.

Trip note: This campground is set along the shore of litte Magone Lake. Numerous dirt forest service roads criss-cross the area northeast of camp.

BEECH CREEK
Site **28**

Campsites, facilities: There are eight sites for tents, trailers or motorhomes up to 16 feet long. Picnic tables and firegrills are provided, and piped water and vault toilets are available. Pets are permitted.

Reservations, fee: No reservations necessary; $4 fee per night. Open June to November.

Who to contact: Phone Malheur National Forest at 503-575-2110, or write at 139 NE Dayton Street, John Day, OR 97845.

Location: From the town of John Day, travel eight miles west on Highway 26, then 16 miles north on US 395 to the campground.

Trip note: This campground is set along Beech Creek.

BULL PRAIRIE
Site **29**

Campsites, facilities: There are 25 sites for tents, trailers or motorhomes up to 31 feet long. Picnic tables and firegrills are provided, and piped water, sanitary disposal services, firewood and vault toilets are available. Pets are permitted. Boat docks and launching facilities are nearby.

Reservations, fee: No reservations necessary; $4 fee per night. Open May to late-October.

Who to contact: Phone Heppner Ranger District at 503-676-9187, or write Umatilla National Forest at P.O. Box 7, Heppner, OR 97836.

Location: From the junction of Highway 26 and 19, drive north on Highway 19 just over two miles from the town of Spray, then 12 miles north on Highway 207. The camp is three miles northeast on Forest Service Road 2039.

Trip note: This campground is set along the shore of Bull Prairie Lake. Boating, swimming,

fishing and hunting are some of the options here. This spot attracts little attention
from out-of-towners.

FAIRVIEW
Site **30**

Campsites, facilities: There are five sites for trailers or motorhomes up to 16 feet long.
Picnic tables and firegrills are provided, and firewood and vault toilets are available.
There is no piped water. Pets are permitted. Boat docks and launching facilities are
nearby.

Reservations, fee: No reservations necessary; $4 fee per night. Open May to late-October.

Who to contact: Phone Heppner Ranger District at 509-676-9187, or write Umatilla
National Forest at P.O. Box 7, Heppner, OR 97836.

Location: From the junction of Highway 26 and Highway 19, drive a little over two miles
past the town of Spray on Highway 19, then 11 1/2 miles north on Highway 207. The
camp is 500 yards west on Forest Service Road 400.

Trip note: This campground is set adjacent to Fairview Springs near Mahogany Butte. A
small, primitive site, known by very few people.

TOLLBRIDGE
Site **31**

Campsites, facilities: There are six sites for tents, trailers or motorhomes up to 31 feet long.
Picnic tables and firegrills are provided, and piped water and vault toilets are available. Pets are permitted.

Reservations, fee: No reservations necessary; $4 fee per night. Open June to mid-October.

Who to contact: Phone the North Fork John Day Ranger District at 503-427-3231, or write
at P.O. Box 158, Ukiah, OR 97880.

Location: From the town of Dale, go one mile northeast on US 395, 1/2 mile southeast on
Forest Service Road 55 and 100 yards on Forest Service Road 10.

Trip note: This campground is set at the confluence of Desolation and Brook Creeks with
Camus Creek, and adjacent to the Bridge Creek Wildlife Area. Small and secluded.

GOLD DREDGE
Site **32**

Campsites, facilities: There are three sites for trailers or motorhomes. No picnic tables,
piped water or firegrills are provided, but pit toilets are available. Motorbikes are
permitted.

Reservations, fee: No reservations necessary; no fee. Open May to September.

Who to contact: Phone North Fork John Day Ranger District at 503-427-3231, or write
Umatilla National Forest at P.O. Box 158, Ukiah, OR 97880.

Location: From the town of Pendleton, travel 64 miles south on US 395 to Dale, then drive
east on Forest Service Road 55 for six miles to the crossroads. Continue east on Forest
Service Road 5506 for 2 1/2 miles to the campground.

Trip note: This campground is set along the banks of the North Fork of the John Day River.
Hunting, fishing and riding trailbikes are some of the options here.

Site 33 ORIENTAL CREEK

Campsites, facilities: There are three primitive tent sites. Picnic tables and firegrills are provided and pit toilets are available. There is no piped water. Motorbikes are permitted.

Reservations, fee: No reservations necessary; no fee.

Who to contact: Phone North Fork John Day Ranger District at 503-427-3231, or write Umatilla National Forest at P.O. Box 158, Ukiah, OR 97880.

Location: From the town of Pendleton, travel 64 miles south on US 395 to Dale, then drive east on Forest Service Road 55 for six miles to the crossroads. Continue east on Forest Service Road 5506 for 10 1/2 miles to the campground. Dirt road for final 2 1/2 miles.

Trip note: This campground is set at 3500 feet elevation along the banks of the North Fork of the John Day River. Nearby trails provide access to the North Fork John Day Wilderness. Hunting, fishing and riding trailbikes are some of the options here, but NO motorbikes are permitted in the Wilderness Area.

Site 34 DRIFT FENCE

Campsites, facilities: There are three sites for tents, trailer or motorhomes up to 16 feet long. No picnic tables, piped water or firegrills are provided, but a vault toilet is available.

Reservations, fee: No reservations necessary; no fee. Open from June to November.

Who to contact: Phone North Fork John Day Ranger District at 503-427-3231, or write Umatilla National Forest at P.O. Box 158, Ukiah, OR 97880.

Location: From the town of Ukiah, drive nine miles southeast on Forest Service Road 52 to the campground.

Trip note: This campground is set at 4200 feet, adjacent to Ross Springs. There is some hunting here.

Site 35 UKIAH-DALE FOREST STATE PARK

Campsites, facilities: There are 25 sites for tents, trailers or motorhomes up to 25 feet long. Picnic tables and firegrills are provided, and piped water, firewood and vault toilets are available. Pets are permitted.

Reservations, fee: No reservations necessary; $6 fee per night. Open mid-April to late-October.

Who to contact: Phone at 503-983-2277, or write at P.O. Box 85, Meacham, OR 97859.

Location: Go three miles south of Ukiah on US 395.

Trip note: This campground is set near the banks of Camus Creek. Good layover for visitors crusing Highway 395 looking for a spot for the night.

Site 36 LANE CREEK

Campsites, facilities: There are nine sites for tents, trailers or motorhomes up to 30 feet long. Picnic tables and firegrills are provided, and piped water and vault toilets are available. Pets are permitted.

Reservations, fee: No reservations necessary; $4 fee per night. Open mid-May to November.

Who to contact: Phone the North Fork John Day Ranger District at 503-427-3231, or write at P.O. Box 158, Ukiah, OR 97880.

Location: From the town of Ukiah, travel 10 1/2 miles east on Highway 244.

Trip note: This campground is set along Camus Creek. There is good hunting in Umatilla National Forest and some fishing. A Forest Service map details the back roads.

Site 37   BEAR WALLOW CREEK

Campsites, facilities: There are nine sites for tents, trailers or motorhomes up to 30 feet long. Picnic tables and firegrills are provided, and piped water and vault toilets are available. Pets are permitted.

Reservations, fee: No reservations necessary; $4 fee per night. Open mid-May to November.

Who to contact: Phone the North Fork John Day Ranger District at 503-427-3231, or write at P.O. Box 158, Ukiah, OR 97880.

Location: From the town of Ukiah on Highway 395, travel 11 miles east on Highway 244.

Trip note: This campground is set at the confluence of Bear Wallow Creek and Camus Creek. One of three camps off Highway 244. The others are campsites 37 and 38.

Site 38   FRAZIER

Campsites, facilities: There are 25 sites for tents, trailers or motorhomes up to 30 feet long. Picnic tables and firegrills are provided, and piped water and vault toilets are available. Pets are permitted.

Reservations, fee: No reservations necessary; $4 fee per night. Open June to November.

Who to contact: Phone Umatilla at 503-427-3231, or write at Ukiah, OR 97880.

Location: From Ukiah, go 18 miles east on Highway 244, then 1/2 mile south on Forest Service Road 5226. The camp is two miles east on Forest Service Road 20.

Trip note: This campground is set at 4300 feet elevation along the banks of Frazier Creek. A popular hunting area with some fishing. It's advisable to obtain a map of Umatilla National Forest.

Site 39   BROOKE TRAILER PARK

Campsites, facilities: There are four tent sites and 20 drive-through sites for trailers or motorhomes of any length. Electricity, piped water, sewer hookups and picnic tables are provided. Flush toilets, showers, a laundromat and ice are available. Bottled gas, sanitary disposal services, a store and cafe are located within one mile. Pets are permitted.

Reservations, fee: Reservations accepted; $10 fee per night. Open all year.

Who to contact: Phone at 503-276-5353, or write at 5 Northeast 8th Street, Pendleton, OR 97801.

Location: From the town of Pendleton, travel 3/4 mile north on Highway 11, then 1/4 mile west on southeast Court Avenue.

Trip note: Waterfowl can be observed at the MacKay Creek National Wildlife Refuge seven miles south of the town of Pendleton. The Pendleton Mills and outlet are in town. Other nearby recreation options include a golf course, bike paths and tennis courts.

Site 40   RIVERVIEW TRAILER PARK

Campsites, facilities: There are 18 sites for trailers or motorhomes of any length. Electricity and piped water are provided. Flush toilets, showers, a laundromat and playground are available. A store, cafe and ice are located within one mile. Pets are permitted.

Reservations, fee: Reservations accepted; $7 fee per night. Open all year.

Who to contact: Phone at 503-276-7632, or write at 2712 Northeast Riverside, Pendleton, OR 97801.

Location: From the town of Pendleton, travel 1/4 mile northeast on Highway 11, then go one block east.

Trip note: This motorhome park is set along the banks of the Umatilla River. Nearby recreation options include a golf course, bike paths and tennis courts.

Site 41   RV PARK

Campsites, facilities: There are 30 tent sites and 31 drive-through sites for trailers or motorhomes of any length. Electricity, piped water, sewer hookups and picnic tables are provided. Flush toilets, sanitary services, showers, laundromat and playground are available. Bottled gas, a store, cafe and ice are located within one mile. Motorbikes are permitted.

Reservations, fee: No reservations necessary; $12 fee per night. Open all year.

Who to contact: Phone at 503-276-5408, or write at 1500 Southeast Byers, Pendleton, OR 97801.

Location: From Pendleton, go one mile north on Highway 11, then one block west on 10th Street. The camp is located 1/4 mile east on 12th Street and 1/4 mile north on Byers.

Trip note: This campground is one block from the levee along the Umatilla River, where people fish and walk. The Pendleton Woolen Mills are around the corner.

Site 42   SHADEVIEW MOBILE HOME PARK

Campsites, facilities: There are eight drive-through sites for trailers or motorhomes of any length. Electricity, piped water and sewer hookups are provided. Flush toilets and showers are available. Bottled gas, sanitary disposal services, a store, cafe, laundromat and ice are located within one mile. Pets are permitted.

Reservations, fee: Reservations accepted; $7 fee per night. Open all year.

Who to contact: Phone at 503-276-0688, or write at 1437 Southwest 37th, Pendleton, OR 97801.

Location: Go one mile south of Pendleton on US 395, then 1/4 mile west on Southgate Place. The park is one block north on 37th Street.

Trip note: This park is set near the Umatilla River. A levee along the river offers walking and fishing opportunities. Nearby recreation options include marked bike trails and tennis courts. The Cold Springs National Wildlife Refuge is eight miles east of Hermiston and offers a large variety of waterfowl.

Site 43
HAT ROCK
CAMPGROUND

Campsites, facilities: There are 40 tent sites and 30 drive-through sites for trailers or motorhomes of any length. Electricity, piped water, sewer hookups and picnic tables are provided. Flush toilets, sanitary disposal services, showers, a store, cafe, laundromat and ice are available. Pets are permitted. Boat docks and launching facilities are nearby.

Reservations, fee: Reservations accepted; $6 fee per night. Open all year.

Who to contact: Phone at 503-567-4188, or write at Route 3, Box 3780, Hermiston, OR 97838.

Location: From Hermiston, go one mile southeast on Highway 207, then 1/2 mile on State Park Road.

Trip note: This campground is not far from Hat Rock State Park, a day-use area with a boat launch along the banks of the Columbia River.

Site 44
BUTTERCREEK
RECREATION COMPLEX

Campsites, facilities: There are 20 tent sites and 24 drive-through sites for trailers or motorhomes of any length. Electricity, piped water, sewer hookups and picnic tables are provided. Flush toilets, bottled gas, sanitary disposal services, showers, a store, cafe, laundromat and ice are available. Pets are permitted.

Reservations, fee: Reservations accepted; $9 fee per night. MasterCard and Visa accepted. Open all year.

Who to contact: Phone at 503-567-5469, or write at Route 1, Box 1929A, Hermiston, OR 97838.

Location: Take exit 182 off Highway 207 in Hermiston.

Trip note: This campground is set along the banks of Buttercreek.

Site 45
SHADY REST
MOBILE HOME PARK

Campsites, facilities: There are six tent sites and 24 drive-through sites for trailers or motorhomes of any length. Electricity, piped water and sewer hookups are provided. Flush toilets, showers, a laundromat and swimming pool are available. A store, cafe and ice are located within one mile. Pets are permitted. Boat docks and launching facilities are nearby.

Reservations, fee: Reservations accepted; $9 fee per night. Open March to late-October.

Who to contact: Phone at 503-922-5041, or write at Route 1, Box 240, Umatilla, OR 97882.

Location: Travel 1/2 mile west of the town of Umatilla on US 730.

Trip note: This campground is set along the Columbia River. Nearby recreation options include a golf course, a marina and tennis courts.

Site 46
DUN-ROLLIN
TRAILER PARK

Campsites, facilities: There are 15 sites for trailers or motorhomes of any length. Elec-

tricity, piped water and sewer hookups are provided. Flush toilets, sanitary disposal services, showers, a laundromat and playground are available. Bottled gas, a store, cafe and ice are located within one mile. Pets and motorbikes are permitted.

Reservations, fee: Reservations accepted; $7 fee per night. Open all year.

Who to contact: Phone at 503-567-6918, or write at 445 East Jennie, Hermiston, OR 97838.

Location: From the town of Hermiston, travel 1/4 mile north on US 395 to Jennie, then go 1/2 mile east.

Trip note: This motorhome park is not far from the Columbia River and Cold Springs National Wildlife Refuge. Nearby recreation options include a golf course, bike paths, a marina and tennis courts.

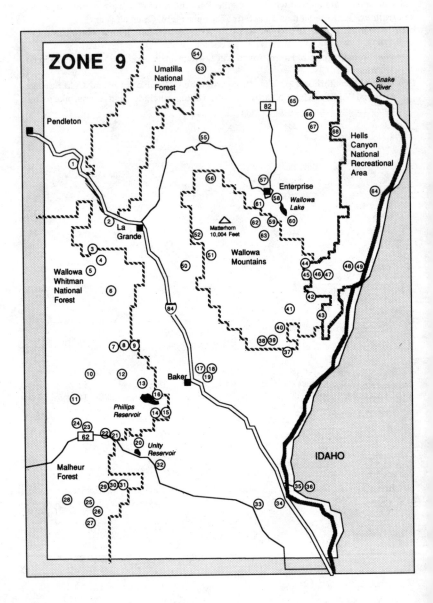

ZONE NINE

WALLOWA

EMIGRANT SPRINGS
STATE PARK

⛺

Campsites, facilities: There are 33 tent sites and 18 sites for trailers or motorhomes up to 30 feet long. Electricity, piped water, sewer hookups and picnic tables are provided. Flush toilets, showers, firewood, a laundromat and playground are available. Pets are permitted.

Reservations, fee: No reservations necessary; $8 fee per night. Open mid-April to late-October.

Who to contact: Phone at 503-983-2277, or write at Meacham, OR 97859.

Location: From the town of Pendleton, travel 25 miles southeast on I-84 to the park.

Trip note: This wooded state park offers group camping and a display about the Oregon Trail. This is a good layover for people driving Highway 84. It's set just south of the Umatilla Indian Reservation.

HILGARD JUNCTION
STATE PARK

⛺

Campsites, facilities: There are 18 sites for tents, trailers or motorhomes up to 20 feet long. Picnic tables and firegrills are provided, and sanitary disposal services, firewood and vault toilets are available. Some facilities are wheelchair accessible. Pets are permitted.

Reservations, fee: No reservations necessary; $5 fee per night. Open all year with limited winter facilities.

Who to contact: Phone at 503-983-2277, or write at La Grande, OR 97850.

Location: Travel eight miles west of La Grande on I-84 to Starkey Road.

Trip note: This roadside campground is set along the banks of the Grande Ronde River at the foot of the Blue Mountains. It is surrounded by Umatilla National Forest.

BIKINI BEACH
CAMPGROUND

⛺

Campsites, facilities: There are five tent sites. Picnic tables and firegrills are provided. Piped water, firewood and vault toilets are available. Pets are permitted.

Reservations, fee: No reservations necessary; no fee. Open late-May to late-November.

Who to contact: Phone La Grande Ranger District at 503-963-7186, or write at Wallowa-Whitman National Forest, La Grande, OR 97850.

Location: Go nine miles northwest of La Grande on I-84N to the Hilgard junction, then 13 miles southwest on Highway 244. From there, go 4 1/2 miles south on Forest Service Road 51.

Trip note: This campground is set along the banks of the Grande Ronde River. If this small camp is full, try the next three camps listed. They are also small, primitive Forest Service campgrounds located just south on the same Forest Service road system. See the zone map.

SHERWOOD FOREST CAMPGROUND
Site 4

Campsites, facilities: There are five sites for tents, trailers or motorhomes up to 22 feet long. Picnic tables and firegrills are provided, and firewood and vault toilets are available. There is no piped water. Pets are permitted.

Reservations, fee: No reservations necessary; no fee. Open late-May to late-November.

Who to contact: Phone La Grande Ranger District at 503-963-7186, or write at Wallowa-Whitman National Forest, La Grande, OR 97850.

Location: Go nine miles northwest of La Grande on I-84N, then 13 miles southwest on Highway 244. From there, go 6 1/2 miles south of Forest Service Road 51.

Trip note: This small, rustic camp is set at 3800 feet elevation, along the banks of Grande Ronde River. Advisable to obtain map of of Wallowa-Whitman National Forest, which details the back roads and side trips available.

RIVER
Site 5

Campsites, facilities: There are six sites for tents, trailers or motorhomes up to 22 feet long. Picnic tables and firegrills are provided. Firewood and vault toilets are available. There is no piped water. Pets are permitted.

Reservations, fee: No reservations necessary; no fee. Open late-May to late-November.

Who to contact: Phone La Grande Ranger District at 503-963-7186, or write at Wallowa-Whitman National Forest, La Grande, OR 97850.

Location: From La Grande, travel eight miles northwest on US 80, then 12 1/2 miles southwest on Highway 244. The camp is 11 miles south on Forest Service Road 51.

Trip note: This campground is set along the banks of the Grande Ronde River. One of four small, primitive camps along Forest Service Road 51 and adjoining road 5125.

WOODLEY CAMPGROUND
Site 6

Campsites, facilities: There are seven sites for tents, trailers or motorhomes up to 22 feet long. Picnic tables and firegrills are provided, and firewood and vault toilets are available. There is no piped water. Pets are permitted.

Reservations, fee: No reservations necessary; no fee. Open late-May to late-November.

Who to contact: Phone La Grande Ranger District at 503-963-7186, or write at Wallowa-Whitman National Forest, La Grande, OR 97850.

Location: From La Grande, go nine miles northwest on I-84N, then 13 miles southwest on Highway 244. The camp is 16 miles south on Forest Service Road 5125.

Trip note: This campground is set along the banks of the Grande Ronde River. Hiking trails are available, detailed on Forest Service map.

ANTHONY LAKE
Site **7**

Campsites, facilities: There are 47 sites for tents, trailers or motorhomes up to 22 feet long. Piped water and picnic tables are provided. Firewood, cafe and ice are available. Some facilities are wheelchair accessible. Pets are permitted. Boat docks, launching facilities and rentals are nearby.

Reservations, fee: No reservations necessary; $5 fee per night. Open July to late-September.

Who to contact: Phone Baker Ranger District at 503-523-4476, or write at Wallowa-Whitman National Forest at Route 1, Box 1, Baker, OR 97814.

Location: From Haines, go 17 miles northwest on Highway SH411, then seven miles west on Forest Service Road 73.

Trip note: This campground is set along the banks of Anthony Lake, where boating without motors is permitted. Several smaller lakes are within two miles by car or trail. These are ideal for trout fishing from a raft, float tube or canoe.

GRANDE RONDE LAKE
Site **8**

Campsites, facilities: There are eight tent sites and four sites for trailers or motorhomes up to 16 feet long. Picnic tables and firegrills are provided, and piped water, firewood and vault toilets are available. Pets are permitted. Boat docks, launching facilities and rentals are nearby.

Reservations, fee: No reservations necessary; $3 fee per night. Open July to mid-September.

Who to contact: Phone Baker Ranger District at 503-523-4476, or write at Wallowa-Whitman National Forest at Route 1, Box 1, Baker, OR 97814.

Location: Travel 17 miles northwest of the town of Haines on Highway 411, then 8 1/2 miles west on Forest Service Road 73. The camp is 1/2 miles northwest on Forest Service Road 43.

Trip note: This campground is set at 7200 feet elevation, along the shore of Grande Ronde Lake, a small lake where the trout fishing can be good. A nearby trail leads north to the Aurelia Mine site. Several other trails are south near Anthony Lake. A map of Wallowa-Whitman National Forest details the possibilities.

MUD LAKE
Site **9**

Campsites, facilities: There are 14 tent sites and seven sites for trailers or motorhomes up to 16 feet long. Picnic tables and firegrills are provided, and piped water, firewood and vault toilets are available. Pets are permitted. Boat docks, launching facilities and rentals are nearby.

Reservations, fee: No reservations necessary; $3 fee per night. Open July to mid-September.

Who to contact: Phone Baker Ranger District at 503-523-4476, or write at Wallowa-Whitman National Forest at Route 1, Box 1, Baker, OR 97814.

Location: From the town of Haines, travel 17 miles northwest on Highway 411, then 7 1/2 miles west on Forest Service Road 73.

Trip note: This campground is set along the shore of little Mud Lake, a small lake located between campsites 9 and 10. Trout fishing can be fairly good here.

Site 10 NORTH FORK JOHN DAY

Campsites, facilities: There are seven sites for tents, trailers or motorhomes up to 22 feet long. Picnic tables and firegrills are provided, and vault toilets are available. There is no piped water. Pets are permitted.

Reservations, fee: No reservations necessary; no fee. Open June to late-September.

Who to contact: Phone North Fork John Day Ranger District at 503-427-3231, or write P.O. Box 158, Ukiah, OR 97880.

Location: From the town of Ukiah, travel 38 1/2 miles southeast on Forest Service Road 52.

Trip note: This campground is set along the banks of the North Fork of the John Day River. This is an ideal base camp for a wilderness backpacking trip. Trails from camp lead into the North Fork John Day Wilderness.

Site 11 OLIVE LAKE

Campsites, facilities: There are six sites for tents, trailers or motorhomes up to 31 feet long. Picnic tables and firegrills are provided. Piped water, firewood and vault toilets are available. Pets and motorbikes are permitted. Boat docks and launching facilities are nearby.

Reservations, fee: No reservations necessary; no fee. Open June to late-September.

Who to contact: Phone John Day Ranger District at 503-427-3231, or write Umatilla National Forest, P.O. Box 158, Ukiah, OR 97880.

Location: From the town of Dale, travel one mile northeast on US 395, then 1/2 mile southeast on Forest Service Road 55. The camp is 26 miles southeast on Forest Service Road 10.

Trip note: This campground is set at 6000 feet elevation along the shore of Olive Lake, located between two sections of the North Fork John Day Wilderness. Nearby trails provide access to the wilderness. Motorbikes and mountain bikes are not permitted.

Site 12 MCCULLY FORKS

Campsites, facilities: There are three tent sites and four sites for trailers or motorhomes up to 16 feet long. Picnic tables and firegrills are provided, and firewood and vault toilets are available. There is no piped water. Pets are permitted.

Reservations, fee: No reservations necessary; no fee. Open late-May to late-October.

Who to contact: Phone Baker Ranger District at 503-523-4476, or write at Wallowa-Whitman National Forest at Route 1, Box 1, Baker, OR 97814.

Location: From the town of Baker, travel 29 miles southwest on Highway 7 to Sumpter. From Sumpter, continue three miles northwest on Highway 7.

Trip note: This campground is set along the banks of McCully Creek. An easy access campground that is free and primitive.

Site 13   DEER CREEK CAMPGROUND

Campsites, facilities: There are eight sites for trailers or motorhomes up to 16 feet long. Picnic tables and firegrills are provided, and firewood and vault toilets are available. Pets are permitted. Boat docks and launching facilities are nearby.

Reservations, fee: No reservations necessary; $3 fee per night. Open early-May to late-October.

Who to contact: Phone Baker Ranger District at 503-523-4476, or write at Wallowa-Whitman National Forest at Route 1, Box 1, Baker, OR 97814.

Location: From the town of Baker, travel 26 miles southwest on Highway 7, then three miles north on Forest Service Road 6550.

Trip note: This campground is set along the banks of Deer Creek, about nine miles from Phillips Lake. The camp is nestled below Elkhorn Ridge.

Site 14   MILLERS LANE

Campsites, facilities: There are seven sites for tents, trailers or motorhomes up to 15 feet long. Picnic tables and firegrills are provided, and firewood and vault toilets are available. There is no piped water. Pets are permitted. Boat docks are nearby.

Reservations, fee: No reservations necessary; no fee. Open May to mid-November.

Who to contact: Phone Baker Ranger District at 503-523-4476, or write at Wallowa-Whitman National Forest at Route 1, Box 1, Baker, OR 97814.

Location: From the town of Baker, travel 24 miles southwest on Highway 7 just past Phillips Lake, then 3 1/2 miles southeast on Forest Service Road 2226.

Trip note: This campground is set along the south shore of Phillips Lake. It is a long, narrow lake, the largest lake in the region. One of three camps on the lake—only campsite 33 has piped water.

Site 15   SOUTHWEST SHORE

Campsites, facilities: There are 18 sites for tents, trailers or motorhomes up to 15 feet long. Firegrills, firewood and vault toilets are available. There is no piped water. Pets are permitted. Boat docks and launching facilities are nearby.

Reservations, fee: No reservations necessary; no fee. Open May to mid-November.

Who to contact: Phone Baker Ranger District at 503-523-4476, or write at Wallowa-Whitman National Forest at Route 1, Box 1, Baker, OR 97814.

Location: From the town of Baker, travel 24 miles southwest on Highway 7, then 2 1/2 miles southeast on Forest Service Road 2226.

Trip note: This campground is set along the south shore of Phillips Lake, a four-mile long reservoir created by the Mason Dam on the Powder River. One of three primitive camps on the lake. Nearby campsite 33 has piped water.

Site 16   UNION CREEK

Campsites, facilities: There are 12 sites for tents, trailers or motorhomes up to 22 feet long. Electricity, piped water, sewer hookups and picnic tables are provided. Flush toilets, firewood and ice are available. Some facilities are wheelchair accessible. Pets are permitted. Boat docks and launching facilities are nearby.

Reservations, fee: No reservations necessary; $8 fee per night. Open mid-April to mid-November.

Who to contact: Phone the Baker Ranger District at 503-523-4476, or write Willowa-Whitman National Forest at P.O. Box 907, Baker, OR 97814.

Location: Travel 17 miles southwest of Baker on Highway 7.

Trip note: This campground is set along the the north shore of Phillips Lake. Easy to reach, yet missed by travelers on Highway 30. One of three camps on the lake; this is the only one with piped water.

Site 17 ALPEN DORF RV PARK

Campsites, facilities: There are 10 tent sites and 30 drive-through sites for trailers or motorhomes. Electricity, piped water, sewer hookups and picnic tables are provided. Flush toilets, bottled gas, showers, a store, cafe, ice and playground are available. Sanitary services and laundromat are located within one mile. Pets and motorbikes are permitted.

Reservations, fee: Reservations accepted; $9 fee per night. Open all year.

Who to contact: Phone at 503-523-7171, or write at Route 2, Box 48, Baker, OR 97814.

Location: Take exit 302 off I-84 in Baker, then travel about 300 feet west.

Trip note: Baker provides the access point for the southern route into Hells Canyon National Recreation Area. Attractions in town include the Oregon Trail Regional Museum, the little Sumpter Valley Railroad, bike paths, a riding stable and tennis courts.

Site 18 MOUNTAIN VIEW TRAV-L PARK

Campsites, facilities: There are 11 tent sites and 49 drive-through sites for trailers or motorhomes of any length. Electricity, piped water, sewer hookups and picnic tables are provided. Flush toilets, sanitary disposal services, showers, a laundromat, ice, playground and swimming pool are available. Bottled gas, a store and cafe are located within one mile. Pets and motorbikes are permitted.

Reservations, fee: Reservations accepted; $10 fee per night. Open all year with limited winter facilities.

Who to contact: Phone at 503-523-4824, or write at Route 1, Box 213A, Baker, OR 97814.

Location: From the town of Baker, go 1/2 mile west on Campbell, then one mile north on Cedar. The camp is one mile west on Hughes Lane.

Trip note: This campground is set near Beaver Creek. See the trip note to campsite 34.

Site 19 LARIAT MOTEL RV PARK

Campsites, facilities: There are 14 tent sites and 20 sites for trailers or motorhomes of any length. Electricity, piped water, sewer hookups and picnic tables are provided. Flush toilets, sanitary disposal services, showers, a laundromat and ice are available. Bottled gas, a store and cafe are located within one mile. Pets are permitted.

Reservations, fee: Reservations accepted; $7 fee per night. MasterCard and Visa accepted.

Open all year, but with limited winter facilities.

Who to contact: Phone at 503-523-6381, or write at 880 Elm Street, Baker, OR 97814.

Location: Take exit 306 off I-84 in Baker.

Trip note: For information about Baker, see the trip note to campsite 34.

UNITY LAKE
Site **20**   STATE PARK

Campsites, facilities: There are 28 sites for tents, trailers or motorhomes. Picnic tables and firegrills are provided. Piped water, flush toilets, showers, sanitary disposal station and firewood are available. Some facilities are wheelchair accessible. Pets are permitted. Boat docks and launching facilities are nearby.

Reservations, fee: No reservations necessary; $7 fee per night. Open mid-April to late-October.

Who to contact: Phone at 503-575-2773, or write at Huntington, OR 97907.

Location: Travel 47 miles west of the town of John Day on Highway 26, then go three miles north on Highway 7.

Trip note: This campground is set along the east shore of Unity Reservoir. Easy to reach and a popular spot when the weather is good.

WETMORE
Site **21**

Campsites, facilities: There are 10 sites for tents, trailers or motorhomes up to 16 feet long. Picnic tables and firegrills are provided, and piped water, firewood and vault toilets are available. Some facilities are wheelchair accessible. Pets are permitted.

Reservations, fee: No reservations necessary; no fee. Open late-May to mid-September.

Who to contact: Phone Unity Ranger District at 503-446-3351, or write Wallowa-Whitman National Forest, P.O. Box 907, Baker, OR 97814.

Location: Travel 41 miles west of the town of John Day on Highway 26 to the campground.

Trip note: This campground is set near the Middle Fork Burnt River. A good base camp for a fishing or hiking trip. The stream can provide good trout fishing. Trails are detailed on map of Wallowa-Whitman National Forest.

OREGON
Site **22**

Campsites, facilities: There are eight sites for tents, trailers or motorhomes up to 16 feet long. Picnic tables and firegrills are provided, and firewood and vault toilets are available. There is no piped water. Pets are permitted.

Reservations, fee: No reservations necessary; no fee. Open late-May to mid-September.

Who to contact: Phone Unity Ranger District at 503-446-3351, or write Wallowa-Whitman National Forest, P.O. Box 907, Baker, OR 97814.

Location: Travel 39 miles west of the town of John Day on Highway 26 to the campground.

Trip note: This campground is set along the banks of Road Creek. Hiking trails are nearby. Easy access with good recreation potential.

DIXIE

Site **23**

Campsites, facilities: There are 11 sites for tents, trailers or motorhomes up to 22 feet long.
  Picnic tables and firegrills are provided, and vault toilets, a store, a cafe and ice are
  available. There is no piped water. Pets are permitted.

Reservations, fee: No reservations necessary; no fee. Open June to November.

Who to contact: Phone Long Creek Ranger District at 503-575-2110, or write Malheur
  National Forest at 139 NE Dayton Street, John Day, OR 97845.

Location: Travel 14 miles northeast of Prairie City on Highway 26, then 1/2 mile north on
  Forest Service Road 365.

Trip note: This campground is set at Dixie Summit at 5300 feet elevation, near Bridge
  Creek. It is just far enough off Highway 26 to get missed by most everybody, yet close
  enough to provide easy access.

MIDDLE FORK

Site **24**

Campsites, facilities: There are 11 sites for tents, trailers or motorhomes up to 22 feet long.
  Picnic tables and firegrills are provided, and vault toilets are available. There is no
  piped water. Pets are permitted.

Reservations, fee: No reservations necessary; no fee. Open mid-June to November.

Who to contact: Phone Long Creek Ranger District at 503-575-2110, or write Malheur
  National Forest at 139 NE Dayton Street, John Day, OR 97845.

Location: From Prairie City, travel 11 1/2 miles northeast on US 26, then one mile north on
  Highway 7. The camp is five miles northwest on County Route 20.

Trip note: This campground is set along the banks of the Middle Fork of the John Day River.
  A rustic spot that is easy to reach.

ELK CREEK

Site **25**

Campsites, facilities: There are five tent sites. Picnic tables and firegrills are provided, and
  vault toilets are available. There is no piped water. Pets are permitted.

Reservations, fee: No reservations necessary; no fee. Open mid-May to mid-November.

Who to contact: Phone Prairie City Ranger District at 503-820-3311, or write Malheur
  National Forest at 139 NE Dayton Street, John Day, OR 97845.

Location: Go 8 1/2 miles southeast of Prairie City on County Route 62, then 16 miles
  southeast on Forest Service Road 13. The camp is 1 1/2 miles south on Forest Service
  Road 16.

Trip note: This campground is set at the confluence of the North and South Forks of Elk
  Creek. It is advisable to obtain a map of Malheur National Forest which details the
  back country roads.

NORTH FORK
MALHEUR

Site **26**

Campsites, facilities: There are five tent sites. Picnic tables and firegrills are provided, and
  vault toilets are available. There is no piped water. Pets are permitted.

Reservations, fee: No reservations necessary; no fee. Open mid-May to mid-November.

Who to contact: Phone Long Creek Ranger District at 503-820-3311, or write Malheur National Forest at 139 NE Dayton Street, John Day, OR 97845.

Location: From Prairie City, travel 8 1/2 miles southeast on County Route 62, then 16 miles southeast on Forest Service Road 13. Travel two miles south on Forest Service Road 16, then take the left fork and drive two miles to the campground.

Trip note: This secluded campground is set along the banks of the North Fork of the Malheur River. Trails and dirt roads provide additional access to the river and backcountry streams. It is essential to obtain a Forest Service map.

LITTLE CRANE
Site **27**

Campsites, facilities: There are five tent sites. Picnic tables and firegrills are provided, and vault toilets are available. There is no piped water. Pets are permitted.

Reservations, fee: No reservations necessary; no fee. Open June to mid-November.

Who to contact: Phone Prairie City Ranger District at 503-820-3311, or write Malheur National Forest at 139 NE Dayton Street, John Day, OR 97845.

Location: From Prairie City, travel 8 1/2 miles southeast on County Route 14, then 16 miles south on Forest Service Road 13. The camp is 5 1/2 miles south on Forest Service Road 16.

Trip note: This campground is set along the banks of Little Wet Creek. A good stream for sneak fishing for trout. There are also some good hiking trails in the area, detailed on the Forest Service map.

TROUT FARM
Site **28**

Campsites, facilities: There are eight sites for tents, trailers or motorhomes up to 21 feet long. Picnic tables and firegrills are provided, and piped water, showers and vault toilets are available. Pets are permitted.

Reservations, fee: No reservations necessary; no fee. Open May to mid-November.

Who to contact: Phone Prairie City Ranger District at 503-820-3311, or write Malheur National Forest at 139 NE Dayton Street, John Day, OR 97845.

Location: From Prairie City, go 8 1/2 miles southeast on County Route 14, then seven miles south on Forest Service Road 14.

Trip note: This campground is set along the banks of the John Day River. A good spot for a trout fishing trip. No other camps are in the immediate area.

ELK CREEK
(#2)
Site **29**

Campsites, facilities: There are six sites for tents, trailers or motorhomes up to 15 feet long. Picnic tables and firegrills are provided, and piped water, firewood and vault toilets are available. Pets are permitted.

Reservations, fee: No reservations necessary; no fee. Open late-May to mid-September.

Who to contact: Phone Unity Ranger District at 503-446-3351, or write Wallowa-Whitman National Forest, P.O. Box 907, Baker, OR 97814.

Location: Travel 49 miles west of the town of John Day on Highway 26 to Unity. From the town of Unity, travel four miles southwest on County Route 1300. The camp is four miles southwest on Forest Service Road 6005.

Trip note: This campground is set along the bank of the South Fork Burnt River. It is a small, obscure camp, yet has piped water and an adjacent stream.

SOUTH FORK
Site **30**

Campsites, facilities: There are 29 sites for tents, trailers or motorhomes up to 16 feet long. Picnic tables and firegrills are provided, and piped water, firewood and vault toilets are available. Pets are permitted.

Reservations, fee: No reservations necessary; no fee. Open late-May to mid-September.

Who to contact: Phone Unity Ranger District at 503-446-3351, or write Wallowa-Whitman National Forest, P.O. Box 907, Baker, OR 97814.

Location: Travel 49 miles west of the town of John Day on Highway 26 to Unity. From the town of Unity, go 5 1/2 miles southwest on County Route 1300, then one mile southwest on Forest Service Road 6005.

Trip note: This campground is set along the banks of the South Fork Burnt Creek. A nice trout creek with good evening bites for anglers that know how to sneak fish.

STEVENS CREEK
Site **31**

Campsites, facilities: There are six sites for tents, trailers or motorhomes of any length. Picnic tables and firegrills are provided, and piped water, firewood and vault toilets are available. Pets are permitted.

Reservations, fee: No reservations necessary; no fee. Open late-May to mid-September.

Who to contact: Phone Unity Ranger District at 503-446-3351, or write Wallowa-Whitman National Forest, P.O. Box 907, Baker, OR 97814.

Location: Travel 49 miles west of the town of John Day on Highway 26 to Unity. Go six miles southwest of Unity on County Route 1300, then 1 1/2 miles southwest on Forest Service Road 6005.

Trip note: This campground is set along the banks of the South Fork Burnt Creek. An option to the other small camps along Burnt Creek.

UNITY MOTEL &
TRAILER COURT
Site **32**

Campsites, facilities: There are three tent sites and 11 sites for trailers or motorhomes. Electricity, piped water, sewer hookups and picnic tables are provided. Flush toilets, showers and a laundromat are available. Bottled gas, a store, cafe and ice are located within one mile. Pets and motorbikes are permitted.

Reservations, fee: Reservations accepted; $7 fee per night. MasterCard and Visa accepted. Open all year with limited winter facilities.

Who to contact: Phone at 503-446-3431, or write at P.O. Box 87, Unity, OR 97884.

Location: Travel 49 miles west of the town of John Day on Highway 26 to Unity. This campground is located in town off US 26.

Trip note: This campground is in town. Possible side trips include visiting Unity Reservoir, Unity Lake State Park and exploring the nearby Burnt River.

BROGAN TRAILER PARK & CAMPGROUND

Site **33**

Campsites, facilities: There are 15 tent sites and 30 drive-through sites for trailers or motorhomes of any length. Electricity, piped water, sewer hookups and picnic tables are provided. Flush toilets, showers, a laundromat and ice are available. Bottled gas, a store and cafe are located within one mile. Pets are permitted.

Reservations, fee: Reservations accepted; $8 fee per night. Open April to late-December.

Who to contact: Phone at 503-473-2002, or write at P.O. Box 23, Brogan, OR 97903.

Location: Drive 24 miles north of the town of Vale on Highway 26 to the town of Brogan. The campground is in town.

Trip note: This rural campground is set on the inner edge of the west's Great Basin. Nearby side trips include visiting Willow Creek, which runs along Highway 26, or Malheur Reservoir, set northwest of Brogan.

FAREWELL BEND STATE PARK

Site **34**

Campsites, facilities: There are 40 tent sites and 53 sites for trailers or motorhomes up to 45 feet long. Electricity, piped water and picnic tables are provided. Flush toilets, sanitary disposal services, showers and firewood are available. Pets are permitted. Boat launching facilities are nearby.

Reservations, fee: No reservations necessary; $7 fee per night. Open all year with limited winter facilities.

Who to contact: Phone at 503-869-2365, or write at Huntington, OR 97907.

Location: From Huntington, travel 22 miles northwest on I-84 to the campground.

Trip note: This campground is set along the banks of the majestic Snake River. One of three camps in the immediate area. See the zone map.

SPRING RECREATION SITE

Site **35**

Campsites, facilities: There are 14 sites for tents, trailers or motorhomes up to 30 feet long. Picnic tables and firegrills are provided, and piped water, sanitary disposal services and vault toilets are available. Pets are permitted. Boat launching facilities are nearby.

Reservations, fee: No reservations necessary; no fee. Open May to October including limited and some off-season weekends.

Who to contact: Phone at 503-473-3144, or write at P.O. Box 700, Vale, OR 97918.

Location: From the town of Ontario, drive 19 miles north on I-84 to Huntington. From Huntington, travel 3 1/2 miles northeast on Snake River Road.

Trip note: This campground is set along the banks of the Snake River. One of three camps in the immediate area.

SPRING RECREATION LAKE

Site **36**

Campsites, facilities: There are 14 sites for tents, trailers or motorhomes. Picnic tables and firegrills are provided. Piped water, sanitary disposal services and vault toilets are available. Pets are permitted. Boat launching facilities are nearby.

Reservations, fee: No reservations necessary; no fee. Open May to October including limited and some off-season weekends.

Who to contact: Phone the Bureau of Land Management at 503-473-3144, or write at P.O. Box 700, Vale, OR 97918.

Location: From the town of Huntington, travel 3 1/2 miles northeast on Snake River Road.

Trip note: This campground is set along the banks of the majestic Snake River. One of three camps in or near the town of Huntington.

EAGLE FORKS

Site **37**

Campsites, facilities: There are seven sites for tents, trailers or motorhomes up to 21 feet long. Picnic tables and firegrills are provided. Firewood and vault toilets are available, but there is no piped water. Pets are permitted.

Reservations, fee: No reservations necessary; no fee. Open June to late-October.

Who to contact: Phone Halfway Ranger District at 503-742-7511, or write Willowa-Whitman National Forest at P.O. Box 907, Baker, OR 97810.

Location: Drive 41 miles east of Baker on Highway 86 to the town of Richland. From Richland, travel 11 miles via a county road and Forest Service Road 7735.

Trip note: This campground is set at the confluence of Little Eagle Creek and Eagle Creek. A trail leaves camp and follows the creek northwest for five miles, a prime day hike. Yet the spot attracts few people.

TAMARACK

Site **38**

Campsites, facilities: There are 10 sites for tents, trailers or motorhomes up to 22 feet long. Picnic tables and firegrills are provided, and piped water, firewood and vault toilets are available. A store, cafe and ice are located within five miles. Pets are permitted.

Reservations, fee: No reservations necessary; no fee. Open June to late-October.

Who to contact: Phone Halfway Ranger District at 503-742-7511, or write Willowa-Whitman National Forest at P.O. Box 907, Baker, OR 97814.

Location: From Baker, drive 23 miles northeast via I-84 and Highway 203 to the town of Medical Springs. From Medical Springs, travel 5 1/2 miles southeast on Forest Service Road 6700, then go 10 miles east on Forest Service Road 6700. The camp is 300 yards east on Forest Service Road 7700.

Trip note: This campground is set along the banks of Eagle Creek. This is a good spot for fishing and hiking trip in remote setting.

TWO COLOR

Site **39**

Campsites, facilities: There are 14 sites for tents, trailers or motorhomes up to 22 feet long. Picnic tables and firegrills are provided. Piped water, firewood and vault toilets are available. Pets are permitted.

Reservations, fee: No reservations necessary; no fee. Open mid-June to late-September.

Who to contact: Phone Halfway Ranger District at 503-963-7186, or write Willowa-Whitman National Forest at P.O. Box 907, Baker, OR 97814.

Location: From Baker, drive 23 miles northeast via I-84 and Highway 203 to the town of Medical Springs. From Medical Springs, go 15 1/2 miles southeast on Forest Service

Road 6700, then 1 1/2 miles northeast on Forest Service Road 7755.
Trip note: This campground is set along the banks of Eagle Creek, about a mile north of campsite 66, which has piped water.

MCBRIDE
Site **40**

Campsites, facilities: There are five sites for tents, trailers or motorhomes up to 16 feet long. Picnic tables and firegrills are provided. Vault toilets are available, but there is no piped water. Pets are permitted.
Reservations, fee: No reservations necessary; no fee. Open mid-May to late-October.
Who to contact: Phone Halfway Ranger District at 503-742-7511, or write Willowa-Whitman National Forest at P.O. Box 907, Baker, OR 97814.
Location: Drive 52 miles east of Baker on Highway 86 to the town of Halfway. Go six miles northwest of Halfway on Highway 442, then go 2 1/2 miles west on Forest Service Road 7101.
Trip note: This campground is set along the banks of Brooks Ditch. A little-used, primitive and obscure camp.

FISH LAKE
Site **41**

Campsites, facilities: There are 20 sites for tents, trailers or motorhomes up to 22 feet long. Picnic tables and firegrills are provided. Piped water, firewood and vault toilets are is available. Pets are permitted. Boat launching facilities are nearby.
Reservations, fee: No reservations necessary; no fee. Open late-May to early-September.
Who to contact: Phone Pine Ranger District at 503-822-3381, or write Willowa-Whitman National Forest at P.O. Box 907, Baker, OR 97814.
Location: From the town of Baker, travel 52 miles east on Highway 82 to the town of Halfway. From Halfway, go five miles north on County Route 733, then 18 1/2 miles north on Forest Service Road 66.
Trip note: This campground is set along the shore of Fish Lake, a good base camp for a fishing trip. Side trip options include hiking out on nearby trails that lead to mountain streams.

TWIN LAKES
Site **42**

Campsites, facilities: There are nine sites for tents, trailers or motorhomes up to 22 feet long. Picnic tables and firegrills are provided. Firewood and vault toilets are available, but there is no piped water. Pets are permitted.
Reservations, fee: No reservations necessary; no fee. Open July to mid-September.
Who to contact: Phone Halfway Ranger District at 503-426-3151, or write Willowa-Whitman National Forest at P.O. Box 907, Baker, OR 97814.
Location: From the town of Baker, travel 52 miles east on Highway 82 to the town of Halfway. From Halfway, go nine miles east on Highway 86, then 13 miles north on Forest Service Road 39.
Trip note: This campground is set between the little Twin Lakes. Nearby trails provide access to backcountry lakes and streams. See a Forest Service map for details.

LAKE FORK
Site **43**

Campsites, facilities: There are 11 sites for tents, trailers or motorhomes up to 22 feet long. Picnic tables and firegrills are provided. Firewood and vault toilets are available, but there is no piped water. Pets are permitted.

Reservations, fee: No reservations necessary; no fee. Open June to late-November.

Who to contact: Phone Enterprise Ranger District at 503-426-3151, or write Willowa-Whitman National Forest at P.O. Box 907, Baker, OR 97814.

Location: From the town of Baker, travel 52 miles east on Highway 82 to the town of Halfway. Drive nine miles east of Halfway on Highway 86, then eight miles north on Forest Service Road 39.

Trip note: This campground is set along the banks of Lake Fork Creek, an ideal jumpoff point for a backpacking trip. A trail from camp follows the creek west for about 10 miles to Fish Lake. It continues beyond Fish Lake to several smaller lakes.

LICK CREEK
Site **44**

Campsites, facilities: There are 12 sites for tents, trailers or motorhomes up to 30 feet long. Picnic tables and firegrills are provided. Piped water, firewood and vault toilets are available. Pets are permitted.

Reservations, fee: No reservations necessary; no fee. Open mid-June to late-November.

Who to contact: Phone Enterprise Ranger District at 503-426-3151, or write Willowa-Whitman National Forest at P.O. Box 907, Baker, OR 97816.

Location: Travel south of the town of Enterprise on Highway 82 to Joseph. From Joseph, go 7 1/2 miles east on Highway 305, then 15 miles south on Forest Service Road 39.

Trip note: This campground is set along the banks of Lick Creek, in Hells Canyon National Recreation Area. Piped water is provided, there is no cost, and it is secluded and pretty.

EVERGREEN
Site **45**

Campsites, facilities: There are 17 sites for tents, trailers or motorhomes up to 31 feet long. Picnic tables and firegrills are provided. Piped water, firewood and vault toilets are available. Pets are permitted.

Reservations, fee: No reservations necessary; no fee. Open June to late-November.

Who to contact: Phone Enterprise Ranger District at 503-426-3151, or write Willowa-Whitman National Forest at P.O. Box 907, Baker, OR 97816.

Location: Travel south of the town of Enterprise on Highway 82 to Joseph. Take Highway 305 east from Joseph for 7 1/2 miles, then go 29 miles south on Forest Service Road 39. The camp is eight miles southwest on Forest Service Road 3960.

Trip note: This campground is set along the banks of the Imnaha River in Hells Canyon National Recreation Area. One of seven camps in the vicinity; see zone map for others.

HIDDEN
Site **46**

Campsites, facilities: There are 10 sites for tents, trailers or motorhomes up to 30 feet long. Picnic tables and firegrills are provided. Piped water, firewood and vault toilets are available. Pets are permitted.

Reservations, fee: No reservations necessary; no fee. Open June to late-November.

Who to contact: Phone Enterprise Ranger District at 503-426-3151, or write Willowa-Whitman National Forest at P.O. Box 907, Baker, OR 97816.

Location: Travel south of the town of Enterprise on Highway 82 to Joseph. From Joseph, take Highway 305 east 7 1/2 miles, then go 29 miles southeast on Forest Service Road 39. The campground is seven miles southwest on Forest Service Road 3960.

Trip note: This campground is set along the banks of the Imnaha River, in the Hells Canyon National Recreation Area. It is essential to obtain a map of Wallowa-Whitman National Forest, which details back roads and hiking trails.

INDIAN CROSSING
Site **47**

Campsites, facilities: There are 15 sites for tents, trailers or motorhomes up to 30 feet long. Picnic tables and firegrills are provided. Firewood and vault toilets are available, but there is no piped water. Pets are permitted. Horse facilities are available.

Reservations, fee: No reservations necessary; no fee. Open June to late-November.

Who to contact: Phone Enterprise Ranger District at 503-426-3151, or write Willowa-Whitman National Forest at P.O. Box 907, Baker, OR 97816.

Location: Travel south of the town of Enterprise on Highway 82 to Joseph. From Joseph, go 7 1/2 miles east on Highway 305, then 29 miles south on Forest Service Road 39. The campground is nine miles southwest on Forest Service Road 3960.

Trip note: This campground is set at the end of the road along the banks of the Innaha River, in Hells Canyon National Recreation Area. A trail is nearby. Obtain a Forest Service map for side trip possibilities.

BLACKHORSE
Site **48**

Campsites, facilities: There are 17 sites for tents, trailers or motorhomes up to 30 feet long. Picnic tables and firegrills are provided, and piped water, firewood and vault toilets are available. Pets are permitted.

Reservations, fee: No reservations necessary; no fee. Open June to late-November.

Who to contact: Phone Enterprise Ranger District at 503-426-3151, or write Willowa-Whitman National Forest at P.O. Box 907, Baker, OR 97816.

Location: Travel south of the town of Enterprise on Highway 82 to Joseph. Travel 7 1/2 miles east of Joseph on Highway 305, then go 29 miles southeast on Forest Service Road 39.

Trip note: This campground is set along the banks of the Imnaha River in Hells Canyon National Recreation Area. A secluded spot in Wallowa-Whitman National Forest.

OLLOKOT

Site **49**

Campsites, facilities: There are 12 sites for tents, trailers or motorhomes up to 30 feet long. Picnic tables and firegrills are provided, and vault toilets are available. There is no piped water. Pets are permitted.

Reservations, fee: No reservations necessary; no fee. Open June to late-November.

Who to contact: Phone Wallowa-Whitman Ranger District at 503-426-3151, or write Willowa-Whitman National Forest at P.O. Box 907, Baker, OR 97816.

Location: Travel south of the town of Enterprise on Highway 82 to Joseph. From Joseph, go 7 1/2 miles east on Highway 305, then 29 miles southeast on Forest Service Road 39.

Trip note: This campground is set along the banks of the Imnaha River in Hells Canyon National Recreation Area. A primitive option.

CATHERINE CREEK
STATE PARK

Site **50**

Campsites, facilities: There are 10 sites for tents, trailers or motorhomes up to 30 feet long. Picnic tables and firegrills are provided. Piped water, firewood and flush toilets are available. Some facilities are wheelchair accessible. Pets are permitted.

Reservations, fee: No reservations necessary; $6 fee per night. Open mid-April to late-October.

Who to contact: Phone at 503-963-6444, or write at La Grande, OR 97850.

Location: From La Grande, drive southeast on Highway 203 about eight miles past the town of Union.

Trip note: This campground is set along the banks of Catherine Creek. A pleasant, easy-to-reach park that is little known to out-of-towners.

NORTH FORK
CATHERINE TRAILHEAD

Site **51**

Campsites, facilities: There are five tent sites and five sites for trailers or motorhomes up to 22 feet long. Picnic tables and firegrills are provided, and vault toilets are available. There is no piped water. Pets are permitted.

Reservations, fee: No reservations necessary; no fee. Open mid-June to late-October.

Who to contact: Phone La Grande Ranger District at 503-963-7186, or write Willowa-Whitman National Forest at P.O. Box 907, Baker, OR 97813.

Location: From the town of La Grande, travel 14 miles southeast on Highway 203 to the town of Union. Drive 10 miles southeast of Union on Highway 203, then four miles east on Forest Service Road 7785. The camp is 3 1/2 miles northeast on Forest Service Road 7785.

Trip note: This campground is set along the North Fork Catherine Creek at a trailhead that provides access to various lakes and streams in the Eagle Cap Wilderness. A good jumpoff point for a hiking trip. National Forest map details possibilities.

MOSS SPRINGS

Site **52**

Campsites, facilities: There are seven sites for tents, trailers or motorhomes up to 22 feet long. Picnic tables and firegrills are provided, and firewood, horse facilties and vault toilets are available. Pets are permitted.

Reservations, fee: No reservations necessary; no fee. Open July to mid-September.

Who to contact: Phone La Grande Ranger District at 503-963-7186, or write Willowa-Whitman National Forest at P.O. Box 907, Baker, OR 97814.

Location: Travel 15 miles west of the town of La Grande to the town of Cove. Drive 1 1/2 miles southeast of Cove on County Route 602, then 6 1/2 miles east on Forest Service Road 6220.

Trip note: This campground is set along the banks of Mill Creek, at a trailhead that provides access to the Eagle Cap Wilderness. A good jump-off point for multi-day backpacking trip. It is advisable to obtain a map of Willowa-Whitman National Forest.

Site 53   JUBILEE LAKE

Campsites, facilities: There are 51 sites for tents, trailers or motorhomes up to 22 feet long. Picnic tables and firegrills are provided. Piped water, firewood and vault toilets are available. Pets are permitted. Boat docks and launching facilities are nearby.

Reservations, fee: No reservations necessary; $5 fee per night. Open July to mid-October.

Who to contact: Phone Walla Walla Ranger District at 509-525-6290, or write Umatilla National Forest at 1415 West Rose Avenue, Walla Walla, WA 99362.

Location: From the town of Elgin, travel 23 1/2 miles northwest on Highway 204, then 11 miles northeast on Forest Service Road 64. The camp is 700 yards south on Forest Service Road 250.

Trip note: This campground is set along the shore of Jubilee Lake. It's a good area for fishing, hiking and hunting.

Site 54   MOTTET

Campsites, facilities: There are nine sites for tents, trailers or motorhomes up to 22 feet long. Picnic tables and firegrills are provided. Piped water, firewood and vault toilets are available. Pets are permitted.

Reservations, fee: No reservations necessary; no fee. Open July to mid-October.

Who to contact: Phone Walla Walla Ranger District at 509-525-6290, or write Umatilla National Forest at 1415 West Rose Avenue, Walla Walla, WA 99362.

Location: Travel 17 miles east of Pendleton via Highway 11 to the town of Weston. From Weston, travel 17 1/2 miles east on Highway 204, then two miles east on Forest Service Road 64. Continue 800 yards on Forest Service Road 20.

Trip note: This campground is set at 5200 feet elevation, adjacent to a trailhead which leads down to the South Fork of the Touchet River. A nice spot, located far from the beaten path.

Site 55   MINAM STATE RECREATION AREA

Campsites, facilities: There are 12 sites for tents, trailers or motorhomes up to 60 feet long. Picnic tables and firegrills are provided, and piped water, firewood and vault toilets are available. Pets are permitted.

Reservations, fee: No reservations necessary; $5 fee per night. Open mid-April to late-October.

Who to contact: Phone at 503-432-8855, or write at Elgin, OR 97827.

Location: From the town of La Grande, drive 20 miles northeast on Highway 82 to the town of Elgin. From Elgin, continue 15 miles northeast on Highway 82, then go 1/2 mile north.

Trip note: This campground is set along the banks of the Minam River. Morning and evening trout fishing can be decent.

BOUNDARY
Site **56**

Campsites, facilities: There are 12 tent sites. Picnic tables and firegrills are provided. Firewood and vault toilets are available, but there is no piped water. Pets are permitted.

Reservations, fee: No reservations necessary; no fee. Open mid-June to November.

Who to contact: Phone Eagle Cap Ranger District at 503-426-3104, or write Willowa-Whitman National Forest at P.O. Box 907, Baker, OR 97815.

Location: From the town of Wallowa, travel five miles south on County Route 515, then two miles south on Forest Service Road 163.

Trip note: This campground is set along the banks of Bear Creek, at a trailhead that provides access to the Eagle Cap Wilderness. Good jump-off point for a multi-day backpack trip.

OUTPOST
RV PARK
Site **57**

Campsites, facilities: There are 40 drive-through sites for trailers or motorhomes of any length. Electricity, piped water, sewer hookups and picnic tables are provided. Flush toilets, sanitary disposal services and showers are available. Bottled gas, a store, cafe, laundromat and ice are located within one mile. Pets and motorbikes are permitted.

Reservations, fee: Reservations accepted; $8 fee per night. MasterCard and Visa accepted. Open all year.

Who to contact: Phone at 503-426-4745, or write at Flora Route, Enterprise, OR 97828.

Location: Go 1/2 mile north of Enterprise on Highway 3.

Trip note: This wooded motorhome park is just outside of the town of Enterprise. Nearby recreation options include a golf course, hiking trails and bike paths.

MOUNTAIN VIEW MOTEL
& TRAILER PARK
Site **58**

Campsites, facilities: There are 20 tent sites and 25 drive-through sites for trailers or motorhomes of any length. Electricity, piped water, sewer hookups and picnic tables are provided. Flush toilets, sanitary disposal services and showers are available. Bottled gas, a store, cafe and laundromat are located within one mile. Pets are permitted.

Reservations, fee: Reservations accepted; $7 fee per night. MasterCard and Visa accepted. Open all year.

Who to contact: Phone at 503-432-2982, or write at Route 1, Box 87, Joseph, OR 97846.

Location: Travel south of the town of Enterprise on Highway 82 to Joseph. This campground is located one mile west of the town of Joseph on Highway 82.

Trip note: This park is not far from Wallowa Lake. Nearby recreation options include a golf course, hiking trails, bike paths and a riding stable.

HURRICANE CREEK
Site **59**

Campsites, facilities: There are eight sites for tents, trailers or motorhomes up to 15 feet long. Picnic tables and firegrills are provided. Firewood and vault toilets are available, but there is no piped water. Pets are permitted.

Reservations, fee: No reservations necessary; no fee. Open mid-June to late-October.

Who to contact: Phone Eagle Cap Ranger District at 503-426-3104, or write Willowa-Whitman National Forest at P.O. Box 907, Baker, OR 97816.

Location: Travel south of the town of Enterprise on Highway 82 to Joseph. This campground is located 3 1/2 miles southwest of the town of Joseph on Forest Service Road 8205.

Trip note: This campground is set at the edge of the Eagle Camp Wilderness. It's a good jumpoff point for a wilderness backpacking trip. It's essential to obtain maps of the area from the ranger district.

WALLOWA LAKE STATE PARK
Site **60**

Campsites, facilities: There are 89 tent sites and 121 drive-through sites for trailers or motorhomes of any length. Group campsites are available. Electricity, piped water, sewer hookups and picnic tables are provided. Flush toilets, sanitary disposal services, showers, firewood and a laundromat are available. A store, cafe and ice are available within one mile. Some facilities are wheelchair accessible. Pets are permitted. Boat docks, launching facilities and rentals are nearby.

Reservations, fee: Reservations accepted; $8 fee per night. Open mid-April to late October.

Who to contact: Phone at 503-432-8855, or write at Route 1, Box 323, Joseph, OR 97846.

Location: Travel south of the town of Enterprise on Highway 82 to Joseph. From the town of Joseph, go six miles south on Highway 82 to the south shore of the lake.

Trip note: This campground is set along the shore of scenic Wallowa Lake. Trailheads that provide access into Eagle Cap Wilderness are nearby.

WILLIAMSON
Site **61**

Campsites, facilities: There are 10 sites for tents, trailers or motorhomes up to 16 feet long. Picnic tables and firegrills are provided. Piped water, firewood and vault toilets are available. Pets are permitted.

Reservations, fee: No reservations necessary; no fee. Open mid-June to November.

Who to contact: Phone Eagle Cap Ranger District at 503-426-3104, or write Willowa-Whitman National Forest at P.O. Box 907, Baker, OR 97817.

Location: From the town of Wallowa, travel eight miles southeast on Highway 18 to the town of Lostine. From Lostine, go seven miles south on County Route 551, then four miles south on Forest Service Road 202.

Trip note: This campground is set along the banks of the East Lostine River. Nearby trails provide access to the Eagle Cap Wilderness. This is another in a series of little-known primitive sites in the area.

SHADY
62

Campsites, facilities: There are 16 sites for tents, trailers or motorhomes up to 16 feet long. Picnic tables and firegrills are provided. Piped water, firewood and vault toilets are available. Pets are permitted.

Reservations, fee: No reservations necessary; no fee. Open mid-June to November.

Who to contact: Phone Eagle Cap Ranger District at 503-426-3104, or write Willowa-Whitman National Forest at P.O. Box 907, Baker, OR 97817.

Location: From the town of Wallowa, travel eight miles southeast on Highway 18 to the town of Lostine. Drive seven miles south of Lostine on County Route 551, then 10 miles south on Forest Service Road 202.

Trip note: This campground is set along the banks of the East Lostine River. Nearby trails provide access to the Eagle Cap Wilderness.

TWO PAN
Site 63

Campsites, facilities: There are nine tent sites. Picnic tables and firegrills are provided. Piped water, firewood and vault toilets are available. Pets are permitted.

Reservations, fee: No reservations necessary; no fee. Open mid-June to November.

Who to contact: Phone Eagle Cap Ranger District at 503-426-3104, or write Willowa-Whitman National Forest at P.O. Box 907, Baker, OR 97817.

Location: From the town of Wallowa, travel eight miles southeast on Highway 18 to the town of Lostine. Drive seven miles south of Lostine on County Route 551, then 11 miles south on Forest Service Road S202.

Trip note: This campground is set at the end of the Forest Service road, along the banks of the East Lostine River. Adjacent trails provide access to numerous lakes and streams in the Eagle Cap Wilderness. At 5600 feet elevation, this is a prime jump-off spot for a multi-day wilderness adventure.

SADDLE CREEK
Site 64

Campsites, facilities: There are six sites for tents, trailers or motorhomes up to 15 feet long. Picnic tables and firegrills are provided. Firewood and vault toilets are available, but there is no piped water. Pets are permitted.

Reservations, fee: No reservations necessary; no fee. Open July to late-November.

Who to contact: Phone Willowa-Whitman Ranger District at 503-426-3151, or write Willowa-Whitman National Forest at P.O. Box 907, Baker, OR 97812.

Location: From Enterprise, drive to the small town of Inmaha. Head 20 miles southeast of Imnaha on Forest Service Road 4240.

Trip note: This campground is set at 6900 feet elevation. Trails are nearby that provide access to Saddle Creek and the Hells Canyon Wilderness. A map of Wallowa National Forest details the trails in area.

COYOTE
Site 65

Campsites, facilities: There are 21 sites for tents, trailers or motorhomes up to 22 feet long.

Picnic tables and firegrills are provided. Firewood and vault toilets are available, but there is no piped water. Pets are permitted.

Reservations, fee: No reservations necessary; no fee. Open mid-May to December.

Who to contact: Phone Enterprise Ranger District at 503-432-2171, or write Willowa-Whitman National Forest at P.O. Box 907, Baker, OR 97818.

Location: From the town of Enterprise, travel three miles east on Highway 82, then 21 1/2 miles north on County Route 799. The camp is another 19 miles north on Forest Service Road 436.

Trip note: This campground is set at 4800 feet elevation, adjacent to Coyote Springs. It is one of three primitive camps in the vicinity.

DOUGHERTY
Site **66**

Campsites, facilities: There are 10 sites for tents, trailers or motorhomes up to 22 feet long. Picnic tables and firegrills are provided. Vault toilets are available, but there is no piped water. Pets are permitted.

Reservations, fee: No reservations necessary; no fee. Open June to late-November.

Who to contact: Phone Wallowa-Whitman Ranger District at 503-426-3151, or write Willowa-Whitman National Forest at P.O. Box 907, Baker, OR 97818.

Location: Travel 15 miles north of Enterprise on Highway 3, then 12 miles northeast on Forest Service Road 46. The camp is 10 miles east on Forest Service Road 431.

Trip note: This campground is set at 5000 feet elevation adjacent to Dougherty Springs. It is one in a series of remote camps set near natural springs.

VIGNE
Site **67**

Campsites, facilities: There are 12 sites for tents, trailers or motorhomes up to 22 feet long. Picnic tables and firegrills are provided. Piped water, firewood and vault toilets are available. Pets are permitted.

Reservations, fee: No reservations necessary; no fee. Open mid-April to late-November.

Who to contact: Phone Willowa Valley Ranger District at 503-432-2171, or write Willowa-Whitman National Forest at P.O. Box 907, Baker, OR 97818.

Location: Go three miles east of Enterprise on Highway 82, then 21 1/2 miles north on County Route 799. The camp is 6 1/2 miles north on Forest Service Road 436.

Trip note: This campground is set along the banks of Chesnimnus Creek. It is the only Forest Service camp in the area that has piped water available.

BUCKHORN
Site **68**

Campsites, facilities: There are six sites for tents, trailers or motorhomes up to 22 feet long. Picnic tables and firegrills are provided. Firewood and vault toilets are available, but there is no piped water. Pets are permitted.

Reservations, fee: No reservations necessary; no fee. Open June to late-November.

Who to contact: Phone Enterprise Ranger District at 503-426-3151, or write Willowa-Whitman National Forest at P.O. Box 907, Baker, OR 97818.

Location: Travel three miles south on Highway 82 from Enterprise, then go five miles northeast on County Route 772. Continue 26 miles northeast on County Route 798.

Trip note: This campground is set at 5200 feet elevation adjacent to Buckhorn Springs. A small, primitive and obscure camp that gets little use.

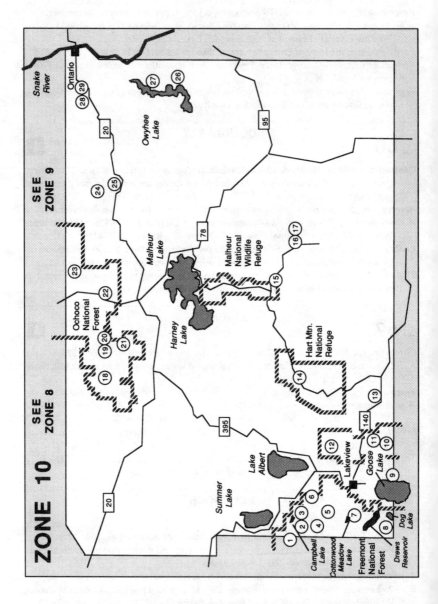

SOUTHEAST BASIN

LEE THOMAS

Site **1**

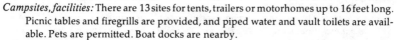

Campsites, facilities: There are seven sites for tents, trailers or motorhomes up to 16 feet long. Picnic tables and firegrills are provided, and piped water and vault toilets are available. Pets are permitted.

Reservations, fee: No reservations necessary; no fee. Open mid-June to late-October.

Who to contact: Phone Paisley Ranger District at 503-943-3114, or write Fremont National Forest, Paisley, OR 97636.

Location: From the town of Paisley on Highway 31, travel one mile west of Paisley on County Route 422, then 27 miles west on Forest Service Road 331.

Trip note: This campground is set along the North Fork of the Sprague River. This is located in the interior of Fremont National Forest. A genuine hideaway.

CAMPBELL LAKE

Site **2**

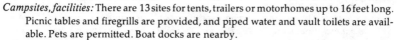

Campsites, facilities: There are 21 sites for tents, trailers or motorhomes up to 16 feet long. Picnic tables and firegrills are provided, and piped water and vault toilets are available. Pets are permitted. Boat docks are nearby.

Reservations, fee: No reservations necessary; no fee. Open mid-June to late-September.

Who to contact: Phone Paisley Ranger District at 503-943-3114, or write Fremont National Forest, Paisley, OR 97636.

Location: From the town of Paisley on Highway 31, travel one mile west on County Route 422, then 22 1/2 miles west on Forest Service Road 331. The camp is three miles south on Forest Service Road 2823.

Trip note: This campground is set along the shore of Campbell Lake. No boats with motors are permitted. Good side trips are available in Fremont National Forest. A Forest Service map details the back roads.

DEADHORSE LAKE

Site **3**

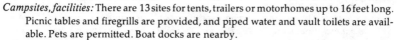

Campsites, facilities: There are 13 sites for tents, trailers or motorhomes up to 16 feet long. Picnic tables and firegrills are provided, and piped water and vault toilets are available. Pets are permitted. Boat docks are nearby.

Reservations, fee: No reservations necessary; no fee. Open mid-June to late-September.

Who to contact: Phone Paisley Ranger District at 503-943-3114, or write Fremont National

Forest, Paisley, OR 97636.

Location: From the town of Paisley on Highway 31, travel one mile west on County Route 422, then 23 miles west on Forest Service Road 331. From there, go three miles south on Forest Service Road 2823.

Trip note: This campground is set along the shore of Deadhorse Lake about a mile from Campbell Lake. No boats with motors are permitted. Good side trips are available in Fremont National Forest.

CORRAL CREEK
Site **4**

Campsites, facilities: There are five sites for tents, trailers or motorhomes up to 16 feet long. Picnic tables and firegrills are provided, and vault toilets are available. There is no piped water. Pets are permitted.

Reservations, fee: No reservations necessary; no fee. Open June to late-October.

Who to contact: Phone Paisley Ranger District at 503-943-3114, or write Fremont National Forest, Paisley, OR 97636.

Location: Drive 67 miles east of Klamath Falls on Highway 140 to the town of Quartz Mountain, then head northeast on Forest Service Road 366 for about 16 miles to the campground.

Trip note: This campground is set along Corral Creek, adjacent to a trailhead that provides access to the Gearhart Mountain Wilderness.

HAPPY CAMP
Site **5**

Campsites, facilities: There are nine sites for tents, trailers or motorhomes up to 16 feet long. Picnic tables and firegrills are provided, and piped water and vault toilets are available. Pets are permitted.

Reservations, fee: No reservations necessary; no fee. Open June to late-October.

Who to contact: Phone Paisley Ranger District at 503-943-3114, or write Fremont National Forest, Paisley, OR 97636.

Location: From the town of Paisley on Highway 31, travel one mile south on County Route 422, then 20 miles south on Forest Service Road 330. From there, go 2 1/2 miles south on Forest Service Road 2823, then 2 1/2 miles west on Forest Service Road 3675.

Trip note: This campground is set along Dairy Creek, about eight miles east of Corral Creek Campground, which has a trailhead that provides access to the Gearhart Mountain Wilderness.

MARSTERS SPRING
Site **6**

Campsites, facilities: There are 10 sites for tents, trailers or motorhomes up to 22 feet long. Picnic tables and firegrills are provided, and piped water and vault toilets are available. Pets are permitted.

Reservations, fee: No reservations necessary; no fee. Open mid-May to mid-November.

Who to contact: Phone the Paisley Ranger District at 503-943-3114, or write at Fremont National Forest, Paisley, OR 97636.

Location: Travel one mile west of the town of Paisley on County Route 422, then seven miles south on Forest Service Road 331.

Trip note: This pretty campground is set along the banks of the Chewaucan River. The first of five camps in this nice area. See the zone map for further details.

Site 7 COTTONWOOD MEADOWS

Campsites, facilities: There are 26 sites for tents, small trailers or motorhomes. Picnic tables and firegrills are provided, and piped water and vault toilets are available. Pets are permitted. Boat docks are nearby.

Reservations, fee: No reservations necessary; no fee. Open mid-June to late-October.

Who to contact: Phone Lakeview Ranger District at 503-947-3334, or write Fremont National Forest at Lakeview, OR 97630.

Location: From the town of Lakeview, travel 20 miles west on Highway 140, then five miles northeast on Forest Service Road 387.

Trip note: This campground is set along the shore of Cottonwood Meadow Lake. It is one of the better spots in the vicinity for fishing and hiking. Boats without motors are allowed on the lake.

Site 8 DOG LAKE

Campsites, facilities: There are 11 sites for tents, trailers or motorhomes up to 15 feet long. Picnic tables and firegrills are provided, and piped water and vault toilets are available. Pets are permitted. Boat docks are nearby.

Reservations, fee: No reservations necessary; no fee. Open mid-May to late-October.

Who to contact: Phone Lakeview Ranger District at 503-947-3334, or write Fremont National Forest at Lakeview, OR 97630.

Location: Travel five miles west of Lakeview on Highway 140, then seven miles south on County Route 60. The camp is another 13 miles west on Forest Service Road 4017.

Trip note: This campground is set along the west shore of Dog Lake. Fishing and boats with motors are permitted. Forest service roads on the east side of the lake provide access to some small lakes and Horseshoe Creek.

Site 9 GOOSE LAKE STATE PARK

Campsites, facilities: There are 48 sites for trailers or motorhomes up to 30 feet long. Electricity, piped water and picnic tables are provided. Flush toilets, showers and firewood are available. Pets are permitted. Boat launching facilities are nearby.

Reservations, fee: No reservations necessary; $7 fee per night. Open mid-April to late-October.

Who to contact: Phone at 503-947-3111, or write at New Pine Creek, OR 97635.

Location: Go 14 miles south of Lakeview on US 395, then one mile west.

Trip note: This park is set along the east shore of Goose Lake. This out-of-the way area attracts waterfowl from the Pacific Flyway.

Site 10 DEEP CREEK

Campsites, facilities: There are nine tent sites and five sites for trailers or motorhomes. Picnic tables and firegrills are provided, and vault toilets are available. There is no piped water. Pets are permitted.

Reservations, fee: No reservations necessary; no fee. Open mid-June to late-October.

Who to contact: Phone Lakeview Ranger District at 503-947-3334, or write Fremont National Forest at Lakeview, OR 97630.

Location: From the town of Lakeview, travel 5 1/2 miles north on US 395, then 6 1/2 miles east on Highway 140. The camp is 16 miles south on Forest Service Road 391.

Trip note: This campground is set along the banks of Deep Creek. Campsite 7 provides a relatively close camping option.

WILLOW CREEK
Site 11

Campsites, facilities: There are 11 sites for tents, trailers or motorhomes up to 22 feet long. Picnic tables and firegrills are provided, and piped water and vault toilets are available. Pets are permitted.

Reservations, fee: No reservations necessary; no fee. Open mid-June to late-October.

Who to contact: Phone Lakeview Ranger District at 503-947-3334, or write Fremont National Forest at Lakeview, OR 97630.

Location: Travel 5 1/2 miles north of Lakeview on US 395, then 6 1/2 miles east on Highway 140. The camp is another 10 miles south on Forest Service Road 391.

Trip note: This campground is set along the banks of Willow Creek, not far from a dirt road that heads north to Burnt Creek. A Forest Service map details the back roads.

MUD CREEK
Site 12

Campsites, facilities: There are six sites for tents, trailers or motorhomes up to 16 feet long. Picnic tables and firegrills are provided, and piped water and vault toilets are available. Pets are permitted.

Reservations, fee: No reservations necessary; no fee. Open mid-June to late-October.

Who to contact: Phone Lakeview Ranger District at 503-947-3334, or write Fremont National Forest at Lakeview, OR 97630.

Location: Travel 5 1/2 miles north of Lakeview on US 395, then 6 1/2 miles east on Highway 140. The camp is another six miles north on Forest Service Road 3615.

Trip note: This campground is set along the banks of Mud Creek. Drake Peak at 8,405 feet is nearby. No other camps are in the immediate vicinity.

ADEL STORE
Site 13 ### & PARK

Campsites, facilities: There are eight sites for trailers or motorhomes of any length. Electricity, piped water and sewer hookups are provided. Flush toilets, showers, a store, cafe and ice are available. Pets and motorbikes are permitted.

Reservations, fee: No reservations necessary; $7 fee per night.

Who to contact: Phone at 503-947-3850, or write at P.O. Box 19, Adel, OR 97620.

Location: From Lakeview, travel 30 miles east on Highway 140 to the town of Adel. The motorhome park is in town.

Trip note: Recreation options in the area include rockhounding, or visiting the Hart Mountain National Antelope Refuge, 40 miles north of town.

Site **14**   HART ANTELOPE REFUGE

Campsites, facilities: There are 12 primitive sites for tents, trailers or motorhomes up to 20
feet long. Pets are permitted.

Reservations, fee: No reservations necessary; no fee. Open May to November including
limited facilities in the winter and some off-season weekends. The road is often
impassable in the winter.

Who to contact: Phone at 503-947-3315, or write at Plush, OR 97637.

Location: Travel 43 miles northeast of Adel on a paved, then gravel road to Refuge
headquarters.

Trip note: This unique refuge offers canyons and hot springs. Some of Oregons largest
antelope herds roam this large area. The closest camping option is in Adel at campsite
13.

Site **15**   PAGE SPRINGS   ▲

Campsites, facilities: There are 15 sites for tents, trailers or motorhomes up to 24 feet long.
Picnic tables and firegrills are provided, and piped water, firewood and vault toilets
are available. Pets are permitted.

Reservations, fee: No reservations necessary; no fee. Open April to late-October.

Who to contact: Phone the Bureau of Land Management at 503-573-5241, or write at 74
South Alvord, Burns, OR 97720.

Location: Travel 61 miles south of the town of Burns on Highway 205 to the town of
Frenchglen, then three miles east of Frenchglen on Steens Mountain Road to the
campground.

Trip note: This campground is set adjacent to Page Springs and the Malheur National
Wildlife Refuge. The Frenchglen Hotel is administered by the state parks department
and offers overnight accommodations and food.

Site **16**   JACKMAN PARK   ▲

Campsites, facilities: There are five primitive tent sites and five sites for trailers or motorhomes up to 24 feet long. Picnic tables are provided, and firewood and pit toilets are
available. There is no piped water. Pets are permitted.

Reservations, fee: No reservations necessary; no fee. Open July to late-October.

Who to contact: Phone the Bureau of Land Management at 503-573-5241, or write at 74
South Alvord, Burns, OR 97720.

Location: Travel 20 miles east of the town Frenchglen on Steens Mountain Road.

Trip note: Set at 8100 feet elevation in the eastern Oregon desert. It is one of three camps in
the area. Campsite 15 is nearby and campsite 13 is about 15 miles northeast at the
southeast end of the Malheur National Wildlife Refuge. No other camps are within an
hour's drive.

Site **17**   FISH LAKE

Campsites, facilities: There are 20 sites for tents, trailers or motorhomes up to 24 feet long.

Picnic tables and firegrills are provided, and piped water, firewood and vault toilets are available. Pets are permitted. Boat launching facilities are nearby.

Reservations, fee: No reservations necessary; no fee. Open July to late-October.

Who to contact: Phone the Bureau of Land Management at 503-573-5241, or write at 74 South Alvord, Burns, OR 97720.

Location: Travel 16 miles east of the town of Frenchglen on Steens Mountain Road.

Trip note: Located at 7900 feet elevation, this campground is set along the shore of little Fish Lake.

Site 18   DELINTMENT LAKE   ◭

Campsites, facilities: There are 24 sites for tents, trailers or motorhomes up to 30 feet long. Picnic tables and firegrills are provided, and piped water, firewood and vault toilets are available. Some facilities are wheelchair accessible. Pets are permitted. Boat docks and launching facilities are nearby.

Reservations, fee: No reservations necessary; $4 fee per night. Open June to mid-October.

Who to contact: Phone Snow Mountain Ranger District at 503-573-7292, or write Ochoco National Forest at Star Route 4, Box 12870, Highway 20, Hines, OR 97720.

Location: From the town of Hines, go one mile south on US 20, then 25 miles northwest on Forest Service Road 47. The camp is another 17 miles northwest on Forest Service Road 43.

Trip note: This campground is set along the shore of Delintment Lake, originally a beaver pond which was gradually developed into a lake covering 57 acres.

Site 19   EMIGRANT   ◭

Campsites, facilities: There are five sites for tents, trailers or motorhomes up to 30 feet long. Picnic tables and firegrills are provided, and piped water and vault toilets are available. Pets are permitted.

Reservations, fee: No reservations necessary; $2 fee per night. Open mid-June to mid-October.

Who to contact: Phone Snow Mountain Ranger District at 503-573-7292, or write Ochoco National Forest at Star Route 4, Box 12870 Highway 20, Hines, OR 97720.

Location: Travel one mile south of the town of Hines on US 20, then 25 miles northwest on Forest Service Road 47. The camp is another 10 miles west on Forest Service Road 43.

Trip note: This campground is set along the banks of Emigrant Creek. One of three camps in the immediate area.

Site 20   FALLS   ◭

Campsites, facilities: There are five sites for tents, trailers or motorhomes up to 30 feet long. Picnic tables and firegrills are provided, and piped water, firewood and vault toilets are available. Pets are permitted.

Reservations, fee: No reservations necessary; $2 fee per night. Open mid-June to mid-October.

Who to contact: Phone Snow Mountain Ranger District at 503-573-7292, or write Ochoco

National Forest at Star Route 4, Box 12870 Highway 20, Hines, OR 97720.

Location: From the town of Hines, travel one mile south on US 20, then 25 miles northwest on Forest Service Road 47. The camp is another 8 1/2 miles west on Forest Service Road 43.

Trip note: This campground is set along the banks of Emigrant Creek. A small and quiet layover for out-of-town visitors.

YELLOWJACKET
Site **21**

Campsites, facilities: There are 20 tent sites and 20 sites for trailers or motorhomes up to 22 feet long. Piped water and picnic tables are provided, and piped water and vault toilets are available. Pets are permitted. A boat launch is nearby.

Reservations, fee: No reservations necessary; no fee. Open late-May to mid-October.

Who to contact: Phone Burns Ranger District at 503-575-2110, or write at Malheur National Forest, Burns, OR 97720.

Location: Travel one mile south of the town of Burns on US 20, then 32 miles northwest on Forest Service Road 47. The camp is another four miles east on Forest Service Road 37.

Trip note: This campground is set along the shore of Yellowjacket Lake. Fishing can be decent, but only boats without motors are permitted.

IDLEWILD
Site **22**

Campsites, facilities: There are 24 sites for tents, trailers or motorhomes up to 30 feet long. Picnic tables and firegrills are provided, and piped water and vault toilets are available. Pets are permitted.

Reservations, fee: No reservations necessary; no fee. Open late-May to mid-October.

Who to contact: Phone Burns Ranger District at 503-575-2110, or write at Malheur National Forest, Burns, OR 97720.

Location: From the town of Burns, travel 17 miles north on US 395.

Trip note: This campground is set in Divine Canyon. Popular spot for visitors traveling up Highway 395 and in need of a stopover. It has easy access.

ROCK SPRINGS
Site **23**

Campsites, facilities: There are nine sites for tents, trailers or motorhomes up to 21 feet long. Picnic tables and firegrills are provided. Piped water and vault toilets are available. Pets are permitted.

Reservations, fee: No reservations necessary; no fee. Open late-May to mid-October.

Who to contact: Phone Burns Ranger District at 503-575-2110, or write at Malheur National Forest, Burns, OR 97720.

Location: Travel 34 miles north from Burns on US 395, then 4 1/2 miles east on Forest Service Road 17. The camp is one mile southeast on Forest Service Road 1836.

Trip note: This campground is set adjacent to Rock Springs. It is far enough off Highway 395 to get completely missed by most long-range travelers, yet close enough to provide a good overnight rest stop if you know of it. Now you do.

CHUCKAR PARK

Site **24**

Campsites, facilities: There are 14 sites for tents, trailers or motorhomes up to 30 feet long. Picnic tables and firegrills are provided, and piped water, sanitary disposal services, firewood and vault toilets are available. Pets are permitted.

Reservations, fee: No reservations necessary; no fee. Open April to late-November.

Who to contact: Phone at 503-473-3144, or write at P.O. Box 700, Vale, OR 97918.

Location: From Vale, drive 56 miles west on Highway 20 to Juntura. Travel six miles northwest of the town of Juntura on a Beulah Reservoir Road.

Trip note: This campground is set along the banks of the North Fork of the Malheur River. The area in general provides habitat for chuckar, an upland game species. Hunting can be good in season during the fall, but requires much hiking in rugged terrain.

OASIS
Site **25**
RV PARK

Campsites, facilities: There are 10 tent sites and 22 drive-through sites for trailers or motorhomes of any length. Electricity, piped water and sewer hookups are provided. Flush toilets, showers, a cafe and ice are available. Bottled gas and a store are located within one mile.

Reservations, fee: Reservations accepted; $7 fee per night. MasterCard and Visa accepted. Open all year.

Who to contact: Phone at 503-277-3605, or write at P.O. Box 277, Juntura, OR 97911.

Location: From the town of Vale, travel 56 miles west on Highway 20. This park is located in the town of Juntura.

Trip note: One of two camp possibilities in this area; the other is campsite 22, which is in a more primitive setting. Other than these two camps, the closest options are almost an hour's drive away.

LESLIE GULCH

Site **26**

Campsites, facilities: There are eight sites for tents, trailers or motorhomes up to 20 feet long. Picnic tables and firegrills are provided, and vault toilets and sanitary disposal services are available. There is no piped water. Pets are permitted. Boat launching facilities are nearby.

Reservations, fee: No reservations necessary; no fee. Open April to late-November.

Who to contact: Phone at 503-473-3144, or write at P.O. Box 700, Vale, OR 97918.

Location: From Homedale, go seven miles west on Highway 19, then turn left on the road to Succor State Park and go 26 miles south. then turn right on Leslie Gulch Road. Access can be limited by road conditions.

Trip note: This campground is set along the east shore of Owyhee Lake. Warm water fishing, waterskiing and hiking are among the recreation options in this high desert area. Campsite 28 provides the other option at this lake. No other campgrounds are located within an hour's drive.

Site **27**
LAKE OWYHEE
STATE PARK

Campsites, facilities: There are 30 tent sites and 10 sites for trailers or motorhomes of any length. Electricity, piped water and picnic tables are provided. Flush toilets, sanitary disposal services, showers and firewood are available. Pets are permitted. Boat docks and launching facilities are available nearby.

Reservations, fee: No reservations necessary; $7 fee per night. Open mid-April to late-October.

Who to contact: Phone at 503-372-2331, or write at , Nyssa, OR 97913.

Location: Go eight miles south of Nyssa on Highway 201, then 28 miles southwest on Owyhee Lake Road.

Trip note: This state park is set along the shore of Owyhee Lake. This is a good lake for waterskiing in the day, fishing for warmwater species in morning and evening. Camp 26 provides the only other camping option at the lake.

Site **28**
PROSPECTOR TRAVEL
TRAILER PARK

Campsites, facilities: There are 28 drive-through sites for trailers or motorhomes of any length. Picnic tables are provided. Flush toilets, bottled gas, sanitary disposal services, showers, laundromat and ice are available. A store and cafe are located within one mile. Pets and motorbikes are permitted.

Reservations, fee: Reservations accepted; $10 fee per night. Open April to December.

Who to contact: Phone at 503-473-3879, or write at Route 3, Box 4634, Vale, OR 97918.

Location: Drive 1/2 mile north of Vale on US 26, then one block east on Hope.

Trip note: One of two camp possibilities for motorhome travelers in Vale.

Site **29**
WESTERNER
TRAILER PARK

Campsites, facilities: There are 10 drive-through sites for tents, trailers or motorhomes of any length. Electricity, piped water, sewer hookups and picnic tables are provided. Flush toilets, showers, a laundromat and ice are available. Bottled gas, a store, cafe and swimming pool are located within one mile. Pets and motorbikes are permitted.

Reservations, fee: Reservations accepted; $6 fee per night. MasterCard and Visa accepted. Open all year.

Who to contact: Phone at 503-473-3947, or write at 317 A Street East, Vale, OR 97918.

Location: This campground is in the town of Vale at the junction of US 20 & 26.

Trip note: This campground is set along the banks of Willow Creek.

Site **30**
WEST GATE
MOTORHOME PARK

Campsites, facilities: There are 10 drive-through sites for trailers or motorhomes of any length. Electricity, piped water and sewer hookups are provided. Flush toilets, showers, a recreation hall and laundromat are available. Bottled gas, a store, cafe and ice are located within one mile. Pets are permitted.

Reservations, fee: Reservations accepted; $7 fee per night. Open all year.

Who to contact: Phone at 503-889-4068, or write at 2511 Southwest 4th, Ontario, OR
   97914.
Location: Go 1/2 mile west of Ontario on US 30, then two miles west on Highway
   201.
Trip note: This park is set near the banks of the Snake River. Nearby recreation options
   include an 18-hole golf course and tennis courts.

INDEX

John Sto[...]

ABOUT THE AUTHOR

Author Tom Stienstra is recognized as one of the West's premier outdoors writers. He is currently Camping Editor for Western Outdoor News, and his column appears in newspapers across the country.

Most importantly, Tom is an avid adventurer. He has traveled throughout the West in search of prime fishing, hiking and camping areas. Among his many adventures are fishing expeditions for Great White sharks, a month-long hunt for Bigfoot, and several 200-mile hikes. He frequently leads seminars on dangers of the outdoors, Great White sharks, bears, and world-class adventures.

A graduate of San Jose State, Tom joined the San Francisco Examiner in 1980 where he has won a number of writing awards, including the McQuade Award, considered Northern California's Pulitzer Prize. His articles appear regularly in Western Outdoors and Field & Stream. Among his previous books are California Camping, Salmon Magic and 101 Outdoor Adventures for the Entire Family.

In Pacific Northwest Camping, Tom brings his entertaining style to the practical aspects of outdoor life. He reveals over 1,400 camping sites across Washington and Oregon, from primitive wilderness areas to urban RV parks, complete with detailed maps. The result is the most complete, useful and entertaining camping guide ever written about the Pacific Northwest.

Other outdoor titles by Foghorn Press.

☐ Rocky Mountain Camping $14.95
☐ California Camping $15.95
☐ 101 Outdoor Adventures for the $12.95
    entire family
☐ Salmon Magic $ 7.95

Send check or money order with $1.50 postage per book to:

FOGHORN PRESS
123 Townsend St., Suite 455
San Francisco, CA 94107
415-546-9695

Please bill my: ☐ VISA   ☐ MasterCard

Card No.: _____

Expiration Date: _____

Telephone: _____

Name: _____

Address: _____

City: _____ State: _____ Zip: _____

Note: All orders sent UPS within 3 weeks